NUREYEV

A Biography

Peter Watson

Hodder & Stoughton
LONDON SYDNEY AUCKLAND

This book is dedicated to
the memory
of my mother

First Published in 1994
by Hodder and Stoughton
A division of Hodder Headline PLC

10 9 8 7 6 5 4 3 2 1

A CIP catalogue record for this title is available from the
British Library

ISBN 0340 596 155

Typeset by Hewer Text Composition Services, Edinburgh
Printed and bound in Great Britain by
Mackays of Chatham PLC, Chatham, Kent

Hodder and Stoughton Ltd,
A division of Hodder Headline PLC
338 Euston Road
London NW1 3BH

Contents

Acknowledgements

Many people have helped in the preparation of this book and I should like to record my debt of gratitude here.

In Russia my researchers and interpreters were Paul Greenwood, Genna Antonovich Druzhinsky, and Alannah Langton. In Ufa, I should especially like to thank Rezida Evgrafova, Mr Nureyev's sister, who gave very generously of her time and patience, Albert Xatkulovich Arslanov, Zaituna Nazretdinova, Vonog-Viktor Petrovich, Pamira Sulemanovna, Alik Biktchourine, Galina Kazantseva, Taisiya Mikhailovna Haltikura Ilchinova, Inna Georgievna Gyckova, Maguera Yamaieva, Nailya Maerlyatova, Irina Ivanovna Formichova, Zoya Mikhailovna Kogan and Alexandra Nikolievna.

In St Petersburg, I owe a debt to Sergei Sorokin, Liuba Miasnikova, Tamara Myasciorva, Zhanna Ayupova, Zoya Grigorevna Arkharova, Faina Ilyenichna Rotxlind, the psychiatrist and expert on homosexuality who refused to be named, Natalia Dudinskaya, Marguerite Alfimorva, Marina Ilicheva, Volodya Evdokimov, Alexander Mikhailovich and Xavier Woodward. In Moscow I was helped by Konstantin Akinsha, Igor Torbakov, Grigorii Koslov, Gabriel Komleva and Yuri Godshelyan.

In London I should especially like to thank Sir John Tooley, Sir Peter Wright, John Lanchbery, Michael Brown, Georgina Parkinson, Antoinette Sibley, Merle Park, Monica Mason, Jennifer Penney, Ken Davison, the staff of the Royal Opera House archive, Mark Bonham-Carter, Bonnie Prandato Robinson, Antelope Films, Barbara Booroff, Leslie Edwards, Anthony Russell-Roberts, Joan Thring, Sheila Pickles, Dame Ninette de Valois, Norman Morrice, Colette Clark, Clement Crisp, Robert Sangster, Edith Gorlinsky, Jan Parry, Lord Rothschild, John and Patricia Menzies, Henry Wrong, Richard Cohen, Rowena Webb and Beth Humphries.

In New York: Peter Martins, Natasha Harley, Earl Mack, Elisabeth Kaye, Clive Barnes, the staff of the Dance Archive, Lincoln Center, Stanley Williams, Lee Walters, John Gingrich, Monique van Vooren,

Lee Radziwill, Elisabeth Kendal, Irina Kolpakova, Todd Merrill, Rhoda Grauer, Bob Colacello, Judy Kinberg, Barry Weinstein, Andrew Grossman, Patricia Becker, Barbara Horgan, Paul Taylor, Violette Verdy, Martin Raeff, Tobias Liebowitz, Rose Curcio, John Springer. I owe a special debt to Marilyn La Vine for permission to use the Marilyn J. La Vine Rudolf Nureyev Collection Archive. In Canada: Sergio Stefanschi, Linda Mabeduke, Veronica Tennant, Brenda and Leighton McCarthy, Robert Johnston, Graham Roebuck. In the Bahamas: David McGrath, Victoria McGrath.

In France: Rosella Hightower, Olivier Merlin, Clara Saint, Pierre Bergé, Yvonne Panitza, Stephan Gambier, Marie-France Polkner, Vivien Roberts, Michel Canesi, Mario Bois, Nina Vyroubova, Dorothy Field, Vartori Bazmadjian, Valentin Vorobiov.

Needless to say, none of the above is in any way responsible for the views expressed in this book.

List of Illustrations

Author's Note

Rudolf Nureyev once said that, by and large, imaginative literature had no power to sway him, that 'words tend to seem dead things; meaningless signs with little to say to me'. But it wasn't true and, later in life, he became a great reader, his favourite authors being Pushkin, Dostoevsky, Byron, Goethe and Schiller. Of these, Pushkin was closest to his heart. And of all Pushkin's work, none was so beloved by Nureyev as *Eugene Onegin*. Indeed, as we shall see, Nureyev's life shared not a few parallels with those of both Pushkin and Onegin. The chapter titles for this book, except for those on the KGB file, have all been taken from *Eugene Onegin*. I have used the English translation, by Charles Johnston, first published by Penguin Books in 1977.

PROLOGUE

A Splendid Joke

And so your faithfullest supporter
Will disappear as fast as smoke:
For Satan, love's a splendid joke

Outside Russia few people have heard of the city of Ufa, in the Urals. Situated on the Belaya, or White river, a tributary of the Volga, and 800 miles east of Moscow, it is in fact quite a large conurbation of 500,000 souls. Its chief industries are the assembly of car and aircraft engines, the manufacture of bronze, and oil refining. The heart of the old city is laid out on a grid pattern and consists chiefly of redbrick offices, or houses built of logs and rarely more than three storeys high. There are two parks in the centre of the city and countless black statues of Lenin, even today. The streets are not unpleasant, being lined with trees, but are otherwise spoiled by a smothering of tramlines and trolley-bus wires. Outside the centre, modern Ufa is a spread-out city, with broad four-lane boulevards radiating in all directions. Small copses of silver birch, set between the all-white concrete apartment blocks, make these suburbs resemble a run-down Aix-en-Provence, or the tougher *banlieux* of Paris.

Ufa, founded in 1591, is the capital of Bashkiria and 5–10 per cent Tartar. In the Second World War, however, many Muscovites and Leningraders were evacuated there and never went home – it might be provincial but it was safe (steamboats sailed the Belaya river until the 1950s). During the cold war, because of its strategic importance in the oil and aircraft industries, Ufa was a 'closed' city. Strangers were not allowed until 1986. Even when they were allowed, they were not always welcome.

Four miles to the south of the city lies the airport. At two o'clock on the morning of Sunday, 14 November 1987, a small group of people gathered in the Intourist VIP lounge in the main terminal building. The room, lined in a dark brown, plastic veneer – imitation mahogany – was dominated by a large television, switched off at that ungodly hour. On one wall was a pale rectangle where a portrait of Lenin had hung until recently. The group in the lounge consisted of an airport official, along with Rezida Evgrafova, her son Viktor, her son Yuri, her niece Guzelle, and Vonog-Viktor Petrovich, a photographer from the Tass news agency. Outside, the temperature was minus 6 degrees centigrade – cold, but not unusually so for a Russian winter.

At five past two, exactly on schedule, flight BL 339 from Moscow touched down. The aircraft had left the Russian capital at 10.20 the evening before. With a two-hour time difference between Moscow and the Urals, the 105-minute flight arrived at a very inconvenient time.

As the aircraft, a TU-154 (similar to a Boeing 727), approached the terminal, and the whine of its engines could be heard inside the VIP lounge, an attendant led Viktor Petrovich outside into the night and down a special staircase reserved for VIPs. A light sprinkling of snow lay on the grass next to the tarmac. Rezida Evgrafova and the others were led off by a second attendant in a different direction. The Tupolev came to a halt, the engines were switched off, and Petrovich noticed that two, not one, gangways were being led to the aircraft. This was most unusual. The gangways were manoeuvred into place and the aircraft doors were opened. Almost immediately, passengers began to emerge from the rear doorway: it was cold and they hurried across the tarmac into the terminal building. For a moment the front doorway remained open but no one appeared. Petrovich stationed himself at the foot of the steps, pulled his coat more tightly around him and gripped his camera in his gloved hand. At last a stewardess appeared, leading a man. He was dressed in a very long coat, with a herring-bone pattern, a green beret, and he had a scarf pulled around his neck. Petrovich guessed that this man was the reason he was here, in the middle of a freezing airfield at a most unsociable hour. This had to be Rudolf Nureyev.

Twenty-four hours before, Petrovich had been only dimly aware that Rudolf Nureyev existed. He had known that Nureyev was a ballet dancer and that a long time ago, in 1961, he had defected to the west. But Petrovich had not known that Nureyev was regarded in the west as the greatest dancer of his generation, perhaps the greatest dancer of all time. He certainly had not known that Nureyev was one of the most famous and flamboyant people in the world and immensely rich. However, the previous afternoon Petrovich had received an urgent telephone call from the Moscow headquarters of Tass, the Russian news agency, to inform him that one Rudolf Nureyev would be arriving in Ufa that very night and that his – Petrovich's – assignment was to photograph the entire visit.

Petrovich wasn't sure what to make of this. Was it a genuine journalistic assignment, or was he being asked – in an unofficial and unobtrusive way – to keep an eye on the dancer on behalf of the authorities? Apprehensive, he immediately phoned the local office of the KPSS, the Communist Party of the Soviet Union, to find out more about Nureyev. But they could not help. Reasoning that if Nureyev had come from the west he must be known to the KGB, Petrovich next called one of the local deputies in the KGB whom he knew slightly, a man called Bulatov. Bulatov's reaction was curious. He gave no sign that he was expecting Petrovich's call but he did happen to have the Nureyev file handy. For about half an hour, he filled in for the photographer exactly who Nureyev was. As the briefing went on, Petrovich realised that he had been right to be apprehensive: he *was* expected to be both journalist and spy.

When Petrovich first fired his Soviet-made 'Blitz' camera at Nureyev, at the top of the aircraft steps, the dancer was startled by the flash. Petrovich later learned that Nureyev had no idea who would greet him in Ufa. After twenty-six years in the west, he had been given permission at the highest level – from President Gorbachev himself – to visit Russia but for forty-eight hours only, to visit his mother, who was gravely ill. The dancer, who was then living in Paris, was accompanied by two officials, one a diplomat from the French Foreign Office and the other from the embassy in Moscow. They were partly bodyguards and partly assistants. The bodyguard element was thought necessary because Nureyev had a residual worry that he might be arrested in out-of-the-way Ufa and thrown into jail. After his sensational defection in 1961 Nureyev had stood trial and been sentenced in his absence to seven years in prison. Theoretically the sentence still stood. He was used to being photographed but, on this occasion, it was understandable that the flashlight should startle him.

Behind Nureyev came the two French diplomats, a tall young man and a smaller, older woman. They were carrying the luggage. Getting over his fright of the camera flash, Nureyev descended the steps and came face to face with Petrovich. 'Dobra dyen,' said the photographer. 'Good day.' He explained that he was from Tass and that his job was to take photographs of the visit. 'Good, *good*,' said Nureyev. 'Great!' He seemed enthusiastic until Petrovich let slip the comment that above all he wanted some shots of Nureyev with his mother. At this, Nureyev's manner changed and he became instantly cold. 'With mother? . . . No. *No!*'

Petrovich backed off, while Nureyev waited for the two French officials to negotiate the aircraft steps. He looked across the apron to the airport sign, which said Ufa in both Russian and Bashkiri. 'Oh, Ufa!' he breathed, 'I haven't been to Ufa for more than twenty years.' He turned back to Petrovich and, in a more emollient tone, asked if there was anyone to meet him. The photographer said that his sister was there, with his niece and nephews – for some reason they had not been allowed out on to the tarmac but were waiting behind the barrier where all the people meeting other passengers were gathered.

Together Nureyev and Petrovich walked across the tarmac to the barrier. Rezida and the rest of the family held flowers, the traditional Russian greeting. Petrovich was aware that this was a poignant moment. A great artist, a controversial man, who had left his mother country in spectacular fashion a generation ago, was back, here in the city where he had had grown up, and among his family.

Rudolf stood before Rezida. Despite the occasion, she wore no make-up and her hair was pulled back to reveal the lines on her face. She was only three years older than her brother, but she looked ten or fifteen. While he had enjoyed the sweetness of the west, her life had been hard, with no promotion at work, thanks to her brother's defection. Nevertheless, they shared the same high cheekbones, and the family resemblance was unmistakable now that they were face to face. She smiled up at him. 'Rudik,' she said in a deep, harsh voice, choosing the name his family had always used when they were children. And she held out the flowers.

Rudolf and Rezida embraced. There were more smiles, of course, but no tears. The Nureyevs never had time for tears. Petrovich took more photographs, then he and the family adjourned to the Intourist VIP lounge. After a few minutes there, for some sweet warming tea, Petrovich went home to Ufa to develop his film: it was nearly 3 a.m. and he wanted to send the prints to Moscow first thing next morning. He arranged to pick up Rudolf at his hotel at nine. He had been given the dancer's itinerary for his stay in Ufa. This itinerary, Petrovich was told, had been agreed with Nureyev and could not be altered. Petrovich – and the Russian authorities, of course – knew exactly where Nureyev would be the whole time. Nureyev had agreed to this partly because without such an agreement he would not have been able to see his mother in the first place and partly because the French embassy also had the itinerary and so they too knew where he was at all times. This minimised any risk of his arrest.

When Petrovich phoned the hotel the next morning, around 8.30, he received a shock. At first he was connected to the wrong room – a German voice answered. Then, when the hotel operator finally connected him to Nureyev's room, there was no reply. Petrovich panicked. Was Nureyev safe? *Had* he been arrested? Or had he already left? The photographer rushed across to the hotel, the Rossiya, and found Nureyev's two-room suite on the second floor. He knocked on the door. There was no reply. He knocked again. Still nothing. He went downstairs and talked to the receptionist. It turned out that, the night before, Nureyev had not gone straight to the hotel from the airport, as had been specified in the itinerary, but had first stopped off at a friend's house – Petrovich never did find out whose. Consequently, the dancer and his French 'minders' had not arrived at the hotel until very late, four or five in the morning. The receptionist thought that it was possible that Nureyev was still sleeping.

Petrovich tried knocking on the room door one more time, and now he did hear movement. The first face he saw was Rezida's; she came out to fetch some tea (many Russian hotels have a samovar on each floor so that guests can help themselves). Next, Rudolf appeared and told Petrovich that he would be ready to visit his mother in about half an hour. He reiterated that he would not allow any photographs with his mother, but added that afterwards he would be visiting friends and his father's grave – and that Petrovich could photograph those parts of his itinerary.

Just after ten, Nureyev appeared downstairs in the hotel lobby, where Petrovich was waiting. The dancer wore the same long coat and scarf but had changed his beret. He was carrying a bowl, which Petrovich assumed was a gift for his mother, and Rezida was with him, together with his great-nephew, Ruslanchik. Petrovich's small car was a *Shestorka*, which means 'Six' in Russian. It was a squeeze to fit four inside but somehow they managed it. In the car Petrovich again asked if he could photograph Nureyev's mother, but it was a mistake. More forcefully than ever, the dancer refused again. 'I understood then that this man had an iron character, that, at the time, only such a man could have defected to France.'

Nureyev's mother's flat was near October Square in a standard, all-white, five-storey concrete apartment block, next to a stream and some silver birch woods. As he got out, Nureyev turned to the photographer and said that he expected to be with her for about forty minutes. At first Petrovich thought he might use the time to take his prints to the office, so they could be sent straight on to Moscow. On reflection, however, he decided against it. He had almost lost Nureyev once and didn't want to risk it again.

It was another mistake. More than an hour elapsed before Nureyev came out. When he appeared, Petrovich noticed the smell of vodka on his breath. But there was no mention of what had taken place in his mother's apartment, though there was 'some sort of emotion visible'. After they had all settled back into the car, Petrovich asked Nureyev what he wanted to do next. 'Let's go to the theatre of opera and ballet,' Nureyev said. As they drove, there was a marked silence about the visit to his mother. Instead, Rezida asked Rudolf what he thought of Ufa. He hesitated for a moment, then said, 'Domodedovo is horribly uncomfortable. It wasn't made for people.' Domodedovo is the Moscow airport from where many internal flights depart. Ufa had obviously not made much of an impact – yet.

After another silence, Nureyev asked Petrovich, 'How much do cars cost?'

As this exchange was taking place they were passing the central market in Ufa. Instead of answering the question, Petrovich asked Nureyev if he wanted to visit the market, to buy some souvenirs. He thought it might produce some interesting shots. The market was a large green and white glass structure near Revolution Street, where there still stood a huge bronze statue of Lenin. They got out and looked around and Nureyev bought some knitted woollen socks. Or he would have done if he had had some roubles, but it turned out he hadn't bothered to change his money. The woman who was serving him wouldn't accept dollars, or French francs, and so, in the end, Rezida paid for the socks.

At the theatre, Nureyev asked for his photograph to be taken outside, then they went in by the stage door. The woman at the desk had no idea who he was, or that he was so famous. When it was explained that Nureyev was a VIP, she insisted on phoning the director of the theatre so that he could act as guide. While they waited, Nureyev and Petrovich browsed through the photos in the foyer, which showed several Ufa dancers, some of whom Nureyev recognised. When the director arrived they all shook hands, and then were shown around the theatre and even allowed on stage. This was the very stage where, thirty years before, Nureyev had first appeared in a professional role, in *Song of the Cranes*. The blue, gold and white theatre decorations (modelled on the Maryinsky, in St Petersburg) had changed not at all. White sheets were still thrown over the seats between performances, as they always had been, as was the practice in St Petersburg. This too might have been an emotional moment, and Petrovich was ready with his camera. But it quickly turned sour as Nureyev began to argue with the director about whether the stage was metal or wooden. Nureyev thought it was metal and would not give way when the director, who must surely have known better, insisted it was not.

While they had been waiting for the director, Petrovich had, at Nureyev's request, rung directory assistance, trying to hunt down the phone numbers of various old friends and colleagues whom Nureyev hoped to meet. Petrovich had been given half a dozen names but had obtained numbers for three only. One was Zaituna Nazretdinova, a famous ballerina who was one of the first dancers Nureyev had ever seen, and whose performances had helped inspire him to study classical ballet. But when Petrovich called her, she wasn't at home. The second number was that of another dancer, Alexandra Nikolievna, whose father had been a dissident. But she wasn't at home either. The third number was that of Pamira Sulemanovna, possibly Nureyev's first partner, when they were both teenagers. No reply.

'Oh, well,' said Nureyev, 'let's go to Zentsova Street.' This was the street, in the old area of town, where he had grown up. When they arrived, it was to find that half the street had been knocked down and a big white block of flats and a hostel built across it, completely changing the landscape. Nureyev clambered through the snow and over the rubble into the yard of one of the houses, the third from the corner. He asked Petrovich to take his picture. 'It is possible his expression changed a bit. He told me that at this place had stood the house where he used to live.'

Next they went to a hill in Ufa where there stood a statue of Salarat Ulaev. The statue wasn't important, but it had been on this hill that the young, the very young Nureyev, years ago, had watched the trains going into and out of Ufa station, dreaming that one day he himself would be carried very far from Ufa, to Kazan, Moscow, Leningrad – and who knows where else? From here you could also see the sweep of the river. The Tartar word for the Belaya river is *Agadel*. Nureyev hadn't forgotten that. He did allow a photograph there.

The next scheduled stop on the itinerary was the Muslim cemetery where Nureyev's father was buried. As a journalist and photographer, Petrovich had high hopes of this part of the visit. It would be emotional and should make a moving picture.

But, at the last minute, as they were getting back into the car, Nureyev changed his mind. 'We won't go to the cemetery,' he said. Petrovich was very upset. He had missed the reunion with Nureyev's mother; now he was to be cheated of the dancer's meeting with his father. As a Russian he was also shocked. Not to visit one's father's grave? It was unthinkable. What *had* gone on in that meeting with Nureyev's mother?

Just as they got into the car, the dancer got out again. Near the *Shestorka* was a tree, a rowan tree, which many people regard as a symbol of Russia. Its berries are dark blue, with red in them, and when the snow falls, little pyramids form on the clusters of berries, making the whole effect very beautiful.

'What tree is this?' asked Nureyev.

'Oh, Rudik!' cried Rezida, 'how can you not remember? It's the rowan tree.'

Petrovich was shocked too that Nureyev could have forgotten something as basic as the rowan tree. What sort of Russian was this man?

Now, instead of going to his father's grave, Nureyev asked Petrovich to take him to the school he had attended. Petrovich told him it was no longer an ordinary school, as it had been in Nureyev's day, but was now – ironically enough – a choreographical school. It didn't matter, said Nureyev, he still wanted to see it. And, since none of his friends were at home, there was not much else to do. The school was at the foot of a hill, near the end of a tram line. As they were getting close, on Sverdlova Street, Petrovich's car suddenly became caught in the tram lines in the centre of the street – and got stuck. However much Petrovich tugged at the steering wheel, the tyres remained obstinately trapped in the rails. It was comical, it was embarrassing, it was deflating. Nureyev quietly said he would go on alone on foot while Petrovich dealt with the problem.

Petrovich had to struggle with the car for several minutes, by which time trams were piling up behind him, their klaxons angrily disturbing the peace. Finally, after still more delay, he managed to wrestle the car free, and out of the way of the trams. As he did so, he saw Nureyev coming back up the hill. 'The school is shut,' the dancer said grimly. 'It's Sunday.'

Petrovich began to see that the great visit was turning into a disaster.

Next they decided to try the Philharmonia (the concert hall). Matters didn't improve. The attendant was a large, gloomy man, who also had no idea who Nureyev was. In response to their request to look inside, he merely grumbled, 'What is there to look at?' When Petrovich showed the man his Tass ID the attendant did allow them to enter but insisted on accompanying them everywhere. Nureyev asked if there were any rehearsals that day, only to be told that there weren't – because it was a Sunday. 'Nureyev was very depressed that everything had worked out as it had, that the choreographical school had been shut and that we had met such a man at the Philharmonia.'

Trying to cheer him up, Petrovich asked Nureyev where he lived in Paris.

'On the banks of the Seine, opposite the Louvre.'

'In that case do you want to go to the Nesterov Museum?'

'Oh yes, what a good idea. I'd love to.'

'We arrived at the museum, and I took out my camera, only to be shouted at by one of the attendants: "You're not allowed to take photographs. Put the camera away!" I said that I couldn't see why, because I was taking pictures of a man and not the paintings. I explained that Nureyev was a famous son of Ufa and a VIP and that he had come from abroad. The woman screamed even louder: "Put the camera away or I'll call the director!" She was a small woman with a repulsive personality. They should take away her salary. It was one stroke of bad luck after another.'

Very little had been achieved, and time was passing. Petrovich dropped Nureyev and Rezida back at the Hotel Rossiya at four. The return flight to Moscow left at six. The two people from the French embassy were waiting for him and Petrovich said goodbye. Nureyev seemed very low.

Next day Petrovich was visited by the KGB, who had phoned and said they wanted to interview him. Petrovich had noticed that Nureyev's room at the Rossiya was not one of the best and had wondered if he had been given a 'special' room – one bugged by the security services. He thought about this again on the Monday, when the KGB officers seemed mostly interested in what Nureyev had said while he had been in Petrovich's car – they appeared to know everything else. But he didn't have much to tell them, he said. Nureyev had been uncommunicative and the trip had been one disaster after another.

Later on, Petrovich concluded that Nureyev's trip had been carefully masterminded. Gorbachev himself may have authorised the visit but there was still a lot of feeling against Nureyev at the time on the part of those in authority, who knew who he was and what he had done. Petrovich came to the conclusion that the choice of a 2 a.m. arrival, on a Sunday, was deliberate. In this way, the visit could be downplayed, the school, theatre and Philharmonia would be closed, friends would be away. Ufa had allowed its famous son to come home, but grudgingly, and unforgiven.

In fact, Vonog-Viktor Petrovich didn't know at the time how unforgiven Rudolf Nureyev really was. But he learned later. Nureyev had denied him the chance to witness the reunion with his mother and, from Nureyev's point of view, his instincts were right. When the dancer had been shown into his mother's room on the fifth floor of the apartment block near October Square, he had been shocked. She was tiny, shrivelled, very weak, suffering badly as he knew from polyarthritis (she died a few months later). She was also incontinent so that, as well as being cramped and shabby, there was a terrible smell in the room. She was eighty-two and seemed encased in a world of her own.

Lilia, Nureyev's deaf-and-dumb sister was also there. So was Boris, Rezida's husband. They had been married in 1961, not long after Nureyev's defection and the wedding had been somewhat marred, to put it mildly. Vodka and *pelmeni*, traditional Russian dumplings, were now served by Lilia, but even so the atmosphere was tense.

Rezida led the way across the tiny room. A weak sun battled through the shabby lace curtains that lined the windows. Rezida bent over the frail body and gripped her mother's wrist. In a loud voice, she said slowly, 'Mother, it's Rudik, your son. He's come to see you.'

She stood to one side, to allow Nureyev to move forward so that his mother could see him. He stood there in his long coat. It was warm in the room and he had taken off his scarf and beret.

His mother was familiar and yet a stranger. He reminded himself that it had been twenty-six years since he had seen her. She had always been small but now she seemed to have shrunk almost to a child's size. Her eyes, always dark and clear when he was a boy, had clouded over and lost a lot of their pigment. Her eyebrows were all but gone. The skin on her face was drawn tightly over her chin and jaw bones. Death was not far away. It was right that he had come.

After a moment, his mother's eyes moved but it was difficult to tell if she looked directly at him. She appeared to chew on something. For a moment longer the silence lingered.

Then, in a frail but clear voice, she addressed herself to Rezida. 'I have no son.'

CHAPTER ONE

Gloomy Russia

. . . gloomy Russia,
where I suffered, where I lived,
where I buried my heart.

On Thursday, 17 March, 1938, as the fast Number Seventeen Trans-Siberian Express pulled away from Angarsk, Farida Nureyev settled uncomfortably into her seat and looked out at the countryside. Aged thirty-three, she was a small woman, with long dark hair parted in the middle and sad, brown eyes set far apart. From her usual expression you could never tell if she were about to laugh or cry. Her high cheekbones betrayed her Tartar ancestry, and she had a pale, powdery skin. She was not unattractive but was a reserved woman and did her best to ignore the other passengers, almost all of whom were men – Communist Party officials, bureaucrats or, this being the year it was, soldiers.

In Siberia it was still winter in mid-March and through the silver birches which lined the track she could occasionally glimpse the ice floes on the Angara river, away to her left. She was looking forward to the train's next stop. Irkutsk was more than sixty kilometres away, forty miles, and a large city where the express would wait long enough for Farida to stretch her legs, get some fresh air and perhaps buy some smoked fish, a delicacy of the area. Irkutsk was also more or less half-way on the Trans-Siberian, 2,950 miles east of Moscow but still 2,780 miles from Vladivostok, her destination. Siberia is an enormous chunk of land whose size is only really appreciated when travelling across it by road or rail. Moscow and Uelen, on the Bering Strait, are as far apart as London and Los Angeles, New York and Tierra del Fuego, Sydney and Johannesburg.

Farida, who lived in the Nuremanovski region of Russia, had boarded the train at Ufa, just west of the Urals and already 800 miles from

Moscow. She was travelling with her three daughters, Rosa, aged ten, Lilia, five, and Rezida, just three. But Farida was pregnant again, hoping hard for a son this time, and was visiting Vladivostok to be with her husband, Hamet, who had found accommodation for his family and wanted them with him. Hamet was a *politrouk*, a political instructor or commissar, in the army at Kalkhin-gole, an artillery base near the Soviet Union's most important Pacific port. In his job he moved around a lot and the family were hardly ever with him.

It was a brave decision of Farida's. In those days Train Seventeen, the fastest express between Moscow and Vladivostok, still took fourteen days, at an average speed of 28 miles an hour (though it could take forty-seven days for the victims of the purges, transported in cattle trucks). Of all Siberian towns, Irkutsk was the most cosmopolitan. In Tsarist times, it had been called 'The Paris of Siberia', after both gold and oil had been discovered there; it had become the most prosperous and fashionable city east of St Petersburg. Gold smuggling, fashionable boutiques and all-night drinking dens were part of Irkutsk's colourful past. It certainly set the place apart from the other drab hamlets that could be glimpsed from the windows of the Trans-Siberian. The train stopped there for forty minutes.

After Irkutsk, the railway veered away from the Angara river, taking a more direct route south to Lake Baikal, which was reached near Kultuk. In later life, Rudolf Nureyev said, 'I like to think about my birth . . . I always think of [it] as the most romantic event of my life.' Certainly, being born on a train *is* romantic but the Trans-Siberian railway, in 1938, was not the glamorous luxury it once had been.

It was built in the 1890s. The company which ran the railway advertised at the Paris Exposition in 1900 that the trains had sumptuous sleeping compartments, dining cars with French chefs, libraries with French and Russian books, a salon with a grand piano and even an entire carriage made up as a church, complete with icons. These claims were almost certainly an exaggeration when they were made but in 1938, twenty-one years after the revolution, conditions were quite different.

Though diesel engines were beginning to replace coal-fired ones, the train Farida was travelling on had an old-fashioned steam locomotive. It was no cleaner than the trains of the 1890s, and in practice rather slower.

One reason why passenger trains were so slow in 1938 was that, under the five-year plans, priority was given not to passengers but to freight – and freight included immigrants, brought out in cattle trucks to settle the sparse areas north of Manchuria, as well as hundreds of thousands of political refugees, sent into forced exile as a result of Stalin's brutal purges. At least thirty-three of some two hundred 'gulags' were located along the Trans-Siberian railway.

Though it was an engineering marvel of sorts, 5,700 miles of track across some *very* inhospitable terrain, the Trans-Siberian had been built on the cheap, and one consequence was that its routes meandered around obstacles because the Tsars had been too mean to blast expensive short-cuts. (There was, for example, only one tunnel west of Irkutsk.) At eight months pregnant, Farida was taking a chance in travelling at all, but on the slow, winding, rocky Trans-Siberian it was really no surprise that, by the time they pulled out of Irkutsk, the infant in her womb was no longer quiescent and Farida was beginning to grow very uncomfortable indeed. The early trains, at that Paris exposition, had advertised a gymnasium, a dark-room for amateur photographers, a barber and a licensed 'dispenser of medicines, competent to treat obstetrical cases'. By 1938 this was all a sick joke. In the lowest class of travel passengers weren't even given a bed; they had to survive fourteen days with just a seat. And the pharmacists had been purged along with everything else.

Fifty miles south of Irkutsk, the express reached Lake Baikal and the prettily situated town of Kultuk. Here the Baikal sturgeon was the basis of a major industry, each fish producing up to eight kilograms of black caviare. Originally, Lake Baikal had been by far the most romantic aspect of the entire Trans-Siberian journey. The largest body of fresh water in the world, it is heavy enough to cause three to five earth tremors a year in the surrounding area, and close enough to Kultuk for the city to have restricted all buildings to five storeys. In summer in the early days, the entire train – passengers, coaches and the engine itself – was ferried forty miles across the water to Mysovsk, where everything was loaded on to the Trans-Baikal section of the railway.

But Baikal is frozen from early January to May, so in winter the passengers would be taken across the ice-bound lake as far as the (British-built) ice-breaker could reach, at which point everyone disembarked and clambered on to horse-drawn sleds which pulled them the rest of the way. Though picturesque, this was not without its dangers, since fissures up to eighteen miles in length could suddenly appear in the Baikal ice due to underwater hot springs. On one occasion an entire railway engine disappeared in this way.

By 1938, however, the rail link between Irkutsk and Mysovsk had been long completed and the Russian-made rails (half as thick as western ones) now skirted the southern curve of the lake, passing through one small town after another – Slyudyanka, Utulik, Murlho, fairly basic places consisting mainly of *isbas*, log cabins. In summer each looked out on to the clear, turquoise-coloured waters of Baikal which, being so large and yet 900 miles from the nearest ocean, was zoologically, botanically and geologically unique, from its emerald green sponges to its *golomyanka* fish, which do not lay eggs but give birth to live young, from its colonies of seals to the stray Manchurian tigers which could still be found in the woods overlooking the lake, from the bristled worms which have survived since prehistory, to the lake water itself, so clear that a dropped coin can be followed by the naked eye for 130 feet.

It was here, in this unique and picturesque spot, near a village called Razdolnaya, hours after they had left Irkutsk, that Farida could hold out no longer. Rudolf was, as he later put it, 'Shaken out of the womb, feet first.' According to Nureyev himself, his sister Rosa was playing in the corridor of the train when she first heard his cries. 'She was so enraptured by the sound of her little brother's loud voice that she stopped in delighted amazement and failed to notice a passenger opening a door which slammed on her fingers.' Years later, as an adult, Rosa's flesh would still show the scars of this incident.

Farida was more delighted than most mothers to have a boy at last, after three girls. She and Hamet were Tartars, distant descendants of the Mongol hordes who, led by Genghis Khan (1162–1227), overran and devastated much of Asia and eastern Europe. And as such, they were Muslims.

In Muslim households, even in Russia in 1938, where religion was outlawed, boys were valued far more than in other faiths. Hamet had longed so much for a boy that when Lilia, his second daughter, was born, in the famine year of 1933, Farida had written to say that she had given him a son (husband and wife were separated on that occasion, too). But her ploy had backfired. Hamet had been so overjoyed that he had arranged some home leave as soon as possible. He was speechless with misery when he arrived to learn the truth. Lilia, too, was speechless – literally. She grew up to be deaf and dumb.

When the Trans-Siberian made its next stop, at Razdolnaya station, Rosa, the eldest child, was dispatched to the telegraph office where she sent word to her father that now, finally, he did indeed have a son. Farida could only hope that, this time, he would believe her.

That, at least, is the official version of Nureyev's birth, in the sense that it is the account Nureyev himself gave in numerous interviews, in his autobiography, published in 1962 when he was twenty-four, and in other books about him. Yet the fact remains that there is *no* Razdolnaya near Lake Baikal, either on or near the Trans-Siberian railway. There are two Razdolnayas actually on the railroad: one lies between Arteushka and Mogocha, 885 miles to the east of Baikal, not far from the notorious Tsarist silver mines and the birthplace of Genghis Khan; the other is a mere hundred miles north-west of Vladivostok. The latter may well have been the place were Nureyev was actually born. The evidence lies in just one interview which he gave to the London *Daily Mail*, on 2 March 1991, when he said, 'My place of birth on my passport is Station Razdolnaya which is on the Trans-Siberian railroad, north of Vladivostok.'

The question arises as to whether Nureyev consistently and deliberately lied about his place of birth and, if so, why? There are certainly grounds for assuming that a birth nearer Vladivostok is more plausible than the more romantic notion. His mother was heavily pregnant when she boarded the train and well knew how long it took to reach the end of the line. It is much more likely that she should have miscalculated by a few hours rather than by several days.

But why then the Baikal story? Put it down to Nureyev's theatrical and romantic nature. The Trans-Siberian railway *sounds* romantic but the reality, in gloomy Russia, was rather different, with one dreary town succeeding another dreary town and thousands of miles of silver birch forest lining the track. Lake Baikal was the only feature which broke the monotony (the same is true even today).

Nureyev was right, in a way, in that the world responded to the Baikal story, absorbing it fully, as he intended. But it serves as an early warning that not everything Nureyev said about his childhood should be treated as gospel.

It is also true that, in 1982, when Rudolf was being considered for Austrian citizenship, evidence was turned up which appeared to show that his birth was *registered* on 17 March but that he had actually been born three days before. Despite requests to the Austrian authorities, the nature of this evidence has not been made available. Three days seems a long time for Farida to have waited.

From Baikal, the remaining journey to Vladivostok took nearly six days. Initially, the route headed north rather than east. This was because the Russians had only recently, in 1935, sold the Chinese Eastern railway, which had provided the most direct route to Port Arthur and Vladivostok, to the Japanese. Given the rapidly deteriorating relations between Russia and Japan, that route was now blocked. The new route took Farida and her family to Ulan-Ude, to Chita, then along the Shilka river to Skovorodino and down the Amur river to Blagoveschensk and Khabarovsk, a mere 200 miles from the Sea of Japan. In the snowy vastness, the occasional camel could be glimpsed, pulling sledges of wood. Chita provided the next highlight, after Irkutsk. For those who knew their Russian history, this was home of the famous Damskaya Ulitsa, or Ladies' Street, where in Tsarist times, the Princesses Volkonskaya and Trubetskaya and other aristocrats had lived in two rows of huts to be near their exiled husbands. In that sense, life had hardly changed in Russia. Near Chita in 1938 there were four 'gulags.'

Khabarovsk, a military centre, was the point at which the Ussuri Line began. When the Trans-Siberian had first been thought of, and construction planned in six sections, the Ussuri – starting from Vladivostok and heading north and west – had been the third section to find finance. Its widespread *use*, however, was fairly new, since the Chinese Eastern railway offered a more direct route to the Pacific coast. This final section of the long journey followed the Ussuri river. At one stage this too had been a colourful stretch – passengers stood a fair chance of seeing a Manchurian tiger stalking the forests which bordered the river and another attraction had been the ginseng farms cultivated by the Goldi tribe, famous for their pigtails. The Ussuri had once shown Russia's orient in all her glory. But by 1938 all that had gone, or been hidden. The Ussuri and Iman rivers were spate rivers and, at times of storm, could swell fantastically, so much that a levee had been built along the entire length of the line, obscuring the spectacular view.

Farida was more than ready to disembark from the train at Vladivostok. Her daughters, too, were exhausted. Vladivostok – the name means 'dominator of the East' – was the Soviet Union's main Pacific port, a city of some 200,000 people in 1938, and wrapped around Zolotoy Rog (Golden Horn) Bay. It had been likened to Naples by early twentieth-century travellers, on account of its heavily wooded volcanic hinterland, natural geysers, and its position on a peninsula surrounded by islands and inlets of great natural beauty. The city's main industries were fishing and whaling but, as a major port, coal, oil and agricultural products all passed through in great amounts. Traditionally, the city had been the only location of any size in the far east of Russia to specialise in science and culture and so in 1938 it was named the capital of Primorsky Kray, the Maritime Territory, and a civil service bureaucracy was added to everything else. Though a long way from Moscow, Vladivostok was a varied, cosmopolitan and not unstylish city. The best season was autumn but the winters were short and usually snow-free. Even grapes grew in the area.

And Vladivostok was, of course, the chief base of the Soviet Far Eastern Fleet. Strategically vital, it was just 400 miles from the nearest tip of Japan and, in 1938, home for many troops of all kinds. Hamet was attached to an artillery unit at Khalkin-gole, to the north and west of the city, near the Lake of Hassan.

He met his family at the station and, after embracing his wife, held his son for the first time. Hamet, like Farida, was thirty-three in 1938. He was a handsome man, reserved like his wife, with whom he also shared the traditional high cheekbones of the Tartar race, and brown eyes set wide apart. He had dark hair, cut ferociously short, and a widow's peak. His strong temper was kept firmly in check. He was not tall but stocky, the classic peasant build, a neat man, always as spick and span as anyone in the army. He had met Farida while they were working in the fields in Kazan.

That day in March 1938, the first thing Hamet did with his family was to take them down to the port, so they could see the sea. After days of being cooped up in a railway compartment he thought they needed the fresh salt air for which Vladivostok was famous, and to gaze out on the picturesque coast and the vast expanse of water, dotted with warships. He and Farida discussed naming their new son. There had only ever been one other man in Farida's life, besides Hamet, and that was the actor, Rudolph Valentino. His silent films had appeared in the early 1920s, when Farida was in her late teens, a brand-new member of the Communist Party in the wake of the successful revolution. She had adored the Hollywood glamour of Valentino and was devastated by his early death. She wanted her son to bear her dead hero's name and Hamet agreed, provided it was Russianised, to Rudolf.

Khalkin-gole was to the north of Vladivostok, about 250 miles away. This base, which was huge, specialised in artillery training. Hamet had quarters on the base where he was a political instructor, a deputy in the political department, known as a *politrouk* or commissar. His classes concentrated on the history of the revolution and the achievements of the Communist Party, events he himself had lived through.

At the time of Rudolf's birth, Hamet was earning a thousand roubles a month. This did not make him a rich man but, since the national average was around 270 roubles a month, it didn't make him a poor man either (ordinary soldiers received virtually no pay – just their keep). As a *politrouk* in the army, Hamet had everything he needed, including a liberal supply of Stalin's favourite *papirosi* cigarettes, so he was free to send home almost his entire wage. Later on in life, Nureyev always referred to his family background as chronically poor but, strictly speaking, this was not true, at least to begin with. It was the advent of war that seems to have hit Hamet's earning capacity particularly hard.

In 1938 the Red Army was expanding rapidly as the international situation deteriorated. Until 1934, the forces had been seen by Stalin chiefly as a means to maintain internal order, and 562,000 men had been judged sufficient. Two years later, however, its strength had more than doubled, to 1.3 million. The rank of marshal had been reintroduced, as had the practice of saluting, two things that had been abolished after the 1917 revolution. The one important way in which the Red Army differed from all other armies at the time was in Hamet's area – of political instruction. The practice dated from the Russian civil war, following the revolution, when Trotsky, as Commander of the Red Army, was forced to accept the services of many ex-Tsarist officers because they alone were capable of countering the technical superiority of the White armies. In order to 'discourage any inclination to conspiracy on their part', Trotsky introduced the system of political commissars to keep an eye on all ranks. From Stalin's point of view, this role grew in importance as the army expanded to meet the international threat. This was because expansion involved taking into the army more and more people from social backgrounds whose revolutionary credentials were at best doubtful. It was also true that the political dimension of the army helped keep it subservient to the central Soviet power.

The organisation Hamet was part of had, by the time he joined, become known as the Political Administration of the Red Army of

Workers and Peasants, or PORKKA. Its members were officially
known as *politrouki*, though they were still referred to colloquially
as commissars. The organisation of PORKKA paralleled, but did not
touch, that of the army proper. It reported to the Central Committee
of the Communist Party and had its own section of secret police. The
politrouki enjoyed enormous powers. They were, of course, Communist
Party members and had exclusive charge of all political instruction of the
Red soldier, 40 per cent of whose time was devoted to political matters.
But the *politrouki*'s influence went wider than that. They also had
responsibility for military discipline, morale and even bravery (awards
for which had also recently been reintroduced). They watched over
military publications and had a hand in promotions and appointments.
Finally, it was the *politrouki* who drew up the regular reports on the
'situation' in the army, reports which more than once led to sinister
purges. Between 1 January 1934 and 1939 the number of *politrouki*
grew from 15,000 to 34,000.

Hamet's membership of PORKKA is intriguing. Both of Nureyev's
parents were peasants by birth and, difficult as it might be for us to
realise it today, the revolution was very welcome to them and they had
both been members of the Communist Party since the early 1920s. For
them, the revolution was, as Nureyev himself put it in his autobiography,
'a miracle . . . Before . . . they had lived constantly near to starvation.
At last there was a possibility of sending their children to school – even
to the universities, which no peasant could ever dream of doing before
the revolution. They became Communists unquestioningly.'

But there was more to it than that and Nureyev must have known
it. Only 3 per cent of the population were ever paid-up members of
the Party, and the proportion of people who were commissars was
much, much smaller. The fact that Hamet was a commissar shows
either that he had more than a passing interest in politics, or that he
was after the privileges that this position carried with it (such as travel),
or both. People did not become party members unquestioningly – for one
thing, not everyone who wanted to join was accepted. And people did
not become *politrouki* without having some sort of political zeal.

There is no evidence that Hamet was involved in any of the purges,
and one of Nureyev's sisters, Rezida, says that his rank was never very
exalted. But the worst excesses of the Terror were taking place at the
time Rudolf was born, and in the years immediately before, when Hamet
was a commissar. Though Hamet may not have attained high rank in
PORKKA, even as a lowly *politrouk* he may not have been able to keep
his hands clean. Purges in the army were widespread and the commissars chiefly responsible for the damage. On 13 March, 1939, four days
before Rudolf's first birthday, Marshal Kliment Voroshilov, using that
lockjaw syntax so beloved of Marxists, singled out *politrouki*: 'These
elite members of the Communist organisation in the army,' he said, in

a speech to the Eighteenth Party Congress, 'are the active cadres, infinitely devoted to the cause of Lenin and Stalin, and during the past two or three years they have conducted themselves as real militants of the Party . . . These political workers, together with the active mass of the cadres of the Party and the Communist Youth in the Army, are carrying out a vast educational work to raise the political level of our army, but also of all sorts of sceptics, grousers and other riff-raff.' By all accounts, Hamet was strict, authoritarian, content to wear a uniform. In Stalinist Russia, no job of any importance was ever given to anyone who was not a party member, save for certain technical positions which demanded specific qualifications. In other words, the sole point of party membership, aside from political conviction, was the power and privilege that went with it. Hamet loved his family and for their sake saw advantages to being a party member and a commissar.

Hamet was not wrong. Whatever shortcomings the Soviet system might have, he recognised that for a peasant, or ex-peasant like himself, the new state of affairs was not as bad – nowhere near as bad – as the system that had preceded it. That is why he and Farida became Marxists and party members in the early 1920s – before they were out of their teens. The problem was that, by 1938, when his longed-for son was at last given to him, the socialist dream had faded, or was fading fast, and in ways that made the world his son would inhabit a far more unpleasant and dangerous place. Gloomy Russia was growing ever more gloomy as the months passed.

In 1938 the single most important fact of life in Russia, perhaps the *only* important fact of life, was that Iosef Dzhugashvili – Stalin – had been General Secretary, and later First Secretary, of the ruling Communist Party since 1922. The Soviet system was two decades old. It could no longer claim to be experimental. The third of the five-year plans, orginally begun in 1928, was just getting under way. The country was starting to come round, after the devastating ravages of the great famine in 1933, but the terror was still very much in force. The west was beginning to look upon Stalinism, as the successor to Marxism and Leninism, with an ever more jaundiced eye.

Much less was known then about Soviet society than today, and the least well informed were the Russians themselves. But on the eve of war, the picture was far from encouraging. Stalin had consolidated his position and that of the Communist Party to the point where the new 1936 constitution allowed for government by decree. Collectivisation had been forced on the people, and had failed; it was partly responsible for the terrible famine of 1933. Collectivisation, or the attempt at collectivisation, decisively and comprehensively set the classes against each other, and this mutual suspicion laid the groundwork for much of what was to follow, in the purges and the terror.

These terrible events took place against the backdrop of economic failure which had shaped Hamet's decision for his career and his family's future. In July 1937, around the time when Nureyev was conceived, *Pravda* declared, baldly, 'The standard of living of the whole working class in the Soviet Union is at a height unknown in Western Europe and America.' This was nonsense. In real terms, the Russians were anything from three to fifteen times worse off than their counterparts in the west. Almost certainly, Hamet and his compatriots were unable to compare themselves with westerners in any detail (otherwise *Pravda* could not have got away with its statement), but the Russians did know that they were worse off than before. The Stalin government could not hide the fact that, between 1928, when the first five-year plan came into effect, and 1938, wages had risen nearly four times but food prices had risen exactly ten times, more than twice as fast.

There were other indicators, too. Whereas in 1928 the average person had space to himself or herself of 5.9 square metres, by 1937 that had shrunk to 4.3 square metres. This question of square metreage still matters today. Nureyev's sister, Rezida, lives in an apartment which measures 9 square metres. When Nureyev defected, his apartment in Leningrad measured 19 square metres and was regarded as palatial. Russians always know instinctively what a room's measurements are.

Then there were taxes. In theory income tax was a mere 2.5 per cent (and incomes of below 150 roubles a month were exempt). But on top of income tax there were 'cultural dues', trade union dues (2 per cent), International Red Aid (1 per cent), five-year plan subscriptions, 'Physical Culture' and so on. Some of these payments were in theory 'voluntary' but in practice many workers paid 30–35 per cent of their wages in one or other form of tax. Since in 1938 the average worker spent 63 per cent of his or her wages on food, that left precious little for fun, or luxuries.

And that, of course, was the point. With life grim and getting grimmer as every month went by, more and more people were questioning the system, whatever *Pravda* said and however little they knew about conditions in the west.

Or they were complaining in their hearts. Very few dared voice their reservations openly, still less their criticisms. For, in parallel with his accretion of power, and alongside the worsening economic realities of life in Soviet Russia, Stalin had perfected his ways of stifling dissent. First came the purges, swiftly followed by the Terror.

The purges went much further than the armed forces. Everything, from factories to entire villages, fell victim to Stalin's brutal whim. Entire families were exiled because one of their number wore a long beard – this being a sign, according to the commissars, of a secret belief in God (priests in the Russian Orthodox Church wore beards). In industry, purging went even further than expulsion. Sometimes, for those whose faces didn't fit, it meant imprisonment and even, in extreme cases, death by shooting.

Some of these purges were 'reported' in the press. Russia was said to have 10,000 dailies at the time but most of these reports were published in *Izvestiia* or *Pravda*, the official papers, which meant that they were less objective or disinterested accounts than examples – warnings – to others of what could happen to the wayward.

Of course the purges were but one aspect of a wider malaise, a deeper wrong. This was the Terror (and the capital letter is well justified). It is no exaggeration to say that March 1938, the very month Nureyev was born, was the height of the Terror, the darkest hour in Russia's peacetime history in the twentieth century. By 1938 no sphere of human life in the Soviet Union, not even affairs of the heart, were outside the scope of official vigilance. In one well-known case, a woman was compelled to divorce her husband because he had been 'unmasked as the author of anti-Soviet utterances'. Citizens were confined to their home districts and forbidden to travel without obtaining internal visas. People found outside their zone without such a visa were punished severely, and multiple offenders could be shot. A wide zone along all frontiers of the USSR was closed to everyone except specialist visa holders. Stealing small amounts of grain could bring ten years' imprisonment. Using a communal boat for fishing, without permission, could result in death, as could throwing stones at farm animals. The hoarding of money meant death. The punishment for striking in the service of the state was death. The horror of these laws has not diminished as the years have passed.

These savage and arbitrary laws affected everyone. But Stalin's form of 'justice' not only had to be done, but had to be seen to be done. And so, beginning in December 1934, a series of show trials began which resulted in thousands, if not hundreds of thousands, of leading officials being killed, and millions – literally millions – exiled to Siberia. Russian prisoners had been banished to Siberia very soon after its conquest in the first half of the seventeenth century (they were known as *kholodniks*, a word based on *xologho*, meaning cold). The system had been reinforced in 1753 after the death penalty was abolished and hard labour was required to exploit the region's great mineral and agricultural resources. Banishment for political dissidents was possible under the Tsars without any form of judicial process, as it was for 'criminal types', who could be banished as a pre-emptive measure before they actually committed a crime. Stalin certainly developed the exile system to new levels of horror but he was only refining an already much abused concept.

Between December 1934 and March 1938 at least eight much-publicised show trials had taken place and, one way and another, 652 prominent figures were executed, including army officers, leading officials of the Communist Party and even some of the judges who had condemned the accused in earlier show trials. As the Trans-Siberian Express with Farida and the children on board rattled through Ulan-Ude and Chita, the most notorious of all these trials was reaching its conclusion. This was the Trial of the Twenty-One, when Aleksei Rykov, Nikolai Bukharin, Nikolei Krestinsky, K.G. Rakovski and other 'right-wing Trotskyists' were put in the dock. All were executed save for Rakovski, who was given twenty years' imprisonment.

In all, it has been calculated that there were 25 million people missing from the Soviet census of 1939. This figure, which applies to the 1929–39 decade, the period of the first two five-year plans, is made up in the following way. There were, on average, 7 million in the gulags at any one time. But they had an average mortality of 12 per cent which, over ten years, accounts for 8 million deaths, making 15 million in total. On top of that, 10 million were simply killed without first being sent to the gulags. The number of detention centres in what has been called the Gulag Archipelago was shown by Allan Bullock, in his book on Stalin and Hitler, as 202, spread all over Siberia. Nureyev himself said that many of the people he met while he was growing up in Ufa had been sent there as political exiles. There was certainly a gulag between Ufa and Sverdlovsk. Gloomy Russia was at its gloomiest in March 1938.

Farida and Hamet must have been aware of these grim factors at the time their son was born. With such numbers involved, 10 per cent of the population, everyone knew at first hand the denunciations, the purges, the terror, the sudden disappearances in the middle of the night which heralded exile in the camps, or worse. Indeed, since both were party members, and because of Hamet's position in the army, they would have been better informed than most.

According to Nureyev, his parents joined the Party in the early 1920s, before the atrocities started. But both *remained* party members throughout the 1930s – in fact, until they died – and long after the purges and the Terror were known about. By the mid-1930s, some 3 per cent of Russians were in the Party and their chief characteristic was a blind and absolute obedience to all orders from superior bodies. However, membership was not automatic for those who wished to join, nor was it unknown for members to be expelled after they failed to live up to expectations. In 1938 the most thorough purge ever *of the Party itself* took place, in preparation for elections to the Supreme Council. At the end of it, Yegov, the Chief of Police, announced that 240,296 expulsions had taken place during the course of that year. Neither Hamet nor Farida was included.

Nureyev was born into a very oppressive world indeed but his father was surviving, participating – even thriving – in that world. Hamet knew how to conform. He understood the vital importance of conforming in Stalin's awful regime.

*   *   *

Farida and the children stayed in Vladivostok for nearly two years. It was a curious time, a pre-war limbo. The area around Vladivostok was picturesque, they were a long way from the heartland of Russia, Hamet had some money in his pocket, and there were trips for the family to make. At the same time, Khalkin-gole, on the Chinese border, was the very area where the future Marshal Zhukov won a series of bloody clashes against the Japanese Kwantung Army in August 1939. So the atmosphere in the Russian Far East was far more edgy than it had ever been in Ufa.

But at least Hamet and his son had a brief chance to be together. As an infant, Rudolf was a stocky child, 'bonny' as the Scots would say, with a sturdy body, strong thick legs and a good round head. He had two features that, as time went by, would stand out, though they were not especially attractive in the early months. One was his large, fleshy lips, which he had for some time and show in many school photographs. His second feature was his eyes – they were large and dark, always wide open, watching, taking things in. Nothing ever passed Rudolf by. He also had surprisingly fair hair, at least to begin with. But those dark, brooding eyes marked him out as his parents' son.

The Nureyevs were called Nureyev by mistake. Rudolf's grandfather's name was Nuri Fasleev. Normally, the Russians make a patronymic by adding *-ev*, or *-evich*, or *-ovich*, on to the first name of the father. Hamet should therefore have been Hamet Nuriev (or Nureyovich) Fasleev. In 1920, however, the Communists brought in an official system of surnames and somehow a mistake was made, and Nuriev, or Nureev, was adopted. What should have been a patronymic became a surname. Nuri has a distinct meaning in Tartar. It means 'bright' or 'shining', like the rising sun.

In the Soviet Union, in 1938–39, the Second World War was further away than it was in France, Holland or Britain but, even so, there was plenty of movement in the armed forces – the purges had seen to that. Indeed, the purges had created an enormous number of vacancies in top positions, and these were hurriedly filled in a way that would shape the Soviet Union in years to come. For example, Alexei Kosygin, an unknown director of a textile factory at the start of the purges, rose to become Deputy Prime Minister of the Russian republic three years later. Leonid Brezhnev rose in thirty months from being a junior engineer in a metal-working plant to party overlord of an entire province. Yuri Andropov became First Secretary of the Communist Party youth organisation at the age of twenty-six. In the army, Georgy Zhukov, a division commander, became Chief of the Soviet General Staff in three years. In the navy, Admiral N.G. Kuznetsov rose from assistant commander of a cruiser to head of the Red Navy in three years, being summoned from Vladivostok to Moscow in March 1939.

Hamet of course was nowhere near this exalted level but, a year after Kuznetsov, he made the same journey, from Vladivostok to Moscow. In 1940 Hamet was recalled to the central headquarters of PORKKA, and the entire family of six scrambled back on to the Trans-Siberian Express for the fourteen-day journey to the capital. (This was not as inevitable as it sounds: in those days you could take the train one way, then *sail* back from Vladivostok to the Crimea. It was longer but was also a refreshing change.)

Farida and the children left the train at Ufa for a few days, to break the journey, to visit relatives and show Rudolf off, and to give Hamet chance to settle in in Moscow and find accommodation. His recall was partly compassionate. Lilia, his second child had now been found a place in a Moscow school which specialised in her disability. (She had fallen ill in 1937, at the age of four, with inflammation of the lungs. This had led to complications, which made her condition worse.)

In Moscow Hamet found accommodation in the centre of the city, on Horoshevskoye Shossé, a broad boulevard leading out to the suburbs. The family occupied a room on the second floor of a two-storey building, which had a courtyard where the children could play. Behind the house was a railway line and, on the other side of the *shossé*, an artillery school. Rosa went to school, Rezida and Rudolf to kindergarten and Lilia to her special deaf and dumb school. It was never hard for the others to communicate with Lilia, despite her handicap; all the family understood her mimes and gestures and she lip-read skilfully. Farida helped ensure that the others always spoke to her loudly and distinctly and looked at her when they said something. She could hear music on the radio so long as it was played loudly; she was in fact very musical, and loved to hum.

To begin with, life in Moscow was good. Or, rather, it was interesting. The climate was harsher than in Vladivostok but, for a political commissar, Moscow was a far more important place to live. For several months the Nureyevs lived a proper family life. Moscow was much closer to Kazan where Hamet's parents lived, and the grandparents often visited. Rosa, now twelve, had begun classes in gymnastics, moving her body to music. Rezida and Rudolf, home for much of the day, became fascinated by the uniformed men who attended the artillery school opposite the house. The men were friendly and would help smuggle them into a nearby cinema which they in fact were too young to attend. The tiny Nureyevs would hide under the greatcoats of the artillery officers and shuffle unseen into the auditorium. From this Rudolf acquired a passion for movies, especially American musicals, which he would never lose.

Their other entertainment was the radio. One song especially was very popular in Russia in 1940 and 1941. This was 'Luba Lubishka', and Rudolf and Rezida used to jump up and down on their mattresses in time to the beat. It was Rudolf's first recorded movement in time to music.

As 1940 gave way to 1941, no one could disguise the fact that the Germans were getting stronger, apparently winning the war with the powers of Western Europe. Someone as lowly as Hamet would not of course have been privy to the Molotov–Ribbentrop pact, the secret non-aggression treaty signed by Russia and Nazi Germany in August 1939, but that treaty was exploded on 22 June 1941 when, at three o'clock in the morning, Hitler embarked on Operation Barbarossa, the invasion of the Soviet Union. His forces attacked along a line stretching from Murmansk in the north to the Black Sea in the south, a distance of some 1,800 miles, and achieved tactical surprise almost everywhere. In the central prong of the attack three thrusts were made – towards Leningrad, towards Smolensk, and towards Kiev in the Ukraine.

The early capture of the Ukraine in September was the personal decision of Hitler – his High Command would have preferred to drive on straight to Moscow. By the same token Stalin, who was no less distrustful of his professional soldiers than the German dictator was of his, sent Voroshilov and Budenny, old comrades from the First Cavalry Army, to take charge in the south-west. Though they were both by now marshals of the Soviet Union, once on the ground they did not see things Stalin's way. Despite overwhelming advice from his professional soldiers, to the effect that his strategy of trying to hold Kiev was putting no fewer than five Russian armies at risk, Stalin remained obstinate. 'Kiev was, is, and will be Soviet,' he insisted, instructing his commanders to hold Kiev and the Dnieper. The result was that, thanks to his obstinacy, Kiev was lost anyway in the middle of September 1941, and nearly half a million Soviet troops were taken prisoner. It was a huge and unnecessary loss, which led to yet more Soviet citizens being sent into active service, among them Hamet Nureyev. Hamet was now transferred out of PORKKA and into the Red Army proper. Instead of being a *politrouk* in an artillery unit, he was now a fully-fledged Red soldier in the same sort of unit. Family tradition had Hamet starting the war as a lieutenant, though according to Zoya Grigorevna Arkharova, personnel manager at the Kirov (and a KGB agent), who handled Rudolf's documentation later on in life, Hamet was only a 'frontier guard'.

Hamet served on the second Ukrainian front, that is to say, the front east of Kiev, where the Russian and German forces became bogged down after Kiev was lost. The Russian counterattack in the south (in spring 1944) consisted of four Ukrainian fronts. The second, under Marshal Koniev, crossed the Dniester in March and reached the Romanian frontier on the River Prut. A month later they raced on to Bessarabia, Bukhovina and Moldavia.

Whatever his exact role in the fighting, Hamet was sent away and Farida was left on her own again with the children. In 1941 both she and Hamet were aged thirty-six, and no longer young. And no longer entirely out of danger, as they had been in Ufa and Vladivostok. For one consequence of the loss of Ukraine was that Hitler's interest in an attack on Moscow was now rekindled. 'In a few weeks we shall be in Moscow,' he told his entourage. 'I will raze that damned city and in its place construct an artificial lake with central lighting. The name of Moscow will disappear for ever.' For a time it seemed as though he might be right. Operation Typhoon, as the assault on Moscow was called, consisted of three infantry armies and three Panzer armies encircling the Russian forces in a pincer operation. The German troops rapidly overwhelmed the Russian defenders in the early stages so that, by the second week of October, senior figures on both sides believed it was all over and that Moscow was lost. According to Marshal Zhukov, on 7 October 1941 there were no Russian troops *at all* between the German front line and the Soviet capital.

Farida knew better than most what was happening. Nearly all civilian radio sets had been confiscated by the militia at the start of the war and people had to rely for news on the press and the street loudspeakers. But the Kremlin bulletins were highly misleading. Thanks to Hamet's earlier status, however, the Nureyevs' radio was never taken and Farida could listen to other, grimmer, accounts of the war – for example, on the BBC's Russian Service.

Of course, people did not need radios to know that German bombers were over Moscow every night and, by the second week of October, a great panic spread throughout the city. On the fifteenth of the month this was made worse by the start of the evacuation of the Soviet government to Kuibyshev, 600 miles to the east. 'Offices and factories were abandoned,' writes Alan Bullock, in his book comparing Hitler with Stalin, 'the railway stations besieged, the roads to the east jammed with cars filled with Party officials. With no police to protect them, stores were plundered, while on Zhukov's orders demolition squads mined the city's bridges and railway stations.' Looting became widespread and the police disappeared from the streets. Even Stalin, by all accounts, succumbed to the fear in the city but his new commander of the Moscow Military District, Lieutenant-General P.A. Artemev (then only forty-three, another beneficiary of the purges), responded by arresting, and even shooting, a certain number of looters and rumour-mongers. It worked, and the panic passed.

But by then Farida had taken her four children and gone. Their house was too close for comfort to two potential military targets, the railway line and the artillery school. After the first bombardments of Moscow, Farida decided to leave immediately. They had no car so could take no more than they could carry (and at that stage they fully intended to return to Moscow when the situation allowed it). They took the radio but among the possessions they left behind was the gramophone and the recording of 'Luba Lubishka'.

To escape Moscow, they first had to brave the mayhem in Kazanski

Square. This is a long broad esplanade on which are found three of Moscow's more important railway stations, including those for Leningrad and the Trans-Siberian Express. Farida and the children were lucky. Because of her prompt action (brought about by having her own radio), they were able to leave the city before the general panic set in and made travel all but impossible. Once on board the Trans-Siberian, for the third time in as many years, their luck changed. In wartime the express was even less worthy of the name, taking half as long again as in peacetime to cover the distance, an average speed, for an express, of 18–19 miles an hour. All the children were under thirteen and Rudolf was three and a half.

Eventually, after nearly two days in the train, they arrived at a village near Cheliabinsk, where they had relatives. The village was called Tchichuna and it consisted of not more than fifteen or twenty *isbas*. Eight hundred and fifty miles from Moscow, in the eastern foothills of the Ural mountains, Tchichuna was more than a thousand miles from Hamet, at the front. But Farida and the children were, relatively speaking, and for the time being, safe.

They were also incredibly cramped. The house where they lived was a traditional log dwelling. You can see these buildings all over Russia even today, in the countryside and the old sections of towns and cities. They are single storey and crudely built, with the logs laid horizontally, and with either wooden planks or corrugated iron as roofs. The houses are built close by one another, in streets which, in general, have no pavements. Mostly, they have no foundations and many have settled in a haphazard way. They are drab buildings unless, as in some cases, they have been brightly painted. Some have ornately carved eaves, known as Russian lace. Often the ground, inside and out, is bare earth, or covered in simple linoleum. Outside, in winter, this quickly turns to mud and slush. For Farida, there was an additional problem. Their dwelling was shared with three other families and they were billeted (it seems the most accurate word) with a very old couple – which meant that there were seven people all in one room. Nor was space the only problem. The old couple were fervent Christians, despite the ban on religion in the Soviet Union. They worshipped every day and believed that all others should do likewise, especially young children. As the youngest child of all in the household, Rudolf was their favourite and also, as they saw it, the person most at risk in a godless world. Accordingly, they offered him cheese if he would say the Christian prayers. This greatly distressed Farida who, though technically a Marxist-atheist, could not shake off her Muslim background entirely. But Rudolf didn't care. He was so hungry he agreed. In later life he had just one other memory of Tchichuna – of being on a green lake in a boat and shouting with fear, though he didn't recall why.

The German assault on Moscow finally took place towards the end of

October 1941, when winter was fast approaching. The rain, mud, ice and snow were a major feature of the battle (as they had been when Napoleon had tried much the same thing 150 years earlier). The Germans felt the weather especially badly because, expecting Barbarossa to be over quickly, they were equipped only with summer kit. The final push began on 15 November but the Russians resisted desperately so that, by the end of the year, a front had been stabilised deep inside Russia, next to Leningrad in the north, about a hundred miles from Moscow in the centre, and along the River Don in the south. Temperatures sometimes dropped to minus 30 degrees centigrade. In the occupied territories the German forces could be very brutal.

Though the fighting was a thousand miles away, conditions were little better in Cheliabinsk. Food was very scarce, meat and fruit non-existent and potatoes which were not eaten straight away had to be buried under the living-room floor to protect them from frost. But not even that was the worst of it. The primitive sanitation system froze for days or weeks on end. The everyday business of living was a severe strain in Tchichuna in the winter of 1941–42.

Hamet, in Marshal Koniev's forces, was stationed near the Dnieper river, between Poltava and Cerkassy, where massive artillery and tank formations were to be assembled. But the family were ever in his mind and, in the spring of 1942, he managed to ease their situation a little: he found them a new place to live. Fortunately, this new move did not involve a long journey, which Farida had come to dread; just 300 miles back down the now-familiar Trans-Siberian to Ufa, where Hamet's brother had a flat going begging. It was only one room, but Farida and the children wouldn't have to share with strangers and there were more relatives in the area than there were in Tchichuna – Ufa had always been regarded as home by Hamet. It was by now clear that the war might drag on for years, Hamet might be separated from Farida indefinitely and, now that they had learned that their house in Moscow had been bombed, an early return to the capital was unlikely. For a Tartar family, Ufa – capital of the Bashkir Republic – was as good as anywhere. It would be a stable background for Rudolf who, Hamet hoped, would grow up to be a doctor or an engineer.

CHAPTER TWO

Virgin Fire

nothing could alter or could tire
this soul that glowed with virgin fire.

The new room was in a house on the corner of Sverdlova and Zentsova
Streets, in the old part of Ufa, and a few streets to the north and west
of the centre. It was a poor area, consisting mainly of log-built houses,
with no pavements and with the streets themselves often unmade. The
Tartars in Ufa were grouped in a small area of about half a dozen streets –
Zentsova, Sverdlova, Aksakava, Kommunisticheskaya and Artchiereke.
The streets were narrow, laid out on a grid pattern, off the beaten track,
but not unpleasant. There were plenty of rowan and birch trees and
the area was on a small hill, which occasionally afforded glimpses of
the Belaya river, off to the north, and the railway station, an imposing
white marble building designed to impress visitors. The 1939 census
had shown that there were about 4 million Tartars in the Soviet Union,
or around 1.6 per cent of the population, but Ufa comprised 19 per cent
Bashkirs, 4 per cent Tartars and the rest Russians. Tartars were a small
minority, but especially visible in the city.

Paradoxically, the Nureyevs' first room in Ufa was not in one of the
traditional log dwellings or *isbas* but in a barracks-type building, several
floors up. There was a table in the middle with the beds built into the
walls. But at least they were sharing with family – that of Hamet's
younger brother.

Generally speaking, wartime conditions in Ufa were safer than points
further west but that is about all that could be said for the city. Its
population was swelled twice over, by evacuees (like the Nureyevs)
but also by the wounded. Several military hospitals were set up in
wartime Ufa, mainly in schools. Apart from the evacuees and the
wounded, the dominant aspect of everyday life was rationing – the only

food not rationed was potatoes and even they were sometimes in short supply. According to Rezida, there was no meat in the shops. 'There was sometimes meat in the *stolovaya* [the market]. You were given rations from the *voenkomst* [the military store, where the families of serving officers were allowed to shop]. In the *stolovaya*, you could maybe get a piece of *kolbasa* [a type of salami] but that was it. There was a nasty black flour, called *rosh*.' Survival often depended on sheer hard work, imagination – and luck. For example, Takhir Valievich Boltacheev, a rehearser at the Kirov who met Nureyev later at the Maryinsky Theatre in Leningrad, was evacuated to Perm during the war, along with the rest of the ballet company and school. He found he could not live on what was available in the Perm shops for a wage such as his, so was forced (but also lucky) to get a second job, unloading coal and salt from the trains in his spare time. He was paid not in money but in salt, a glass of salt per shift which, fortunately for him, was valuable enough to exchange for food.

Farida was badly affected by the advent of war and the straitened circumstances that followed. Before the war, Hamet had been well enough paid and could look forward to the future with confidence. But now he was just a regular soldier, or rather a conscript, albeit an officer. His pay had dropped significantly, there were four children to feed, and the future was uncertain, to say the least. Farida began to lose her looks and her face took on a 'troubled' expression, which it never lost.

This may have been a natural reversion for her. She had been orphaned when she was seven, her father and mother dying in fairly quick succession (but of natural causes) in 1912. She was then brought up in her elder brother's family, where she worked as a nanny. As a result, she never went to school. She did teach herself how to read and write Arabic – as a Tartar, that was her first language – but she wrote very bad Russian. 'Indeed,' says Rezida, 'you could go so far as to say that she didn't write Russian at all.' Unable to read the local newspapers, ordinary shop or road signs, or the notices for what was playing at the cinema, Farida missed the comforting presence of her husband. As her children grew up, and became more and more at home with Russian, Farida was in the minority even in her own family.

Daily life revolved around the 'Russian stove', which was in the 'kitchen' – more of a corridor really – off the main room and which was shared with other families in the building. Hot water was always on the go here, for tea. General fare consisted of soup, meat in the good times, and noodles. Until the war there had been fruit but from 1941 to 1945 there was none. Curiously, in wartime and immediately afterwards, the Russian markets were *more* expensive than the shops. This was because the produce was fresher and arrived via a more localised distribution network. The choice, therefore was often between staler, cheaper food in the shops, with little queueing, and fresher, more expensive foods, including meat, in the markets where there were often long queues. In wartime, families received a ration of 400 grams of bread per day and an allowance of powdered egg, made in America.

At public holidays the local delicacies were prepared, Farida's favourites being cabbage or carrot pies. She was also known for her excellent bread rolls. She had learned to cook when she had been brought up in her brother's family, and in 1921 she had baked biscuits and buns good enough to sell. Other favourites included *pilmeni*, Russian ravioli but with thicker pasta than in the west, and usually eaten with *smetana*, sour cream, topped with a cold tomato sauce.

Rationing highlighted the Nureyevs' problems but it was not the only difficulty. Rezida recalls that, like the others, she had one change of clothing only, a dress and a skirt and blouse, which had to be washed in strict rotation, so that she always had something clean to wear. 'There was,' as she tactfully put it, 'a lack of splendour.'

Everyone had their hair cut extremely short. Rudolf and Rezida were fairer than the others in their family, and rather proud of the fact, so much so that they wanted to wear their hair long, to show off their colouring. But Farida would not hear of it. Everyone in wartime Russia had a military haircut – it was almost an act of patriotism. Rudolf was allowed to keep a single lock of his hair at the front of his head but as for the rest – he and Rezida were shorn like everyone else.

While they were young children, Farida tried to get Rosa, Rudolf and the rest to speak Tartar – in fact, she nagged at them. But the younger ones, Rezida and Rudolf especially, resisted, preferring the Russian which was spoken at school and by most other people. Rezida, who spoke some Tartar, was also embarrassed by her accent: another reason to prefer Russian. This appears to have been the main sign of tension within the family, though in theory there might have been much more. After all, Hamet and Farida were communists and party doctrine stipulated equality of the sexes. At the same time, the Nureyevs were Muslims, and Islam has rather different ideas on that score. The Nureyevs were not a devout family – that would *not* have gone down well in the Party – but they did observe the holy festivals of Islam and, most importantly, followed all the Islamic cultural traditions. This meant that although Rudolf was the only male in the family until his father came back from the front in 1946, he never had to work hard at household chores. His mother and his sisters always did everything.

Rezida, who had a much harder time of it as a child, remembers that childhood more fondly than Rudolf did. Those early years, she says, were hard but fun. 'We didn't have any terms of endearment for each other within the family. Mother was always troubled, and those romantic nicknames you read in novels were never heard in our family. We quite simply called Rudolf "Rudik". There was no place in our family for whims or fancies. We had the usual bouts of flu and I remember that both Rudik and I went down with mumps – but I don't remember whether I caught it from him or whether he caught it from me. Mother used to say that it was never peaceful when the two of us were together. We would dare each other and make bets.'

Nureyev's own recollection of these years was somewhat bleaker. 'We shared a room of nine square metres with my uncle and another family. I can't find words to describe the psychic upheaval that set up in me: three families in a single room, of nine square metres. Yet I can remember no disastrous scenes. We must have achieved a miracle in sharing that nightmarish existence without getting to the point where we couldn't bear the sight of each other.' He seems to have been more affected than his sisters by the lack of food and by the great length of the winters in that part of the world. And just as Rezida recalled Farida as always being 'troubled', so Rudik remembered her as sad. 'I don't remember a single occasion when she laughed out loud.'

The low point was reached in 1944, when Hamet had been gone for nearly three years and when he was most at risk, during the Red Army's thrust towards Romania. Two episodes underline how far the family had sunk. In the first place, they had to sell some of Hamet's civilian clothing, to pay for food. The children did their best to make light of it. As they crawled into bed at night, after dinner, they would joke that 'Daddy's belt tasted quite sweet, don't you think?' What it did for their father's standing in the eyes of the younger children is macabre to contemplate. Who was this man who was so unimportant that his clothes could be sold off? The second episode, remembered vividly by all the children, concerned the time when food was so short that Farida was forced to visit relatives to obtain potatoes. According to Rezida, the relatives lived at Osanova, a village about forty kilometres away. It was winter and she was walking as there was no form of transport available to her. She had her toboggan with her as well as some tea and sweets and she took with her a quilt with which she would wrap up the potatoes that were the object of the journey. Normally, she would have taken Rosa with her but since this trip was so long – a day's hike in either direction, involving an overnight stay with the relatives – the eldest daughter was left in charge of the others.

Just before she reached Osanova, Farida found herself pursued – and very nearly surrounded – by a pack of wolves. It was winter so it never really got light that day and their yellow eyes were unmistakable in the early evening gloom. At that time there were many stories about wolves being so starved in the forests that they were forced to raid villages. These were no doubt partly true and partly exaggeration but that was precious little comfort to Farida and she was terrified. Nonetheless, she showed admirable presence of mind – setting fire to the quilt and brandishing it at the wolves. This seems to have done the trick and the creatures slunk away.

As Rudolf told this story later, in his autobiography, he made it appear as if his mother was begging the potatoes from their relatives, as if even among the family the Nureyevs were the poorest of the poor. Rezida remembers it rather differently. Farida was the wife of an army officer and therefore had the right to shop at the army stores. As a result, she had access to certain things that their relatives didn't – for example sweets. According to Rezida, Farida was actually visiting the relatives to *exchange* some goods from the army stores, for potatoes. She says it was quite a common practice in wartime for army families in the towns and cities to go out into the countryside to trade goods. It was a way of breaking out of the rationing system. The relatives were Hamet's sister's family. It was an exchange among equals, rather than begging on Farida's part.

Nureyev believed that growing up during wartime, when nearly every family was mourning a son, a brother or a husband, and when hunger and starvation were paramount, had permanent effects on him, one effect being that imaginative literature was never able to sway him. 'Words tend to seem dead things; meaningless signs with little to say to me, no more exciting than our daily drama. Whereas music . . .' This was a dramatic and romantic theory but there may have been a simpler explanation. His mother couldn't read Russian, and they had left Moscow with only the few things that they could carry. The Nureyev household was hardly one in which books were common or plentiful. And at the same time, he came from a musical family. Hamet always liked to listen to Farida sing; in Ufa, Rosa went to music school and later continued her music studies at the School of Arts, Rezida liked dancing and always wanted to play the piano and even Lilia liked to hum. The only form of entertainment they had at home, apart from a few toys and chess and draughts, was the radio.

There was another thing too, which may help explain his choice of career. There was no religion in the Nureyev household, just as there was no religion in most households under the Soviet system. A major outlet for emotional, passionate, involvement was therefore blocked. It is no surprise that music meant so much to all the Nureyevs, not just to Rudolf.

While they had lived in Moscow, Rudolf and Rezida had been sent to kindergarten together. (In their early years, Rudolf had been closest to Rezida, because of their ages. Later, he became closer to Rosa who shared his interests in music, and indeed fostered his tastes.) In Ufa, he was again sent to kindergarten which, fortunately, was also located on Sverdlova Street, just opposite the apartment. It was a simple log building and was known as a Bashkiri kindergarten, where many of the pupils were Tartars. With the children off her hands, Farida was free to go to work for at least some of the day. At first she worked in a bread factory, as an unskilled worker (though she was, as we have seen, an accomplished baker). Later she transferred to a mining factory, a small place not far from where they lived where the work was seasonal and Farida was taken on only during the summer. Her earnings were low but better than nothing. She still had time to be with the family.

There are mixed reports of the Ufa kindergarten. According to Albert Xatkulovich Arslanov, one of Rudik's earliest friends, who met him at kindergarten in 1943 and remained friendly until they were both adults, Kindergarten Number One, as it was called, was a good school. It began between eight and nine in the morning, when the pupils were dropped off by their parents, and the children remained there all day, not just for the mornings as is common with kindergartens in other countries. Some of the tuition was in Russian, some in Tartar but that was mainly for appearance's sake. Although Kindergarten One was a Bashkiri school, according to Arslanov, everyone lapsed into Russian at break time. There was some formal tuition in reading and writing but, as with most kindergartens, the majority of 'lessons' consisted of instructive games and sports. Even Rezida played football.

The school happened to be exceptionally good musically. Every summer a camp was run by the school librarian, and it was here that Nureyev first danced. According to Rezida there was a pianist called Tuturoza who taught in the school and it was she who first noticed Nureyev's, and Arslanov's, aptitude for dance. They were included in the school dance group and given their own costumes. The troupe would dance Tartar, Bashkiri and Russian folk dances, wearing bright traditional costumes, produced by a nearby sewing factory. The Tartar costume consisted of a pointed hat, and a large smock which was light in colour. A sash hung over the smock and underneath, large puffed-out baggy trousers were worn. Though the children were very young, they were a colourful band and quickly became known in drab, wartime Ufa. They were twice photographed for a cinema magazine, at performances when the whole kindergarten turned out to watch. Nureyev and Arslanov quickly became the 'stars' of this little troupe.

Since it was still wartime, and because there were many hospitals in Ufa, Nureyev and Arslanov often performed in front of wounded soldiers. Sometimes there were as few as five or six soldiers, who couldn't even get out of bed – they had legs missing, or other serious injuries. 'We didn't just dance,' says Arslanov. 'We would sing and read them poetry.'

The troupe's fame seems to have spread quickly. After the cinema magazine, they were filmed for a 'trailer film' (a short film to be shown before the main feature), and were able to go and see themselves at the Octyabr cinema opposite the Ufa Opera and Ballet Theatre. This was a large cinema and the episode must have been a huge boost for the young dancers' self-confidence.

The extraordinary thing about these recollections of Arslanov is how at variance they are with Rudolf's own memories. In his autobiography he says that he remembers his first day at kindergarten vividly but it appears to have been a totally different place. For a start, he said that he had no suitable clothes: the family was so poor just then that his mother had to carry him to school on her back, because he had no shoes to wear. Worse, he had to borrow Lilia's cape, complete with 'wings'.

Turning up for his first day with no shoes and in his sister's clothes was humiliation enough, but more was to follow, for the children began to make fun of him and sing about him in Tartar. 'We've got a bump in our class,' they chanted, 'we've got a bump in our class.' Rudolf's grasp of Tartar was less than perfect but you didn't need to be a genius to catch the gist of what they were saying. When he got home after his first day at kindergarten, he asked his mother for a precise explanation. Embarrassed on his behalf, he said, she explained that the word 'bump' was slang for 'beggar'. Rudolf says he didn't feel this humiliation as keenly as that of being dressed in his sister's clothes, but it cannot have made his transition to kindergarten easy.

This does not seem the sort of story anyone would make up about themselves, but it is extraordinary that Arslanov does not recall it – an episode that would surely have lodged in anyone's memory. Rezida flatly contradicts the claim that Rudik was ever dressed in his sisters' clothing, even as hand-me-downs, or that he went to school without shoes. Since the kindergarten was almost exactly opposite the house in any case, there wasn't far to walk to school.

What *did* happen, however – and this is an episode that Nureyev himself seems to have forgotten – was that the other children started calling him 'Adolf'. This was due to the similarity of his name, but also to his temper, which was already clear, and which was likened by his schoolfriends to the rantings of the Führer. Nureyev hated this nickname and it is not surprising he should have found it distressing. The Nazis were occupying a large part of Russia, brutally mistreating women and children. And, with the Second World War being called, in Russia, the Great Patriotic War, 'Adolf' carried overtones of treason.

After his first day, Nureyev's main impression of kindergarten was how much 'richer' everyone was than he. It was on the first day, he says, that he first became aware of class differences. This seems a misuse of the term, certainly in comparison with the west. But Nureyev meant that even in provincial Ufa he met children who were much better off, better dressed 'and above all better fed'. He put it down to the fact that they had never suffered the indignities of evacuation, but that wasn't the whole picture. If these children's fathers were working in industries vital to the war effort they would have been at home with their families *and* earning much the same as before the war. There is no getting away from the fact that Rudolf's father had a better job before the war than he did during it. The Nureyevs were not just poorer than other families they came into contact with in Ufa but they had come down in the world. This fact helped condition Nureyev's feelings about his father.

By his own account, at this stage of his life, between the ages of five and seven, Rudolf was obsessed with food, or rather the lack of it. Arslanov makes no mention of it, nor Rezida, but for Rudolf it was all-important. Indeed as time went by the issue came to symbolise for him the difference between the classes. They had breakfast at kindergarten (as well as lunch) and he noticed that many of the 'richer' children never ate all their food, because they were well enough fed at home. He, on the other hand, would by his own account always arrive at school late. When his teacher enquired why, he always gave the same answer: he had to have breakfast first. When she replied that he was supposed to eat breakfast at kindergarten, there was, as he put it, a breakdown in communication. He was ashamed to admit that he needed *two* breakfasts, that he simply couldn't let that chance pass him by. He even claimed that in his second year at kindergarten he fainted from hunger. There had been no food at home the night before and Farida had gone off in search of potatoes again. In her absence, Rosa had put the younger children to bed early, before dinner time and without eating. Next day he had felt dizzy and fainted in class.

No one else remembers this incident and what Arslanov says tends to contradict it. He says that during their years together at kindergarten Rudolf and he were known as 'Eat' and 'Look', because on most occasions when it came time to eat, in their homes, their families had to go looking for them. Rezida also confirms that on non-school days she would sometimes eat lunch at a friend's, or the friend would eat with the Nureyevs. In other words, their childhood in this regard was not at all as traumatic as Rudolf pretended.

In 1945, at the age of seven, Rudolf and Arslanov transferred from kindergarten to proper school. Soviet schools didn't have names the way western schools do, based on some famous alumnus or local figure, or on their location. They simply had numbers. Rudolf's was School Number Two, on Sverdlova Street near the end of a tram line. The school no longer exists – ironically, it was knocked down to make way for Ufa Ballet's choreographical school.

Rudolf makes little mention of this school in his autobiography, so the school cannot have been so bad by Soviet standards. Standards were not high. In those days equipment, even equipment as basic as exercise books, was in notoriously short supply. Soviet schools were different from western schools in much the same way that the Red Army was different from western Armies – in terms of politics. Politics had been a feature of school life – even primary school life – since 1934 at least.

In February of that year all headmasters had been 'enjoined' to include the decisions of the party congresses and the reports of Stalin to those congresses in their school curricula. The instruction was sanctimonious in the extreme:

'The party, and political-ideological organisational questions, will form the centre of study in all classes on the basis of the masterly report of Comrade Stalin. . . . In the infant classes the master will proceed by means of commenting on extracts which he will insert in his lesson. . . . Masters who teach physics, chemistry, biology and mathematics will always find matter for their educational work in the decisions of the Congress.'

There was a history, too, of the authorities simply co-opting pupils as apprentices in industry whether they liked it or not. A million had been earmarked in 1940, just before war broke out, and during wartime a further 9 million were co-opted. This was gradually discontinued after the war ended but even in 1947, when Rudolf was nine, more than a million secondary school children were 'chosen' for the apprentice scheme and had no say in their careers. Rudolf, fortunately, was too young to be affected.

Like everywhere else, the Ufa schools were attended in shifts. The school day was split into three and, in general, the young children attended in the mornings, the nine to thirteen-year-olds in the afternoons, and the older pupils in the evening, not finishing until around seven. For Rudolf, this didn't happen straight away, even though schools in Ufa were particularly overcrowded, due to the large number of makeshift hospitals in the area that were housed in schools. School Number Two was very full, so full that Nureyev and Arslanov were among a batch of pupils transferred out of it for a while to School Number Sixty-Four, at Aktsatva Street (this school does still exist). This school had been modernised. The original building was a long, single-storey log-built construction, in much the same style as the houses in the area. But it also had a second storey built out of brick. Arslanov remembers his time at School Sixty-Four as hard but happy: 'We got a good education.' But there was no dancing. 'At that time we didn't dance as regularly as we did at kindergarten.'

This was now late in 1945. At the end of that year an event occurred which was to shape Nureyev's life permanently. He was seven, nearly eight and the incident can be pinpointed accurately – it took place on 31 December 1945, New Year's Eve. In Nureyev's words, 'it was love at first sight but only through housebreaking'. Somehow, as a holiday treat, Farida had managed to obtain a ticket – just one – to a special gala performance at the Ufa Ballet that night. Despite its otherwise provincial character, Ufa was home to a very good ballet company. It was Soviet policy for every republic to have one, and sometimes two, ballet companies. At one time, there were no fewer than thirty-three in the USSR, and it was the same with philharmonic orchestras and with dramatic theatres. In 1945 the strength of the Ufa company was reinforced by refugee dancers evacuated from the Bolshoi in Moscow and the Kirov in Leningrad.

Although she only had one ticket, Farida took three of her children (Rezida says she didn't go). Why Farida should take the others is difficult to fathom, unless she knew Ufa and had an idea of what might happen. After years of war, a gala performance in Ufa before the days of television was a major event and the performance was a sell-out. A huge crowd gathered in front of the theatre, some people no doubt hoping for black-market tickets, some hoping to sneak in, some hoping for a glimpse of the stars, others just hangers-on. There had been four years of rationing, four years of greyness, four years without relief from the misery brought on by the killing and absences of wartime. People were desperate for a little respite, an escape, a change – however brief – from the drudgery of everyday living. As Nureyev himself described those years, 'The Russians' boundless spiritual resources, the profundity of their inner life – the sheer capacity that they have to cut themselves away from the sordidness of their daily struggles is for me perhaps the strongest explanation of the enormous success which almost any manifestation of art can command in the Soviet Union.'

Farida and the children were not the last to arrive that night. As they stood in front of the theatre more people milled around behind them, pushing them forward, towards the doors. Perhaps Farida had hoped to find more tickets to buy but soon she was unable to move, the crush was too strong. More and more people joined the crowd and conditions deteriorated. The children, who could not see what was happening, were alarmed. As the crush increased, Farida and the others were pressed closer and closer to the doors of the theatre. Now Farida grew anxious. She only had one ticket. If they were turned away, how would they escape the crowds? And who should go in? Rudolf and Lilia were too young to go anywhere by themselves. But Farida could not abandon them. It was a dilemma.

Suddenly, when Farida was in sight of the doorman checking the tickets, the crowd behind her surged forward – and the doors collapsed under the pressure. The doorman himself ran ahead of the crush and those at the front of the crowd were swept through the doors and into the theatre. Inside, there was chaos. The foyer and corridors were soon filled with people milling in all directions. Everyone, that night, wanted to celebrate the New Year, the first year of peace, in style.

Farida didn't hesitate. With so many people everywhere, she gripped Rudolf's and Lilia's wrists and led them forward, with Rosa bringing up the rear. They found the auditorium and sat in the first seats they came to. With such a crush who could tell if the real ticket holders would get anywhere near their seats?

It was the first time Rudolf had ever been in a proper theatre. The rows of blue velvet seats, the gold and white stucco on the walls, the sparkling chandelier hanging from the ceiling were all new to him, as were the sounds of the orchestra tuning up, which floated from the pit. He looked around at the boxes and the tiers of seats above him, at the little lanterns that lit the deeper recesses of the auditorium. He gazed, enthralled, at the mass of people jamming the seats and, that night, filling the aisles. The buzz of anticipation communicated itself immediately to him. And above all there was the blue curtain, surrounded by a gold-painted proscenium arch, concealing . . . what? It was very different from the shabby *isbars* on Zentsova Street.

For that New Year's Eve performance, people sat everywhere. Few were in the seats they had bought tickets for and many ticket-holders never got in at all. Once the crowd was in place, nothing would budge it.

Eventually, about half an hour late, the lights went down, the audience hushed and the conductor appeared. And then the music began and the blue velvet curtain rose. The ballet being performed that night was *The Song of the Cranes*, a Bashkir story about good and evil in which a shepherd, representing innocence, defeats the plottings of a cruel, cunning rich man to possess the girl. It was a fairly new ballet, created during the war with music by Lev Stepanov and Z. Izmagilov and with choreography by Nina Anisimova. It was also the first specifically Bashkiri ballet.

The young girl was danced that night by Zaituna Nazretdinova, a small, dark, very beautiful local ballerina with flashing eyes and sinuous arms. As the music swirled around the auditorium, as the fortunes of the young girl rose and fell, only to rise again, as the dancers twirled and twisted in time to the cadence of the instruments, as the leading ballerinas unfurled their arms and the men leapt the height of a young boy off the stage, the seven-year-old Rudolf Nureyev sat stock still, enthralled. Here was a new world, a magic place far from Ufa, far from poverty, far from the cold. But, in its way, it was just as real. Here was a place of passion, of elegance, of joy. It was a painted place but it held a deeper truth, too. In the theatre, people – actors and audience – were *moved*. 'From the moment I entered that magic place,' he said later in his autobiography, 'I felt I had really left the world, borne far away from everything I knew by the dream staged for me alone . . . I was speechless.'

Nazretdinova took several curtain calls that night. In Ufa, in winter, in wartime, real flowers were a rare commodity. But paper flowers, lovingly cut and crafted, floated down from the gallery and began to cover the stage. This enchanted Nureyev almost as much as the dancing and the music.

The final curtain came down. The little lanterns were turned up and Nureyev, along with everyone else, went out into the cold December night, that would soon be a January morning. For once, he forgot all about food.

After that night there was no going back. From then on, he always said he felt 'called' to dance.

But he was still only seven. He now knew he wanted to dance above all else but he didn't know how to become a classical ballet dancer – indeed, it is doubtful that, at that stage, he fully understood what classical dancing was.

This was a frustrating time, for at School Sixty-Four there was little dancing. Fortunately, that year there was a reorganisation in the schools at Ufa, brought about by the fact that the war was over and more and more wounded soldiers could go home. As a result, Nureyev and Arslanov moved back to School Two, which now became an all-boys' school, and Rezida was moved from School Two to School Forty-Five. Rudolf and Rezida now began to grow less close; instead Rudolf warmed towards Rosa. She was already at a special music school and talked to him constantly about the history of music, even allowing him to accompany her to lectures. These introduced him to the world of music, and dance, outside Ufa.

In School Two, Nureyev and Arslanov picked up where they had left off. There was a new teacher there, called Asabakova, who taught them sailors' dances, and she spotted Nureyev's quick talent. Arslanov remembered: 'We used to put on performances. For example, we danced at the railway workers' club. It was near the railway station and had its own stage.' There are many of these clubs in Russia. A large profession or trade union has a club in each big town or city and on public holidays there would be a little performance, put on by children. The audience here would have been composed of railway workers and their children.

The Soviet Union may well have had thirty-three ballet companies in those days, and dance may well have formed an important part of the Russian psyche, as Nureyev said, but that did not mean that all Russians were passionate balletomanes. Another schoolfriend from those years, Marat Saidashev, recalls that,

'Rudik was somehow different from the rest of us – like a white crow. But he was not popular . . . he could never have become our [gang's] leader. Other boys were always playing tricks on him, to bring him down to size. And although he was athletic, he was athletic in a different way. Near Number Two school was a ski jump on the banks of the Agidel river. We already had a number of well-known acrobats in school because our sports master, Dmitri

Dmitrovich, was always pushing us, so that there was a big cult of sports in the school. So much so that none of the boys would avoid the ski jump – we could all do it. Except Rudik. As we all went off to the ski jump, with Dim Dmitri as we called him, Rudik would stay behind, doing his pirouettes. How he endured our slights!'

Fortunately, at least to begin with, Nureyev was a bright pupil. Taisiya Mikhailovna Halturika-Ilchinova, his teacher for almost five years, remembers him as small for his age, not given to hooliganism unless provoked and then, although he was small, he gave as good as he got. In fact, she says, in the early years he was noted for his obedience and if he didn't get the best grades it wasn't because he wasn't able. She often noticed that, sitting in class, Rudolf would be immersed in his own world. The other boys were envious, and would pick on him and shove him around. 'He was already someone special.' Among non-dance subjects, he particularly loved English, and this was a love driven by another teacher, Elena Kuzminichna Troshina. She had grown up in Shanghai and studied in Cambridge and London. Elena Kuzminichna spoke of all these places in English, so that Rudolf came to identify the language with exotic travel and interesting places abroad.

Already, then, by the age of seven or eight Nureyev was emerging as a special child, certainly in comparison with other pupils in Ufa, or School Number Two. He was 'difficult', in that he knew his own mind and refused to participate in the normal games activities. And he was seen as giving himself airs and graces, in preferring dance to escapades and in dreaming about far-off places, rather than being satisfied with Ufa. He commanded a degree of respect, however, just because he knew his own mind, and because he was athletic enough to defend himself if bullied.

Despite his friendship with Arslanov, and their shared love of dance, Nureyev also described himself, not simply as different but as solitary. In his autobiography he says that he spent all his free time in one of two ways. He would sit by the radio and soak up all the music on offer (praying that someone important would die, because then the normal programmes would be replaced by a daylong diet of Tchaikovsky or Beethoven). Or, he would climb up a small hill near his home, to what he called his private observation point. This was a hillock which looked north and east and provided a good vantage point from where he could look out across the river, the very river where the other boys were ski-jumping, towards the railway station. He loved to watch the trains coming and going (he retained a fascination with trains all his life), and the people of Ufa going about their everyday business. His favourite time of all was Saturday because on that day he could see the men, who would be at work the rest of the week, walking to the steam baths in their bathrobes or pyjamas. Some even carried the traditional Russian bundle of birch twigs, with which to beat themselves. These baths are still widespread in Russia. In a country where few people had hot running water, the steam baths were crucial. Once a week, people would spend up to two hours in the *banias* (they would even take their lunch). They would spend a quarter of an hour in a sauna, followed by a plunge into icy flowing water. This contrast may be heightened by a light beating with birch twigs, which bring the blood to the surface of the skin, causing the bather to feel the heat more, and thus sweat out more of the body's impurities. The process would be repeated several times over a couple of hours. The experience is exhausting and invigorating at the same time, a purgative that would become a feature of Nureyev's own life later on.

The memory of those Saturdays, when Nureyev sat on the hill and watched the trains steam in and out of Ufa, would stay with him all his life. They were the roots of the dream which would eventually lead him far beyond his home town. But there was another element, too, a darker factor. Nureyev was free to dream because his life was, to an extent, and so far as Farida was concerned, on hold.

It cannot be overlooked that, during the war, he was the only male in the household, a spoiled younger brother whose sisters doted on him and shared among themselves the drudgery of everyday life. Rudolf was no less special at home than he was at school. Farida gave her son free rein partly because he was the only boy and partly because she assumed that when Hamet came back from the war he would take his precious son under his wing. There was much anticipation of this great event in the Nureyev household among the older children who remembered him, but in 1946 the waiting came to an end. Hamet arrived home.

At least, Nureyev and Rezida say that he did. In the Red Army there were three general mobilisations, in 1947, 1949 and 1951, so they may have got the year wrong. Or perhaps, as a major and a former *politrouk*, Hamet was given another privilege (though Rezida says he was demobilised). After serving on the second Ukrainian front, he had been moved north, at first to Schetzen in Poland. He had not been part of the attack on Berlin that ended the war in Europe but he moved into the city not long afterwards. So although he had escaped the worst of the fighting, he had seen some of the most ravaged areas of the war zone and returned to Ufa a changed and chastened man.

If Hamet had changed, so had his family in the five years he had been away. For a start they had moved house yet again – twice. Not very far, it is true, from 60 Sverdlova Street, to 37 Sverdlova Street, and then to 40 Zentsova Street, which was between Sverdlova and Stalin Street, subsequently renamed Communist Street. The family occupied the third house from the corner. It was a one-storey *isba*, the logs 'greyish-brown' according to Rezida, but their room (they were still in one room) was bigger now, fourteen square metres as opposed to nine. And they had windows on two walls, a great luxury, and a yard, separate from the house, where the lavatory was located. At last they had something to themselves.

Hamet's return was a severe shock for the younger children, an uncomfortable rupture in their familiar, closed world. Nureyev had simply forgotten he had a father, since he had left for the war when the boy could barely speak. But Hamet was even a stranger to the other children, to such an extent that they referred to him, in Russian, as *vy* (the equivalent of *vous* in French) rather than *ty* (*tu* in French). This lasted for about six months and Hamet understandably became very cross, the more so as Rezida and Rudolf, with rudimentary Tartar, could not properly pronounce the word in that language for 'father'. They had mastered 'mother', *Enkyai*, but simply found *Etkyei*, father, too much. After six months it had become second nature to refer to Hamet as *ty* but *Etkyei* would not come. Hamet never got used to this and it always angered him.

Then there was the question of their tempers. Who knows if there is such a thing as a Tartar temperament but in the Nureyev family there were three very hot tempers indeed – Hamet's, Rezida's, and Rudolf's. Each was quick to be aroused, and as quickly calmed. But Rudolf's temper was the strongest of all. It was, as Rezida remembers, 'a nightmare'. 'If, for example, we were playing draughts, then everything would be fine until he started to lose. He didn't like to lose but I liked to win. At the time I didn't understand that I had to make concessions, that I had to compromise. He was better at chess but I didn't play. We didn't have any other games. We usually played in the mornings because we were on the second shift at school.'

There were other reasons for Rudolf's cool reaction to Hamet's return. He now recalled that this was the man whose clothes they had sold to buy food, a man who obviously could not feed his own family. This was the man who, in marked contrast to the fathers of many of Rudolf's fellow pupils, had not been able to maintain his income during the war, allowing the family to slide down the social scale into poverty. So far as Rudolf was concerned, Hamet was responsible for Farida's 'troubled' condition. Then there was the simple fact that, until Hamet's return, Rudolf was the only male in the household, the sole recipient of his mother's, and his sisters', favours. All that changed overnight. On many occasions, he now came second. As a result, far from being a role model for Rudolf, Hamet had to prove himself. Relations were very tense.

In fairness to Hamet, his return to Ufa cannot have been easy. He was a taciturn man, a man who, according to Rezida, avoided the neighbours and kept himself to himself. More than that, however, the war had come at a particularly bad time for Hamet, in career terms. He had been thirty-three in 1938, when Rudolf was born, and a *politrouk*, a member – albeit a junior one – of a very privileged elite. He was not well off but he was comfortable, more than he can ever have hoped for as a peasant in the fields of Kazan before the revolution. When he came back from the war he was forty-one, no longer young and just one of millions of ex-soldiers who had to adjust to ordinary provincial life. He had no privileges and four children to support. Rezida confirms that her father did not leave the army by choice and says that 'It would have been better for us if father had remained in the army.'

He had three jobs as a security guard in quick succession, first in a scientific research establishment, then in the economics department of an industrial school, before settling down in an electrical apparatus factory (eventually he became head of security there). This was a revealing choice of job, maintaining his military links, exchanging one uniform for another. For Hamet was a man's man, he enjoyed male company and conventional manly pursuits. He liked hunting and he liked fishing and, not long after his return, he bought a dog with which to go hunting at weekends. This was a liver-coloured spaniel named Palmo. The children liked having a dog but Palmo never became a toy: he was Hamet's hunting companion and that was that. Hamet even had Palmo's tail docked despite the objections of his children, who thought the practice cruel. Another reason Palmo never became a toy was that their neighbours also had a dog, which had badly bitten both Rudolf and Rezida. It was called Trezor, and was big and black and much more ferocious than Palmo. Rudolf liked to stare Trezor into submission before feeding it scraps of leftovers. On one occasion, while he was holding his face close to Trezor's snout, the creature jumped up and bit him on the lip, drawing blood and giving him a scar which lasted all his life, resembling at times a hare-lip. When Rezida had tried to slap Trezor to scold him for biting Rudolf, the dog had bitten her hand into the bargain. For the Nureyevs dogs were not playthings.

Then there was the fact that Hamet was still a committed communist (indeed, a Stalinist as Nureyev once described him). Hamet involved himself in local party affairs as soon as he arrived in Ufa and this too shaped his relations with his son. As an eight- and nine-year-old, Rudolf was hardly sophisticated in his political understanding. But it didn't take a genius to see that political animals and creative animals are very different creatures, with different aims and very different attitudes. Hamet's rapid immersion in party politics had a chilling effect on his son.

Neither could Hamet entirely shake off his Muslim background. He would allow himself the occasional vodka at home, a Russian rather than a Tartar practice, but his Islamic roots showed most in his attitude to his children in general and to his son in particular. For Hamet, even more than for Farida, Rudolf was the favourite child, the child on which all his hopes for the future were pinned. Rudolf would be the one to take full advantage of the Soviet system. Rudolf would be the doctor or the engineer. Rudolf would be the man to set an example to other men.

So when Hamet found that Rudolf wanted to dance he was very unhappy, to put it no stronger. Hamet found out straight away because, having had no father before, Rudolf saw no reason to hide his passion, and would practise at home in front of the mirror whenever he could. 'He was spinning all the time,' says Rezida. 'Always prancing. We all watched him.' To Hamet, dancing was not a man's world and in any case he thought the arts as a whole too unreliable as a source of income. However, to begin with he had no idea of the strength of his son's feeling for dance and Rudolf was barely eight. He was just a child and would no doubt change as he grew older.

Rudolf did change, but not in the way his father expected. When Hamet had come back from the front, his son's grades in school were still good. In those days, all children across Russia were marked according to the same system, from '1', *neudovletvoritelno* (unsatisfactory) to '5', *otlichno*, (excellent). In Rudolf's first years at school he scored '4s' and '5s' in all subjects and did so easily, without much homework. However, after that New Year's Eve visit to *The Song of the Cranes* he began to spend more and more of his time either dancing in the folk dance troupe with Albert, or in dreaming about the dance and listening to music. His grades began to suffer, to such an extent that Hamet twice visited Rudolf's school and asked Taisiya Mikhailovna to dissuade his son from spending so much time on dance. 'He was worried,' says Taisiya, 'that as a man Rudolf would not be able to put food on the table for his family.' But she never relayed these messages to Rudolf. 'I knew I'd be wasting my breath.'

The family at this time appears to have been happy enough and relations between Rudolf and his father, though strained in regard to dance, were good enough in other areas, thanks mainly to the blatant favouritism which Hamet employed towards his son. By today's standards this was quite remarkable. For example, it was Lilia's job to wash the floor each day. The room wasn't large but in winter they burned coal in the stove, which produced a lot of smoke, soot and dust. Rezida helped her mother with the shopping and, when she was a little older, had to make the soup every day before her mother returned home from work. Farida and her daughters did the washing together on Sundays though Rosa did the lion's share. Rudolf had only two duties: to fetch kerosene from the market, for the stove they cooked on, and to fetch bread. These tasks were hardly arduous (he didn't need to go for kerosene every day) but even they appear to have been arranged to appease Rudolf's sisters, for Hamet used to complain, 'Why must we send Rudolf for bread when I've got three daughters?' His was not a modern attitude, nor even a Marxist's.

In fact, Rudolf – so spoiled in other ways – didn't mind going for bread.

The queue was long, and he was not expected home for a while, so he would arrange to fetch the loaves when his dance classes were on. He would go to class, sweat for an hour, then dash to the bread store just before it closed, picking up whatever loaves were left. The Nureyevs always ate stale bread.

Between the ages of eight and ten Rudolf and his father coexisted like this civilly enough, and with Farida making life at home as comfortable and family centred as possible. She now worked in a milk factory very near the house, which enabled her always to be on hand for the children when they needed her. Though as reserved as Hamet, she opened up more with the children and was a great practical joker. On one occasion, in teaching Rezida to thread a needle with one eye closed, she placed a finger over her daughter's eyelid. Rezida did not realise the finger was covered in soot – and walked around the house for a while with a black eye, much to everyone's amusement.

Hamet tried to interest Rudolf in what he thought of as manly pursuits. Not long after his return, he acquired an allotment a little way from the house, on which he started to grow potatoes. The children were supposed to help weed this patch in the mornings before attending the second shift of school but Rudolf was never keen. Nor did he much relish his father's invitation to go hunting or fishing. On one occasion his father took him into the wood and, while he took Palmo and his rifle to search for game, he left his young son trussed up in his shoulder-bag, hanging helplessly from a tree. In the gloom of the forest, Rudolf's imagination played havoc with his peace of mind and he always hated hunting after that. He also thought his father had been very cruel.

He could not see the point of fishing, either. The waters of the Agidel river were so polluted by the oil in the ground around Ufa that the fish were all but inedible. Every attempt by Hamet to influence Rudolf in his direction backfired.

Their relationship was not helped by the fact that Hamet sometimes beat Rudolf. He beat all his children from time to time: 'He beat us out of love,' explains Rezida, but Rudolf, with the worst temper, didn't agree. He always hated constriction of any kind.

As with many parents, Hamet's behaviour towards his son produced exactly the opposite effect to that intended. Though Rudolf was not popular among the other boys of his neighbourhood (always fighting with a certain Kostia, who lived across the yard), he was a peripheral member, with Albert, of a large gang of boys who gathered in the yard by Arslanov's house. The chief role of this gang in Rudolf's story is that, one day, all the nine- and ten-year-olds who were 'hanging out' together in Arslanov's yard decided to visit the House of Pioneers. Now the Pioneers were, in one way, rather like the Boy Scouts in the west. Every town had a house, where all manner of activities went on. In an age before television, and when it was fairly safe for children to be out on the streets after school, the Pioneers were very popular. Most children lived in much the same cramped conditions as the Nureyevs lived, so on the grounds of space alone the Pioneers offered a welcome and much-needed escape.

Inevitably, this being Soviet Russia, the Pioneers had a political edge to them. Children of nine to fourteen were eligible and the Pioneers were regarded as a precursor to the Komsomol, for the fifteen- to twenty-eight-year-olds (the Komsomol itself was regarded as preparation for party membership proper). Every school had a 'Pioneers' room', containing a picture of Lenin, a small museum of the history of the proletariat and of Russian history. (*Every* room in school had a little dedication to one of the heroes of the revolution, for example Kirov.)

But though the Pioneers might have an ulterior purpose, that didn't stop many of their activities being fun for nine- and ten-year-olds, who were not yet all that bothered by the finer points of Marxism-Leninism. And for Rudolf his arrival at the House of Pioneers was no less important than his visit to the *Song of the Cranes* three years before.

For the house, on Karl Marx Street, offered lessons in dance. The classes were free and Rudolf could not believe his luck. The teacher there was a step up from what he had been used to in school, for she adapted for her pupils a number of dances, not just from Bashkir, but from all the Russian republics, using Pioneer *Gazettes* published in Leningrad and Moscow, which showed the various steps and costumes. This was a welcome change for Rudolf, freeing him from dancing exclusively local dances. In a very short time it enabled him to show his teacher what he was capable of.

She was a hard teacher, however, and soon quarrelled with Rudolf. When he turned up late for his lessons, or made some sarcastic comment in class, or swore (as he already did, a lot), she would threaten to send him to the Matrasov Colony. This was, in effect, a local Borstal for juvenile delinquents. She routinely referred to Rudolf as a hooligan – but never threw him out. She recognised that he had problems at home, and that he had talent. Already she had heard the gossip from Rudolf's earlier schoolteachers in Ufa, that Rudolf was good enough to send to Leningrad to learn classical ballet, but she had heard that about young pupils before. (This was to become a pattern in Rudolf's life: that he would be regarded as a hooligan but was too talented to let go. It says a great deal for the Russians' understanding – and tolerance – of the artistic temperament.)

Very soon, after a few months, the teacher reached the conclusion that there was little else she could impart to Rudolf, and she referred him to yet another, more experienced, teacher. This was Anna Ivanovna Udeltsova. She was a small, fair-haired woman with a high-pitched voice, and remarkable in her own right. Already sixty-one when Rudolf was ten, she was cultivated, well read, very musical and had herself danced 'years and years ago', as she would put it, in the *corps de ballet* of Diaghilev's Ballets Russes de Monte Carlo. Although she spent most of her time in Ufa, where her husband worked in a factory, she made the journey to Leningrad each summer to see what was new in the world of dance. Culturally, she kept up. Not only was she able to introduce Rudolf to the basics of classical ballet but she could take up where the twenty-year-old Rosa had left off, imparting all the romance, all the history, all the colour of the international ballet world. 'It was Udeltsova who first talked to me of Anna Pavlova,' Rudolf said. 'She had probably met her in the Diaghilev days. She told me what Pavlova brought to the world; how that greatest of ballerinas religiously trained to acquire her irreproachable technique but how, by the very atmosphere she distilled around her, she threw a veil over all outward manifestation of technique, creating an impression of utter spontaneity each time she danced.' This was the aspect of Udeltsova's teaching that meant the most to him from the start. And in a sense, he was already used to it in his own way. He had been hiding his art from his father for years.

Rudolf had already been to Udeltsova's class, just to watch. He had been taken by Rosa, herself then at teacher training college. A fellow pupil of Udeltsova's, Alexandra Nikolievna, known to Rudolf and Rosa as Shyrochkoy or Shura, remembers Rudolf being brought, because Rosa then left him in Shura's care. 'He looked at everybody with big eyes. He was a small child – but watched, and copied everything we did.'

Anna Ivanovna's classes were given at the House of Teaching, Ufa's teacher training college, and Rudolf was brought before her there. As a test, she told him to dance a *gopak* and a *lezghinka* and various folk dances that by now were second nature to him. A *gopak* is a type of folk dance in which the dancers stand with their hands on their hips and dance in a circle. In a *lezghinka* the men begin on tiptoe, then suddenly sink to their knees. A piano was all the accompaniment Rudolf had and his performance lasted less than a quarter of an hour. When he had finished, Udeltsova seemed for a moment to be stunned, saying nothing and remaining absolutely motionless in her chair. Eventually, when she did speak, she rambled at first, saying that she had spent more than thirty years teaching children to dance. She had seen all sorts, she said. She beckoned him to come closer. In her high-pitched voice, a small woman's voice, she said, 'This is the first time I have been able to say what I am going to say. Rudolf Hametovich, you have a duty to yourself to learn classical dancing. You have an innate gift and with such a gift you must prepare yourself to join the students at the Maryinsky Theatre.'

Rudolf blushed as Udeltsova gave her verdict. Many adults who had seen him dance before had praised him, and even mentioned the Kirov Ballet School in Leningrad (calling it by its old name of Maryinsky was very incorrect, politically). But even a child of ten could see that there was a difference between Udeltsova's informed opinion and that of an ignorant neighbour or railway worker. She offered to give him lessons twice a week, for free. This was not unimportant as his father would certainly never have agreed to pay any fees, however minimal. (Hamet had already told Rezida, who wanted to learn the piano, that although he wasn't opposed to the idea, the family couldn't afford the lessons.) Without bothering about his father's reaction, Rudolf accepted Udeltsova's offer immediately. He had learned enough by now to know that the traditional starting time for students at the big ballet schools was ten. There was no time to be lost.

Udeltsova's offer did not mean that Rudolf was the only person in her class. Far from it. The class was quite large and differed from those in a proper ballet school in that people of different standards and different ages attended together. At times there were up to sixty adults, though twenty-five was more usual, and some six or eight other children, including Albert Arslanov, who had also been accepted by Udeltsova at the same time. But the two boys were the youngest in the class.

Alexandra Nikolievna, who had been with Udeltsova for about a year when Rudolf arrived, confirms that she taught them much more than dance steps. 'Udeltsova was a simply wonderful person, such as you don't find these days. She gave us so much. She introduced us to literature and to music, always saying that we should read this or that. At first Rudolf stooped, as if to conceal himself, so that he wouldn't be noticed too much. But that was only for a short time, about a month and a half.'

Rudolf and Albert stayed in Udeltsova's class for about eighteen months. During that time he and Shura became very close and this friendship may have helped determine his character in an important way. For her father had been 'repressed', sent to the gulags, because of his dissident views. One consequence was that Shura's mother didn't like her mixing with other children, in case they picked on her. Her father's rejection clearly mattered to Shura. At the end of Udeltsova's classes they would round off the evening with a singsong, classical songs and songs about Stalin. Shura had a fine voice and joined in the Stalinist songs with extra gusto, to prove that *she* was not tainted with her father's dissident views. For the first time, at the age of ten, Rudolf saw close up the cruel reality of politics in Russia. He grew fond of Shura – and she was a victim of the system his father had once been part of. Indeed, was part of again.

Already, Rudolf was interested in the other arts, too, beyond dance. Shura confirms that, even at this age, they would visit the Nesterov Museum on Gogol Street. He was also beginning to show a penchant for perfection in the dance and, when he danced with Shura and she did something that fell short of what he hoped for, he would pull her hair. He even pushed her off the stage at least twice. She seemed not to mind, as if she deserved such 'criticism'.

Rudolf enjoyed Anna Ivanovna's classes more than anything he had done before. During the eighteen months he spent with her, he learned the very basics of classical ballet, the correct 'five positions', his first *pliés* and his first *battements*. He was also taught that while there have been times when the Italian, Russian or British ballet have been paramount, the art form as such began in France in the eighteenth century, which is why the basic language of classical dance is French.

It was in Anna Ivanovna's class that Rudolf's virgin fire really began to show itself. For example, once when she came to class but was clearly ill he would not allow her to teach and insisted that the senior pupil, a woman called Tanya, take her place. 'But obviously,' says Shura, 'since it wasn't Anna Ivanovna we were all noisy and undisciplined. Eventually Rudik could no longer contain himself; although he was the youngest in the class, he jumped into the middle of the hall and screamed, "What are you playing at? Don't you know Anna Ivanovna is ill?" We pulled ourselves together a little and quietened down. But a little while later we were noisy again, and Rudik shouted, "I've told you already! Anna Ivanovna is ill!"'

Rudik did not disappoint Udeltsova. According to Shura, he never had the restraint of the other dancers in her class. 'He danced the mazurka, the polka, and the waltz. I remember a girl who had ringlets and huge, blue eyes, like a doll. I think she was called Sveta. Between them they had the four biggest eyes you ever saw. And they looked good together but even she had that restraint. He didn't. When he talked to people, his face was a mark [set, immobile]. But when he danced his countenance shone.'

This lack of restraint sometimes led to problems. Although Arslanov says that both he and Rudolf were strong swimmers, Shura claims that, as a boy, Rudolf didn't like swimming. He would go to the beach at the river, but never went in. Once, on a windy day, Shura and he were making for a cave they knew and Rudolf was dancing and jigging on a narrow path at the top of the high riverbank. He became unbalanced and would have fallen, perhaps fifteen feet, down into the river had not Shura grabbed him by the trousers. 'He sat down, the scar on his lip went pale, his nostrils flared. Then he got up. "Home?"

'So we went. On the way back, he said, "You did a great deed today. You saved a Pioneer." He was proud. It was his way of saying thank you.'

While he was in Anna Ivanovna's class, Rudolf's relations with his father deteriorated still further. Hamet simply didn't grasp the passion his son had for the ballet and no one was allowed to discuss it at home. In consequence, Rudolf was forced to lie. He would say he was at the House of Pioneers when he was dancing. The minute Hamet left the house, Rudolf would go to the mirror and beginning practising his steps. His mother and all his sisters knew what was going on, so they too were part of the charade. In a Muslim household, this stand-off between the two males was especially traumatic. The Russian phrase to be in love with the ballet is literally translated as 'to be ill with ballet'. It is an apt description of what was happening in the Nureyev household.

Hamet would occasionally try to get closer to his son. Rezida remembers yet another hunting trip at around this time, on this occasion in summer. Hamet insisted that Rudolf accompany him, as well as Rezida, in the hope that the time spent together, out of the house in each other's company, would spark something between father and son. But Hamet's idea of fun was to walk to Krasny Yar. This was forty minutes away by bus (say fifteen miles). When they got there, they stayed out all night, sleeping in a haystack. Next day, when the hunting proper began, Hamet couldn't help himself and became much more interested in the chase than in his children, who were now in the way. Rudolf spent the whole trip in a sulk and father and son returned even more estranged than before.

Besides the five basic positions, Anna Ivanovna taught Rudolf the seven movements in ballet. Again the language is French, beginning with *plier*, meaning to bend. The others were *étendre*, to stretch, *relever*, to raise, *glisser*, to slide or glide, *sauter*, to jump, *élancer*, to dart, and *tourner*, to turn. But after eighteen months, Anna Ivanovna thought that Rudolf had made so much progress that she could teach him no more. She referred him to another teacher in Ufa, Elena Konstantinovna Vaitovich. Vaitovich was a complex character. Before the revolution, her father had been an officer in the Imperial Army and her mother a member of the court. She herself had been a young ballerina with the St Petersburg (Imperial) Company, possessed of a remarkable jump, or *elevation*. After the revolution, when the company was renamed the Kirov, she had been kept on and had become a soloist. It was no mean achievement, to have shone under both political systems and Vaitovich was something of a celebrity in Ufa, where she had moved after her retirement from the stage.

Vaitovich accepted Rudolf into her class. She was an even better technician than Udeltsova but she had other advantages which suited Rudolf even more. In the first place, since she taught in the Pioneers, there were no adults in her class. She only taught children, whose age and standard were similar to Rudolf's. She was also less strict, more tolerant of the idiosyncrasies of her pupils, and this of course fitted Rudolf's temperament much more successfully. Third, she was also ballet mistress at the Ufa Theatre of Opera and Ballet and therefore success in her class offered the tantalising possibility of being taken on – eventually – as a professional. Finally, there was the quality that had distinguished her as a ballerina, the ability to jump.

The jump is a controversial matter in classical dance. For many people without a thorough grounding in ballet the jump is the most obviously spectacular element in dance, the most obvious skill which dancers, male dancers especially, have over ordinary mortals. On the other hand, there have been very many dancers, including male dancers, who have never had a big jump and yet have been regarded as the finest artists of their time. For many balletomanes, a big jump is simply unnecessary.

Neither of the two great Russian dancers in the post-Second World War period, Vakhtung Chaboukiani or Konstantin Sergeyev, had big jumps. Rudolf wasn't aware of this at the time but Vaitovich certainly was. Her own ability to jump had been somewhat neglected, simply because female parts in classical ballet rarely call for elevation. But given Rudolf's abilities, she wasn't going to neglect *his* jump. And as she told him more and more about Chaboukiani and Sergeyev, he began to see a way to make himself stand out.

Later in his career, there was controversy about Rudolf's elevation. Some said it was magnificent, others that, although it wasn't actually all that big, it *felt* big. In Ufa, however, in Vaitovich's class, Arslanov (who was also now a pupil) had no doubt about Rudolf's jump. 'His jump even then was good. This made some people jealous of him. He used to have the habit of bending his fingers back – he was naturally very flexible. All that natural talent . . . it made the others jealous.'

Rudolf stayed with Elena Konstantinovna for just over a year. His first partner was Pamira Sulemanovna, a fellow Pioneer and just as poor. An exile from Azerbaijan, her father never came back from the war; her mother sold her own blood to buy food.

'We used to do "stool routines" together. At first they were very short, because we were so young. We began concerts at the *agitpunkt* (agitation centres) and while the House of Pioneers was being repaired we took lessons at the DOSAFP (Army Sports Federation). Rudik was a good partner, strong, reliable and very mobile. The boys used to wear wide trousers in the concerts (*sharovari*) and we girls had skirts with tassles on them. For rehearsals of course we just wore shorts and singlets – Rudik's shirt, I remember, was light blue and his shorts were black and none too clean. His hair was always a mess in those days and fell forward over his head. He didn't bother with his appearance and as a result didn't stand out in any way. Certainly, I never thought of him as handsome, not then. He was normal. There was no real sign of beauty but his eyes shone when he smiled. I didn't like the colour of his hair.

'We did study classical dances, not just folk dances. We danced *Song of the Cranes* and *Aida*. But mainly it was character dancing. It was very difficult for Rudik because his parents were against him dancing. He would always arrive late, running, with a large bag. He used to go out to get bread, but then came to the lesson. Basically, we were being groomed for the *corps de ballet* in Ufa but Rudik, however late he was, would stay on after our class, and attend the class for soloists.

'We had dancing exams twice, when the local Minister for Culture, Cumunov, came along. Rudik and I performed *Dance of the Dolls* and the Caprice Waltz. In the *Dance of the Dolls* he had to catch me and he never collapsed once. We were very harmonious.'

Dancing did not lead to close friendship with Pamira, however. Already, Rudolf was single-minded. His virgin fire burned only for the dance. 'There was a staircase in the House of Pioneers,' says Sulemanovna, 'and underneath the staircase, on the ground floor, there was a mirror. Here Rudik used to practise his exercises while looking at himself in the mirror. He would hold a position and shout, "Pamira, come and look! Come and look!" He looked very graceful. It's obviously something he was born with.'

By now the House of Pioneers was a second home for Rudolf, as it was for so many children in Ufa at that time. Before the war, certain 'Pioneer Palaces' had been run with 'almost oriental luxury', with the one in Leningrad being housed in the Anitchkov Palace, the former residence of Alexander III. However, after Krupskaya, Lenin's widow, had drawn disapproving attention to the privileges attaching to many Pioneer halls, they had been downgraded, at least so far as the physical fabric of their buildings was concerned, and the Ufa House of Pioneers was certainly no palace.

Inna Georgievna Gyckova, a friend of Rezida's, who knew the Nureyev household when Rudolf was a boy, was in the House of Pioneers at the same time, in the entertainers' class (conjuring, ventriloquism, juggling, and so on). She says her class had the air of a children's secret society, with inductions every so often. At these inductions, new members would be given a special tie and had to make a one-word oath of allegiance to the class, that word being 'Circus.'

The regime was not informal, surprising as that may sound. At least in the Ufa house, there were pictures of Stalin everywhere, even a weatherproof one overlooking the playing field. And there were propagandist, realist paintings on the walls, with such titles as 'The Morning of our Motherland'. As Pamira remembers, 'Of course we sang songs about Stalin, read verses about Stalin. And it wasn't bad music.' When they were not dancing, or playing sports, a uniform was insisted upon. This consisted of short-sleeved shirts, pale or white, with a dark blue skirt, or trousers for the boys, which had to be properly pressed. And there had to be pockets in which the Pioneers must carry a handkerchief. The boys were supposed to wear ties as well, but here Rudolf seems to have bent the rules. He found that, provided he *arrived* wearing a tie, he could then take it off and no one would mind though, Pamira says, none of the others boys dared do this. The uniform was topped off by 'accurate' haircuts. All hair was carefully checked: the boys' had to be kept very short and the girls' kept in place with dark blue or black ribbons.

Vaitovich had choreographed some of her own ballets, which the children danced as part of their training and performed at matinées in schools and clubs around the city. Rudolf's first performance for Vaitovich was in just such an offering, when he was cast as a bear cub in an opera, *Little Frost*. But they also prepared one bigger ballet all year and then mounted it on stage at the Ufa Theatre of Opera and Ballet, the very theatre where Rudolf had first been enchanted by *Song of the Cranes* on New Year's Eve 1945/1946. The Pioneers' production was performed during the school summer holidays (this would have been 1951 or 1952) and was a matinée attended not just by all the children at the Pioneers but by the public. In the year Rudolf was studying with Vaitovich, the ballet was *Feya Kokol* and he was judged sufficiently good to be given the leading role.

By now, everyday living was getting easier in Ufa. Wartime shortages had continued until about 1947, especially in regard to food. Pamira Sulemanovna confirms that until then they had sometimes eaten nettle soup and, to vary the diet, invented a dish of potato shavings – the vegetable was eaten raw but in finely chopped form it seemed to taste differently. Rationing ended in 1947 but queueing for food didn't. Even in the early 1950s one of the perks of being a dancer, or dance student, was the extra food. In Ufa, dancers at the House of Pioneers were treated to a special beetroot pie every time they had a class. In the Nureyev household the food situation had improved because of the allotment Hamet had acquired. It had taken a year to produce the first potatoes – and it was only potatoes – but it was enough.

Life was improving in other respects, too. Pamira and Rudolf had discovered a way to sneak into the theatre without paying. 'Through the puppet theatre there was a corridor and on the right a door that was never locked. This led to the scenery store, and beyond that to the wings. And there could be found a door which led through to the auditorium We never got caught. Rudolf and I would try not to let anything new pass us by.' 'I remember Rudolf had his favourite dancers,' says Arslanov. 'Zaituna [Nazretdinova], of course, but also Guzel Sulemanova, and Levshitz Yasha – he was jealous of Yasha's jump. Then there was Volodya Grigoriev. He was a character dancer whom Rudolf liked. The theatre proper closed in the summer, but we kept going, watching the operetta that filled in, and of course the circus, every time it came to town.' Another way that life improved was that Rudolf and Albert joined the local library. However many books he read at that stage (and Arslanov says they read a lot), Rudolf never dreamed of *owning* books.

By now, too, Rudolf was an avid cinema-goer. There were about fifteen cinemas in Ufa at the time, showing both Russian and western films. He saw Marlene Dietrich in *Blonde Venus*, many of Garbo's films, *Lady Hamilton* with Vivien Leigh, Eisenstein's *Potemkin* and *Ivan the Terrible*.

Not that it was all plain sailing. During his first year with Vaitovich, Rudolf learned with great interest that a group of children was to be selected from throughout Bashkir and sent to Leningrad, to be tested for entry into the famous Leningrad Ballet School. This, of course, was the very school that friends, and the parents of friends, and even Udeltsova, had been saying that Rudolf ought to go to. Here was the opportunity he had always dreamed about. Normally, in the Nureyev household, dance was never mentioned or discussed in front of Hamet. On this occasion, however, Rudolf had to break the convention – he begged his father to visit the House of Pioneers, speak to Vaitovich herself and make sure his son was included in those children being sent to Leningrad. Hamet refused. Already opposed to Rudolf's dancing, this request only showed that his son, far from giving up on his ambition to become a dancer, was becoming ever more serious about it. Hamet angrily insisted his son forget all about Leningrad, and the ballet school.

Later in his life, Rudolf said that he realised, when he was a grown man, that his father didn't really object; it was just that the family couldn't afford to send Rudolf away. But this is disingenuous. It may have been part of the reason, but if Rudolf had been accepted into the school, it would have been on a scholarship. It would not have cost Hamet anything and there would have been one less mouth to feed at home. No, this episode further damaged relations between father and son, the more so as, despite this setback, Rudolf wouldn't let go of his dream. Independently, he himself approached the responsible official at the Ufa Opera, which was sponsoring the group, to see what arrangements needed to be made. The conversation didn't last long. Almost as soon as the young lad walked in the door he found that while he had been embroiled with his father, trying to persuade him to speak to Vaitovich, the opportunity had come and gone. The chosen children had already left for Leningrad.

It took Rudolf several days to recover from this, and in some ways he never did. His relations with his father suffered permanently. But the episode produced an effect on Hamet, too. His son's request had shown him just how strong the desire to dance was, and so he chose this moment to put his foot down. Hamet was no fool and although he wasn't aware of the full extent of his son's deception in the preceding months, he realised that something had been going on. Only by completely forbidding Rudolf to dance, so Hamet felt, could he stifle his son's absolute obsession with ballet. The boy was a baby no longer and it was, Hamet decided, time for him to pay more attention to his studies, to try to become an engineer or scientist, or even a doctor.

There is no doubt that a good part of Hamet's objection to his son becoming a dancer was economic. True, there were more than thirty state dance companies in Russia at the time but that didn't change the fact that, as Hamet saw it, dancers were over the hill at forty, especially male dancers. Life had been hard for Hamet and it was natural, and honourable, for him not to want his own offspring to go through such hardship if they could avoid it. In his view, Rudolf was an intelligent and good-looking boy. He, Hamet, was a party member (eventually he became leader of his 'cell' in Ufa), and a war veteran. These qualifications of Hamet's, despite the family's economic plight, combined to give his son as good a start as he could hope for in Ufa. If Rudolf wanted to enter any of the professions, his father's political standing would go a long way to ensuring that his wishes would prevail. It was not an advantage to be squandered lightly.

But was there something else? Was Hamet, however dimly, or however reluctant he was to admit it to himself, aware that his son might be a homosexual? As an army veteran, a war survivor, a man who had travelled from Vladivostok to Berlin, he was a man of the world. There is a saying in Russian: 'A homosexual in the army is like a man in a woman's *bania*.' Hamet knew full well that homosexuality was not unknown in ballet companies. Albert Arslanov denies that there was anything homosexual about Rudolf while they were close friends. 'No, absolutely not. I have heard that he was homosexual, but I never saw any indication of those tendencies while he lived here in Ufa.' But Hamet may have wanted to take no chances.

Sexual orientation may not matter very much in the west in the 1990s but the situation was very different in Russia in the 1950s (indeed, it is very different in Russia in the 1990s). In the years when Rudolf and Arslanov were growing up, attitudes to sexuality itself, not just homosexuality, were very complicated. Russians have always been more puritanical on sexual matters, attitudes that can probably be traced to the Orthodox Church, which has always been more restrictive than western churches, for example in the representation of the human body in art. In the aftermath of the Second World War, two factors were paramount in the Soviet Union so far as sex was concerned. The first was that the entire country was very inhibited sexually. Dr Mikhail Stern, in *Sex in the Soviet Union*, published in 1981, quotes a number of statistics and vignettes which are depressingly revealing about the quality of life in those days. There was, for example, no real equivalent of the word 'orgasm' in Russian, which was a term mainly employed by doctors. Almost the only term in everyday language was virtually untranslatable, the verb *konchat*, meaning 'to finish'. This, says Stern, is a truly sad comment on sexual relations. He adds: 'There is even a very common expression used these days to refer to the sexual act, the primary meaning of which is "to beat" (*trakhnut*).'

Stern further reports that, before the 1960s, and certainly during the 1930s and 1940s, puritanism was widespread in Russia. 'Imagine,' he writes, 'a country where the model of great lovers that one studies in school is the militant couple Lenin and Krupskaya.' This is certainly what Nureyev studied. There was a whole Stalinist campaign, Stern says, to de-eroticise love, to stress the importance of friendship at the expense of love, all in the interests of the revolution; the early communists firmly believed that the family was 'the enemy' of the revolution. (This may sound absurd now, but it was the atmosphere in which Nureyev grew up.) As a result of the communist attitude to love and sex, says Stern, sex surveys and even sex education were banned, and normal methods of therapy, like psychoanalysis, were forbidden. It was therefore no surprise that in the 1930s at least the effects of this repression were seen clinically. Stern reports that, in the 1930s, cases of *penis captivus* became quite common. This is the condition where the couple, because of spasms during intercourse, remain 'soldered together'. 'These cases, which are in general very rare, are caused by vaginismus (an involuntary contraction of the levator muscle of the anus, which is also a constrictor of the vagina).' In the USSR such cases occurred relatively frequently on account of the fear and sense of guilt surrounding all matters of sex. A very simple technique – rectal touch – permits an immediate relaxation of the woman's muscles. 'The doctors were and still are unaware of this, which is to be explained by the Soviet context.' Stern, remember, was writing in 1981.

That 'Soviet context' includes a fierce disapproval of homosexuality. In aiming to destroy the family, Leninist legislation in the 1920s had in fact 'liberalised', as we would now recognise the term, some aspects of sexual behaviour. For example, abortion had been legalised. Under Stalin, however, the 1930s saw a progressive tightening up again. In 1936 abortion was made all but illegal again and, two years earlier, homosexuality had been declared a criminal offence, carrying a penalty of three to eight years, 'a triumph,' according to Gorky, 'of proletarian humanism'. This law was not rescinded until May 1993, in the face of bitter opposition from the President of the Academy of Medical Sciences and the Chief of Police, who argued that homosexuals had been born with a form of mental disorder and tended to pervert children. The *Great Soviet Encyclopedia*, written in the 1930s, envisaged a 'radical cure' for homosexuality, in which the testicles of heterosexual men would be transplanted into homosexuals.

The attitude of the criminal law was paralleled in everyday life. Until very recently, the word 'homosexual' was very rarely used in Russia and was regarded as an insult. The press never discussed the practice, which was widely regarded as a synonym for total perversion. As Stern points out, 'The *Soviet Medical Encyclopedia* gives no definition of lesbian love; it merely gives the geographical location of the island of Lesbos.' To give some idea of attitudes in Russia, and how little they have changed, a survey carried out in 1989 showed that 33 per cent of people thought that gays ought to be shot, 30 per cent said they should be imprisoned, 30 per cent favoured forcible medical treatment, and 6 per cent advocated 'assistance' of some sort. In central Asia (including Ufa, but not Leningrad) 'those advocating capital punishment exceeded 85 per cent'. In the everyday Russian language there are several swear-words which liken a person insulted to a passive homosexual. It is commonly thought that Armenians (a generally despised group) have strong tendencies to homosexuality. Even worse, says Stern, many Russian homosexuals 'often think of their proclivity as a pathological phenomenon, a fatal illness which will strike them down'. 'Gay' in Russian is *galooboy*, the literal translation of which is 'pale blue'.

A particularly Russian gloss on this whole issue arises from the fact that Soviet medical science even today still makes a fundamental division of homosexuals into 'active' and 'passive', depending on their preferred sexual positions. Moreover, they associate 'passive' with 'inborn' and 'genuine' homosexuality, and 'active' with 'acquired' homosexuality. As a result, the stigma is more attached to the 'passive' than the 'active' form.

According to Stern, homosexuality was more common in the army and navy and in the camps (in previous centuries, under the Tsars, there had been special laws to prevent homosexuality in the armed forces; those convicted could be burned at the stake). Surveys have shown that, in the Soviet Union, the three most homophobic groups are pensioners, housewives and members of the armed forces, with Muslims even less tolerant than these. Nureyev's father would have been familiar with this gloomy picture, as he would with perhaps the most sinister aspect of all. As Stern puts it, 'More vulnerable to blackmail, the terrorised homosexual constitutes a choice target for the secret police, who will often try to make him one of their agents.' With his knowledge of the purges, and his fear that they could return at any moment, Hamet would have been especially concerned that his son avoid any risk of that nature. Homophobia was a recurrent issue, stirred up time and again by populist politicians and reported gleefully by many sectors of the press, intent on an easy boost to circulation.

In the general moral climate of the time it is easy to see why Hamet would have been worried. Even after the war, with the cold war just beginning, Russia was still very much a Stalinist society. In the 1950s a Leningrad publishing house refused to use a photograph of the Venus de Milo in a brochure on aesthetics, calling it 'pornographic'. And it was impossible for a young man to escape contact with homosexuals in Russia. The lack of hot running water in private homes, and the ubiquitous presence of *banias*, ensured that this minority, though much persecuted, had an institutionalised network of meeting places, which enabled it to survive.

Hamet wasn't simply prejudiced. He was also realistic.

It was now, aged nearly fourteen, that a truly difficult part of Rudolf's early life began. His parents, his father especially, had made no bones about his dancing: it was forbidden and that was that. Rosa, his closest ally in the family, had left home, to attend teacher training college in Leningrad. But though deprived of her comfort and support, Rudolf was determined to continue dancing.

So he had to lie to his parents about where he was. This was hard because dancing required practice, endless practice, and that meant time away from his lessons. His grades suffered, slipping from 4s and 5s to 3s and even 2s. A stream of letters was sent by the teachers to Hamet, complaining about his son's 'indifference' to his work. 'Nureyev works less and less . . . his behaviour is appalling . . . he is always late for classes . . . he jumps like a frog and that's about all he knows. He even dances on the staircase landings.'

Hamet's refusal to allow Rudolf to go to Leningrad, as part of the group to be considered for the Kirov Ballet School, was little short of a declaration of war between father and son. Hamet could not have wounded Rudolf more if he had tried, and Rudolf's temper – his fire – was kindled. Rudolf was very intelligent and, as Arslanov confirms, could have scored high marks – '4s' and '5s' – without doing much in the way of homework. His low marks were deliberate, an easy and direct way to get back at Hamet.

Arslanov also confirms that Rudolf was a good draughtsman. 'He didn't study drawing but he could do it if he needed to. When we were in the eighth grade [aged fourteen] we had to draw Lomanosov [a local bigwig]. Rudik's drawing was published in the school newspaper, it was so good. By then he also played the piano a bit.'

Meanwhile, he continued to dance. He was by now a very good folk dancer and contributed considerably to his school winning all the national dance competitions that they entered. But these competitions, and the glory that went with them, occurred only infrequently. More prosaically, Rudolf spent his early teens travelling from village to village with the folk dance troupe. This was before the age of television and any spectacle was well received. The troupe would arrive with all the scenery and musical equipment jammed into two trucks. On arrival the trucks were unloaded, then lined up in a row with their sides let down, to form the stage. A curtain formed the backdrop, kerosene lamps were hung from trees and buildings to provide lighting, and the villagers brought their own stools.

Rudolf was already an instinctive performer. He himself recalls one incident when he was dancing – on the makeshift stage on the back of the trucks – when he became embroiled in the long trailing ribbons that were part of his costume. In no time he was trussed up like an animal in a trap, with no means of escape. Rather than fight his way free, in an undignified and graceless manner, he merely pretended this was the normal ending of the dance. 'Miraculously, it worked; the peasants accepted it that way and I scored a big success.'

Bit by bit, Rudolf's adult personality was appearing. Besides his appetite for performing and his stage presence, there was also his love of musical performances by others, a passion that all his friends and acquaintances would remark on later in life. Alexandra Nikolievna recalls one evening in Ufa around this time when about thirty children went to a concert some way outside the city. Rudolf insisted on staying to the very end despite the fact that to get home again, they had to cross the river by ferry and the ferry stopped running before the concert ended. Bridges were rare in Ufa in the 1950s – there was just one pontoon bridge across the Belaya. According to Alexandra:

'The concert finished somewhere around ten or eleven. The ferry had already stopped. We searched for the ferryman. By the time we had found him, and persuaded him to take us children across the river, it was already very late and we were still in Nizhnegorodka. To make matters worse, among our number were four girls younger than we were, whom Rudik and I had to see home. Only after that did we go home ourselves – and it was by now between two and three in the morning. The next day I asked, "Well, then?" Rudik said, "I got a good beating."'

Apart from his temper, Rudolf's sheer toughness was also beginning to show itself. Rezida, Alexandra and Gyckova, Rezida's friend, all confirm that, as a boy, Nureyev had a 'problem' with his legs. Rezida says that varicose veins ran in the family, that Farida, Rezida herself and Rudolf all suffered. This sounds implausible, given the kind of dancer Rudolf was to become, but according to Alexandra,

'I remember one occasion very well. Rudik had to go about in *valenky* [a form of soft boot made partly with felt]. Even in April. That was all he could wear on his feet. They were aching badly. I recall he came to dance lessons, stretched his legs out and closed his eyes. The teacher said, "Rudik, are your legs aching?" He: "Yes, they're aching." She: "Perhaps you won't be joining us today." He: "No, I will be." And he proceeded to join in with such aching legs. And on the way home he walked slowly-slowly. He preferred to go home by tram, because he was aching.'

In 1953, when Rudolf was fifteen, a crucial change came over the musical-dance world in Ufa. This was the opening of a 'Studio', as it was called, a special class whose purpose was to prepare young dancers for the *corps de ballet* at the main theatre. This was held at the House of Pioneers in the mornings, from 8 a.m. to noon, and pupils were required to pass an audition. Rudolf was one of the first to be admitted, as was Arslanov, who applied at Rudolf's urging. This was a much more professional class than either boy had attended before. Vaitovich was one of the teachers, together with Zaituna Nureevna Bakhtiyanova, but the guiding force was Victor Cranstovich Parinas, head ballet master at the Ufa Theatre. He brought in various other dancer-teachers who had been sent from Leningrad to Ufa, so that Rudolf and the others now drew the benefit of their experience. Among these teachers were Nayim Valerevna Batacheva and Abdyraxaman Lukjulovich Kumisnikov, who later taught in Copenhagen, Berlin and Vienna. In other words, Ufa may have been provincial but it wasn't a backwater. As Arslanov puts it, 'At the time we joined the studio, the ballet in Ufa was strong. We were perhaps even the third ballet in the USSR [after the Bolshoi and the Kirov]. We had a good repertoire and many dancers from the Leningrad Choreographical School.'

At much the same time that the studio was formed, there was change in the teaching staff at Rudolf's regular school. Until this point, Rudolf's maths teacher had been a man called Sobanov, the director of Number Two School. In 1953 he was replaced by a woman called Sorabranovna, who demanded more preparation. According to Arslanov, this didn't suit Rudolf, who was 'too proud'. As a result, he left School Number Two (as he was perfectly entitled to do) and transferred to the 'School of Working Youth'. This was a special type of school created for those in their final grades at school who wanted to go to work and yet continue their studies. It was open all day and at night, so that students could fit their studies around their other commitments. This suited Rudolf perfectly, for it meant he could attend the studio from 8 a.m. until noon, then go to the School of Working Youth and still be free in the evenings.

The free evenings were all-important because, although Rudolf and the others were not yet ready for the *corps de ballet*, there were bit-parts in a number of productions which did not require dancing and were filled from the ranks of the studio classes, to give the students early stage experience. In this manner Rudolf made his professional stage début, in a production where he was required to sit on the roof of a hut for one entire act. He was fifteen at the time and although his part was no more taxing than it sounds he loved every moment.

The classes at the studio continued, and the teacher who most caught the students' eye was no longer Vaitovich but Zaituna Nureevna. She was young and had a very chic way of dressing, at least by Soviet standards. As Pamira Sulemanovna puts it, 'She always used to turn up in new outfits. She was neat but strict, insisting that we [the girls] all wear white socks and specially sewn dresses. We all learned a lot about style from her. She showed us you could be stylish *and* disciplined. We danced in plimsolls for the first year of the studio, then we changed to proper ballet shoes, so we could learn points. To begin with there were about sixty of us, but it was gradually whittled down to ten or so.'

Of course, by now there was no hiding the fact from Hamet that Rudolf was embarked on a career, a life, in dance. His move to the School for Working Youth was impossible to conceal, as was the fact that he left home before eight every morning, to attend the studio. Nor would his appearances on stage at the theatre have gone unremarked. He was learning French, the language of ballet, and English as well. Everything about Rudolf showed that he was going to be an artist, not an engineer or doctor.

After Rudolf's attempt to travel to Leningrad had provoked a direct confrontation with Hamet, the two males in the Nureyev household had maintained cool relations. Now that he was appearing on stage, however, Rudolf saw a way to make his point, to both impress his father *and* rub in what he could achieve. When, in the second year of the studio, he became part of the *corps de ballet*, dancing a small role in the *Song of the Cranes*, he started to earn a salary of 200 roubles a month. This was not a lot, but it was something: it was enough to build on. In the summer of 1954, when Rudolf was sixteen, he and Arslanov went with the Ufa Ballet on a short tour of Ryazan. They shared a room, took breakfast and lunch in the theatre canteens where they appeared, and dined only on tea and fish-paste sandwiches, the cheapest there were. They bought sugar and cherries, and some of the ballerinas could make jam. They lived well, had fun, and all could take some money back for their families.

This gave Rudolf an idea – to try his first piece of private enterprise. Introducing himself (somewhat grandly) as 'an artist from the Ufa Opera', he approached various workers' collectives and offered to give them a weekly lesson in folk dancing, for 200 roubles a month. Later in life Nureyev showed himself to be a very astute businessman and this was the first sign of that side to his talents. His approach worked with enough of the collectives for him eventually to earn as much as his father.

Now at one level, of course, this was an aggressive act. His father had specifically said that one reason he objected to dance as a career was that it 'couldn't put bread on the table'. Yet here was his son, aged sixteen, earning as much as he was, at forty-nine. Rudolf was putting his father in his place in no small measure.

Rudolf put pressure on Hamet in another way too. While he had been travelling with Albert, or 'Alka' as he was called by then, he had discovered the pleasures of masturbation. On his return home after the tour, he had been in the yard of his home, in the lavatory, masturbating. His father had approached the lavatory, and had waited outside for a while. When he grew impatient he knocked on the door and told his son to hurry up. At this point Rudolf deliberately gave himself an orgasm so loud that his father could not help but hear. This too was an aggressive act, an unbelievably cruel act, an act which, given the general attitudes to sex in Russia in the 1950s, can only have been very distressing for Hamet, reinforcing his long-standing fears and prejudices. Rudolf discussed the matter fairly openly later in life.

A state of war between father and son was firmly established at all levels.

That wasn't enough, of course. The end of Rudolf's schooldays were approaching and bit-parts and bit-teaching were not a career. Something more was called for. Here, in a pattern that was to be echoed later in his career, an older woman came to his aid. She was Irina Alexandrovna, the pianist who played in Vaitovich's classes at the Pioneers, who went on tour with the folk dance troupe in the two trucks, and who also accompanied the classes at the studio. She had formed a soft spot for both Arslanov and Rudolf and had even taught Rudolf the piano, or at least its rudiments. She had a small flat on Gogol Street not far from the Nureyevs, with 'a cat as big as a dog'. Alka and Rudolf took to dropping in for tea and to listen to music.

Irina Alexandrovna thought that Rudolf had talent, and she was well known in the Ufa musical establishment. She set about persuading a number of influential people, prominent citizens in Ufa (party secretaries, administrators at the theatre), to write to the Ministry of Culture in Moscow, saying that Rudolf's dancing was good enough to justify a scholarship at the Leningrad Ballet School. Letters were sent out a few at a time, over a period of a few weeks, to keep up the pressure on Moscow.

It did no good, in the sense that a reply from Moscow was not received. But Irina Alexandrovna's enthusiastic support underlined Rudolf's determination to become a dancer and influenced his choice when a conflict of major proportions loomed a few weeks later. This occurred a short while before he was due to take his final school exams, when he should have been doing his revision. He was offered a very small role in a ballet called *Polish Ball*. This was a real dilemma. The part itself was small but it was a dancing role and if he accepted he needed to attend rehearsals as well as all the performances. There would be no time to prepare for his exams: he would risk failing and another fight with his father.

Even so, the result was a foregone conclusion. Rudolf would dance in *Polish Ball*, rehearsals would take precedence over revision, and the exams could look after themselves.

He told Rosa, but no one else at home. On the night of *Polish Ball*, the theatre was full but no one from home attended. His performance was a success: although it was a small role he made no mistakes and got through the evening to become a proper dancer, who had appeared on stage. Afterwards, he was so excited he didn't sleep a wink all night.

A few days later, in early June, he sat the dreaded exams. Rudolf was so certain he had failed that he didn't dare visit the board on which the results were announced. Instead, he asked Arslanov to look for him. His name wasn't there.

He had expected an explosion. He got ice instead. His failure was never discussed openly in the family, though Farida and Hamet knew perfectly well what had happened, and *why* it had happened. Hamet was now head of security in the milk factory and a prominent figure in the local Communist Party. This made his son's failure especially hard to bear, not to mention the fact that he needn't have failed, that he was bright enough to have sailed through the exam. To Hamet it meant that his son was already a wastrel and battling him at every turn. He couldn't bear to face him.

Avoidance of the issue was made easier by the fact that, just then, Ufa Opera offered Rudolf a position on a month-long tour of Bashkir. It involved a succession of walk-on parts but it meant being an actor full time, for a month at least, and it meant he could get away from the atmosphere at home. He accepted, as he himself put it, 'with joy'.

The tour was not especially memorable. He enjoyed travelling and watching the more experienced dancers but most of all he took advantage of the way of life – living in hotels, having all his meals found for him, rehearsing incessantly so that there was no time to spend his wages. As a result, when he returned home, for the first time in his life he had money in his pocket, even after giving his mother what she needed. He still hadn't heard from Moscow about his scholarship, but he often thought about it.

Moscow. Suddenly, he realised that he now had a freedom he had never enjoyed before. He had a little money. The Ufa Theatre was now closed for the summer. Things were still awkward at home. He decided he would go and see the Russian capital for himself.

He went, of course, by train (though in an interview he said he went by bus). At last he had a real reason to visit Ufa station, rather than simply to watch the locomotives haul other people to exotic destinations. Arslanov went with him.

In the mid-1950s Russian railways were going through yet another phase of 'rationalisation' and the fifty-four directorates were being amalgamated into thirty-one larger units. Freight still had official priority but for passengers there were now three classes of travel, 'hard' (which Rudolf and Arslanov took), 'soft' and 'courier', small fast trains essentially for party officials on important business. Electrification was under way and speeds had improved a little since 1938 though it still took the Trans-Siberian nine days to get from Moscow to Vladivostok. At an average speed of 42 k.p.h. (26 m.p.h.) it took Rudolf and Arslanov thirty hours to travel the 800 miles from Ufa to Moscow.

Nureyev loved Moscow. 'Perhaps my first adult impression of Moscow was rather like a vast railway station [he could only afford to travel *to* the capital; once there he was forced to sleep on public benches or in station waiting rooms]. Never had I encountered so many races on the streets, so many different types of human beings – from Asia, Siberia, the Balkans and every conceivable province.' The two boys had arrived in the middle of August. This was convenient for sleeping on public benches, since it was warm throughout the short nights, but very inconvenient in other ways, since many theatres and concert halls were closed. And so Rudolf and Arslanov walked Moscow, seeing all the sights. 'I walked and walked until my legs simply refused to carry me any farther. Three days and almost three nights of walking . . . Moscow, that sprawling, enormous town where, as I soon found out, one meets the strongest conformism, a total acceptance of the Kremlin as a true symbol of the heart-beat of the country, and also the rebellious younger generation who take an ironic view of the staunch, middle-aged, unquestioning Stalinist man.' Since his own father was a Stalinist man, Rudolf was strengthened by his Moscow experience. He discovered he wasn't the only one who felt as he did about Russia in general, and Stalin in particular.

According to Arslanov, the one place they visited more than once was the Tretyakov Museum, which housed both modern paintings and pictures by Russian artists showing life before and during the revolution. There was an opulence in the paintings at the Tretyakov, a *Russian* opulence that Rudolf had seen nowhere else except in the theatre. He loved it, for the fact that it showed different possibilities.

The one spot off the tourist track which he visited was Horoshevskoye Shossé, where the family had lived during the war. The cinema was no longer there; it too had been bombed.

Three days after they had arrived, they boarded the train for Ufa, using the same station the whole family had travelled from thirteen years earlier when they had evacuated the city. Having walked for three days and nights, the young boys dozed the whole way back, slipping in and out of reverie. Rudolf now knew what life was like outside Ufa, in the more sophisticated world of Moscow. He had always felt instinctively that the world was full of possibilities. Now he had seen some of them for himself. As he travelled home, he knew there was no going back.

* * *

Back in Ufa relations between Rudolf and Hamet did not improve. Indeed, they got worse. For one thing, Rudolf was stronger now. He had always had an inner strength but now – well, he might not be the man of the world that his father was, not yet, but he had seen Moscow in all her glory, in all her guises. Another reason for the deteriorating relations was the fact that, during the winter, he was offered more regular employment by the ballet of the Ufa Opera. Although he had no formal training at any recognised ballet school, he was offered a position in the *corps de ballet*. Again he accepted without consulting his parents. He was sixteen and a half.

One perk of this new position as a permanent member of the Ufa Opera Ballet was that he was allowed to attend the classes of the regular dancers. This offered further training of a kind. Once again, he was not taught formally: no one ever said, 'Do it this way, Rudolf', or, 'Rudolf, this is correct.' Instead he was forced to imitate what the other dancers did. But he already had a good memory for steps, a memory that would not desert him as he grew older, and in any case he now had a lure. That winter, six months after Irina Alexandrovna had helped organise the letters, Rudolf finally heard from Moscow. He *would* be allowed to audition for the Leningrad School, but not until the summer. That, at least, allowed him time to prepare himself.

Arslanov was also in the *corps de ballet* and he confirms that relations with Hamet continued to be bad. As a member of the *corps*, Rudolf's salary was now at least equal to his father's. To Rudolf, who believed inside himself that he would not remain in the *corps* for long, the ballet, even in Ufa, offered the chance to earn more money than his father had ever dreamed of. Already his dancing paid better than security work – and medicine, for that matter. And then there was Hamet's own job. He had only ever put just enough food on the table for *his* family. The Nureyevs had never had any luxuries and now, aged forty-nine, his mother was still out at work in a milk factory. What did Hamet know?

In the early months of 1955, while the opera and ballet season lasted, Rudolf was hardly ever at home. He and his father were simply not speaking. In the mornings Rudolf attended classes. In the afternoon there were rehearsals, or fittings, or matinées. In the evenings he was at the theatre, whether he was performing or not. Guest stars – interesting people – were always passing through, for a few nights at a time, bringing with them new interpretations of familiar roles and stories from the outside world. Each night the theatre was a brightly lit, colourful, fantastic, romantic world, a million miles from the drabness of everyday Ufa. Given the chance, in 1955, who would *not* have loved Ufa Theatre?

At home, every now and then, Hamet would try to force chores upon Rudolf, to make it difficult for him to attend class, or even a performance. And Rudolf was still only seventeen. But this was so out of character for a Muslim who, hitherto, had adored his only son, that these episodes always ended badly, with Rudolf and Hamet screaming at each other, and the boy storming out of the house. These altercations made Rudolf's temper worse and, in class or backstage, he began to acquire a reputation as a firebrand, as an uncouth peasant. When he was in one of his vile moods, he swore at almost everybody, and at almost every opportunity. In 1955 swearing wasn't unknown, of course, but it was nowhere near as commonplace as it is now.

Towards the end of the season, some time in May, Rudolf was called into the office of Victor Cranstovich Parinas, the ballet master. He was a small, neat man, a bit of a pedant normally. 'Rudik,' Parinas said. 'I have received eleven marks against you for bad behaviour.' The scar on Rudolf's upper lip turned white. What was coming next? 'I really should throw you out of the company altogether,' Parinas went on. Rudolf's mind went back to when Zaituna Nureevna used to threaten to send him to the Matrasov Colony. He stood and stared at Parinas. Suddenly, the ballet master smiled. 'But instead, I'm inviting you to stay with the company as a fully-fledged dancer.'

This was an honour. In fact, it was more than an honour. It would mean better pay, better than his father's, and, besides the greater variety of roles he would be given, the chance at last to move away from Zentsova Street, into a communal flat for dancers his own age. This offered the chance of peace – of sorts – with his family. Perhaps Hamet would now concede that Rudolf was not a wastrel, that his talent was as genuine as his passion.

But . . . at the same time there had been his all-too-brief trip to Moscow. There was the Leningrad possibility around the corner. There was also the fact that, twice now, with Nureevna and with Parinas, despite his wayward behaviour, despite his ferocious temper and foul mouth, he had not been fired or sent away, but had been promoted. Informed people had recognised his talent, a talent so promising that they were prepared to make great allowances for his behaviour.

There was something else, too. That year the Republic of Bashkir was making a selection of dancers to take part in an important event, a festival celebrating a decade of Bashkir art, to be held in Moscow. All the best dancers, and ballet company officials from all over Russia would be there, watching. It would be the perfect opportunity for Rudolf to show his skills before an audience that really counted. If he could contrive to be selected for the Bashkiri *Dekada*, as it was called, then there was a good chance that, with his talents, he might be selected either for the Leningrad school, or one of the Moscow companies, the Bolshoi even. He had been to Moscow now, and knew what life could offer, outside Ufa. If, on the other hand, he accepted Parinas's offer, it would mean going on summer tour with the Ufa company and being away when the *Dekada* took place. All this went through Rudolf's mind as he stood there in the ballet master's office. Rudolf might have failed his school exams but he could be bright, phenomenally quick-witted when he needed to be. He now realised that a calculated gamble was called for. The situation demanded it.

And so, to the utter astonishment of Victor Cranstovich Parinas, Rudolf turned down the offer of becoming a full-time dancer in his home town.

It was a foolhardy risk in many ways. But, just occasionally, fortune really does favour the bold. A couple of weeks later, when the commissioner from the local Ministry of Culture, who was in charge of the auditions for the *Dekada*, was in Ufa, events played into Rudolf's hands. Everything had been made ready for the audition the minister was to watch – with one exception. The soloist had failed to appear. This was a disaster for everyone since if there was no performance no one from Ufa could be chosen. The director called the company together on stage, explained the situation and asked for a volunteer to take on the part. It was, as Rudolf himself was the first to admit, a 'situation you would expect to find in a romantic novel or film'. But he hadn't given up the chance to dance in the Ufa Ballet to let such an opportunity pass him by. Before the director had finished speaking, Rudolf stepped forward.

It was part of Rudolf's natural talent that he had a very retentive memory for dance sequences. On top of that, he had been forced to train himself on many occasions by imitating other, more senior, dancers. Almost without knowing it, he had picked up many of the soloist's steps during rehearsals. On that day, before the commissioner, all Rudolf required was a short session with the ballet master and he was ready to go on. In doing so, he saved the day not just for himself but for the entire company.

The circumstances of his elevation to the soloist's role were almost enough in themselves to ensure his place in the Moscow festival. As the man who had rescued everyone, he should at least be allowed to go, if only as a member of the *corps*. But that wasn't Rudolf's style. He had seized the opportunity the moment it was offered and wasn't about to squander it now. That day, in front of the commissioner, he danced with such a passionate intensity, with such conviction, with such zeal, that this feeling communicated itself to the audience which, at the end of his performance, applauded enthusiastically. (Many of the prominent citizens who had petitioned Moscow on his behalf the year before were in the auditorium.) Rudolf was selected for the *Dekada*, not as a *corps de ballet* member, but as a soloist.

His second visit to Moscow was somewhat different from his first. According to Pamira Sulemanovna, who was also on the trip:

'We stayed at the Hotel Aravat and although I was very shaken by the noise and bustle of the city, Rudik took me by the arm and led me forward. We were on Sverdlova Square, near the Bolshoi, and went down into the metro. He led me on to the escalator, hurrying me. If it hadn't been for him I would never have been able to get into the train, I was so scared. He seemed so confident. It wasn't until I read his [autobiography] that I realised he had been to Moscow before and so wasn't disoriented like the rest of us.

We had free passes into all the theatres of Moscow during the *Dekada* and we went to Nemirovicka Danchenko. I think *Swan Lake* was on. We went up to the gallery because we didn't have tickets. Suddenly I saw Rudik, who had grabbed one of the empty seats in the stalls. I watched and thought that at any moment somebody would come up and throw him out, but nothing happened. He sat and watched the whole performance in the stalls. We went to museums as well as theatres. We dashed all over the place.'

Rudolf loved Moscow just as much the second time. However, the *Dekada* itself did not prove the success he had hoped. There were no fewer than three rehearsals the day they arrived and the schedule continued to be heavy in the days that followed; it was this that helped prevent Rudolf making the impact he had anticipated. It must always be remembered that he had not really had any proper classical training at that point and so, although he was naturally strong, and young, he had not consolidated his strength through systematic exercises. And there was always that old, mysterious problem with his legs. With the demanding rehearsal programme in Moscow, he tired himself and landed heavily after a pirouette, spraining his toes. Later that day his foot swelled so much that he couldn't put on an ordinary shoe, let alone a ballet slipper. So although he was able to dance in the performance, he did not do so with the distinction, or the panache, that he had hoped.

On the contrary. Pamira says that when the Ufa troupe was written up in one of the newspapers someone else, a female dancer called Olga Toroshuna, was singled out as a future star. 'A little bit was said about me, and about Nina Ivanova, but there was no mention of any of the others. We were annoyed by the fact that so much was written about Olga – but it was said that her aunt had written the piece.' Either way, there was no mention of Rudolf.

Pamira also says that there was a viewing, a special rehearsal, for officials from the various choreographical schools, on the lookout for fresh talent. That led nowhere either, and by now Rudolf was growing desperate. His calculated gamble was not paying off.

Once more, however, Irina Alexandrovna intervened. She was in Moscow with the troupe, fulfilling her usual role as pianist for their rehearsals and classes. She looked upon Rudolf as her protégé and had entertained just as high hopes for him from the *Dekada* as he had himself. Now she set about making up for the setback. She seems to have had almost as much influence in Moscow as she did in Ufa because, after a week, by which time Rudolf's toes had healed, she arranged an audition for him with the great Asaf Messerer. Rudolf was impressed. This meeting would be his first with one of the truly great figures of Russian ballet. Messerer was a Bolshoi dancer and one of Russia's most famous ballet teachers – but he was more even than that. He was the man responsible for several technical advances in classical ballet, especially in mime, and he had helped push forward the importance of the male dancer. Messerer was also the teacher of the legendary Galina Ulanova, whom many consider to have been the greatest Juliet ever. She attended Messerer's classes daily.

On the day in question, Rudolf found Messerer in the rehearsal room of the Bolshoi, high up near the roof. This was Rudolf's first time backstage in that great theatre, with its enormously wide stage. *Bolshoi* is Russian for 'big' or 'grand', and the Bolshoi Theatre has been appropriately described by Clive Barnes in a book the New York Times published to coincide with the 50th anniversary of the revolution, as a cross between 'a fortress and a cathedral'. Messerer told Rudolf to take a seat and that he would audition him at the end of the class. And so, for forty-five minutes, the boy was given the treat of a lifetime, a close-up of *both* Ulanova and Messerer in action. But then, unfortunately, towards the end of the class Messerer was called away on an urgent personal matter. Rudolf hung on for a long time, 'and could have wept with frustration'. But Messerer never came back.

He had in fact been called away from Moscow – but he hadn't forgotten Rudolf. He arranged for the young dancer to be auditioned by someone else from the Bolshoi on the very next day. This time Rudolf danced as arranged. At the end, the man told Rudolf that, if he wished to enter the Moscow Ballet School he would be eligible for entry at the eighth-year stage. Rudolf was more than delighted. Ballet students traditionally started at the age of ten so, as a seventeen-year-old, he could expect to be admitted to the sixth or seventh grade at most. That the man thought he was eligible for a year above that was praise indeed. 'It was almost a miracle,' Nureyev wrote later.

But . . . there always seemed to be a 'but' in Rudolf's career. There were problems with Moscow Ballet School, for it was a school only, not a residential college. Young dancers had to find their own accommodation and pay for their own food: these matters were not covered by scholarships. Rudolf knew very well that even if his father could have afforded to send him to Moscow, he wouldn't. In a sense, the offer of a place there was worth-less.

But after the setback of the *Dekada*, the audition had fired Rudolf's spirits all over again, especially the official's view that he was worth admitting to the eighth grade. Rudolf now turned to Alik Biktchourine, a Ufa dancer who had trained at Leningrad and was in Moscow for the Bashkiri festival, although he himself was dancing in *Giselle* at the Bolshoi at the time. As a native of Ufa, and a more senior figure, he had made himself known to Rudolf and Pamira's troupe. As a fellow Muslim, he felt a certain kinship with Rudolf, one that was reciprocated. Rudolf went to Biktchourine, explained his dilemma, and asked if the older dancer could help him get an audition for the Leningrad School while he was here in Moscow.

There *were* officials from the Leningrad School in Moscow for the festival. Coincidentally, these were none other than Batacheva and Kumisnikov, who had taught Rudolf in Ufa a few weeks before. They may already have seen Rudolf dance in his troupe's official performance and dismissed him. Nonetheless, Biktchourine persuaded both men to audition Rudolf on his own. They did not go overboard like the man from the Bolshoi, nor did they say anything 'miraculous', such as that he could skip a grade. But they did say that when they returned to Leningrad, they would speak to the director, Chelkov, and recommend Rudolf for the Kirov School.

In his autobiography, Rudolf says that he took the bull by the horns at this point. Instead of returning to Ufa with the rest of the troupe, he used his fee for the *Dekada* to buy a ticket to Leningrad, where he immediately followed up on the Batacheva and Kumisnikov offer. But this is not how Pamira remembers it. 'When we got back to Ufa, Rudik came up to us after a lesson . . . we were sitting on a settee and then Rudik suddenly got up and said, "Everybody, listen. I am going to study in Leningrad." This upset me for some reason. I still don't know to this day why I cried so much. It may have been because I too wanted to study, or perhaps that I was sorry to see Rudik go.' Arslanov also recalls that Rudolf went back to Ufa, and then on another tour of Ryazan with the Ufa Ballet Company. He remembers clearly Rudolf buying each of his sisters a pair of fashionable *slattern valenkii*, felt boots, on that tour.

Perhaps Rudolf romanticised his acceptance into the Kirov School. It certainly seems unlikely that he would have left Ufa for the *Dekada* in Moscow, then decamped to Leningrad, and stayed. Even if Batacheva and Kumisnikov had endorsed his application enthusiastically, rather than offering a mere recommendation (as seems to have happened), he needed a scholarship. That had to be offered from Leningrad, approved by the Ministry of Culture in Moscow then at a local level in Ufa. It would have taken time.

Either way, in the third week of August 1955 Rudolf boarded the train out of Ufa yet again. In his hand he held a ticket for Leningrad. One-way.

CHAPTER THREE

This Freakish Stranger

. . . this freakish stranger,
who walks with sorrow, and with danger

According to Nureyev himself, he arrived in Leningrad on 17 August 1955. He always felt that the number seventeen played an important part in his life – and would point to the fact that he had been born on 17 March 1938 and that he defected on 17 June 1961, though there are doubts about both dates. In Moscow the trains for Leningrad leave from a station on Kazanski Square, just across from the terminal where the Trans-Siberian Express arrives. Having checked the timetable, and finding that trains left every half-hour or so, he plumped for the first available coach, only to find that it was filled with peasants and he had to stand all the way. Worse, this was a stopping train, not an express, and it took sixteen hours to reach its destination, rather than the usual eight.

After such a long and disagreeable journey he was even more dismayed, as the train approached Leningrad, to see that the city was covered with dark cloud, as if some terrible storm was about to break. This was August, high summer. He took his raincoat out of his bag and prepared for the worst. In fact, the clouds were industrial effluent, which always hung over the manufacturing suburbs of the city. This was not how a romantic country boy had imagined the city of the Tsars.

Leningrad station, where Rudolf arrived, is located at one end of Nevsky Prospekt, the wide, very long main street of the city which leads all the way to the River Neva and to the Hermitage Museum. It is one of the most famous and beautiful streets in the world, criss-crossed by narrow canals, and lined with churches and cathedrals, grand hotels, small parks and elegant eighteenth-century mansions. Rudolf decided to save all that for later. Without even finding a place to stay, he made straight for the Ulitsa Rossi, Rossi Street, named after Carlo Rossi, the Italian architect who had designed the street and the Pushkin Theatre which stands at one end. This is where the ballet school was located.

The street is very pretty. At the other end from the theatre is a small circular park, one side of which gives on to the Fontanka canal, the other to a striking eighteenth-century arch decorated in yellowy-cream stucco. As one looks at the theatre, from the park, the ballet school is on the right, separated from the Pushkin by the theatre museum and library. If only the authorities gave it a lick of paint, the Ulitsa Rossi would easily rate as one of the prettiest small streets anywhere.

Although he was only seventeen, in ballet matters Rudolf already had an old head on young shoulders.

'In Leningrad [unlike Moscow] the college was already established and most of the students lived there, either paying for their room and board or subsisting on scholarships, as I had hoped to do. I might add that the existence of the college attached to the Kirov since its early days is an important factor in creating the feeling of unity, the almost monastic dedication which you find there and which forges the Kirov into the strong, unique ensemble that it is.'

As he opened the glass door into the small foyer of the college, Rudolf fancied that he could hear the footsteps of his illustrious predecessors – Vaslav Nijinksy, Konstanin Sergeyev, George Balanchine. But in fact all he could hear were the noises of cleaners and decorators. In his hurry to get to the school, he had arrived too early, and the annual redecoration was still going on. Term would not begin for another week.

But he had travelled more than a thousand miles, standing for much of the way. He was undeterred, and accosted the first person he saw who didn't look like a decorator. It was a fellow student, another boy who had arrived early, and from him Rudolf asked urgently if he knew where he might find Comrade Chelkov, the head of the school. This was the name Batacheva and Kumisnikov had mentioned after his audition in Moscow. Before the boy could reply, Rudolf felt a tap on his shoulder. He turned to see a big, red-faced man, balding but with grey hair. 'I'm Chelkov,' he said. 'What do you want?'

With more than a touch of swagger, Rudolf told him that he was the artist from Ufa, who had been auditioned in Moscow in the summer and had been recommended by Batacheva and Kumisnikov. He had arrived to take up his studies.

Chelkov, on this occasion at least, was gentle with the boy, who must have been exhausted after standing for sixteen hours in the swaying, crowded train. He told Rudolf to come back in seven days' time, on

24 August, when classes were due to start and he could be examined properly.

And so Rudolf was given an unexpected holiday, a week in which to explore Leningrad, as he had explored Moscow the year before. Moreover, he found that he was not alone in the city. Udeltsova was there, making her annual visit to keep in touch with what was happening in the world of dance, music and literature. She was staying with her daughter, a psychiatrist.

With the daughter's help, Rudolf found lodgings near the Kirov Theatre and, during the next few days, set about walking the city. Leningrad is made for walking, being a mixture of open spaces, arrived at unexpectedly, and more intimate side streets following the curves of the canals. The buildings are not as high as those of Paris but, like that city, Leningrad is full of half-hidden courtyards, glimpsed through archways. The predominant colours are cream and ochre, pale earthy colours which give the city a unity matched only by Paris. And then, of course, there is the River Neva, slow-moving and wide, wide enough to dominate the huge palaces and museums that line its banks. Rudolf found in Leningrad 'a city which could subtly match all one's moods: often nostalgic, melancholy, clinging to its past, suddenly under a ray of sunshine it would emerge cheerful and smiling, its ancient stone façades timeless and alive'. The great cathedrals and churches, with their onion domes, lay dotted around the city like exotic blooms in a formal garden.

In the evenings Rudolf would visit Udeltsova, who had a nostalgia all her own, looking back to the Russia of Tsarist times. She had been exiled to Ufa before the revolution. Gradually, during that week, her stories conveyed to Rudolf the great intellectual upheaval that had taken place in Russia during those years, as she mentioned name after name of people who had fled rather than live under Leninism. There were lighter moments, too, especially when she talked of her sister, who had been married to a rich Moscow merchant. After the revolution, she was frightened to show off her jewels, but equally frightened to leave them at home. When she went out she wore every stone she owned, but concealed *beneath* her clothes. This may have calmed *her* nerves but not those of her husband, who always carried a pistol with him wherever they went, just in case. Sentimental Muscovites thought he was jealous of his pretty young bride 'but in fact it was the remains of their wealth he was so zealously protecting'.

During that week, when Rudolf was relaxing in Leningrad and Udeltsova talked and talked of a different time, a change came over him. No city in Russia had altered so much after the revolution as had Leningrad. The more Rudolf learned about this, the more he realised, for the first time, that there was nothing inevitable about the Soviet system, that it was by no means the only way of life in the world.

His favourite academic subject in school, apart from dance, had been geography but in School Number Two it was taught in a fairly basic way. The other possibilities around the world were never explored; many were never even mentioned. His parents were Stalinists but also ignorant ex-peasants. His father had been to Berlin but only in wartime. As he listened to Udeltsova revisiting her past, Rudolf began to think of Leningrad in a different light.

St Petersburg achieved the peak of its cosmopolitan fame at the end of the nineteenth and the beginning of the twentieth centuries. It was visited by the fashionable people of Europe and America, being well served by fast international trains and the best steamship lines. By train it was only forty-six hours from Paris and twenty-eight from Berlin; the trains in those days achieved speeds in excess of 60 k.p.h. From London a regular steamship service left Tilbury every Friday night, travelling via the Kiel canal.

Arriving, passengers were spoiled for choice among the top hotels. As Suzanne Massie has pointed out, in her book on old Russia, the Astoria especially catered for British travellers, boasting a fine library of English-language books, ranging from Chaucer to D.H. Lawrence. The telephone system in St Petersburg was the best in existence at the time. The telephone book contained the seating plans for all the theatres (there were four ballet companies in those days), as well as details of fashionable milliners, florists and other specialities, such as *chocolatiers*. Doctors, lawyers and even the crack regiments had their own section, an early form of 'Yellow Pages'.

The restaurants were no less exotic. The most famous French restaurant was Donon's, though Dominique's was known for its draught beer. Privato's was generally regarded as the best Italian eating place though Palkin's boasted organ music. In Leiner's, a cosy delicatessen with sawdust on the floor, Diaghilev, Benois and Stravinsky argued and planned while eating caviare, Black Sea oysters and the most delicious pickled mushrooms in the world. The imperial palaces could be visited by well-connected foreigners, provided they left their passports at the entrance. The changing of the guard took place every day, as in London, though a little later, at noon. If anything, the household cavalry was smarter than in London for, in addition to their sparkling uniforms, each regiment boasted mounts of matching colour: the Horse Guards were black, the Gatchina Hussars dapple-grey, and the Chevaliers Gardes chestnut. Horse races took place in spring and summer, and there were news vendors on every corner, with the foreign papers available at Wolff's and Violet's.

At the Maryinsky Theatre the new operas and ballets of Tchaikovsky, Borodin and Rimsky-Korsakov were produced impeccably, not to mention the works of Wagner. The finest German, Italian and French singers and dancers came to St Petersburg. Rimsky-Korsakov himself was a regular conductor. Sarah Bernhardt made several visits to the Mikhailovsky Theatre. Each of the four opera houses remained open for an eight- or nine-month season, such was the demand.

In 1910, when Udeltsova was already twenty-two, Nicholas II built the Narodny Dom, or People's Palace. The most significant feature of such palaces, the fashion for which spread quickly throughout the country, was that they could be used as a concert and opera theatre with extremely low-priced seats. But the palace also contained a non-paying choir school, a free library and a number of lecture halls. In St Petersburg, the Narodny Dom accommodated 3,000 in the concert hall and the admission to the standing enclosure cost the equivalent of one penny. The best national and international companies were booked for the Dom and they were immensely popular. According to a report in the London *Times*, the auditorium was filled with 'crowds of working people, artisans and soldiers who are given the opportunity of becoming acquainted with a great variety of standard operas, both Russian and foreign'.

No other country was as lavish in its support of the performing arts as Russia, all thanks to the Tsars. One of the brightest jewels in St Petersburg, one of the institutions the Tsars and the city was most proud of, was the Imperial Ballet School, the forerunner of the institution Rudolf was about to enter. He had some idea of the school's history but only from tendentious post-revolution Marxist tracts. But Udeltsova had been there before the revolution and her memory was undimmed.

In imperial days, acceptance by the school was already very difficult. Fewer than 10 per cent of applicants were successful. The children were given a rigorous medical examination, in which their spines, hearts and hearing were the main focus of attention. They were asked to sing a scale and required to read music. For those who passed these tests, and were admitted, the first two years were regarded as probation (a little like admission to holy orders). During this time, the pupils continued to live at home but were otherwise supplied with everything from the school. After two years, if they qualified, they entered a world apart, where their life really did become as secluded and regulated as life in a monastery or a convent.

But a lush form of monastery or convent. A doorman in imperial livery stood guard in the lobby. Portraits of the Emperor and of great ballerinas from the past hung in all the corridors. The school had its own chapel, painted yellow and white, the imperial colours, its own theatre, where the annual examination took place, and which was shared with pupils of the Imperial Drama School. The ballet school had its own hospital with its own doctors and nurses who specialised in the type of injury sustained in dance.

All the pupils had to wear uniforms. The boys had three – black for everyday wear, dark blue for holidays, and grey linen for summer, with a high velvet collar on which was embroidered a silver lyre, encircled with palms and surmounted with the imperial crown. The boys also had two overcoats, one for winter with a heavy astrakhan collar, patent-leather boots, and six changes of underwear. The student-ballerinas wore serge dresses with tight bodices and a white fichu of lawn, black alpaca aprons for every day and white tucked aprons for Sundays, with white stockings and black pumps. Juniors wore brown bodices. Pink was given as a mark of distinction and a white dress was the highest mark of all. The students even had a special uniform for taking walks.

Rudolf loved all this talk of clothes. He was not merely clothes conscious but loved *texture*, the feel of things, quite apart from their colour or shape. He loved it too when Udeltsova explained the routine of the Imperial School. It wasn't what he would experience but he was still avid to know what had gone before, what the other possibilities were.

The Imperial Ballet School had been spacious. The dormitories slept anywhere from twenty-five to forty, but in spaces that had been designed for fifty. Each pupil had his or her own cubicle with his or her own icon above the bed. The sexes were strictly segregated, of course, and even when they did meet, for ballroom dancing lessons or at rehearsals, they were forbidden to talk to teach other and were even instructed to keep their eyes lowered.

The daily routine was strict but not unpleasant. Pupils arose at 7.30 and had to exchange yesterday's handkerchief for that day's fresh one. All girls up to the age of fifteen had their hair brushed every day by a maid. Once a week, on Fridays, they were taken to the steam baths, where maids in white linen shifts scrubbed them on wooden benches. Every Saturday they were examined by a doctor. Being dancers, their feet were well cared for: a chiropodist was in constant attendance.

In every sense they were considered as part of the imperial household. In recognition of this, the Tsar or his family would often send expensive delicacies to the pupils' dining table. Only people used to the finer things of life, it was felt, could be expected to dance in a graceful way. That appealed to Rudolf.

This protected species remained in the imperial school for eight years. They were taught far more than dancing – maths, history, languages, manners. As seniors they were taken to the theatre and given lessons in elocution, acting and singing. They were taught make-up, in mock theatrical dressing-rooms, with mirrors edged in lights, just like the real thing.

Of course, dancing was the main reason they were at the school. For several hours a day, while their teachers played the violin, they went through their exercises, the boys in black trousers and white blouses, the girls provided with tasselled shawls to keep them warm during the breaks. As a high honour, the pupils who excelled were asked to water the floor, which settled the dust and kept the surface from being slippery.

After the first year the pupils took part in real productions at the Maryinsky, to give them stage experience. This was, and is, a lovely theatre, pale green on the outside, with blue, gold and white hangings adorning the boxes inside. There are sparkling crystal chandeliers, and chairs upholstered in blue velvet. Designed in 1860 by Albert Cavos, the Maryinsky is both gay and cosy. The pupils of the Imperial School were taken to the theatre in their own carriages, which seated six. They were accompanied by their governesses, a maid and a beadle in livery. Long vehicles, which accommodated fifteen, were used for grand occasions and their arrival at the theatre was part of the spectacle. In the theatre they were provided with their own dressing-room. Before the revolution, the Maryinsky was a near-holy place. Special carriages also fetched the artists and took them home after each performance; every ballerina was given a carriage to herself.

Udeltsova knew how to tell a story. By Rudolf's day it was a changed world. But that wasn't the point. From the way she spoke, she made being a ballet dancer *exciting*. Some of the traditions of the Imperial School may have changed but, listening to Udeltsova talk, Rudolf saw more than ever that it was still a glittering world.

It was Anna Ivanova Udeltsova who also explained to Rudolf how St Petersburg, and its ballet school, had changed since her day. After the war of 1914 and the revolution of 1917 the city's name had been changed, to Petrograd at first. For a time the very existence of the ballet was threatened, and many dancers had already gone abroad (including Nijinsky and Balanchine, as well as Diaghilev, ballet's greatest impresario). Some revolutionaries wanted to close down the imperial theatres, which they considered to be extravagant and frivolous luxuries of the court and aristocracy. Fortunately, Lenin didn't agree and his first Commissar for the Arts, Anatole Lunasharsky, saved the day, by re-establishing the imperial theatres as academic theatres and endowing them and their attendant schools with central funds. The intake of the schools was changed, of course, and many of the traditions abolished (such as maids combing the ballerinas' hair). But the central preoccupation with excellence was maintained. Indeed, the Leningrad school was actually strengthened during the 1920s, following the defection of so many dancers, and it was renamed after Agrippina Vaganova, a legendary teacher under whose guidance the school continued to produce amazing dancers – Galina Ulanova, Marina Semenova and Natalia Dudinskaya among the women; Alexei Yermolaev, Vakhtung Chaboukiani and Konstantin Sergeyev among the men. The Vaganova School was less opulent than the Imperial School, more austere. But it was no less distinguished.

By the time his week of waiting in Leningrad was over, Rudolf felt both sad and excited. Sad that so many of the colourful traditions had been lost, but excited that he now knew so much about the institution he was about to join. It all served to strengthen his determination to do well.

The twenty-fourth of August finally arrived, and in the morning Rudolf presented himself at Rossi Street. He was not alone. Young dancers from all over the Soviet Union, and from abroad too, presented themselves every August (and still do). Some, like Rudolf, hoped for scholarships, others had parents or, if they were from the socialist countries of Eastern Europe, governments who were willing to pay for room and board, if only their candidates could scrape in. On different days of that week, dancers from one particular region would be assessed. It would be Georgians one day, Ukrainians another. On the twenty-fourth it was the turn of the Latvians.

The steps outside the Vaganova, on Rossi Street, were crowded not just with children but with their mothers too, for some of the applicants were very young. Pupils entered the Vaganova in three tranches. The earliest started at nine, for an eight-year course. Some older children were taken at thirteen, for a six-year course. It is said in Russia that children who enrol on this course sometimes progress more rapidly because they arrive with a more mature intellect and can profit from instruction more readily. (Certainly ballet experts in most countries now accept that children should not begin instruction any younger than nine.) At the Vaganova, a small proportion of exceptionally gifted students are admitted for a two- to three-year course. This is the entry for which Rudolf was to be assessed, which confirms that Batacheva and Kumisnikov, when they had seen him in Moscow, had been as impressed as Messerer's colleague from the Bolshoi, who had offered him a place in the eighth grade.

Rudolf pushed past the mothers and their children, climbed the few steps into the lobby, and saw from a notice underneath a framed photograph of Semenova that he was to be examined by Vera Kostrovitskaya. Vera Sergeevna Kostrovitskaya was – according to Marguerite Alfimova, a ballerina of Rudolf's generation, who graduated from her class – very strict on the technical side of dance. She was systematic, methodical and very demanding and didn't hesitate to send anyone who didn't match up to her high standards back down to a younger class, until they had mastered the basics. She left the teaching of expression, the dramatic side of dance, to others and so she was in many ways the worst possible assessor Rudolf could have had, since his strengths lay in his expressive power whereas his weaknesses, due to lack of training, were in his technical ability. Alfimova herself, who later became one of the Kirov's better dancers, failed one of Kostrovitskaya's classes and was relegated for a year.

Rudolf, however, had heard very good reports of Kostrovitskaya, whom he believed at the time to be the best teacher in Russia. He later said that he arrived at the Vaganova knowing nothing about ballet technique – but was that entirely true? There were, after all, several people back home in Ufa who had trained in Leningrad. In Moscow, at the Bolshoi, Messerer's colleague had said he could skip a year. If accepted at the Vaganova, at seventeen, he would be put on a three-year course. In other words, he had to be good enough to be thought able to benefit from such a short course.

The examination took place in one of the rehearsal rooms on the ground floor, beyond the commissary where the pupils who were already members of the school were collecting their sheets, pillows and uniforms. There was just piano accompaniment, and Kostrovitskaya sat on an uncomfortable-looking chair underneath the lunette windows. Rudolf was nervous. As he watched some of the other pupils limbering up, he could not help but notice their crisp, clean movements, the product in most cases of years of classical training. When it came to his turn to dance, his whole manner betrayed that he had had very little classical training up to that point. His style was soft and fluid compared with the others, almost none of his movements the product of a sure and conscious technique. This had its good side, for it meant that his dancing retained its individual flavour; that he still showed the passion with which he had first embraced dancing as a boy. In his performance there was no hint of dry routine.

But that wasn't the main point. The point was: was his natural spontaneity, his expressive ability, capable of being harnessed to proper training? Or was it too late? Batacheva and Kumisnikov had felt he was worth the risk, but would Kostrovitskaya agree?

He had performed some exercises but knew he was better in an actual role, with the possibility for expression, for feeling. He had danced *Song of the Cranes* often enough and he went back to that now. He used up the entire room, devouring the space with his own brand of dance, and showing off his elevation. Time and again he had been told that his movements fitted perfectly the phrasing of the music and he could only hope that Kostrovitskaya would notice, and not be too worried by his obvious weaknesses in technique.

And then he was done. He stood, panting and sweating, looking across at the woman who was to decide his future. He held himself upright, a proud stance, but he didn't approach her. Already he was aware that he had a stage presence and he wanted her to feel it. For a moment she remained seated on her chair, looking at him with her hands in her lap. Then she got up and came towards him. She walked slowly. She was a small woman, wearing ballet pumps that were adapted with low leather heels. Those heels clicked on the floor of the rehearsal room.

She stood before him, close. He tried to read her face but could not. Her eyes raked across him, taking in his sweating forehead, his still-heaving chest, the fact that, even for a short audition, he was exhausted, having poured himself into his performance.

Eventually she spoke. 'Young man,' she said in a voice loud enough for the pianist to hear, 'you will either become a brilliant dancer – or a total failure.' Rudolf was too breathless to say anything before she added, 'And most likely you'll be a failure!'

What did *that* mean? It meant that Rudolf was in. It meant that Vera Sergeevna, the great mistress of technique, had responded to the passion in this young dancer. It meant that, in just a short time, he had achieved the near-impossible. He had caused her to forget, or overlook, his technical shortcomings, which were her own forte, to recognise what this raw, unbridled dancer *might become*. She had realised that Rudolf would have to work harder than anyone else, to perfect his technique and build his muscles, and that he might fail. But she had seen the stage presence, the embodiment of the Tartar temperament; she had witnessed, amid the fluidity of his movements, the fanaticism and iron control inside him, without which no great dancer is made. And she had judged that he was worth the risk.

Rudolf left the room to change into some dry clothes. He still had to pass the medical examination (that hadn't changed since before the revolution). But that didn't worry Rudolf. He had stood for sixteen hours in a train compartment to get here. He knew he was fit. He had made it. He was going to be a classical dancer in the world's best school. Vaganova records show that he arrived with a ski jacket, a dark brown costume, 'very tattered shoes' all carried in a briefcase rather than a suitcase.

Leningrad – St Petersburg – had not always been the world's best school, nor had the Kirov always been the world's best company. Nowadays we accept classical ballet as an art form in which the Russians excel, but although the Imperial School was founded in the eighteenth century, ballet as we know it was an Italian invention and developed in its modern form in France.

Catherine de Medici took the court dance from Italy to France when she left Florence to marry Louis XIV in the second half of the sixteenth century. At that time there was no real distinction between opera and ballet – the 'spectacle' consisted of both, plus poetry declaimed aloud from the stage. This appealed enormously to the French king, who liked to dance himself and performed in several early ballets. The first appears to have been *Le Ballet comique de la reine*, produced in 1581 by Baldassarino Belgiojoso, who had been Catherine's valet. The

French court took up the king's passion, and the French mind codified the dance, with Louis XVI setting up L'Académie Nationale de la Danse in 1661. From that time on, an unbroken line of dancers and teachers may be traced all the way down to the present day where, at the Paris Opéra Ballet, Louis's Académie still exists.

To begin with, the French ballets were essentially mythological stories, but included comedies as well as romances. It was all fairly sedate, technically speaking. The other advance which the French made in the seventeenth century was the inclusion of more acrobatic dancing in the familar kind of court spectacle. At that time the gypsies and acrobats in the popular circuses performed a quite different kind of movement to music, at fairs and festivals, and French dance experts had the vision to see that a marriage between the two styles could work.

Until the early eighteenth century, dancing was essentially a male preserve. For one thing, the sexual mores of the day insisted that women wear long dresses and keep their legs and feet hidden. While such fashions were followed, dance – for women at least – could never be more than a set of elaborate patterns drawn horizontally on the stage. It was both impossible and unthinkable for women to *jump* in their dresses. However, in 1721, the ballerina known as La Camargo caused a scandal by shortening her skirt – just a few inches – so that her feet and ankles were visible; the costume she wore was portrayed by Nicolas Lancret in a famous painting. This minor change at least freed the ballerina's feet to do more interesting things and it was La Camargo who invented the *entrechat*.

As a result of this, dresses began to shorten still further, as dancers and choreographers exploited the technical possibilities of free legs. This change also promoted the ballerina at the expense of the male dancer. Experiments continued throughout the eighteenth century, culminating just after the French revolution, when Maillot, the costumier at the French Opéra, invented tights, freeing the legs completely. Like everything else, this created a scandal at first, and in some places they were banned. Eventually, however, even the Pope allowed them to be used in the theatres under his jurisdiction, so long as they were coloured blue, so as not to suggest that they were flesh.

At the same time as La Camargo was shortening her skirt, the five positions, the basis of ballet technique, came into general use, encouraged by an Italian dancing master who recognised that when the feet were turned out the line of the body was more graceful and certain steps were easier to execute from that starting point.

After Camargo the next great influence in France was that of Jean-Georges Noverre. Born in Paris in 1727, Noverre, possibly the son of an aide-de-camp of Charles II, was initially destined for a military career, but fell in love with the dance. He was a better choreographer than he was a dancer (his first ballet had décor by Boucher), but he

Peter Watson

was best of all as a theoriser of dance. Until Noverre, dance had been a mainly visual affair, what we would today call *divertissements*, without form or meaning. It was Noverre who, in *Lettres sur la danse et les ballets* (1760) insisted that dance was a dramatic art, which, like other art forms, needed an introduction, development and a climax; that it should *express* a dramatic idea.

Noverre was something of an itinerant but he did spend eight years in Stuttgart, where the art-loving Grand-Duke of Württemberg placed a huge company at his disposal, with no fewer than a hundred in the *corps de ballet* and twenty principals. Stuttgart thus became a great centre of ballet activity, especially when revolution curtailed the performing arts in France, and many great dancers flocked to work with Noverre. Among them were Mademoiselle Heinel, who invented the pirouette, Pierre Gardel and Auguste Vestris, who brought in the *rond de jambes*. Noverre also dispensed with the mask which, until then, had been customary wear for dancers.

In stifling developments in Paris, the revolution did more than drive the ballet to Stuttgart. Many French dancers fled to Milan, where at that time two men were responsible for a revival of the dance at La Scala. The first was Salvatore Viganò, a nephew of the composer Boccherini, who developed the Milan *corps de ballet* to new heights, fashioning it into a creative ensemble in its own right, and not just as a backdrop for the principal dancers. But the more important of the two Milanese was Carlo Blasis. Blasis was a pupil of Gardel and of Jean Bercher (known to everyone as Dauberval), and therefore a direct artistic descendant of Noverre. And like him, Blasis may be regarded as one of the fathers of classical ballet. His contribution was threefold. His famous *Treatise on the Art of Dancing* codified the developments of dance to that point. Second, he stipulated that dance, as well as having all the emotional force of dramatic theatre, should take its physical form from nature and anatomy. He advocated that dancers study painting and sculpture, to emulate the forms they found in great classical art and, as a result, he invented the 'attitude'. This is a way of finishing a series of steps so that the figure is not simply left standing upright on the stage but instead poses in some more graceful way – Blasis himself took his ideas from Giambologna's statue, *Mercury*. His third innovation was the creation of an Academy of Dancing in Milan, in 1837. It was the Milan academy which became the model for all the others and set the basic pattern for ballet training which exists to this day. Pupils were not admitted before the age of eight or after twelve (fourteen for boys). They were attached to the school for eight years, during which time they did three hours' practice every day, with one hour of mime. It was Blasis who introduced the *barre*.

By 1837, when the Milan academy opened, the whole of Europe was swamped in the romantic movement, which had momentous consequences for the ballet. It was an age of extreme artificiality, whose idols were Heinrich Heine and Walter Scott. The greatest productions were the dramas of Victor Hugo, the enormous paintings of Delacroix and the music of Hector Berlioz – though so far as ballet was concerned the French poet Théophile Gautier was the central figure. He was not merely a passionate balletomane but a fulsome and ubiquitous critic and an inventor of plots. It was a time when, in Arnold Haskell's apt phrase, 'The fairy, the wili, the witch, and the vampire swept away the heroes of antiquity, the pale German moonlight of Goethe replaced Olympus.' In ballet the ballerina had now entirely replaced the male dancer. 'Woman was idealised, and the man must be content to remain in the background and lift her when necessary.'

This period saw some fine ballets, most notably *La Sylphide* and *Giselle* (originally visualised by Gautier), which was so popular that it entered, and remained in, the permanent repertoires of Paris, London, Milan and St Petersburg. These ballets were aided by the one great technical development of the period, *les pointes*, the use of the tips of the toes. This was perhaps the greatest technical development of all, enabling the ballerina to appear to float above the stage, delicate and artificial, ethereal at the same time every night, the perfect embodiment of the romantic movement.

But there was a price to pay for such complete identification of an entire art form with a single movement. In the first place, the emphasis of the romantic was so concentrated on human frailty and on the supernatural qualities that sex appeal completely disappeared from the stage. This was fine for a while, perhaps, but then romanticism gave way to other nineteenth century 'isms' – realism at first (helped by the invention of photography), then impressionism. As romanticism sank, so did the ballet. This was particularly true in France where, towards the end of the nineteenth century, the ballet became little more than a notorious pick-up place where the young bloods of the day were allowed to flirt with the 'rats', as the ballerinas in the *corps de ballet* were known, in the intervals of the performance. The tawdry circus that the ballet had become is nowhere more evident than in the canvases and pastels of Edgar Degas. The French themselves refer to this as *La Décadence*.

By the end of the nineteenth century, there was only one country where the ballet had not fallen into disrepute. Russia.

There is a mention of Russian dancers at the court of Louis XIV, when some 'Muscovites' arrived to learn the art and distinguished themselves by their lack of attention. Peter the Great (1672–1725), the first of the Tsars to pay particular attention to ballet, had a general policy of westernising Russia (and especially of Frenchifying it). He wanted to make Russia more modern, less backward. He forced the boyards (aristocrats) to shave their beards and instituted costume reforms. His enthusiasm was taken up by Empress Anne, who founded the academy in St Petersburg which Rudolf was about to join. Anne considered dance so important that it was included in the curriculum of the army cadets. She, like Peter, was disturbed at the segregation of the sexes in Russia, which smacked of oriental backwardness.

But it was under Catherine the Great (1762–96) that the ballet made its greatest advances in Russia. As with Louis XIV in France, she made it popular at court. The difference was that, in Russia, with its vast estates thousands of miles from the centre, many nobles, in emulation of the Empress, set up their own companies out of season when they were at home. Ballet in Russia both was, and was not, a court art. It also became an art of the people, achieving a depth in the country that it never had in France or Italy.

By the same token, the central schools, especially the Imperial School in St Petersburg, became more important, as the guardians of national standards. Under Anne, foreign teachers were brought in – people such as Franz Hilferding, the influential Austrian dancing master who worked throughout Europe. The first graduates were produced in 1742 but the school did not have a Russian director until Ivan Valberg took over in 1794. International standards were maintained by the importation of the best foreign talent – Charles Didelot, Louis Dupré and even Marie Taglioni. Naturally, Russia soon began to produce her own ballerinas, especially under the influence of Didelot, who returned to St Petersburg to teach and stayed for twenty-one years. His pupils included Elena Andreyanova, who became one of the finest early Giselles, and Avdotia Istomina, who moved her audiences and inspired Russian poets.

But the depth of Russian ballet, its geographic spread across the vast steppes of eastern Europe and central Asia, was only one of the reasons that Russian ballet held up when it was in decline everywhere else. The other reason was that a small number of exceptional foreigners made St Petersburg their home, maintaining the tradition that Hilferding and Didelot had begun.

The first and most important was Marius Petipa, a Frenchman from Marseilles. He was a soloist with the company from 1847, then ballet master, and from 1869 to 1903, chief ballet master. He ran the Imperial Ballet for fifty years, choreographing some of the great classical ballets. He devised *Don Quixote* in 1871 and *La Bayadère* in 1877, then developed the symphonic form of dancing and worked with Tchaikovsky and Glazunov on the first great symphonic ballets, *Sleeping Beauty* (1890), *Swan Lake* (1895) and *Raymonda* (1898). Despite his influence, and the length of time he spent in the imperial capital, Petipa never properly learned Russian (which shows how successful Peter the Great's Frenchification had been). Petipa was aided by Gustave Johannsen, a Dane and a great teacher, and their skills were later enhanced by those of Enrico Cecchetti, a virtuoso Italian.

(*top*) Hamet, Rudolf's father: 'dancing doesn't put bread on the table'.

Farida, Rudolf's mother: 'she always wore a troubled expression'.

(*top*) Rudolf always wore a hat, even from an early age.

(*bottom*) A younger Farida, with Lilia, Rezida and Rosa: not Russians but descendants of the Tartar hordes'.

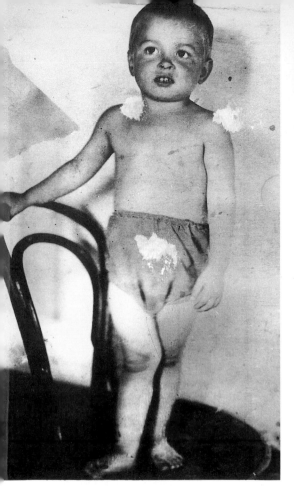

(*top left*) Rudolf aged eighteen months in Vladivostok. (*top right*) Rudolf, as a boy, with toy pistol and his mother's troubled expression. (*below*) Rudolf's kindergarten class: he is in the middle row, fourth from left.

(*top*) Rudolf, left in
Bashkiri costume.

Rudolf at the 'Bashkiri
Dekada'.

The late starter in full flight.

With Alla Sizova, before he became handsome. The authorities tried to make them a partnership, but the more beautifully they danced together, the more they loathed each other.

Rudolf, far left: Pushkin, third from left; his teacher always wore a tie.

Rudolf, second from the left, at the Vaganova graduation (inset of theatre union card).

With Irina Kolpakova in the late 1950s.

A solo in La Bayadere; Rudolf, controversially, shortened this costume to make it more revealing.

With Erik Bruhn, South of
France, 1961.

With Erik in New York, a rare
public display of affection. 'But
Erik could be very cruel.'

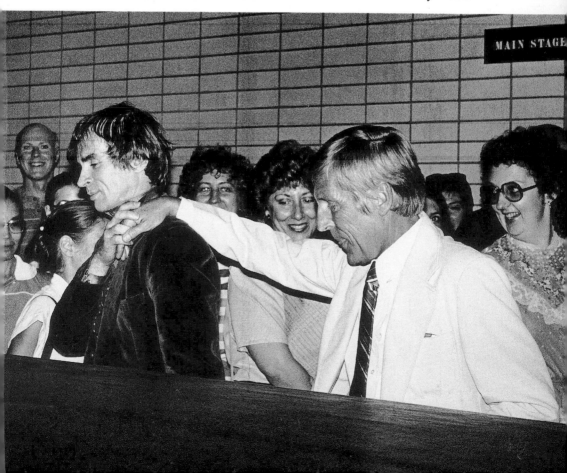

MAIN STAGE

Rudolf in his
'Christmas tree'
outfit, with the De
Cuevas Ballet,
Paris, 1961, with
Nina Vyroubova.

With Rosella Hightower in the South of France, Summer 1961.

By the end of the nineteenth century, then, ballet in Russia was still very much alive, far more so than was true anywhere else. But by now Petipa had been the dominant force for fifty years and his influence was growing stale. There were great dancers – Mathilde Kchesinska, Vera Trefilova, Olga Preobrajenska – but somehow the new works were not quite up to them. The Imperial Theatre was thus fortunate in that, in 1904, Michel Fokine, a graduate of both the dance and drama schools, as well as a musician and a painter, took over as chief choreographer. Fokine was a revolutionary in his art but ever mindful of the traditions of Noverre and Blasis. He agreed with Isadora Duncan, then making waves in America, that ballet was too much in thrall to *les pointes* and too wedded to the three-hour ballet. Change had to come.

In his first ballets, *Nuits d'Egypte* and *Eunice*, he abolished both and the scandal was such that he was nearly forced to flee the theatre. But Fokine was right to make changes. He had injected new blood, new grey matter rather, into the Imperial Ballet and before long a new generation of great dancers was dazzling the St Petersburg balletomanes – Anna Pavlova, Tamara Karsavina, Vaslav Nijinsky, Olga Spessivtseva and others.

Fokine also acted as a bridge to yet another extraordinary talent. In St Petersburg he was a member of a group of remarkable young men who were led by Alexandre Benois. Benois was first and foremost a painter, and a very good one too. But he also designed scenery and costumes for Fokine and even took a hand in working out storylines. At the university he led a discussion group, or club, where artistic matters were endlessly argued over. One of the young men on the edge of this group was Serge Diaghilev. He was in the capital to study law, though his chief ambition was to become a composer. He had suffered an early setback when he met Rimsky-Korsakov, who told him he had no talent for composing. With exemplary panache, Diaghilev simply changed tack and, before long, he and Benois had launched their own series of books, *Mir Isskoustva* (The World of Art).

At first, Diaghilev had not been interested in the ballet but he showed himself so good at organising the World of Art project that he was offered an administrative post in the Imperial Theatres. The man who offered him the job, Prince Serge Wolkonsky, was eager for reform and, on the face of it, Diaghilev should have been a success. Unfortunately, he had already made enemies in St Petersburg, traditionalists who couldn't stomach the new theories of art expounded in the World of Art. When he tried to impose his radical views on a new production of Delibes's *Sylvia*, which was entrusted to him, the company threatened to go on strike. Wolkonsky did his best to mediate but Diaghilev refused to compromise, and was dismissed.

This made two setbacks in short order. Diaghilev was dismayed but not defeated. He managed to mount a number of art exhibitions, with increasing success and, in time, built on that, bringing Russian painting, then music, then opera, to Paris. In this way he found his true *métier*, as an impresario of distinction. Finally, in 1909, he brought his Ballet Russes to Paris, and then to London, and revolutionised the whole art form. His productions were a fantastic success but ironically, in calling attention to Russian ballet with his company's name, he was actually taking the spotlight away from St Petersburg, at least for a while.

The other irony is that Diaghilev was a non-dancer, a non-composer and a non-artist, yet he influenced everything that he touched. 'He was a Maecenas who did not spend his own money,' says Richard Buckle in his biography of Diaghilev, 'an impresario who ignored public taste, a businessman who lost money.' His artistry lay in the use of advisers and experts. Through this he became like a Russian nobleman who ran his company – *his* company – like an aristocrat of old. His influence was felt everywhere: from the ideas which were to be adopted and developed, to the choice of collaborators, to their wooing so that they *would* collaborate. He offered his criticisms of all the other creative individuals along the way to the finished work. He became an expert on stage lighting, and acquired a vast knowledge of theatre history. He wouldn't create a costume but would modify it, crucially. He would change elements in a colour scheme, spend hours on the tone of the lighting. He was a one-off.

In Paris, his productions at first adapted music that was already written, but a year later began the great collaboration between Diaghilev, Fokine, Nijinsky and Stravinsky. In 1910 *The Firebird* was produced to great acclaim, followed by *Petrushka* in 1911 and *Le Sacre du printemps* in 1912. A ballet legend was formed and, with Benois, Bakst and Goncharova – all Russians – providing the designs, Diaghilev could be said to have put three Russian art forms, dance, music and painting, on the international map.

Diaghilev created a world. Until 1910 his company was a travelling branch of the Imperial Theatre and the dancers joined him during their long vacation. After the *Giselle* scandal, when Nijinsky was dismissed from the imperial service after altering his costume to make it more revealing, Diaghilev decided to create his own company. Even so, until the First World War and the October revolution, the Ballets Russes lived up to its name, since the supply of highly trained Russian dancers was unfailing. During the war, Diaghilev's reputation was high enough to ensure that his company had no trouble surviving, but after the revolution its composition began to change. French, English and Irish dancers joined the company, among them Ninette de Valois, Alicia Markova and Anton Dolin.

After Fokine, Nijinsky choreographed several ballets. None of them was successful except *L'Après-midi d'un faune*, which caused a great scandal. It was attacked by *Le Figaro*, which called it wicked, and was defended by Rodin, who thought it beautiful. In the Diaghilev company, however, the real heir to Fokine was not Nijinsky but Léonide Massine, who had attracted Diaghilev's attention in Moscow and was brought in to dance a new ballet, *Joseph's Legend*, commissioned from Richard Strauss. Massine, like Diaghilev, had an enormous appetite for all the arts and was very well read. His own ballets were immediately successful and produced great collaborations with, among others, Picasso. After Massine, Diaghilev turned first to Bronislava Nijinksa, Nijinsky's sister, then to George Balanchine. A pupil of the Imperial School, whose works in post-revolutionary Russia had been considered too adventurous, Balanchine had left Soviet Russia with a small group of dancers. His more abstract style caused a sensation but by then, unfortunately, ballet audiences had dwindled, a decline in large part brought about by Nijinsky's retreat into madness. Diaghilev's last choreographer was Serge Lifar but after a short while he was offered the post of choreographer and *premier danseur* at the Paris Opéra, the original home of ballet. He accepted with alacrity. It was the last chapter for the Ballets Russes and Diaghilev knew it. He died in Venice in 1929.

In Russia itself the ballet was again moving in a different direction from the ballets of other countries. After the revolution, the theatre and the school had been reorganised. Vaganova had been brought into the school and F.V. Lopukhov into theatre. Lopukhov kept the best of Petipa, Fokine and other renowned choreographers and at first adapted new works to old music. But an experimental period began in 1929 when the first Soviet ballet appeared called *The Red Poppy*. This was followed in 1930 by *The Golden Age*, and *Bolt* was produced a year later. Both had music by Shostakovich.

By now the first fruits of the Vaganova system were appearing, with the earliest generation of Soviet-trained dancers – Natalia Dudinskaya, Tatiana Semenova, Konstantin Sergeyev, Galina Ulanova, Vakhtung Chaboukiani and Alla Shelest. Ironically, during the purges and the show trials, and in the run-up to war, a new series of ballets was developed: very different from those of Fokine, they had great drama and strong plots. The first of these was *The Fountain of Bakhchisarai* (1934), followed by *Laurencia* (1939), and *Romeo and Juliet* (1940). The war does not seem to have had much effect on the fecundity of Soviet ballet, and soon afterwards another generation of dancers began to make its mark. These included Yuri Grigorovich, Ninel Kurgapkina, Leonid Jacobson and Olga Moiseeva, and a new series of ballets, often with a military theme, was produced: *Tatyana* and *Militsa*, both in 1947, *The Bronze Horseman* in 1949 and *Taras Bulba* in 1955, the year Rudolf arrived in Leningrad.

The mid- to late 1950s, as Rudolf prepared himself for serious training, saw the experimental ballet, *Spartacus* (1956), produced by Jacobson, Grigorovich's *The Stone Flower* (1957), *Choreographical*

Miniatures (1958), and Sergeyev's production of *The Thunderclap* (1958). The last of these was dedicated to the struggle against racism. These three men were as good choreographers as they had been dancers.

In some ways the history of ballet is more important than that of other art forms. With painting, with books, even with music, the work can be put down in permanent form. With ballet, although there is a system of notation for steps, it bears little relation to what is performed on stage. Even in an age of video, ballet remains the most evanescent of all art forms, essentially gone the minute the performance is ended. In such a world, the passing on of skills, of information, of insight, *from person to person*, is all-important. In such a world, history is present today as nowhere else. The people Rudolf was about to be taught by had themselves been taught by the great names of the past, in an unbroken line going all the way back to Petipa, Blasis and beyond. Ballet is a repeated, secular form of the laying on of hands, and treated with the same dignity and respect as its equivalent in the church.

Thanks to Udeltsova, and the fact that Rudolf had arrived in Leningrad a week early, he now had a rudimentary grounding in ballet history. And from that history, Rudolf now knew three things. He now knew in what way St Petersburg was special, how it was different from anywhere else, yet how it fitted into the international world of dance. He now knew that there was a division in ballet, between the Soviet system and the systems elsewhere. And he now knew from the experience of Diaghilev, the most important figure in twentieth-century ballet, that what counted was *being* different and being sure of oneself and one's abilities. It was Diaghilev who had made the difference. In later years, Rudolf would be compared time and again with Nijinsky. In many ways, he had far more in common with Diaghilev.

Classes started on 1 September. When Rudolf first arrived, he was shown to his living quarters. Behind the main school building are a number of courtyards around which are grouped the four-storey dormitories, painted in ochre and cream. He was given a bed in the dormitory named after Zodchevo Rossi (Architect Rossi), on the first floor, which slept twenty. His room overlooked the archway where the food and coal were delivered. Sergio Stefanschi, a dancer from Romania who shared the dormitory with Rudolf, says that the new boy was very quiet and serious to begin with. He was conscious of being a late starter and of having to work harder than everyone else, so as to catch up. He was interested only in dance, and not in any of the other things that interested boys his age, such as sport or girls.

Nureyev was not the only dancer to enter the Vaganova from Ufa that year. Pamira Sulemanovna had been accepted, as had a male dancer

called Zhena Cerebrov. Sulemanovna had been accepted after Rudolf
and without a formal audition. In late summer, on a tour of Kalinin,
her prowess had been recognised. A minister of culture, who had seen
her dance in the *Dekada*, had recommended her to the Vaganova. She
did not remain long in Leningrad, unfortunately. Her mother fell ill and
she was obliged to return to Ufa to look after her. Cerebrov stayed,
though he was never close to Rudolf. He eventually became a dancer
in Perm.

The dormitory where Rudolf lived was well lit and airy, with wide,
arched windows. But it was not spacious – there was just a chair
between the beds, and no lockers. The courtyards were planted with
small trees which were very ragged in winter but made the school
much more pleasant in spring and summer. Each dormitory had a
master in charge. Every night before bedtime, the students had to
report to him, stating the time they wished to be awakened, according
to their schedule of classes, which could begin at any time from 8
until 10 a.m. Stefanschi says that despite this the boys would get
up at 6.30, 'because there was only one washroom for all the boys
and we used to have to stand in line, thirty-nine or forty boys, to
wash and brush our teeth. There were no showers, just a washbasin
and lavatory. For showers we were allowed into the *bania* near the
Fontanka canal once a week when it was closed to the public, for
cleaning.'

Breakfast from 8 to 10 a.m., consisted of tea, cereals and cakes and
was served in a large canteen which was also used by dancers from
the Kirov. The two groups were not allowed to talk to each other,
a restriction Rudolf says he admired. 'We owed them respect and
admiration; they in turn had no right to tease us or look down on us
for being such nonentities compared to them.'

In a normal day which began at eight, there were academic lessons
in the morning and dancing in the afternoon. On standard days the
curriculum was like that of any school – chemistry, maths, geography,
and so on. This side of the teaching staff was thirty-three strong as
everyone understood the need to give the pupils a general education.
Sixty-five graduates were produced each year (forty-five to fifty girls,
fifteen to twenty boys); only half a dozen would be taken by the Kirov,
and perhaps twice as many by other companies. That left plenty who
would fail completely.

On non-standard days there were lessons in literature, or lectures
with slides from curators at the Hermitage. The theory was that the arts
would form a large part of the pupils' lives, and they needed an intelligent
understanding of ballet in the overall scheme of things. Van Gogh was
an early enthusiasm of Rudolf's in these classes but, Dostoevsky and
Pushkin apart, he was not then as interested in literature as in other
artistic subjects. At that stage, he said, he only wanted to learn about

things that affected him directly – painting, for example, which was related to set design.

At noon, the pupils took their lunch. This usually consisted of soup, vegetables, a meat or fish course, and a very sweet pudding. Even during rationing Vaganova pupils had been given meat, since dancers need protein to build them up. During the lunch break, the rehearsal studios were taken over by the Kirov dancers. This was wonderful for the students: it gave them a chance to see Dudinskaya, Kolpakova, Sergeyev and their other heroes and heroines close up.

The dance faculty at the Vaganova consisted of more than seventy teachers and a breakdown of their areas of work gives as good a guide as any to the shape of the teaching. Over half, forty-two, taught classical dance. Seventeen taught character dancing and five specialised in the *pas de deux*. In addition there were seven history teachers, four who taught acting skills and one who taught an hour of fencing each week to the graduating class, for balance. Rudolf always said that the ballet classes in Leningrad school were so concentrated, well prepared and absorbing that one session there was worth double anywhere else. This was the heart of the course.

For the younger pupils, starting when they were nine, Vaganova had devised an eight-year course that built up the dancer's strength and technique without strain. This was based on a thirteen-point code: thirteen forms of step or exercise designed to strengthen the various parts of the body – such as the instep or the knee joint – but at the same time teaching grace and elegance. The last of the thirteen points was *épaulement*, a misunderstood word but one which many people think separates the Vaganova from elsewhere and comprises its great secret. As used by Vaganova, *épaulement* meant the practice of always holding the head and shoulders in line with the sweep of the spine. The purpose of this, she maintained, was to make the body always look as long as possible. This aided turning but also made the human form more graceful, more delicate, more beautiful. At Rudolf's advanced level, or his supposedly advanced level, he was not taught these basics specifically but they were so much a part of the culture of the school that he picked them up very quickly.

Except for learning the *pas de deux*, dance was taught in segregated classes, for no other reason than this made it easier to concentrate on essentials. By Rudolf's time, there was no segregation outside classes and dormitories.

The afternoons were given over to dance, although on two days a week, from three to five, came lessons on the history of ballet and the history of music. Rudolf was particularly taken by these, and was moreover eternally grateful to Marietta Frangopoulos, the Greek woman who taught the history of dance, because she spent a great deal of energy showing how different dancers, and different musicians, had interpreted a role, or a piece of music, in their own way. She built the theatre museum in Leningrad and taught Rudolf a lesson he never forgot: that art is not written in stone, that there are all manner of possibilities, different opportunities for the artist alive today to elaborate upon, or even replace, what has gone before. She also introduced her students to the work of George Balanchine, whom she greatly admired.

The last part of the afternoon was sometimes spent in 'character' work, studying folk dances, sailors' dances, the colourful roles in classical ballet, such as the villains, but excluding the grand roles of prince and princess. On other afternoons there would be repertoire classes, when the students learned specific roles, rather than steps. They were also taught how to bow, to fight, to fall, and so on. These lessons took place on the stage of the school's own tiny theatre.

Piano lessons were given later in the day. The school had eighteen professors of piano, including the sister of Shostakovich, and twenty-six musical coaches who taught different instruments. Rudolf loved the piano and would carry sheet music with him at all times. At night he kept whatever score he was studying under his mattress since there was space between the beds only for a chair, on which his uniform and wash things were kept.

At seven came dinner, much the same as lunch but without the soup. Sometimes the evenings were enlivened by an invitation to the theatre or, better still, by walk-on parts as extras. This tradition had been preserved since imperial times because it obviously gave the students stage experience.

The overall atmosphere of the school had softened somewhat since Karsavina's day, in the early years of the century. 'In my time,' she wrote, in *Theatre Street*, her memoir, 'we did ballet in the morning, and ballet in the afternoon. In the evenings when our time was free, we chose ballet again. The windows of the studio were too high to see the outside world, so there was nothing else to do but practise our ballet.' By the 1950s, it was realised that many of the young pupils, dedicated as they were, were spending large amounts of time away from their families. The school therefore did what it could to provide a family atmosphere: it was important they have something to feel part of.

This was good, so far as it went. But, in fostering this atmosphere, the Vaganova naturally fostered conformity. For students to feel they belonged, they had to share things, perhaps too many things. For a solitary soul, a nonconformist, this could spell trouble, and for Rudolf it did.

He himself said that it started inconsequentially enough. He began skipping breakfast. It meant an extra thirty minutes in bed (and sleep is always important for a dancer). More important, it meant he avoided having to eat with everyone else, which he hated. It did not go unnoticed, of course, and marked him out as difficult, out of the ordinary.

But Rudolf's reputation as a nonconformist, as a difficult loner, really came to the fore with his fight against Chelkov. This man was universally detested by all the pupils at the Vaganova. Known as 'Square Face', on account of his jaw line, he was an irritable man with a very red complexion and was very, very strict. He was administrative director of the school, not artistic director, and the whole place ran like clockwork. But he had many unpopular peccadilloes. For example, he insisted that all the pupils stop whatever they were doing when he walked by, and that the girls curtsy and the boys bow. He was fanatical about haircuts and every time he had his own hair trimmed – there wasn't much but he kept what there was under strict control – he would take with him all those boys whose hair he thought needed attention. He once called to Natalia Makarova in front of several other pupils and handed her a napkin, saying 'Take off the make-up.' It was not so much *what* he did as the humiliating way in which he did it.

That alone was enough to make him the most hated person in the school, but he also had an unenviable reputation as a bad teacher. According to Stefanschi, Chelkov was aware of this shortcoming and compensated by always allocating the best pupils to his own class.

As director of the school, Chelkov had naturally heard of Kostrovitskaya's verdict on Rudolf, that he would either be a brilliant dancer or a complete failure. It therefore surprised no one when he took Rudolf into his class. The cunning in this move was plain to see. Given Kostrovitskaya's views, if Rudolf were to fail, then he himself would be blamed, for not having enough talent in the first place. However, should he succeed then his teacher, Chelkov, would reap a great deal of the credit.

It didn't quite work out like that. There is no doubt that, in his first year at the Vaganova, Rudolf was a very raw individual indeed. He might be a talented dancer but he was also a seventeen-year-old Tartar peasant who had few manners, a foul tongue, and an opinion of his own abilities that came across as confidence or arrogance, according to taste. The Vaganova uniform for boys at the time was a grey military-style shirt with a stiffish white collar, grey trousers and a brown belt. Rudolf, who took little interest in his own appearance at that stage, never wore his tie, had his own thick belt, which he pulled very tight to show off his narrow waist, and trousers which, as a result of always being tucked under his belt, invariably rode too high up his ankles. He *looked* like a peasant and this incensed Chelkov, who could not have been more different. An altogether smoother, more sophisticated, more fastidious Leningrader, he soon despaired of knocking the rough edges off this backward Bashkiri. 'Chelkov was unfair on me from the start,' Rudolf wrote later, 'and seemed bent on humiliating me whenever possible. Some of the boys he would encourage, constantly patting them on the head and urging them not to strain themselves. Me, on the other hand, he always treated like a backward foundling from the local orphanage:

"provincial good-for-nothing" he would call me. "Don't forget," would come the reminder, "that you're here out of the goodness of our hearts and the school's charity." . . . After a time I felt no obligation to him whatsoever. I was always placed so far back in class that my leotard started to wear out behind through constant rubbing against the back wall during practice.' He later told friends that Chelkov referred to him as 'the village idiot'.

Relations between Chelkov and Rudolf soon deteriorated badly, though to be fair to the older man there were other reasons than sheer chemistry for why this particular student rebelled so quickly. In the first place, as a seventeen-year-old, Rudolf had to move quickly in his training, and show rapid progress if he was to make the grade as a professional dancer with an established company by the time he was nineteen. This was a crucial birthday, for at that age he would become eligible for military service and, at the height of the cold war, it would be hard to escape unless he had been a great success. (Albert Arslanov didn't escape; he did his military service in 1956.)

There were still other reasons for Rudolf's frustrations. Most of the boys in the higher grades, who were his age, had been at the school for years, so were very friendly with one another. They no longer lived in the school but either had apartments of their own, in Leningrad itself, or shared smaller dormitories, which slept six, on the ground floor. The boys who shared Rudolf's dormitory were younger than he, a good deal younger in some cases, and were willing to accept restrictions on their lifestyle that he found irksome and absurd. For example, boys living in dormitories were not allowed out in the evenings, an unacceptably petty restriction for someone of Rudolf's age.

This matter came to a head one evening over a production of *Taras Bulba*. That night Rudolf simply ran out of the school and went to the Kirov, to see the ballet. This was hardly a hanging offence but it was strictly forbidden for those who slept in the dormitory to leave the school in the evening unless they had been given an *official* invitation to the theatre. In practice, all the students had to do was to put their names down on a list, but Rudolf hadn't even done that. Rudolf looked at it differently. 'I hadn't come all the way from Ufa to stay indoors every night when it was obviously an important part of my education to watch ballets.' And he *was* seventeen.

When he returned, Rudolf found that his bed had been removed from the dormitory and that his meal tickets, which he had left on his bedside chair, had disappeared. None of the other students in the dormitory spoke to him – they just watched his every move in silence. But Rudolf was not going to give them the satisfaction of asking what had happened, still less of apologising to anyone for an action on his part that was perfectly reasonable. So that night he slept on the floor, not in the dormitory itself but in a quiet, out-of-the-way corner. He forsook breakfast the next morning and went straight to class as if nothing had happened.

It was a bravura performance but, this time at least, it didn't work. The first class that day was literature and, early on, the teacher asked Rudolf to stand up and answer a question in front of the whole class. He stood up – and promptly fell down again. He had fainted. When he came round, he was seething in anger. He was convinced he had fainted because of his ill-treatment (though he had himself chosen to forgo breakfast, for which he didn't need a meal ticket). Clambering to his feet, with the other students milling around him waiting for the doctor to arrive, Rudolf turned on the teacher and, in front of the whole class, shouted that he had been punished the night before by having his bed removed – all because, as a ballet student, he had chosen to go to a ballet performance. Giving the teacher no time to intervene, he added that the next time (and there obviously *was* going to be a next time) he would expect to be punished as though Russia were still being governed by Alexander the Great. This was especially provocative, implying that the Vaganova was hopelessly backward. In the past Alexander would send people into exile in Siberia for even a slight infringement of the code of behaviour – and Siberia was where Rudolf had come from. This was hardly a mollifying speech, but Rudolf's temper was flying now and he gave the teacher no time to recover. He asked that the teacher excuse him, saying that he proposed to visit some friends in Leningrad where he could get something to eat and a warm bed in which to sleep. And, for the second time inside a day, he left the school without permission.

This latest outburst soon had the entire school buzzing about Rudolf's 'Tartar temperament' and it was only a matter of time before he was summoned to see the principal. Chelkov did not even have the courtesy to offer Rudolf a seat. As soon as the boy entered his office, 'Square Face' started shouting at him, ordering Rudolf to give him the names and addresses of any friends he had in Leningrad. This may sound unreasonable but Rudolf was still, technically, a minor under Soviet law, and legally in Chelkov's charge. If Rudolf were to play truant at the school, Chelkov needed some idea of where he might be.

Rudolf refused to give Chelkov any names. The principal insisted, and glared at Rudolf. It is not entirely clear whether Rudolf *had* any friends in Leningrad at the time but he now compromised, and gave Chelkov the name of Udeltsova's daughter, the psychiatrist, who lived in Leningrad and whose flat he had visited in the days before term began.

But Chelkov was no fool. Suddenly, he leaned forward across his desk and snatched Rudolf's address book out of his hand. The boy was shocked. No one had ever invaded his privacy like that. But he was too slight, as well as too junior, to do anything about it.

The incident left its mark. It was this encounter which brought to a head Rudolf's departure from Chelkov's class. Normally, a student doesn't see the director of his school all that often. But when that director is also a teacher, whom the student sees every day, it is a different matter. About a week after the tussle over the address book, Nureyev asked to see Chelkov again. Knowing what he intended, the young man was calm, despite what had gone before. For once, revenge and self-interest coincided.

This time Chelkov motioned him to a seat, but didn't speak. He just sat there, looking at Rudolf. Rudolf detested the man but had the good sense not to let his temper show this time. Coolly, he informed the director that he found it irksome, not to say a waste, that he had to study sixth-grade lessons when he had officially been admitted to the eighth grade, as he had in Moscow. He said it wasn't simply the fact that the mainly younger boys in the same class were beneath him – he admitted that his technique was still somewhat raw. But he said he felt he learned faster than anyone else and this was what mattered. If he stayed in the sixth grade, the army might catch up with him before he graduated to full dancer status. If he moved to the eighth grade straight away, however, then he would graduate in time to try for what he most wanted, to be part of the great Kirov company.

'Chelkov looked at me in utter amazement,' Nureyev said later. There was a long silence. Finally, the director choked out, 'I've wasted enough time on you. Now you can have your own way. I *will* send you to a teacher in the eighth grade – someone who won't even bother to glance in your direction.' Chelkov may have thought he was being clever. If he had sacked Rudolf from the school after only a few weeks, when he had been the boy's teacher and director, it would have been almost as embarrassing for him as for Rudolf. But by promoting the boy as the boy himself wanted, when he clearly was extremely raw so far as his technique was concerned . . . well, maybe this Nureyev would bite off more than he could chew. Quite possibly, he would not be able to adjust to the new advanced class and would simply fail, all by himself.

The man Chelkov chose to teach Rudolf was Alexander Pushkin. Later, Rudolf found out that, in introducing the boy to his new teacher, Chelkov had said, 'I'm sending you an obstinate little idiot – a weak-minded evil boy who knows nothing about the ballet. He has poor elevation and can't sustain his positions correctly.' He added that if Rudolf made no improvement with Pushkin the school would have no choice but to 'throw him out'.

CHAPTER FOUR

The Comrade of So Many Days

The Comrade of so many days,
Oh! her young dove, the natural hearer
Of secrets, like a friend but dearer

There was something patently absurd about Chelkov's introduction.
For one thing, Rudolf's elevation was *not* poor. But, at least to begin
with, the director's words seemed to have an effect. For some weeks,
Pushkin did not even look at Nureyev. And for a while, Rudolf was out of
his depth in Pushkin's more advanced class. Marina Ilicheva, who was in
Pushkin's female class at the time, recalls Rudolf's arrival. 'I remember
the day we were told a Tartar had arrived and that he was a very talented
boy. I thought that he would be dark-skinned, you know, like a Tartar is.
Everybody talked about this very gifted and talented boy. When he was
pointed out to me, I immediately said that he didn't look very much like
a Tartar.' But she soon became frightened of Rudolf, 'because he could
be ungracious and scathing with people'. And, 'we were all shocked by
his lack of training. He couldn't do even the most basic things.'

There were eight other students in the eighth-grade class and they
were very good indeed, especially a fellow Tartar who bore an uncanny
resemblance to Rudolf. Rudolf stood at the back of the class and tried
to imitate what the others were doing. In that respect it was like being
back in Ufa.

But Pushkin was very different from Chelkov. Pushkin had himself
studied under Nikolai Legat, the man who had taken over at the
Maryinsky from Petipa in 1904. He had also studied under Pavlova's
coach and became a principal dancer at the Kirov for twenty-eight
years, from 1925 to 1953, retaining a magnificent jump to the end,
even when, according to someone who saw him dance, 'his belly
stuck out like an old man's'. He had also been teaching since 1932.

His secret lay in two things. He let dancers develop in their own way, emphasising their strong points. This maintained their self-confidence. And he insisted that dancers listen to their muscles. The muscles would have a 'memory' of what had gone before, so if the dancer knew the 'feel' of his or her muscles in the correct position, all he or she had to do was regain that 'feel' and the correct position would be adopted.

In addition, and again quite unlike Chelkov, Pushkin was very gentle – one of his students even wrote a dissertation on his gentle manner. He lived in a small flat in the school itself, which he shared with his wife, Tseniia Iosifovna Iurgenson, a former ballerina who was much younger than he and a flamboyant character in her own right, coming from a distinguished family of Leningrad publishers. The apartment was cheerful, decorated in red, with old mahogany furniture, mirrors and eighteenth-century divans. In fact, the apartment had become a sort of unofficial common room for the senior students, more cosy than the school proper, where tea and bouillon were consumed in gargantuan quantities and ballet was endlessly discussed. In class Pushkin sometimes took off his jacket, but never his tie.

Even so, Pushkin cannot have found Rudolf easy. As Marguerite Alfimova puts it, 'Rudolf already understood that he was an unusual appearance on the scene and he demanded a suitable relationship on account of his worth. Quite simply, he stood out.' Marina Ilicheva noticed that, even then, 'He was hostile to reprimands from the teachers. He didn't want to listen to anybody.'

This was not an easy combination for others to assimilate. Rudolf always had an instinctive understanding of theatre, of the *effect* which a performance must have. In the company he was now keeping, he knew that small advances in technique were not strictly relevant to what he wanted to do. He had to learn that technique, yes, but he had to *impose* himself on this class, on Pushkin, and on the school and anyone else who might be watching. He believed he had enormous talent, but knew that he didn't have much time to make other people agree.

And so, from the first, he spiced his dancing with a certain swagger. This took some nerve, all the more so as Rudolf had not yet filled out to be the mature man he became. As Alfimova puts it, 'You can't say that he had an ultra-beautiful body. He had short-ish legs – he wasn't tall for a dancer. There were dancers with better bodies, that were more graceful. His legs were quite compact.'

This combination, of swagger and the raw quality that never left him soon caused the others in his new class to pick on him. At one point they were so annoyed by his attitude that they grabbed hold of him and dragged him across the rehearsal room, to the mirror that lined the wall. 'Look at yourself, Nureyev,' one teased. 'You'll never be able to dance – it just isn't possible. You're simply not built for it. You have nothing – no schooling and no technique. How do you have the nerve to work with us in the eighth grade?'

Christmas 1955 came, however, and Rudolf was still there, still hanging on in the eighth grade. Pushkin paid him no more attention than he paid the others, but he didn't throw Rudolf out either, as Chelkov had expected (and perhaps hoped). Rudolf's technique had improved slightly but what impressed Pushkin, and everyone, was Rudolf's ability to learn. When he had insisted to Chelkov that he learned faster than the other boys in the sixth grade, he had been right. Quite simply, he had an amazing ability to absorb what he saw. He could remember new steps after seeing them only once, so he could put himself through lessons as often as he wanted until he got it right.

But it wasn't only that. Marguerite Alfimova watched Rudolf from her parallel class. 'He knew *how* to study, that's what distinguished him. He didn't only train at lessons. He soaked up the atmosphere, the culture and the music. He danced all variations of a dance, including the female parts. He used to practise before and between lessons, when the rest of us were resting.'

Slowly, he was catching up with the others in the eighth grade, or that's how it appeared. But a vital change came over his relationship with Pushkin as the end of the first academic year approached. Rudolf had settled down so far as the school in general was concerned, and was now allowed out at night, as he wished. It wasn't as if he was prowling the pavements, or drinking, or going to night clubs, of which there were precious few in Leningrad. Every night he would either be at the Maryinsky, watching ballet or opera, or at the Philharmonia, the concert hall on Arts Square, opposite the Russian Museum, listening to a concert, or at one of the other theatres in Leningrad. Alfimova sometimes went with him. 'Nothing passed him by,' she said, echoing the words of Pamira Sulemanovna in Ufa.

But in class there was a disappointment in store for Rudolf as the academic year came to an end in May. In the eighth grade, each pupil had to prepare a variation of a well-known solo part, to be performed on the main Kirov stage. Rudolf had been looking forward to this so was very distraught when he found that he had been left out. Pushkin didn't think he was quite ready.

It was not in Rudolf's character to accept this setback without trying to have the decision reversed. Secretly, he began to work on a variation that was all his own, which no one else, Pushkin included, had ever seen him dance. His phenomenal memory for steps meant that he knew what to dance, provided he could get it right technically.

He chose the man's variation from the *pas de deux* of Diana and Actaeon, which comes from the ballet *Esmeralda*. For days he crept into the rehearsal room when it was empty, early in the morning or late at night, practising, practising, practising, inspecting critically the steps he was making in the mirror. Finally, he thought, he had it right.

One afternoon, after class, he took a deep breath and approached Pushkin. He begged that he be allowed to show his teacher his variation.

Pushkin was not a tall man though he had a high forehead. He looked up at the eighteen-year-old. 'You'll miss dinner.'

Rudolf shrugged.

And so, with the two of them alone in the big room, Rudolf danced in front of his teacher. As he danced, the sun cast long shadows across the room. Leningrad's 'White Nights', the period when the sun never sets, were not far away. Based on Victor Hugo's *Notre Dame de Paris*, *Esmeralda* was first produced in the early nineteenth century and is the story of a gypsy girl caught up in a love triangle between a friend of the King's and a captain of the King's guard. Actaeon's solo had been reworked by Vakhtung Chaboukiani in 1935 and contained some prodigious jumps which Rudolf would either bring off, to impress his teacher, or not, leaving him in no doubt that he was right to have omitted him from the exam.

The solo lasted little more than two minutes. There was not even a piano to accompany Rudolf so that the only sounds were his own breathing and his footsteps on the rehearsal-room floor as he came down from the many jumps created by Chaboukiani.

When it was over, Rudolf stood where he had finished, breathing heavily. It was the same rehearsal room where he had danced for Kostrovitskaya. Pushkin walked over to the *barre*, took his pupil's towel and carried it across to him.

'Well?' said Rudolf impatiently as he towelled his hair dry. 'May I dance?'

Pushkin patted his arm and walked away. As he went he called back over his shoulder: 'Yes, Nureyev, yes. You may dance.'

And so, one of Rudolf's ambitions was to come true. He would dance on the stage of the Kirov. It was a long way from the backs of those trucks in Bashkir.

There was something else that may have played a part in Pushkin's decision. By then he had Rudolf's overall exam results for the year. These are preserved in the display case devoted to Nureyev in the Leningrad Choreographical School. (They were not displayed until 1992.) In his first year at the school Rudolf had been very difficult, and had used every moment to develop his dancing technique. Yet his exam results were most impressive. The school marked its pupils on the standard national marking system, as used in schools throughout the country, from '1' (unsatisfactory) to '5' (excellent). During the year, Rudolf had obtained at least a '4' in every subject except drawing, and in the final examination had obtained three '5s' and two '4s' out of six subjects. He had shone in literature, geography, physics, botany, history and English. And all without trying.

As the day for the dancing exam approached, Rudolf learned something that gave the occasion a tension, a needle, that he had not anticipated. By chance, another of the eighth-graders, one of the fellow pupils who had dragged Rudolf in front of the mirror and laughed at him, had chosen the same variation from *Esmeralda*. The exam took on the atmosphere of a competition between these two: one a popular, established member of the class, the other a raw but pushy outsider.

Rudolf went second, and therefore had the benefit of having seen his rival dance before him. The rival was good, technically very accomplished, but Rudolf had taken the trouble to read about the ballet. Actaeon was a mythological creature, but the ballet was the creation of Jules Perrot, an acrobatic French dancer born in 1810 who had an extremely ugly face but, according to Gautier, was delightful to look at 'from the waist downwards'. Perrot's feet and knees were extremely slender and the contour of his legs somewhat feminine. He was the greatest dancer of his day, brilliant at mime and had a superb elevation, all the more surprising because of his unmuscular legs. Rudolf set out to make the same kind of impact: Actaeon was not a man but a god; however high he jumped – and he must *really* jump – he had to land as if there was no substance to him. Rudolf had, in the days before the exam, worked hard at making his many jumps even more prodigious than Pushkin had seen, and his landings softer than ever.

The two minutes were soon over. As he finished, and Rudolf stood panting on the stage, there was complete silence all around him. No one applauded, or made flattering remarks. There was just a deathly hush. But no one had laughed either, or said anything disparaging, and that was what mattered. 'In that most demanding of all schools, I knew that silence in itself implied approbation.' It had taken Rudolf a whole year but at last he felt he belonged at the Vaganova. He had made his mark.

Rudolf went home during the 1956 summer vacation, then on to the Crimea where he took a mud cure for his legs. When he arrived back in Leningrad for the new term, he found he had been allotted to one of the smaller dormitories, which slept six, on the ground floor of the school. Among his room mates were Sergio Stefanschi and a Finnish dancer, Leo Ahonen. They observed that Rudolf was as raw as ever in his general manners, but this term there was a new warmth between him and his teacher, Pushkin.

The importance of Alexander Pushkin in Rudolf's life is hard to overestimate. It went far beyond his teaching skills, crucial as they were, to his own personality. Pushkin was really the first significant man in Rudolf's life who was not hostile. Until that point, all the most encouraging and positive figures, either in Rudolf's home life or in his career, had been women: Farida, Rezida, Rosa, Tuturoza, Asabakova, Udeltsova, Vaitovich, Nureevna, Irina Alexandrovna, Kostrovitskaya. Some may see a link between this preponderance of influential women and Rudolf's later sexual orientation; others may feel that such explanations are too glib. Either way, Rudolf certainly seems to have had a need for the type of relationship Pushkin could provide.

A crucial aspect of Pushkin's technique was to encourage dancers to be themselves. In Rudolf's case, this meant accepting his huge and instinctive appetite for the big roles. Inexperienced as he was in a formal sense, he had nonetheless indulged in theatre-going on a massive scale. Unlike many better-educated colleagues of his own age, he had actually seen a great many roles being performed, not just in the ballet but in the opera and in dramatic theatres as well. These fleshed out his understanding of the more important characters and stimulated his desire to try his own interpretations. He begged Pushkin to teach him *Swan Lake, Giselle, Le Corsaire.* His teacher not only obliged, but lent him the music as well. Rudolf wanted to understand all aspects of a ballet, not just his own role. Pushkin was touched by this enthusiasm.

Rudolf's love of all the arts had been set very early on – ever since he and Pamira Sulemanovna had sneaked into the Ufa Theatre via the scenery store, to watch whatever was on. But if his taste for the arts was catholic, that was the limit. As a boy, as a teenager, and as a man, Rudolf had no interests outside the arts except, later on, for sex. Most important, he had no interest in politics, though that is putting things a little too simply perhaps. In 1956 Stalin had been dead three years, after thirty-one years at the head of the Soviet system. Under Khrushchev, the personal life of Russians was a little easier – Beria and his KGB thugs, for instance, had been kicked out of office. But the cold war was still at its height, the Communist Party still ruled the roost and in such a climate to be apolitical was not as easy at it sounds, or as it is today. To be apolitical meant not to be part of the group, and not to be part of the group meant that you were *anti* the group.

This became clear in Rudolf's case in relation to his membership – or rather his non-membership – of the Komsomol. He had joined the Young Pioneers because it was compulsory, but that wasn't true with the Komsomol (for fifteen to twenty-seven-year-olds). The Komsomol was a far more serious organisation than the Pioneers, and in the late 1950s had close links with the KGB. In 1958 Aleksandr Shelepin succeeded Ivan Serov as chairman of the KGB. Before that, Shelepin had held high office in the Komsomol and one of the major changes he introduced to the KGB was to flood it with young Turks from his old home, including Vladimir Semichastny who would succeed him, in 1961, as chairman.

In the Vaganova, meetings of the Komsomol were compulsory for party members and encouraged for everyone else. At these meetings political questions were discussed in minute detail, a way of both keeping politics at the forefront of everyone's mind, of showing the 'correct' way of thinking, and of identifying those individuals unsympathetic to this way of thinking. In short, it was a form of political/psychological terror and control.

At Komsomol meetings in the 1950s and for a long time afterwards, the name of Pavlik Morozov was continually glorified. This boy became a Hero of the Soviet Union at the age of fourteen, at the time of the collectivisation and dispossession of 10 million peasants in the early 1930s. It came about in this way. In the village of Gerasimovka, Morozov's father gave shelter to some fleeing *kulaks*, as the more prosperous peasants were derisively termed. Whereupon Morozov, 'recognising his duty to Soviet society,' betrayed his father, who was summarily shot. This was the sort of conformist behaviour the Komsomol approved of but the contrast with Nureyev's own relationship with his father, where the situation was in a sense reversed, could not have been more marked. Every time Rudolf thought of his father, the ugly side of the Soviet system stared him in the face. Rudolf, as an individualist by temperament, realised very early on that an artist, to be worthy of the name, needs to be his own man. But for him the espousal of art and the eschewal of politics also had a more personal meaning. It went against everything his despised father stood for.

In his second year at the Vaganova, following his success on the stage of the Maryinsky during his exam, Rudolf's strengths and weaknesses became even more marked, and even more of a talking point for the others at the school, both students and teachers. On the positive side, his reprimand to Chelkov was borne out by events. He *did* learn fast.

His manners, however, did not improve. In class he would throw something – anything he could get his hands on – if the steps didn't go right. The only person he ever listened to was Pushkin. The two became even closer and Pushkin didn't call Rudolf Rudik, like the others did, but had his own name, Rudenka. If Rudolf had made a mistake, or was agitated because he couldn't get a particular step right, Pushkin would speak quietly. 'Now, Rudenka, get up on one leg. Now do a pirouette. Now you are collapsing . . . well, then, why are you getting so confused? Try to do it precisely.' Somehow the fact that Pushkin never got flustered, never lost his temper, never raised his voice, calmed Rudolf down. By breaking down the steps into their components, he allowed Rudolf to see where he was going wrong.

Gabriel Komleva, later a star at the Kirov, who was on the 1961 tour to Paris with Rudolf, was also at the Vaganova when he was there. She too noticed the paradox that began to develop with Rudolf in the second year (which was the ninth, and final, grade). 'He acquired a great deal of knowledge about culture, but retained a side to him that was very uneducated. He never read newspapers, for instance. And he would come out with swear-words and scathing comments that would upset people around him. There was permanent conflict. He studied badly, in the sense that he wouldn't listen to anyone. He just wanted to dance.'

Komleva also says that in those early years Rudolf had a problem with pas de deux. 'He found the pas de deux very hard. At the school he was never a master of this and used to hold the ballerinas badly. Generally, he got on badly with women, because he never paid them enough attention. As I was a better than average dancer I was often assigned to be his partner, because it was easier for him.' Nothing could change the fact that he had started late. It would plague him for years to come.

In that second year at the Vaganova, however, he did begin to make a few friends. At school there were Stefanschi and Ahonen (neither of them Russian). Their dormitory had a window that gave on to Rossi Street. The window was sealed in winter, save for a small *koshka*, a flap that let in fresh air. But when the White Nights came round the three of them would escape through the window at all hours, to sample the joys of the festival.

More important were the friends he made through music. In Ufa most of the music he had heard had been folk music and ballet music – Tchaikovsky, of course, or sometimes a Beethoven symphony played on the occasion of a distinguished party member's death. The full range of musical expression, the fact that it could be so *joyful*, was a new discovery for Nureyev.

In first place was the Philharmonia. In the centre of Leningrad, just off the Nevsky Prospekt, beyond the Grand Hotel, is a lovely square filled with trees and bounded on all sides by theatres, museums – and the Philharmonia, the concert hall. The Philharmonia is not large. The stage is barely more than a dais, and the main auditorium, which faces a splendid organ, is surrounded by magnificent white columns which support a gallery where you can watch the concert or look out through lunettes at the skyline of the city. The Philharmonia is intimate. The Maly Theatre, across the square, specialised in modern ballet in the 1950s, but Rudolf was not as interested then as he later became in the abstract forms of contemporary choreographers. His life was classical ballet.

With his evolving love of music, Rudolf also discovered in Leningrad a wonderful shop, a type of shop that had never existed in Ufa. Called Noti, (HOTbI in Russian) and located opposite the Cathedral of Kazan, on the corner of Nevsky Prospekt and Griboedova canal (named after a Russian novelist), this was a music shop. It had a splendid light over the door with a bronze sculpture entwined around it, and inside there was a red marble floor, a crystal chandelier and column after column of mahogany drawers. This was before the age when record players were common, at least in Russia, and the shop sold mainly sheet music. But the chief attraction of Noti, for Rudolf, was the piano in the middle of the shop. Customers who were thinking of buying a particular piece of music were allowed to play the piano, to see whether they liked the piece and to make sure they would be able to play it. At times Rudolf would sit and play the simpler pieces. The more complicated compositions he would try to persuade more experienced musicians at the school to play for him. The shop mounted occasional promotions, and professional musicians visited the shop to play. If there were no pianist available, Rudolf would simply hum the notes. In this way, he became familiar with the works of Mozart, Schumann, Rachmaninov, Prokofiev and Debussy. At that time the most romantic composers appealed to him.

Rudolf had discovered Noti towards the end of his first year at the Vaganova but during the second year his visits were more common, almost daily in fact. Before long, he came to know the shop's manager, a woman in her mid-thirties named Elizaveta Mikhailovna Pashe. All the significant women in Rudolf's early life were a good deal older than he was and Elizaveta Mikhailovna was no exception. Very soon their relationship became more than one of shopkeeper and customer. She knew that he was a pupil at the ballet school, but recognised that Rudolf was out of the ordinary even for a student of such a famous school. She began to look forward to his visits and was disappointed on the days when he didn't come. When he did, and if there were no one else in the shop and she had some free time, she herself would play the piano, letting Rudolf listen to his favourites. Since he was so keen to hear everything she would tell him in advance when she was expecting professional musicians to call in, searching for certain sheets. Rudolf would be there, and Elizaveta Mikhailovna would persuade the musicians to play. It was a kind of easy conspiracy between the two, luring musicians into the shop and persuading them to play, so that Rudolf could listen.

In early 1957 Elizaveta Mikhailovna took their relationship a step forward: she invited Rudolf to her home, for dinner. He accepted. There he met her husband, a quiet, bearded man, who was as passionate about poetry as Rudolf was about ballet. Elizaveta's husband read aloud from the poets and introduced the young dancer to some of Europe's great writers – Molière, Lamartine, Shakespeare, Goethe. On his lips, words no longer seemed dead things.

As the year wore on, Rudolf gradually fell into the habit of going to the Pashes' flat every week for dinner. It was small but cheerful, a welcome change from the school. Through her shop Elizaveta Mikhailovna had a wide circle of friends, most of them artists or intellectuals, whom she now introduced to Rudolf. It was his first experience of a salon. Politics was rarely the chief subject of discussion for these literary and musical types. But, by nature none of them was in the Komsomol, or the Party, so by implication they were free thinkers. Not dissidents necessarily, but not conformers either. Collectively, they had a big influence on Rudolf.

It was through the salon that Rudolf also met and befriended Tamara Myasciorva. She was unusual in his life at that point in that she was an attractive woman of Rudolf's own age. He described her as a 'tall, handsome nineteen-year-old girl with big brown eyes'. She was not an artist but a scientist, and the granddaughter of a very famous scientist indeed, a member of the Scientific Academy. Tamara and Rudolf became instant friends and she dubbed Elizaveta 'Columbovna', because she had 'discovered' Rudolf.

While he had, in a way, discovered a 'home' away from the Vaganova in his second year, his progress inside the school was still far from straightforward. Marina Ilicheva reports that, in 1957, the senior students were practising *The Red Poppy*. This is a popular Soviet ballet, first produced in 1929, with a revolutionary theme, about a Soviet ship's captain, whose craft is in a Chinese port. The captain shows mercy to the 'coolies' unloading his ship, an act which stimulates unrest in the harbour, leading eventually to violence and, in time, the victory of the proletariat. The red poppy is the symbol of liberty. Ilicheva was dancing the heroine who, in a dream, sees herself and the hero surrounded by butterflies. 'Six or seven boys were attempting to be butterflies. They were all from the oldest class and they studied with me. At first these boys were practising alone but then others appeared, Dolgushin and Rudik among them . . . I can boast only of the fact that he was working at the time in the background compared to myself. He danced. All of us students were completely shocked by his total lack of training. He did everything wrong, even then.' But she adds something no less interesting. 'Even when he graduated from the choreographical school, he still had many imperfections, but it was also true that he in some way deliberately didn't want to rectify these imperfections. He wanted to do everything in his own way. He constantly tried to transgress something, to change something.'

So perhaps Ilicheva was wrong to be shocked by Rudolf's apparent lack of technique. The fact is, he knew exactly what he was doing. He knew he was backward technically, he knew it would take time to rectify. He would work as hard as he could, learn as fast as he knew how, put his musical and dance training above everything else, to the *exclusion* of everything else. But he also knew what made him different, what separated him out from the others. He had a stage presence, but it was more than that. He had an intensity, an emotional force which, quite simply, overcame his technical imperfections. It communicated itself to audiences and to the more knowledgeable teachers. His interpretations needed to improve – that is why he was so hungry for all the arts, to sample the best that others could offer. But, from that second year, when his technical imperfections continued to be tolerated, when even Pushkin gave him so much attention, he realised something else about his gift. No one else had it.

Despite his membership of Elizaveta Mikhailovna's salon, Rudolf was very lonely inside the Vaganova during his second year. That, at least, is what he said later in life although Stefanschi and Ahonen certainly regarded themselves as his friends. His manners were still coarse and unpredictable and maybe that had something to do with it, causing the others in his class to shun him as much as he shunned them. Certainly, he made no new friends over a celebrated incident with a watering can. It was the tradition at the Vaganova for the youngest, or least senior, pupil to water the floor, to sprinkle drops of water around the rehearsal room to settle the dust, making it easier and pleasanter to practise. When it was his turn, Rudolf sprinkled the water – but only for the area of the room where he himself would dance. (This had once been an honor in imperial times but the tradition had changed.)

Pamira Sulemanovna says Rudolf did strike up a friendship of sorts with Alla Osipenko – based on ice-cream. Osipenko, six years older than Rudolf, had been one of Vaganova's last pupils and graduated in 1950. 'In the 1950s and 1960s,' according to Gennady Smakov in his book on Russian dancers, 'Alla Osipenko was the most decorative ornament on the Kirov stage, with a more western artistic profile than her illustrious colleagues.' A superb technician, with a wonderful physique and stage presence, like Rudolf she preferred highly dramatic roles where she could add her own interpretation. Sulemanovna says that in those days there was a little ice-cream stall run by an old *babushka* opposite the Sattikov-Shedrin public library on Nevsky Prospekt, in a basement. Rudolf loved to buy 100 grams of ice-cream there whenever he could but he was no match for Osipenko. 'She was virtually an ice-cream addict,' says Sulemanovna. 'She could surely eat more than half a kilo.'

Alla and Rudolf would bump into each other at the ice-cream stall and stroll down the Prospekt eating, and discussing ballet. She had a better classical figure than he did, and as a result was more restrained technically, but other than that their views on ballet coincided. And they both had an interest in the west, though she always remained in Leningrad.[1]

Once while he was buying ice-cream in 1957, Rudolf bumped into Gyckova, his erstwhile friend from Ufa. She was studying engineering in Leningrad and they arranged to meet, to attend the Philharmonia together. Gyckova confirms that Rudolf appeared to have no friends even then, after more than a year at the school, with whom he could attend concerts. His friendship with Tamara was just beginning and there was a Cuban dancer called Nina Martines who was studying at the Vaganova and whom Rudolf liked. But that was it.

Gyckova also appears to have been the first person to spot that Rudolf was homosexual. She herself was attractive, so were Tamara, Pamira and Nina but, all the time Gyckova was in Leningrad, 'he never treated me like a man should treat a woman. He was completely indifferent to the female sex. One day he said to me, "How good that all *that* [meaning sexual attraction] has already passed between us".' Since Rudolf was now beginning to show the good looks that would help him become famous, this remark bothered Gyckova. Indeed, she was so upset that when Rudolf took her to Elizaveta's salon a little later, she asked a fellow guest, Liuba Miasnikova, an exceptionally attractive Leningrader who was also to become a good friend of Rudolf's, if he was 'indifferent' to her. 'Oh yes,' Liuba replied. 'I have never seen any interest of that sort from him.'

The whole time Gyckova was in Leningrad she never saw Rudolf in love. 'He could be attentive – yes. But no more. And so one day, I plucked up courage and asked him if he was a man.' Rudolf was upset by the question and the two of them argued. He felt she shouldn't have invaded his privacy in such a direct way. But afterwards, as Gyckova put it, 'he allowed himself to say that he was not a man in the sense that I had meant it'.

In late spring 1957 Rudolf completed his second year at the Vaganova, in the ninth grade, from which the better pupils graduated to the *corps de ballet* of the Kirov or other companies around the country, according to merit. During that last year, the graduating students mounted a series of ballets and gave matinée performances on stage at the Kirov. These were attended by the balletomanes of Leningrad as a way of introducing them to the emerging talent.

There is no record of Rudolf dancing in any of these productions during the 1956–57 academic year, which must mean that Pushkin had decided early on that, although he was *in* the ninth grade, Rudolf was not yet ready to graduate. And in fact at the end of that year he was told that, next year, he would be repeating the ninth grade. This did not distress him. He knew he needed another year of training, that technically he wasn't ready, and he was confident that, under Pushkin, he would continue to learn fast.

During the last weeks of term he enjoyed the White Nights festival in Leningrad, with Stefanschi and Ahonen, then went home to Ufa for the vacation. His mother by now was something of a local celebrity and, at the age of fifty-two, becoming eccentric. She was still working in the milk factory but now had charge of the yoghurt section. Her yoghurt was so good that it had drawn the attention of the national press, and her picture had been published, alongside a mountain of yoghurt cartons.

She took her job very seriously and would even waken Rezida or any of the other children who happened to be at home, in the middle of the night, saying that she was going down to the factory to move her latest batch of yoghurt to a fresh spot, where it would keep for longer. The children were made to accompany her, to their deep embarrassment. Hamet was head of security at the same factory and also by now head of the local Communist Party cell. This did not make father and son particularly close.

That summer Rudolf took what had by now become his annual mud cure in the Crimea, for his legs, then returned to Leningrad for the new term. By this stage, Pamira Sulemanovna had returned to Ufa permanently: both her mother and her sister had fallen ill and, lacking a father, she was obliged to look after them. She hated leaving the school but Rudolf wrote to her for several weeks after she left, providing details of life in Leningrad and at the school. He told her he had been to see *Zolushka* (*Cinderella*) and had a lot to say about the music of Prokofiev.

In that final year Rudolf also took a highly unusual step: he went to see Chelkov for discussions about sex. This would appear to suggest that the director and he had settled their differences. For if Chelkov had still wanted to get rid of Rudolf, and if it was becoming clear to those who knew the young Tartar well that he was homosexual, nothing could have been easier. To Russians in the 1950s, homosexuality was still regarded as a diabolical perversion and had it become known that one of the older pupils was 'tainted' in this way, and living in close proximity with younger boys, there would have been a scandal.

Two incidents may have provoked this move. One was Gyckova's challenge, which forced Rudolf to examine his sexuality, not least for how it might affect his art. Another was the fact that he had been accosted, sexually, in broad daylight. Near the Vaganova, at the east end of Rossi Street, was the Pushkin Theatre. Between the theatre and the Nevsky Prospekt lies a small park, Ekaterina Square, which boasts a statue of the Empress. This square, or public gardens, was and is a gathering place for homosexuals. One Sunday, walking back to the school, Rudolf was approached by a man who, without warning, placed his hand on Rudolf's crotch. This was 1957, Rudolf was nineteen, and nineteen-year-olds were more innocent then than they are now. So Rudolf may simply have approached Chelkov for advice. He may also have been frightened as well as puzzled, since he heard a group of dancers from the school planning to go to the gardens, as a group, and attack the homosexuals they found there. Gay-bashing was by no means unknown in Leningrad. Stefanschi says he never saw Rudolf make a pass at anyone while he was at the school though there were boys – like Alexandre Minz – who did so.

Rudolf later told close friends in the United States that he arrived in the west 'effectively' a virgin (we shall explore what 'effectively' means later on). Certainly, by 1957 it would appear that his sexual experience was confined to masturbation. Chelkov may have been a shoulder to lean on.

For his part, Chelkov may well have known that Rudolf didn't get on with his father and may have merely been trying to fulfil that role for Rudolf in certain specific, problematic areas. The Vaganova, after all, did try to be a family of sorts.

In the last months of 1957, with Pushkin's help, Rudolf worked hard to perfect his technique without sacrificing that emotional intensity and creative intelligence which was his unique gift. After Christmas the pattern changed in an exciting way. Between January and May the graduating class mounted no fewer than nine ballets as matinées, on stage at the Kirov. This year, Pushkin decided, Rudolf was ready. Rehearsals began after Christmas and the first performance took place on Friday 15 February, when Rudolf danced the duet from *Swan Lake* with H. Usaeva, a fellow graduate who never became well known. After that, came five performances in which he danced the Nutcracker Prince, from *The Nutcracker*, between 19 February and 6 April. He also danced as one of the Prince's friends in a performance of *Swan Lake* on 21 March, four days after his twentieth birthday.

It was after the final, April performance that Rudolf drew his first review. Here is the way a local newspaper, *Theatre Life*, put it at the time. Headlined SUN IN BLOOD, the piece began.

'Leningraders always wait impatiently for the introductory evenings at the A.Y. Vaganova Choreographic School. On such evenings the theatre buzzes with an air of festivity, animation and anxiety.

'In the spring of 1958 they awaited this event. There goes the last bell. The lights are dimming. The concert has started. One number follows another. The spectators greet the aspiring ballerinas and male dancers with warm applause. The greatest success is Nureyev's. High and light jumps, vertical twists, genuine temperament, rare flexibility and suppleness – all point to the fact that before us stands a dancer with magnificent natural qualities.'

Rudolf, Rudik, had begun to metamorphose into Nureyev. And the praise went beyond *Theatre Life*. During those nine matinées, word spread among the Leningrad balletomanes that a rare talent was about to break on the scene. Audience numbers rose steadily throughout March, and their enthusiasm grew, to the point where Nureyev was met outside the stage door by young girls carrying flowers. This was most unusual for a mere student. Tamara, Luiba and Elizaveta were among this group. All recognised, even then, that they were present at the birth of an extraordinary career. A French journalist visiting Lenningrad cabled her editors to say she thought she had just seen the best dancer in the world. Came the reply: Master your emotions:

After the matinées came a short break while the graduating students took their final examinations. Rudolf chose three pieces for this performance which, like the matinées, took place on the stage of the Maryinsky. He selected the Diana and Actaeon he had danced to impress Pushkin, the *pas de deux* from *Le Corsaire* and a solo from Nina Anisimova's *Gayane*. Again, Rudolf stole the show – though this wasn't easy: Yuri Soloviev was also graduating that year. What impressed the audience was not simply Rudolf's stage presence ('animal magnetism' was the cliché used), but the fact that, as one Soviet reviewer put it:

'he looked nothing like a graduating student. The public was confronted with a mature artist with his own style, approach, and even individual technique, strikingly singular against the severe background of the Kirov. It would be fair to say that if there ever was a *danseur noble* totally alien to the entire Kirov generation of "academicians" from Konstantin Sergeyev to Boris Bregvadze and Vladilen Semyonov, it was the young Nureyev. He was an odd bird in the flock indeed, not only because he was not a "neat" dancer [which he was never to become] but also because the viewer was so transfixed by the sweeping scope of his movements, his confidence and feline grace, that even the most vigilant eyes failed to catch his technical imperfections. They were in fact of no importance, given the thrill of his presence.'

In the middle of this exciting time, reality reared its ugly head. Chelkov called Rudolf into his office and told him that, upon graduation, he would return to Ufa, to dance in the ballet there. This was as a repayment to the Republic of Bashkir, which had helped fund his studies. There was a logic to this, but Rudolf was not prepared to recognise it. Alfimova was standing in the corridor outside the director's office while this meeting was going on, and she heard raised voices. 'Then the door opened and Rudolf came out. He was furious. He was so angry he threw his briefcase across the hall. It was a brown briefcase, with hammered corners, the sort that everybody had. "No!" Rudolf screamed, "I'm *not* going back to Bashkiria." And he stormed off.'

But term was not yet over and he had to sit on his frustration if he was to graduate at all. He determined to fight his battles one at a time. The next step in the graduation process was to show off the dancers with partners. Careers could not be built on solos. And so, in June, Rudolf twice danced the duet from *Corsaire* with Alla Sizova. Sizova had a fiery temperament and style herself but, by common consent, Rudolf provoked her to even more dramatic performances. Alfimova saw them a lot in that final year and confirms that they danced beautifully together. But she also adds: 'There was no contact between them outside dancing. I even remember that Alla said it was very difficult being with him, but she wouldn't say why.' Despite this, the rave reviews continued. Tamara was in the audience for Rudolf's first performance with Sizova. 'Already, by this stage, the ballet world, the balletomanes, had started to talk about Nureyev, using such terms as "astonishing".'

Given these successes, it is not surprising that Rudolf was chosen to represent the Vaganova at the national contest of all the Soviet ballet schools, held that same month, in Moscow. It was the first chance to distinguish himself on a truly national basis and he was very excited. The evening before he was due to leave for the capital, he visited Liuba Miasnikova and her twin brother Leonid, at the flat they shared in Tchaikovsky Street. Like Tamara, Liuba was a scientist, in her case a polymer physicist. It was during the White Nights, 'small clouds were racing at top speed through a transparent-looking sky and flying so low you felt you could reach up and touch them with your hand'. That evening they talked about 'everything' and Rudolf, for once, did not feel alone. 'Nowhere else, up till now, had I ever found such a tranquil, cultivated atmosphere.' The Miasnikovas specialised in *blinis* and after a *blinis* supper, with cherry jam, Rudolf walked back to the school at one o'clock in the morning as near content as he had ever been. As he walked he watched the clouds race by overhead, 'as if they knew where they were going'. Next morning he left for Moscow in a 'perfect' frame of mind.

It didn't last long. At one point, early on in rehearsals at the Tchaikovsky Philharmonia Hall, Rudolf leaned across the footlights to ask for Pushkin's critique of the dance he had just been practising. One of the Kirov teachers (not a Vaganova teacher) was also on stage at the time and, because of the glare of the footlights, could not see who Rudolf was talking to. He thought the young man was just chatting, and wasting time – and ordered him from the stage. This was humiliating in front of the other contestants and Rudolf was furious.

But, as he and others would discover later, this seems to have been just the spur he needed. He had chosen the programme he wished to dance with great care. It was in fact the same as he had danced in his graduation performance back in May. He had selected these pieces because each had a very different mood and called for high technical ability. It was not just a clever choice; it was a showman's choice.

The contest took place the very evening after he had been ordered from the stage, when he was still feeling piqued. Later he described his performance as 'wild and violent' but technically superb. On this occasion, however, we do not have to take his word for it. His *pas de deux* from *Le Corsaire* was so magnificent that the audience demanded he repeat it. It was the first time in his career that he had danced an encore (after which, the applause was even louder). It was no surprise, as *Theatre Life* subsequently reported, that he won first prize.

And that recognition at last changed his standing. 'For the first time since I had entered the Leningrad Ballet school [i.e. as he was just about to leave it] I could feel the conspiracy of silence around me breaking up; teachers and model students all came to see me after the performance to offer congratulations.' Even Feld, the lead conductor at the school, who had hitherto kept his distance, told Rudolf how impressed he had been by the different moods the dancer had conveyed in his performance. This was praise indeed, from one equal to another.

Rudolf's success that day was such that he was included in a special film made to commemorate the contest. He again chose the *pas de deux* from *Le Corsaire*, using the same costume of dark tights, a bare torso with a red and yellow bandana over one shoulder. What stand out are the prodigious jumps with their light landings – as he intended.

The events in the Moscow contest were marked not just by his colleagues at the Vaganova but by others too, and in the days that followed, he was approached by both the Bolshoi and the Stanislavsky companies, each offering him a place as a soloist as soon as his final year at the Leningrad school was over. These offers were a great honour, for they meant he would skip the usual period in the *corps de ballet* which is the traditional next step for the successful graduate. Everyone seemed to have forgotten the threat to send him back to Ufa.

Though he was flattered by the offer, the Stanislavsky held no allure for Rudolf; he felt the standards there were provincial. But the Bolshoi was a different matter. There was a great rivalry between that company and the Kirov, a rivalry that was to some extent a reflection of the rivalry between Moscow and Leningrad. Traditionally, Muscovites are seen as dowdy, greedy, rude but vigorous. In pre-communist days they were led by a conservative, orthodox clergy and a grasping merchant class, the *meshchanstro* – tough, vodka-drinking families who had risen from being peasants, on the backs of their own kind. They were isolationists who both hated and feared Europe.

St Petersburg, on the other hand, symbolised for Moscow all that was new, progressive, stylish – and dangerous. Traditionally, St Petersburg looked down on Moscow, the symbol of red tape, backwardness and provinciality. And it was not so different in the Soviet era. Following the assassination of Sergei Kirov, the popular Politburo member who ran Leningrad, the Terror came to the city in no uncertain fashion (some 600 people were killed) and this set many intellectuals against Stalin. Zhdanov was brought in to solve the problem and succeeded; but he hardly won the hearts of the locals and neither Stalin nor anyone else in the Moscow government was ever entirely happy with the city.

The situation wasn't helped when Moscow was made capital of the Soviet Union in 1918, with the result that, in time, the Bolshoi began to get more funds. It prospered at the expense of the Kirov and although the differences took time to show themselves the strengths of the Bolshoi had finally become apparent in 1956, when the (ex-Russian) New York impresario, Sol Hurok, had taken the Bolshoi on a tour of the west. They had been rapturously received everywhere.

All this made the Bolshoi offer to Rudolf very tempting. The situation at the Kirov was more complex. Naturally, as the star pupil of his year, and with such successes in his various performances, Rudolf *assumed* that an offer would be forthcoming. But when? And what would the offer be? His talents were undoubted but the ballet authorities in Leningrad were also more familiar with Rudolf's faults. There is no doubt that, at this time of great success, his confidence did spill over into arrogance. Alfimova watched it. 'He understood his uniqueness and didn't hold himself back very much. Perhaps his education was to blame. Educated people know how to control themselves. But he, being emotional, didn't consider it necessary to control himself.'

He had heard nothing from the Kirov by the time he returned to Leningrad. He had heard nothing when, about a week later, he danced the last of the graduating class's special performances. It was 29 June 1958 and again he chose the *pas de deux* from *Gayane*, variations from *Laurencia*, and the pas de deux from *Le Corsaire*. Again his partner was Alla Sizova.

That night there was the same wild applause as there had been in Moscow. But there was something else as well. After the performance, Natalia Dudinskaya, the greatest ballerina of her day in Russia, and the star of the Kirov, arrived backstage and sought out Rudolf's dressing-room. Dudinskaya was forty-seven at the time, and Rudolf just twenty. Nonetheless, she came straight out with her message for the young dancer: she would like to dance a full-scale *Laurencia* with him. Such an offer was virtually unprecedented and little short of miraculous. But it was also a cool piece of theatre. Dudinskaya knew that Rudolf was not a simple person. She said later that she understood he was 'complicated', but in a certain way: 'He certainly knew what he was worth. He was slightly guilty of knowing what he was worth.' In other words, he was arrogant. But she also knew what *her* offer was worth. It would be the making of him.

It is worth pausing for a moment to consider who, exactly, Dudinskaya was, for it is fair to say that, in the history of ballet, there had never been anyone quite like her in Russia. Not Pavlova, not Ulanova. In some ways she eclipsed Taglioni, even Fonteyn. To explain we need to return, briefly, to the war.

Shortly after Hitler had mounted his drive on Moscow in 1941, the German Army Group North broke through the outer defences of Leningrad and, on 8 September, cut the city's last land link with the rest of the Soviet Union, leaving Lake Ladoga (and the air corridor) as the only means of communication. Stalin responded by sending Marshal Zhukov to take command and attempt to save the city. By the time Zhukov arrived, however, on 13 September, Hitler had already decided not to storm Leningrad but to starve it into surrender.

The story of the siege of Leningrad has been told many times and the fate of the 3 million souls in the city is a moving tale. Conditions soon deteriorated and the only lifeline was the thin layer of ice on Lake Ladoga, across which lorries – only half-loaded for fear of breaking the ice – slithered for a hundred miles to the nearest railhead. The German bombardment was unstinting. One factory, the Kirov Works, was hit by 700 bombs and 4,000 shells. Private telephones were disconnected, newspapers vanished, water gave out, the sewage system failed, only factories and headquarters had electricity. Trams stopped, theatres and cinemas closed, as did shops, which had nothing to sell. Fuel gave out. Wooden houses were demolished for firewood, and maple leaves used for tobacco. Each week the food ration sank until, by November, it was down to 250 grams of bread a day for workers, with others receiving half that. This was the equivalent of five slices but, since the bread was 20 per cent glucose, sawdust, bark and leather, it provided only 460 calories (the minimum for subsistence is 3,000). Ever more desperate measures were followed. Cotton-seed oil cake, intended as shipping fuel, was used as food. Sheepgut was turned into jelly, pancakes were made from wallpaper paste, soup by boiling buttons.

It was not at all unusual for people to eat cats and dogs, despite the heartache this caused. Even so, by February 1942 5,000 people were dying every day. A small number of specially adapted lorries spent their whole time picking up corpses. There were no funerals. Workers collapsed at their benches, women died in bed, leaving young children to fend for themselves. Corpses lay along the icy canals with no one to bury them.

By some miracle the radio kept going, and loudspeakers in the streets warned when the bombers were coming. A hospital for the wounded was destroyed at Smovorsky Prospekt, and a bomb hit stage left at the Kirov, near the main entrance.

Dudinskaya was the prima ballerina in Leningrad when war broke out. Born in 1912 in Kharkov in the Ukraine, she grew up with a mother who had her own private ballet school, which Natalia attended from the age of seven. In 1923, at the entrance exams for the former Imperial Ballet School, Talia (as she was known) astonished Agrippina Vaganova with her vast repertoire. Talia joined the Maryinsky as a soloist in 1931 but her later development was delayed until she formed an artistic marriage with Vakhtung Chaboukiani, which at last began to stretch her dramatic abilities. In addition to her phenomenal technique her dancing took on a new urgency, a new depth. Chaboukiani choreographed *Laurencia* specifically for her and with this role, first performed on the eve of the war, she achieved unrivalled popularity with audiences.

In August 1941 her career, like everyone else's, was disrupted by the Kirov's evacuation to Perm in the Urals, and it was here that her later partnership with Konstantin Sergeyev (which would ultimately lead to marriage) began to flourish. He had been dancing with Ulanova in the 1930s.

As with the other Allied armies, the Red Army had what it called concert brigades during the war, units of entertainers who travelled around performing in front of the troops to aid relaxation and boost morale. In August 1943, at the height of the siege, and despite the great danger the decision was taken to fly a concert brigade into Leningrad. Dudinskaya and Sergeyev were chosen and at first recalled to Moscow, where the flight began, using the latest military intelligence on the fighting. The siege had been partly lifted at the beginning of 1943 but the narrow supply corridor along the shore of Lake Ladoga was still ravaged by heavy guns. The Soviet offensive to clear the corridor would not come until January 1944.

Despite the risks, the flight was uneventful and they landed safely. In Leningrad Dudinskaya stayed with Vaganova. There was little time for rehearsal. The bombed green and white Maryinsky Theatre was closed. Performances were therefore scheduled for the Philharmonia.

'We did two concerts at the Philharmonia,' says Dudinskaya.

'When Sergeyev and I came out the first time to dance *The Nutcracker* the whole of the stalls stood up because they wanted to show their thanks for the fact that we had come at such a terrible time. It was a dangerous time, because they were bombing a lot. We had to go everywhere by foot because none of the transport system was working. We were in Leningrad for two weeks. The snipers started at 4 a.m. [when, in Leningrad in August, it was already light], and there was never any warning. The beginning always claimed victims. After that, people ran into the stairwells of houses.

The bombing would occur during rehearsals and during performances. I saw many dead people. When the artillery started firing on us during *The Nutcracker* the performance was stopped for forty minutes. Everyone dashed for the shelters – and then they *all* came back. Not a single person left. I wasn't frightened at first, but I was when I saw the corpses. Despite everything I saw, I was pleased that I had come. I was pleased that I had danced with tears in my eyes. I was the sun, a light for those people who were here in Leningrad.'

After that, of course, Dudinskaya and Sergeyev became more than mere dancers; they were local heroes, fixtures in the national heritage, an emotional focus around which people had been proud to rally in their darkest days. As Tamara Myasciorva put it, 'We had the Bronze Horses, the Hermitage, the Russian Museum – and Dudinskaya and Sergeyev.'

Rudolf was flattered by Dudinskaya's offer – who could fail to be? And it at least implied that Dudinskaya assumed that he would be offered something by the Kirov. But a formal offer didn't come and Rudolf found he was thinking more and more about the Bolshoi. The Bolshoi, after all, had Galina Ulanova, the one dancer who could rank with Dudinskaya, perhaps even eclipse her. But that wasn't the only factor. 'It seemed to me that the Bolshoi was too restricting for its artists to express themselves to the full – always with the exception of Ulanova . . . For lesser artists the Bolshoi's policy can often prove disastrous, turning them into mere athletes, record-breakers with marvellous muscles of steel but no heart and no deep sensitive love for the art they serve.' Rudolf was worried that the Communist government had turned the Bolshoi into a national showplace, to impress important foreigners and tourists. And he knew, without being told, that as a result the Bolshoi would always be subject to closer government scrutiny.

But at least they had made an offer . . .

A few days after the approach from Dudinskaya, she says she found Rudolf sitting on one of the sofas in the corridors of the Kirov, pondering his dilemma. He rehearsed for her the strengths of the Moscow company, and its weaknesses. In reply, she gently pointed out three things. One, that some of the greatest *artistic* successes of Russian ballet since the revolution (she mentioned *Romeo and Juliet* and *Laurencia*) had been produced at the Kirov long before they had been taken up by the Bolshoi. Two, that it was still a golden period for the Kirov. The company had an extensive repertoire and it was the policy of her husband, Konstantin Sergeyev, to produce every ballet in the repertoire at least twice a year, to keep them alive. 'The scenery is always ready here,' she said, putting her hand on Rudolf's arm. And three, very gently now, she reminded him that he had a difficult personality. 'Anything might happen in Moscow.'

She stood up and brought the meeting to a close. 'Don't be foolish,' she whispered. 'Don't choose the Bolshoi. Stay here and we'll dance together.'

That seemed to be that, and Rudolf returned the Bolshoi contract to Moscow, unsigned. He graduated formally in early July and the school closed for the summer vacation. This year he preferred not to go home straight away. Provincial Ufa held little allure for him after the glitter of the past few weeks. Instead, he hung around the company, which would not finish its season until the end of the month. He didn't dance again, not in a proper role or in front of an audience. But he did rehearse. As with the Bolshoi, the Kirov has a complete second stage in the roof of the building. There are only two rows of seats but, to give the dancers the feel of the theatre proper, the rehearsal stage is raked in the same way and even has a full-sized orchestra pit.

He discovered the scenery store – where everything was kept ready, as Dudinskaya had said. A sort of mini-railway led down a slope from the back of the stage into the scenery bays. With his love of trains, this special railway always fascinated him. It was on the 'male' side of the theatre, under the men's dressing-rooms (the women's were on the other side of the stage) beneath the long corridor which led to the stage door. Rudolf just loved being *in* the theatre. Of course, he watched every performance. If only the company would make an offer . . .

In August the theatre closed and the ballet and opera companies took themselves off for the summer break. Rudolf was still very much on his own. Tamara and the Miasnikovas had gone on holiday, Elizaveta was away, Gyckova had gone back to Ufa. He couldn't face his home town and there had been too little time to make any new friends inside the Kirov proper. He decided to take some sun and another mud cure in the Crimea. He took himself off to the Black Sea, alone, where he could relax his muscles and do nothing.

No sooner had he arrived than a telegram arrived from the Ministry of Culture in Moscow. He read it in mounting horror. The text informed him that he was to report to Ufa – Ufa! – and to dance in the opera there. He was beside himself with fury and dismay. Chelkov had been right and the grim news had finally caught up with him. Only weeks earlier he had been the toast of Moscow and Leningrad. Now this.

But there was something else, too. In the telegram he recognised the hand of his rivals and enemies in Leningrad. That made him determined to fight. Cancelling his holiday, he took the first plane to Moscow and went straight to the Ministry of Culture. The woman he met there was uncompromising. The Ministry was not used to having its decisions queried, she said. Nureyev must return to Ufa and repay his debt.

Rudolf was now very upset indeed. But he wasn't going back to Ufa without a fight. Apart from anything else, it would mean facing his father, who would regard a return to Ufa as confirmation that his son had failed. The only other person Rudolf felt comfortable with in Moscow was the director of the Bolshoi, so he walked up to the theatre and told him what had happened. The director grew excited at the news. He was perfectly aware that Rudolf had returned unsigned the contract that had been sent from Moscow. But the Bolshoi was a more political company. If Rudolf was no longer a member of the Kirov, and hated the thought of returning to Ufa, the director was sure he could swing it for him.

That was better – far better – than a return to Ufa, and Rudolf accepted. By now the Miasnikovas had returned from their vacation, so he went back to Leningrad to fill them in on all that had happened while they had been away. They were a sort of family to him and he could relax there. While he was in Leningrad, however, he happened to visit the Maryinsky and the director, hearing he was backstage, asked to see him. Rudolf didn't much want to make this visit. The way the company had treated him – not making any formal offer gracefully, allowing Dudinskaya to do it in a roundabout way, and then the telegram from the Ministry – suggested that the Kirov authorities were not only against him but cowardly too.

The director's office was on the male side of the stage, above the scenery railway Rudolf was so intrigued by. He knocked on the door and was told to enter. He stood just inside the door, wondering what to say and fearful of any new bombshell that might be about to drop. But the director was remarkably relaxed. He waved Rudolf to a seat, smiled and, without preamble or histrionics, said, 'Why are you making such a fool of yourself, Nureyev? There was never any question of throwing you out of the Kirov. Unpack your things again. You're staying. Your salary is waiting to be collected.'

Rudolf was flabbergasted. A week later his contract arrived from the Bolshoi and he was obliged to return it a second time. It did not make him popular in Moscow.

Note

1 Around this time, April 1957, Ninette de Valois, artistic director of Britain's Royal Ballet, arrived in Leningrad, where she visited the Vaganova school and picked out Ninel Kurgapkina as a future star. In the evening she saw Dudinskaya in *Laurencia*. Later on, Nureyev told de Valois that this was his first performance in the ballet. Alas, the dates do not coincide. De Valois saw her *Laurencia* on 7 April 1957. Nureyev made his début in *Laurencia*, with Dudinskaya, on 20 November 1958 (see below, p. 125).

CHAPTER FIVE

The Hollow Sequence

It's agony to watch the hollow
sequence of dinners stretch away,
to see life as a ritual play,
and with the decorous throng to follow
although one in no manner shares
its views, its passions, or its cares!

Rudolf was the first dancer in the history of the Kirov to go straight from the school to being a soloist. That simple, but extraordinary, fact shows how much the company had its wires crossed over his personality. Even though he was a soloist, however, Rudolf was still a newcomer to the company, which meant that he did not immediately qualify for all the privileges a soloist could eventually expect.

His living conditions, for example, were primitive in the extreme, worse even than the dormitory in the Vaganova. For the first six months – the second half of 1958 – he was compelled to live in the *kollectiv* reserved for people who were connected with the theatre. Mostly, they were truck drivers and manual labourers and eight of them lived in one room on beds that were nailed to the wall like shelves, one above the other. It was an ordeal for all concerned, and not unlike being back in Zentsova Street. Rudolf had a coarse tongue at the best of times. But even he learned some new words in the *kollectiv*.

But although his living conditions were still primitive, Rudolf was at last receiving a decent wage. According to Tamara, the Kirov *corps de ballet* in those days received about 80 roubles a month. (Irina Kolpakova got married when she was in the *corps* and wasn't earning enough to be able to afford a ring.) Rudolf as a soloist got about 200 roubles and star dancers like Dudinskaya and Sergeyev earned about 500 (the rouble had been devalued in respect to the pre-war currency). Since the minimum wage in the Soviet Union at that time was 30 roubles a month, Rudolf was well paid. According to Arkharova, the KGB officer at the Kirov, ballet wages were settled by a wages committee which discussed each person's entitlement every year.

Rudolf now started to send about half his salary home to his family. Like many things Rudolf did, this was a double-edged gesture. At about this time, his mother began to experience fainting spells and pains in her legs and, before long, would give up work. So the money was especially welcome. On top of that, Rudolf was now out-earning his father quite easily, and by sending so much money home he was rubbing in his success, at his father's expense.

Though he kept in touch with his family, he never talked about them to his friends in Leningrad. Tamara felt that he was still 'the black sheep – or odd one out – in the family. None of the others studied art in any way. For them he was the ugly duckling who turned into a swan they couldn't understand.' Rudolf was as much of an outsider in his family as he was everywhere else.

He was still living in the *kollectiv* when the great night arrived, 20 November, 1958, when he was to dance opposite Dudinskaya in *Laurencia*. This ballet, based on a play by Lope de Vega Carpio, *Fuente Ovejuna*, had been choreographed by Chaboukiani specifically for Dudinskaya. Set in fifteenth-century Spain, its plot is centred upon a woman whose rage, when a tyrannical lord exercises his *droit de seigneur* on her wedding day, inspires a revolt. Nureyev danced the role of Frondoso, her fiancé.

Once again, during rehearsals for the ballet, Pushkin came into his own. It was clear to him that although Rudolf had learned the part technically – he had been taught by Igor Belsky, interestingly enough, one of the Kirov coaches particularly well informed about the west – his time in the *kollectiv* was depriving him of proper sleep, he was exhausted, and his interpretation of the role was suffering. The night before the performance Pushkin moved Rudolf into his own flat so that he could get a good night's sleep.

There is some mystery about that night. Later on in life, Rudolf always made a point of saying that the night he had spent in Dudinskaya's flat, and the times he had stayed with the Pushkins, he had always slept on the sofa – and nothing more. Whether his western interviewers knew it or not, when he said this he was responding to persistent Leningrad rumours that, in fact, he had slept with both Dudinskaya and Pushkin's wife.

Nureyev never slept with Dudinskaya. But Pushkin's wife, Tseniia Iurgenson, was a different matter. Much younger than her husband, with wavy blonde hair, Tseniia was very attractive and somewhat exotic by Leningrad standards. She came from a cosmopolitan family of publishers and had herself danced character roles at the Kirov, where she had met Pushkin.

Both Pushkin and Tseniia knew how important the *Laurencia* performance was for Rudolf's career. It could, quite simply, make or break him. If he danced well, some of Dudinskaya's greatness would rub off on him. If he let her down, he would let himself down even more.

Pushkin had done all he could to train Rudolf for the role he was to play. But by now he and Tseniia knew Rudolf well, and were aware that there was one aspect of his life that was missing. It contributed to his ever-present tenseness and was hampering his emotional maturation. What was absent from Rudolf's life was sex. This was an important gap, artistically speaking. No one could be sure how large a gap it was, but it surely made a difference, robbing his personality of an essential ingredient, that final layer of understanding he needed to play a passionate lover, and preventing his performances from delivering a complete realisation of his ideas. *Laurencia*, no less than other ballets, is about love and its effects on the heart.

Though Pushkin was a quiet man, he was not unsophisticated and he had been in the theatre for many years. That he was less conventional than his outward appearance is shown by his choice of wife. Both shared a view of what Rudolf needed to complete his training and the fact that he was living in a dreary *kollectiv* and not getting enough sleep provided a perfect opening for their plan. They invited him to spend the night before *Laurencia* at their flat and, while he was there, and with Pushkin's full knowledge and approval, Tseniia Iurgenson seduced him.

It worked. Dudinskaya was not especially beautiful. She had large eyes, though her chin was rather big and square. But her skin was perfect, a pale backdrop which made her features very expressive. Later she said that Rudolf had held her very well and that his more exotic presence fitted perfectly with her more straightforward, ethereal appearance. The high point of the evening was in the *pas de six*, which forms part of the wedding celebration, before the grandee delivers his psychological blow. Until then the choreography is very free – violent, almost – but in the *pas de six* it suddenly becomes restrained and classical; the contrast is striking. The main characters therefore matched the choreography. As the performance came to an end, Dudinskaya was relieved that Rudolf had danced so well, because it vindicated her choice. The band of supporters he had attracted while at the choreographic school attended that night and applauded wildly.

Afterwards he lay in bed, too excited to sleep, until he felt an arm through the window, tugging at his foot. It was Yuri Soloviev, who had graduated at the same time as Nureyev, albeit only into the *corps* at the Kirov. As a fellow performer, Soloviev knew how Nureyev must be feeling. 'You can't go straight to bed after a performance like that,' he said. 'Come out and we will walk with you.' 'We' turned out to be Soloviev and his mother. Rudolf loved that, the fact that Soloviev had the kind of mother who would walk through a November night in Leningrad. And it set a pattern: from then on Rudolf never went to bed after a performance, but would take hours to wind down.

Next morning everyone complimented him, saying he had a great future. Only Pushkin, of all people, voiced any criticism. He pointed out that when Rudolf had arrived on stage the night before, he had been too diffident. In future, Pushkin said, making no reference to any other recent events, Rudolf should strive to make an entrance, a 'clean start' as he called it. He stressed that the best way to draw attention to oneself on stage was by use of the *port de bras*, the carriage of the arms. If held forward slightly they created a sense of anticipation, denoting that *this* dancer was about to *do* something, and it would draw the eye of the audience. This was a lesson Rudolf never forgot. He would never again be accused of not making an entrance.

Early in 1959 Rudolf was able to move out of the detested *kollectiv* and into his own flat – or, rather, a two-bedroomed flat which he was to share with Alla Sizova. This apartment was itself a reflection of conventions inside Russia at the time. Despite its prim attitudes about sex, the Soviet system saw nothing unusual in having these two young ballet stars sharing the same living accommodation. Sizova had graduated at the same time as Nureyev, they had danced several performances together in their last year at the Vaganova, and now the powers-that-be considered that, in time, these two might make an excellent couple, on stage. If they happened to hit it off off-stage, that would only help their dancing partnership, so why not make it easy for them? In its way it was much the same attitude as Pushkin and his wife had had on the night before Rudolf danced with Dudinskaya.

But on this occasion the whole idea was a disaster from start to finish. To begin with, Rudolf and Sizova argued about who should have which room. One bedroom was 19 square metres, the other 17. This may not sound much to westerners but it was a vital matter to Russians and there was no question of Rudolf playing the gentleman here. He had been deprived of space all his life, and he took the larger room. Sizova was livid and determined to get her own back.

That winter, the latter half of 1958 and the early months of 1959, Rudolf danced minor roles as well as repeating Frondoso in *Laurencia*. Three times, for instance, he danced as one of four boys in *Red Flower*, on one occasion when Kolpakova and Sokolov were playing the main parts. He also shared the limelight with Dudinskaya, Moiseeva, Yastrebova and Vikulov in *Raymonda*.

Meanwhile, the relationship – off-stage – with Sizova had gone from bad to worse. 'It was surprising,' says Rezida. 'The more they danced beautifully together, the more they didn't like each other in real life.

Maybe it was intensified by the fact that they lived in the same apartment.' In fact it was intensified, in the first instance, by the arrival of Rosa to share Rudolf's room. She had come to Leningrad to study at the Lesgaft Institute but Sizova disliked her even more than Rudolf. She told friends that the basis of her dislike was that Rosa had 'an improper lifestyle'. She refused to elaborate but others say that there were rumours at the time that Rosa had an illegitimate child.

At one stage, Zoya Arkharova, the KGB agent in the Kirov, bumped into Rudolf in one of the corridors of the theatre.

'Rudik, come here,' she said.

He stopped.

'I congratulate you.'

'What on?' he growled.

'On the marvellous flat they have given you.'

'Do you think I need that hovel?'

'What? Do you know how many people who lived through the blockade are living in communal apartments? Do you know how many people don't have their own flats? You have just jumped about a couple of times on stage and they give you an apartment like that – and then you're not happy! You pig!'

She walked away and left him standing. Later she was told by one of the porters that Nureyev just stared after her for a long time, without moving.

So, if his manners *were* improving, they still had some way to go. It was certainly true that, even as a full member of the Kirov, Rudolf did not find friendship easy. Tamara confirms that he liked Ninel Kurgapkina, a dark, rather muscular dancer, who later partnered Baryshnikov a lot, and Nikita Dolgushin, who was six months younger than Rudolf and different in every way – he was tall, cool, from a family of Leningrad intellectuals, and was once described as 'a living statue'. But, as Tamara puts it, 'that was it'. Twice in early 1959 Nureyev walked off stage during rehearsals because the conductor was not playing a tempo he liked.

Even Gyckova, his loyal friend from Ufa, now began to lose patience with him. On one occasion they were walking together in Leningrad, near St Isaac's Cathedral, when they bumped into a student who was on Gyckova's engineering course. They stopped to talk but after a few sentences Rudolf intervened. 'What *is* this, Gyckova?' he said. 'Is this deliberate? Do you assemble your friends deliberately to annoy me?' And he walked off. Gyckova felt that his boorishness was a protective reaction. 'He once said to me that he didn't *want* to get close to Leningraders, because he didn't want their "nostalgia".' True as this might be, it didn't help. Whenever they went to the cinema Rudolf would always turn up at the last minute, just as the lights were going down. He would claim that he had been rehearsing and though this was true, it was, Gyckova felt, not the whole truth.

If he was very late, she or someone else would have bought the tickets.

The break between them came with two specific acts which showed, she concluded, that Rudolf had not behaved as a true friend. One concerned another dancer called Kostya who, Rudolf felt, was as good as he if not better. Unfortunately, in 1959 Kostya was forced to return to Novosibirsk for personal reasons. 'This was nearly 2,000 miles from Leningrad and Kot, as we called him, couldn't afford the fare back. It was as simple as that. I mentioned it to Rudolf and said that I was going to send Kot the money. Rudolf overruled me and said he would do it. Later, I learned that he never did.' The second incident concerned the birthday of a mutual friend of Rudolf's and Gyckova's, called Valya Monashkina. Valya, whose brother worked at the ballet, was having a party and all those invited were giving her presents. Rudolf was invited but had a rehearsal which clashed with the party and couldn't go. He gave Gyckova his present for Valya and asked her to pass it on, on his behalf. Gyckova refused. 'It was a box of sweets, so pitiful, so pathetic, so wretched. I would have been ashamed to give it to anyone. I grew very tired of Rudolf. He simply could not meet me other than to pour out everything evil which had accumulated in his soul during the day. I was forced to make the break.'

The 'evil' she was referring to involved any number of incidents which took place during rehearsals at the Maryinsky – with the conductor, say, or the costume designer, or other dancers. And there was always the ever-rumbling problem with Sizova. Their relationship deteriorated even further when Sizova retaliated against Rosa's arrival in the apartment by moving in her own mother, father and sister Nina into her room. What had been intended as a cosy home for two rising ballet stars thus became a battleground between two families, totalling six in all. The whole situation turned into a bitter farce, with one family hogging the bathroom, while the other occupied the kitchen.

It was against this extraordinary background that Rudolf's second big night at the Maryinsky was scheduled to take place, on 7 April 1959, nearly five months after his début. Once again, the ballet was *Laurencia*; once again Dudinskaya was to be his partner. This ought to have pleased Rudolf and it did, but only up to a point. The amount of time between these two dates illustrates the fact that, in those days, the Kirov gave only fifteen performances a month. The company had fifteen soloists and twenty 'first dancers', each one entitled to, and expecting, a principal role in a ballet. Simple mathematics dictated that soloists and principals could only hope to dance about five times a year. Even Dudinskaya had to take her turn in this queue. The company gave fewer foreign tours then than it does now and the standard was so high that some dancers preferred to stay at home when the company went on tour, since that gave them more opportunity to dance big roles. As Tamara put it, 'If Kolpakova went on tour, then Ter-Stepanova stayed in Leningrad. We could have *Swan Lake* here in Leningrad and *Swan Lake* abroad, all done by the same company and equally good.'

Rudolf's second *Laurencia* was a watershed in more ways than one. On the day before the performance he rehearsed all day long, going through the technically difficult parts time and again. However, since he was still a relative newcomer, Belsky, the Kirov teacher, insisted that he work on into the evening until everything was absolutely right. In early April, winter still lingered. It was cold outside, growing dark, and Rudolf was exhausted by a hectic routine that had gone on for hours. That morning, there had been the usual altercation with the Sizovas. Rehearsing his steps in the *pas de six*, where he had to jump and turn, he made a mistake – and in landing tore a ligament in his right leg. This was not a minor injury – the tear went right through to the bone, and he screamed in agony. His scream was for more than just the physical pain. He knew that a tear of that kind was sometimes irreparable. A tear of that kind had even ruined careers.

The Kirov's own doctor was called and he recommended that Nureyev be taken to hospital immediately. At the hospital, Rudolf's worst fears were confirmed. The specialist examined the ligament, probed the extent of the damage, and pronounced that Rudolf could not expect to dance for three years. Rudolf was in despair. He had danced one leading role and now his career might be over for good. The doctors left but Rudolf was forced to remain in hospital overnight. He couldn't sleep and next morning felt even worse. The first signs of spring were showing on the trees of Leningrad but all he could think about was his maimed right leg and the fact that he wouldn't be dancing on his beloved Kirov stage that evening.

Later that day Pushkin came to see him. The older man had heard about the accident when he arrived at the theatre that morning, and had come straight round. He examined the wound for himself – he had seen a few in his time – but was more concerned about Rudolf's mood. His protégé was beside himself with worry. Sitting at Rudolf's bedside in the hospital, Pushkin took a decision: he would move Rudolf out of the apartment he shared with Alla Sizova, and into his own home. Tseniia liked Rudolf. In fact, she more than liked him. The young man was clearly a star in the making, but also something of a lost soul in Leningrad. He knew his own mind in many ways but was a loner who might just respond to a stable home. The Pushkins' friends were all in the arts – dancers, musicians, writers, actors. They overlapped with the salon of Elizaveta Mikhailovna.

Again, Pushkin was right. It was an atmosphere in which Rudolf thrived. The Kirov doctor came every day, exploring the way Nureyev's wound was healing and giving him gentle exercises. Tseniia saw to it that the doctor's instructions were adhered to and fed Rudolf the best foods then available in Leningrad – she knew where to lay her hands on eggs, fish and steak, for the protein he needed to rebuild his torn muscles.

There was no repeat of the seduction but, between them, the Pushkins worked a minor miracle. After three weeks, Rudolf was fit enough to attend class again. In another three weeks he was strong enough to begin full-scale rehearsals for the rescheduled *Laurencia*. Rudolf's will had something to do with this extraordinary progress, of course. How could he face his father again if his career had come to such an ignominious end so soon after it had begun?

But there was more to this incident than Nureyev's recovery from illness and the Pushkins' part in it. The critical nature of the illness and the close proximity brought about by living in the Pushkins' flat, produced a great intimacy. It was exactly what Rudolf needed. Under the influence of the Pushkins, Rudolf not only recovered physically but began to grow intellectually. 'And his manners at last began to change,' says Tamara. 'It hadn't been all that easy at the beginning. But now he learned beautiful things. He began to read a lot. He read the *Mockva* [a newspaper]. *Master and Marguerita* was serialised in the *Mockva* in those days. He definitely changed.'

But he still had his enemies. Not long after he recovered from his injury, he learned that several young dancers from the Kirov had been invited to travel to Moscow to audition for the privilege of being allowed to compete in an International Festival of Youth in Vienna. His name had been left off the list. He was perplexed and angry. By now he was used to being an object of envy, and he knew that some of his fellow dancers were bitterly jealous, resenting particularly the privileges he had earned without being a member either of a *kollectiv* or of the Komsomol.

But if he was used to having enemies, he was also used to fighting for himself. He went to see the director of the Kirov and argued that, as the youngest soloist in the company, and because he had danced only two roles since he joined, he had the strongest case of all for going to Moscow to be auditioned for the Vienna festival. Not for the first time, his forthright approach worked, and his name was added to the list.

One problem was followed by another. When the Kirov dancers reached Moscow, Rudolf was distressed to find that the rehearsal space reserved for them was at a fencing club close to the hotel. The proximity was convenient, but that was all that could be said for the club. There was no mirror, no *barre* and no proper dancing floor. None of the other dancers thought of this as a problem but Rudolf did. He had recently recovered from serious injury and he knew well the value of proper rehearsal. Without a *barre* and mirror, faulty positions could not be identified, or corrected. He announced his intention of finding somewhere else to rehearse – alone if necessary.

For some of the others, this was too much. One of the teachers (Rudolf would never name him) turned on the dancer and openly accused him of nonconformism. This was designed to be a dreadful accusation but Rudolf pleaded guilty. Something snapped inside him and he turned on his accusers, arguing forcefully that there was a point to nonconformity, that an excellent technique was all very well, that good technique was where the Russians stood out, but he added that great technique wasn't enough. To the astonishment of the others, who had never heard an exchange like this before, he argued that the emphasis on technique was, in effect, killing the ballet in Russia because people were tired of seeing one faultless dancer after another, but each faultless in the same way. What Russian ballet needed was dancers with Russian technique – and then something extra, something each dancer could bring to the ballet that was his – or her – own.

This speech of Rudolf's almost certainly made him some friends. His generation was the first of the post-war dancers, and they could see how, despite the cold war, old ideas were bound to die. But these friends were secret friends; they lacked the conviction to speak up in public, whereas his enemies, being in the majority, had no such inhibitions. Criticism of the raw man from Ufa did not go away.

On this occasion, however, Rudolf had the last laugh. He was chosen to go to Vienna.

In his autobiography, Rudolf devotes two lines to Vienna. He says it seemed to him 'the gayest, most beautiful and hospitable city I had ever seen'. But it was also the occasion of a great triumph, and a terrible fight with Sizova – a fight that she won.

The triumph came when Sizova and Rudolf danced a duet in the competition. Their choice was *Choreographical Miniatures*, a piece by Grigorovich which they had danced before in Russia and which was really more of a *divertissement* than a ballet proper. The couple won first prize, a huge honour both for them and Russian ballet, given that other contestants represented France, Italy, Great Britain and the United States (the Russian dancers also included Kolpakova and Soloviev from Leningrad and Ekaterina Maximova and Vladimir Vassiliev from Moscow). Unfortunately, the winning pair were given only one medal and one certificate. Both of them wanted the medal and neither wanted the certificate, and a furious tussle ensued. Sizova had been handed the medal at the presentation ceremony, while Rudolf had been handed the certificate, and she now refused to let Rudolf even touch the medal. She hadn't forgotten or forgiven him for taking the bigger room in the apartment they 'shared'. He was angry and tried to snatch the medal from her but she anticipated his move and held on to it. The whole episode, which should have been a high moment in their careers to date, only made their relationship even worse. The presentation was spoiled even more when, after their fight, it turned out that the organisers had decided to give *several* first prizes, so the argument had been over nothing.

On the way back to Russia, Rudolf proved a nonconformist yet again, this time by accident. They were travelling by train and the route took them via the Ukraine, where they had to change trains in Kiev after a wait of half an hour. True to form, Rudolf, whose father had been in Kiev during the war, refused just to sit on his luggage on the platform and stare at the track; instead he took a taxi for a quick look at a city he had never seen before. He was accompanied by another more adventurous soul from the Kirov orchestra. Unfortunately, on their way back to the station the taxi was held up in traffic and the two men missed the train. With anyone else this would have been a trivial incident – there was another train barely half an hour later. But Rudolf knew that, for him, this would be seen as yet another example of his difficult nature. 'I told my friend that I was ready to bet he would find the entire orchestra waiting for him in Leningrad, laughing and joking about him missing the train, while my own absence would be construed in a completely different light by the company.' The two recalcitrants arrived in Leningrad just a few minutes after the rest of the troupe – and Rudolf was proved correct. The musician's colleagues viewed his lapse as a joke. With Rudolf, however, the view taken was so severe that several of his fellow dancers told him they thought his 'insubordination' would be the end of his career. Indeed, they were so certain that Rudolf would be fired after the Kiev incident that some had begun to divide up his forthcoming performances among themselves. The chief divider of the spoils was the director of the Kirov Komsomol.

Rudolf was being somewhat unrealistic. After all, with Sizova he had just won an international prize, a high honour. He could not have been fired just then, even for gross insubordination, let alone missing a train. And of course, nothing of the kind happened. But the awkward sequence of difficult situations continued. He continued to be difficult and denunciations of his behaviour continued to snowball.

In that second year at the Kirov his main fight occurred with Yuri Grigorovich, a relatively young choreographer. Grigorovich had made a great success with *The Stone Flower*, Prokofiev's last ballet which had first been staged by Léonid Lavrovsky, then reworked, much more successfully, by Grigorovich. Now he had created *Legend of Love* in which Rudolf was to play the hero Feshad. When Grigorovich first saw Rudolf dance he was very impressed. 'I couldn't even imagine that something like that was possible in the theatre', he said later. Rehearsals took place in the theatre while, at the same time, and sometimes on the same day, Rudolf was rehearsing *Laurencia* at the choreographical school. Now the theatre and the school are a good fifteen minutes walk apart, perhaps more, so Rudolf had to get his timings right if he was to attend both rehearsals promptly.

This time he was to have a new partner, Alla Shelest. Shelest, who was forty in 1959, was never as well known in the west as Ulanova or Plisetskaya, but in Russia she was considered by many people to be the equal of both of them – indeed it was said she had better technique than Plisetskya and that her *claque* equalled Ulanova's. A great tragic actress, Shelest had been a soloist at the Kirov since before Rudolf was born, and was perhaps best known for her extraordinary stage presence, which is what fascinated Rudolf. He was anxious to perform well with her, to show that he could shine even when Dudinskaya was not his partner.

While all this hectic toing and froing was going on, Vakhtung Chaboukiani arrived in Leningrad to mount a production of *Othello*. Chaboukiani was of course one of the Soviet greats, a hero of Rudolf's childhood, when Vaitovitch had held up him and Sergeyev as models for young dancers. Chaboukiani did not have an especially big jump but he did have the ability to hover in the air. He too had become a star overnight, as the slave in the *Corsaire pas de deux*, and his partnership with Ulanova had passed into legend. Since giving up dancing he had become a successful choreographer. While he was in Leningrad, Pushkin persuaded Chaboukiani to give Nureyev some lessons. Naturally, Rudolf was thrilled although, strictly speaking, he didn't have the time. To make matters worse, it was never explained to Chaboukiani that Rudolf had other rehearsals to attend, and so the classes sometimes ran on.

Inevitably, there came a day when there wasn't time for Rudolf to squeeze everything into the available hours. He couldn't run, let alone walk, between the school and theatre, and he couldn't find a taxi. He arrived late for Grigorovich's class.

Grigorovich was something of a star himself, and used to being treated as such. Like Chaboukiani, he had been a successful dancer and now he was a successful choreographer. He had, therefore, started the rehearsal without waiting for Rudolf. There was a tense atmosphere among the other dancers on the second stage of the Maryinsky, for the chief object of the rehearsal was Rudolf. 'What's this?' Grigorovich shouted, the minute Rudolf appeared. 'Taking the liberty of being late?'

The wording was deliberate, and perhaps intended to wound. Everyone knew that Rudolf's chief concern was his freedom.

His temper flared. This version of *Legend of Love* was being created around him, by the most talented choreographer in Russia. Grigorovich was being provocative, but Rudolf, though late, had an excuse. He could have apologised and explained. It would all have been quickly forgotten.

But that wasn't Rudolf. He said one word – 'Shit!' and flounced out. And forfeited his chance of dancing in the first night of *Legend of Love*.

Nureyev said that, from the middle of 1959, when he returned from Vienna, his enemies stepped up their campaign against him, to the point where there were almost daily denunciations of this or that aspect of his behaviour. But the fact is, he was an iconoclast in all areas, so his critics had no shortage of material to work with.

There were, for example, his innovations in costume which recalled what Nijinsky had done. Up to that point, each role in a Kirov production had its own costume. Whoever danced Albrecht in *Giselle*, for example, or Solor in *Bayadère*, wore the same outfit – whether it was Sergeyev, Soloviev or Nureyev. Only minimal variations were customary, usually in colour. Sergeyev wore red, Nureyev wore orange, but otherwise the costumes were identical. Rudolf changed that. Most controversially, he shortened men's tunics. Previous designs had been longer, covering both the dancer's groin and his bottom. They were also symmetrical. Rudolf may have been copying western costumes, which he had seen on his trip to Vienna, but he now shortened his own clothes, so that his tunic stopped at the waist, allowing greater freedom of movement. He also drew the hem to one side, so that instead of being parallel with the stage, it fell from one hip to the other. This had the effect of both revealing, and drawing attention to, the groin and it provoked great controversy at the time. Others in the company said the Rudolf was combining boastfulness (regarding the size of his equipment) and salaciousness. Leningrad, which thought of itself as so sophisticated in many ways, was still prim in matters of sex.

On another occasion he tightened the costume for Solor and introduced a turban with a feather in the top. The effect was striking and, in time, other dancers would copy it. But not just then. In fact, after he wore this costume for the première, an anonymous note was pinned to the company noticeboard which read: 'Rudolf Nureyev, this is the last time. Do that again and you will be dismissed.' The note-writer felt that, in making these changes, Nureyev was not so much making male dancing more sexy as breaking a near-holy tradition.

In retrospect, many of the controversial incidents Rudolf was involved in at the Kirov may now be seen to show him in a good light. For instance, there was a teacher at the Kirov called Boris Chavrov, who was generally respected. It came as a shock when, one day, Rudolf referred to all the others dancers as *Chavrovchivka* – little Chavrovs. He was simply mocking their lack of individuality. But not all of the incidents can be seen in a good light. On one of the mornings in the week, for example, he would attend a special class for soloists and principals, where the older dancers, like Sergeyev, Chatilov and Boris Bregvadze worked with the younger generation, Soloviev, Vikulov and Rudolf. On occasion, Nureyev would simply stand in that part of the room where, Bregvadze say, had always stood. When they objected, he would simply shout 'Shit!' and leave the room. This incensed everyone without, it has to be said, achieving very much.

Despite being steeped in controversy, both on and off the stage, Rudolf continued to progress at the Kirov. His talent was not just self-evident: it forced itself on everyone. Throughout 1959 and 1960 he was gradually given more taxing roles – the Nutcracker Prince, Armen in *Gayane* (a ballet about love on a collective farm, in which he starred with Kurgapkina),

Solor in *Bayadère*, Blue Bird in *Sleeping Beauty*. He was sent on a short tour to Cairo. More unusual, however, were his appearances with Alla Sizova in a series of evening entertainments, called *Choreographical Miniatures* (which they had danced in Vienna). The casts in these evenings were often very good – Shelest, Soloviev, Sokolov, Chernishev – but it became the practice for Sizova and Nureyev to dance last. This was partly because the Kirov was still intent on promoting the young couple as *the* partnership of the future, and partly because Nureyev by now had an enthusiastic group of fans, who attended every performance, deluged the stage with flowers afterwards, and would throng the stage door in the late evening, no matter how cold or wet it was. His looks were now beginning to mature and his stage presence, aided by Pushkin's expert tuition, stood out from everyone else's. He looked upon his fame almost scientifically, as part of the business of being in the theatre. Very early on he noticed that, when Dudinskaya was scheduled to dance, the theatre sold out on the first day the tickets went on sale, whereas when he danced it took three days. Because of her flight into Leningrad during the siege, she had become more than a dancer – she meant something even to people who were not balletomanes. He realised he must try to achieve a similar sort of fame.

People forget now that the late 1950s were the first time in history, on both sides of the iron curtain, when 'youth' had its own identity, based chiefly on the fact that teenagers had money for the first time, and were free to exercise choice in the way they spent that money. Nureyev (and Sizova too), though they might not be 'stars' as Dudinskaya, Sergeyev and Shelest were stars – revered by all ballet lovers, irrespective of age – nonetheless had their own following. The enthusiasm of these followers, not to mention their economic power in being able to buy seats, was not overlooked by the Kirov management, which always needed to have an eye on the future.

They were not wrong, for right at the end of 1959 Rudolf achieved his first notice in the western press. The *Atlantic Monthly* ran a special issue on the arts in the Soviet Union. This included a very moving account of the siege of Leningrad by the poet Olga Bergolts and an article entitled 'Talent and the Ballet', by Yuri Slonimsky, probably the best of the Russian ballet writers. Ostensibly this was about the Soviets' search for young ballerinas, and it explained how all sixteen Soviet Socialist Republics were being combed equally thoroughly. There was a measure of propaganda in the article, which compared Tsarist Russia unfavourably with the Soviet regime: 'Today our ballet organisation comprises thirty theatres and sixteen state schools . . . more than five thousand ballet artists are on the staffs of state theatres.' But only one young ballerina was mentioned by name: Kathy (Ekaterina) Maximova, a rising star of the Bolshoi, who had been on the Vienna trip with Nureyev. Far more space was devoted to a male dancer and in much more dramatic terms. 'On December 14, 1959,' wrote Slonimsky, 'the inhabitants of Leningrad literally besieged the Kirov Theatre trying to attend the performance of the well-known ballet, *Giselle*, though the performers were only beginners. The part of Albert was danced by the Bashkir, Rudolf Nureyev . . . Nureyev has an extraordinary natural talent. The height, the length, and the timing of his jumps are phenomenal. The vigorous whirling movements are thrilling. Nureyev's nervous, somewhat exalted artistic constitution lends to everything he does an unprecedented, original character. His Albert is unlike anyone's we have ever seen. Having made Giselle fall in love with him as a whim, he then loses control over himself. The second act, in his version, unfolds like the effects of the torments of love, and we witness the gradual purification of the hero's feeling and the elevation of his soul. The main theme of the ballet comes clear to us in Nureyev's meaningful dancing. In a word, new people are interpreting even the deepest past in a new way. They are viewing this past in the light of modern techniques.'

The article showed a picture of Rudolf at the Vaganova and recorded that Natasha Makarova and Nikita Dolgushin danced the same role two weeks later. But the theatre was besieged only when Rudolf danced. There could be no question of the Kirov firing its young star, who was already such a crowd-puller.

That summer another honour was bestowed upon him when he was one of the dancers chosen to perform in front of the Soviet Premier, Nikita Khrushchev. The occasion was a reunion of Soviet intellectuals and took place in June at N.A. Bulganin's villa some sixty miles outside Moscow. It had a large, attractive garden, where the performances were to take place and, besides Rudolf, the glittering company included Kurgapkina (with whom he would dance a variation from *Don Quixote*), Marshal Voroshilov, commander of the Tenth Army and one of Stalin's few friends to have survived the purges, Khachaturian, Shostakovich, and Richter, the pianist, who was also performing.

Rudolf was not at his best that day. The stage that Kurgapkina and he were provided with was too small for anything but the *adagio* from *Don Quixote*. But the high point, unexpectedly, turned out to be Voroshilov, who gave a rendering of some Ukrainian folk songs. The marshal had an excellent voice and soon even Khruschev joined in. As Rudolf later wrote, 'They both knew every word of every folk song and thoroughly enjoyed singing them.' It was a beautiful day and the singing lasted until dusk. It was a privilege for someone as young as Rudolf to be present on such an occasion.

Wherever Nureyev went, however, and however well he was received, however interesting a time he had, when he returned to Leningrad it was to yet more sniping. It was not that the Kirov was especially bad in this regard, for we should never forget that the political system encouraged people to keep watch on each other. Every mishap, every transgression, by anyone, not just Nureyev, was reported to the Kirov director. It just happened that Nureyev was more of an individualist than most.

Two types of transgression were regarded as especially important by the authorities. The most serious form of misdemeanour, in those cold war days, was the allegation that one had met foreigners. This carried overtones of spying and was not allowed, at least in an unsupervised capacity. There was even a special department of the KGB to prevent this happening. It was known as the 'First Directorate' and to fall foul of the 'First' was something everyone tried to avoid.[1] Even if you bumped into a foreigner accidentally this had to be reported. Too many 'accidental' meetings would look suspicious. The 'First' had its own suite of offices on the second floor of a building in Nevsky Prospekt.

Anything to do with the conformist communist state went against the grain with Rudolf by now. It didn't suit his nature and it reminded him all too forcefully of his father, and Hamet's former role in Soviet, indeed Stalinist, affairs. Nureyev would not allow himself to be dictated to in this manner. He was avid for new experiences, new theatrical experiences especially, and he rarely missed a chance to visit any touring company: ballet, opera, straight theatre or even musical comedy. He was forever catching a plane or overnight train to Moscow and in this way even managed to see a touring production of *My Fair Lady*.

When he could, he got to know the artists. He wasn't trying to make a political point, but he must have known the risks he was running. He always said that he simply wanted to immerse himself in theatrical life. The Soviet press was heavily censored, and what newspapers were published were very slim. News about the outside world, including the outside theatrical world, was very thin on the ground. Personal contact could, to an extent, rectify that.

Everyone concurs in a saying that Nureyev was a highly intelligent man. It will not do, therefore, to accept his version of his behaviour at face value. In going out of his way to approach foreigners, Rudolf may well have been hungry for information about the theatre world outside Russia but he was also sending signals, signals to anyone watching, that he was willing to take risks, to push his situation to the limit.

This is underlined by his behaviour regarding the touring show of *My Fair Lady*. After it had played Moscow, the cast travelled to Leningrad where, on 27 May 1960, the entire troupe attended the Kirov to watch Nureyev dance Basil in his very first *Don Quixote*. The evening was another triumph for him and, at the end, his circle of young fans covered the stage in red roses. Nureyev, with his inborn sense of theatre, asked that the roses be given to the cast of *My Fair Lady*. It was a gesture of thanks (accompanied by a note in English, a language he was now brushing up) for the enjoyment their show had given him. This was a touching move on his part and, in reply, as he may well have anticipated, the cast invited him to have supper with them. He had the sense, on that occasion at least, to forgo their hospitality. There was a line and he knew he mustn't overstep it, but that only shows he was aware of the game he was playing. Signals were being exchanged.

The other line which people had to beware of transgressing in the 1950s in Leningrad related to homosexuality. It may be difficult for us to understand in the west, in the 1990s, but in Soviet Russia in the late 1950s there was in many people's minds a conceptual link between homosexuality, mixing with foreigners, and the KGB.

Unsupervised meetings with foreigners were not allowed for the simple reason that foreigners were likely to harbour anti-communist views, and too much exposure to such influence might rub off on native Russians. The link to homosexuality was twofold. Since homosexuality was so frowned upon in Soviet Russia, foreigners – with their more liberal attitudes – might provide partners for Russian gays. Second, the KGB profited from this state of affairs, both in the west and inside Russia itself. In the west, as is now well known, the Russian security services' favourite method of recruiting agents was to suborn someone into a sexual, usually a homosexual, act, which was photographed, and then blackmail that person into co-operating. The same method was used inside the country.

The ubiquitous communal flats played an important part in all this. Groups of homosexuals living together were known as *soseds* or *sosedkas* and if the KGB got to hear of them they would immediately question their members. If a man confessed, then his fate largely depended on what use he was to the KGB. If they could use him, they would. Otherwise, he would stand trial. The penalty was imprisonment for five to eight years and some 1,000 people were sent to prison every year in the 1950s. In prison they were the lowest of the low and known as *Opushgonny* – the downcast. As in other cities and countries, there was an underworld of gay life in Leningrad. One meeting place, as we have seen, was Catherine's Square, near the Pushkin Theatre. Other meeting places were at the *banias*, notably those at Baltiskaya station and Moskovsky Perenlok.

It was a twilight world, and gays lived an uncertain life, risking denunciation at any moment. One bad report was not enough. Two would be noted and sometimes reported to the man's employer. If the man was particularly effeminate or camp, he could lose his job. If, however, someone was reported for homosexual behaviour by three separate sources, he would be prosecuted.

Gays, and lesbians for that matter, were well aware of the dangers, and many would get married and even have children to disguise their sexual orientation. But there were still risks. If a gay made an approach to someone who turned out not to be homosexual, then almost certainly he would be beaten up and reported to the police. The police would never prosecute the person making the assault; it was always the gay who was punished.

There was some relaxation after 1959 but it was very slight; homosexuality remained a criminal offence in Russia until 1993.

In the ballet, a privileged world, the situation was a little easier but still risky. Very few people will talk about the matter, even today, but one person who did so was Arkharova, the KGB functionary in the Kirov. She remembered one episode inside the company:

'We employed a man as part of the lighting team. He came to us straight from technical college, he looked a very earnest man and worked well. Then it was said that he was having relations with foreigners. He was a bad man. He used to buy things from them and re-sell them. Once Yura Morozov came up to me and said he had seen two men having sex in the cloakroom – and one of them was the lighting man. [This is how the denunciations worked.] We of course sacked him – not for having sex in the cloakroom but for selling goods that had belonged to foreigners [though he wasn't dismissed until he was discovered having sex]. Later, I found out that he was working at the choreographical school and I made sure he was dismissed from there too. He then went on to work in a shop [she was determined to track his career!]. You could say that he was a criminal I caught in the act. There were undoubtedly similar acts of homosexuality between the dancers but we didn't investigate such things.'

From Arkharova's account, it becomes clear that, for many Russians, 'relations with foreigners' was a kind of code, for nonconformism in general and homosexuality in particular.

So far as Rudolf's sexual orientation was concerned, it should first be noted that he was a dancer, a rising star, and that to an extent his position was privileged. However, three episodes are known which confirm that it was apparent to many people that Rudolf was, as he put it to Gyckova, 'not a man in the sense that [she] meant it'.

The first was an observation of Arkharova's.

'I was standing at the bus stop in front of the theatre, waiting for a bus. I noticed that two young girls were laughing and pointing at somebody. I looked and I saw Nureyev waiting in a queue. The girls were giggling and then suddenly one jumped into the queue, kissed Rudolf, and then went back to her friend. They had obviously had some sort of bet and dared each other. He smiled but that was all. He never responded to women, not like that. He was a figure apart, never making friends with anyone. There *are* homosexuals in the ballet world, and not only in the ballet world.'

The second incident was related by someone Rudolf did form a friendship with, one Sergei Sorokin, a balletomane. Sorokin says that, as early as 1959, Rudolf was convinced that the composer, Tchaikovsky, was not killed by the father of a woman he had 'dishonoured', as was always believed, but was in fact homosexual and had committed suicide rather than have his family suffer ignominy once this became known. This theory has gained much credence in the 1990s, but in 1959 it was new, certainly in Russia and really only accepted within the gay community in Leningrad. Rudolf's enthusiastic espousal of this theory marks him out as sympathetic to, and familiar with, that community, even if he was not, at that time, a practising homosexual.

Where Arkharova's account is incomplete and partial (and shows the reticence that marks this area even today) is in her failure to mention that the *very top man* at the Kirov, on the creative side, was gay.

Konstantin Sergeyev was the archetypal Soviet homosexual in that he had married Dudinskaya, thus fulfilling the general public's romantic dreams about their on-stage partnership. In fact, this was done as a disguise (so it would not have been unthinkable for Nureyev to have slept with Dudinskaya when he spent the night at her flat). Sergeyev's homosexuality was well known to all the more worldly dancers at the Kirov who, in the 1950s and 1960s, would watch his official limousine bring him to the theatre in the morning, then go off in a different direction to pick up Dudinskaya, who would arrive at the Maryinsky twenty minutes later. The nature of their relationship was an open secret inside the theatre.

Sergeyev was an attractive man, pale with beautiful deep-set eyes. His big successes had come in *Raymonda* and *Giselle*. By the time Nureyev joined the Kirov, Sergeyev was already dyeing his hair, an action which, in so far as it betrayed his homosexuality, was a risk – it was the sort of sign the anti-homosexuals of Leningrad were on the lookout for. He also had an affected, rather 'actorly' manner. But he was protected to some degree by being a strong party man, so was able to promote his protégés inside the company. He was different from Rudolf in all respects save one: he always wore a wrap or shawl thrown over his shoulders and neck. It made him appear very dashing and, later on, Nureyev copied it.

Sergeyev didn't like Nureyev and it is possible that the misunderstanding that had arisen over whether the young man was to join the Kirov was, at base, Sergeyev's doing. And Rudolf, of course, detested Sergeyev. This came out clearly one day when Irina Kolpakova invited him to go and see Sergeyev and Dudinskaya dancing *Giselle*. 'What's to look at?' replied Rudolf. 'You can go to any restaurant and see a waiter with the same mannerisms.'

Two theories were put forward in Leningrad as to why Nureyev continued to make progress at the Maryinsky, despite the controversy he aroused and despite the fact that the top man didn't like him. One was that Sergeyev eventually hoped to seduce Nureyev and therefore blew hot and cold in his attitude, giving him plum roles one minute and sending him away from Leningrad the next, in an effort to 'soften him up'. The other theory is that Nureyev's homosexuality was known to the KGB, that he had been caught, and then suborned to work for the security services. According to this theory, it was Nureyev's task to infiltrate 'the nest of homosexuals' inside the theatre, allow himself to be seduced by Sergeyev and then blackmail the artistic director into promoting him. This, according to the Leningrad rumour factory (which has never accepted that Nureyev was a better dancer than, for example, Soloviev or Dolgushin), accounted for Nureyev's rapid rise within the company. On this scenario, Nureyev was allowed to remain a member of the Kirov, and a practising homosexual, so long as he provided reports on the others within the company. And this was a psychological burden that, gradually, became too much for him . . .

No details to support this latter theory are contained in the KGB files which the author obtained in the course of his researches for this book. Nor does it square with what we know about Nureyev's love of freedom and his hatred of his father's role in the Stalinist system; nor with Sergeyev being a party man. The KGB already had all the control they needed inside the Maryinsky.

That there was a love–hate relationship between Nureyev and Sergeyev appears far more likely. Rudolf's 'difficult' personality is much better understood as a product of his genetic make-up, and his upbringing in Ufa, than as any complicated pact with the security services. That is certainly how the Kirov management, including Sergeyev, appear to have viewed it. For example, Rudolf's gesture towards the cast of *My Fair Lady* did not go unnoticed. On the next occasion a western company was in town, this time the American Ballet Theatre (ABT) in September 1960, the Kirov were ready. They arranged for Nureyev to dance in Berlin.

This was a blow for Rudolf in more ways than one. A short time before, hearing that ABT were coming, and that the Danish star Erik Bruhn would be part of the company, Pushkin had told Nureyev that he thought Bruhn one of the greatest classical dancers of the day, if not *the* greatest. Knowing that he wouldn't be able to see Bruhn in Leningrad, Nureyev flew to Moscow, where the entire ABT Company had been invited to a performance of *Sleeping Beauty* at the Bolshoi. If he couldn't see Bruhn dance, then at least he would try to meet him and talk to him.

Nureyev, who had a ticket for the Bolshoi show, turned up at the theatre clutching a photograph of Bruhn from a dance magazine, so that he would know who to introduce himself to. Unfortunately, on this occasion, the ABT were closely guarded. On the sixth of that month, at the Moscow House of Journalists, William Martin and Bernon Mitchell had given 'perhaps the most embarrassing press conference in the history of the American intelligence community', when their defection from the USA was formally acknowledged and they made a number of damaging allegations about the American National Security Agency, the outfit for which they had hitherto worked. Nureyev's 800-mile round trip had been wasted – except that it had taken him to a city writhing in torment over the defection. Individual Russians were defecting to the west every few months but those going from west to east, in groups, such as Burgess and MacLean, and Martin and Mitchell, attracted far more headlines.

Before he left Moscow, Nureyev obtained an 8mm camera and some film, and asked a friend to film Bruhn while he was in Russia, so that Nureyev could study his performance when he returned from Berlin.

Who knows how things might have turned out if Bruhn and Nureyev had met in Moscow or Leningrad? Certainly, so far as Nureyev was concerned, the tour he was required to make while Bruhn was in Russia turned out to be a fiasco. The fact that the Berlin engagement was a festival allowed the management (that is, Sergeyev) to present the visit as an honour for Nureyev, but that is not the way he saw it. For one thing the festival was usually reserved for dancers from the satellite countries – Poland, Hungary, Romania, Czechoslovakia – and not Russia proper. And Berlin was only part of the assignment. For a month after the festival, Rudolf was forced to tour throughout East Germany – with a circus! They covered 3,000 miles in a bus, thirty small towns, dancing in run-down or bomb-damaged theatres and even, on occasion, in cafés. Conditions were cramped and cold and the low point was reached when the entire company was forced to sit in the broken-down bus without heating throughout the night, awaiting repairs. Routinely they would arrive in towns barely half an hour before the performance was due to start.

Nureyev found it a 'hateful' month and later on, told his assistant Joan Thring that he first considered defecting on that tour. He was glad to return to Leningrad. Here, however, more bad news awaited him: he was not scheduled to dance again for three months. He was in despair. The powers-that-be in the Kirov (Sergeyev again) were making fun of him. The one bright spot was the film he had had made of Bruhn. This, he was truly impressed by. He later told John Percival, ballet critic of *The Times*: 'It was a sensation for me. He is the only dancer who could impress me out of my wits. When I got back . . . he had been dancing there and one of the young dancers said he was too cool. Cool, yes – so cool that it burns.'

He took the opportunity to go home. In Ufa he bumped into Pamira Sulemanovna.

'They were showing a ballet film at the cinema at the time. It was

Song of the Cranes. We lived in the country then, a steamboat ride away but that was so boring we used to walk all the way into town instead of taking the boat. We were just walking past the Bashkiri Hotel, opposite the opera theatre, when I heard someone call out "Pamira!" I looked across the road and saw Rudik. He was wearing dark-tinted glasses, which had only just come on to the market. That's how much he wanted to look good – and indeed he did look good. I ran up to him and talked a bit with him. Then I explained that I had tickets for the cinema and that I was late, and then I left. He just stayed where he was, standing and watching. It was obvious that he hadn't expected that I would talk to him for such a short time.'

Pamira manages to inject a lot of emotion into this one short episode, making Rudolf appear both presumptuous *and* solitary. But perhaps she was right.

He saw his mother, of course, in Ufa. By now she was showing signs of the illness that would dominate her later years – mysterious pains in the joints of her legs. But, to an extent, she seemed to have come round to accepting her son as a dancer. All the people in Ufa who remember her from those days say she was proud of Rudolf. But his relations with Hamet never improved.

On Rudolf's return to Leningrad he found to his dismay that, before he was scheduled to dance again at the Kirov, he must go off on yet another provincial tour. This time it was to Ioshkar-Ola, in the north of Russia. Such a tour was not welcome. Every dancer's main worry is cold – not simply the brute fact of coldness itself but the stiffness that goes with it, and therefore the threat of injury. Rudolf told Sergeyev that he preferred to travel to Ioshkar-Ola by plane rather than train. He would even pay his own way. But the plane didn't materialise (Sergeyev's doing all over again). So it was yet another damned train.

On the train he discovered something else which upset him further. His companions on this latest tour were the selfsame circus he had toured East Germany with. The Kirov had gone too far. They could make fun of him once, but this was too much. He was being kept away from Leningrad for months on end, away from the knowledgeable balletomanes who can make or break a career.

So when he arrived at Ioshkar-Ola he was already fuming. Then, on his arrival, he found that he was expected to dance on his very first night in the frozen north. This was hardly the most considerate requirement, and a decision quickly formed in his head. Coolly, he did as he was asked, but that was it. After the performance, he handed in his notice – and clambered on to an all-night train to Moscow, since there wasn't one to Leningrad. He had had enough of being made a fool of.

Naturally, word of Rudolf's latest infraction had reached the Maryinsky before he did, and he expected fireworks. What he didn't expect was that the explosion would come, not from the theatre management itself, or from Sergeyev, but from the Ministry of Culture. He was summoned to report to the Ministry, in Moscow, where he was kept waiting for nearly an hour. That in itself told him the news would be bad. Were they now determined to send him back to Ufa, as had been threatened before? Eventually he was called into an office where sat a dour bureaucrat with a moustache. That was bad news, too. Good news would have been relayed by the minister herself, Ekaterina Furtseva. The man did not rise as Nureyev entered. Instead, he read from a piece of paper in front of him. It was a verdict. As a result of his insubordination, the man said, Nureyev was to be doubly punished. In the first place, he would never again be permitted to cross a foreign frontier – this included the eastern bloc as well as the west. And he would never again share in the honour of performing before the high-ranking big-wigs of the Soviet government.

Nureyev could scarcely believe what he was hearing. As it happened, he had thoroughly enjoyed his afternoon dancing before Khrushchev and listening to Voroshilov's singsong. But he thought he could live well enough without a repeat of that honour. The other punishment was a different matter. The other punishment hit home. He, above all others, enjoyed the company of foreign artists. He, above all others, loved the style of the west, from Erik Bruhn to sunglasses, from Van Gogh to *My Fair Lady*. And he alone knew that, deep inside, he was considering defecting. This punishment was all the more terrible because it was right on the button.

In fact, it was sharper even than that. For it had just been announced that in the following year, 1961, the Kirov would be making its first tour to the west since the end of the Second World War. The climax of the tour would be Covent Garden, in London, where the Royal Ballet was, at that time, perhaps the greatest rival to the Kirov. Before that there would be another stop, in a western city that was yet more beautiful than London, and was the very home of ballet: Paris.

And now, this bureaucrat had told Rudolf that he wouldn't be going.

Note

1 There were four chief directorates in the KGB. The first looked after foreign intelligence, the second was responsible for internal security and counterintelligence, the third comprised the border troops, and the fourth looked after communications and cryptography. A fifth directorate investigated dissidents.

CHAPTER SIX

. . . the Muse Came Too

When I defected from their union
and ran far off . . . the Muse came too.

Nineteen sixty-one was a good year for the Kirov. There were no fewer than twelve new productions, by Leonid Jakobson, Rostislav Zakharov, and Sergeyev himself. The roster of ballerinas alone shows the depth of talent – Ninel Kurgapkina, Irina Kolpakova, Natalia Makarova (who graduated that year), Nona Yastrebova, Lyuba Voishnis, and last but not least, Alla Shelest. Conditions within the company had improved throughout the 1950s. In 1951 the Soviet government had doubled artists' rates of pay. In 1954 and again in 1958 a group from the theatre had gone abroad to socialist countries. But 1961 was the most exciting time for the dancers, giving them their first chance to see the west. In the world of classical ballet, Paris and London were the most important cities in the world outside Leningrad.

Russians in those days were not completely cut off from the west. Certain foreign films were allowed, French ones especially since there was a thriving Communist Party in France. The French actor Gérard Philippe, for example, was even better known in Russia than in the west. And of course there were many smuggled books and magazines available for those who wanted them. Marina Ilicheva remembers Nureyev reading Hemingway and Remarque in 1960–61, when those authors were banned, along with books by Bulgakov, a Soviet writer whose works were very difficult to get hold of.

At the same time, politics entered everything in Soviet Russia and the Kirov Ballet was no exception. At the Maryinsky the Communist Party was strongly represented, the chairman of the 'cell' during Nureyev's time being Nikolay Yatskovsky, a member of the orchestra. He was later replaced by Nikolayevna Rizhovaya though Sergeyev himself, as we have seen, retained strong party links. The Komsomol was especially strong in the ballet, where the secretary was Misha Domarov, himself a dancer. Arkharova was in charge of political education, taking seminars in the theatre itself on the history of the party and politics generally. Attendance at these seminars was compulsory for party members and voluntary (that is, encouraged) for others. People from every part of the theatre, including cleaners, usherettes, dancers, singers and musicians, all attended. All except Nureyev. According to Arkharova, he never came once.

With a foreign tour in the offing, attendance at political meetings became even more important. It wasn't the job of the political commissars to select people for tours; that was Sergeyev's responsibility. But the commissars could – and did – stop people going who had already been selected. Everyone had heard stories about dancers, musicians – even opera stars – failing mysteriously to get their exit visas in time, or even being pulled off planes at the last minute. The Soviet authorities were torn between the prestige that such tours garnered, showing what artistic heights the Soviet system had achieved, and running the risk of defections.

The year 1961 was a climactic time for defections. Throughout the 1950s, a year rarely went by without some movement in either direction: Petrov in 1950, Burgess and MacLean in 1951, Reino Hayhanen in 1957, Pavel Monat in 1958; 1954 and 1959 had been busier than most – three in each case. But in 1961 there were six defections, and much related activity, such as the arrest of George Blake, and of Heinz Felfe, the trial of Peter and Helen Kroger, and of Konan Molody (Gordon Lonsdale), and the building of the Berlin wall. The security services were particularly nervous about the Kirov's tour. Burgess, MacLean, William Martin and Bernon Mitchell had gone *from* the west but at that stage the overall tally stood at these four versus fourteen who had defected in the opposite direction (Kim Philby did not disappear until January 1963). When Pyotr Derybin defected in 1954 he confirmed that the Russian security services had a special unit, OS2, whose business was the assassination of defectors. It was known in the trade as the 'Department of Blood-wet Affairs'.

Paradoxically, after all that had gone before, in the early months of 1961 Nureyev danced more for the Kirov than he ever had before. He danced Bluebird in *Sleeping Beauty* at the end of January (Makarova also danced in that performance), he appeared as the Nutcracker Prince twice in February, and once opposite Shelest in *Laurencia*. In April he twice danced Prince Siegfried in *Swan Lake*. For the *Sleeping Beauty* performance, his parents at last came from Ufa to see him dance. He got them front-row seats and, as they arrived, their presence was announced over the loudspeaker system an accolade that was not conferred on every ballet star. Afterwards, the senior members of the Kirov administration entertained them and, on this one evening, Hamet was finally proud of his son. It was one of many ironies in Rudolf's life that Hamet's change of heart was to be so short-lived. But Rudolf was irritable. Around him the company was preparing its foreign tour and he was not included. The tour was part of a cultural exchange so far as the British were concerned: the Royal Ballet was to visit Russia at the same time. The arbitrary and capricious nature of the authorities was under-lined when, not long before the tour was scheduled to start, Alla Shelest, at the time the biggest female star the Kirov had, apart from Dudinskaya, was told she would not be going to the west. It began to look as if she and Rudolf were being kept back to hold the fort in Leningrad while the others enjoyed the pleasures and applause of Paris and London.

But about a month before the company's scheduled departure, there was a crucial change in the Kirov. Strictly speaking, the company's leading dancers at that time were Konstantin Sergeyev and Natalia Dudinskaya and, not having performed in the west before, they were as anxious as anyone to dance in Paris and London. But by now they were both middle aged. Towards the end of April, there came word from Georges Soria, the Kirov's Paris impresario, that Sergeyev and Dudinskaya were too old to star on such a tour. Soria's telex reminded the Kirov management that Paris audiences were notoriously demanding, and would not turn out in sufficient numbers to see a male star who was over forty and a female who was ten years older. In the early 1960s, in film, music and fashion, there was a cult of youth throughout the west. Soria was adamant. The cast list *had* to be changed.

This news threw the Kirov into turmoil. The programme couldn't be changed to suit younger dancers whose repertoire was more limited than Sergeyev's and Dudinskaya's, since tickets had already gone on sale in France. The only alternative was for the company to select a young soloist to take over Sergeyev's repertoire. Nureyev had no real hopes of being selected: Sergeyev hated him as much as he hated Sergeyev. And Nureyev needed no reminding of what he had been told at the Ministry of Culture – that he would never travel abroad again. On the other hand, the programme for Paris included *Swan Lake, The Sleeping Beauty, Giselle, Don Quixote, La Bayadère* and *Taras Bulba*, all roles that Rudolf knew and some of which he had been dancing that year or the year before, to great success. Added to that, he was known for his ability to learn roles quickly, and there was barely a month to go before the first night. It was like a re-run of the time when the Ufa soloist for the *Dekada* had injured himself and been unable to perform; when Nureyev had saved the day at the last moment. But this time events were on a much grander scale.

The Kirov management had to swallow its pride, as did the Ministry of Culture. At the end of April, Nureyev was told he had been chosen for Paris.

He was thrilled. His international travels so far had taken him to

Vienna, Cairo and East Berlin, nowhere to compete with the great cities of the world. He spent the next weeks locked in rehearsals, with both Sergeyev and Pushkin helping him improve his technique. During this month, Zoya Arkharova noticed a change come over Nureyev. 'Normally, he was dishevelled and slovenly. However, before the tour the theatre photographer took some pictures of him for documentary purposes, and he looked a completely different person. Suddenly, he appeared a very handsome lad, wearing a white striped shirt that was clean and decent. He asked for some copies to give to his mother. I said I couldn't spare any just then but that I would have some ready for him when he got back from the tour so he could send them home.' Arkharova mentions this incident as evidence that Nureyev was intending at that stage to return to Leningrad. She took the official KGB line that he was 'trapped' in Paris by the west, though her evidence could also be used to show that Rudolf wanted to send his mother some good photographs of him so that she could remember her son in a particularly handsome guise.

Paradoxical as it may seem, even in these critical circumstances it was still by no means certain that, when it came to the crunch, Nureyev would be allowed to leave. The decision was not the Kirov's but the government's, with input from the local Communist Party.

In communist cold war Russia the bureaucracy surrounding a foreign tour by such a company as the Kirov was extraordinary. Up to 400 people might travel – dancers, orchestra, stage hands, administration, costume and make-up people, security – although for the Kirov's 1961 tour 'only' 140 actually travelled. Incredibly, for each of these individuals, a *karaxteristic*, or 'character description', had to be compiled, and in the Kirov that was Arkharova's job. These character descriptions were exactly that: assessments of the personality of each individual going on the tour. Anyone who got a dubious *karaxteristic* was refused permission to leave. Initially, they were written by the managers of each group – ballet, choir, orchestra, and so on – and then submitted to Arkharova. She kept an exercise book on each member of the Kirov, in which she would write her impressions and observations, based on her own encounters with individuals, notes on their performance in party meetings or in her seminars, and any newspaper clippings if they were performers. Arkharova added her own gloss to what the managers said to produce the final assessment from within the theatre.

Theoretically, these character descriptions then had to be checked by Rachinsky, the administrative director of the company, but in practice he left everything to Arkharova. She forwarded them to the local PartBureau (party office), who checked them again and passed them next to the president of the NestCom (the party committee for all Leningrad). Both the PartBureau and NestCom had the right to add comments if they wished, and to recommend, or withhold, the right to travel abroad. Next the *karaxteristics* were sent to the committee of the District Communist Party (for all Leningrad and its surrounding administrative region). This sat every Thursday, when it would add its opinion to everyone else's. The District Committee also had the authority to issue exit visas. These had everything on them. One one side were basic details – name, date of birth, photograph – and on the reverse details of the person's place of work, where he or she had studied, and a list of relatives (to remind the bearer of the travel document of who would suffer, should he or she not return). Meanwhile, the theatre secretary of the PartBureau would visit the Maryinsky and interview anyone he wanted, who was scheduled to be going abroad. He would ask specifically political questions. Arkharova, having been on the District CP Committee for Foreign Travel for more than ten years, knew what sorts of question were asked and would help her favourite dancers by coaching them in the right answers. For example too much interest in a foreign language was frowned upon; why was it necessary?

When the *karaxteristics* had cleared the District Committee, Arkharova would take one set to Communist Party headquarters in the Smolny area of the city (where Lenin had his HQ during the revolution) and a second set was sent to the Ministry of Culture in Moscow. The Ministry authorised foreign (as opposed to internal) passports, and the tickets. These would be collected from Moscow and taken to the Border Department in Leningrad. A separate authorisation from the Border Department was needed for each traveller, for each country being visited. All these documents were then taken, together with the tickets, to Intourist, for yet further authorisation. In other words, the traveller needed an exit visa from the Party, a passport from the government, and written permission to leave the country from the Border Department *and* from Intourist. As a measure of the red tape involved, no fewer than sixteen photographs were needed for each person for each country to be visited. For the Paris–London trip, Arkharova needed to collate 32 photographs for each of the 140 people – a total of 4,480 photographs.

The company was scheduled to fly to Paris on 11 May. Rudolf rehearsed right up to the morning of the last day. That afternoon he took a *bania* near the Baltiskaya station. In the evening, he had dinner with the Miasnikovas in Tchaikovsky Street. The *Bely Noche*, or White Nights were not far away and in Leningrad it remained light until quite late. After dinner, they all strolled along the Moika canal, one of the most beautiful in the city, and ended up at St Isaac's Cathedral. The conversation was of Pushkin, the greatest of the Russian poets, whose works Rudolf loved and with whom he felt a certain kinship, in that the great man's relations with his parents were explosive, and he had a volatile temper. (There were also some marked differences between Rudolf and Pushkin but, on that evening at least, he overlooked them.) On the eve of his visit to the cradle of ballet, Rudolf was in danger of succumbing to the nostalgia for Leningrad that he had vowed he would avoid.

*   *   *

Next day he was accompanied to the airport by his sister, Rosa.[1]

Arkharova was there too and handed out the travel documents at the last moment. This was always a nervous time: the moment when people found out they had been refused permission to travel. Two KGB men, known locally as '*v shtatskomm*', 'the men in civvies', were travelling with the company. They could be seen in conversation with the local Leningrad party officials on duty in the terminal building.

But the departure was uneventful. Rudolf was given his documents like everyone else. He kissed Rosa and boarded the plane. The Tupolev taxied to the runway. Nureyev was terrified of flying and hunched forward in the 'brace' position even before the aircraft left the ground. But the plane took off without incident and, four hours later, arrived in Paris.

The novelty of the Kirov's arrival in the French capital had an edge to it. In 1954, when the Bolshoi had arrived, the political situation in Indochina had deteriorated rapidly, to the point where the visit was summarily cancelled and the company left without performing. This time, the balletomanes had been prepared. In June 1961 an article in *Dancing Times*, by Natalia Rosslavleva, had introduced the best of the dancers. She singled out Irina Kolpakova ('the last ballerina to be graduated by Vaganova herself'), Vladilen Semenov ('the "danseur noble" of the company') and Nureyev ('fiery, temperamental, with an excellent schooling'). The latter phrase wasn't really true, and little did anyone know that Nureyev had nearly been left out of the tour.

A blue coach met the dancers at Le Bourget airport and took them and their luggage to the Hôtel Moderne on the Place de la République in the third *arrondissement*, north of the Hôtel de Ville and Le Marais. Nureyev was given a room to share with Yuri Soloviev, 'cosmic-Yuri' as he was called in view of his jump and in the wake of Yuri Gagarin's successful first manned space flight in April 1961.

There were three days available for rehearsal, before the first night of the Kirov 'season', which would last for two weeks at the Palais Garnier, home of the Paris Opéra Ballet in central Paris, and two weeks in the Palais des Sports, in the south of the city, near the Porte de Sèvres. For most of the company, the three rehearsal days were spent at the opera house, on the main stage, to give everyone the feel of the place. The Paris Opéra building is an elaborately carved stone jewel in the heart of Paris, where the Boulevard des Capucines crosses the Avenue de l'Opéra, just north of the Place Vendôme. It has perhaps the most magnificent foyer of any theatre in the world, with elaborate stone staircases and balustrades, fabulous lanterns, carved ceilings and huge mirrors. There is an enormous raked stage and a four-tiered auditorium dominated by a huge chandelier surrounded by two concentric circles of smaller chandeliers. On these grounds alone it deserves to be called the home of ballet.

Nureyev was surprised that, although the French dancers were rehearsing nearby, only three of them ever came to watch the Kirov. These were Claire Motte, Pierre Lacotte and Jean-Pierre Bonnefous. Their presence, however, was all-important. Among the Russian dancers, hardly any spoke French (beyond *pirouette* and *plié*) and Nureyev was no exception. But he did speak English, very passable English at that stage, and was virtually alone in the company in being able to communicate with the French dancers, who also spoke some English.

They all fell to talking and, on the Kirov's second evening in Paris, the French dancers invited Nureyev out. According to the Kirov/KGB rules, Nureyev should have refused. The dancers, musicians and others had been divided into groups of ten, each with a leader who was supposed to keep an eye on everybody's whereabouts at all times. People were instructed not to go anywhere alone: they must always be in groups of two at least, and preferably four. Even if Nureyev thought this rule arbitrary and silly, he knew what he was doing in breaking it. To flout the 'security' regulations was bad enough but to do it on the opening night was a very provocative move. But, since he wasn't dancing, and had seen *Sleeping Beauty* many times, Rudolf took himself off to a rival entertainment. Yehudi Menuhin was giving a Bach recital at the Salle Pleyel. Bach was emerging as Rudolf's favourite composer, as his own skill at the piano improved, so for him it was an obvious way to spend the evening. To the authorities, it might look as though Rudolf was not conforming but to him he was merely satisfying his curiosity, exploring the opportunities Paris had to give. Why else visit a city?

In fact he didn't go off with the French dancers at the first opportunity, as was said later. On the night of the dress rehearsal there was a reception at the Russian embassy, which Nureyev attended. He was gratified to meet Ekaterina Furtseva, the Russian Minister of Culture, at the party. She was making waves herself at the time, having just come from the Cannes Film Festival where she had appeared as by far the most 'chic' Russian official ever seen in the west. *Time* magazine had devoted a whole article to her – her recent weight loss, her dress sense and her excellent relations with Khrushchev, and who had taken a personal interest in Rudolf's inclusion on the tour. At the reception she singled out Nureyev and told him that she hoped she would see him dancing much more in the future. This was a most interesting comment in the circumstances, and one to which we shall return.

Nureyev was not appearing until the third night of the season and before he even appeared on stage his circle of French friends was extended. Through Claire Motte, he met her husband, Mario Bois, a publisher who was friendly with Shostakovich and unusually well informed about the Soviet Union. He met Pierre Bergé, Yves Saint Laurent's right-hand man, a balletomane and opera-goer. Bois, Bergé and the others took Rudolf to Montmartre, Montparnasse and the Louvre, and introduced him to the sophisticated milieu that surrounded couturiers, *parfumiers*, the whole milieu of *haute couture*, which overlapped both the ballet world and the homosexual nexus. Nureyev was both drawn to this world and repelled by it. 'The streets had the atmosphere of a perpetual party. I felt a physical attraction for the city – and yet a kind of nostalgia. For while Paris looked gay and the people on the streets looked interesting and so different from our drab Russian crowds, they also had a hint of decadence, a lack of solid purpose.'

His own very solid purpose in Paris, of course, was to dance. On that tour the Kirov danced three programmes at the Opéra. The first was *Sleeping Beauty*. This was well, but not rapturously, received. The discipline of the company was singled out in reviews, as was the great musicality and youthful energy of the dancers and a 'sweetness' of style. But if anything the performances were regarded as *too* sweet. Audiences in the west were by now used to a bit more bite in the choreography, more modern references. And the scenery was damned as embarrassingly over-elaborate and old-fashioned.

The second programme, the one in which Rudolf danced, consisted of eight pieces from three ballets – *La Bayadère*, *The Nutcracker* and *Taras Bulba*. The audience for that second first night was no less distinguished than for *Sleeping Beauty*. Both André Malraux, France's first Minister of Culture, and the Russian ambassador, were there. But on this night the critics went overboard. Olivier Merlin in *Le Monde* even went so far as to wonder whether the Kirov had deliberately made their first night sugary in order to thrill all the more with the second programme. He was, in truth, not a little sugary himself, writing that, when the curtain went up, all was dark save for a thin sliver of moon. As the eyes adjusted to the gloom, a dim silhouette in white could be seen moving slowly in time to the music, down an incline. That figure was followed by another one, also in white, then another, then another. This is now a famous opening to the Kingdom of the Shades scene from *La Bayadère*, when as many as thirty-six ballerinas appear in this way. But that was the first night anyone in the west had seen it, and Merlin for one was bowled over.

He was even more impressed when first Olga Moiseeva and then Nureyev, as Solor, appeared. 'I will never forget his arrival,' Merlin wrote, 'running across the back of the stage, and his catlike way of holding himself opposite the ramp. He wore a white sash over an ultramarine costume, had large wild eyes and hollow cheeks under a turban topped with a spray of feathers, bulging thighs, immaculate tights. This was already Nijinski in *Firebird*.'

It may have been a bit soon to make such a comparison but Nureyev's dancing that night certainly matched his appearance. Merlin was especially taken with his *tours en l'air*, not just because they were so high but also because he managed a *saut de chat* (a rapid crossing of the legs) at the summit. Rudolf covered the stage, commanding it, Merlin wrote, continuing with his double *tours en l'air*, pirouetting as he landed, or doing the splits in mid-air at other times, never forcing anything, remaining supple and natural all through. It was, Merlin concluded, 'a moment of pure emotion'.

Solor is a little like Albrecht in *Giselle*, or Orpheus. He is an Indian warrior who loves the *bayadère* – a temple dancer – but treats her badly. In the last act he dreams that he seeks his beloved (now dead) in the Kingdom of the Shades, and they dance together linked by a long scarf. In Paris, Nureyev's strong masculinity and magnificent stage presence was mixed with a tenderness for Moiseeva that was palpable, the very embodiment of grief and sadness.

Merlin was almost as enthusiastic about Sizova, Irina Zubkovskaya, Soloviev and the choreography of Jacobson, Vainonen, Sergeyev and Chaboukiani, and, from that night on, the Kirov's tour was marked as a great success.

But it was Nureyev who was noticed before the others, and not only by Merlin. Claude Bagnières, in *Le Figaro*, wrote 'Au premier chef il faut citer l'aérien Rudolf Noureev', remarking on his brilliant virtuosity and supreme elegance. *Ballet Today* said the company made an 'excellent impression', but, paraphrasing Merlin, the magazine added:

'What stood out was the musicality which inspires the dancers. With them, nothing is hurried. There is no faking, and what is remarkable is that both with the *corps de ballet* and with each individual dancer slow movements are very beautiful, and movements are no less impressive when they are speeded up – for they never become forced.'

Again Moiseeva was singled out, and Sizova among the ballerinas. From the men only Soloviev ('a fine dancer') and Nureyev ('a male star of high quality') were mentioned by name. Yet another paper described Nureyev as a 'phenomenal aerian'. Elsewhere, under a picture of him jumping, the caption read: 'The ballet of Leningrad have their man in space.' One periodical even commented on 'the slim beauty of his fingers'. No detail was overlooked.

What Merlin and the others didn't know, since they were unfamiliar with the choreography, was that Nureyev that night had introduced some steps of his own into the ballet. Marina Ilicheva was in the wings and she noticed that, once again as she put it, Nureyev simply *had* to introduce something that was all his own.

'In that part of *Bayadère*, the ballerina dances the steps first, and then the man is supposed to follow her, with exactly the same steps. But Rudik performed a new trick; he danced the steps *twice*, but twice as fast. It looked more difficult and of course it was, and drew attention to him. To an extent the gimmick came off and he always did it after

that. In the precise terms of the choreography it was incorrect
– but it was very effective. Everybody backstage grumbled, and
complained that it shouldn't be done that way, but we resigned
ourselves to it. The audience appreciated it very much.'

There might be grumbles backstage but the reaction of the audience,
and of the critics, did not go unnoticed by the Kirov management, or
by Georges Soria. After that first night, and however 'difficult' Nureyev
might be, and however much the fact annoyed them, Sergeyev and the
rest of the hierarchy realised that they had a major star on their hands.
This is doubly clear from the subsequent press coverage in Paris of
the Kirov dancers off-stage. When a contingent visited the offices of
L'Humanité, the Communist Party newspaper, the group included Niazi
(the conductor), Sergeyev, as artistic director, Moiseeva, Osipenko,
and Kolpakova. The only male dancer present was Rudolf. On other
formal occasions, the same group was wheeled out with little variation
– Moiseeva, Kolpakova, Sergeyev and Nureyev.

Nureyev's willingness to take part in these formal events belies the
allegations that he was unhelpful or completely egotistical (and the
photographic evidence is there, in the French newspapers, to prove
that it took place). He was not a nonconformist for the sake of it and
he always made himself available to help the company's public image.

But he was determined to get the most out of Paris. On the very night
that he so enraptured Olivier Merlin and Claude Bagnières, Claire Motte
brought a girlfriend of hers backstage. This was Clara Saint, a young
redhead who had been born in Chile but had lived in Paris since she was
five. The daughter of a painter, she was very beautiful and a passionate
balletomane. These two immediately hit it off and Nureyev announced
that he was free that night after the show; did they all want dinner? They
left together straight after the performance, ducking into the back seat
of a car provided by his new-found French friends, who were waiting for
him. From there they watched the rest of the Kirov climb back into the
blue bus. That night they went to Les Deux Magots in St-Germain. The
food was good and there was a fine mix of intellectuals, artists, actors, and
the usual rich hangers-on. It was the kind of café society that Udeltsova
had told him had once existed in St Petersburg, and he loved it.

Les Deux Magots was so crowded that Nureyev and Clara did not have
the chance to say much, though he did find out that she had been engaged
to Vincent Malraux, son of the French culture minister who had been
killed the year before in a car crash. However, Nureyev liked her so
much that, two nights later, he invited her to the Kirov's performance
of *The Stone Flower*. He was not performing himself but it was one of
his favourite ballets; he persuaded Clara to accept. This was no problem
on her part because she had the use of a box almost at will and the couple
sat in that, accompanied by some of her Parisian friends.

For any non-Russian this would be unremarkable. In the climate of the times, however, this simple act of friendship was seen as massively provocative by the Kirov authorities, many of whom, that evening, sat in another box only a few feet away. The sight of Nureyev shunning his Russian colleagues and very obviously enjoying the company of stylish – even flashy – Parisians was especially galling. During the intermission two of the Kirov officials visited Clara's box and asked Nureyev to step outside. There they started to criticise him for mixing with 'undesirable' people. Not surprisingly, this had the opposite effect to that intended and later in the evening Nureyev and Clara had supper entirely alone at a small students' restaurant just off the Boulevard Saint-Michel.

Nureyev saw as much of Clara as he could after that. But their liaison only enraged the Kirov authorities all the more. In the first instance he was sent for by Sergei Korkin, the director, who told him, 'If you see any more of that Chilean deserter, I shall have to punish you severely.' This was typical authoritarianism, always trying to make out that inconvenient people were worse than they really were. How could Clara have been a deserter? Deserter from what?

Naturally, this cut no ice with Nureyev. He went on meeting Clara as he pleased. There was so much in Paris to explore. He and Clara spent hours in Au Nain Bleu, a toyshop in the rue St Honoré, looking for the best electric train set he could find. They spent three hours in a wig shop, buying a blonde wig, a brown wig, and a black wig. Rudolf was dumbfounded by his first visit to Gallignani, the famous bookshop in the rue de Rivoli. He had never seen so many art books, and was even more astonished to find that it was a shop, and not a library, that he could actually *buy* the books on show. He immediately bought a large book on impressionism. Clara had noticed how knowledgeable he was on painting but that afternoon he told her the story of how he and Arslanov used to swap the books they borrowed from Ufa library.

Clara did not feel they were being followed in Paris, but she did sense that they were breaking the rules in their jaunts. 'I asked all the time why he was not going with the others. He always replied, "No, no. It's all right."' (See below, p. 157 and 173, for a quite different version.)

As the dancer all Paris was talking about, Nureyev's self-confidence told him that he was untouchable, at least while the Kirov was in France. With each performance, his stature grew. Indeed, his fame had even crossed the English channel. *Dance Magazine* relayed the rumours about him to its readers and a few British critics, like Nigel Gosling of the *Observer*, travelled to Paris and returned with rave reports.

In a cunning piece of theatrical management, the Kirov authorities put Nureyev on stage on nights when he was not scheduled to dance, and when his name was not in the programme. This was clever because word of what was happening soon went round Paris, and those who had been disappointed at not having tickets to see the new sensation could now hope that they would see him. The ploy ensured that all evenings seemed as thrilling, or at least began with an air of expectancy. The entire season was a complete sell-out.

In effect, a sort of gavotte was being danced between Nureyev and the Kirov managers: the more they used him to promote the company, the freer he felt to follow his own inclinations in Paris. And much as he loved Paris, he was not blind to its shortcomings. On 9 June he called Tamara Myasciorva in Leningrad. He had been buying costumes, he said, and he was particularly fond of a light blue one he had acquired to dance the lead role in *The Legend of Love*, a favourite of his, but a ballet that was danced only in the Soviet Union. He told Tamara then that he was looking forward to London. He had had enough of Paris, he said. The French audiences were 'all fools', whereas the English 'really understood ballet'.

But there was still a week to go before the company moved on. By now they had vacated the Opera building and moved into their second home, the Palais des Sports. This was bigger but not as fashionable. The audiences were younger, less knowledgeable, but also more appreciative.

The Kirov was not the only ballet company in Paris that summer. In fact, there was a veritable festival of dance. To begin with, there was the Marquis de Cuevas Ballet, which specialised in classical works. There was also the Berlin Opera Ballet, the Cuban People's Ballet, the National Folk Ballet of Mexico, the Ballet Peruano de Lima, the Ballet National du Katanga, and folk dance groups from the Lebanon, Madagascar and the Niger. Enough to make any dance fan happy, and Nureyev was hardly ever in his room.

One of his more interesting encounters took place during that last week, when the company was in the Palais des Sports. Nureyev eagerly accepted an invitation to meet Raymondo de Larrain, a close friend of Clara's and head of the Marquis de Cuevas Ballet, a private ballet company headquartered in Paris, owned by the marquis until his death earlier that year. The avowed purpose of the meeting was for de Larrain to show Nureyev some costumes. Clara knew that Nureyev was unhappy with his Kirov costumes and wanted to buy yet more western ones to take back to Leningrad. However, during the meeting an argument broke out between the two men.

De Larrain, a small man with sharp features and a large pointed nose and who looked not unlike Jean Cocteau, started off aggressively by criticising the Kirov's production of *The Sleeping Beauty*, arguing mainly that the costumes and scenery were drab and old-fashioned. This was hardly new. The newspapers had pointed out exactly these shortcomings on the morning after the first night. But de Larrain went further, saying that even the choreography of the ballet was poor. Finally, he launched into a similar tirade against Prokofiev's *The Stone Flower*. It was, he said, cold.

Nureyev took this in good part for a while. After all, he liked the freedom in the west, especially the freedom to express oneself, which appealed to his own iconoclasm. In any case, it was difficult to stop de Larrain once he got started. But Nureyev liked *The Stone Flower* and he knew from the reception the Kirov had received in Paris that the choreography was *not* poor – on the contrary it was exciting and fresh to western eyes. And so, once the other man had finished, Nureyev gave as good as he got. He told de Larrain that the de Cuevas costumes were in some respects superb – very elaborate – but that their very quality often got in the way and distracted the audience's attention from the dancing. He could see that the de Cuevas dancers were suffocating physically beneath their fancy costumes, and suffering psychologically with the 'overdone scenery'. This was a nice allusion to the fact that in the Kirov's best-received programme, the eight pieces taken from three ballets, the company used *no* scenery whatsoever. *Touché*.

The best ballets, Nureyev said, talking in English as quickly as he could, in the way that de Larrain did, were those that conveyed a single mood, and a simple message. But that message needed to be conveyed subtly, not by 'lavish paraphernalia' encasing the straightforward attributes of the human body. Then Nureyev struck home. He said he had left the de Cuevas performances 'feeling uneasy and distressed at the general lack of emotional depth'.

Coming so soon after his bout with Korkin, it may have seemed as though Nureyev were fighting with everybody. In fact, de Larrain, a bit of a bully himself, recognised that there was force in what the Russian said, the two parted as friends and Rudolf was later invited to a party at de Larrain's flat. It was to prove an important exchange.

However, in that last week of the Paris tour, the atmosphere at the Hôtel Moderne was very tense. Everyone could feel it but Nureyev was the sole object of attention. Marina Ilicheva was only one of many who noticed it. 'He appeared less and less frequently at the hotel. Conversations were taking place and they talked of Rudolf being up to something. Unpleasant things were said although he never missed class and danced superbly.' Two members of the KGB, the 'men in civvies', kept watch outside the hotel, day and night, ready to follow Nureyev wherever he went. Clara Saint may not have felt that they were followed, but they were. Since he had now been expressly forbidden to associate with foreigners, any fresh infringement could result in Nureyev being sent home.

The company's last performance in Paris, a *soirée de ballets*, was given on Thursday, 15 June. That morning, in *Le Monde*, Olivier Merlin bade a fond farewell to the company. Under a headline which read, 'THE LESSON OF THE KIROV,' he wrote that his own 'horrid bourgeois liberalism' was troubled by the hermetic nature of the Kirov's off-stage life. He was vexed, he said, that the Slav sensibility of the Russians had been subsumed by socialism, and that the Kirov had, off-stage, kept itself to itself, as if walled up. He felt that an opportunity had been missed, for the French to get to know the Russians better, and that for their part the Russians had deliberately declined to enjoy the 'troublants trottoirs' of Paris. At the same time, he paid tribute to the 'all-powerful dream' of the Kirov management, people who were, he said, of Tolstoyan dimensions, and he thanked them for bringing their 'inestimable fortune' to Paris.

He ended as he had begun, more than three weeks before. The previous night there had been a performance of *Swan Lake* (this had been introduced as an extra attraction when the company moved from the Opéra to the Palais des Sports). 'Yesterday evening,' he wrote, 'they [the Kirov] gave perhaps the most marvellous interpretation of *Swan Lake* that I have ever seen', and he particularly praised 'Alla Osipenko and Rudolf Nureyev, whose names are already joined with those of Karsavina and Nijinsky in the firmament of the sylphs.'

Whether he knew it or not, Merlin could hardly have written a piece more calculated to irritate the Kirov management. The one man who had broken out of the 'walls' which surrounded the company, the one man who found Paris's 'troublant trottoirs' the most fascinating places he had ever been, the one man who was giving his 'Tolstoyan' superiors Dostoyevskian problems because of all this, was the man who, time and again, Merlin praised above all others. It was as if Merlin knew what was going on backstage at the Hôtel Moderne, and was taking Nureyev's side. The *Le Monde* reviewer may well have been unconscious of the battles raging inside the Kirov, but his article only made those battles worse.

That Thursday, Nureyev again danced Solor in *La Bayadère*. His performance had lost none of its edge and the audience, like all the other audiences before it, was thrilled. And because this was the last night, the applause went on even longer than usual. True to form, however, Nureyev did not stay for the party afterwards. It was his last chance to escape with his French friends and enjoy the nightlife of Paris. They went back to Les Deux Magots, in St-Germain, scene of his first dinner in the city. But afterwards, he and Clara detached themselves from the others and walked by the Seine. Nureyev was not unaware of the effect his actions were having inside the company and he told Clara that he might never see Paris again. So he wanted to make the most of his last night. Sleep was out of the question.

They walked down rue Bonaparte, along the quai des Grands Augustins, across the Pont de l'Archevêché and back along the quai des Orfèvres. By now, it was nearly three o'clock in the morning. But it was a warm night and they found a bench near the Pont Neuf, and continued talking. Even now, Nureyev did not show a nostalgic side. Clara remembers that he didn't talk about Russia, about the past, Leningrad or his family. He was sad to be leaving Paris, he said. But mainly, he looked forward. He looked forward to England, the English style of ballet, to the English audiences and how they might differ from the French ones. He was anxious to see the English school of ballet, Margot Fonteyn and all the other dancers for he had heard, he said, that the ballet was better in England than in France. He never once asked Clara about herself. He was, she says, a complete narcissist.

As they sat on their bench, facing the quai Voltaire, the sun rose to their left. The sky was clear – it was going to be a glorious day. They continued talking. They talked until 6 a.m. When the smell of roasting coffee began to waft across the Seine, they stood up and said their *au revoirs*; not adieu because Clara had already told Nureyev she would follow him to London, to see him and to watch him dance there, at Covent Garden. She would arrive in a few days' time.

They parted on the Pont Neuf. Clara lived with her mother on the quai d'Orsay, on the left bank, and she returned home and went to bed. Nureyev walked north, along the Boulevard de Sebastopol towards the Place de la République. It was about seven when he arrived. The pavement in front of the Café République was wet, having just been doused by a green truck splashing the gutters, and the sun glistened from the stones. A waiter was wiping the marble-topped tables, while another lowered the green and white striped awning. The smell of warm bread filled the air.

Part of Nureyev hated to leave Paris but, as he had told Tamara, and Clara, he was looking forward to London. Given his personal success in Paris and what he had been told about London audiences being more knowledgeable, he dared to hope for an even better reception at Covent Garden.

His heart sank somewhat when, outside the hotel, he saw the blue bus that had met the Kirov dancers at the airport, and which had ferried most of them on their communal sightseeing trips. Suitcases were already laid out in rows alongside the bus. The BEA flight didn't leave Le Bourget until 10.15 a.m. but he would have to pack before he could grab breakfast.

Soloviev was in the room when Nureyev got there. He looked sheepish and whispered that, while Rudik had been out, the KGB men had asked Yuri to go through Nureyev's belongings to see if there was anything compromising, anything they could use against him. Nureyev was shocked by this, but decided to make light of it. 'That's funny,' he told Yuri, 'they asked *me* to do the same with *you*!' They both laughed.

The bus left shortly after eight for the half-hour ride to the airport. On the bus, the tickets for the flight to London were handed out. This was unusual, for normally one official handled all the tickets (like Arkharova, in Leningrad). Nureyev was travelling in black trousers, a blue jacket, with a beret. He put his ticket in his inside pocket.

Le Bourget was Paris's main international airport at the time but, in

1961, in an age before jet travel, it was fairly small, a collection of square concrete and glass structures, described by one local journalist as *le plus paisible*, the most uneventful of places. There were no separate arrival and departure levels, just one biggish hall.

Inside the terminal building, the company was met by a number of French balletomanes, carrying flowers. The Kirov season had not only been a success, but was sufficiently unusual, and welcome, to merit a real send-off. Suddenly, amid this unofficial ceremony, there appeared Bogdanov, one of the administrative staff, who began collecting all the tickets again. This seemed to be a return to normal practice, but it was curious. Why? Nureyev fished in his inside pocket and handed back his ticket.

He was standing near the bar, from where passport control and the entrance to the departure lounge could be seen. At the bar, the Soucoups, were Georges Soria, the Kirov's Paris impresario, who had come to bid the company farewell, and Pierre Lacotte, who had arrived specifically to say goodbye to Nureyev. Olivier Merlin was also there, dressed in motorcycle leathers (his Harley Davidson was parked outside). Merlin had been especially complimentary to Nureyev in his articles but Nureyev wondered why the journalist was at the airport. A departure was dull copy, surely. Was there some other reason? Did he know something Rudolf didn't?

In this frame of mind, Nureyev suddenly thought back to the curious business with the tickets. Why had they been given out and then taken back? He had held his ticket for London in his hand, but no longer had it. Then there had been that business with Yuri in the hotel bedroom, the unwelcome attentions of the KGB. What was going on?

Before he could sort all this out in his mind, or order a coffee at the bar, or speak to Merlin for that matter, to ask why he had come, Nureyev was approached by Sergeyev. The older man was smiling. 'Rudi,' Sergeyev said softly, 'you won't be coming with us now. You'll join us in London in a couple of days. We've just received a wire from Moscow saying that you are to dance in the Kremlin tomorrow. So we'll be leaving you now and you'll take the [Aeroflot] Tupolev which leaves at 12.30.'

Marguerite Alfimova was standing nearby with Ksenya Ter-Stepanova, and after Sergeyev had approached Nureyev, she says she saw him turn 'an earthy-grey colour'. Whatever had been said, 'You could see that it had turned his world upside down.' At first she thought he was just tired, since he had been up all night, but then she heard him cry out, 'Khvatit mne vrat!' This is a slang phrase and means 'Stop telling me lies!'

Nureyev had a point. The above version is what he wrote in his auto-biography. However, according to Rezida, who discussed the episode with him on his return to Ufa in 1987, what Sergeyev actually said was, 'Rudolf, your mother is ill. You've got to go to Ufa and on the way stop in Moscow to do a concert for Khrushchev's government, and spend the night there.' Rudolf did not mention this in his autobiography, perhaps because he didn't want to involve his mother in the events of Le Bourget. But if these words were said, they were a give-away. Not only had the Ministry of Culture told him, not long before, that he would never again perform in front of high government officials but if his mother was so ill that he had to hurry back from Paris, how could there also be time for him to waste a night in Moscow? It didn't add up.

That this was a critical moment in his career Nureyev had no doubt. Quite apart from the suspicious circumstances of Sergeyev's little speech, and its dubious and inconsistent contents, Nureyev was familiar with the case of Valery Panov. Panov had been on a tour abroad for the Bolshoi in 1955, had been enjoying the west much as Nureyev had been, and was asked – instructed – to return to Moscow. After he went back he had been 'grounded' and never allowed out again. The Russians have a special phrase for it which, literally translated, means 'in constant residence in one place'.

Nureyev realised that the same thing was about to happen to him. Only worse. Panov did not have Nureyev's temperament. There had been a campaign inside the Kirov against Nureyev and his lifestyle for three years now, and this was the moment of climax, carefully orchestrated to wrongfoot him. His rivals and enemies had finally got their way. He was being humiliated, and in the most public fashion.

Sergeyev was to blame, of course. The artistic director had never liked him and could scarcely have been pleased when he had been forced to replace himself with none other than the man he most loathed. How much it must have crucified Sergeyev to see the success – the triumph – Nureyev had enjoyed in Paris, a success which should have been his. For Nureyev, it all came together. Sending him home now, now that he had tasted the sweetness of the west, the sweetness of success, was the cruellest blow imaginable. Locked away in Russia, in all likelihood in some remote, drab spot, Nureyev would wither. It was a form of death.

Nureyev had half expected *something* to happen but, now that it had, he felt winded and so played for time. He looked about him. Soria and Merlin were still at the bar, apparently unaware that anything was going on. Could that be true? He looked back at Sergeyev and smiled. If he wasn't coming to London just yet, he said, playing along with the story, he wanted to say goodbye to the other dancers. As it happened, the Moscow-bound Tupolev, which was scheduled to leave at 12.25 p.m., was delayed for forty-five minutes due to mechanical trouble, so Sergeyev could hardly object.

Nureyev walked away from the bar area to where the main soloists were standing in a group. Quietly, he repeated to them what Sergeyev had told him. They were surprised but most of them immediately grasped what he himself had understood only moments before – that this was a ploy. There was no Kremlin appointment, and even if there were, it was a decoy. Once back in Russia, Nureyev would never be allowed out again. Irina Kolpakova didn't believe the Sergeyev story for a minute. 'They took the best for London and Paris. The tour was far more important than dancing in the Kremlin.' The more he thought about it, the more Nureyev realised how serious his situation now was. The embargo would not only apply to his travel; it would apply to his dancing as well – for a great star who cannot travel would provoke too many awkward questions about the wonderful Soviet system. He would be sent into internal exile.

Several of the ballerinas had started to cry by now, as they realised the full implications of the dilemma that Nureyev faced. Others told him they would go to the Soviet embassy in London and complain *en masse* about his treatment. They would argue, they said, that his lifestyle, though individualistic, was not politically motivated, was not a criticism of the regime. They would say that Nureyev's talent simply needed to follow its own course.

Nureyev turned to Pierre Lacotte, who was also nearby. 'Terrible news,' he whispered. 'It's all over. They're sending me back to Russia. I will never dance again! For pity's sake, save me! I'm going to end up in Siberia.' He took from his pocket a dagger which Lacotte had given him the day before as a gift. 'See this,' he said, still whispering. 'If you don't help me, I'm going to kill myself. Look at this ticket. It's for Moscow, not for London . . . Save me!'

Lacotte went to tackle Sergeyev, but Sergeyev turned on him. 'Rudolf isn't being punished. His mother is gravely ill. He must see her as quickly as possible.'

Lacotte didn't know who to believe. But he did notice that all the dancers were coming up to Rudolf, and saying goodbye. Some were crying. As he said later, 'All seemed certain of never seeing [Nureyev] again.'

All Lacotte could think of now was to prevent Nureyev being taken through to the departure lounge, where he would be beyond the reach of any help. So he kept talking to him. Olivier Merlin was brought in on what was happening, and proposed making a 'getaway' on his Harley Davidson, but the presence of the 'guardian angels', as Lacotte called the men in civvies, prevented that. Next he thought of calling André Malraux, in the government, but it would take ages to get through. Malraux made him think of Clara Saint, who had been the fiancée of Malraux's late son. Discreetly, he wrote her number on a piece of paper and, under the guise of tying his shoelace, he passed it to Jean-Pierre Bonnefous, the other French dancer in the terminal. Bonnefous went off to make the call.

But what could Clara do, and what should Nureyev himself do in the interim? The two KGB agents, whose hats and faces he knew so well, were talking to Sergeyev. As Nureyev looked across to them, one of the agents moved over to stand by the main door of the terminal building, blocking any exit.

But now Nureyev saw his chance. As the KGB man moved across to the main doorway, he turned his body away from Nureyev. The second man was still talking with Sergeyev and drinking coffee at the bar. He too had taken his eyes off his quarry. The other dancers were just beginning to move through to the customs area and passport control to board the BEA Viscount for London.

In that moment, Nureyev moved. Quietly, rapidly, he stepped behind a pillar. It was square, with a white marble veneer and was just thick enough to conceal his figure. It wasn't a real hiding place but it bought a little time. On top of that, everyone in the company had suddenly moved forward towards passport control and the KGB people were temporarily disoriented. They ran to where the last remaining dancers were going through into the departure lounge in a bunch, thinking perhaps that Nureyev was concealed in the middle of them. But, without a boarding pass, there was little chance that Nureyev could have got away with such a ruse and the KGB agents soon realised that. They knew he must be somewhere in the terminal building, and it didn't take them long to find him. They closed in and, with Nureyev between them, shifted back to the bar.

Then Clara ran into the terminal building. She had been asleep when Bonnefous had called. 'Rudolf gave Pierre and me your number,' he said. 'I'm at Le Bourget. Please come right away. There's trouble. Rudolf asks that you come. *Le plus vite que possible.*' It had taken her barely twenty-five minutes to get dressed and drive from her apartment on the quai d'Orsay to the airport. There had been no time to put on any make-up.

When she arrived, Bonnefous was the first to see her, and he led her to Nureyev. She remembers that there was a tall man either side of him, men she recognised from outside the Hôtel Moderne. Nureyev looked tiny in comparison. He was wearing his beret, with a white shirt which made him look very pale, black trousers and a navy blue jacket.

But he was also surrounded by a lot of other people, too: journalists, balletomanes, officials from Georges Soria's organisation, Aeroflot personnel. Bonnefous had quickly told Clara what was happening – that the rest of the company had already gone through passport control, to catch the London flight, which left at 10.15, and that Nureyev was being sent back to Moscow on the 12.25. Everyone milling around seemed to know that they were in the middle of a crisis but no one, so far as she could see, was actually *doing* anything.

She approached Nureyev. 'I've come to say goodbye,' she said loudly, in English. They embraced, watched closely by the KGB men and everyone else. Nureyev whispered back, in English, 'I want to stay. I want to stay.'

'Are you sure?'

'Yes. *Yes!*'

Clara broke off the embrace. 'Goodbye, Rudolf,' she said, speaking loudly again.

Her first thought was: how much time do we have? From the others milling around, she found that the Moscow Tupolev had mechanical problems and wasn't scheduled to leave before 1 p.m. It was now just after 10.00. That gave her a good hour, at least, before Nureyev would have to go through passport control.

She still wasn't sure what to do next when she saw a blue sign which read POLICE DE L'AÉROPORT.' An arrow pointed up some stairs to the first-floor gallery. She followed the sign and found the office. Inside, were two men. Like the KGB agents, they were in civilian clothes. Quickly, she explained her mission.

'There's someone downstairs, a Russian dancer who wants to stay in France.'

'Are you sure he's a dancer?' said one of the men.

'Oh yes. I've seen him dance. He's a star. All Paris is talking about him.'

'You're sure he's a dancer? And he wants to stay in France?'

'Yes, I'm sure. Please help him.'

A pause. Then, 'We can't go looking for him. He must come to us.'

'But he's guarded! There are two men from the Soviet embassy.'

'That's your problem.'

These men were impossible, but Clara wouldn't give up. 'He can't come up the stairs, don't you see? But he does want to stay in France.'

Another pause, as the two policemen looked at each other. Then the same man spoke again. 'Go back downstairs. Have a coffee at the bar. We'll follow you in five minutes. Tell your dancer friend who we are and that *he* must come to *us*. We can't go to him.'

Clara didn't know whether to believe them, but she had no choice other than to do as they said. She left the office, went back down the stairs and returned to the bar.

Nureyev never took his eyes off her, trying not to let his anxiety show.

Clara ordered a coffee. She was on edge, too. Would the men do as they had promised?

Her coffee arrived.

Yes! The two police were descending the stairs now, smoking and chatting like two ordinary members of the public. They ambled towards the bar and ordered coffee.

She waited until they were in position, and then approached Nureyev again. She wanted to say goodbye a second time, she told the KGB men. The guards looked on as the couple embraced once more.

'Two men at the bar,' she whispered. 'Smoking and drinking coffee. Police. They can't come to you. You must go to them.'

She stood back. 'Au revoir, Rudi. Bon chance.'

She returned to the bar, to talk to the journalists who were still there. She could see – or imagined she could see – Nureyev trying to inch away from his guards. They were having none of it. She could see the airport police looking in his direction, then across at her. Why didn't Nureyev act? There were only about five or six yards between him and the police. How long would the police wait at the bar? Did they still believe her story? Had Nureyev changed his mind? Was he going to make a fool of her?

Then Nureyev jumped. Or rather he ran. Quickly, very quickly, he covered the five yards in no time. He stood in front of the policemen and gasped, in English, 'I want to stay! I want to stay!'

One of the guards followed him and lunged forward.

But the French police were a match for him, stepping between the guard and Nureyev. 'On est en France, ici,' said one.

That rough gesture by the guard provoked the French police into action and they now, none too gently, escorted Nureyev upstairs, followed by the straggling journalists and hangers-on. Seeing what was happening, the other Soviet agent ran to a telephone, to call the embassy.

Upstairs, outside their office, the police were attentive and polite – this sort of thing didn't happen every day. But they were forced to explain that defection wasn't quite as simple as it sounded. They said that, eventually, Rudolf would have to put his request in writing, by filling out an official 'sanctuary permit', but before that could be done, according to the French rules, he would have to spend forty-five minutes alone, in a special room, to reflect on the decision he was about to take away from all the pressure.

Nureyev agreed and was led to the room, which was next to the security police's own bureau. It was explained to him that the room had two doors. If he decided to return to Russia after all, one door led back to the departures area and the waiting Tupolev. If he decided to stay in France, the other door led directly into the headquarters of the Sûreté's airport office.

All of this unusual activity had attracted a lot of attention, from other passengers, bar staff, airline personnel, and Olivier Merlin, who was still in the airport building. But the police now sent them away. To Clara they explained about the forty-five minutes' wait. 'Go back to the bar,' they said. 'Have a sandwich, a cognac.' She decided she would use the time to put on some make-up.

Nureyev said later that the room where he had to wait was white, completely plain. There was no decoration – just the two doors he had been led to expect.

Then Mikhail Klemenov, one of the secretaries from the Soviet embassy, arrived. He climbed to the second floor and screamed at the police, 'Nureyev is a Soviet citizen! You must hand him over to me.'

It was hardly the best tactic.

'This is France, *monsieur*,' said one. 'And *Monsieur Noureev* has placed himself under our protection.'

Klemenov wouldn't give in. 'You've arrested him!' he shouted. 'This is illegal!' Eventually the police relented and Klemenov was allowed into the room, alone with Nureyev. Seeing him arrive, Clara had followed the Russian official up the stairs. She stood outside the room where she heard raised voices but could only distinguish one word. This was Nureyev saying over and over, *'Niet! Niet! Niet!'*

After a while, Klemenov left the room, pulled the door shut behind him and, looking grim, left the airport.

In the room, Nureyev now had forty-five minutes to make up his mind about his future. It was an extraordinary moment. Few people can have been in quite that position, with two such stark choices in their life, symbolised by identical doors.

Naturally, he thought of his family. His mother most of all. If he stayed in the west, would she be persecuted by the KGB? He had little doubt that she would. Would he be able to get money to her? He doubted that, at least for the moment. And she would miss what he had been sending from Leningrad. He thought of Rosa, Rezida and Lilia. He pitied Lilia, his deaf and dumb sister, but he would miss Rosa most. He thought of his father. Hamet was now the head of security at a large factory and a leader in his local Communist Party cell. He would be the most embarrassed, and the most angry, if Rudolf opted for the west. Hamet would never get over it. He was a strong man – but this could kill him.

Nureyev thought of Pushkin and Tseniia, of Tamara, Liuba, and her brother. What would happen to them, if he defected? He thought of the *banias* of Leningrad, of Noti and Elizaveta, Saint Isaac's, the Hermitage, the Neva itself. He had never wanted to feel nostalgia for Leningrad and he knew that if he was to survive in the west he must put Russia behind him. As usual, some lines of Pushkin came to mind:

> From all sweet things that gave me pleasure,
> since then my heart was wrenched aside;
> freedom and peace, in substitution
> for happiness, I sought

That would be the way to look at it, if he defected.

He thought of the Kirov. It had given him something to aim for, and a superb training. But life there had become a hollow sequence, too.

On the other hand, what awaited him in the west? He would be alone. He had always been alone but this would be different. He would not be a member of any company. He would have no family, no roots, and in all likelihood would be shunned by many of those he was fondest of. As a dancer he might just fade away. Either way, there were risks, terrible risks.

He stared at the doors, the plain, indistinguishable doors which symbolised his future. The situation was both absurd and wonderful. The sort of thing that can only happen in a fairy tale, the opera – or the ballet. Something like this could never happen in Russia. He heard voices outside, French voices, and thought back to his three weeks in Paris. In that time he had done little more than glimpse the possibilities of the west. It was still largely unknown. But, as he listened to those French voices, he also realised that his fear of the unknown west was less than his fear of the familiar Russia. The familiar was drab, conformist, collectivist. The west might be unknown but it was already clear to him that, for an individualist, life was easier. Indeed, individualism was encouraged.

There were still a few minutes to run, but his mind was made up. He rose from his seat and approached the door. He turned the handle and pulled it towards him. On the other side, the two policemen looked up and, for the first time, smiled.

At 1.10 p.m. the Tupolev left Le Bourget for Moscow. It was forty-five minutes late. Nureyev was not on board.

Note

[1] Later reports said that his mother was there too. If true, this would be very revealing (see below, p. 172). Nureyev himself never mentioned it, though he may have kept silent to protect her.

CHAPTER SEVEN

The KGB File: 1 – The Defection

That is the 'official version' of Nureyev's defection, the sanitised version; the partial version, according to some of the participants. As with the account of Nureyev's birth, it is more or less the story he stuck with for the rest of his life. The KGB file, however, gives a somewhat different account of events. Before we come to that, we need to consider two things. We need first to ask ourselves why, if the events described in the last chapter are not accurate, Nureyev should have lied about them all his life. And we need to re-examine the chain of events which led up to his defection with a more sceptical, a more realistic eye, to see whether they really do sustain a different interpretation.

The first point is the more easily answered. Though Nureyev was not especially close to his family, and although he didn't have many friends inside Russia, such family and friends as he did have would have come under very grave pressure had it become at all clear that his defection had been planned, or organised in any way in conjunction with the foreign security services. Events, as we shall see, actually played into Nureyev's hands but even so, it was vital for him, all his life, to maintain that his defection was a spur-of-the-moment gesture, one that was moreover provoked by the mishandling of the Le Bourget departure on the part of the Kirov management. In taking this line, Nureyev was protecting those that he left behind. It also painted him as someone who only reacted to a situation he was presented with, rather than an architect of the events himself, which would have meant that he would have to accept some of the responsibility for what followed.

Now let us turn to the chain of events which preceded the 1961 tour of the Kirov. With Nureyev dead, it is difficult to know exactly where to begin with this chronology but what is certain is that for three people, Sergio Stefanschi, Sergei Sorokin and Linda Myasnikova's brother, Leonid, the news of Nureyev's defection, when it came, was no surprise. Stefanschi and Nureyev were both fascinated with the west. Both were well aware that many Russians, dancers and others, had left the Soviet Union in previous decades, and both accepted that, when the time came, they would make the same move. It was accepted between them. With Sorokin, Nureyev specifically discussed defection. He never gave Sorokin a date and left him with the impression that it would be later, rather than sooner. But defection, and life in the west, *was* discussed. And Rudolf also discussed the matter with Leonid Miasnikova, about a week before the Kirov left for Paris.

We have already mentioned the 'signals' that Nureyev was sending, to such people as the cast of *My Fair Lady* when they toured Soviet Russia in 1960. Is this fanciful? Not at all. To repeat, 1961 was the height of the cold war. There were six defections that year, the Berlin wall was built, George Blake was arrested, and the Portland spy ring was blown. None of this directly relates to Nureyev, but it was all part of the climate of the times, which were very edgy. Contacts with foreigners were forbidden, or strictly controlled in Russia, for precisely the reason that, in extreme cases, they could lead to defection.

Afterwards, Nureyev always said that he had contact with foreigners simply because he was interested in different art forms, different interpretations, that he was mad about the theatre, *all* theatre. This was perfectly true, but it wasn't the whole truth. He was playing a game. In 1961 the United States was just as interested in propaganda victories as was the Soviet Union. Although on balance more people travelled from east to west, the much-publicised defection, in 1960, of Bernon Mitchell and William Martin, from America *to* the USSR, was especially important to Nureyev. Rudolf quickly realised that it would make the USA keen to obtain a comparable propaganda coup of its own and, as we have seen, the press conference when Mitchell and Martin went public with their attack on the National Security Agency took place in September 1960, the very month when the American Ballet Theatre was in Moscow. The press conference was embarrassing for ABT and of course quite deliberate on the part of the Soviets. Its impact on Nureyev was profound and it is interesting to note that Nureyev told Rosella Hightower that it was after he saw Erik Bruhn in Moscow, in the month of September 1960, and watched the film of him dancing, that he started to take private lessons in English, in Leningrad. Bruhn had appeared with the American Ballet Theatre. To learn English therefore made sense. Bruhn, Nureyev felt, was the only dancer he could learn from. From that moment the idea of defection took firm hold in his mind.

Nureyev was extremely intelligent, decisive, and very conscious of history, especially in ballet. He was aware that the Bolshoi had visited Paris in 1954, and America in 1956. There was a reasonable chance, therefore, that the Kirov would also go on foreign tours. Such tours are arranged well in advance, so it is possible that the Kirov/Royal Ballet exchange was known about as early as September 1960. It certainly was in London. And if Bruhn was the 'pull' factor in Nureyev's mind, the behaviour of Sergeyev and the rest of the Kirov management was the 'push' factor. They treated him so badly in 1960 that his immediate future inside the Kirov seemed bleak.

But to defect to where? The initial clues here are Bruhn and the fact that, from autumn 1960, Nureyev was learning English. He had clearly devoted quite a bit of energy to this in the five or six months before he left on tour. Everyone – Clara Saint, Pierre Lacotte, Olivier Merlin, Mario Bois, Margot Fonteyn, Colette Clark, people already encountered or who will be mentioned later – confirms that Nureyev's English, though it could be idiosyncratic at times, was good when he arrived in the west. Good enough to make himself understood by dancers, choreographers and musicians; good enough to give newspaper interviews. He was supposed to be uneducated, by Kirov and Leningrad standards. Yet in Paris he was the dancer who found communication with westerners most easy.

Let us jump ahead slightly in the narrative, and consider the fact that when Nureyev arrived in London, to meet Margot Fonteyn, she was surprised to find that he was familiar not only with the names of the main dancers in the Royal Ballet but with many of the *corps de ballet*, too. Why?

The truth of the matter is that, as well as learning English in 1960–61, Nureyev was also studying the Royal Ballet. The best classical company outside Russia at that time, it went to America regularly where it was, if anything, even more highly regarded than in London. If he could learn, as a dancer, from Erik Bruhn, then as a dancer he would also need a 'home'. The Royal Ballet was the leading candidate. When he went back to Leningrad in 1989 (see below, p. 427), he let slip to a Russian reporter that his main thought, when he was trapped at Le Bourget airport, was how he could dance for the Royal Ballet.

That he was sending out signals to foreigners cannot really be doubted, in view of his reprimand by the man at the Ministry of Culture. Nureyev had just come back from a tour of deepest Russia when he was punished by being told that he would never be allowed to go abroad. This punishment does not sensibly fit the crime, unless what he was really being punished for was taking an unhealthy interest in foreigners, in foreign ballet companies, and in the English language.

The importance and purpose of Nureyev's signals was to make it known that, if and when he did reach the west, as a member of a Russian touring company, he would be receptive to approaches from western security services and/or western ballet companies. Making it known, as he did, that he could speak passable English, gave more specific signals as to where he would like to go.

It is also interesting in this context to recall that some of the regulars at Elizaveta's salon were scientists (Tamara Myasciorva, Liuba Miasnikova). Three of the Russians who defected in 1961 –

Lencharsky in Britain, Klotchka in Canada and Golub in Holland –
were not 'political' defectors, in that they were not military personnel
or spies, but scientists. Lencharsky defected so that he could practise
his religion. Klotchka defected because he wanted greater scientific
freedom. (A winner of the Stalin prize, he had criticised an article on
physical chemistry in the Soviet encyclopaedia as 'ludicrous', which led
to trouble with his superiors.) Golub had simply holidayed in Holland
and liked it. The scientists in Elizaveta's salon knew the details of each
of these events, from the scientific grapevine.

Then there is the report, made just once but never repeated, that,
when Nureyev left for Paris his mother came to see him off. By this
time Farida was not well and it was a long way for her to come. If she
did go to Leningrad, it can only have been for one reason. She knew
that she might never see him again.

We may ask whether, when he arrived in Paris, on the first leg of a
two-stage tour of the west, Nureyev had *pre-selected* himself as someone
the CIA, or MI6, might target as a candidate for defection. The answer
is that Nureyev had probably done all he could to identify himself as just
such a target. Indeed, he had done more than enough: he had gone too
far and had fallen foul of the Soviet authorities. Only through luck was
he in Paris at all.

The KGB file is in no doubt over this matter, and gives details of
what was done to lure Nureyev to the west. Before we come to that,
there is one other part of the preamble which we need to consider first:
Nureyev's behaviour in Paris.

Once again, Rudolf's own version of events has been accepted at face
value, when it doesn't really stand up to scrutiny. On his account, he
was simply enjoying the freedom that Paris had to offer, as any normal
person would have done. But Nureyev *wasn't* normal; he was a Russian,
on a KGB-supervised tour at the height of the cold war. The truth is that,
in Paris, Nureyev's controversial behaviour was stepped up a gear. He
knew two things. He knew that it was dangerous for *him* to approach
the western authorities. This would not only have drawn the wrath of
the KGB who were actually on the tour, and brought in the embassy;
it might have resulted in him being 'sedated' and bundled back on board
an Aeroflot plane, much as had happened to Colonel Strygin in Burma in
1959. Even if Nureyev had succeeded, the consequences for his family
and friends back home would have been hideous. (Golub's wife had been
kidnapped by Soviet agents in Holland after he announced that he was
defecting.)

It followed that the western security services had to come to him.

That the Russians were aware that something might happen in Paris
seems evident from Furtseva's comment, at the embassy reception
early on in the tour, that she hoped to see far more of Nureyev's
dancing in the future. She would have been all too well aware of the

punishment meted out by her own subordinate only recently. She would also have been aware of the signals Nureyev had sent out in Russia, and her change of tune was designed to reassure him that there *would* be more foreign tours, so that he didn't need to contemplate what she knew he was contemplating. At the time of her remarks Nureyev had not yet danced in Paris. He was not yet the star that he so quickly became.

But the most important aspect of this preamble is surely Nureyev's own behaviour in Paris. A few weeks earlier, he had been told, firmly, by the Ministry of Culture that he would never be allowed out of Russia again. Now, through luck, he was here in France. If he really had no plans to defect, and despite what Furtseva told him, the best way for Nureyev to ensure that he *was* included on future foreign tours was to behave impeccably on this one, to behave in as 'politically correct' a manner as possible. That meant dancing to perfection, which he did, and conforming in every other way, which he did not.

For a highly intelligent man, he behaved in a very unintelligent way, in a manner which seemed designed to ensure that this was his last tour of the west, and which would remove any chance of his ever studying under Erik Bruhn. Unless . . .

There was yet another aspect to Nureyev's behaviour in Paris – his flamboyant spending. He bought costumes, he bought wigs, he bought art books, he bought an electric train set. But think about what he *didn't* buy. He didn't buy what every other member of the Kirov bought – personal everyday clothes, such as stylish jeans, which they couldn't get at home, which they could show off in when they got back, and which they could sell for fantastic sums if they wanted to. He made a point of calling friends in Leningrad – knowing that the calls would be listened in to – and making disparaging statements about Paris, saying how much he was looking forward to the audiences of London. It was the *audiences* of London that he drew attention to. He was the dutiful Kirov ballet star, working for the good of the company. He was showing that he wasn't taken in by the west, by Parisian audiences who were shallow and ill-informed. His conversations were purely professional, when anyone 'normal' would have told his friends what Paris was like, what was in the shops, what people were wearing, and so on.

Finally, consider two vignettes. First, Marina Ilicheva's comment that '[Nureyev] appeared less and less frequently at the hotel. Conversations were taking place *and they talked of Rudolf being up to something*. Unpleasant things were said' (italics added). Second, there was that late encounter with Soloviev in their bedroom at the Hôtel Moderne, when Soloviev said that he had been asked to search Nureyev's things for the KGB. Nureyev made light of this in his autobiography but what if Soloviev had found something? We shall return to this in a moment but if Soloviev *did* find something, and Nureyev realised that he had, he would also have realised that the KGB were on to him. In Ilicheva's words, they would have known what he was up to. Furthermore, if the KGB realised that Soloviev had told Nureyev what he had been asked to do, then, in that double world, they would have known that Nureyev also realised they were on to him. This is important because it would explain the change in ticket routine on the way to the airport. The KGB must have been very worried that, after his discussion with Soloviev, Nureyev would abscond in Paris. They needed him at the airport for what they planned. So they gave him a London ticket to reassure him.

Everything points to one thing. Nureyev was planning to defect in London. Under Ninette de Valois the Royal Ballet had gone from strength to strength, outstripping the French, Italian and American companies. In Margot Fonteyn it had the only western star who could rival Ulanova and Dudinskaya. In Frederick Ashton it had one of the top choreographers in the west. Britain was strongly allied with the United States, and their security services often worked together, and so there was some hope, if Nureyev played his cards right, that his material needs would be looked after, at least for a while. There was also the possibility of him joining the American Ballet Theatre, where Erik Bruhn was a star.

This much is supposition. The KGB file, however, makes it clear that the meeting with Clara Saint was a set-up. This file consists of 2,348 pages in five volumes, but by no means all have been made available to the author 'as they are not very interesting', and certain names, as we shall see, have been either censored or changed.

When one reads the file (in translation, in the author's case), one is struck first by its vagueness in several areas (Clara Saint is referred to as Clare Sene), and the thinness of the material on which many conclusions appear to be based. One finds oneself asking just how *good* the KGB really was. Second, there is the self-serving nature of much of the material, as if either the organisation is *still* trying to spread disinformation, or that the lower levels are trying to give the higher levels what they want to hear. Whatever the true reason, one should approach the contents of the file with the utmost caution.

The involvement of Clara Saint would have been quite a clever move by the Americans. She was neither American, nor French, nor British and therefore had no obvious links to any of the security services which might be involved in any plan to 'lure' Nureyev to the west. Even according to the file, Clara Saint was not a proper CIA agent in the accepted sense of the word.

But she was well-connected in Paris political circles, being a wealthy Chilean who, via her late finacé Vincent knew his father André Malraux, the French Minister of Culture. According to the file she was 'recruited' by a 'Mr Wilson' who was a CIA man whose cover was as the London-based editor of the *Baltimore Sun* newspaper. Wilson had asked around in Paris, coming across her name from various balletomanes, including the photographer Serge Lido.

Once Saint had made contact and, as the KGB supposed, the young couple had made love, she was to report back to Wilson. The file records claim that she was observed at several meetings with the CIA man at a café on Rue du Départ. Wilson met Rudolf only once at that stage, also in Rue du Départ, on 28 May. After Saint 'recruited' Rudolf, so to speak, she was to introduce him, casually, to a Mr James, an Englishman who had a good reason for being in Paris, since he worked for the British impresario, Victor Hochhauser, who was organising the London end of the tour. James was making himself known to the Kirov in Paris, prior to its arrival in Britain. If all went according to plan, James, as the PR man in London, would quite naturally introduce Rudolf to the journalist from the *Baltimore Sun*, and the defection could proceed from there.

In other words, Clara Saint was to make the first approach, during pillow talk. If Nureyev turned down this overture, then not much had been lost, because none of the security services had revealed their hand. If, on the other hand, Nureyev took the bait, he would be introduced to Wilson in London, on an apparently legitimate basis. Clara was to accompany Nureyev to London and if, at any time, he changed his mind while he was in Paris, Saint was simply to say that *she* wasn't going to London. Wilson, and James, would know what that meant.

Once Nureyev reached London, it would be quite natural for James to meet up with him again, having already seen him in Paris. During the course of the Kirov's stay in the British capital there would be plenty of opportunity, and plenty of time, for journalists to interview the Kirov stars, so a meeting between Nureyev and Wilson, organised by James, would not be difficult to arrange. Clara's presence in London was required to reassure Nureyev and to comfort him during his ordeal. James, of course, was perfectly placed to advise Nureyev on the work that might be available for him in the west. The KGB file says that Wilson was observed paying $250 to Clara Saint in Paris in July 1961. This suggestion is recorded as reaching Moscow in two ways: by a report from Paris after the meeting itself had been observed, and from a KGB resident in Washington DC who claimed to have been given the same details by a mole in the CIA several months later, including confirmation of the sum.

Whatever the KGB files may suggest, Clara Saint denies their account completely. She never slept with Nureyev, she says. She was not paid by the CIA and she had no conversations about Rudolf's defection before the call from Le Bourget airport, either with him or anyone else. The names Wilson or James mean nothing to her. In fact, the whole thing is made up, she says with considerable irritation. She says that on their last night together in Paris, before Nureyev was supposed to leave for London, they walked the streets all night, did not go to bed at all, and Nureyev said that he thought he might never return to Paris. Whether the information in the KGB files is true or false, Saint is to be sympathised with. If false, she faces the frustraton of knowing she can never persuade everyone that certain things did not happen. If true, while she has nothing to be reproached with, she faces the frustration of never being at liberty to tell her story.

There is one other matter that has never been properly addressed, least of all by Nureyev himself. Why did the Soviet authorities want to send him back to Russia from Le Bourget? Why did everything happen so suddenly? There is no doubt that it was sudden, or that the reason Sergeyev gave was phoney. And there is no doubt either that Sergeyev would have got a great deal of personal satisfaction from sending Nureyev back home and in disgrace. But why did they have to skip London? Nureyev had been the star of the show in Paris, a sensation. A lot of London balletomanes were looking forward to his arrival. If he were to dance, success would be assured. And the 'season' lasted only a few weeks. If he were to mix with Londoners the way he mixed with Parisians – well, that would be awkward but would it really be such a disaster when the benefits of him dancing were so great? In 1961 London was even more important than Paris.

No, the sudden change of policy which occurred at Le Bourget was brought about by the KGB's discovery that Nureyev was planning to defect shortly after his arrival in London. How did they know? Yuri Soloviev told them. He had gone through Nureyev's things in his room on that last night, and discovered the names of both Wilson and James. Nureyev hadn't bothered to come back to the hotel after the last performance, before spending the whole night out. The KGB thus had all the hours of darkness to check out Mr Wilson and Mr James. In 1961 the Russian security services had penetrated both the French and British intelligence networks and, once they found that Wilson was involved, Nureyev's plans would have been known beyond doubt. Soloviev always felt guilty for what he had done, with results that we shall see.

There were other matters, too. According to the file, Rudolf was observed to have spent the night with Pierre Lacotte, a French dancer-choreographer, and with Raymondo de Larrain (for more detail on this see Chapter 10). Certainly, Strizhevsky, the more senior KGB man on the tour, had been told by Moscow on 14 June, two days before they left for London, that Rudolf was being recalled. Strizhevsky was also told that Rudolf was to be informed of this decision only at the last moment, at Le Bourget airport. There is one final piece to the jigsaw, provided by Joan Thring, Rudolf's assistant in London in the 1960s and 1970s. She confirms that Rudolf told her he had intended to defect in London.

So the situation that faced Nureyev at Le Bourget airport was somewhat different from that he portrayed in his autobiography, though no less urgent. When he returned to his hotel that Friday morning and talked to Soloviev, he realised that the KGB knew more than he thought. This is what made the situation so bleak, *this* is why he went grey when he was told he was being put on a plane for Russia. It was much more serious than he ever let on. If he went back in these circumstances, he might face jail – or worse. That is why he showed the dagger to Pierre Lacotte. He wasn't joking.

But, being extremely quick-witted, and tough, Nureyev also realised that, in a sense, the problem he now faced also harboured the solution. If he suddenly made a break, if he defected here at Le Bourget, then part of the situation might be retrieved. This would be a genuine impromptu business. Indeed, the KGB could be said to have brought the whole thing on itself. And in any case he now had no choice. Either he went back to Russia, and to oblivion, or he made a jump for it right here.

After he jumped, of course, there was every incentive to say that it was done on the spur of the moment. In a very real sense that was true. But more importantly, it protected everyone. It protected his family and friends, because it appeared that what he had done involved no real thought or preparation and meant that they weren't involved in any way. In a curious way it also protected the KGB and even Russia itself, because in occurring so suddenly his defection could never be said to be truly political.

It worked. The west bought the story and the KGB was also willing to let the story be accepted. The only allowance they had to make was not to victimise the family too much – otherwise questions might have been asked. If Nureyev *had* jumped without thought, his family and friends could not be blamed too much.

But, in the inner recesses of the Soviet government, in the KGB, of course, and in the Party, the truth has always been known. This accounts for Nureyev's rough treatment when he went back to Ufa in 1987. There were other consequences too, one of which can be mentioned here. One of the few people who knew the real truth early on was Hamet, Nureyev's father. That is why Rudolf didn't visit his father's grave in 1987. Hamet despised his son and Rudolf knew it.

CHAPTER EIGHT

Fervid Hero

Always our fervid hero tended
pure passion's flame, and in a trice
would launch into self-sacrifice

While Nureyev had been in the first-floor office at Le Bourget, deciding
what to do, the BEA Viscount for London had taken off. The crowd at
the airport had thinned, but hadn't dissipated entirely, as the journalists
waited for news of the defector. After the forty-five minutes had elapsed,
Clara Saint climbed back up the stairs and was called into the police
bureau. The inspectors wanted to know if Nureyev would have a place
to stay, and what he would do for food and clothing. Clara had anticipated
all this, and had a place in mind where Nureyev could stay for up to a
week. She was able to reassure the policemen and so they agreed to let
the situation be formalised. This meant that Nureyev had to go to the
Ministry of the Interior on the Place Beaubourg in central Paris and fill out
the necessary forms. It was tedious but important, and to save Nureyev
yet more anguish from the waiting journalists, the airport police agreed
to let him out by a back way. Clara acted as a decoy. She returned to the
crowd outside the door and kept them talking while Nureyev escaped.
Then, when she was certain he had gone, she revealed all. Which is how
only *her* picture, and not his, appeared in the newspapers the next day.

On the way to the Ministry, Nureyev had an anxious moment when
the police escort suddenly changed direction to avoid a traffic jam.

'The Russian embassy?' he said nervously.

The policeman next to him was a stolid figure. 'Non.'

Nureyev was at the Ministry for a couple of hours that afternoon. He
phoned Clara from there but she had the presence of mind to tell him
not to come to the flat she shared with her mother on the quai d'Orsay.
As she had anticipated, the KGB already knew where she lived, and

had stationed two men right outside. They wore raincoats and soft felt trilbies.

Clara had liaised with Olivier Merlin, who had hurried back to Paris on his motorcycle. They had a mutual friend who was away from Paris, Jean-Loup Puznat, who had a big apartment that Nureyev could use. It overlooked the Luxembourg Gardens. This was perfect for there was no obvious link to Nureyev and, provided his new-found friends did not allow themselves to be followed, he was safe. He was taken to the apartment in the early evening and, soon after, both Clara and Claire Motte arrived with the evening papers. He found he had made the front pages, even in London (together with 'The "K" Summit', when Kennedy met Khrushchev in Vienna). Claire had to read the text to him, since his French wasn't up to it.

Three hundred miles to the north, the rest of the Kirov company had checked into the Strand Palace Hotel in London, around the corner from Covent Garden. The entire company was agog at the news of Nureyev's defection, which they had been told about on their arrival at Heathrow airport. Once again the Russian officials had given conflicting explanations for why Nureyev had been recalled. One said no one was missing. Bogdanov repeated the claim he had made in Paris, that Rudolf was wanted to dance for Khrushchev in the Kremlin, on the premier's return from Vienna. BEA said they had been told that a passenger was 'unwell'. Another official, Feodorov, had given Farida's grave illness as the main reason. As the London *Standard* remarked, it was difficult to know who was telling the truth. But then, not even Sergeyev had known that Nureyev had defected until he landed in London. As soon as he did hear, he realised that it would take the shine off the Kirov's season at Covent Garden. However good they were, the whole world would want to see the dancer who had, as every paper put it, 'made a leap for freedom'. When the box office for the Kirov had opened in April, people had queued for three days, and 10,000 tickets had been sold on the first day.

Behind the headlines, Rudolf's first night in the west as an exile was remarkably calm. He was tired, not just from the emotional turmoil of the day, but also because he hadn't been to bed the night before; instead he had sat up talking with Clara. Not for the first time, he found his beloved Pushkin a comfort. Dostoevsky, preaching a eulogy on the fiftieth anniversary of Pushkin's death, had spoken of Onegin as a restless wanderer, travelling unsatisfied from one country to another. *Eugene Onegin* contains the lines, 'He roamed the world, his lyre behind him.' As a Russian, as a Siberian, if there is such a thing, Nureyev knew better than anyone that exile is seldom easy.

The next day, the morning papers across the world carried the news of his defection. It was page one everywhere, from *L'Humanité* in Paris, to the *Daily Express* in London and the *New York Times* in America. In Russia there was a news blackout.

Late in the morning the Ministry of the Interior sent a car to fetch him, to complete yet more formalities, among them the issuance of his *titre de voyage*, a form of identification since he now had no passport. Nureyev later recalled that, before giving him this document, the man at the Ministry had one important question: what would be the dancer's future source of income while in France? All credit to Nureyev for having an answer; he had discussed it with Clara, Claire and Olivier Merlin the evening before. Claire had spoken with Raymondo de Larrain and Rudolf felt fairly certain that he would, in the first instance, be offered something by the Marquis de Cuevas Ballet. The man from the Ministry seemed satisfied by this and handed over the *titre de voyage*.

That weekend the press was full of speculation and comment on Nureyev's defection. The *New York Times*, which told its readers that Nureyev had been with the Kirov for ten years, and had been promoted to lead dancer only one year before, also said that it understood the dancer had arrived in Paris with the idea of defecting. He had, the paper said, discussed defection with several of his (unnamed) French friends. The paper didn't follow up on this lead, or on another that romance with Clara Saint was the real lure, but it may have been nearer to the truth than it knew, and perhaps this is what prompted Victor Hochhauser to say he was suing Nureyev for loss of earnings. It was a curious thing to do, since he could never have enforced any writ that might have been issued. Was he just making a noise to deflect unwelcome attention away from his role in the defection?

The *Sunday Telegraph* in Britain speculated that Serge Lifar was the lure for Nureyev, that a career with the Russian in charge of the Paris Opéra was what had prompted him to leave. The paper also quoted a Covent Garden spokesman who played down Nureyev's talent. The spokesman conceded that Nureyev was to have danced *Sleeping Beauty* and *Swan Lake* but emphasised that he had *not* been scheduled to dance on the first night of either ballet.

In Leningrad, Tamara heard the news about Nureyev on the BBC World Service, which, along with the Voice of America, was the chief way the Russians got their 'unofficial news' in those days. The Russian press and broadcasting organisations were silent on the matter for the time being, but Tamara heard the news on the very day it happened. 'At first I didn't believe it. I personally didn't understand what "political asylum" was. I found such a thing absurd as Rudik had never taken any interest in politics whatsoever. He was interested in anything *but* politics.'

Likewise, Sorokin heard the news on the BBC. He was distressed but perhaps less surprised than most. 'I had expected Rudolf to stay abroad later on. But not at that time.'

In Ufa, Pamira Sulemanovna heard the news 'from somebody who whispered it to me . . . They read it out on the radio, the fact that he had stayed in France [a reference to someone else hearing it on the BBC World Service]. Everyone was talking about it, but in whispers. People said he was a discredit to the country, and that if he came back he would be locked up. I just couldn't see the reason why he had left, why he had stayed over there. Later I heard that he had gone to Turkey and that no one was taking him into their company. I was worried that he would be a poor man, wandering the streets. It upset me. I didn't know that he was all set up over there, and was working. We generally didn't talk about it. We were scared.'

The defection was a particularly bad blow for Rezida. The family was phoned on the day that it happened but what hurt was that she got married that year and the news marred the ceremonies. Also, she was chosen as the one to go to his flat in Leningrad to clear it out. She found the flat filled with postcards from all the places he had travelled to, and with sheet music. She threw most of it away. Rezida was sent to Leningrad because Rosa had been the one to tell Hamet and Farida and they had been badly affected. Hamet aged immediately; his hair went grey, his face hardened, he became even more taciturn than usual. (He, of course, knew more than most, though he kept it to himself.) Farida tried not to show that she was hurt, putting a brave face on things but, more than anything, she was worried about whether he would have enough work, rather than what other people would think, or whether he had been a discredit to his country.

Rezida, who still hoped that Rudolf might return in time for her wedding, actually phoned him in France. First, she simply rang the KGB in Moscow, introduced herself and asked if they had her brother's number in Paris. The man who answered said, 'Hold on, I'll look.' He came back and gave her a number but it turned out to be wrong. The next day she rang again and asked for the same man – only to be told that he had been dismissed for giving her information, even though it was wrong information. After telling her this, the second KGB contact hung up on her.

Rezida did, eventually, find Rudolf's number, and rang him. He was at pains to say he was not a traitor, and he described how it had happened. She told him that the Russians would try to lure him back.

'He said that he would come back when he had seen the "bright lights". He said he would come back here when he had seen the whole world. He wrote [in his autobiography] that the Soviet authorities had "fixed up" these conversations, but in my case it isn't true. I don't know if the authorities organised mother's

Maude Gosling: Rudolf's London 'mother' and the 'lioness-in-chief' at the end.

Nigel Gosling: 'seeing Rudolf dance was like a wild animal let loose in the drawing room.'

Ninette de Valois: inspired by Rudolf's bow.

With Frederick Ashton, seated, and Cecil Beaton, during the rehearsals for Marguerite and Armand.

Fonteyn said: 'When I'm on stage, I don't see Rudolf, I see Albrecht.'

With Fonteyn in Giselle: the legend is minted.

With Roland Petit, Margot, and the pre-Beatles haircut.

'I should have married her'.

(*bottom*) Lovers?

The scar on his lip only added to his beauty.

'Our job', he told Monica Mason 'is to make it look difficult'.

(*top left*) With Fonteyn in Romeo and Juliet, 1967. Oblivious of Lynn Seymour's sacrifice.

(*top right*) With Merle Park.

With Leslie Collier and Jennifer Penney (back), Merle Park and Antoinette Sibley (front). Half the Royal Ballet ballerinas were in love with Rudolf, the other half with Erik.

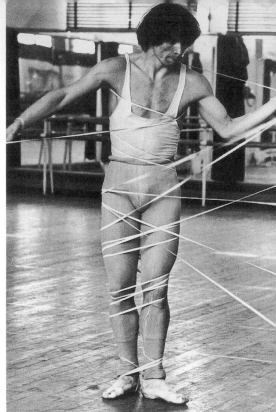

With Carla Fracci

Rudi van Dantzig's 'The Ropes of Time'.

Rudolf with Joan Thring. 'You crack good whip' he told her.

conversations with him but I just called him. I didn't think that he would have a better life there. We suffered. We were still confused. We were still under the sway of the propaganda that said life was better here than over there. We didn't know that things were better over there than they were here, that there were more possibilities. We thought that a man could die of hunger over there, but that here nobody died of hunger . . .'

After Nureyev's defection, Farida stopped working. She was already ill with polyarthritis that would gradually spread throughout her body. Her hands and arm had already been giving her trouble but now there was further deterioration.

There *was* a plan to send Farida to France, to try to bring her son back but this was vetoed by the KGB. No doubt with her poor health, Rudolf would have tried to keep his mother in the west, a development the Soviet system could well do without. But Farida and Rezida did travel to Moscow to see Ekaterina Furtseva, the Minister of Culture, to discuss Nureyev's personal habits and preferences, in case these could be used in some way to lure him back. It came to nothing.

Arslanov heard from someone at Ufa Theatre. 'I remember that they told me he had defected in England and it was only later that I discovered he had defected in France and then gone to England. I heard the details from Rosa when I went down to Leningrad in 1962. She was in his flat, the one he had shared with Sizova, and from where she ran a kindergarten. Of course, everybody in Ufa knew about the defection and it was psychologically very difficult for the family. The authorities didn't hinder their work – but they refused to help them either and Hamet, especially, found that hard. They now moved house, from Zentsova Street to Oktobr Prospekt. Hamet also came under pressure in the local party.' According to one neighbour, Nailya Maerlyatova, 'The party organisation started a campaign against him. At the meetings they would taunt him and rub salt in his wounds. "He grew up a traitor," they would say. "You didn't bring your child up carefully and you have no place among us communists." It even went so far as saying he should not be part of the collective. My husband intervened on his behalf but he was the only one. I believe that the pressure in the Party was partly to blame for Hamet's early death [in 1966, aged sixty-one].' Hamet went to the KGB, that he might contact his son (Arslanov went with him). Only a telephone call was allowed.

Farida's collapse was also due to the strain. 'They all worried with one heart,' as Maerlyatova put it. 'Their mail was interfered with [the KGB file confirms this], there was no economic advance, the hardship continued.' Arslanov was also told that Tchichuna had been flattened *because* Rudolf had defected.

But not everyone shunned the Nureyevs. Some friends named Saidishev had relatives in Moscow, who had access to the foreign press. They forwarded everything they could. Taisiya Mikhailovna Halturika-Ilchinova, Nureyev's former teacher, was one of the few who thought he had done the right thing. 'Had he stayed here the most he would have received would have been a three-room apartment.'

In Leningrad, at the Kirov, according to Arkharova, the PartBureau summoned the director, Rachinsky, and the artistic director, Sergeyev, to an emergency meeting and instructed them to give a full account of what had transpired and *why* it had transpired. Sergeyev was suspended, but only briefly. Naturally, all photographs of Rudolf were taken off the walls. His very existence would be omitted from all Soviet ballet works for decades to come. Pushkin received several visits from the KGB – and went down with an attack of hives.

Neither Farida nor Rezida need have worried about Rudolf going hungry, or not being able to earn his living as a dancer. His first contract with a western company was signed within three days of the incident at Le Bourget. He was to receive FF30,000 ($6,000) a month to appear with the Marquis de Cuevas Ballet in Paris.

The Marquis de Cuevas, a Chilean, had two fortunes to lavish on ballet, his own and his wife's – she was a daughter of John D. Rockefeller. Having run one ballet in America, he determined, in 1953, to take Europe by storm and spent half a million dollars on a coming-out party in Biarritz which he himself attended wearing a wig of grapes and which Renée (Zizi) Jeanmaire graced virtually naked on a camel borrowed from a nearby circus whose entire cast she also brought to the party uninvited. In Paris, de Cuevas lived at 7 quai Voltaire where he received visitors in bed, surrounded by Pekinese and overlooked by two nudes, one by Salvador Dali and the other by Botticelli. Rosella Hightower recalls attending a dinner for twenty given by de Cuevas, where he suddenly whispered to her that he had no money to settle the bill. She had just a few francs on her but he borrowed them anyway, took a taxi to the nearest casino and won enough before the dinner had ended to avoid any embarrassment.

De Cuevas had died a few months before Nureyev defected and his company had been taken over by his nephew, Raymondo de Larrain, with whom Nureyev had discussed costumes only a week before. He was introduced to his future partners, of whom the most famous were Nina Vyroubova and Rosella Hightower. Vyroubova was of Russian extraction. She was older than Nureyev but had been trained, in Paris, by exiles who had taught many of Nureyev's own teachers. Rosella Hightower, an American Indian, had been brought up in Oklahoma but preferred Europe. Rehearsals began immediately in a room near the Salle Pleyel, which was important to Nureyev because he needed to keep fit. In order to keep his whereabouts secret they would all take a taxi to the Hôtel Plaza, which was then home to many South Americans, run through the kitchens to the service entrance, where the same taxi would be waiting to pick them up again. This way they could ensure they were never followed.

But the ramifications of what Rudolf had done were still working themselves out, and although the French authorities had been very good in allowing Nureyev to stay in their country it should not be forgotten that France in those days had a sizeable – and powerful – Communist Party which favoured good relations with the USSR. The communists now began to make trouble. Theirs would be an intermittent but unpleasant campaign against Rudolf over the next months. It began in that very first week, when Raymondo de Larrain received a number of abusive and anonymous telephone calls, accusing him of sheltering the 'traitor' Nureyev in his company. The callers were obviously telephoning de Larrain because Nureyev was in hiding and they couldn't find him. But the KGB did – they were not a security service for nothing. Two days after he had moved into the apartment overlooking the Luxembourg Gardens, the men in felt hats were stationed outside.

It was nerve-racking and a totally new situation for de Larrain but, like Nureyev, he was not easily intimidated. He promptly hired two bodyguards for his new star, so that Rudolf had 'company' when it came time to leave the apartment for rehearsals. Nor did de Larrain bother about the expense of the bodyguards. Their presence, like Rudolf's, was pure gold so far as publicity for the company was concerned.

To begin with, Nureyev's life was very regimented and circumscribed. He went straight to the theatre every morning, rehearsed, took lunch at the restaurant next door, then returned home, where he remained for the rest of the day. At that stage, no one was very sure what the KGB agents who were following him might do, and no one wanted to take any risks. The press continued to follow his every move and he gave a number of interviews in which he said that his life now was not so very different from life in the Soviet Union. Not seeing the irony in this, more than one journalist reported that Nureyev was homesick, disappointed with life in the west. Nothing could have been further from the truth.

Meanwhile, the Soviet authorities were not accepting his defection without a fight. They informed the French government that if Nureyev were allowed to dance at the Paris Opéra Ballet, which was a totally subsidised and therefore national company, then all cultural exchanges between France and the Soviet Union would be severed. Given the size of the Communist Party in France at the time, this would have been a most unpopular move.

In London, at the Strand Palace Hotel where the Kirov were staying, feelings had hardened against Nureyev. The always hysterical British tabloids had, as sometimes happened, got the wrong end of the stick and had taken up the report that he had defected to be with Clara Saint. Marina Ilicheva says the other dancers found this painful and offensive. The person who felt most strongly, by all accounts, was Alla Sizova.

Having danced so much with Nureyev, and despite the fact that she couldn't stand the sight of him off-stage, she realised that she no longer had a partner.

There was a meeting in London to crack the whip and prevent any further thought of defection among the other dancers. Komsomol meetings were stepped up. The secretary, Chernishev, insisted on discussing Nureyev at Komsomol meetings, where his behaviour was dissected and his motives criticised. While the ordinary members of the Kirov saw something of London, Sergeyev and Dudinskaya and the principals and soloists hardly got about at all. As Dudinskaya put it later on, 'Rudik had been such a success. His defection meant that Sergeyev was short of dancers. Rudik was supposed to have danced *Swan Lake, Sleeping Beauty* and *La Bayadère* in London. Sergeyev and I had to train Vikulov for *La Bayadère*, Soloviev for *Swan Lake* and Oleg Sokalov for *Sleeping Beauty*.' Sergeyev came through with flying colours because the performances were met with great acclaim. That was also a tribute to the overall high standards at the Kirov. Soloviev was a particular success. 'It's possible,' says Ilicheva, 'that he jumped higher even than Rudolf. He really took off, soared, and yet it was a gentle jump.' But they all spent so much of their time in rehearsal while they were in England that neither Sergeyev nor Dudinskaya saw anything of London.

Ironically, while the Kirov were playing *Sleeping Beauty* in London Nureyev opened with the de Cuevas company in the same ballet on Thursday, 22 June. (The programme carried an advert for Aeroflot, showing the selfsame Tupolev which was meant to carry Rudolf back to Moscow.)

For the first night, the Théâtre des Champs-Elysées was surrounded with police and all Babylon, all Paris, was there, according to Roger Grenier in *France-Soir*: Serge Lifar, Alicia Markova, Liane Daydé. The auditorium was also filled with plain-clothes policemen, just in case.

Nureyev was on edge, and not just because it was his first appearance with a western company. Throughout the day telegrams had been arriving, one every fifteen minutes, from the Kirov dancers in London. Each one begged him to return home. Each one urged him not to disgrace himself, and the company he had left. They were hard to ignore.

The de Cuevas performances were arranged so that Nureyev danced Florimund on one night and the Blue Bird the next night. On that first night, after the second intermission, wrote Grenier, there was a silence, a clash of cymbals – and then Nureyev jumped into the spotlight. It was the most 'insolent' jump Grenier had ever seen, he said. But Pushkin would have been proud of the entrance Nureyev had made. His appearance, in a striking blue and gold costume, with a blond wig, was a different matter. It made him look like a Christmas tree, as he later put it, and his eye make-up made him resemble Elizabeth Taylor in *Cleopatra*. It was the type of effect de Larrain loved but Nureyev hated. However, only he seemed to mind that night. His performance was stopped four times by 'tumultuous' applause. He took thirty curtain calls and the clapping lasted for fifteen minutes. At the end he was in tears.

Besides the celebrities in the audience, Grenier noticed a number of White Russian exiles, who had made Paris their home in earlier decades. He listened to two old Russian women talking as they left the theatre afterwards.

'He is *so* beautiful!'

'Frankly, I am very pleased he is here, poor boy. But he has not found himself yet.'

'No, he seemed troubled.'

'Yes. It's going to be hard for him.'

'When I think of all the people there tonight, who know nothing about dance . . .'

'Ah yes. All the same, he danced well, the traitor.'

Despite this initial success, Nureyev immediately felt that there was something lacking in the French company. What was missing, he sensed, was the sort of dedication to dance that he himself had and which was taken for granted in Leningrad. He also felt that this applied as strongly to audiences as to the dancers. He was used to the rapport that existed between the performers and the audience in the Maryinsky, and its absence in Paris bothered him. It caused him to dwell on his own roots and reminded him of the invisible but very real strength of the Kirov, despite his problems. These were not just romantic shilly-shallyings, but real worries. In that first week as a 'westerner' it crossed his mind more than once that defection had been a terrible mistake.

The one undoubted bright spot was Rosella Hightower. He found her to be 'a kindred soul'. Already an international star, Nureyev nevertheless found that she was always willing to learn, and more than willing to assimilate those parts of the Kirov technique which she felt she lacked and could benefit from. Like himself, she was confident of her own abilities and the tradition which lay behind them, enough to be always flexible, always learning, always adding to what she knew and to what she could do. She was, he said, 'an inspiring partner'. She found him distant. His jump was good, she felt, but not natural. He admitted as much when he told her that 'Pushkin broke me and put me back together again.' But she loved his *port de bras* and adapted it for herself.

Of the two roles he was dancing in *Sleeping Beauty*, the Blue Bird interested Nureyev most. He had always found it a difficult role, technically, but his main interest was in its interpretation. In Leningrad it had been danced in much the same way since the time of Petipa nearly a hundred years before. The bird was always graceful, with soft and flowing arms, or wings. Nureyev had different ideas. He wanted to give the bird more

energy and a slight awkwardness, as if the Blue Bird really does want
to fly, to break loose from his familiar world. It was not too dissimilar
from his own plight, and that made him doubly anxious to try his new
interpretation now that he had broken free of the Kirov.

His first performance with de Cuevas was Florimund, so he got
his chance on the second night. The circumstances were not ideal.
Normally, on days when he was dancing, Nureyev followed a strict
routine. He would get up late, take class for two hours, lunch on
steak, for protein and strength, then rest again. He insisted on being
alone. He would see no friends, read no newspapers, make no telephone
calls *before* a performance. He found it comfortable, and necessary, to
retreat into himself, to think about the role he was to dance, and his
forthcoming performance. To shut out the real world helped him create
one of his own.

But, in Paris, in 1961, Nureyev was a celebrity. He was the man of the
hour, the man drawing the crowds to the de Cuevas Ballet and de Larrain
wanted his pound of flesh. Nureyev was forced to give interview after
interview. Speaking of France, he told one interviewer, 'I shall never
return to my country, but I shall never be happy in yours.' To another
he said he had no intention of going to America, nor was he attracted by
modern dance. He said that he would remain in France with de Cuevas.
To another he said he was considering an offer from George Balanchine
to join the New York City Ballet. He was polite but found the tendency
of the French press to treat him as a freak irritating.

On the second night that he danced, before Blue Bird, he had to give
yet another interview in his dressing-room. The journalist arrived just
before the performance, and she, like most of the others, was more
interested in his appearance and his adjustment to life in the west, than in
his dancing. But she was more than a journalist: as well as her notebook,
she also brought with her three envelopes from the Soviet embassy in
Paris, which she handed to him. She said that one envelope contained
a letter from his father, the second a telegram from his mother, and the
third a note from Pushkin.

Nureyev was stunned. It was the first direct communication he had
received either from Russia, or from his family, since the defection. To
have them delivered just before the performance of a role in which he
would seek to show just what he was capable of, was calculated to knock
him off his stride. Should he leave the envelopes unopened until after the
performance? Not Rudolf. He tore first at the envelope which contained
the note from Pushkin:

'The letter from Pushkin was shattering. The one man who really
knew me well didn't seem to understand me. He wrote that Paris
was a city of decadence whose rottenness would only corrupt me;
that I would lose not only my dancing technique but all moral

integrity if I stayed in Europe. The only thing left for me to do was to come home immediately.'

Upset, Rudolf turned next to his father's letter. It was short and to the point. Typical. Hamet said he found it difficult to believe a son of his could betray the fatherland and that there was no excuse for what Nureyev had done. Nureyev had been standing while he read this. He sat down. His father was still his father. Proud, unforgiving, hard. The wording of the letter tore into Rudolf – his father hadn't used the word 'traitor', but he clearly regarded his son as one. The letter steeled Rudolf. He and his father had never got on. Neither was going to change now.

That left his mother's telegram. He slipped his thumb under the flap of the envelope. Would she be kinder? He took out the paper. The message was short. There were no pleasantries, but no remonstrations either. Come home, she said. Come home, she begged. Rudik, come home.

Home? Where was that? Could it be that not even his mother understood him? Ufa had never been home. He had always longed to escape from Ufa. To Leningrad? To do what? The Kirov would never take him back, and no other first-class company would want him now. His parents missed him, he could concede that. But they didn't know the west. No doubt they had been told all sorts of things about the west by people in authority, unflattering things no doubt, as Pushkin's letter revealed. But, at heart, his parents were still ignorant peasants who knew nothing of the world outside the Soviet Union.

A voice over the Tannoy system told him there were three minutes to go before the performance. For a moment his heart softened as he thought of his mother all those miles away, in a different world. She would be thinking of him, just as he was thinking of her. But then his heart hardened again. They had not sent him their love, not even his mother. They had not sent him any news about the rest of the family. They had not expressed any interest at all in his own well-being. Indeed, who could say if his mother had really sent that telegram? Maybe the KGB had sent it.

He put the letters to one side and asked the journalist to leave. He had forgotten she was there. He had to complete his make-up. He *must* concentrate.

As he looked at himself in the mirror, and added some dark lines to his eyes, he became more convinced that the Soviet authorities had prevailed upon his parents to send those letters. They were so matter-of-fact. *Anyone* could have written them. His mother, surely, would have known how comforting some little personal detail would have been. The whole episode seemed so controlled, so calculated, so cold. He put more shadow under his cheek bones. The Blue Bird had to look dramatic. He sat back and looked at the overall impression he made in the mirror. The de Cuevas costume was more striking than the one he had used in the Kirov production and he was pleased with the effect. He was determined that his first Blue Bird for a western company would be memorable. He would show his talent as a dramatic artist, not just as a superb technician. He had no intention of allowing himself to become 'decadent', as Pushkin put it.

In *Sleeping Beauty*, the Blue Bird does not appear until the third act. Nureyev looked as striking that night as he had done the night before, as he waited in the wings, practising, keeping warm. Besides the blond wig, he wore a small coronet and a brilliant blue tunic, set off with diamanté, and fingers of satin which hung down from his waist. Another concoction of de Larrain's. Two thousand people had crammed into the Théâtre des Champs-Elysées, expecting fireworks.

They got them, but not quite in the way they had anticipated. No sooner had Nureyev walked on stage that night than a shower of shouting and whistles engulfed the audience. But these were not balletomanes saluting a new star; they were Communist Party members intent on making Rudolf feel uncomfortable, or worse. About twenty had bought tickets for the upper circle and they made the most noise. 'Traitor!' they yelled. 'Back to Moscow!' They also dropped programmes, paper bombs with pepper in them, and tiny tear-gas bombs down into the stalls to irritate the eyes of the richer spectators. Although Nureyev didn't know it, a second group had stormed the stage door of the theatre at the very moment he made his entrance. Dotted about the theatre were still other, smaller pockets of five or six protesters who didn't show themselves at first. Only after the first twenty in the upper circle had been ejected by police did these others add to the mayhem, with one or two throwing glass bombs on to the stage.

Nureyev was determined not to be intimidated, and kept on dancing despite the danger from the broken glass. Many in the audience shared his view and they now tried to drown out the protesters, by applauding wildly and cheering. The sounds of Tchaikovsky sank between the caterwauling and the cheering but still Nureyev attempted to dance. Segments that normally took three minutes, took fifteen that night. In carrying on regardless, Nureyev was making a political statement of his own.

Something else happened that night, which he never mentioned. Obsessed with making an impact, he changed his last steps without telling the rest of the cast. Suddenly and without warning, he abandoned *Sleeping Beauty* and danced the coda from *Taras Bulba*. In the fervid atmosphere, only the balletomanes present, and the other dancers, knew what he was doing. The coda to *Taras Bulba* is far more spectacular than the final part of *Sleeping Beauty* and produced exactly the effect that Nureyev wanted. But Nina Vyroubova, his partner that night, was furious and, as the curtain came down she attacked him, screaming that he was unprofessional, a scene-stealer, a selfish good-for-nothing, and much worse. He frosted over completely, she said later, and they didn't speak to one another again for five years.

Of course, when news of this fracas on the second night appeared in the papers, the remaining seats for the de Cuevas performances were sold out. In fact the protests continued – sporadically – throughout the week. Nureyev was upset, the more so by several threatening letters that he received. But he knew he mustn't show his feelings publicly and told one interviewer that he found the disturbances stimulating. 'All that excitement is amusing.'

Less amusing was an attack on Nureyev by Serge Lifar. A few days before, when Nureyev had first defected, Lifar had taken a different line, saying that Nureyev was the unquestioned star of the Kirov. He had even awarded him the Nijinsky prize. Now he changed his tune. In an interview with *Izvestiia*, which was soon relayed back to the west, he described Nureyev as a 'traitor and opportunist', who would soon sink into oblivion. This was the only mention the Soviet press made of the episode at the time and, conceivably, they distorted what Lifar had said. As director of the national company, which stood to lose a lot if the Soviets banned all cultural exchanges, he was perhaps being diplomatic in criticising Nureyev, and may not have meant what he said. His own memoirs, published in 1983, make no mention of the incident.

A different kind of criticism came from the veteran historian of ballet, Arnold Haskell. Haskell then wrote a regular column, a sort of diary, in the *Dancing Times* and he began one entry by remarking that Nureyev's defection had made not one whit of difference to the Kirov's performances in London. The company was so strong, he said, that it could easily survive the defection of one soloist. Haskell, in those early months at least, was inclined to view Nureyev as a 'crazy mixed-up dancer' who had defected on impulse because the adulation he had received in Paris had turned his head. He did not see much of a future for Nureyev, 'when he ceases to be a nine-day wonder'. Nureyev's problem, as Haskell saw it, was that he would have *less* freedom in the west to express himself than he had enjoyed in Russia. 'A dancer who defected some years ago and who, for a time, was a sensational success is now appearing in cabaret!' As he went on, Haskell's prognosis became gloomier and gloomier.

'He [Nureyev] was quoted as saying that he had followed Nijinksy's example in leaving Russia in 1912 and that he too wanted to dance without the regulation tunic! It is only too obvious that his head has been badly turned and certain French journalists, impresarios and dancers, who pride themselves on "helping him to freedom" have shown themselves to be irresponsible, if not downright wicked . . . I also hope that the public in Paris and elsewhere will not further turn his head by making him into a hero, a freedom fighter and the like. It degrades the word freedom and makes the young man ridiculous.

Another lesson emerges from this sorry affair. The free-lance dancer, permanently removed from the discipline and background of his school and tradition, rapidly deteriorates. The star needs the company far more than the company needs the star. Nureyev, if accurately quoted in the French press, mentioned Nijinsky as an example – and that in itself is significant. Nijinsky left the Diaghilev Ballet at a time when his reputation was unique, to many he *was* Russian ballet. Yet the Diaghilev Ballet continued to flourish and at a time when it had not the wealth of Russian talent to draw upon. The dancer with the deeper roots in his national tradition goes the furthest.'

Let us hope that Rudolf didn't read this obituary too soon after he renounced the Kirov. In fact, his instincts were sound and his head had not been turned (at least, not much). For example, initially he had been offered a three-year contract by de Larrain but had opted for six months instead, not wanting to attach himself too permanently to a company which, he felt, was not the best. This was a hard-headed decision, difficult to make in the circumstances, but it confirms his excellent judgement regarding his career. At the same time, he fully realised that he risked becoming a nine-days' wonder and, instead of worrying unnecessarily, he had his own proposal for dealing with it. In July there was a gap in the company's programme so he decided to take himself well away from the Paris limelight, before the press tired of him. He went to the south of France for a few days' holiday.

Raymondo de Larrain, Clara, and he stayed at La Réserve, a swish hotel in Beaulieu with a private beach. Press photographers from Paris snatched the occasional picture of him and Raymondo sunning themselves on the terraces at La Réserve but they utterly missed the one episode of real drama – when Nureyev nearly drowned.

It occurred as he was swimming out to the raft, which was anchored to the sea bed about 50 metres offshore. Theoretically, Nureyev was a strong swimmer, at least he should have been if the stories about him swimming in the Belaya river at Ufa are true, for the river there had a strong current which he had grown up with. But as he swam out from the La Réserve beach that day, he got into difficulty. One of the people already sunning himself on the raft was the young British football pools heir, Robert Sangster. Sangster, a strong swimmer himself, noticed someone making an awkward splash in the water, and dived in to help. He pulled the young man back to the beach and only afterwards was Sangster told whose life he had saved. Nureyev was embarrassed by the incident and Sangster, a modest man, never made much of it. A Pioneer was saved a second time.

After the break in Beaulieu, Rudolf returned to Paris to find the city in full swing. Clara Saint found that Nureyev took to café society instinctively. She had to find him a tailor who could provide him with '*le smoking*' (jacket). He was at that point, she says, a complete narcissist, interested in no one but himself. He now moved out of the flat overlooking the Luxembourg Gardens, into de Larrain's own sumptuous quarters in the rue St Père. Despite the move, he still received abusive telephone calls and nasty letters, but de Larrain had withdrawn the bodyguards, since the Soviet embassy had withdrawn theirs. The next scheduled performances were to be in Deauville, on the Normandy coast, during the fashionable summer racing season and, towards the end of July, rehearsals began again.

During those days, while he was waiting for the Deauville season to start, Nureyev was surprised to receive one communication which made a great change from the abusive and threatening letters that were now delivered almost daily. This was an approach from the American photographer, Richard Avedon, who wanted to take Nureyev's portrait. Nureyev was flattered. At least, he was to begin with. He already knew who Avedon was and he felt that for such an eminent artist to approach him in this way was recognition. When the session took place, according to Clara, Avedon got Nureyev drunk (a new experience for him), and proposed a series of nude photos. Nureyev agreed but, once he had sobered up, immediately regretted what he had done. Rudolf later said that he thought of Avedon as his first true 'occidental' friend. This was complete eyewash, published in his autobiography to flatter Avedon, in the hope that he would never publish the more revealing nude shots that he took that day. (To date, Avedon never has.)

Anyone who is familiar with the paintings of Eugène Boudin will have some idea of Deauville, on the northern, Calvados coast of France. There is a broad beach with a boardwalk, several large hotels and houses built in the traditional half-timbered wattle and daub Normandy manner. There are smart shops, chic restaurants, summer outposts of the exclusive Parisian clubs. Everything comes alive in August, for the races, which attract a fashionable international clientele. Around the races swirls all manner of 'fast' action, from gambling to sailing to theatre.

Nureyev was scheduled to dance more 'Sleeping Beauties' in Deauville at the theatre near to the casino and the baths. It was important from his point of view, for though Deauville could not be called a significant cultural centre, in August it was a showplace. Many rich benefactors – from London, Switzerland and America, as well as France – stayed there. This was the kind of audience he had to succeed with if he was really to make his mark in the west.

As usual, on the first night he arrived at the theatre about two hours before the performance to check his costume and begin work on his make-up. Nureyev liked to take his time with make-up, partly because he found it relaxing, but also because, as he put on the paints and lip-glosses, the eye-shadow and hair lacquer, he also donned the character he was to dance that night. It was a process that helped him to concentrate. Everything went well until, about half an hour before the curtain rose, the telephone in his dressing-room rang. It was a long-distance call, international. Now, 1961 was well before the age of direct dialling and when he heard that the call was coming from Russia, Nureyev was immediately nervous. Who was it and how had they found him in Deauville? Was it bad news? Was it a coincidence that the call was coming through just before his performance? He thought back to those letters he had been given by the journalist, at the Théâtre des Champs-Elysées.

'Rudik? Rudik? Can you hear me?'

He could hear very well, and he recognised the voice. How could he fail to; it was his mother. He was immediately torn in his feelings – her familiar voice, the childhood that it brought back, the smells and sounds of Ufa, already a lifetime away from Paris, Beaulieu and Deauville. The practical jokes she used to play on his sisters. The troubled expression she always had on her face. At the same time, it was half-past six in Deauville, which made it half-past ten in the evening in Ufa. His mother didn't have a telephone, so where was she calling from at such an hour? She was not a worldly woman, would not know there was a four-hour time difference between the Urals and France. She would not even know where or what Deauville was.

It was lovely to hear her voice. But once again, she must have been put up to this.

They talked. This time she did mention other members of the family but mostly she again begged her son to come home. He listened, trying to imagine her face as she talked, the heavy eyebrows, the brown eyes, the parting in the middle of her hair. But, when she had finished, he said, 'Mama, you have spoken a great deal. You have told me about my sisters. But there is one thing you have not asked.'

'What is that?'

'You have not asked me if I am happy.' Nureyev had first thought of this when he had read his mother's telegram in Paris. Now he was determined to face her with it. 'Ask me if I am happy.'

'Rudik, are you happy?'

'Yes.'

The Deauville season was a success. There were no disturbances during the performances and many invitations afterwards to dine with this or that member of the international set who made the pilgrimage every year. Rudolf was particularly taken up by the Comtesse de Ribes. More important, one of the people in the audience the first night he danced in Deauville was Maria Tallchief, an American ballet star of Osage Indian descent who had once been married to George Balanchine, and was at the time just coming out of an affair with Erik Bruhn. In a stormy scene with Bruhn, during the Jacob's Pillow festival in Lee, Massachusetts, the Dane had called off their partnership, off-stage at least, and Maria had replied, 'All right, I'll find a new partner. There is a Russian that has just defected. He is in Paris and I'll find him. *He'll* be my new partner!'

She wasn't being entirely serious, and was in fact in Deauville with her young daughter and her daughter's nurse, relaxing. But, by a great coincidence, here was the Russian, in the same small town. Tallchief was very impressed by what she saw that first night and arranged to take company class with de Cuevas the next day. Once there, making contact wasn't difficult. Tall and dark, Tallchief had a magnetic stage presence of her own and in no time she and Nureyev were fast friends. She would meet him after performances and introduce him to Ciro's or other fashionable eating places, such as the Ferme St-Siméon along the coast at Honfleur.

At dinner he was more than anxious to talk about Bruhn. He told Maria how he had sat near Erik one night in Moscow and yet not been allowed to talk to him. And how he had made a film of Erik dancing. Maria told Nureyev she would be happy to arrange a meeting, once he could find the time.

After Deauville, the de Cuevas Company was scheduled to make a short tour of France, which included Biarritz and La Baule, both on the Atlantic coast. Rudolf, however, wasn't going. He was nothing if not thorough, and he knew himself. These towns had small theatres, with small stages, and he needed a large stage if he were to display his talents properly. There were other reasons, of course. Rudolf was a showman and that meant not only not appearing on small stages, but not appearing in the less fashionable spots, and not being always readily available. It might add to his reputation for being difficult but it would help make him sought after.

Besides, he was anxious to visit Copenhagen. Bruhn was not his only reason for wanting to see the Danish capital. To begin with, for a ballet dancer Denmark is by no means an out-of-the-way place. August Bournonville (1805–79) was born in Copenhagen but was awarded a ballet scholarship to Paris where he studied under Vestris and Gardel. He was eventually taken into the Paris Opéra but returned to Denmark where he signed a contract for eighteen years, as director, soloist and choreographer of the Royal Danish Ballet. During his long tenure he created a style of dancing, taken from Paris but which was more buoyant and fleet and which characterises Danish dancing to this day, making the Royal Danish Ballet one of the top five or six companies in the world. Bournonville created more than fifty ballets, among them *Napoli*, *La Ventana* and, his most famous work, *La Sylphide*. The Danes have a repertoire that is significantly different from elsewhere.

There was a third reason for Nureyev to go to Copenhagen: Vera Volkova. Volkova was an extraordinary woman who, though a fine dancer, was most well known as a teacher. Born in St Petersburg in 1904, she had studied with Vaganova and toured Japan and China, where she taught the young Margot Fonteyn in Shanghai. In 1936 she had married an English painter and architect, Hugh Williams, and moved to the Sadler's Wells in London where she taught a whole generation of British dancers. (And where, according to Fonteyn, her hilarious English kept the dancers in stitches, when they had the breath for it. 'Leg does not know is going to arabesque' was a piece of advice she once gave to Fonteyn.) In 1950 Volkova moved to La Scala and in 1951 became artistic adviser to the Royal Danish Ballet, where she remained until her death in 1975. For Nureyev she had one other attraction above and beyond all these. She was a childhood friend of Pushkin's.

Nureyev's route to Copenhagen took him via Frankfurt, where he had been commissioned to dance *Le Spectre de la rose* for a television programme. This turned into a bit of a disaster because the producer had assumed Nureyev knew the role, when in fact he didn't. They cobbled something together, helped by Pierre Lacotte, but it was not a happy experience. The music was provided by gramophone records, and the tempos were not all they might have been.

Maria Tallchief had accompanied Nureyev to Frankfurt – he seemed a solitary soul even then, and she thought he might welcome the company. An American magazine tracked them down and sent another Russian exile, Vaslav Orlikovsky, a choreographer, to watch him dance and interview him. Orlikovsky blew hot and cold, saying that while on stage Nureyev was the reincarnation of Nijinsky, and very disciplined, off stage 'he was his own worst enemy', the 'most ambitious man' Orlikovsky had ever met, 'sloppy, rude, moody . . .' He noted that Nureyev spoke Russian in a coarse way, 'showing he must have been brought up by the poorest of the poor'. In the hotel room, Orlikovsky said, Nureyev lay back listening to Mozart's *Requiem*, Brahms's Symphony No. 4, and Scriabin's *Symphonie divine*, all played full blast, while Tallchief massaged his feet. No one, said the interviewer, was allowed to talk while the music blared around the room and Nureyev, having just discovered Scriabin, played *Symphonie divine* ten times in a row.

Orlikovsky said Nureyev was a boy, that he had no concept of belongings and that everything was strewn around the hotel room. At that point he didn't seem certain that he should have defected. 'Perhaps I was wrong to jump,' he said. He told Orlikovsky he had a good idea of what he would find in the west – in other words, he *had* made enquiries. He resisted questions about his family, saying that anything he said could make it uncomfortable for them. And he then told his interviewer a complicated lie. He said his father had taught him folk dancing when he was very young and that he had been part of a ballet troupe that had gone to Leningrad seven years before. 'We played the Kirov Theatre,' he said, 'and this is where Sergeyev saw me first. He asked me if I would remain there. It was exactly what I wanted.'

He hoped to dance in Copenhagen and London, he said. He wanted to work under Balanchine and at Covent Garden. He did *not* want to stay in France.

Orlikovsky had taken him to a Russian restaurant, but the 'boy' had hardly touched his food. He had, however, consumed enormous quantities of vodka and had drunk until his eyes had become glassy. Then he had left with Tallchief and, as Orlikovsky said his goodbyes, he watched them sit on a bench overlooking a river and a factory, holding hands. The river had reminded Nureyev of the Neva. 'What a hopeless romantic!' Orlikovsky had concluded. 'I love him but he's going to have such troubles in his life.'

After the débâcle with *Spectre*, Tallchief thought she might cheer up Nureyev with a phone call to Erik. She got through and told her former lover that she was planning to come back. She then said, 'Guess who I'm with?' and put Nureyev on the line. On this first encounter both men were lost for words. All Nureyev could think of to say was 'Hello.'

They left Frankfurt by car, driving first to Amsterdam, which was more or less on the way, so that Nureyev could see more of the west. In Amsterdam he called Tamara. She already knew that he was dancing with de Cuevas because she had managed to get hold of a copy of *L'Humanité*, the communist newspaper, which had carried a highly tendentious account of the 'Bluebird' evening when the disturbances had taken place. It was an awkward conversation. In 1961 all phone calls into and out of Russia stood a chance of being tapped by the KGB. 'All that could be transmitted,' said Tamara, 'was that he was alive and he was working. Happy or not happy – you couldn't talk about those things. He understood that he couldn't tell me how happy he was in the west – I might have suffered if he had. He knew that every word was dangerous. He merely told me the dates he was dancing, and where.'

By the same token, she could not tell him what was happening at the Kirov. 'There was total silence. If his defection had happened any earlier, they would have shot everybody in the theatre. The KGB had interviewed Sergeyev when he came back from London, and he had been suspended, but only for a short while because the other, replacement dancers had been such a success. Then they turned their attention to Pushkin. They knew that Rudik had not just studied with Pushkin, but that he had lived with him as well. There was even a rumour that Rudik had slept with Tseniia, Pushkin's wife. They were trying to get Pushkin to go to Paris at this time, to try to persuade Rudik to come home. But, about this time, Pushkin's health began to suffer. He didn't go to Paris and he wasn't punished. I couldn't tell Nureyev any of this.'

Nureyev and Maria arrived in Copenhagen as lovers. Though he was predominantly – almost exclusively – homosexual, Nureyev told several people important in his life that he had slept with three women, and indeed made two of them pregnant. The first woman had been Tseniia Iurgenson, the second was Maria Tallchief and the third . . . he would meet a little later in life. He made no mention of Clara Saint.

CHAPTER NINE

This Angel, this Proud Devil

Whether from heaven or from hell
this angel, this proud devil, tell
what is he?

When they arrived in the Danish capital, Maria and Nureyev checked into the Hotel Angleterre. They phoned Bruhn at home from the bar and invited him to join them. It is important to stress Bruhn's position in the world of classical dance at that time. Born in 1928, and therefore ten years Nureyev's senior, Erik shared certain similarities with the younger man. He too had three sisters older than himself. His father, Ernst, had been an irrigation engineer in Russia, who had escaped at the time of the revolution. A solitary withdrawn child, the boy was sent to dancing school by his mother because his sisters were already there and she felt they might ease his way in making friends. Like Nureyev he did not make friends easily as a child. At dancing school it soon emerged that Erik had more talent than anyone else and he was recommended for the Royal Danish Ballet School. His formal début as a dancer took place on 4 May 1945, a propitious date in some ways. Two minutes before his solo, the British liberating forces appeared at the gates of the Tivoli Gardens – and the entire audience left the auditorium to meet them. As a result, his steps were watched by no one. 'And a good thing too,' he said later. 'I fell several times.'

Despite this hiccup, Bruhn was soon noticed in Denmark and then outside it, first in London, and then in New York where he was invited to join the American Ballet Theatre. He danced with all the major ballerinas – Sonia Arova, Alicia Alonso, Violette Verdy, Nora Kaye – but his greatest success came as Albrecht in *Giselle*, opposite Alicia Markova in 1955 at the Metropolitan Opera House in New York. The critics went overboard that night, all agreeing for once that this was a performance that made history. From that day, Bruhn was regarded as the best male dancer, certainly in the west. He had been called upon to appear with Danny Kaye in the film, *Hans Christian Andersen*, and to star on the Ed Sullivan show, in *Swan Lake* in 1957.

In 1959 he had been invited to join New York City Ballet (NYCB), whose co-directors were Lincoln Kirstein and George Balanchine. It was there that he had met Balanchine's ex-wife, Maria. For a year or so, Bruhn was a great success at NYCB and his relationship with Maria, both on and off stage, deepened. Then things started to go wrong. First Balanchine turned against him, feeling that Bruhn was now too much of a star, which contravened the choreographer's well-known and often stated principles, that NYCB should have no star system: the *ballets* were the chief attraction. At the same time, Bruhn began to grow uncomfortable with Maria, feeling she was making too many emotional claims on him. Some months before Rudolf defected, Bruhn and Maria had agreed to separate. This was when she had stormed off, vowing to find another partner.

And so when Erik arrived at the bar of the Hotel Angleterre in Copenhagen on that summer afternoon in 1961, the psychological situation between these three dancers was already somewhat complicated. For a start, Nureyev had replaced Erik in more ways than one.

It was late afternoon and the bar was very dark. Nureyev, Bruhn later told John Gruen, who wrote the Dane's biography, was dressed in a sweater and casual trousers. 'I sat down and looked at him more carefully and saw that he was very attractive. He had a certain style about him . . . a kind of class. It was not a natural elegance, but somehow it worked.' It was an awkward hour, in which Erik and Maria covered their embarrassment with a lot of laughter. Nureyev was not as taken with Erik as Erik was with him. For a start, he hated Erik's laugh.

Nevertheless, one of the reasons Nureyev was in Copenhagen was to see Erik in class and at rehearsals. Gradually, a routine was worked out which enabled Nureyev to be with Erik *and* with Maria. In the mornings, Rudolf would take the company class, where he could practise and watch Bruhn, and where Maria was also present. In the afternoons he took his own private class with Volkova, while Maria and Erik sometimes rehearsed together for an upcoming ballet they had agreed to do. And in the evenings Rudolf and Maria would go to see the Royal Danish Ballet where Erik was sometimes, but not always, appearing.

The classes, which ought to have been straightforward, in fact complicated the situation. Rudolf seemed very strange to the Danes – his technique was very different – and he didn't seem intent on making friends. He would always stand at the front of the class, while Erik practised at the back (nothing could have epitomised better what different dancers they were). Also, Nureyev was disconcerted that the others in the class did not defer to Erik, as the greatest artist among them.

After a while Maria suggested that Nureyev actually give a class himself. It would be interesting to see what lay behind his technique. And so Rudolf gave the Danes a Russian *barre*. Everyone found it unusual, so much so that Erik, the star, was forced to stop in the middle because his muscles were aching.

Nureyev had mixed feelings about Copenhagen at this point. He did not think the Bournonville style was for him. And he was secretly disappointed with Volkova's class. She had taught Semenova, Dudinskaya, Irina Kolpakova and he had therefore expected a familiar Russian routine, with Volkova pressing him forward in ways he was familiar with and would accept. What he wasn't prepared for was to find Volkova old-fashioned. He soon began to feel that although the old woman (she was fifty-seven) had studied with the great Vaganova, she had done so at a relatively early time in Vaganova's career and had not progressed as her mentor had done. He had little to learn from her.

To add to this confusion, Nureyev found that his feelings for Erik were getting in the way of his feelings for Maria. The other two were spending far more time together now, as their performances drew close (they were to dance *Miss Julie* and *Don Quixote*). Nureyev wasn't happy with this. One morning, he was watching Erik and Maria rehearse on stage. There was a break and Maria returned to her dressing-room to fix her clothing. While she was away, Rudolf approached Erik and asked quietly if the two of them could have lunch together – alone, without Maria. There was, said Nureyev, something he had to say. Erik agreed and Nureyev went off to Maria's dressing-room. He was direct as only he could be, and told her that he and Erik would be having lunch together, without her. She asked why. Again, Nureyev was direct; brutally so in fact. He had fallen in love with Erik, he said. That was why he wanted to lunch alone with him. He had to tell him.

Maria exploded. She shouted and screamed. She swore. She threw tubes of make-up at him. She tried to hit him. Until then a sort of equilibrium within the trio had been possible because Maria, spurned by Erik, had captured Rudolf. She had slept with both men. Now they had both spurned her, and for each other. Still screaming, she ran from her dressing-room. Rudolf swept after her. Erik, who saw both leave, ran after Nureyev. Unhappily, the whole episode occurred just as the rest of the company had finished its morning class. There was an audience of perhaps forty people for this bizarre scene.

When the three of them stopped chasing each other, Maria at first would not be consoled. She threatened to leave. This would have been very embarrassing for Erik so, as a gesture, he agreed to cancel his lunch that day with Nureyev. He begged Maria to stay, and even agreed to see more of her himself between then and the performances. He suggested the three of them have dinner together that very evening. For the time being, the situation was patched up.

Following this setback, Maria seems to have extracted herself with dignity, and perhaps in a way that Bruhn did not expect. In their performances on stage, when they took place, she outdanced him. Given the complex emotions then existing beneath the surface between Bruhn and Tallchief, it is perhaps no surprise that, after these incidents in Copenhagen, they never danced together again.

Falling in love with Erik was scarcely less traumatic for Nureyev than for Maria. He was twenty-three, a late starter in sexual matters, as he was in classical dance. Mikhail Baryshnikov, who was to follow Rudolf in the Pushkins' affections, recalls being told by Tseniia Iurgenson that even as late as twenty Rudolf would lie on the floor of their apartment listening to Bach and playing with a train set. Rudolf had known at least since his conversations with Gyckova, during his second year at the Vaganova when he was eighteen or nineteen, that he 'was not a man in the sense that [she] meant it.' And he had probably felt that way for some time. Nevertheless, the only sexual encounter he had allowed himself inside Russia had been that one night with Tseniia Iurgenson, when she had taken the initiative and it was obvious why she was doing it. In a very real sense, the episode was part of his training.

In Russia, the rest of the time, he had repressed his homosexuality, giving it no expression for one very simple reason: it was dangerous. Nureyev had hated Stalin's Russia but in sexual matters things had not changed so very much under Khrushchev. The surest way to be suborned by the KGB was to get caught as a homosexual. That threatened Nureyev's love of freedom too much.

So too did Sergeyev. The way he ran the Kirov, dispensing favours to young men who took his fancy and then withdrawing those favours when it suited him, did not at all attract Nureyev. The occasion in Ekaterina Square, when he had been accosted by a homosexual was frightening. He had reached school in a terrible state, only to find some other boys planning a 'gay-bashing' excursion to the very spot where he had been approached. Yet part of him had enjoyed the encounter. No wonder his manners hardly improved and he was always tense. He had to keep his sexuality under firm control and masturbation was the only release.

Then there had been his encounter with Bruhn in the Bolshoi Theatre in September the year before. Encounter is perhaps too strong a word, for they didn't meet, though Nureyev saw Erik from a short distance. He didn't fall in love with him then and there but Erik was a man who managed to remain cool both off-stage and, when Nureyev later saw the film he had commissioned, on-stage too. He was as different from Nureyev as could be and yet was a great – a very great – dancer. At the time of the Bolshoi near-meeting Nureyev was being sent away, to East Germany. It stared him in the face that the authorities in Russia would always have the power, and the ill-will, to do this sort of thing.

That month there had been the famous defectors' press conference in Moscow, and talk of defection was in the air. When Nureyev returned from Germany and saw the film of Bruhn, he wondered about the Dane's sexuality. If Nureyev were to defect then, being the calibre of dancer he was, the chances were that he would meet Bruhn. Indeed, he could *request* a meeting. Bruhn was older than Nureyev, and had a lot to teach him. Would they get on? You can't force these things.

By the time he reached the west, Nureyev was still very inexperienced sexually. Clara Saint confirms this. He slept with Maria for a variety of reasons. She was attractive; she was willing; she had slept with Erik. Nureyev was solitary and he was sex-starved. He fully realised that, even in the west in 1961, it was easier – and safer – to be heterosexual than homosexual. Finally, of course, Maria was a way of reaching Erik, the one dancer who could give Nureyev not only technical advice but advice on his career. Bruhn should be able to help Nureyev, especially now that he had danced with the de Cuevas company and knew that it did not feature in his long-term plans.

There was therefore a great deal of psychological background to Nureyev's meeting with Erik. But none of it compared to the actual meeting. For Bruhn was not only a very attractive man, physically, he was also far more complex than Nureyev had suspected. He had a light side and a dark side. He was an angel, as Pushkin would have put it, and he was a devil. He had a wicked, cutting, sarcastic sense of humour, and a dark, Danish, depressive element in his nature. Like all good dancers he ate sensibly, but he drank wildly – whisky, vodka, wine. He was a heavy smoker. Although he had a cool nature, he was also a committed sensualist who aroused strong passions in the dance world. Many ballerinas around the world were secretly in love with him. Just as many detested him and thought him malign. He had a high opinion of his intellect.

He was also a genuine bisexual. He had had several long-term relationships with females, including the dancer Sonia Arova as well as Maria. But he enjoyed the intimate company of men.

For Nureyev, as for so many others in the dance world, Erik was irresistible. Besides his personal charm, for Nureyev he also appeared to have all the important parts of his life in place. He was famous and respected in his own country, Denmark. He had danced with many of the great companies in the world including Balanchine's NYCB, the ABT, the Berlin Opera Ballet, and had partnered Sonia Arova, Lupe Serrano, Alicia Markova and Yvette Chauviré.

Nureyev had held himself back, sexually speaking, for years by now. Denmark, like most Scandinavian countries, was at that stage the most liberal environment there was for sexual matters, including homosexual matters. Nureyev was suddenly released – and for a while could not control the flood of feeling that came out. He had never been in love before.

Although Rudolf had his reservations about Volkova's method of teaching, she was still Russian, had spent her life in the ballet, and knew everybody. So he enjoyed her company. Bruhn was immensely fond of her too; he considered her his primary influence. Being Russian, but having travelled, she fully understood and sympathised with Nureyev's sexual confusion, and saw that he needed Erik as much sexually as he did in other ways. Nureyev and Eric could relax at Volkova's more than anywhere else.

There are two versions of what happened next. According to Rudolf, while he was at Vera's one night the telephone rang. She went through to the next room to take the call, but soon came back to say that it was for him, long distance. He had rather come to dread the words 'long distance', after the calls from Russia at awkward moments, but Volkova reassured him that this call wasn't from Russia. It was from London.

Nureyev was nonplussed. London might have played an important part in his plans for defection, but it hadn't worked out and, so far as he was aware, he knew no one in Britain. He went through into the next room and took up the receiver. 'Yes?'

'It was a small, composed voice,' he wrote later. 'Nothing imposing. "It's Margot Fonteyn here. Would you like to dance in my gala in London? It's to be in October, at Drury Lane".'

Nureyev was surprised – but flattered. This was an honour, surely, for Fonteyn was known all over the world, at least to ballet fans. The British ballet was, with the Russian, the best in the world at that time. However, his first thought was for practicalities. This was still a post-war world – just – and the cold war was at its height. There were travel restrictions in force and even stronger laws against earning foreign currency and transferring it from one country to another. Would he be able to get permission from de Cuevas for the gala? No less important, would the British allow him in?

Fonteyn was diplomatic. The gala, she said, was something she did every year, and was produced in aid of the Royal Academy of Dancing. All those who agreed to perform, gave their services free. Nureyev didn't mind. Indeed, he thought the lack of fee might make things easier – there would be no need for tedious red tape over pay. But both realised there would be other complicated matters to arrange and Fonteyn suggested he fly to London to discuss them.

Nureyev was against this. In the first place, he was growing tired of the incessant media circus which dogged him everywhere (he had been found in Copenhagen and his picture, and Erik's, was everywhere). In Britain, he knew, the Fleet Street tabloids were more hysterical than anywhere else. He didn't look forward to their attentions. And in the second place, he couldn't really afford the air fare. His salary from de Cuevas was hardly princely and certainly did not allow him to make jaunts by air at the drop of a hat. In 1961 air travel was not cheap.

Here too Fonteyn was his equal. To his first objection, she suggested that his visit be incognito. She would tell no one, Nureyev would arrive unannounced and he would be met by her own driver who would take him direct to London, where he could stay with her. Second, she said she would contact just one British newspaper, the *Observer*, whose ballet critic was a good friend of hers. She said she thought that if Nureyev agreed to give them one exclusive interview, they would pay for his trip, and he would not be chased from pillar to post by a pack of reporters. The interview could appear only after he had already left London.

Rudolf was impressed by the practical and down-to-earth nature of Fonteyn, and he agreed there and then. He said it might take him a few days to get a visa but he would do his best.

While he waited for the British embassy in Copenhagen to provide him with the necessary documentation, he expected the news about his trip to break in the papers. The embassy and the *Observer* surely both leaked like sieves. But the news didn't leak. Fonteyn was as good as her word and the *Observer* stumped up the cash for his ticket. Unfortunately, when he arrived at Heathrow, Fonteyn's driver, Linley, was nowhere to be seen. There was no one to meet him, not even the press, and he sat in the arrivals hall at Heathrow for three hours. By then he knew it as well as he knew Le Bourget.

After an hour, he telephoned the Fonteyn house in Thurloe Square (opposite the Victoria & Albert Museum) and simply announced 'Here Nureyev.' Fonteyn was shaken that her driver had not made contact, and even more so when, after another hour, Nureyev called again, this call coinciding with the arrival back home of the driver, empty-handed. Linley was sent back to Heathrow a second time, and again failed to make contact, perhaps because Rudolf had got tired of waiting and travelled into London by taxi. It was not a good start.

According to Fonteyn, she had originally intended to have Ulanova dance in her gala but the Russian authorities had vetoed that, since she had to dance at an important state occasion in Moscow. Then, at a meeting called to decide what to do, with Margot, the Duchess of Roxburghe and Colette Clark, co-chairing the gala, Colette Clark had mentioned Rudolf, adding that he had just finished a season with the de Cuevas Ballet. Margot thought this an excellent idea and Colette Clark then spent some weeks trying to find Nureyev, who was eventually run to earth at Volkova's. However, what then happened was not quite as Rudolf recalled events. In the first place, Volkova acted as an emissary of Rudolf's, while Colette Clark played the same role for Fonteyn. The two stars did not actually speak on that occasion.

To begin with, Nureyev insisted on dancing with Margot, but she had never seen him and didn't want to risk her reputation with an unknown quantity. In addition, she had already invited John Gilpin to dance with her in *Le Spectre de la rose*.

Colette came back to say: 'Vera says he's adamant about dancing with you, and that he's marvellous.'

'He sounds rather tiresome to me,' said Margot.

'No, they say he's extraordinary,' insisted Colette. 'Michael Wishart says that he has such a presence he only has to walk on the stage and lift his arm and you can see the swans by the lake. I think it would be wonderful if you danced with Nureyev as well as Gilpin.'

'The more I hear of him the worse he sounds.' Fonteyn was not about to give in. 'I don't mean as a dancer, but why should he decide to dance with me when he's only twenty-three and I've never even met him?'

Colette was insistent. 'Vera thinks he's a genius. She says he has "the nostrils".'

In the end, according to this account, Rudolf caved in and asked if he could dance with Rosella Hightower instead. At least she *had* danced with him and knew what he was capable of. But he had another request: would Frederick Ashton choreograph a solo for him? Ashton agreed, but circumspectly, being as unfamiliar with Nureyev as Margot was.

When he got down from the taxi in Thurloe Square, Nureyev was surprised to find that the Fonteyn home was, in fact, an embassy with a small coat of arms, in red, gold and blue, over the front door. In addition to being a world-famous ballerina, Margot Fonteyn was also wife to Tito de Arias, the Panamanian ambassador to Britain. She was standing on the steps when Rudolf arrived. '[He] seemed smaller than I had expected, probably because I was standing above him on the doorstep. He had a funny, pinched little face with that curious pallor peculiar to so many dancers from Russia. I noticed the nostrils at once.'

They had tea (five sugars for Nureyev), sizing each other up. He was very polite, she wrote in her memoirs, sitting up straight but trying to be relaxed. His English was limited but he made himself plain – concise, was the way she described it. Only when he suddenly laughed at something she had said, did she see a different side to him. 'His whole face changed. He lost the "on guard" look, and his smile was generous and captivating.'

Rudolf, for his part, had been apprehensive. He had thought she might be grand. But the pair of them hit it off from the very beginning. He found her warm, straightforward and completely unfussy. She might be the most famous dancer of her day, but she knew that the practicalities of life were always important. She gave him a room and left him to lead his own life as he wanted. That appealed to him. 'From the first moment I knew I had found a friend,' he wrote later. 'This was the brightest moment of my life since I came to the west.' Which seems hard on his relationship with Erik, or simply untrue.

That evening, Nureyev's first in Britain, Margot was dancing. But, ever thoughtful, she had arranged for him to see a performance of *Giselle* at the Ballet Rambert. Afterwards he was introduced to Marie Rambert herself, who had known Nijinsky at the time when he was working on *The Rite of Spring*. Nureyev found Madame Rambert 'an amazing vital little person who talked so fast I felt dizzy'.

Here again we have a sanitised version of the truth. Colette Clark, Fonteyn's friend who, in the star's absence, took Nureyev out that night, says that Marie Rambert and Nureyev took an instant dislike to each other and would only speak through Clark. It was all 'hideously embarrassing,' she said and afterwards, when they went to the Brompton Grill, then a very fashionable restaurant opposite Brompton Oratory and near the Fonteyn house, the table was tense until Margot appeared. She soon had everyone laughing, 'even Nureyev'.

Clark remembers Nureyev as being self-obsessed and 'withering'. He hated the way all the houses in London 'were the same' and all he wanted to know that night was how good the other male dancers were in the gala. 'He wanted to know whether they would be his rivals.'

Margot and Colette compared notes towards the end of that day. Margot said she liked him 'nine-tenths'. Her reservation, such as it was, stemmed from the fact that she thought his face reflected every thought he had, and changed rapidly. Once or twice she had caught a very cold look, and that had chilled her.

The next day, while Margot was busy again, Nureyev explored London on his own, by bus. His first stop was the National Gallery in Trafalgar Square; he then went on to the Tower of London, ending up with a walk in Hyde Park, which took him back near to Thurloe Square. He was both impressed and disappointed by London. He liked the buildings, the wide-open streets, all the parks. But he had expected it to be more like the city of Dickens.

On that second night, Margot herself was dancing *Giselle* at Covent Garden and was able to get him a ticket. He was taken by 'Alexander Bland'. Bland was the byline of the *Observer*'s ballet critic but was in fact two people, Nigel Gosling, who was also the paper's art critic, and his wife, who had danced under the name of Maude Lloyd. They were the ones who had funded his trip and that night would provide the basis for their article on Nureyev, the first in a British newspaper. Nureyev had arranged to meet him at seven but there was no sign. At five past he appeared, wearing a dark sports shirt and tight trousers. He bowed and apologised, saying he had been asleep, and reappeared five minutes later in a well-cut dark suit. The Goslings had seen him dance in Paris, and been wildly impressed. Close up, Nigel Gosling registered how tough Nureyev appeared. They arrived at Covent Garden just as the curtain was going up.

Nureyev found himself surprised by Covent Garden. Most theatres he knew by then were dominated by great chandeliers hanging from the main part of the ceiling, over the stalls. This certainly had been true of Ufa, the Maryinsky, and even the Bolshoi in Moscow. It was true of the Paris Opéra and the Royal Danish Theatre in Copenhagen. Covent Garden had no such thing – instead it had little pink shaded sconces all around the theatre. Nureyev thought this rather comical: it made the theatre more like a café. He was also distressed when the safety curtain was lowered during the interval. He had never seen this before; in Leningrad it wasn't lowered until after the audience had gone home. In Britain it was a law, strictly enforced, that the safety curtain had to be lowered once *during* each performance, while the audience were in the theatre, to prove that the device was working, and could be seen to be working. That was a real iron curtain, he wrote later.

His feelings about the performance that night were mixed. He noticed that the main difference between the British style and the Russian style lay in the acting. At the Kirov everything was expressed more or less in the dancing, whereas here at Covent Garden the acting was, in a sense, added on. To him, this was much less natural than the system he had been taught – less 'pure', he thought. At the same time, he could see that it was more dramatic and, on occasions, more moving.

But these were his only caveats. He was very impressed indeed by Fonteyn herself. Here was a musical dancer of the highest order, who moved to the rhythm instinctively, whose every muscle and bone in her body was filled with the nuances of the music. He was also impressed by the overall standard of the company. Having intended to defect in London, and having researched the company in the Kirov's excellent library, he was familiar with the names of many of the dancers. The Royal Ballet was certainly of a higher standard than the ballets in Paris, or in Copenhagen, or what he'd seen of the American Ballet Theatre in Moscow (save for Erik). Moreover, by the end of the performance he found he didn't mind the lack of a chandelier nearly as much as he had done, and the café atmosphere of the theatre was beginning to work its magic. He didn't say anything to anyone when Fonteyn met up with him after the performance, but privately he felt that, of all the places he had seen so far, London was indeed the one he would like to dance in. It was right that he had intended to defect here, he thought. It was the only real rival to the Kirov, at least in Europe.

When she wasn't working, Fonteyn was an attentive host and, over the next few days, she introduced him to many of the leading lights in the Royal Ballet. He met Sir Frederick Ashton, Dame Ninette de Valois and Sir David Webster, and he was taken to the school in Baron's Court, where he took class. Here, however, he was still in disguise –

at least theoretically. Margot had given him the name Roman Jasman, which belonged to a real Polish dancer who had also been engaged to appear in her gala. The device fooled few, especially when, on one occasion, Rudolf suddenly broke out and performed an amazing series of steps. People stared, among them Svetlana Beriosova and David Blair and broke into spontaneous applause. Nureyev charmed them by saying, 'I show off.' He paused and smiled. 'Only do once. Second time, fall over.'

Amazingly, while he was in London, no one in the press found out he was there. He returned to Copenhagen with his incognito intact. And Gosling had his scoop.

Nureyev was almost as apprehensive about his return to Denmark as he had been about his arrival in London. He fully realised that he mustn't let his feelings for Erik intimidate the other man. Bruhn did not welcome that sort of attention. Indeed, it was Maria Tallchief's overwhelming emotion for Erik that had got in the way of their relationship so very recently. At the same time, Nureyev was an exile, very much on his own, without a family or a company to act as his anchor. He was strong – very strong – but he was also anxious to experiment with all the freedoms the west had to offer, sexual freedom not least. He was therefore both surprised and flattered when, on his return from London, Erik asked him to live in his house in the Gentofte suburb of Copenhagen. It would save Rudolf a lot of money, of course, but that wasn't the only, or even the primary, reason for the invitation. Erik had decided it was more prudent, for both their sakes, to keep their private life private. If they were going to share the same bed, it was easier to live under the same roof.

For the next three months the two men lived in each other's pockets. They were seen at all the best Copenhagen restaurants, at parties, at receptions, gallery openings, first nights at the theatre, book launches. And they took class together. At that time, when Erik was more famous than Nureyev, Rudolf was more in love with the older man than the older man was with him. It wasn't just age; his technique was more refined, more polished, less raw. In class they did the same steps but their dancing could not have been more different. What Nureyev most responded to in Erik was his self-assurance, his poise, his self-control. In class they never spoke to one another, never corrected one another. Erik had his way of doing things, a way that had made him the best in the world, and it was not Nureyev's way.

Much as he admired Erik's approach and technique, much as he wanted with all his heart to be *like* Erik, Rudolf found it difficult to take at times, and he would explode in class, complaining out loud that the Danish way of doing things was not the Russian way. Erik always calmed him down, explaining that there was the Danish school and the

Russian school and that they were different. One was not necessarily better than the other. Nureyev found this hard to grasp at first.

Rumours about the couple began to circulate in Copenhagen. The rumours were not always flattering and not always true. Many people seem to have thought their friendship was phoney, an act got up for the cameras, to further their careers. They were so different, both as people and as dancers, that they could not really be friendly, could they? Others thought that the younger, less experienced Nureyev was 'bleeding' Erik, the older man of the world, taking everything from him and giving little in return.

This wasn't true. For nearly three months the couple enjoyed each other's company and Nureyev, at least for a while, felt settled. Erik was becoming the emotional anchor he had lacked. For the first time, Nureyev knew tenderness. His preferred sexual position was as the passive partner, the recipient. As one later lover put it, Nureyev's whole life was spent searching for a husband. Later on in life he would change, crudely, and let his potential partners know that, if their sexual equipment was larger than his, they would make love to him and, if not, the position would be reversed. But with Erik he was always the passive partner and this was very important psychologically. For one thing, in adopting this position, he was acknowledging to himself, in the Russian tradition, that he was an instinctive, a born homosexual. The discovery of the anus as an erogenous zone was also a surprise. It would encourage his promiscuity later in life.

Only two problems disturbed this idyll in Copenhagen. The first was Erik's mother. Nureyev didn't get on with Ellen – they had taken a violent dislike to each other on sight, and never got over it. Erik put it down to the fact that she was a Scorpio and Nureyev a Pisces. This was something else that Nureyev picked up from Erik – a fascination with astrology and horoscopes that never left him. The second problem arose when Erik received a letter from the Soviet embassy in Copenhagen. About a year before, when he had been touring Russia with the American Ballet Theatre, Bruhn had received an invitation from Gosconcert, the state-run agency in charge of cultural contacts with foreign countries, to appear for a season with the Bolshoi. He had accepted with pleasure, feeling enormously flattered. When the letter arrived, it was in Russian. Erik handed it to Rudolf to translate. He wasn't expecting the bombshell it contained, for as Nureyev read, it became clear that the Bolshoi had changed its mind, and Erik's appearances there were to be 'postponed'. Gradually he realised that his relationship with Rudolf had not gone unnoticed and the KGB had exacted its price.

This was very upsetting for both men and they began to think about leaving Copenhagen for somewhere more cosmopolitan, somewhere bigger where they and their relationship wouldn't be so obvious. As luck would have it, the Russian letter was soon followed by a phone call, this time from Anton Dolin in London, asking if Erik would be prepared to partner Sonia Arova, a Bulgarian-born dancer who had trained under Serge Lifar in Paris, in a group Dolin was putting together for a two-week season in London. Now, Arova had been Erik's first love, before Maria, so this proposal was not exactly risk-free, emotionally speaking. However, she was living in Paris at the time, and they could rehearse together there. Paris was a good distance from Copenhagen, it was a city Nureyev knew and liked, and sexually it was about as liberated as you could get. Erik accepted.

They travelled by train, Nureyev apprehensive that his travel papers would not be sufficient, and that the KGB would kidnap him *en route*. Neither fear proved justified, but when they arrived in Paris Rudolf was knocked off his stride by Arova. He thought there was a marked resemblance between her and Maria Tallchief! In fact, Nureyev needn't have worried. Their time in Paris was golden, and for two reasons. In the first place, Erik and Sonia got on very well and their dancing seemed better than ever, putting all of them in a good mood. Second, now that he was away from Copenhagen, and his mother, Erik was much more relaxed. With his dancing going well, with domestic pressures removed, *he* suddenly started to fall for Rudolf much as Nureyev had fallen for him earlier on. Arova was making no emotional demands on him (she had realised some time before that Erik was a true bisexual), and so, for the first time in his life, Nureyev was properly loved. This was not what he had specifically come to the west for, but it was liberating none the less.

Clara Saint saw a change come over Nureyev now. Their friendship was already beginning to fade, as she tired of his moodiness and narcissism. On his first visit to Paris, as a member of the Kirov, Saint says she hadn't guessed Rudolf was homosexual. He never once sent her flowers, never paid for anything in fact and, in general, he seemed like a raw student. He drank tea, and ate soup. But now she found him very obviously Erik's lover, and they were both drinking heavily, vodka and wine. She admired Erik as a dancer but didn't care for the influence he was having on Nureyev. She and Rudolf went to a Russian restaurant, Dominique's in Montparnasse. The waiters were all old White Russians but nonetheless Rudolf made Clara order. She thought this was curious until she realised that he was ashamed of his peasant Russian accent.

At about the end of September they all travelled to London. Erik and Sonia performed first, at the Golders Green Theatre and the Streatham Hill Theatre. At one of the performances, Ninette de Valois sat in the audience and, afterwards, asked Erik to join the Royal Ballet for the forthcoming season. Rudolf was green with envy.

The next month Rudolf was back in London for Fonteyn's gala. There was nothing anonymous about his arrival this time. Nigel Gosling, for the *Observer*, attended at least some of the rehearsals. He also took on Arnold Haskell, whose piece on Nureyev, saying he was spoilt and would be just a nine-days' wonder, had attracted a lot of notice. Gosling was one of the few people who had seen Nureyev dance in Paris and had also seen the Kirov in London. Writing as 'Alexander Bland', he pointed out that Nureyev could not have been spoiled all that much for his reception in Paris was actually *less* rapturous than Soloviev's in London. He also said that when he had congratulated Nureyev on his performance at the Palais Garnier, the Russian had said, 'Ah, but you should see Soloviev.' This, commented Bland, did not sound like the behaviour of a spoiled child.

John Lanchbery, the Royal Ballet's principal conductor, was at the very first rehearsal with Nureyev, as were Frederick Ashton and a pianist. Nureyev had chosen the music himself, Scriabin's *Poème tragique*, and Ashton had devised a completely new piece for the young newcomer. The first thing Ashton did was to ask the dresser to fetch from the wardrobe room the cloak that was used in *Giselle*. While they were waiting, Ashton, with a slight smirk on his face, announced that he was going 'to try a bit of cock-teasing.' When the cloak was brought, Ashton had Nureyev wrap it around him, then sent him right to the back of the stage until he could go no further. He bade the pianist start the piece. After a few bars, he indicated to Lanchbery the moment at which he wanted the curtain to rise. Then he shouted to Nureyev to run forward.

He did so.

'No, no,' said Ashton. 'I want you to run, to *really* run. Be wild and don't stop until you get to the footlights.'

They started again, and this time Nureyev ran so fast that the cloak billowed out behind him. Ashton smiled.

When they turned to the dress rehearsal for the Black Swan *pas de deux*, Nureyev became very difficult. However slowly Lanchbery played the music, Nureyev called out, 'Slower! Slower!'

'I can't go any slower, Rudi,' Lanchbery cried. 'It won't work dramatically.'

Nureyev stopped. 'When I dance in Russia, always going slower.'

Whereupon a voice came from the wings. 'Come on, Rudi. How often have you danced this in Russia?' It was Erik, calling Nureyev's bluff. There was no more talk of slowing the music.

Margot and Colette Clark watched some of the later rehearsals. They were, Fonteyn reports, a riot. Nureyev was earnest, most anxious to please, to make his mark. Already in those days he was concerned about catching cold, and would keep stopping, either to put on his leg-warmers, or to take them off. At intervals he would change his shoes. At each change, his breathing could be heard, which sounded to Fonteyn like a 'sibilant "Ho".' She and Colette were creased up with laughter most of the time.

But they were laughing with him, not at him. He showed great strength, not just strength of character, and they warmed to his dedication. Margot finally fell for him completely when at the end of one rehearsal she asked him if he shouldn't preserve some of his strength for the actual performance. He looked at her with amazement. 'In Paris,' he said, 'I never once finish variation!' When she asked if it might not be better if he did, 'He considered the point as though it were an original idea.'

Finally, the day of the gala arrived. It was an afternoon performance, not at Covent Garden itself but at the Drury Lane Theatre nearby, where many musicals were staged. Anticipation was so high in the ballet world that Covent Garden had to keep a doorman at the main entrance all day, to remind people that the performance was not there but at Drury Lane. Before the curtain went up Margot visited all the dressing-rooms to wish the artists good luck and to see if they had everything they needed. Rudolf was in a panic. 'They send the wrong wig!' he cried, and indeed they had. He was scheduled to dance the Black Swan *pas de deux* with Rosella Hightower and he was holding a blond wig, very like the wig he had worn for the de Cuevas first night, when he had described his own appearance as 'a Christmas tree'. It was too late to change but Nureyev never wore a wig again.

Though it was an afternoon performance, the audience was glittering. Cecil Beaton and Diana Cooper were among those in the stalls.

As the opening bars of *Poème tragique* were heard, the auditorium settled and, a moment later, the curtain rose for London to get its first glimpse of the Russian. Exactly as in the rehearsal Nureyev's first steps in London were his wild run the whole depth of the stage, full tilt, and his striking red cloak billowed behind him. He had now perfected his run and was able to stop suddenly right on the edge of the footlights. This was a striking piece of theatre, as Ashton had known, old-fashioned cock-teasing in fact, and the entire audience gasped. The gasp was so loud that, for a moment, Nureyev was disconcerted and was force to ad-lib a few steps because he had forgotten what he was supposed to do. But he soon picked up again and the effect was – well, it was a shock. It was a shock even for Erik because this was actually the first time he had seen Nureyev on stage. 'Seeing Rudik on stage was a shock. He had a tremendous presence and it was inspiring. I must confess I was not taken with his Black Swan [with the blond wig] – something was still missing. But the Ashton work was superb.'

Others thought so too. Cecil Beaton confided to his diary that he felt 'rejuvenated' by the experience (he was fifty-seven), as though an electric current had been switched on. 'My very blood stream was altered by the thrill of what was being performed.' At the end of the gala, a crowd mobbed Nureyev and Rosella outside the stage door. People were not content with Nureyev's autograph; as a Russian defector they wanted to touch him and would stop at nothing to do so. Rosella was carrying her costume over her arm and it was badly torn in the crush. It took all Margot's skill to get Rosella into the car that was waiting for them, and away to safety. This episode had a marked effect on Margot.

That evening there was a party at the Fonteyns' house in Thurloe Square, for the cast to celebrate and relax. Beaton had been invited.

'I kissed [Nureyev] on the cheek and forehead. He was very surprised but I felt the consistency of his smooth, poreless, vellum skin, and was pleased that I had made such a public fool of myself. When I talked to Freddie Ashton about the dance I could not keep back the tears in spite of kicking the door hard behind me. Perhaps it is something other than this afternoon's experience that reduced me to such a state of hysteria.'

Nureyev's manners were still somewhat raw. Fonteyn tells the story of how one 'old woman' approached him and gushed that, before she left, she just *had* to speak to him. Why? he asked bluntly. (In fact, this wasn't an old woman. It was David Carritt, the art dealer, who then worked for Christie's.) But he did teach Colette Clark the twist that night. He began by saying 'Adopt fourth position.'

Margot always remembered that Nureyev stayed very late at the party, talking as best he could in his limited English. Eventually, as the last guests were leaving he approached her and asked if her driver might take him to the King's Road. This was a part of London, in Chelsea, that was fast developing as a stylish, bohemian area, full of clothes boutiques, restaurants and night clubs. Nureyev was already aware of where 'the action' was in London.

When the guests had gone and Margot and Tito were unwinding over a last drink, by themselves, she asked him what he thought of the Russian. Tito remarked that he had said something very odd.

What was that?

'I asked him what he was doing in Copenhagen,' Tito had said. 'He had frowned and replied, "Is story better not told".'

CHAPTER TEN

The KGB File: 2 – The Secret Trial

It was a mark of the esteem and affection in which Nureyev was held by some people in Leningrad that before he danced in the gala with Fonteyn he received a telegram at Drury Lane wishing him good luck. This was from Russian balletomanes, who had heard of the forty telegrams he had been sent by the dancers at the Kirov, on the occasion of his first night with the de Cuevas in Paris, urging him to go home. On 17 March 1962, Rudolf's twenty-fourth birthday, a group of his fans and followers – women mostly – gathered in the 'Sever' (North) café, on Nevsky Prospekt. This was an act of homage, a commemoration. They talked of Rudolf, ate his favourite ice-cream, and reminisced. Some ten to twelve of these loyal aficionados kept up this memorial for many years. As time went by, although the Soviet press maintained its silence on Rudolf, the more independent Yugoslav and Polish newspapers carried snippets of news. These would be collected throughout the year and brought to the Sever meetings. Rudolf retained a following.

But there was another side. In autumn 1961 Nureyev stood trial – in his absence – in Leningrad. As a defector he was accused of treason. The trial was 'open' in the Soviet context, in that witnesses were allowed. But that was as far as it went; members of the general public were excluded. The giving of evidence lasted from at least 19 September to 3 November and more than 90 pages of the testimony were made available to the author. Under the judicial system used, there was one judge and two jurors; the jurors only had half a vote each, whereas the judge had one, so could not be outvoted. Among those giving evidence were, in the following order: Pushkin; Sergeyev; Alla Osipenko; a certain Terasov, a stage worker and probably a KGB agent; Grosinsky, head administrator; Virsalodzy, ballet master; Fidler, a soloist; Tseniia Iurgenson; Strizhevsky, a 'KGB worker' (one of the 'men in civvies' who observed the Paris tour); and Korkin. Ten witnesses, at least.

Pushkin reiterated that Nureyev had lived with him, 'like one of the family'. He told the court that the boy was 'very nervy', that he was awkward in his dealings with people, but that he had never noticed 'any far-sighted political viewpoint held by him . . . I think he took the decision to stay [in the west] in a fit of passion'. Osipenko said that Nureyev

'wasn't respected by the collective as a person. We condemned him for his cheek and swear words and conceit and for other things. He treated the people around him with disdain. He was rude and coarse to everybody. Authority didn't exist for him. He was a gifted, talented dancer. He knew this. He considered himself to be irreplaceable . . . In France a lack of discipline manifested itself. He used to go out alone and would come back late to the hotel . . . he had relations with homosexuals. Bockadoro [perhaps the other KGB officer on the tour] said that he [Nureyev] had told French people that the theatre wouldn't give him work, that he wasn't free to do what he wanted.'

Terasov, the stage worker and one of the KGB's people inside the Kirov, said like everyone else that Nureyev was a talented dancer but that he had formed very close French friends. He thought Nureyev was closer to Claire Motte than to Clara Saint. Grosinsky said he had been told the day before they left Paris that Nureyev wouldn't be going to London, and that when Nureyev was told, at the airport, he kept saying, over and over, 'Kak Tak?,': 'How can that be? How can that be?' Tseniia Iurgenson repeated what Pushkin had said, but added that, in the interim, ie., since the defection, Nureyev had called her. It is not clear from the testimony whether this was meant to imply that Nureyev was missing Russia, and his friends, or just keeping in touch.

But the most interesting testimony came from Strizhevsky, the KGB man on the tour. He said that he had been told, on 14 June – forty-eight hours before the flight to London – that Nureyev was to be sent to Moscow. These orders, which came from the Ministry of Culture in Moscow via the Soviet embassy in Paris, stipulated that Nureyev was not to be told until the day of his departure. Korkin confirmed this in his testimony, also saying that he had registered a protest, on behalf of the theatre management, since Nureyev had been such a success in Paris, but that he had been overruled. Korkin was then told, by Moscow, that Nureyev was to be informed of the decision only at Le Bourget airport. When he was told, according to Korkin, Nureyev said, 'Etoro ne mozket but' ('It can't be so').

The court also heard two intriguing pieces of testimony, which were both recordings. One was between N. Karbopel, the general secretary in the French department of the Soviet Ministry of Foreign Affairs, and a certain Nemchun, a Soviet embassy worker in Paris. The other was between Mikhail Klemenov, First Secretary at the Soviet Paris embassy, and a senior editor of *Russian News*, who was not named in the documents made available. From these discussions it emerged that Nureyev had let it be known, to theatre people he met, as well as newspaper people, that he didn't want to return to the Soviet Union. Nureyev was also observed having sexual relations with Pierre Lacotte, who tried to persuade him to stay in France. Lacotte was, apparently, the most forceful of contacts, urging Nureyev to defect, and accusing him of being 'faint-hearted'. These witnesses also claimed that Nureyev had relations with Claire Motte, and with Raymondo de Larrain. Apparently, during his discussions with de Larrain, it had been agreed that, following his return to the Soviet Union, de Larrain would invite him to dance with de Cuevas. In view of France's relations with the Soviet Union, there were high hopes that this would work. On this account, even Rosella Hightower said to Nureyev, while he was in Paris, 'The west is waiting for you.'

The jurors in this trial, it should be said, although they were 'ordinary' men and women by Soviet standards, were of course party members with 'sound' views on communism. They proved this with their verdict: not only did they find Nureyev guilty of treason but they called for a heavy sentence – fourteen to twenty years' imprisonment.

What followed was curious. The judge decided to lighten the sentence. He did so because of the testimony of Tseniia Iurgenson. The authorities did not know at that stage (and may never have known) that Nureyev had slept with Tseniia, but the judge took the view that, because Nureyev had telephoned Tseniia, he was missing Russia and was in two minds as to whether he should return. The judge reduced the sentence to six to seven years, and made an order that, if Nureyev *did* return home, his case would be reopened and 're-analysed'. This was intended to send signals to Nureyev that, if he did the decent thing, he could expect still more lenient treatment.

Although the proceedings in the court were closed, in the western sense of the word, the authorities were well aware that the verdict would get back to Nureyev. The witnesses – Pushkin, Tseniia, Sergeyev, Osipenko – would be bound to relay what had happened and the ballet world would soon be awash with the news. In fact the news did not percolate to the general public in any detail, although Nureyev soon learned what had happened. As he was so bright, it did not escape him that the message being sent out of Russia was barbed. In being so 'lenient', the court was in effect inviting him back. He could have every hope, they were saying, that when his case was re-analysed he would be allowed to defend himself, argue his corner, and in all likelihood end up with 'only' a few years' exile, after which . . . who knows?

On the other hand, if he *didn't* respond to this offer, what then? Nureyev himself was in no doubt. He may or may not have known at that stage about Department OS2, and the 'travelling executioners', as they were called. But he fully realised that if he stayed in the west and became ever more successful, then the higher his profile, the greater the likelihood that he would become a target for kidnapping, and worse.

CHAPTER ELEVEN

Queen of Secrets

the moon
through heaven's expanse serenely flying,
that queen of secrets and of sighing

Although *Poème tragique*, the Ashton sequence he had danced at
Margot's gala, was a short piece, that did not deter most critics from
writing full-scale reviews of Nureyev's performance. 'A true genius,' is
how Oleg Kerensky described him in the *Telegraph*. 'The new Nijinsky?
I never saw him dance but Nureyev is the most exciting dancer I have
ever seen. The Black Swan *pas de deux* stopped the show and had to
be repeated. It is not often we can hail a new star of such brilliance.
It must not be long before he is seen here again.' 'Alexander Bland'
in the *Observer* said Nureyev was a 'Balletic missile . . . something
utterly different, a strange haunted artist whose medium happens to
be dance'. He had a savage intensity, said Bland, that produced a shock
akin to 'seeing a wild animal loose in the drawing room.' Richard Buckle,
the most flamboyant of the London critics, compared Nureyev not to
Nijinsky but to Chaboukiani. Calling him the 'Rimbaud of the Steppes',
his view was that Nureyev *should* join the Royal Ballet. 'He would enjoy
the discipline.'

Buckle was responding to a campaign, organised by the Covent Garden
gallery, to bring Nureyev to the Royal Ballet. The campaign had 2,000
signatures.

But not everyone was impressed. One critic described *Poème tragique*
as 'Ashton's tawdry show', and *Ballet Today* said Nureyev's appearance
in the piece had been 'unhappy', adding that almost every aspect of his
début was ill-fated. The music was unrhythmic, the costumes gauzy, his
face had an 'inappropriate feminine cast', his hair suggested an English
sheepdog, and his 'haphazard' arm movements, which were supposed

to express the anguish of the soul, 'in fact expressed nothing at all'. His technical shortcomings were surprising in a lead dancer of the Kirov, his *plié* especially being weak. *Dance and Dancers* couldn't make up its mind. It said he was no paragon, like Bruhn, no overnight sensation, like Soloviev, and that his faults could not pass unnoticed. Yet the magazine's reviewer concluded, 'Make no mistake; this is the sort of dancer on whom legends alight.'

A few days later, Richard Buckle had the idea of asking several leading lights in the ballet world what they thought of Nureyev, mainly because so many had disagreed with the moderately critical line of his earlier article. Perhaps the most considered assessment came from Tamara Karsavina, who had seen both Nijinsky and Nureyev. She agreed with Buckle, and one or two others, that Nureyev landed badly. She thought he danced many steps better than Nijinsky, and that he had a better line than the earlier star; but she also said he lacked Nijinsky's 'gift for pausing in the air'.

In a sense, however, the critics didn't matter, and the public didn't matter. Only one person mattered to Nureyev. He wanted to dance for the Royal Ballet and therefore he had to impress Ninette de Valois, the artistic director. Her reaction, characteristically enough, was different from everyone else's. She was at the gala of course and, later on, recorded her reactions in her memoirs, *Step by Step*:

> The dances that he executed on this occasion left me dissatisfied. I did not feel that they told me anything about the dancer. Eventually he took his bows in front of the red curtain. I saw an arm raised with a noble dignity, a hand expressively extended with that restrained discipline which is the product of a great traditional schooling. Slowly the head turned from one side of the theatre to the other, and the Slav bone-structure of the face, so beautifully modelled, made me feel like an inspired sculptor rather than the director of the Royal Ballet. I could see him suddenly and clearly in one role – Albrecht in· *Giselle*. Then and there I decided that when he first danced for us it must be with Fonteyn in that ballet.

A few days later de Valois called Fonteyn into her office and asked her if she would like to be his partner. Fonteyn's instinct was to say that it would be like mutton dancing with lamb. But something inside her told her to wait, and to give de Valois an answer the following day. When she got home that evening she discussed the plan with Tito. He was a worldly man and told her she was being naïve. It was clear, he said, that the young Russian was going to be a big hit next season. She had better be a part of that bandwagon or risk ending her career in eclipse. This was showman's talk coming from a diplomat, but none the less she phoned de Valois the next morning to accept the offer.

Nureyev hadn't even been consulted.

After his triumph at the gala, Rudolf rejoined the de Cuevas Ballet in Hamburg. This was a dismal anticlimax for he found that his role in *Sleeping Beauty* had been cut and he was to dance only in the second act. But that wasn't the only bad news. It turned out that the company wasn't performing in Hamburg's fine opera house as he had assumed, but in a cabaret theatre in the notorious Reeperbahnstrasse, a red-light area. Rudolf was very upset by this: it reminded him of the times when he had danced with the circus in East Germany and reinforced his view that the de Cuevas company, though it had helped him when he most needed help, was not an 'establishment' company, was part of no fine tradition. He was not looking forward to the performance.

He need not have worried. Shortly after he arrived, the phone rang in his hotel room and he was told that the performance had been cancelled. A stage-hand had pressed the wrong button during a runthrough and had set off the fire sprinklers. The sets were drenched and the stage had been flooded. Rudolf was angry and relieved at the same time, but in his autobiography he didn't give the real reason why the sprinklers had been set off. It was yet another demonstration against him, by communists. That at least was the conclusion of Olivier Merlin, *Le Monde*'s ballet critic, who was closely following Rudolf's career. In an article he wrote the following week, Merlin revealed that every time he wrote something favourable about Rudolf he – Merlin – received anonymous hate mail, inspired, he thought, by the Soviet embassy. He realised that Rudolf himself must be receiving far more and that this emphasised the young dancer's solitude. Merlin developed this theme in his article, saying presciently that Rudolf had already outgrown de Cuevas and he wondered what was the right course for the future. Covent Garden was too rigid (he characterised it as 'le style horse guard'), Paris was difficult because of 'the diplomatic situation', Copenhagen was 'Bournonville, Bournonville et encore Bournonville'. Nureyev had no work permit for the United States. 'At the moment,' Merlin concluded, 'Nureyev is at sea, and not just in Hamburg.'

Rudolf went first to Munich, to see Erik dance in *Swan Lake*, then returned to Paris, where to his delight he learned in the space of a few days that he was to dance in *Giselle* with both Margot Fonteyn and Yvette Chauviré. Chauviré was a French star whom he had seen dance in Russia; she had scored such a big hit with her 'Dying Swan' that she had been asked to repeat it three times.

But he already had other ideas, too. Or rather, he and Erik did. It was a natural extension of their relationship that they should want to dance together, on stage. In between their other engagements, they decided to form a little company of their own. Not only would this enable them to dance together; it would give both of them the chance to try their hand at choreography. They discussed partners and eventually decided on Rosella and Sonia. By now Sonia was perfectly at home with Erik's domestic arrangements with Rudolf, so much so that the three of them rented an apartment together overlooking the sea at Cannes. Rosella was based in Cannes, where she was just starting her own school, and had her own studio – almost as big as the Bolshoi stage – which was permanently available for them to rehearse in.

Cannes was agreeable in winter. Warm but relatively deserted, it seemed at times as though they had the whole Croisette to themselves. Both of the men devised deliberately difficult new pieces for them all to dance, to extend themselves. Erik's was a 'Fantasia on a Spanish Theme', using a Bach toccata, while Rudolf created a new version of the *adagio* in *The Nutcracker* and a *pas de quatre* to music by Glazounov. The difficulty of the pieces – which has been confirmed by Sonia Arova – was to prove important.

All four dancers were now sufficiently well known in France for every performance to be sold out in advance. Before the first night took place, however, Rudolf created yet more controversy. Rosella and he had been invited to dance in a version of *La Fille mal gardée*, in Marseilles. The new version had been created by an Italian choreographer, Lazzini, whom Rudolf admired, but what really struck home that evening was the nature of the Marseilles crowd. Before the ballet had gone very far, a cacophony of catcalls and whistles rose above the sounds of the orchestra. It seemed that the communists of the south were not to be outdone by their comrades in the north. As in Paris, others in the audience joined in the uproar, and started to cheer and applaud. There was no clear victory for either side that night, as there had been in Paris, but it helped add to the mystique surrounding Rudolf.

Following this uproar in Marseilles and before their Cannes début, Rudolf rejoined the de Cuevas company for the last part of its tour, in Italy. Nina Vyroubova noticed that Rudolf was already changed – he was more princely. Erik, she felt, was having an effect. In Italy they danced in rapid succession in Turin, Genoa and Bologna, ending up in Venice. Italy was surprisingly cold, and when the company reached Venice it had been snowing. In his autobiography, Rudolf wrote: 'The canals ran smooth and grey between the fantastic fairy-tale houses on which every detail of carving and iron-work was edged with white.' The hotel was so cold that Rudolf was forced to leave his room and walk about to keep warm.

La Fenice Theatre in Venice is a jewel but it is also fairly small. When the end of the tour came and Rudolf bade goodbye to the de Cuevas company, he was not sorry to go. He had no certain future, apart from the new company which he shared with Erik, and his *Giselle* with Fonteyn in February, but he now knew deep inside him that he needed a bigger world than de Cuevas was able to give him. It had been a great prop, but it was no longer enough.

*   *   *

The Cannes performances with Erik, Rosella and Sonia opened on 6, January 1962 and were repeated a few nights later. They then moved to Paris, where they appeared at the Théâtre des Champs-Elysées on 12 and 13 January. Although the theatre was packed with an enthusiastic audience, critical reception was less keen. The idea of the evening was simple: the Company of Four, as they thought of themselves, was the dance analogy of a musical quartet, an ensemble of four soloists who would provide a full evening's entertainment without the need for full orchestration, or elaborate sets and scenery. Besides the new pieces devised by Erik and Rudolf, there were excerpts from *Raymonda* and *The Flower Festival at Genzano*. Marie-François Christout, writing in *Dance and Dancers*, summed up the evening:

> The recital may have been of more interest to a sociologist than a dance critic. It resolved itself into something in three more or less equal parts – dancing, hysterical applause from a roaring mob, and intervals. That such artists should lend their talents to this type of circus enterprise seems utterly regrettable.

Perhaps the critic was exaggerating as much in her way as the 'mob' was in its. Neither Erik nor Rudolf nor the others had wanted a circus atmosphere but, after Marseilles, it was inevitable.

Olivier Merlin was there too, and as usual was both more sympathetic and more perspicacious. The performance was excellent and Rosella Hightower, he said, had never been better. But he concentrated his attention on Rudolf. He saw that he had been helped by Erik, who was not a jealous man. Erik, he said, was a better choreographer than Rudolf. Rudolf was trying too hard to be a noble dancer, like Erik, whereas he should strive to be more exciting, as was more natural for him. Don't be so haughty, he lectured Rudolf. Let's have the occasional smile. Merlin seems to have truly understood Rudolf in those days. He concluded this review by remarking that next day Erik and Rudolf were off to New York, where Rudolf's great hope had to be Balanchine. He had detected a Balanchine influence in Rudolf's own choreography, he said, and that pointed to where the young man's future lay.

At that point, Nureyev was besotted with Erik and, in dancing terms, wanted to match him step for step. Erik was flattered even though the two men were fighting a lot. Everyone found Nureyev's moods difficult. If he had a bad day, he simply wouldn't speak. He wouldn't say 'Hello' or 'Good morning' but would barge around the rehearsal room. Sometimes this would be taken to ridiculous proportions. He wanted a car, so he bought one. But he couldn't drive. He asked Rosella to teach him and chose the haute Corniche, above Monte Carlo, as the place to learn. Conceivably the most dangerous road in Europe, this is where Princess Grace was killed, but Nureyev liked the view. Rosella declined to risk her neck and Nureyev did not have his driving lesson; not then, anyway.

Though he had been right about the departure of Erik and Rudolf for New York, what Olivier Merlin didn't know when he wrote his article was that, during the last performance of the evening, Erik had injured himself. Moreover, since the pieces were very ambitious and technically demanding, they had quickly tired out all the dancers. As a result, Erik's injury was serious. This was a disaster, as Erik had been booked to appear on the *Bell Telephone Hour* on NBC, dancing the *Flower Festival pas de deux* with Maria. Sonia Arova, who went to New York ahead of Erik and Rudolf, was deputed to suggest to NBC that Nureyev replace Bruhn in the TV slot. This was very generous and meant that, once NBC agreed (which they did immediately), Rudolf was seen by millions of Americans.

Rudolf disliked flying at the best of times but that first flight across the Atlantic was one of the worst experiences he ever had. As the plane approached America, the weather got rougher and rougher. By the time the DC8 was over New York, the storm was so bad that the aircraft was diverted to Chicago. There they were forced to wait in the plane for three hours until the storm had abated, before flying back to Manhattan. He arrived exhausted.

No one was really expecting Nureyev on that trip, so for once he was left pretty much to himself. He appeared on NBC on 19 January 1962, but not a single US newspaper, daily or Sunday, reviewed his performance. There *was* a report that he was to appear in a Hollywood film about Nijinsky (the first of many abortive projects), in which Nureyev would dance but the star would be Horst Buchholz. But the real highlight of that short trip, as Olivier Merlin had foreseen, was a meeting with Balanchine.

Nureyev's obsession with Balanchine needs some explanation. George Balanchine was a fellow Russian and a graduate of the Kirov School. He had worked under Diaghilev and set up his own company in New York. Balanchine was probably the most respected figure, worldwide, in ballet at that time, and conceivably the most important artist in ballet history in the entire post-war period. W.H. Auden once described him as the most intuitive person he had ever known. 'Ideas come to him as images, not abstractions . . . He's not an intellectual, he's something deeper, a man who understands everything.'

Balanchine was omnivorous. Bernard Taper, in his witty biography, described him in this way:

'He liked Braque, Pushkin, Rockefeller, Stravinsky, Sousa, Jack Benny, Piero della Francesca, fast cars, science fiction, TV westerns, French sauces, and American ice cream . . . He patronised only the best and costliest tailors, but the clothes he fancied

were a sort of Russianised version of a Wild West dude's garb
– bright pearl-buttoned shirts, black string tie, gambler's plaid
vest, frontier pants. On him, these surprising outfits appeared
natural and elegant. He lived for almost fifty years in America
and remained enthusiastic about it the whole time. He loved the
way it looked, sounded and smelled; on occasion he would even
remark what a pleasure it was to pay taxes to support a country
it was such a pleasure to live in.'

On ballet, Balanchine told Taper that, 'It's like coffee, it never tastes
as good as it smells.' But his whole life was dedicated to improving ballet.
Born in St Petersburg in 1904 as Georgi Melitonovich Balanchivadze,
he took to dance when he accompanied his sister to an audition at
the Imperial Ballet School, and he tried too, having little better to
do. He was accepted; she wasn't. By the time he was sixteen he
was producing his first choreography. He left Russia in 1924 and was
almost immediately taken up by Serge Diaghilev of the Ballets Russes,
where he became ballet master. The list of painters Balanchine worked
with on Ballets Russes was extraordinary: Rouault, Utrillo, Miró, Gris,
Ernst, de Chirico, Braque, Derain, Tchelichev and Matisse. By then he
had de-Russianised his name.

In 1928, a year before Diaghilev died, Balanchine produced *Apollo*, a
highly classical ballet at the height of the jazz age and his work changed
for all time. He had found his own 'language' to work in. After Diaghilev's
death, he was rootless for several years, working in Britain among other
places, and with Bertolt Brecht and Kurt Weill. But in the mid-1930s he
teamed up with Lincoln Kirstein, a well-educated and wealthy American
balletomane, and migrated to New York. Together, the two men started
the American Ballet School and a company of the same name, which
enjoyed brief stardom when it was taken on as the Metropolitan Opera's
in-house ballet company. The good fortune didn't last, however, despite
Stravinsky himself acting as conductor on occasions, and in 1938 the
company ceased to exist.

Balanchine spent several of the war years choreographing Hollywood
musicals, including *On Your Toes*, *The Boys from Syracuse* and *An
American in Paris*. In 1946, following Kirstein's return from the war
– where he had been involved in tracking down art which the Nazis had
looted – the two men created a new company, Ballet Society. This did
well and, in 1948, became the New York City Ballet.

But Balanchine was far more than the artistic director of a single
company. He was known as the very embodiment of a quintessentially
modern form of choreography which was not so much 'abstract' (a term
some critics used, though he himself disliked it) as plotless. Balanchine
stood for everything that the classics were not. *He* had moved on, he
had invented a new language for dance, changing it for all time. The

mantle of Petipa and Fokine had passed to him, being transformed in the process. His world was very different to the one Nureyev had inhabited, though he had been told about Balanchine since his earliest days at the Vaganova. Like all dancers, he recognised Balanchine's genius, his sublime creativity, the new forms of beauty that he had fashioned, the fact that there was no one else quite like him. Dancing for Balanchine would complete his artistic growth, help make him whole and be a different kind of recognition. More, Balanchine was surrounded by people of talent, people like John Taras, ballet master of NYCB and a choreographer himself. Taras had worked with Erik and with Maria Tallchief; he knew British ballet well, and was very familiar with Russian music. There was a sense in which Rudolf would feel at home at NYCB.

Barbara Horgan was then assistant manager of New York City Ballet and one of her jobs was to give away seats that hadn't been sold, to distinguished members of the public. One night Betty Cage, the manager, told her that she was sending Nureyev to the theatre 'alone.' Horgan found him charming and showed him to his seat. Subsequently she was standing backstage when Balanchine came up to her and said, 'We're going across the road, to Castellano, for a drink with Nureyev. Come on.' (This was near NYCB's old home on 55th Street.) At the bar they spoke in Russian but Balanchine translated for Horgan and, since she had a 'semi-crush' on both men, she listened closely.

After a few preliminaries, Nureyev broached the subject closest to his heart: that he wanted to dance for Balanchine. Balanchine, says Horgan, was diplomatic. Nureyev was young, his life was changing rapidly, he was not yet settled in the west and oughtn't to make up his mind in a hurry. Besides, he said, we don't have stars in my company. The *ballets* are the stars. And then he added a sentence that Nureyev never forgot. 'Why don't you go off and dance your princes, and when you get tired of princes, come back, and we'll see.' Later on in life, Nureyev could never tell his version of this story without adding, 'Well, I never got tired of princes – and the princes never got tired of me!'

He must have been disappointed at the time but he was not the type to lick his wounds. And in any case he had to get back to London to start rehearsing *Giselle*. His role, Albrecht, was that of a prince.

Some idea of the anticipation which was building up in regard to *Giselle*, and which shows de Valois's innate showmanship, may be had from the fact that no less than 70,000 applications were received for tickets for the three performances which Fonteyn and Nureyev were to give.

To begin with, Nureyev stayed with Margot – Erik would be joining him later. She found the young Russian more at peace with himself than before. This may have been Erik's doing. After all the chopping and changing between Paris, Copenhagen, Venice, Hamburg, Cannes and New York, Nureyev found the atmosphere at Covent Garden both businesslike and steadying. In professional terms, this was the first time such a thing had happened since his defection. The agreement with de Valois was that Rudolf would dance three performances of *Giselle* with Fonteyn and would be allowed nearly a month in which to rehearse. This was perfect for him. It was the sort of time-frame he had been used to at the Kirov but, after all the hard work, he would dance three nights, not one. There was a good chance for him to get the role exactly right.

Another reason why Rudolf was now more settled was due to Margot herself. They had got on from the very start, as people. But now they were dancing together – and here Margot's exceptional nature was crucial. She was of course by far the senior dancer. She was very experienced, world-famous and quite a bit older. It was not unlike the situation he had had with Dudinskaya. In the foyer of Covent Garden, near the box office, was a notice which made it clear that prices were more expensive on the nights Fonteyn was dancing. She might be on the verge of retirement but there was still no one who could pull in the crowds like she could.

Giselle was a special ballet for Rudolf. He had already danced it six times in Leningrad, in a version that was substantially different from that of the London ballet and into which he had introduced several modifications. His interpretation had drawn great acclaim from both critics and audiences in Leningrad. He had hopes of a similar reception in London.

While Fonteyn and Nureyev were rehearsing he had time to watch other performances by the Royal Ballet. The British, he felt, were very conservative with the classics. Both *Sleeping Beauty* and *Swan Lake* were much closer to the original Maryinsky versions than those of either the Kirov or the Bolshoi. But for Nureyev this was not necessarily a good thing. He felt that for a theatrical work to be kept alive, to have some effect on the audience when it was performed, it had to develop. He noticed, by way of contrast, that the British were always trying new versions of Shakespeare, who was one of their own, so to speak. He preferred that attitude.

But if the Royal Ballet was inflexible as a whole, such criticism did not apply to Margot. She, Rudolf found, was infinitely more flexible than other people. For him this was part of her greatness. However famous she might be, however experienced, however *old*, she showed herself as always willing to learn, even from someone as young as he. They were allowed twelve rehearsals for that first performance of *Giselle*, an unusually high number, and this gave them plenty of opportunity to explore each other's style and stamina, their strengths and weaknesses.

He surprised her. He was young, he was wild, he was not well educated in the usual sense. But he had a thoughtful attitude to the roles he played, was an instinctive dramatist, and had done his historical research. He knew, for instance, that the long peasant *pas de deux* was extraneous to the story and that it spoiled the dynamic of the first act. He pointed out that it had been written by a different composer, and he thought it should be dropped. Much the same arguments, he felt, applied to the mime scene by Giselle's mother. His reasons impressed Fonteyn and she phoned Colette Clark to say that Colette had been right, and she should have danced with Nureyev at the gala. The only reservation Fonteyn had about Rudolf, which she confided to Tito, was whether or not he was some sort of spy. In 1962, cold war paranoia was at its height and a wild, controversial defector would be the perfect cover for a double agent. Tito, being a diplomat, took a more practical view. He told Margot her imagination was working overtime.

The more she saw of Rudolf in rehearsal, the more relaxed he appeared. He was growing in confidence, had a less pinched look about him and the colour was returning to his face. There were only two tricky moments in this run-up to the great début. One was when he confessed to hating *cold* roast beef, a favourite of Margot and Tito. It seemed that Rudolf had never eaten cold meat in Russia and he wasn't about to start now. He had gone short of hot meat as a child and would spend the rest of his life making up for it. (At a restaurant, he would often pick up a steak and hold it close to his cheek, to test how warm it was.)

The other moment occurred after Margot had noticed that he seemed ill at ease one day.

He had nodded and said, 'I am like dying.'

'Why?'

'Four days I hear no music.'

'Poor Rudolf,' Fonteyn said later. '[He was] literally fed on music, and he was like a starving man in the silence around him.'

The friendship between Fonteyn and Nureyev, though young, was beginning to deepen. Tito recognised this and left them alone as little as possible. Colette Clark recalls that when he came back suddenly from a trip abroad, Fonteyn was very cross. This was despite Nureyev making no secret of his homosexuality when Fonteyn was around. At one stage in their rehearsals he was particularly jovial. 'Had letter from Erik,' he said.

Nor did she seem fazed by his exceptional coarseness. His favourite word, in any language, was 'Shit!' If something wasn't going right in rehearsal, he would explode. 'You shit, Margot! You shitty, shitty, shitty, shit!'

She would stand there, in her warm-up clothes, her hands on her hips. 'Rudi,' she would say softly. 'Just tell me *how* I'm a shit.' This was not the sort of language she was used to, or that he was used to hearing from her. He would beam and the episode was over.

Just as a deep friendship was beginning to flourish between Rudolf and Margot off-stage, they were also beginning to work out a new form of relationship between male and female dancers. Until Rudolf, most male dancers – even Erik – had played a subordinate role in ballet. In Balanchine's phrase, 'Ballet is Woman'. One effect of this was that, in rehearsal, the man – whose chief function until that time was to hold the woman – would accommodate his partner's wishes. But Rudolf, as in so much else, was different. Instead of meekly standing by and going along with whatever solution to whatever problem Margot had, he was forever making suggestions or offering advice. 'Don't you think this way better?' he would ask, then proceed to show her. Never forget he had taught himself all the main female roles in Leningrad and knew exactly what he was doing. In a sense, their rehearsals became a form of negotiation, as Fonteyn put it, each teaching the other something new, each learning from the other. This had important consequences, not just for their technique and for the basis of their relationship, but for the emotion they could invest in their roles. 'What mattered to me most,' said Fonteyn later, 'was the intensity of his involvement in the role. Two hours went by in no time at all. I was Giselle and he Albrecht.'

With his unrivalled knowledge of both male and female parts he was able to show her, 'with infinite exactitude', how she could improve certain steps. She was impressed with Rudolf in those rehearsals in much the same way as Giselle is impressed with Albrecht. A perfect example of this occurred one day when Margot was having difficulty with her *fouettés*. Rudolf, with his hands on his hips, asked, 'What is your mechanic for *fouetté*?' Margot was dumbfounded by the question and had never thought of their 'mechanic', as he put it. She just did them. Unable to give an answer in words, she tried again. 'Left arm is too back,' said Rudolf simply, and got on with what he was doing.

For Margot it was a revelation. 'With that one simple correction, I recovered my old form easily.'

After that, she scrutinised his technique minutely, watching the extraordinary thoroughness and exactitude with which he rehearsed each step. She was not the only one to remark on the great paradox in their rehearsals – that he, the wild, spontaneous Tartar, should care so much about technique, whereas she, the cool English matron, should be so much more interested in emotion.

After four hours' rehearsing, he would be exhausted, pale and edgy. 'I *hate* weak people!' he announced on one occasion, just after rehearsal had ended. 'All should be killed!' He was referring to anyone who was less hard on themselves than he was on himself. But after several cups of sugared tea and a hot steak he would mellow, though never completely.

Ballet Today said that there was more interest in *Giselle* 'than any comparable occurrence since the war'. Nureyev was in great demand from newspapers for interviews and photographs. Cecil Beaton was one of those who went to photograph him. Although Beaton had made such a public fool of himself on their previous encounter, Nureyev apparently did not remember him. The dancer was in a furious temper and however much charm the photographer turned on, it did no good. 'It was lucky that this trapped fox did not bite me,' Beaton entered in his diary, 'but merely glowered into the lens.' He had never, he said, had such an unresponsive sitter.

Frederick Ashton added to the sense of anticipation. Interviewed shortly before the performance, he acknowledged that 'changes have been made', adding that it would have been pointless to have squeezed Nureyev into some preconceived mould as Albrecht. Those changes, when they were seen, would become the stuff of controversy.

A few days before the big night a furious row broke out in Fleet Street over the fact that Lord Snowdon, Princess Margaret's husband, who was a photographer, had been allowed into the rehearsal to take pictures for the *Sunday Times* colour magazine, which was appearing for the first time that month. The other papers, notably the *Observer*, which felt it had done pretty well by Nureyev when he needed help, felt slighted and wrote cutting comments about 'non-titled' photographers not being given the privileges Snowdon had. Covent Garden responded by inviting the rest of Fleet Street to a runthrough but just such a fracas was exactly what *Giselle* needed. Scandal always helps.

Finally the first night arrived. It was Wednesday, 21 February 1962. When *Giselle* had first been produced, in Paris in the 1840s, it was as a vehicle for ballerinas. Giselle was seen as an unattainable sylph who leads men to destruction. Under Diaghilev, male dancing rose in importance and the character of Albrecht, the lover who betrays Giselle's love, became more important and more interesting. It was not a heroic role but it did lend itself to several psychological interpretations.

That night, Nureyev followed the interpretation he had worked out in Leningrad. This was not completely his own invention – other Russian dancers had tried much the same thing, but it was the first time it had been seen in the west. Instead of playing Albrecht as a dashing young hero, Nureyev was much more vulnerable. To begin with, he was a callous, callow prince who is unconcerned with the effects of his actions. After Giselle's death, however, he is shocked into a transformation – anguish, remorse, sorrow. John Percival, for *The Times*, put it well. 'The detailed naturalism of his acting in the first act came as a revelation; so did the way he soared through the solos in the second act. His *cabrioles*, especially, were not only far higher and travelled farther than any British dancer had managed, but he gave an illusion of pausing in the air at their highest point [he had, in other words, responded to Karsavina's comparison of him, with Nijinsky].' Percival added: 'His slight build and boyish appearance added to the effect of his performance; even more striking were the wild grace of his dancing and his complete absorption in every moment of the action.'

The *Telegraph* critic who was there that night, later wrote,

'From his first entry it was plain that something was happening to
the old role. Instead of the customary confident march down to the
footlights, Nureyev – whose reputation for flaunting panache had
preceded him – crept on almost surreptitiously, half-hidden by his
cloak, to disappear into hiding before the audience had time to raise
a hand clap. When he re-emerged, his slim, vulnerable figure with
its touching pretence of arrogance marked him as much a centre
of pity and sympathy as Giselle herself.'

But it was more even than that. As several critics were to remark,
Rudolf had developed a manner in which he gathered himself for his
spectacular leaps. He was not an impala or a gazelle, jumping easily,
but more like a lion, marshalling his strength, so that you appreciated
the effort as well as the result. He brought an *edge* to dancing that hadn't
been there before.

Nureyev had also achieved what in hindsight was a remarkable
synthesis of the Russian and English styles in dance. His mime, his
acting and his steps were all of a piece. He didn't suddenly break into
dance; he moved in the same way throughout, completely in character.
The result was an unforgettable Albrecht – a weak character shaken into
strength by his own mistakes and thoughtlessness.

Nureyev also wrought a transformation in Fonteyn. Until that night
she had never been totally successful in the ballet. She hadn't danced
Giselle as much as some other roles and where she had once had
a youthful, fragile poignancy, she was now a mature woman, quite
unlike the vulnerable near-child that Giselle is. But that night Nureyev's
conviction, his attention to detail, the complete way he fulfilled *his* role,
challenged and stimulated her to do the same – and she did. She was a
young girl again, titillated, bewildered, and finally devastated by what
was happening to her.

At the end of the ballet, Albrecht is alone on stage, lying exhausted
by the grave of Giselle. The music dies away as the curtain falls. That
night as the red and gold velvet curtains came down, the Royal Opera
House at Covent Garden was completely silent for four seconds. In that
silence Mark Bonham Carter, the member of the Ballet board who was
doing the counting, heard Lydia Lopokova utter two words in her deep
Russian whisper. Or rather she uttered one word twice. 'Lurvely,' she
said. 'Lurvely.'

Then came the applause. As with the gala performance, Nureyev was
applauded 'within an inch of his life'.

But for once the applause did not mark the end of the evening. That
night there were thirty curtain calls, during the course of which a legend
was being minted. As the couple stood there, breathing heavily and

acknowledging the applause, the shouting and the stamping of feet, Fonteyn was handed a big bunch of red roses. The cheers mounted, Fonteyn smiled at Nureyev, detached a rose from her bouquet and gave it to him.

'The young, dishevelled Russian gazed at it with the purest rapture and suddenly, his eyes gleaming with tears, swept down on to one knee, caught Fonteyn's hand and kissed it fervently. For a moment he was not just Rudolf but Albrecht again, who had had his prayers answered and his beloved Giselle returned to him. The audience responded as if Mafeking had been relieved. No one else, I swear, could have got away with it. That sudden total gesture of arrogant abnegation.'

It was a gesture, said Clive Barnes, whose quote this is, that took the curtain call to new heights. *Dance and Dancers* later wrote that this single gesture, more than anything else, created the ballet boom that was to last for nearly two decades.

For Ninette de Valois, watching from the wings, there was a pleasing symmetry about Nureyev's gesture. It had been his *bow*, rather than his dancing, that had first captivated her, which had led her to invite him to dance this very evening. And now a second bow, admittedly more extravagant, had captured the hearts of the first-night public.

Only two people did not join in the general adoration. One was Erik. In one thing Olivier Merlin was wrong: Erik could be very jealous and that night he sensed that something important was happening, something he was being left out of. As soon as the performance was over, he ran from the theatre.

The other person was David Blair, the dancer who had expected to take over as Fonteyn's partner when Michael Somes retired. He was in the pub across the road from Covent Garden, buying drinks and bemoaning, 'That should be me over there, that should be *me*!' Blair's was a tragic story, for he took Rudolf's arrival very hard, drank heavily and died young.

But if Nureyev had captured London, he was more and more captivated by Fonteyn. As he was discovering, there was far more to Margot Fonteyn than met the eye. She would soon become the most important woman in his life.

Margot Fonteyn's real name was Peggy Hookham. How or why the change occurred was a considerable mystery, even to her, though it is hard to imagine a great romantic heroine named Peggy Hookham. Her father was English and her mother half-Irish and half-Brazilian, a woman who was always insistent, Margot said, on good manners. Brought up in Ealing, west London, Peggy made her stage début at the age of four when she played a 'Wind' in the babies' ballet of the local ballet school's annual show.

When she was eight her father accepted the position of chief engineer of the British Cigarette Company in Shanghai, which the family reached by sailing to New York and taking a train across North America to Seattle, where they joined the SS *President Jackson* bound for Shanghai by way of Yokohama and the Inland Sea. In Shanghai, Peggy's mother found an old Russian ballet teacher to take up where the Ealing school had left off.

After a little more than a year in China, Peggy and her mother travelled back to Britain, this time by way of the Trans-Siberian railway. In 1929 the journey would take a 'mere' fourteen days, compared with several weeks, if they sailed. They went first to Mukden and then to Chang Chun,

'where we left the Chinese coaches and boarded the wide-gauge Russian train which stopped at Harbin before reaching the frontier at Manchoulti. It was spacious and comfortable, the roomy carriage converting into a sleeping compartment at night. I didn't much care for the restaurant car cuisine, but of course my mother had brought lots of tins of sardines and Heinz baked beans, still favourite foods today.'

Fonteyn recalled this in the mid-1970s, when she was in her fifties.

'The fascinating journey was broken by stops at little village stations where peasants brought incredibly delicious farm butter and hot fresh bread for the passengers to buy. Also roast chickens and wild flowers, of which the plum-red lilies-of-the-valley made an unforgettable impression, their smell so sweet and strong, redolent of the pure air and clean earth in which they grew. It came as a surprise one morning to draw the blinds and look out on to the clear vista of Lake Baikal after travelling through the endless miles of forest. Our train skirted the lake all day . . . Not everyone travelled that line as comfortably as we did; there were coaches of what was called "hard class" accommodation, consisting of bare wooden shelves, lower and upper level, on which soldiers and peasants sat for days at a time, cushioning the unfriendly surfaces with their thick clothing and what bundles they carried with them. At one of the stations there was a lot of shouting and excitement at the discovery of a stowaway clinging to some underpart of the carriage between the wheels. He was a sad pale youth who had travelled a couple of hundred miles undetected.'

After that trip home, Peggy remained in China with her family until 1933. In Shanghai in those days there was a good deal of artistic activity and in the last months Margot's mother began to take her daughter's dancing very seriously. She was now being taught by another Russian, George Goncharov, who had trained and danced at the Bolshoi and who, as an *émigré*, had formed a small troupe to dance excerpts from the classics in – of all places – the night clubs of the Far East. He had two partners, George Toropov and Vera Volkova.

After Peggy's father's contract came to an end, and they had moved back to London, her mother found her an even better teacher, the woman who had taught Alicia Markova, and who ran a school at the Pheasantry in the King's Road. Soon after, however, Peggy's mother moved her yet again, this time to the Vic-Wells School in Rosebery Avenue, Islington, north London. Peggy herself was at first upset by this move, for she felt she wasn't ready yet for such rapid promotion, but she was wrong. Her mother had read the situation correctly and knew she was putting her daughter in the right place at the right time.

Two remarkable women were behind the Vic-Wells. The first was Ninette de Valois. Born in Ireland in 1898, Edris Stannus (as she was christened) moved to England at the age of seven where she took up 'fancy dancing' and was taken to see the Ballets Russes. At fourteen she was 'on the boards', touring the country with a troupe known as 'The Wonder Children'. She performed in most of the music halls, at a time when, in Britain at least, ballet *was* a music hall act. It had been different in the eighteenth century, and would soon change again, but Edris Stannus was not atypical of her time.

Like Balanchine, Edris, who had now changed her name to de Valois, tried her hand at choreography. She trained under Cecchetti and in 1923 she was invited to join Diaghilev's Ballets Russes. She remained for two years but, just as the rest of the company was cosmopolitan, so de Valois was stubbornly British and believed that Britain needed above all its own classical ballet company. On leaving the Ballets Russes she started her own dancing school in Kensington and then approached Lilian Baylis, the second key female figure in the history of British ballet. Baylis ran the Royal Victoria Hall, better known as the 'Old Vic', which offered all thirty-seven of Shakespeare's plays at prices the working class could afford; it was not unlike the Narodny Dom in Leningrad. De Valois suggested that the Old Vic needed a ballet troupe, and Baylis agreed.

The few evenings of ballet that were put on in the first years – 1926 to 1928 – proved so popular that W.B. Yeats invited de Valois to help the Abbey Theatre in Dublin where she became director of ballet. Her next step was to buy her own theatre for ballet, a shell called Sadler's Wells in Islington. Sadler's Wells had started life in 1684 when Dick Sadler found a well in his garden and shrewdly marketed the water as medicinal. People arrived in such numbers that he decided to offer entertainments as well. In time the entertainments proved more popular, and by all accounts more medicinal, than the waters.

The success of de Valois and Baylis attracted other figures including the young choreographer Frederick Ashton, who had been born in Ecuador, the composer/conductor Constant Lambert, and George Balanchine, all of whom had worked for Ballet Russes. Balanchine, unfortunately for Britain, was refused a work permit and decamped to the United States.

The first full evening of ballet took place at Sadler's Wells on 15 May 1931, and consisted of small pieces choreographed by de Valois herself. By the beginning of 1934, however, the company was able to offer two full-length nineteenth-century classics, *Giselle* and *Coppélia*. During that year, Fonteyn made her début. 'One evening,' wrote 'Alexander Bland', in his history of the Royal Ballet, 'sharp eyes might have noticed among the Snowflakes [in *Nutcracker*] a small dark girl with a slightly oriental face which would change instantly from gaiety to sadness, and a specially soft, easy way of moving . . . she appeared in the programme as Peggy Hookham, but a few months later this was changed into the stage name of Margot Fontes, soon to be modulated into Fonteyn.'

From then on, Fonteyn's fortunes were bound up with the Sadler's Wells Ballet. Her first serious role was in Ashton's *Le Baiser de la fée*, to music by Stravinsky, and she took over as Odette in *Swan Lake* in 1936. This was the beginning of an upswing in British ballet that was to last until the 1970s. In February 1939 she danced Aurora in *The Sleeping Princess* to great acclaim and was one of those in the company who, in May 1940, were very nearly cut off in Holland when the Germans invaded. De Valois was woken at 4 a.m. on the morning of 10 May by the sound of aircraft and guns. Annoyed, she asked who was disturbing her sleep. 'Excuse me, Miss de Valois,' said one of the *corps de ballet*, 'but I really think it must be the Germans.' Their retreat to the coast, by bus, took two days and ended in a midnight walk through woods. They were taken to Harwich in a cargo boat. There were no casualties, but costumes and scenery for six ballets were left behind, plus the only manuscript score for *Horoscope*, which was lost for ever.

In wartime the home of the company was in Burnley but the news wasn't all bleak. Ballet, like the theatre in general, was popular with both civilians and military personnel keen to have a break from hostilities, and the company was very profitable; for a while, the ballet profits subsidised the opera.

At the end of the war the decision was taken to move de Valois's company to Covent Garden. (Lord Keynes, chairman of the Council for the Encouragement of Music and the Arts, the forerunner of the Arts Council, was married to a dancer Lydia Lopokova, and was himself a noted balletomane.) The reopening of the Covent Garden theatre, on 20 February 1946 was, according to the official history of the Royal Ballet, 'a symbol of the beginning of peacetime, as opposed to the mere ending of the war'.

In the late 1940s, de Valois was made a CBE and the company toured in both Eastern and Western Europe. But it was its first tour to the United States and Canada, under Sol Hurok, that really made it a world-class company. This took place in the autumn of 1949, beginning in October in New York with a season at the 'Met', which was then located on Broadway between 39th and 40th Streets. Hurok insisted on as many full-length ballets as the company could offer, and they brought *Swan Lake, The Sleeping Beauty* and *Cinderella*. The tour was an outstanding success. Queues formed all round the block for tickets, and the reviews were ecstatic. 'This was ballet in all the grandeur of pageantry and finish of technique,' wrote one critic. On the opening night applause broke out for Oliver Messel's designs before anyone had even danced a step.

That Met season confirmed Fonteyn as a great star. 'In one performance,' writes Bland, 'she was precipitated from national adoration to international adulation, a "ballerina among ballerinas" with a special place among the world's superstars.' The success was felt by everybody in the company, and then and thereafter the Royal Ballet, as it became in 1956, had a special relationship with New York audiences. Many felt, quite simply, that the company danced better there than in London. Following that first triumphant tour, the company visited America every two or three years until the early 1970s. Tours would last up to nineteen weeks and cover thirty-two cities. Living together for so long, the dancers on tour always sharpened up their performances. The Royal Ballet even had its own train to travel in.[1] It was called the 'Sol Hurok Special' (there was actually a board on the front of the engine saying that). Leslie Edwards remembers it breaking down one night and the entire company walking up and down the track in their dressing gowns.

In 1951 de Valois was made a Dame of the British Empire and Fonteyn received the CBE. Her career soared gloriously upward but in private there was a shadow. Fonteyn, like Nureyev, always jealously guarded her private life but the fact is that, as a young dancer, this Queen of Secrets had been deeply in love with Constant Lambert, the conductor and musical director of the company, who was already married. He rates only three brief mentions in her autobiography but their relationship, never acknowledged publicly, is one reason why she had not married and why she had not had children. Lambert died in 1953 and, at the age of thirty-four, Fonteyn was completely alone. Another affair with the French choreographer, Roland Petit, had not worked out either.

In September 1953, just as the curtain was about to go up on *The Sleeping Beauty* at the Met, the stage doorman brought a visiting card to her dressing-room. The card read: 'Robert E. Arias, Delegate of Panama to the United Nations'. It had been some time since Fonteyn had seen Arias. They had met sixteen years before, in 1937, when Tito – as he was always called – was a student at Cambridge and Sadler's Wells had been performing there. Fonteyn had fallen for him but he had sailed back to Panama for the long vacation, leaving her to nurse a broken heart until she was on the same tour the following year, when they took up as before. After that there was total silence until he had called her out of the blue while she was on tour in America in 1951. Then silence again for two years until he delivered the card.

Three times she had allowed herself to be treated like a doormat, but the card arrived at an opportune time. Now thirty-four, Fonteyn had always imagined retiring at thirty-five. Her love for Lambert, and then for Petit, had not been returned in the way she had hoped to have love returned, she was childless, and alone. Many men were intimidated by her fame and she did not take lovers easily. Although Tito was obviously a philanderer, he was a charming man and had once carried a torch for her. He now invited himself to her dressing-room after the performance but she had another dinner engagement that she could not break. He called her next day, came round for breakfast – and asked her to marry him. This was gloriously, impulsively romantic but, since he was already married, with three children, she did not think he was entirely serious. But the next day he sent her a hundred red roses, and the day after that he phoned from Panama to say that his wife had agreed to give him a divorce.

There followed a bout of serious wooing on Tito's part – suppers at El Morocco, a chauffeur-driven car placed at Fonteyn's disposal, fantastic gifts such as a diamond bracelet, extravagant parties in her honour, for which the invitations were sent out by means of thirty-word telegrams to every guest. Tito followed Margot on tour, and took her to meet his famous friends across America, including the actor John Wayne. When they were forced to be apart – he was, after all, Panamanian ambassador to the United Nations – he bombarded her with reams of remarkable love letters.

But the central truth about Roberto de Arias was that he was a philanderer. In order to be a successful philanderer (and Tito was *very* successful) a man needs considerable charm. Arias used all his charm on Fonteyn. He had decided that he needed a famous wife. Realising that on account of her age she was vulnerable, he put all his energies into catching her.

Faced with such attention, Fonteyn was at first wary. She had lost the original spark which had flared in 1937 and, try as she might, she could not will it back. Eventually, however, she abandoned the search for 'wild passion' and realised, or pretended to realise, that Tito made her complete. On that basis, she agreed to become his wife.

They were married in February 1955 and honeymooned in the Bahamas. Shortly afterwards, Tito took up a new appointment as Panamanian ambassador to the Court of St James and a new life began for Margot. She was an ambassadress and, from 1 January 1956, when she was honoured in the New Year lists, a dame. She might have retired then and there but the wholesale changes to her life seem to have given her a new lease of life. Through Tito she met Aristotle Onassis and holidayed with Sir Winston Churchill on the Greek millionaire's yacht. She met Castro. At their home in London the mix of politicians and artists proved irresistible. They entertained not only John Wayne, but also King Hussein of Jordan, Vivien Leigh, Marilyn Monroe and Maria Callas. Tito also had another set of friends, rather dubious Central Americans: gunrunners, wheeler-dealers, property speculators – but Fonteyn had a soft spot for them, too. She wasn't like that herself, and that was the point. There was a definite attraction of opposites.

Altogether, it was a busy, heady life and Fonteyn loved it. All the more because, apart from dance, it was all she had. In 1961, after five years of marriage to Tito, she knew that Tito's first love was politics, and politics in Panama was not, shall we say, straightforward. She had herself been jailed and then deported for aiding, or at least being present at, one of her husband's plans for revolution in Panama. This side to Tito was both dangerous and absurd.

Life said the insurrection was 'one of the funniest fiascos of recent history.' Someone else described it as 'the revolution that couldn't shoot straight.' When Tito decamped to Brazil he left behind a briefcase which showed that he had a cheque from John Wayne for $682,850, for a 'shrimp business.' At one of the Fonteyns' weekends at Chartwell with Churchill, Viscount Montgomery had offered his services for Tito's 'next revolution'. In one light, Tito was colourful; in another, he was sinister and pathetic .

There was also the fact that Tito's philandering had never stopped. He was a 'lovely, sexy man', as one of his many admirers put it, 'but he was not much of an egg. He was naughty.' By the time Nureyev arrived in London to dance *Giselle*, Fonteyn could no longer ignore the truth. Not only did Tito not love her. He never had.

Note

[1] In her memoirs, Fonteyn tells a story about this train. She was with Moira Shearer, and they had had dinner together after the performance in a small American town. Late at night they reached the station. They asked the ticket inspector where the special train was, but he hadn't heard of any special train. He asked to see their tickets – they didn't have any. He asked what time the train left – they didn't know. The ticket collector scratched his head. 'So you are looking for a train that doesn't have a departure time, for which you don't have tickets, and which appears not to exist. I don't suppose you know the destination by any chance?' They did not.

CHAPTER TWELVE

Misunderstanding, Noise and Blame

So now be off to Neva's brink,
you newborn work, and like a winner
earn for me the rewards of fame –
misunderstanding, noise, and blame!

Although many critics shared the public's reaction to Fonteyn and Nureyev in *Giselle* – that they were wonderful – a sizeable minority dissented from the wild adulation. Several thought that Nureyev had been cavalier with the choreography. In particular, he had introduced a set of 'relentlessly repeated' *entrechats*. They were saying, in effect, what Vyroubova had said in Paris: that Nureyev would do anything for effect. The *Financial Times* critic thought, perversely, that Fonteyn and Nureyev constituted an 'ill-matched' pair and that, in contrast to Fonteyn's fully worked-out performance as Giselle, Nureyev's Albrecht was an 'immature sketch'. Immature or not, his endlessly repeated *entrechats* were widely imitated in the months that followed. Nureyev was not the only dancer who liked to show off.

The Russians no less than anyone else had noticed the rapture with which the performance had been received, and they responded with pique. The Russian cultural attaché in London tried several times to persuade Sir David Webster to shed Rudolf from the Royal Ballet. These moves came at a time when Sol Hurok was in London, holding talks with Webster about the Royal Ballet's forthcoming tour of North America. Webster and Hurok flew to Moscow (separately, but they were in the Russian capital at the same time) to discuss the matter. At the end of the month the Soviet authorities announced a ban on Maya Plisetskaya and Nicolai Fedeyechev coming from the Bolshoi to the Royal Ballet as guest artists, a ban which extended to Asaf Messerer, who was to have given lessons at Covent Garden. And there would be no exchange tour that summer with the Bolshoi.

Hurok was worried about 'his' north American tour but the Soviets appeared to accept the argument that, while the Paris Opèra Ballet and Covent Garden received public subsidy, and to that extent were 'national' theatres, Hurok was wholly private. Khrushchev himself, according to Vladimir Ashkenazy, settled matters with Hurok. As we shall see, the Russian president had his own reasons for wanting Nureyev to travel as much as possible.

The London public did not stop to reflect on these matters. For later performances of *Giselle*, black-market tickets were changing hands for £25, four times their face value. By now, Fonteyn and Nureyev had not only perfected their roles, they had actually rehearsed their curtain calls. Over the years, wrote Clive Barnes, this would become an essential coda to their performances. 'In slow, stylised fashion, Fonteyn turns to Rudolf and offers her hand. He takes it and, coyly bending, kisses her fingers. But only on that first night – recorded for posterity by G.B.L. Wilson – did he fall to one knee.'

Talking to him after the performance, Barnes discovered that Nureyev had been deeply influenced by Stanislavsky. He didn't mime his roles, he said. 'You must have a basis, a reason, for every gesture. Otherwise the audience will see that what you are doing is wrong.' And he quoted Zeffirelli, that the great heroes of the classics are 'modern men'. Nureyev's Albrecht was a modern man, he said. Besides being a prince, he responded to life with all the bewilderment that any ordinary man feels.

The première of *Giselle* that February night, which sparked the Fonteyn–Nureyev partnership, was part of a wave of change overtaking London, and Britain. The *Sunday Times* colour magazine was perhaps the most visible sign of these changes. The Saddle Room, the capital's first discothèque, had opened just before in 1961, the same year that saw the launch of the satirical review, *Beyond the Fringe*. The Establishment, a new kind of club, had just opened, together with any number of 'bistros'. Nineteen-sixty-two was the year of *That Was the Week That Was*, a satirical television programme, of Truffaut's *Jules et Jim*, the first issue of *Private Eye* and Arnold Wesker's *Chips with Everything*. These changes would culminate in the 'swinging Sixties' (and how dated that sounds now). They were social, cultural, intellectual, stylish, political, moral (1961 was the year when the Gaming Act was liberalised) but, above all, sexual. Throughout the world, not just in Britain, the 1960s were associated with what came to be called the sexual revolution.

There is a sense in which this was inevitable. Many old taboos had been broken during the Second World War, not necessarily because of any basic change in people but simply because in wartime, with so many young people away from home and faced with the possibility of imminent death, old practices fell by the wayside. As early as 1956 reviewers had remarked on the 'casual promiscuity' in John Osborne's play *Look Back in Anger*, a harbinger of what was to follow. *Lolita* was published in 1958 and then, in 1960, came the trial of *Lady Chatterley's Lover* with its celebrated exchange by the prosecuting counsel, who asked members of the jury whether it was the kind of book they would allow their wives, or even their servants, to read. Paul Raymond's 'Revue Bar' opened in Soho in 1962, and 1963 was the year when the Profumo scandal broke, displaying casual promiscuity among the highest and mightiest in the land.

Writing a history of 'the revolution in English life in the fifties and the sixties', Christopher Booker called his book, *The Neophiliacs*: the lovers of the new. So Nureyev's arrival in London was exactly on schedule. His good looks, his pre-Beatles hairstyle (their first hit was in 1963) may not have been as important as his dancing skills, but they weren't entirely irrelevant.

Sexually, although the situation for homosexuals was easier in the west than it was inside the Soviet Union, it was much less liberal than it is today. And it wasn't Denmark. Nureyev's remark to Tito at Fonteyn's party, after the gala, that his *ménage* with Erik was a story better not told, may have been a throwaway shot, but it shows that he was well aware of circumstances in Britain at the time. Change was coming but 1961 is longer ago than, perhaps, we think.

In London, for example, gay life was more discreet than it had been during the war (or more oppressed, depending on your point of view). In the late 1950s there was one internationally famous gay pub, the Fitzroy Tavern in Charlotte Street, which retained a boisterous, bohemian atmosphere *and* immunity from the police (due, it was said, to its hefty contributions annually to police benevolent funds). There was also the A&B Club (Arts & Battledress, denoting its wartime origins), and the Rockingham. Between 1945 and 1955 the number of prosecutions in Britain for homosexual behaviour actually rose from just under 800 to just over 2,500 annually, more than one thousand of whom went to prison, the same number as in Soviet Russia, which had four times the population. Men were often imprisoned for acts with other consenting adults which had been 'committed' several years earlier. Such cases often made sensational headlines when they featured well-known names, like Lord Montagu of Beaulieu, or John (later Sir John) Gielgud.

In September 1957 the Wolfenden Report was published in Britain, which recommended that sexual acts in private between consenting adults (over the age of twenty-one), no longer be a criminal offence. Thereupon Britain entered a kind of limbo, for the recommendations of Wolfenden did not become law until ten years later, in July 1967. During those ten years, when Nureyev first arrived in the UK, being homosexual still carried risks although the exact nature of those risks was changing all the time. It continued to be an offence, even if in 1964 the Home Secretary called on chief constables throughout the country to consult him before prosecuting homosexuals for acts in private.

In 1962, however, attitudes of even supposedly informed people could be amazingly crude. That year saw the publication of a 'report' by sociologist Richard Hauser, called *The Homosexual Society*, which characterised homosexuality as a 'stress-related disease', analagous to bed-wetting. The author reprimanded homosexuals for being self-centred and for living 'an eternal life of parties and excitement without any need to settle down', and for mostly being unwilling to make any contribution to society. Hauser thought he could distinguish more than forty 'homosexual types', including the Demoralised Married Man, the Call-Boy, the Sugar Daddy, the Cottage Type, the Prison Queer, the Body Builder and the Woman Hater. Hauser concluded that he 'knew of no other minority among whom self-pity and self-righteousness were so rampant; which was so lacking in a sense of values outside its own circle, or so bereft of loyalty to its own country'. He referred to the break-up of homosexual partnerships as being followed by 'terrible tragedies of an adolescent type [which] shake otherwise mature people for about five days'. Hauser regarded himself as a scientist.

Erik was able to help Nureyev find his way through the minefield of gay life in the west at that difficult time. He was familiar with both Britain and the United States and, as a Scandinavian and a bisexual, he knew the range of experiences – and risks – that Nureyev might have to face. Where he couldn't help him was over the stresses of exile. The banning of Plisetskaya and Fedeyechev showed that the Russians were not going to let Nureyev's defection pass by without consequences and Nureyev was distressed to hear, amid the euphoria over *Giselle*, that Tamara Myasciorva had been expelled from Leningrad University on his account. She had been in her fourth and final year of a teacher training course but the university authorities decided that, as the friend of a defector, she was not after all teacher material. There was more. Liuba Myasnikova had also been punished: banned from travelling to all foreign conferences, as retaliation for her friendship with Nureyev.

But life had to go on, and in mid-March Nureyev flew to New York to make his official American début, this time in his own right and not as a substitute for Erik. The performance took place, not at one of the great theatres in Manhattan but at the Brooklyn Academy of Music, where he was a guest artist with Ruth Page's Chicago Company. Page had danced for Diaghilev, for Balanchine, at the coronation of Emperor Hirohito of Japan in 1928 and since 1934 had been ballet director of the Chicago Grand Opera Company. Soonia Arova was Nureyev's partner that night and they danced the *pas de deux* from *Don Quixote*. Though attended by the now-familiar publicity, this was a very different affair from *Giselle* at Covent Garden. Provoked by the massive press coverage of his defection and subsequent triumphs, the entire New York dance world crossed the

Williamsburg bridge over the East River. Balanchine was there, as was Danilova, and so was the well-known balletomane, Shelley Winters.

If the occasion was different, so was the reaction. These professionals were distinctly cool to the young Russian. As the ubiquitous Clive Barnes put it, in the *New York Times*, 'New York does not give up its scepticism without a fight, and, after all, who did this young Russian think he was, just because he had leapt over an airport barrier? It takes more than that to impress New York.'

The critics did not speak with one voice. The *Christian Science Monitor* thought that Nureyev lacked the 'pure classic perfection' of Erik Bruhn, that he was less brilliant than Soloviev, but that nevertheless he was 'amazing, on the threshold of a career of blazing glory, that will make ballet history'. He had a quality of mystery, said the paper, and before him only Nijinsky and Babilée had that. Their highest compliment was that he encouraged the spectator to see the beauty of the steps, not the skill of the performer. The *New York Herald Tribune* critic had fewer reservations, especially after he gave up counting the curtain calls. He concluded that Nureyev promised to be 'one of the most compelling dance figures of our era', with 'an animal magnetism that invites something very close to hypnotic adoration'.

However, the doyen of the New York critics, John Martin (who was known, therefore, as 'Dean Martin'), was not so impressed. In fact, he was not impressed at all. He considered that the 'reds' had packed the theatre with stooges as part of a Soviet plot to destroy Nureyev's career by means of unthinking idolatry, which would cause him to grow soft very quickly. He started by criticising Nureyev's physique, saying he was too short, and sloppy. 'Day after day he was told he was the best in the world and in his naïvety may have believed it and blamed the Kirov for not telling him so.' After carping at his performances in Paris and London, Martin went on to say that, in Brooklyn, Nureyev's dancing was

'talented, winning, uneven in style, unfinished in technique, a little gauche in deportment. He is not the best of the lot, nor even as good as the best. At the moment he is a long way from being a great dancer . . . In his audience at Brooklyn there were perhaps a score of male dancers of all nationalities and backgrounds who could have performed that particular pas de deux more accurately, with more polish, if not perhaps with as much talent.'

Martin concluded that it had been a tragedy that Nureyev had defected, that the Kirov was the one company that could give him the discipline he needed. Instead, he had 'thrown himself to the lions'. He concluded on one bright note – that Nureyev had befriended Erik Bruhn, 'who may really be the greatest male dancer in the world . . . If young Nureyev can listen to him . . .'

Rudolf did his best to ignore this obituary. In an interview he gave after the performance he said that 'It would be perfect for me if Mr Balanchine would accept my working for the Royal Ballet for part of the year and the New York City Ballet part of the year.' Another line had been cast over the biggest fish in modern dance, but again Balanchine refused to respond.

The prospects were more exciting in London, where Rudolf and Erik were to dance in many of the same roles. After the early *Giselles*, Nureyev had moved out of Fonteyn's house in Thurloe Square, to share a flat with Erik in Eaton Place. To begin with, it was fun living together in London. Nureyev even brought over the car he had nearly wrecked when he had tried learning to drive on the Corniche above Monte Carlo. Again naïvely, he thought that maybe Erik would teach him to drive but it turned out that Erik couldn't drive either. They had a go anyway, with disastrous results. 'Every time Rudik was at the wheel,' Bruhn told John Gruen, 'I was such a nervous wreck that I would open the door and throw up. When *I* was driving, the same thing would happen to him. The car [which was brand new] looked like it had been beaten with a hammer. People would scream at us and call us killers.' Eventually, Fonteyn got to hear of it. She was appalled. What they were doing was not only dangerous but also illegal. With her connections, she arranged for someone from the Automobile Association to give them instruction and arrange for the driving tests. Erik admitted that he was the more terrified of the two, and let Nureyev take his test first. He disappeared, with the man from the Ministry of Transport, and came back a short while later, having been awarded his licence. Amazing. Now it was Erik's turn. The examiner took him to a hill and asked him to drive to the top, where there was heavy traffic. Erik was terrified, not yet feeling confident enough to drive surrounded by buses, lorries, and so on. He asked the examiner if he would go ahead and stop the traffic, to make it easier for Erik to join the flow. The man looked at Erik in consternation, then asked if he had read the *Highway Code*. Erik had no idea what the man was talking about. 'I thought he was referring to some Agatha Christie novel. I said, "No, I haven't, I never read detective stories".' Later, when Erik was asked to park the car, he said he would rather not since it always ended up either too near or too far from the kerb.

It says a lot for Margot Fonteyn's influence that, despite everything, Erik, like Nureyev, was given a licence.

As the weeks went by, however, Erik was growing increasingly uncomfortable on the professional side. Hitherto, he had been the star, the focus of attention. He was ten years older than Nureyev and felt that he had earned his fame. Now, in early summer 1962, he was dancing the same roles as Nureyev – in *Giselle, Swan Lake, The Sleeping Beauty, Les*

Sylphides, Don Quixote – and although he was getting just as much critical acclaim, if not more, it was Nureyev who seemed to attract incessant media attention. For example, when Erik danced *Giselle* with Nadia Nerina, the partner Ninette de Valois had chosen for him, *Dance News* wrote: '*This* is what we have been waiting for.' Other critics remarked that, where Nureyev was concerned, there was something 'untidy' about his feet.

Yet it was Nureyev who was lionised by the non-specialists, who was invited everywhere. There were articles on Rudolf's polo-neck sweaters which, it was said, were becoming all the rage. Gayle Fitzpatrick, a fashion designer, imitated his caps and cuban heels in her products.

He met, and fell for, Peter O'Toole, on whom he modelled himself for a while. He met the Burtons, Albert Finney, Tom Courtenay, Jane Fonda. There were queues outside Covent Garden for Fonteyn/Nureyev performances that were longer, and longer-lasting, than any seen since before the war. In June the poet Stephen Spender was only one of many celebrities attracted to the ballet by the publicity. He went to see *Giselle*. Fonteyn, he said in his memoirs was a very individual dancer, in contrast to others:

'She has a thistledown movement, seeming to float rather than leap, and her real personality is felt all the time and has great appeal. Nureyev has a blue-period Picasso quality. He danced well, but his most moving moment was when he took the curtain call. She handed him her rose, which he held up with his right arm extended. He is best in repose, which seems odd for a dancer.'

Later, Spender went to dinner at Margot's. 'She appeared and was just the same as on stage. Nureyev appeared a gaunt, haggard beatnik with untidy hair and considerable charm.'

Three weeks later, Noel Coward went to see the same couple in the same ballet. He confided to his diary that 'She was marvellous and he, of course, remarkable, but I thought too pleased with himself. I had already made a vow never to see *Giselle* again. It is a ghastly ballet and I loathe it, and so help me God that was the last time.'

Erik's discomfort was due not simply to jealousy, though. Another problem was his partner, Nadia Nerina. There was little wrong with her as a dancer (as *Dance News* had written), but she didn't have the stamp of Fonteyn and, as Nureyev's equal, Erik felt he had been short-changed. And Covent Garden itself was not as relaxing as he had expected. He detested what he saw as the centralisation of the entire company around de Valois. 'I mean, I wanted a zipper changed on the top of my costume, and they had to go and check with Madame de Valois. It was ridiculous.'

Rudolf was uncomfortable with the publicity in a different way.

Although he wished to be *part* of the Royal Ballet, and badly wanted the security of a company, he realised that all the publicity would keep him apart from the other dancers, make *them* feel uncomfortable with him. But he was already caught. If he avoided publicity, that only increased his reputation for being 'difficult'.

There were those who equated Erik and Rudolf. One was Walter Terry, the critic for the *New York Herald Tribune* who, on the day that Stephen Spender went to *Giselle*, sent home a piece entitled 'Teenage Squeals'. This began, 'A beatnik and a prince have taken London by storm. They are alike in that both are artists of the ballet, both tremendously potent box office material. Both are bringing a new audience to the ballet, especially the demonstrative balcony area.' Terry noticed that the more sophisticated balletomanes, in the orchestra stalls, 'lingered' longer for Bruhn but that the 'flower-pelters' in the high balconies were all for Nureyev. This admirably demonstrated the differences in the reception of the two men.

And, one can say, Erik had a point. Even Clive Barnes, who was to be Nureyev's staunchest critical defender in years to come, took issue with him that summer. In May Nureyev had caused controversy at a gala when he had introduced a new male solo into *Swan Lake*. This was, in John Percival's words, 'a dreamy, melancholy number intended to show the hero's mood', and it was danced when normally he is just walking about the stage. Barnes went for Nureyev, describing him now as a problem child. 'Ever since he arrived at the Royal Ballet he has been encouraged to change things around to suit himself . . . He invents his own choreography for *Swan Lake*. Unfortunately he has no talent for it.' Barnes thought Nureyev's innovations patchy and that 'overall, he has made it worse, not better'.

Barnes wasn't the only one. P.W. Manchester, in an article entitled 'The Problem of Nureyev,' went further: 'Wandering the earth with a few trick *pas de deux* is death to an artist and very quickly loses its novelty . . . What he does is remarkable, wonderful . . . but in five, even three year's time, will it seem quite so remarkable, will it be enough? I think not. He will be an ageing little boy . . . He will never fulfil his promise.' Harsh words, but even within the company Erik and Nureyev divided people. Half the female soloists (like Georgina Parkinson) were in love with Nureyev, and the other half (like Antoinette Sibley) with Erik. Nadia Nerina made perhaps the best comment. In one performance of *Swan Lake* she suddenly burst into a big grin (as Nureyev could do) and, instead of doing thirty-two *fouettés*, a female step, did thirty-two *entrechats*, a male step. If we all make changes to suit ourselves, she was saying, where will it end up?

There was a darker side, too. Fonteyn noted that people were already putting her and Rudolf together as a couple off-stage as well as on. In 1975, when she published her memoirs, she still felt unable to say that

Nureyev's lover at that point was a man. 'The fact remains,' she wrote, 'that Rudolf was desperately in love with someone else at the time.' That love was already complicated and Nadia Nerina for one was disturbed by the whole set-up. At one stage, for example, Rudolf began to turn up at all the rehearsals she was having with Bruhn. They would be in the middle of some steps when Rudolf would suddenly point things out to Erik, giving him advice and telling him what was good and what wasn't. She felt that Rudolf was forcing his personality on Erik. 'Erik was always very cool and collected,' she said, 'and would come to rehearsals prepared in his mind as to what he was going to do . . . he would always appear meticulously dressed for our rehearsals. On the other hand, Rudy would come in looking like a ragbag and slop about. Their personalities were totally different.'

More specifically, she felt that Rudolf was a bad influence on Erik, that he unsettled him, and she decided to make a stand. One day she simply said that *she* wasn't going on until Rudolf left the rehearsal room. He glared at her, but then left rather sheepishly (Rudolf always understood firmness in others). 'When he closed the door behind him,' Nerina said, 'I could still see him with his nose pressed against the door window watching us.'

It worked, in that Rudolf stopped coming to their rehearsals. On the other hand, Erik became more and more upset – Rudolf was obviously getting at him at home. 'I'll never forget [Erik] saying to me after he had been with us for two months that he was not a classical dancer. I remember replying that I had never heard such a bunch of rubbish in all my life, and that he was the greatest classical male dancer I had ever seen.' Nerina clearly feared that Rudolf, so very different from Erik, and receiving such massive publicity and adulation, was causing Erik to lose confidence in himself. For Nerina matters were not helped when, after a while, Sonia Arova appeared in London and the three of them, Sonia, Erik and Rudolf, formed a kind of trio. Nerina never said whether this trio was sexual, just that it was 'altogether too complicated for me.' Certainly, the threesome made Nerina and her husband so uncomfortable that they stopped mixing with the others socially.

Clive Barnes took up where Nerina left off. He told John Gruen that he was not at all sure that in those days the Royal Ballet realised that Erik and Rudolf were living together:

'It took them a long time to understand that relationship . . . The competition was fantastic, but at this time they were very different dancers. To some extent Erik was caviare to the general. I mean, every dancer and certainly the elite critics knew that Erik was the world's greatest male dancer. In a way, Erik was a kind of cult hero. He was not at that time a superstar. Interestingly enough he gained that status *after* Rudolf.'

These conflicting and explosive emotional and professional forces came to a head in late spring 1962 when Ninette de Valois and Frederick Ashton decided to invite Rudolf to become a permanent guest artist with the Royal Ballet. Erik had hoped very much to have been given the same opportunity. He was not happy in either Denmark or New York and standards in Paris were nowhere near as high as in London. But de Valois and Ashton decided to have just one foreign dancer and, as Barnes put it, 'Rudolf was more useful.'

'I remember Erik coming around,' said Barnes, 'and we did an interview with him for *Dance and Dancers*. It was just at the point when that decision had been made and Erik was shattered. I had never seen him look so much like the Prince of Denmark. Erik was very hurt and he felt very rejected . . . he felt his international career was shattered.'

Nonetheless, despite the rivalry, despite the fights and flare-ups, the three months which Rudolf and Erik spent in London deepened their relationship. Its very intensity even frightened Erik. Rudolf was much younger, much less experienced, more openly passionate – and had come from an authoritarian regime where homosexuality was even more criminal and stigmatised than in Western Europe. The fact that Rudolf had responded so strongly to that film of Erik in Russia, and had in effect come looking for him after his defection, underlined his passion but also suggested to Erik, who had his mystical side, that the two men had been predestined to meet. The image he himself used to John Gruen was of two comets colliding. This implied an explosion, but also that there was some impermanence to the relationship. 'The initial collision is attractive and exciting,' said Erik, 'but I have to follow my instincts about it and my instincts invariably guide me into many different directions.'

Rudolf's relations with the Goslings was also developing. He enjoyed the cosy dinners at their house in Victoria Road, Kensington, when, after the meal, they would sweep away the dinner things and screen movies. These were, as he dubbed them, their 'Roxy' evenings. Rudolf loved to catch up on all the old black and white movies he felt he had missed out on as a boy in Russia. He was also developing a taste for blue movies, as we shall see.

With so much going on in the background, Bruhn was relieved when his engagement with the Royal Ballet was finished. He was glad to go, and set off for Italy on a tour with the Royal Danish Ballet. After that, he joined John Cranko at the Stuttgart Ballet. Cranko, who had been a choreographer with the London Festival Ballet, had taken over in Stuttgart a year before and was already beginning to make fundamental – and generally very successful – changes which would eventually lead the company to international fame. Besides Bruhn, Cranko had invited Yvette Chauviré from Paris, Georgina Parkinson from the Royal Ballet, Erika Slocha from Vienna – and Rudolf.

And sure enough the tension returned. It took its toll on Erik in spectacular fashion. The high point of the week was a gala at which he was to star. In the rehearsals, however, the bad atmosphere that had so upset Nadia Nerina in London reapppeared. It was partly the simple presence of Rudolf who, now that he was free, seemed unable to control his homosexuality. As virile as he was on stage, he could be equally camp off it. This side of him had simply never been allowed to surface in Russia but in the west Rudolf at times seemed to revel in it. In class there was tension too because Rudolf, though always respectful of Erik, could often be very caustic about other people. The combination of high camp and professional bitchiness was not attractive.

Erik knew that Rudolf and he were becoming figures of fun, that people were making jokes about them behind their backs. For a *danseur noble* this was hardly a comfortable situation. If it were to become public, who could say what damage it might do to his image? And on top of everything there were the emotional and sexual demands that Rudolf was making on him. For a normal person the sexual demands might not have been onerous – indeed they would in all probability have been intensely pleasant. But for a dancer, who needed his rest and who was ten years Rudolf's senior, they were wearing.

The emotional demands were worse. Rudolf loved Erik and was impressed by him (it always mattered to Rudolf, to be impressed by people). He once said that western dancers are well prepared technically, 'but they do not on the whole have the intellect the Russian dancers have. In the west the intellectual father is the choreographer, who does all the thinking.' That didn't apply for a moment to Erik. But it was in Rudolf's nature that all his friendships, all his relationships, must be demanding. He challenged everyone, from the beginning and at every opportunity. This wasn't wrong; indeed without it Rudolf would not have made the mark he did. But, alongside Erik's cooler nature, it was less mature. Rudolf had turned his back on his father, so perhaps it was only natural that, once he could enjoy the freedom of the west, he should fall in love with an older man. But, as Erik put it, after the initial collision and explosion he found the sheer intensity of Rudolf's feelings overwhelming. When that also brought about a change in the way he was seen as a dancer – something had to give.

He fell ill, and took to his bed. Or he said that he did. Many people thought he was playing a game. Kenneth MacMillan, who had choreographed one of the ballets Erik was to dance, and John Cranko, visited him in his room. Neither of them believed he was really ill and accused him of lying, of playing the temperamental star. That made Erik even worse, and he threw them out. Before anyone else could visit him, he dressed, packed his things, got into his car and left. He said goodbye to no one, not even Rudolf. He left Germany altogether, driving north to Copenhagen. But despite what MacMillan and Cranko thought, he *was* ill, even if that illness was psychosomatic. He now developed spasms in his back which were so painful, and so restricting of movement, that it took him a week to reach the Danish capital. During that time, no one knew where he was.

He felt better when he arrived home but the tension had not eased entirely. He was due to dance in yet another gala performance, to celebrate the hundredth anniversary of the Tivoli Gardens (Europe's first 'theme park'), at which he was to appear before the King and Queen. His partner at the gala was to be Sonia Arova and so, before he had been in Copenhagen long, she arrived. Arova was soon followed by Rudolf, and the three of them again stayed in Bruhn's house in Gentofte. The threesome that Nadia Nerina and her husband found so distasteful was renewed.

At least in the privacy of Bruhn's house, the tension between Erik and Rudolf was relatively hidden and their equilibrium seems to have re-established itself, so much so that when Arova tore a ligament and was unable to rehearse for several days Rudolf agreed to dance *her* part with Erik. This was a friendly gesture, but it was bound to provoke sniggers. After the gala, as Arova was leaving, she noticed that the two men were again having a stormy time.

The fighting might have continued, but tragedy struck. Erik's mother died. He had rushed to hospital when he heard she had been taken ill with a blood clot. He arrived, asked where his mother was, and was directed to a room. When he entered, expecting her to be alive, he was devastated to see her body covered by a sheet. Rudolf, who was with Vera Volkova at the time, went home to Gentofte – and now showed his best side. He missed his own mother and fully empathised with Erik's loss. He was considerate. Scheduled to leave Copenhagen the next day, he cancelled his plans and stayed on so that Erik would not be alone in the house. In so doing, Rudolf fully redeemed himself in Erik's eyes. As a result of that experience, Erik always felt bound to Rudolf far more than to his other ex-lovers.

CHAPTER THIRTEEN

In Love with Fame, by Freedom Smitten

In love with fame, by freedom smitten,
with storm and tumult in his head.

In the autumn of 1962 a Polish newspaper reported in a small article that Nureyev had bought a villa at La Turbie in the South of France, over-looking Monte Carlo. The article said he had paid $1.2 million, but though the fact of the purchase was true enough, the price quoted was way off – the villa cost him about FF 300,000 (£30,000 or $42,000). However, this newspaper was monitored by friends of Rezida in Moscow and they relayed it to her. The news brought about a change in Farida's attitude. Until that point, she had faithfully believed all the Soviet propaganda about the west, and thought that her only son risked starvation and crucifying poverty. But, after Rezida had told her mother about the article, Farida replied, 'Well then, let him live there. In the name of God.' She was not the Stalinist her husband was.

Hamet never discussed it. Rezida, who was married and living away from home by this time, thought that her father had, from the first, never imagined that Rudolf would come home. 'Perhaps father just knew more about the west.' Rudolf got word through to them, to invite his mother (but not his father) to the west but, says Rezida, 'the authorities would not allow her to leave'. Rezida went with her mother to the local KGB headquarters to explore the possibility of her mother leaving Russia. 'Call him over here, if you miss him,' they were told. 'Let him come himself.' But, says Rezida, Farida would have none of it. 'You want to lead him, through me, to prison. I will not call him.' She had heard of the Leningrad court verdict, of course, but wasn't taken in.

The economic and work situation of the Nureyevs in Ufa didn't change much, one way or the other, but they *were* watched. 'Nobody said anything to my face,' says Rezida, 'but I was under the control of the security services. In the factory where I worked I was the manager's assistant and one day he fell ill for quite a long time. I thought I would fill in for him but they put another person there instead, letting me understand that I was offensive because my brother was abroad and a traitor. Because of Rudik, my son suffered more. At school much was made of the fact that his uncle was a "traitor" and both his teacher and the headmaster took it out on him. They wouldn't let him join the Pioneers. I later learned that even the headmaster of Number Two School had come under pressure after Rudik defected. Many in the local Party wanted to know what sort of teacher he was, that he could bring up a traitor.'

As justified a 'traitor' the KGB devised two plans to get back at Rudolf. In one he was approached to see if he would work six months in the west and six months in Russia. If he hadn't fallen for the original deception, why should he fall for this one? The other plan was for both his legs to be broken. The KGB file contains some amusing internal exchanges reflecting on the effect this would have on Russia's international image. Some people clearly didn't care – they just wanted to prevent Rudolf dancing and to dissuade others from following his example. But they seem to have lost the argument.

Still, Nureyev's purchase of the La Turbie villa showed that *he* was doing all right, economically speaking. He had plenty of work, had spent part of the summer in Italy, dancing with the Royal Ballet and with Fonteyn, before returning to America to appear for a second time on the *Bell Telephone Hour*. The cold war was such a part of life in those years that he received more press attention when he went – as a customer – to a performance of the Bolshoi in New York, having bombarded Plisetskaya with flowers. The newspapers wanted to know whether he would be allowed to meet the cast. He was told firmly that they did not want to meet him.

From New York he went to Chicago. In his early years in the west Ruth Page in the United States was especially welcoming. He stayed with her when he performed with her company. In Chicago, he taught the *Le Corsaire pas de deux* to Arova. She was the third pupil in this role, after Fonteyn and Lupe Serrano, with whom he had danced it on the Bell television programme. As John Percival has remarked, this *pas de deux* was Rudolf's first small but brilliant contribution to the Royal Ballet's repertory. It was also, as Rudolf appreciated, a role that began to attract a new type of audience to the ballet. 'It is,' to quote Percival again in his book on Nureyev, 'full of big jumps for the man, and in this more than any other role Nureyev was able to display the soaring quality of his technique. In the solo the lithe springiness with which he leaped to revolve in the air, the smoothness of his pirouettes and the crispness of his final circuit of the stage all contributed to a sense of exhilaration. Then his long, high grand *jetés* in the finale always caused a gasp by the way he appeared to hover in the air at their peak.'

Back in London, he had been commissioned to film *Les Sylphides* but what everyone was really waiting for was the announcement of a new ballet by Ashton, specially created for Fonteyn and Nureyev. After Margot's gala, after *Giselle*, this was a natural progression, the perfect step forward in theatrical terms. The announcement was duly made. The new ballet was to be called *Marguerite and Armand* and it was based on Alexandre Dumas's romantic story of a tragic Parisian courtesan, *La Dame aux camélias* (the same story as Verdi used in *La Traviata*). The music was by Liszt, the sets were to be by Cecil Beaton, and the ballet would open on 15 December 1962. Covent Garden was besieged.

And then the opening had to be cancelled. Covent Garden announced that Nureyev had injured his foot. This was true enough, for he had danced *Les Sylphides* with one ankle in a bandage and in excruciating pain. But a spokesman also let it be known that he 'would rather deal with *ten* Callases than one Nureyev'. So was the new boy acting up? It seemed so, for no sooner had Covent Garden gone public with the news that *Marguerite and Armand* was to be delayed than another announcement was made, this time from Lucia Chase of American Ballet Theatre in New York. Chase said that Nureyev would dance with her company *in Chicago* over Christmas. Nureyev's critics naturally blamed him for this juicy piece of double-dealing, for it appeared that he had invented his foot injury to get himself off the hook of his London commitment; that he preferred Chicago, at least at Christmas time, to London. In fact, the misunderstanding was all the fault of the Covent Garden management. Nureyev's Chicago plans had been known about for some time and London had gone public with the news about *Marguerite and Armand* before he had signed any kind of undertaking with them and on the arrogant assumption that he would be bound to put Covent Garden before Chicago. But the double-dealing was worse than that, for the Royal Ballet management had used Nureyev's illness as an excuse for cancelling a performance that they knew they would have to put back anyway, for other reasons. They had counted on Rudolf's reputation for wildness to draw the flak. David Webster and his staff did not come out of this episode well.

Unable to dance for the time being, because of his foot injury, Rudolf took himself off to Australia. It was somewhere fresh to see – he had told Rezida he wanted the bright lights – and Erik was there, dancing with Arova, so the threesome resumed once more. Rudolf, still worried that he might be kidnapped by the Soviets, arrived in Australia under an assumed name. While there he and Erik were observed having dinner together by Michael Powell. 'It was', Powell wrote in his memoirs, 'like watching an eagle mate with a pigeon.'

Between Australia and Chicago his autobiography was published. Since he was not yet twenty-five, this could be considered somewhat premature, but he was persuaded by the argument that it would be good for his career, and that was paramount for Rudolf, even more than his love for Erik. Though the book was necessarily not long, and in some places his story had been 'improved' in the telling, it nonetheless gave a clear view of Rudolf, his views on the differences between western and Russian ballet, and the pressures that led him to defect. The book was written in collaboration with 'Alexander Bland' – i.e. the Goslings. They were forming a firm friendship with Rudolf; Nigel Gosling was not a little infatuated with the Russian dancer himself.

Rudolf danced five performances in Chicago with Lupe Serrano – in *Le Corsaire*, *Themes and Variations*, and *La Fille mal gardée* – and enjoyed a better reception than in New York. However, he ran into yet more trouble at the beginning of 1963, when he was due to return to Paris, to dance at the Opéra. The Russians had other ideas. The French were told firmly that, if Nureyev was granted the honour of dancing at the Opéra, other Russian-French cultural exchanges would be cancelled. In no time, the Paris invitation was rescinded – but the French were not alone in their attitude. Ruth Page told John Percival that several New York companies were worried about reprisals so that, in the early days, they chose not to invite Rudolf to dance with them. It was shameful but, perhaps, realistic.

Luckily for Rudolf, London, like Chicago, was not intimidated. In early 1963 he was welcomed back to Covent Garden, where he danced Etiocles in John Cranko's *Antigone* and the leading male role in Kenneth MacMillan's plotless ballet, *Diversions*. Both of these were fast, powerful roles where his physique and technique were seen to advantage.

All his life, Rudolf would have a certain number of female friends whom he could rely on, scattered about the cities he visited most often. In London there was Margot, and Maude Lloyd (Gosling), and in early 1963 he befriended Lee Radziwill, who was then a princess (Rudolf adored titles), married to Prince Stanislas Radziwill. They lived quite near Eaton Place, in Buckingham Place, where they planned to give Rudolf a birthday party that year. Lee was the sister of Jacqueline Kennedy and, with his nose for café society, which Rudolf had learned from Margot, he began to spend as much time at her house as he did with Fonteyn or the Goslings. Joan Thring, who was to become Rudolf's assistant, observed that Lee was 'besotted' with Rudolf and convinced herself that the couple had an affair in the mid-1960s. Her chief evidence for this was the fact that, in the spirit of the times, Lee tried to set Joan up with her husband, 'Stash.'

What everyone in London was waiting for, however was the 'postponed' première of *Marguerite and Armand*, scheduled now for March. Marguerite Gautier, the heroine of Dumas's book, had always fascinated Frederick Ashton, who looked upon himself as a romantic man obsessed by romantic figures. Ashton – born in Guayaquil, Ecuador, in 1906 –

was British to the core though, as Peter Williams the journalist and critic put it, his South American years had given him a Latin bloom and he spoke perfect Spanish. He had seen Pavlova dance in Lima in 1917 and, having failed to shine as a banker in the city, returned to his first love under Léonide Massine. Ashton had read a great deal about Marguerite, the beautiful but fatally consumptive courtesan who renounces her aristocratic lover to preserve his reputation, then dies before he can redeem himself in her eyes. In real life Marguerite had been based on Marie Duplessis, but the idea for the ballet did not occur to Ashton until, quite by accident, he heard one day on the radio a sonata by Liszt. 'And I sat there, and I saw the whole thing could be contained in this music. Margot seemed to me the epitome of Marguerite, and Rudolf seemed to me the epitome of Armand.' Ashton was also taken with the idea that Liszt himself had had an affair with Marie Duplessis, and he was fond of quoting her words beseeching Liszt to take her with him to Italy: 'I will be no trouble to you. I sleep all day, go to the theatre in the evening and at night you may do what you will with me.' The story contained a form of womanhood that, in Ashton's eyes, was fast disappearing.

The Liszt music, the Sonata in B Minor, was orchestrated by Humphrey Searle, and the lighting was by William Bundy. But, so far as the general public was concerned, *Marguerite and Armand* was the creation of four people: Ashton, Fonteyn, Nureyev – and the designer of the scenery and costumes, Cecil Beaton. Beaton worked on *Marguerite and Armand* just before he left for Hollywood where he designed the famous film, *My Fair Lady*. So it could be said that he was at the peak of his powers (though not yet knighted, like his friends, Olivier and Ashton). His experience with this ballet was not altogether agreeable, however. He invited Rudolf to his house one afternoon in January. This was a ruse to 'show him friendliness and perhaps strike up a relationship that might make our working together more agreeable – or even more satisfactory'. Like the photography session in early 1962, the meeting was not a success, and Nureyev created a bad impression. 'He was impolite and surly, never showed enthusiasm for the pictures he liked, only disdain and anger for those he hated. He was only drawn to full-length portraits of himself.' Beaton was even harsher in a note he wrote in his diaries:

In many ways Nureyev reminded me of Greta [Garbo], the same wild untamed quality of genius, of not fitting. But Greta is subtle and sensitive and has a sense of humanity, even if she is utterly self-centred. He has no pity, no concern for others. He is ruthless and says, "If they were dead I not mind." I felt very much as if I had brought an animal from the woods into my room. I felt at any moment the furniture might be violently kicked, tables and chairs turned upside-down, the whole place reduced to a shambles. It was quite dangerous.

Beaton concluded by saying that he felt he had played the Russian like a fish (presumably in the sense that the fish hadn't broken the line and got away) but that he had failed to establish any rapport. In that sense, the meeting had failed, at least from Beaton's point of view. His assistant, Eileen Hose, disliked Rudolf.

Matters did not improve during rehearsals. Beaton had chosen to set the ballet in a semicircular gilded cage, derived, according to his diary, from a Second Empire gilt firescreen that had caught his eye as he began work. He put red camellias on most of Margot Fonteyn's gowns but she was embarrassed to wear them. In the original story, the courtesan Marguerite wore red camellias five days a month, when she did not receive visitors, and white ones twenty-five days a month, when she did. Fonteyn, 'for reasons of modesty', insisted on white ones. Nor did Fonteyn like the hat that Beaton designed for her, and disposed of it as soon as he was out of the way. 'I could have kicked her,' he wrote. But the ugliest scene at rehearsals came when Rudolf almost refused to wear the costume which Beaton had designed for him. He said the tailcoat made him look like a waiter and insisted on cutting the tails so short that Beaton loathed the result. De Valois calmed everyone down but it was hardly the best preparation for the big night.

That the *Marguerite and Armand* story suited Fonteyn and Rudolf was never in doubt and as the first night approached the London press worked itself into a frenzy speculating on the precise nature of the romantic attachment between these two when they were off-stage. They were so beautiful together, so talented, and spent so much time in each other's arms with hardly anything on . . . how could they not be lovers? Whatever may have happened later, nothing happened just then. Rudolf was still very much in love with Erik. He was still wreathed in smiles on the days that he received a letter. Lee Radziwill recalls bumping into Rudolf in a mews near where they both lived, and finding him very worried because Erik had refused to destroy some passionate and frankly erotic letters Rudolf had sent him. He wasn't worried that the letters might fall into the wrong hands, just that Erik was not totally in his control. He had never had a relationship like this before.

A few days before the first night, Nigel Gosling, writing as Alexander Bland, published an interview with Frederick Ashton in the *Observer*. Ashton was a little upset with Rudolf, because he would keep talking about Balanchine all the time and Ashton thought that Rudolf should have more manners – or else just decamp to New York. But, at least in this interview, Ashton outlined his working methods. With this ballet, he said, contrary to his usual practice of starting at the beginning and working forward methodically, he had chosen to start with the highlights. On the second day, Fonteyn was rehearsing with Michael Somes, who had been cast as the stiff father of Armand and who, in a highly emotional confrontation, pleads with Marguerite to give up his son, to save his reputation and that of the family. Margot and Michael were old partners, and knew each other well and the rehearsal was going famously, with much emotion being generated. 'I saw the door [to the rehearsal room] open a crack,' said Ashton, 'and Rudi looking in very cautiously, in his scarf and everything. I could see him tiptoe around behind me as we went on working, and when we began to come to the end of the scene he started stripping off his coat and things and just at the right moment he flew out from behind me into Margot's arms; it was wonderful.' Fonteyn later gave her own version of this moment. 'As Michael and I played the scene over, an electrical storm of emotion built up in the studio. We came to the end, and Rudolf tore into his entrance and the following *pas de deux* with a passion more real than life itself, generating one of those fantastic moments when a rehearsal becomes a burning performance.'

What Ashton never revealed was that even he was afraid of this extraordinary twenty-five-year-old. At one point in the rehearsals, Rudolf kept asking for the music to be played slower and slower. Eventually, Jack Lanchbery left the rostrum and stood next to Fred in the stalls. 'This is wrong musically,' he said to Ashton. 'Who wrote this piece, anyway, Liszt or Nureyev?'

Ashton lit a cigarette, got up and said, 'Sort it out with him.' And sauntered out of the auditorium.

Expectations were building. One critic wrote that Covent Garden had given *Marguerite and Armand* enough publicity to win a general election (the real one came the following year, but election talk was in the air). More photographs were taken of this ballet than any other Fonteyn had worked on. Beaton himself took a great many since the set designs called for blow-ups of photographs. Rudolf nearly punctured this elaborate build-up when he was interviewed on radio and, instead of talking in a misty-eyed fashion about Dumas, Paris and the drama of consumption, he said baldly and with not a little glee that he had modelled himself on Robert Taylor, the Hollywood actor.

Marguerite and Armand opened on 12 March 1963 with Margot, Rudolf, Michael Somes and Leslie Edwards in the principal roles and the Queen Mother and Princess Margaret in the royal box. About two hours before the curtain went up, Rudolf visited Margot in her dressing-room and gave her a small, white camellia tree. She was very touched. They had been dancing together barely a year and that tree, for her, 'seemed to symbolise the basic simplicity of our relationship in the midst of so much furore'.

As the curtain goes up in *Marguerite and Armand*, Marguerite is seen alone on the stage. She is dying and, in her consumptive delirium, she looks back on her life with Armand (briefer even than the time Margot and Rudolf had been dancing together). These flashbacks are shown through high projections on screens at the back of the stage. While this is happening, Armand enters and moves in a distracted way – mourning – before these visions of his life with Marguerite. When she sees his face she reaches out – but in a spasm. Then, for a moment and behind a gauze screen, their earlier life together is recaptured realistically on stage. Marguerite sits on the same couch, alert and beautiful, camellias at her breast and surrounded by admirers. Ashton said this scene was suggested by a reception for Ulanova in Peru at which only the men turned up. The orchestra sounds a major theme of the sonata and Armand enters. He is handsome, masculine, vital, intense. The duke, her present lover, watches with the others as Armand approaches Marguerite and kisses her hand. She coughs slightly but no one pays any heed, it is a minor thing. They dance together – gaily – and she coughs again. Suddenly they are alone and Marguerite sinks into Armand's arms. The duke returns, to find them embracing, and takes her away. As she leaves, Marguerite throws a camellia to the floor near Armand. Another man starts to pick it up but, observing Armand's interest, backs away. Armand seizes the flower and dashes off.

It is spring. The couple are leading an idyllic life in the countryside, away from Paris in Bougival. Their dancing reflects their simple joy. Afterwards, Armand goes off, to ride, and Marguerite sits alone, contemplating a happiness she had not thought possible. The music turns stern and portentous – and Armand's father appears. At first Marguerite does not comprehend what the father is saying, but he is unrelenting and soon his message is painfully clear. She must give up Armand. She is unsuitable and conflicts with the life he had planned for his son. Armand's sister is to be married but the sister's suitor will call off the match unless Armand's unsuitable liaison is abandoned. Marguerite refuses at first, and implores the father to stop his demands. For a time, both are implacable.

But Marguerite is ill, weaker than she was when she and Armand met. She tires – and faints. Armand's father softens, but only for a moment. As she recovers, his point made and having produced the effect he intended, he leaves. Marguerite takes to her bed.

Armand returns and the couple dance with a furious, blind passion. We guess, though Armand doesn't, that this may be their last time together. The dancing gets faster and faster, displaying more and more brilliance and virtuosity, but ends on a calm note, with the couple sitting quietly together. Then she rushes off stage and, before we have time to study Armand's reaction, the scene ends in a blackout.

We are back in the glitter of Paris. Marguerite is back with the duke. She is adorned in diamonds and camellias. However, although she is clearly at home in this sophisticated world and once more the centre of attention, she rests on a couch and coughs repeatedly. She is now very ill.

Armand enters. He is shocked to find her in such company, and she is devastated that he should see her in this way. He grabs her diamond necklace and throws it away. She tries to escape but he throws money in her face. No one has told him of his father's intervention, so he thinks she has left him for all this glitter. He stands, cleansing himself of her tainted company. As Armand is doing this, his father enters and offers help to the tiring Marguerite. She rejects this.

In the last scene a nurse and Armand's father are comforting Marguerite. She has a fever, and can see only Armand. He enters in a black cloak, seizes her, kisses her and lifts her up. She makes a few steps on hobbled point – and dies. Armand places her gently on the floor as his father turns his back on his son. Armand lifts Marguerite's arm, still not comprehending that she is dead. It falls away from him, to the floor.

As with *Giselle*, the fall of the curtain was followed by a brief pause in which the theatre was completely still. The grief on Rudolf's handsome face as Armand realises that Marguerite is dead, the moment when his beautiful eyelids close, as he presses her lifeless hand to his cheek, was truly moving.

And then the applause came. Hand-clapping, feet-stomping, cheers and whistles. Flowers began to rain down on stage as Rudolf stepped back to let Fonteyn curtsy and bow low, alone. As one curtain call followed another, as the emotion in the auditorium rose and the couple relaxed, they could be seen talking. What Margot said was, 'Well, now do you think you will stay another year, even though you are so unhappy with us?' Smiling to the audience, he spoke to her almost out of the side of his mouth. 'Margot,' he whispered. 'You know I will never be happy anywhere.'

The reviews of *Marguerite and Armand* mirrored its reception in the balcony. Writing in *The Times*, Clive Barnes said: 'the swiftness of the ballet gives it an hallucinatory quality and a sense of flying passion, of a tragedy fitfully illuminated by flashes of Keats' "spangly doom" . . . Here is the true romantic agony distilled into a brief ballet, far more pungent in its effects than any Giselle.' He added, "It shows as never before Fonteyn the dance actress. . . . The power she first tested out in *Ondine* and later in *Giselle* is here seen at full stretch . . . Even to a greater extent than Fonteyn's Marguerite, Armand is derived from Nureyev . . . he has never been seen to such advantage in the west . . . he goes through *Marguerite and Armand* like a fiery arrow shot by destiny. The wild theatricality of Nureyev, the charge he can give the simplest pose or movement, the impact of his dancing, are used to telling effect.'

No one else has ever danced *Marguerite and Armand*. Created for Nureyev and Fonteyn, in many people's minds it came to symbolise their relationship. Very different in background, Marguerite and Armand fall in love, but are prevented from loving by social constraints. The embargo on other dancers may also be seen as a great tribute by Ashton, who did not want to sully their performances by giving the work to others. And yet . . . Ashton had been upset during the rehearsals, by Rudolf's constant talk of Balanchine. He thought it ill-mannered, ungrateful and insensitive. It was one reason why he never again created a role for Rudolf.

From Leningrad, there was mixed news. Thankfully, Tamara's exile from university was now over. She had been reinstated the previous December but Nureyev only found out now. Her father, who was a minister in the government, had discovered what had happened and complained to his colleagues in the Ministry of Higher Education. Tamara would be allowed to sit her exams next time around.

Liuba Miasnikova still faced her ban, however. It would last for ten years.

And Rudolf himself was attacked in *Izvestiia*. The Soviet press at last broke its two-year silence on his defection, but only to denounce him as a traitor, to his art and to his country, adding smugly that he was now 'decaying' as a dancer. It reported yet more comments by Serge Lifar, on Rudolf's 'moral degradation', saying that he was 'unstable, hysterical and vain', that he drank whisky until five o'clock in the morning instead of working. The communist press in Paris always repeated such tendentious nonsense gleefully. Rudolf was distressed only in so far as others, at home, might believe it. He was content to remind himself that Lifar was a Nazi collaborator.

Marguerite and Armand had been the right move theatrically, for Ashton, for Fonteyn, for Rudolf, and for Covent Garden. But there had been yet another reason for doing it. That spring the Royal Ballet took 160 souls and 500 tons of scenery on an American tour. As we have seen, these tours were regular affairs – every other year. Hitherto, they had begun in late autumn and continued through Christmas. This was the first spring tour and, with the new Russian sensation as a permanent guest artist, and a brand new ballet created especially for Fonteyn and him, hopes were high that the tour would be every bit as successful as earlier ones. Sol Hurok had overcome his nervousness about Russian retaliation (he imported the Kirov, Bolshoi and many Russian musicians, as well as the Royal Ballet). He had seen for himself the reaction to Fonteyn and Nureyev in London and knew that if he didn't bring this partnership to North America, someone else would.

America was ready. Clive Barnes, in his 1982 book on Rudolf, tells a very funny story about the chain of events in March 1963:

'I remember meeting [Rudolf] for a late lunch in a South Kensington café in 1963. I was writing a story on him for the *New York Times* Sunday magazine in preparation for a forthcoming visit by the Royal Ballet to New York. He explained to me that he could not eat, and merely toyed reflectively with a Negroni cocktail – a drink he was at the moment fond of. He had, he said, already had two lunches that day – one with the representative of *Time* magazine and another with a reporter from *Newsweek*. Both wanted to prepare a cover story on him, and this unsophisticated child of Soviet nature understood immediately that if *Time* did it, *Newsweek* wouldn't, and vice versa. He shrewdly realised that it would be better for all concerned – particularly himself – if each party were kept in ignorance of the other's activities until it became too late.'

The ploy worked. Nureyev appeared on the covers of both *Time* and *Newsweek* in the same week. Politicians apart, the double cover remains an extreme rarity.

Joan Thring helped set up these lunches. Her life had come full circle now. An Australian, she had arrived in London in the 1950s and, because her husband was an actor, she had worked in theatrical publicity (starting at the top, with the Oliviers). She had handled the Kirov's publicity on the London leg of its 1961 tour, meeting them at the airport after Rudolf had defected (see above, p. 180) but now she was handling Rudolf. They had met throught the Covent Garden grapevine. She remembers that the *Newsweek* reporter was terrified of Rudolf's temper and was anxious to avoid upsetting him. The lunch was at La Popotte. 'May I bring my photographer?' the *Newsweek* man pleaded.

'Is he good-looking?' asked Joan.

'No.'

'No.'

Rudolf arrived in his Mercedes. (A little later he swapped this for Joan's Triumph Herald. The police were following him just then because he had jumped a red light five times, *in front of* the police. Joan's car was less conspicuous and Rudolf thought she looked better in a Mercedes than he did anyway.) He was then drinking negroni (gin, sweeet vermouth and bitters) and the interview started in the bar. All went well until the reporter, feeling bolder, criticised Rudolf's treatment of Joan, who had left. Whatever happened, it did not make into the reporter's copy.

Rudolf's relationship with Margot developed on the North American tour. 'Little Genghis Khan,' as Fonteyn called him by now, 'was in fact growing up like a lion. I learned that the secret when he snarled was to make him laugh and, thank heaven, he found silly things amusing, such as the sign 'Dead Slow', which I suppose *is* hilarious to someone approaching English with a clean eye. It wasn't long before he could make puns, too. In most *pas de deux* there are some lifts where the girl's arm is round the back of the boy's neck. If I put my arm too high, Rudolf finds it killingly uncomfortable and says, "Necrophilia! Necrophilia!" even in the middle of a performance.' (A more characteristic usage was changing the title of the ballet *Blown by a gentle Wind* to *Blowjob in the Wind*.)

Although David Blair opened the Royal Ballet's season in America, with Fonteyn in *Sleeping Beauty*, it was Rudolf who drew attention, in *Marguerite and Armand*, *Le Corsaire* and *Giselle*. New York owed nothing to London in its response to the great couple. After the first night of *Marguerite and Armand*, the bravos were 'shattering' and 10,000 carnations were strewn over the stage. After *Giselle*, 'the fans stood and screamed for half an hour.' When they danced the Black Swan *pas de deux* from the third act of *Swan Lake*, the applause held up the performance for five minutes. 'Shattered ear drums are a dime a dozen,' wrote Walter Terry in the *New York Herald*. 'This is the hottest little team in showbiz.' On the black market, $15 tickets were selling for as much as $73.

But *Le Corsaire* overshadowed everything. Based on Byron's poem, *Le Corsaire* is about a pirate who frees the woman he loves from slavery, though the resemblances between the ballet and the written work are slight. Although *Le Corsaire* was originally a three-act work, Russian companies and the Royal Ballet often performed just the *pas de deux*. Introduced by Fonteyn and Nureyev in London in November 1962, it really took off in the United States. As Fonteyn later recounted it:

'In New York,' she wrote in his memoirs, 'we danced the *Corsaire pas de deux*, which we had already done in London. Then it had been programmed like a one-act ballet, with intermissions before and after. I was upset, thinking that people would feel cheated to get only ten minutes of dancing. I went to Ashton in great distress to complain. He simply said, "Well, it will be all right. Ten minutes of *Corsaire* and twenty minutes of applause. What are you worrying about?" I was full of apprehension until the performance came.'

She need not have been.

'Rudolf's Corsaire is the stuff of which legends are made. The first step of his variation, when one clearly saw him sitting high in the air with both feet tucked under him, exactly as though he were flying on an invisible magic carpet, was beyond description. One watched with a touch of disbelief . . . no one has ever danced *Corsaire* like Rudolf, and it is permissible in this case to use the adjective "sublime." It was so exciting to watch him from the wings that I lost all nervousness for myself, and danced with a glow of exhilaration and joy. In New York the applause lasted for twenty minutes – in fact, it only stopped when the curtain rose on the following ballet.'

After the performance, Jacqueline Kennedy tried to go backstage to pay her compliments, but now Hurok did get nervous. As wife of the President, Mrs Kennedy wasn't just any fan and Hurok was worried that the Russians might take offence. He refused to let her backstage and even locked the door to Rudolf's dressing-room. For Mrs Kennedy Hurok made up a story, saying that he was concerned that she might fall and hurt herself amid the 500 tons of scenery, wiring and scaffold. Mrs Kennedy agreed and Hurok for ever after boasted about the way the President's wife had obeyed him. But Rudolf was livid.

Not everyone joined in the chorus of approval. One anonymous Royal Ballet dancer was quoted in the press as saying that Nureyev was 'very unpopular' at Covent Garden. 'Many dancers don't like him,' said this source. 'He's flashy but technically no better than anyone else.' Among the American critics, there are no prizes for guessing who led the assault – John ('Dean') Martin, who had so viciously attacked Rudolf after his Brooklyn début. This time his review was entitled 'Rudolf Nureyev: Pluses and Minuses', and he remained distinctly unimpressed. In fact, his diatribe must rate as one of the worst ever written. Rudolf's Blue Bird was indifferent, Martin said, his *Swan Lake* and *Giselle* 'a disaster'. It had been a black day for the Royal Ballet when Nureyev arrived as a roving *cause célèbre*. De Valois had not made many mistakes in her career 'but when she does it's a beaut'. Nureyev was like the man who came to dinner: he stayed to take over and he was jeopardising the very ballet company she had started. His partnership with Fonteyn was an unhappy experience 'whatever the ballet', since he had repellent mannerisms and his psyche trailed across the stage like lava. Martin insisted that the box office retained a 'frigid indifference' to Rudolf and that on nights when he danced but Fonteyn didn't, the theatre was *not* full (his italics). He said that Rudolf was, albeit unintentionally, a 'disintegrating force', meaning that the general (i.e. uninformed) public was so besotted with him as to be blind to other, better dancers. Not even Fonteyn was immune to his sniper fire this time. Writing of her partnership with Nureyev, Martin sniffed that 'she has gone, as it were, to the grand ball with a gigolo'. And then he included the phrase that was to cause so many to decide that the Dean had finally joined the damned: 'It was a tragic facility that allowed him to escape from the Soviet agents at the Paris airport, who were shipping him back to Russia.'

Not even Arnold Haskell, himself one of Rudolf's sternest critics, could stomach that. He wrote to *Saturday Review* saying that there was no place for bad manners in such a periodical. 'Alexander Bland' was even stronger, accusing Martin of being malevolent, vulgar and – worst of all – provincial. The riposte seems to have worked. Martin was rarely heard from again.

Normally, the Royal Ballet's American tours took in Washington, but not that year. However, Fonteyn and Nureyev, along with Frederick Ashton, Michael Somes and John Lanchbery, the conductor and musical director, were invited by Jackie Kennedy to take tea at the White House. They were flown down from New York in a private plane and shown around the public and private apartments of the first residence by the

President's wife herself. After tea, as she showed them into the Cabinet Room, she said, 'I will just see if the President is busy.'

'While she went to the Oval Office,' said Fonteyn later, 'Rudolf took the opportunity to find out what it felt like to sit in the President's chair.' Kennedy did join the party and made some tactful remarks to Fonteyn about her husband's understanding of Central American politics. For Jackie, who had heard about Rudolf from her sister Lee in London, this was the beginning of a long-term friendship.

Back in New York, the glitter continued. Sol Hurok always gave the entire company of 160 a welcoming party on the roof of the St Regis Hotel. Tito joined Margot when he could, contributing his showbiz and diplomatic friends. One evening at a restaurant with Fonteyn, Rudolf was spotted by a woman who was obviously part of the exiled Russian community in Manhattan. She bore down on him and began speaking volubly in Russian. After a while, and in the middle of her gushing, she suddenly stopped and looked at Fonteyn, who was wearing a fashionable white hat, with a wide brim. The woman turned back to Rudolf and said, in English, 'Who is that? Your mother?'

It was on that first tour of America that Rudolf discovered two great ballet teachers. The first was Valentina Pereyaslavec at the Ballet Theatre School in Manhattan. A small woman with a powerful personality, and a voice to match, Pereyaslavec had the gift of making her pupils *want* to please her. Rudolf recognised the cleverness and importance of this, relishing the fact that it made the hard work in class much easier, since her pupils naturally pulled out their best. No one was allowed to talk for the entire hour and a half as she bellowed out instructions and – occasionally, in a quiet voice – praise. At the end of class the exhausted dancers would applaud her, and she would curtsy. Then she left, ahead of everyone else. Her classes were themselves theatre and this is what the genuine performers responded to.

The other teacher was Hector Zaraspe, an Argentinian of great charm and something of a comedian. According to Fonteyn, whom Rudolf took along for a lesson, Zaraspe liked to tell the story of how, when he first arrived in Manhattan, he spoke very little English. One day on the subway he was strap-hanging between two enormous Americans. He was of slight build, and when the time came for him to leave the train he had to push past the burly frames of his fellow strap-hangers. At first he spoke timidly but one of the men glowered down at him and shouted, 'Whaddya say?' Zaraspe, even more timidly, repeated. 'I said, ex-squeeze me, please.'

The New York season lasted from 17 April to 19 May. The tour then took in Baltimore, Philadelphia, Boston, Detroit, Toronto, Chicago, Seattle and Portland, ending at the Hollywood Bowl in Los Angeles on 7 July. In Chicago, they took over the Shuma Hotel, made famous by Al Capone. In Los Angeles Hurok threw another massive party, at the Bel

Air Hotel. In Toronto Rudolf was off on one of his late-night walks, trying out a few steps in the middle of the highway, when he was arrested by the police. He took a few playful kicks at one of the arresting officers, and was observed by passing motorists, who cheered and applauded. He was taken to the cells and left to cool off for a while, before being released without charges being brought. The Canadian police seem to have been understanding about the whole affair.

As Fonteyn said, these extended tours, where 160 people lived and worked in each other's pockets for weeks on end, always sharpened the rivalries and romances within the company. And no relationship aroused as much curiosity and interest as her own with Rudolf. She wrote later:

> As I was obviously very fond of Rudolf and spent so much time with him, it was food for scandal to those who liked it that way. I decided there was little I could do but wait for it to pass. The truth will out eventually, I thought. Meanwhile, I worked with Rudolf and often went out with him. But I hardly ever saw him go home. He always walked off into the night, a lonely figure diminishing in perspective down a desolate street. There was something tragic in his departing step after the uproar of laughter and gaiety over supper. It is frequently so with stage people, who pay for coming out in the limelight by going home in the rain.

This was typical Fonteyn: an acute observation, but only half right, the sentiment wilfully distorted. For there were several things Fonteyn left out of her analysis. The first was that Rudolf always got so keyed up for a performance, and was so exhilarated *by* a performance, that he could not sleep for hours after the curtain had fallen. He *had* to go out, wherever he was. He was the perfect night owl, drifting from night club to night club in search of stimulation. Then there was the fact that, in the mid-1960s, Rudolf was overwhelmed by a mixture of fame, wealth, sexual freedom and continuous travel. He still loved Erik but they now spent a great deal of time apart. Rudolf was a handsome man, and demanding, who found that others would accede to his demands, do things for him, including sexual things. In the United States, although there were many places that were far more backward, sexually, than in Europe, this was not true of the big cities where the Royal Ballet appeared. These had a more active, and a more liberal homosexual life than much of Europe. On that first North American tour Rudolf began to experiment with the promiscuity that was to form such a feature of his private life in years to come. When he went off into the night, cruising, he may well have been a lonely figure, as Fonteyn described him, but he didn't stay alone for long.

One reason, perhaps the main one, why Rudolf kept his private life to himself was because it had nothing to do with the other parts of his life. He might be becoming a promiscuous homosexual in private, and as time went by not a little camp, but he was a heterosexual, monogamous prince on stage, and saw nothing odd in that.

By the same token, all this was separate from his feelings for Fonteyn. And their feelings for each other were very strong. She herself told Colette Clark that she had to be 'half in love with Rudolf' to dance with him as well as she did. And Clark says that 'they were always kissing and cuddling'. It would seem that the 1963 tour was the beginning of the romance between Fonteyn and Nureyev. That relationship was still new; she was young enough to attract, and be attracted by, younger men; Rudolf was maturing rapidly and, not least in importance, Tito was still philandering. Rudolf told friends that Margot had the kind of body he liked in a woman. He found it 'very feminine'.

That summer a smaller company, made up of Royal Ballet and ABT dancers, went on a world tour that took in Athens, Nice, Cannes, Israel and Japan, ending in Honolulu. Joan Thring, who helped organise this jaunt, remembers being buttonholed by Rudolf a short while before the tour, to ask if Erik could be included in the party. He didn't want to be separated for the six weeks that the tour lasted. Eventually Erik was found a slot – he would give class every day. Then, when they were all in the plane waiting to leave for their first destination, Athens, Rudolf approached Joan and asked, in a loud voice and in front of everyone else, 'My hotel room; it has double bed?' Joan said she didn't know. 'I want double bed,' shouted Rudolf. Joan retaliated by saying that, so far as she knew, they were all booked into hotels of international standard and that *all* the rooms would have a double bed. Rudolf stared down at her and uttered one word. 'Pizducka!' He then went back to sit with Erik.

Joan, being a feisty Australian, followed Rudolf back to his seat and, cannily, asked Erik what *Pizducka* meant. 'It turned out that it was every filthy Russian word rolled into one.' But Erik was so embarrassed that Rudolf at least on this occasion apologised. Thereafter, Joan always called Rudolf *Pizda*. She wasn't sure what it meant exactly, 'but it seemed to fit'.

During that tour, Joan and Rudolf brought down to a fine art the business of getting visas for him. Since he had no passport, he needed visas for everywhere. 'Usually,' says Joan, 'while the others were at the farewell party, Rudi and I would be closeted with the local British ambassador, getting this document or that, so we could actually get into where we were next going.'

At the end of the tour during a rest day on the beach at Honolulu, Rudolf approached Joan. He stood over her.

'Rudolf, you're blocking the sun.'

'I think you crack very good whip,' he replied, without moving. 'I like you look after me.' Pay was not discussed. She said yes anyway.

*   *   *

On 3 October 1963 Erik turned thirty-five. This is a psychologically crucial age for a male dancer, for he knows that, from now on, his physical powers must decline. It is one of the ironies of the dancer's art that, at the moment he matures intellectually and emotionally, his physical powers begin to fail him. It must count as one of the great opportunities of Rudolf's career that he and Erik were lovers at this stage. *He* could benefit from Erik's ageing, since he was just twenty-five.

Rudolf was lucky in other ways too. In September 1963, Ninette de Valois retired as artistic director of the Royal Ballet and Frederick Ashton took over. For his first production as director, he asked Rudolf to mount his own version of *La Bayadère*. When the Kirov had appeared in London, in the days following Rudolf's defection in Paris, one of the most popular ballets had been the Kingdom of the Shades scene from *La Bayadère*, in which *he* should have starred. The scene the Kirov had danced was the one in which the spirit of the dead heroine appears to the hero, together with her companions – 'rank after rank of remote but radiant figures weaving and bending like a field of corn in the moonlight'. (This was the scene that had so enraptured Olivier Merlin in Paris.) There was some apprehension at Covent Garden that Ashton should entrust the *entire* ballet to Rudolf's young shoulders, but he proved to have a phenomenal memory for the Kirov steps and to be excellent as a teacher. This more than offset his volatile temperament.

Rudolf's problem, or challenge, was to teach the Royal Ballet not just the steps of the ballet but a new style. He wanted more of a Kirov – or Russian – effect than the British company was used to: more attack on the part of the soloists, more discipline in the *corps*. Crisp rather than lyrical. The ballet was mystical enough as it was; it had to be danced with *force*. As several critics noted, the *corps* of the Royal Ballet now entered its strongest phase and *Bayadère*, and Rudolf, had something to do with that.

Again, expectations were building: £8 tickets were changing hands for £45 on the black market and a great fuss broke out when this was revealed. Ballet lovers from the balcony who found even £8 steep, were incensed that rich people who had only discovered ballet in the past few months were pushing up prices in this way. Then, just five days before the première, on a Friday night when Margot and Rudolf were dancing *Marguerite and Armand*, and before anyone could take any curtain calls, Ashton stepped out to make an announcement. During the performance, he told the audience, the news agencies and radio services had reported the assassination of President Kennedy. Ashton asked that everyone should stand for one minute as a tribute to the President's memory. 'There was a gasp and then a frozen silence as the minute dragged by,' wrote John Percival in his biography of Rudolf. 'Then, with no curtain calls, the theatre emptied swiftly and solemnly.'

Rudolf took the assassination badly. Although he had met Jackie through Lee, he always preferred Jackie. She was not in love with him, didn't want anything from him, and of course was much more famous than her sister.

La Bayadère, set to music by Ludwig Minkus, was choreographed by Marius Petipa and first produced at the Maryinsky Theatre in 1877. Mikhail Baryshnikov has called this ballet 'one of the great, if not the greatest, classical works in the history of ballet. It is Petipa's idea of life in the beyond . . . Poetically, it is unmatched in the classical repertory.' Most westerners were unaware of it until the Kirov toured with it in 1961, so the full ballet was quite an event. The narrative tells the story of an Indian *bayadère* – a temple dancer – called Nikiya. She is loved but badly treated by the warrior, Solor, who breaks his pledge to her and marries someone else. She is then poisoned by a confidante of her rival, and dies. Solor realises in the last act that he has loved Nikiya all along, and dreams that he seeks her in the Kingdom of the Shades. As in *Orpheus* and *Giselle*, she eludes him but he pledges never to forsake her again. The most powerful scene in the ballet is the last act, in which more than thirty shades descend upon the stage down a long ramp, parallel to the audience and all in profile. They execute simple steps but the prolonged repetition is so effective that an ethereal atmosphere spreads across the entire stage.

Margot played Nikiya, Rudolf was Solor, of course, and Merle Park, Lynn Seymour and Monica Mason were the three soloists. There was one minor disaster early on, when Rudolf slipped and lost his footing. As one critic said, two thousand hearts leapt into two thousand throats. Other dancers might have recovered, and continued dancing – but Rudolf ran off stage. This had only happened once before in London, with the French dancer Jean Babilée, and the anti-Nureyev claque tut-tutted away in prim self-satisfaction. Mr Temperament was at it again. But despite this, on the first night, most people felt that the whole company had absorbed the Russian flavour of the work completely, producing a ballet of classical simplicity that was to endure for many years. Moreover, the last act showed off the *corps de ballet* to great effect, which never failed to win a round of applause for its first ensemble, and this did no harm to Rudolf's popularity within the company. It also opened up a new course for him, as producer and coach.

Rudolf's success in *Bayadère* contrasted markedly with Erik's situation. He was again working with Balanchine in New York. He still didn't get on terribly well with the older Russian and, to make matters worse, had a health scare which necessitated a stomach X-ray. As a result, he left New York City Ballet prematurely. Then, early in 1964, Erik made his long-awaited début at the Paris Opéra, in *Giselle* with Yvette Chauviré. Here, he was somewhat put out to be described as the teacher of Nureyev. Though it was intended as a compliment, it made him feel old.

Rudolf attended the second night rather than the first. This was more sensitive than it sounds for he was such a celebrity by now that his presence might have detracted from Erik's opening. Rudolf went backstage after the performance, where Erik found him to be rather down. 'He avoided the press and said that he didn't want to see anybody but me.' Once with Erik, however, Rudolf relaxed and the two of them decided to sneak off together to Maxim's. Of course, Rudolf was recognised but they managed to enjoy the evening all the same. They ordered Russian caviare and a bowl was put before them. They were so hungry they ate the entire bowlful and could barely afford the bill when it came. 'Pity the Marquis de Cuevas isn't here,' said Rudolf. 'He would have won the money at the casino.'

During the dinner it became clear why Rudolf was so quiet. He told Erik that he had been asked to dance *Giselle* with Margot in Australia. Erik asked what the problem was, and Rudolf replied that, having seen *Erik* just dance *Giselle*, he didn't think he could dance it any more. Rudolf might have all the celebrity he could want but he was acute enough to see the depth in Erik's performances, a depth which, he felt, was lacking in his own. He both admired Erik and was jealous of him.

In fact, they were jealous of each other.

CHAPTER FOURTEEN

Private Tastes

His father died; and (as expected)
before Onegin there collected
the usurers' voracious tribe.
To private tastes we each subscribe.

Just before Christmas 1963 Rudolf was knocked down in the street by a
motor scooter, and for a time he didn't know how serious the injury to his
ankle was. Instead of going home to Eaton Place, he stayed for a few days
with Margot. Interviewed around this time, she was quoted as saying
that Rudolf was mature artistically but immature emotionally. She said
little more but was referring to an incident that took place while he was
staying with her, in which he had tried to take their relationship further.
She had been tending to his ankle one day when he had made a reference
to Bougival. This was, in a way, romantic but as Margot saw it, also immature. Bougival is the place in *La Dame aux camélias* where Marguerite and
Armand spend time together in perfect happiness. As a gesture by Rudolf
it ought to have been touching, but it struck a false note. He knew it, she
knew it, and was annoyed. Worse, she was embarrassed. It seemed
to epitomise Rudolf at his arrogant worst; he was being not so much
romantic as saying, in effect, that he could have anything and anyone.

Well, he couldn't. At that time, Tito had been having an affair with his
secretary and Margot had kicked her out twice, and Rudolf knew it. But
that didn't mean that she herself was fair game. She suggested Rudolf
move back to Eaton Place.

Because of his injured foot, Rudolf had to miss the first night of a new
production of *Swan Lake*, directed by Robert Helpmann, to which he had
contributed three new dances. He did appear in a television spectacular
transmitted live from Covent Garden in February and in a number of
other ballets before going on the Australian tour that he had spoken

to Erik about. This was a physically tiring time – they danced *Giselle* or *Swan Lake* three times a week, in Sydney and in Melbourne. Lupe Serrano also danced.

In Australia Rudolf was now spending more time with Margot than he was with Erik. More to the point, perhaps, Margot was spending more time with Rudolf than she was with Tito. The intervening weeks, since Rudolf had made that reference to Bougival, had been very important for Margot, emotionally speaking. Before the Australian tour she had spent a few days in Panama with Tito, who was now a candidate for the National Assembly, the country's parliament. A general election was scheduled for 17 May.

What she never said in any of her writings, but Panamanian friends and Joan Thring confirm, is that she discovered that Tito was now having an affair with the wife of one of his political colleagues. Tito had never said that he wanted Margot to retire – he liked her money too much for that. But he hinted at it and Margot now saw that if Tito was elected to the National Assembly, he would have a regular income and need to spend more time in Panama. Where his affairs would continue. For Margot there was nothing wrong with life in Panama, in itself, except that if she retired Tito would really be in control – and where would that leave her? His philandering would just get worse. It was in this reflective state of mind that she left for Australia.

When the two dancers reached Sydney they were besieged, as they were everywhere now, by the press who wanted them to explain the 'secret' of their partnership. In her memoirs, Fonteyn said that she really did not know the answer. Nureyev always denied in public that they had slept together, adding that if they had, it would have spoiled their dancing; that they retained a spark on stage precisely because they had not consummated their relationship off-stage. This was neat, too neat (although several of their friends, like Joan Thring and the ballet photographer and writer Keith Money, believe that there was never anything sexual between them). Twice in as many pages, Margot wrote that Rudolf was happy on that Australian tour, happier than she had ever seen him. It was in any case a curious thing for Fonteyn to say, apparently apropos of nothing at all. It was put to the author by friends of Fonteyn's that she was in fact writing in code, that what she meant was that *she* was happy on that tour: happy to be with Rudolf, away from London and the rest of the Royal Ballet, and away from Tito's tawdry affairs.

Nureyev was dancing more strongly than ever now. When they had first danced together, he had performed *Giselle* only a few times and he showed what Fonteyn called an amateur's enthusiasm. 'He had since gone through the period of losing his natural excitement for each performance, and was now learning to manufacture spontaneity. He did it by getting angry – it is easier to dance in a rage than in cold blood, and I noticed him looking around for an excuse, no matter how flimsy, to shout one or two profanities before an important evening.' Fonteyn loved this. Rudolf's strength, on stage and off, impressed her and stimulated still stronger feelings for him.

Rudolf could not have been more different from Tito. Tito, outwardly sophisticated, urbane and charming did not so much love his wife as feed off her fame and money. Rudolf might have a temper, might prefer men to women most of the time, sexually speaking, might be one of the coarsest people she had ever met, might have come from nowhere, but he was gloriously funny, astonishingly honest, a perfectionist in his art and, so far as she was concerned, generous with his time, his affection and his money, which was his own.

One night in Sydney, in the last week of April, they walked back to their rooms in the hotel, holding hands as they sometimes did. As they came to Margot's room, she opened the door with one hand without letting go of him.

For the next three and a half weeks they were effectively man and wife. Nureyev made one comment about this period of his life. 'To have made love as a man and as a woman,' he once told an interviewer, 'that is special knowledge.' What he didn't say was that, in 1964, he had both experiences, with Erik and Margot, at more or less the same time.

For Fonteyn the crunch came at the end of the Australian tour, when Tito had promised to meet her on her way back from Sydney, in Miami, for her birthday (18 May, the day after the election). When she reached Miami he wasn't there. When she reached him by phone he said it was impossible for him to leave as the votes were still being counted. She went on to Panama, where she found not only that he had very little time for her (she said she felt 'lost in the political jabbering') but that his affair with the wife of Alfredo Jiminez, his political colleague, was the talk of all their friends. On the flight back to London, Fonteyn felt depressed and sick in her stomach. In Australia she had never felt happier. The contrast was stark.

After Australia, her next performance with Rudolf was in Stuttgart for a very different version of *Swan Lake* staged by John Cranko. Shen then went on to Rome. While she was there, she and Joan Thring, who now worked for both Margot and Rudolf, spent a lot of their time trying to contact Tito by phone, but it became clear he wasn't at home. In fact, he wasn't even in the country. He had gone for a mountain holiday – with the wife of Alfredo Jiminez.

This was the first of two decisive events for Margot. Tito had not been able, or willing, to meet her for her birthday in Miami (and in 1964 she was forty-five), but he *could* spare the time to take his new mistress away. She, Margot, was being made a fool of. The second decisive event occurred when she discovered, on her return to London, that she was pregnant. Fonteyn never told anyone about this, except Rudolf, but he told several of his lovers and his American agent in later years, Andrew

Grossman, that Margot had become pregnant by him. (Joan Thring confirms that Fonteyn saw a doctor that summer for an unspecified obstetrical problem.) What Margot did discuss with her friends in London was her decision to leave Tito. It wasn't that she harboured any thoughts of marriage with Rudolf. The differences in their ages and basic nature precluded that. And she did not intend to have his child, either. She could do without *that* scandal. But she did love Rudolf in a way that she had never loved Tito, not since 1937 anyway. Her love was returned by Rudolf, in his way, and that was a cleansing thing, purifying after Tito's cheating and philandering. What she had with Tito, she realised, was second best, and Rudolf had taught her, on stage and off, to only go with the best. She might never find the right man but Tito was the wrong one, at least for her. Separation from him would make her life more honest. It might even help her art.

On 9 June 1964 Margot and Rudolf had agreed to dance a specially choreographed *pas de deux*, by Kenneth MacMillan, for the opening of Yehudi Menuhin's music festival at Bath. The day before, they rehearsed as normal and then went out with Joan Thring to eat. When they returned to the St Francis Hotel they were met by the Menuhins. Diana Menuhin approached Joan Thring first and said, very quietly, that Tito had been shot but was still alive. Joan first turned to Rudolf. 'Go to your room,' she said, 'and stay there till I come for you.' Rudolf was not used to doing as he was told but on this occasion something in Joan's voice made him obey. In the hotel lobby, Joan now told Margot, 'There's a problem with Tito.' She didn't elaborate, but said she had to call Tito's brother, in Panama. Margot took this news fairly calmly and went to her room with Kenneth MacMillan and Barry Kay, the designer. There were no phones then in the hotel bedrooms and Joan had to call from the lobby. She got through to Tito's brother who said that he was being operated on as they spoke and that if Margot wanted to see him alive she had better get on the first available plane. Joan then asked if they knew who the assassin was and why he had tried to kill Tito. The brother told her what he knew and repeated the name of the assassin twice, so she could be sure she had it. He had asked that Joan call him, not Margot, he said, so that he could make it clear *why* Tito had been shot. This wasn't a political assassination.

Joan returned to Margot's room. How much should she tell her and should she tell her when they were alone, or with others in the room? She decided to let the others stay. It was a mistake. As soon as she started to tell Margot what Tito's brother had said, Margot began to scream and yell. She ran from the room, still screaming, and fled down a long corridor that led to a ballroom. Joan ran after her, calling to the others to fetch Rudolf.

When Joan reached Margot she was standing in the centre of the ballroom, where the lights were switched off, wailing. Rudolf arrived, went up to her and held her. She calmed down. Rudolf didn't like Tito and, like Joan, didn't know whether Margot had been wailing for her husband or herself, but she calmed down when he held her.

Joan stood close. The first question Margot asked was, 'Who did it?'

Joan knew that Margot often didn't like all the unpleasant aspects of a problem spelled out at once. But this seemed a straightforward, if detestable, situation.

'Alfredo Jiminez.'

Margot started screaming again. 'No! You've got it wrong. No! *No!*'

'I haven't got it wrong,' said Joan softly. 'I asked them to repeat his name twice.'

Margot knew then what she had already suspected, that this wasn't a political assassination attempt at all. It was the logical conclusion of Tito's years as a flagrant philanderer.

'Margot, I need to organise a plane. Shall I do it?'

'No, no,' said Margot, calming down again. 'Let me think about it for a while.'

It was extraordinary. At that moment of maximum drama, Margot was in two minds as to whether she wanted to see her husband. It was a crucial moment of absolute honesty on her part, when all pretence had been dropped.

Joan arranged the ticket anyway, and called Covent Garden to alert Lynn Seymour that she might have to replace Margot the next night in Bath. And of course Margot decided later in the evening that she *would* fly to Panama the next day.

She wrote in her memoirs that she read the newspaper reports of the shooting on the plane and only in that way did she learn the shocking truth: Tito was paralysed. She said that she also caught up on the circumstances of the shooting. According to the press reports, it was a political crime. One of Tito's deputies, Alfredo Jiminez, had asked Tito to register him as one of the substitute deputies. Tito had said he would, but only if Jiminez gained the requisite number of votes. Otherwise another deputy, who did have enough votes, would have to be chosen. Jiminez had worked for Tito, and thought he owed him greater loyalty. To him, it seemed that Tito was hedging. He had put a gun in his pocket and driven through Panama City until he saw Tito in his car, which had stopped at a red light where Calle 50 and Via Brasil intersect. Jiminez got out and fired six times at Tito from point-blank range. Two bullets entered Tito's right arm and chest, puncturing a lung. A third bullet grazed past his shoulder and lodged against his spine, near the neck.

Of course, Margot was relieved that none of the newspapers had got on to the true story. Their Panamanian friends must have closed ranks.

When she reached Panama she was met by Archbishop McGrath, the religious leader of Panama, and taken straight to Tito. She arrived at the hospital at about eight o'clock at night. The ward was enormous, empty and dark. Tito was lying, not on a bed, but on some kind of table, and he was covered by a sheet. His right arm was in a plaster cast and there seemed to be drip-feeds everywhere. As she approached the table she saw the tube through which he breathed coming out of a hole in his neck.

'Darling, I am here,' she whispered.

Tito opened his eyes and turned them towards her without moving his head. 'Their expression indicated that he recognised me and understood my words. He even tried the very faintest of smiles,' she wrote later.

Margot remained in Panama for two weeks, during which time Tito continued to improve; or she thought that he did. She visited Tito every day and had consultations with the doctors. But she also uncovered something truly shocking, something it was amazing that the press had not printed. *Jiminez's wife had been in the car with Tito when he was shot.* Joan Thring and all their Panamanian friends were also amazed that this extraordinary story never leaked out.

In her memoirs Fonteyn says that the doctor who had undoubtedly saved Tito's life, Dr Gonzalez-Revilla, suggested to her that Tito be transferred as soon as possible to Stoke Mandeville hospital in England for rehabilitation treatment. This is a specialist clinic with rare facilities for the treatment of paraplegics. Such a move may well have been the doctor's recommendation, but the real force in having Tito transferred, only four weeks after the shooting, was Margot herself. She knew that he might suffer a thrombosis at any time but she was prepared to take the risk because she was more worried that there might be *another* attempt on Tito's life. This is an interesting admission. Since he was known to be paralysed, it is unlikely that Tito would ever have been a force in politics again. But if the motive for the original shooting was romantic revenge, Jiminez would not want his wife feeling sorry for Tito. Margot wasn't prepared for what actually happened. During the journey back to Britain, Tito caught pneumonia and the infection spread, attacking his vocal cords and damaging his ability to speak. Margot felt guilty about this ever after and her guilt helps to explain a lot about what subsequently took place.

Fonteyn's rapid change, from such happiness in Australia, to profound distress now, barely a month later, was as clear to her friends as the difference between night and day. But life had to go on and Margot had to go on dancing. It was not merely a question of her being emotionally and artistically committed; there was now the added worry of finance. Tito wasn't earning and his treatment needed to be paid for.

There was never any question of her leaving him now, of course, not in her own mind. She *could* have left him, and there was no shortage of friends who believed that she should let the real reason for the attack be known, and then go her own way. For some of those friends, the more callous perhaps, Tito had only got what he deserved. It was surprising that someone else's husband had not done the same thing long ago. But no, Margot wouldn't leave. Although she was the same person off-stage as on, as all her friends point out, there *was* a sense in which, even off-stage, she was a production. She was a famous ballerina, a famous English ballerina whose best-loved roles were Giselle, Ondine, Odette-Odile – innocent, pure, ethereal, otherworldy creatures who nevertheless lead their lovers to doom. Here was life imitating art with a vengeance. Fonteyn knew instinctively how she had to respond to this crisis.

Her surviving friends confirm that, after the shooting, Fonteyn changed completely: 'she changed overnight.' Having made up her mind to leave Tito at the end of May/beginning of June, she now became fiercely loyal to him, put him and his needs above everything except her dancing, which now took on a new urgency since she needed to provide the income.

Rudolf, at that time, was one of her harsher critics. As one friend put it, 'He really chewed her out.' But she was implacable and Rudolf, a forceful man who acknowledged strength of purpose in others, accepted her decision, however much he disagreed with it. He loved her, and knew that she loved him, but he also knew that sex was over between them. For her part, she had never fully accepted her feelings for Rudolf. Now she denied them more than ever.

The consequences for Rudolf were complex. Margot was almost certainly the last woman he slept with, although Joan Thring says he had a couple of inconsequential girlfriends later on. But the fact that the sexual relationship with Fonteyn was cut short meant that it was one of the few aspects of Rudolf's life that he couldn't fully determine or control. As a result, he always remained half – and maybe more than half – in love with Margot. The way Margot coped with her misfortune, her sheer strength, impressed him. Not many people did that.

After seeing Tito settled in Stoke Mandeville, Margot joined Rudolf and the smaller touring company in early July at the Teatro Nuovo in Spoleto, Italy, where they were to dance in the first performance of *Raymonda*. This is a glorious ballet – at least it has glorious music, by Glazounov. It was first produced at the Maryinsky in 1898, with choreography by Petipa. In the story, Raymonda is separated from her betrothed, Jean de Brienne, who is away at war but expected home at any moment. Before he can return, however, a sinister Saracen, Abdérâme, arrives and woos Raymonda ardently. Jean arrives home, challenges the Saracen to a duel – and wins. It is a simple, but winning, story.

Rudolf's achievement with Raymonda was rather more than he was given credit for. It was only thanks to his phenomenal memory for ballet steps that the work could be recreated at all – because he had never danced the entire ballet when he had been in Leningrad, just the male *pas de quatre* from the last act. And he had never played the lead. There were other problems, with the Italian designer who was too modern for everyone's taste, so that after the festival the ballet was withdrawn for a while from the Royal Ballet's repertoire.

Before that decision was taken, there were still more dramas. The day before the première, Joan Thring took a call from the hospital at Stoke Mandeville, recalling Margot. There was no more medical information, just the bald statement. Margot recalled: 'Rudolf came into the room. The *Raymonda* production was very important to him – it was the first three-act ballet he had ever staged and no one was standing by to replace me at the première the next day. But, realising the extreme gravity of the situation, he was unusually gentle and seemed dreadfully upset for me as he said, "You must pack and leave right away. Don't think about the ballet. The drive takes two and a half hours so you must leave in half an hour".'

Doreen Wells replaced Fonteyn, very successfully, but for Rudolf the importance of *Raymonda* lay in the experience it gave him in choreography. His vivid memory meant that he should be able to resurrect classic ballets and give them his own stamp. That set him thinking.

The row over the sets produced one important piece of fallout. The Spoleto festival is called the Festival of Two Worlds, because it seeks to bring American and European artists together. Another figure at Spoleto that year was Paul Taylor, the choreographer of modern dance. He was sitting watching one of Rudolf's rehearsals when the argument broke out and the set designer stormed off. Taylor approached Rudolf and told him that if he didn't want the sets, Taylor could use them. Rudolf thought this both very funny *and* practical. The two men soon became firm friends. It was during this festival that the celebrated 'spaghetti affair' took place. Rudolf attended a buffet given by the opera director Gian Carlo Menotti, at which he was invited by a waiter to help himself to spaghetti. 'Nureyev does not help himself,' Rudolf replied and threw his wine over the man.

Meanwhile, in Stoke Mandeville, Tito had suffered the thrombosis that had always threatened. Indeed, technically he had died, in that his heart and breathing stopped. But he had been resuscitated, even though at one point his temperature had reached 108 degrees – unheard of, certainly in adults. Margot returned to Spoleto in time for the last performance and then accompanied Rudolf to the Baalbeck Festival where *Raymonda* was continued.

In the autumn Rudolf went to Vienna where he had been asked to stage *Swan Lake*. He, Fonteyn and Nicholas Georgiadis, the designer, were to share a fee of 600,000 Austrian schillings. By now Nureyev was developing as a designer of ballets in a marked direction. For example, he would keep to the basic structure as worked out by Petipa, 'because it's so logical.' But he would introduce changes, which were always intended to give the male a bigger role. Petipa lived at a time when ballerinas were

Roland Petit's Paradise Lost. Clearly not Milton.

Rudi-mania.

Sol Hurok: 'The Last Impresario.'

Wallace Potts:
'Everyone liked
Wallace'.

Surveys showed he was
even more famous than
his friend Elizabeth
Taylor.

His princes didn't
forsake him, nor his
princesses. With the
Snowdons.

EXIT

With Leslie Caron, without hair cut.

With his bodyguard in New York. Rudolf was under 'executive checking' by the KGB, from 1961–1979.

Douce Francois, who once dressed as a man to get into Rudolf's good books.

Rudolf's companion
on the set of Exposed.

With Michelle Phillips in Valentino. But there was no love lost between them.

Make-up in Valentino. Rudolf was also buried in his evening clothes.

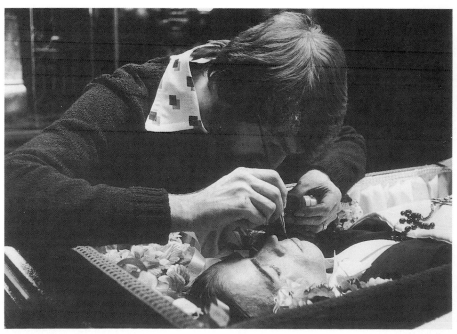

'If you've got it, flaunt it.' With Baryshnikov.

Robert Tracy, far right, with Rudolf in Don Quixote on Broadway, 1983.

Rudolf called him his 'ganymede' but as soon as the AIDS scare began Robert changed his behaviour and never slept with Rudolf again.

Homage to Martha Graham. Booed in Paris in the 1950s. Rudolf brought her back in the 1980s – to great acclaim.

Tea, with five sugars.

The French stars Rudolf discovered: Isabelle Guerin and Laurent Hilaire. 'We are not pots of flowers.'

Lee Radziwill: the 'Princess of Nothing'.

With Monique van Vooren, Regine's, New York, 1983.

the main attraction in ballet and, naturally, this did not suit Rudolf. But there were other changes, too, intelligent changes. Rudolf believed that ballets should have a strong point of view. It helped the audience identify with the characters and they came away feeling that they had seen a piece of thought as well as everything else. In his Vienna *Swan Lake*, for example, Rudolf made the prince the focus of the story, the swan becoming merely a projection of him.

In an interview he gave at this time, Rudolf showed how familiar he was with ballet history and how he updated that knowledge and applied it to his own day. He said that when Taglioni had adopted *les pointes*, it was no coincidence that the ballet was the *Revolt in the Seraglio*. 'She put men down,' he said. 'Even the soldiers in that production were women. In most productions of *Swan Lake* there is no chance for Siegfried to develop – all he can do is mope around with his eyebrows sloping like a house roof. That is why I revive the classics – for me.' And he attacked Balanchine. 'Balanchine never creates for men. He even emasculates men.' He then attacked the Royal Ballet. The school turned out great technicians, he said, but dancers with little emotion. Some people, he said were like umbrella pines, they developed but put all around them in the shade. Others could flourish in the forest. Who *can* he have had in mind?

His *Swan Lake* was extremely lush. The sets and costumes were sumptuous, in Nureyev's favourite autumnal colours. Margot danced superbly – never better, according to the local critics – and a young dancer named Anthony Dowell was 'engaging' as Benvoglio. It was during these performances, in October, that Margot and Rudolf earned eighty-nine curtain calls – throughout the evening, not just at the end – a record that stands to this day.

But it wasn't all plain sailing in Vienna. Joan Thring, who had stayed in London to organise some future work for Margot and Rudolf, got a frantic phone call from the management at the theatre. Rudolf had suddenly turned on Margot and had twice kicked her out of rehearsals, telling her to 'Fuck off!' in front of the entire company. This was all most embarrassing. No one spoke to Dame Margot like that. Would Joan please come and sort it all out? Joan did not think anything needed sorting out; Margot and Rudolf were both professionals and all would be well within hours. Still, the theatre management begged her to fly to Vienna on the next plane.

When she arrived, the first crisis was that there was no hotel room for her. Lord Snowdon, who was in Vienna photographing Margot and Rudolf for *Life* magazine, came to the rescue. He had a very grand suite, and allowed Joan to use his dressing-room.

As she had predicted, the problems had sorted themselves out by the time she arrived, but the reason for the fights on that occasion were more substantial than usual. If you look at Snowdon's pictures of Margot and Rudolf in Vienna at that time, you can see that he captured more than, perhaps, he knew. You see a very fragile, rather sad Fonteyn and a frenetic Rudolf, desparately trying to cheer her up. Besides all her problems with Tito, Margot had arrived in Vienna having had a miscarriage.

This was not surprising, in the circumstances. No doubt all the worry and travel had brought it about but it was, in its way, fortunate. She was forty-five and had intended to have an abortion. However, as a woman without children, that might easily have been more upsetting than what actually happened. As it was, she did not have to suffer the indignity of consulting doctors and persuading them to operate. She did not tell Rudolf that he had made her pregnant until it was too late – and that is why he was so furious with her in Vienna. He told several people later in life that he would have loved a child. He regretted losing his temper as soon as it happened, which is why Snowdon's pictures show him as so manic. After what they had been through, perhaps it was no wonder that their performances in Vienna should have been so moving, and earned such a marvellous reception.

Although they didn't know it at the time, this production also marked the beginning of the end of Rudolf's intimate relationship with Erik. Bruhn travelled to Vienna to watch Rudolf at work, and the two men naturally discussed the ballet in some detail. But although Erik liked Rudolf's choice of music (which included Tchaikovsky's original Black Swan music) the two men didn't see eye to eye over the ballet. Although they had had their fights and disagreements before, their artistic views coincided far more than they diverged. In this case, however, the disagreements were fairly fundamental. It didn't matter then, but it would come to matter. It would come to matter very much.

The year 1965 was the start of the Nureyev decade. By now, at the age of twenty-six, going on twenty-seven, he was a major celebrity, the man who had – almost singlehandedly – begun to draw a new audience for ballet. Despite its successes in the war and after, ballet at Covent Garden had, in strictly commercial terms, by then been overtaken by opera. The prices for opera tickets were higher than for ballet tickets and the audiences were richer and more fashionable. On opera nights, the crush bar at Covent Garden sold three times the amount of champagne as it did on ballet nights. All that changed when Rudolf and Margot danced. The prices on the evenings they danced were the same as for opera evenings, and so too was the consumption of champagne. De Valois gave an interview at this time in which she said that, thanks to Rudolf, the applications from boys to join the Royal Ballet School had almost doubled.

Surprisingly, it was only after Rudolf's arrival that Margot began to make any real money – and just as well given what happened to Tito. Rudolf was a natural businessman but he was ably abetted by Sandor

Gorlinsky, the impresario, who became his manager. Born in Kiev in 1908, Gorlinsky had moved with his family to Berlin but pushed on to Paris in the mid-1930s after the rise of the Nazis. In Paris he promoted ice shows and dance bands but, on holiday in Ostend in 1938, noticed the Royal Palace Hotel standing empty. He persuaded Billy Butlin to let him revamp the building as a pleasure-ground but before he could go very far war broke out. He transferred to Britain where, for the duration, he ran hostels for agricultural workers.

In 1946, however, his career really began when he sent a postcard to Benjamin Gigli the opera singer, who was living in Naples. Gorlinsky had overheard some British soldiers recounting how they had heard Italian opera during the war and wanted to hear more. Gigli wrote back to say that he was interested but drew Gorlinksy's attention to the fact that he had sung before Hitler and Mussolini. He didn't want to be accused of collaborating with the enemy. Gorlinsky didn't think it mattered, travelled to Naples by jeep and signed up the entire Naples opera company and delivered it to David Webster at Covent Garden.

By 1950 Gorlinsky was acting for Sir Thomas Beecham, Sir Malcolm Sargent and Sir John Barbirolli, and brought to Britain Arturo Toscanini, Tito Gobbi, Renata Tebaldi and Renata Scotti. But his greatest coup was Callas, who he lured to Covent Garden in 1952. After she divorced her husband, Gorlinsky managed all her affairs, so well that he was soon taken up by Alfredo Kraus, Montserrat Caballé and many others. He once flew 10,000 carnations from San Remo to London, at a cost of £115,000, to decorate an opening of *La Forze del Destino*. He was as tough as nails and that is what Rudolf liked.

After Vienna, Rudolf returned to London where he had his tonsils out. This was a nightmare for Joan Thring. When he couldn't dance, he had to be entertained. In the Eaton Place flat he had an antique train set which he played with. It had rails and worked on paraffin, making it extremely dangerous and, indeed, the two of them set the flat on fire one night. Joan was thankful when Rudolf could go out again. In those days, Rudolf liked the Sombrero, a restaurant/club in High Street, Kensington, the Arethusa, in Chelsea, and especially the old Caprice in Curzon Street. On one occasion, Joan organised a dinner there for Rudolf and Sean Connery, who was then starring in the James Bond films and was married to Diane Cilento, an Australian, like Joan. Everyone was excited when Marlene Dietrich rang up and invited herself to this dinner. Joan arrived early, to make sure everything was in order. It was, except that Dietrich was already there and was sitting\nearby at a table for two. 'What are you doing?' asked Joan. 'Waiting for Rudolf,' said Dietrich. 'We're having a *tête-à-tête*.' 'Oh no, you're not,' said Joan.

Dietrich took it in good part except that after all the others had arrived, she kept saying how much she preferred the company of peasants, how peasants were 'real' people, just like potatoes were the only 'real' food.

This was meant to be a flattering reference to Rudolf's background. Connery, who had a peasantish background himself in the rougher end of Scotland, looked around the restaurant, at the *foie gras*, the Dover soles, the carcasses of duck and upturned champagne bottles. 'Ah yes,' he said. 'But only peasants who can afford to eat at the Caprice.'

At another party that autumn, Rudolf was astonished to be greeted by a stunning brunette, with long eyelashes, what used to be called a 'full' figure, and a deep voice. 'Rudolf,' she breathed, 'I've been a fan of yours since I was a little boy.' It was April Ashley, known in London for being the first in Britain to undergo a sex-change operation.

While convalescing after his tonsils operation, Rudolf spent Christmas in Toronto, where Erik was dancing with the National Ballet of Canada opposite Lynn Seymour. Rudolf turned up at their rehearsals unannounced, dressed in sleek boots and a black fur coat. He took Erik and Lynn out to dinner that first night, trudging through deep snow. However, when they reached the restaurant, the *maître d'* refused to seat them because Rudolf was wearing a turtleneck sweater rather than a tie. Rudolf lost his temper, grabbed the *maître d'* by his shirt and, according to Seymour, in her memoirs, jabbed the man's nose into his fur collar. 'Feel this!' he shouted. 'If the coat isn't worthy of your restaurant, then nothing is.' And he led the way outside, where he started pelting the restaurant windows with snowballs.

Seymour was highly amused, but Erik wasn't. He had seen it all before. The two men had a fight in the snow, Erik stormed off and Rudolf took Seymour back to their hotel for dinner.

Bruhn had been asked to mount a production of *La Sylphide* and, once they had made up, Nureyev sat in on the rehearsals. It was just as well: again, Erik injured himself, pulling a muscle. He managed to dance that night (it was New Year's Day), and another dancer replaced him on 2 January. But Rudolf, with his facility for learning new roles in no time, took Erik's place on 5 January. Before the curtain went up the house manager made the announcement: 'Rudolf Nureyev,' he said, 'will replace Erik Burke.' Behind the curtain Rudolf and Lynn were shaking with laughter but for Erik it was a different matter. He made a rapid recovery.

Shortly afterwards, Rudolf rejoined Margot in Washington, where they were invited to dance at the inaugural celebrations for President Johnson. It was an honour, but not quite as thrilling as when the Kennedys had been in the White House. The other entertainers were Harry Belafonte, Carol Channing, Julie Andrews and Barbra Streisand, but the loudest and longest applause of the evening was for Margot and Rudolf. This was despite the fact that Rudolf had danced at the gala with his foot in a bandage – he had slipped on some ice in Toronto and hurt his ankle. Back in London he injured it again, by jumping off a bus! This was more than annoying. Rudolf was always superstitious about his ankles and believed that Pisceans were born with a weakness in this part of their anatomy. He decided to miss out a couple of performances in London because he didn't want to forego that spring's big new opening. This was Kenneth MacMillan's new ballet, which was being taken on the 1965 tour of America: *Romeo and Juliet*. The first night was set for 9 February.

The drama behind this ballet was probably greater than for any other comparable production, though the whole truth didn't emerge for nearly twenty years. To begin with, there had been plans for Britain and Russia to exchange choreographers – Ashton for Lavrovsky, who would bring his *Romeo and Juliet* west – but this had proved impracticable. Ashton therefore invited Kenneth MacMillan to take on the production. MacMillan gave the story his own twist, stressing the family side of the drama, and relegating the public scenes to the background. This was all perfectly legitimate but what produced the drama was that, just as Ashton had a special relationship with Fonteyn, so MacMillan adored Lynn Seymour. From the beginning, MacMillan choreographed the main roles for her and for Christopher Gable. It was an important ballet for all of them. It was MacMillan's first full-length effort for Covent Garden, and it was the first complete ballet to be modelled on Gable and Seymour. Once it become known inside the company that the ballet was going forward, these three became inseparable. Between them they worked out a new, modern, but completely credible version of the familiar plot. MacMillan told the designer, Nicholas Georgiadis, that he wanted a realistic Verona, 'where young horny aristocrats roamed the town full of romantic, adventurous spirits'. MacMillan had seen Franco Zeffirelli's stage production starring Judi Dench and John Stride and wanted to achieve much the same effect at Covent Garden.

For MacMillan, the ballet – the story – really revolved around Juliet. To him, she was the key, the catalyst of the tragedy, a self-willed girl who dominates the more poetic Romeo, though she falls in love with him in an uncontrollable way. 'Romeo is a nice normal fellow,' MacMillan told Seymour, 'but it is Juliet's decisive personality and rebellious temperament that provokes the affair.' This suited Lynn Seymour very well, since it accorded with her own personality much more than it did with, say, Fonteyn's. Indeed, the whole production seemed tailor-made for MacMillan, Gable and Seymour. In her memoirs, Seymour says that they took to referring to *Romeo and Juliet* as 'our ballet'.

There was only one problem: Seymour was pregnant. She had been married to the photographer Colin Jones in 1963 and was told in late 1964 that she was going to have a baby, at almost exactly the same time that the *Romeo and Juliet* project was finally given the go-ahead. She was distraught. Ambitious dancers do *not* have children in their mid-twenties. As it happened, her husband was going to Leningrad with Nigel Gosling, to take photographs for the book Gosling was writing about the city. So Seymour was left alone in London. While her husband was away she made up her mind that there would be plenty of time, later, to have children. But 'Juliet was mine. Juliet was the bonding of my relationship with Christopher Gable. Juliet was a priceless gift from Kenneth, glazed especially for me. Juliet, the classic heroine of the theatre, was the culmination of all my fantasy roles as a dancer.'

She trailed across London, from doctor's surgery to doctor's surgery, trying to find someone who would perform an abortion. Always she was given the same reply – only if she was physically or mentally ill could the termination be legal. When she complained that she *was* mentally traumatised, she was invariably referred to a therapist. Finally, the Covent Garden administrator gave her the address of a 'clinic' (as she put it) in north London. The operation would cost £500, which she raised by borrowing against her weekly salary of £40. The operation took place at eight o'clock one Friday morning at the end of 1964 and she was back at home by the afternoon. MacMillan stayed the night, since her husband was away and didn't know what was going on.

Seymour was at rehearsals three days later and the old magic resumed. MacMillan, Gable and she hit upon the idea that the last act, when Juliet is dead, should not be fey and beautiful, but tough and ugly, as death is ugly. 'You're just a lump of dead meat,' MacMillan told her, and they conceived the manoeuvre that, in the last scene, her legs should be visible, and wide open, rather than primly crossed. 'The death scene was crucial to Kenneth. His lovers were not united in death. They did not die in each other's arms. "Two beautiful young people are dead," he said. "Two beautiful lives have been totally wasted".' That was the effect he wanted.

One afternoon in early December 1964 a Covent Garden press release announced baldly that the Royal Ballet's top attraction for the 1965 season would be *Romeo and Juliet*, starring Margot Fonteyn and Rudolf Nureyev. Sol Hurok, the American impresario who was bringing the Royal Ballet to North America the following spring, needed a big new vehicle for Fonteyn and Rudolf. The Royal Ballet board had agreed.

Seymour's reaction may be imagined. Her abortion, which of course had been kept a closely guarded secret, had been for nothing. MacMillan took it even harder. Unable to sleep, and privy to the sacrifice Seymour had made, he appeared at the theatre gaunt and haggard with hollows under his eyes. Glen Tetley, the American choreographer, was in London just then and he, like others, wondered why MacMillan didn't withdraw the ballet. But that might have done even more damage. In fact Seymour's plight was even worse than anyone had first imagined because, with the part of Juliet being modelled on her, she was obliged to teach Fonteyn and other ballerinas 'her' role. And, when the cast lists were announced, she found that she was cast only as the *fifth* Juliet. Her humiliation was complete.

By now, the calls from either Farida or Rosa had become routine. Rudolf wasn't upset by them and Joan Thring struck up quite a relationship with Rosa over the telephone (it would be a different matter when they met later on). Rosa was forceful and her personality came down the line as strongly as Rudolf's did on stage. Always the message was the same: 'they', meaning the authorities, had promised to forgive Rudolf, if only he would come home. He would use the conversations to try to get as much information about his family's material circumstances as he could, but it wasn't easy.

Once or twice, he tried to send things to them. He couldn't send money; it was too dangerous. Once, Maude Lloyd (Gosling) took a mink coat for Farida, wearing it under her own raincoat. The plan was for Maude to meet a local Kirov dancer and hand it over. The meeting took place but Maude and the dancer were forced to sit on a park bench for more than two hours until the dancer was satisfied that they weren't being watched. Then the switch occurred. Even then, however, Joan received an irate phone call from Rosa, complaining that what they had done was very dangerous. Farida could neither wear the coat nor sell it, too many questions would have been asked. They had had enough problems as it was, disposing of the coat. She made them promise never to try to do such a thing again.

A second visit, by Lee Radziwill, was more successful. She travelled to Leningrad with her young daughter and met up with Rosa and her daughter, Guzelle. The two girls got on very well and a number of minor exchanges, of items hidden in boxes, hair lotion and so forth, were possible.

The first night of *Romeo and Juliet*, on 9 February 1965, was a great success. Margot and Rudolf took forty-three curtain calls and the applause, led by Princess Margaret, lasted for forty minutes. The first and last of Margot's curtain calls were made to Tito, who had been brought from Stoke Mandeville in a wheelchair. Margot's new persona was being minted, and one of those most enthralled by the change was Joan Thring. She had been to Stoke Mandeville with Margot and seen what went on. When anyone but Margot entered the room, Tito would smile. When she arrived, his eyes 'were filled with venom'. According to Joan, Tito hated Margot having such control over him and she, although she felt guilty for damaging his vocal chords, partly relished the fact that she now did have complete control. So much so that she even allowed the ex-secretary, and ex-mistress, to visit Tito. Her performance on the first night of *Romeo and Juliet* was masterly in every way. And the curtsies to Tito were the greatest performance of all – completely phoney.

The reviews were ecstatic. *The Times*, in a reference to Rudolf's recent injury, said that he danced better on half a foot than most men did on two. But everyone was praised that night. In the same week, the Royal Opera had premièred a sensational production of *Arabella*,

Richard Strauss's last collaboration with Hofmannsthal, so 'the Garden' was enjoying wild success on all fronts. Not a hint of the drama and personal sadness that had gone on behind the scenes was made public.

The success was repeated when the company took *Romeo and Juliet* to North America in April. That year the company visited seventeen North American cities, finishing in Vancouver on 25 July. Several American dance writers now repeated Ninette de Valois's arguments about Rudolf's effect on dance, but citing even more impressive statistics. Ten years before there had been 75 dance companies in the United States, now there were 225. Washington and Los Angeles now had their own resident companies, and so did Boston which, in 1929, had banned females from dancing on stage in bare legs. Some of this was put down, quite rightly, to the efforts of such people as Martha Graham, Balanchine, Cranko and Béjart. But again Rudolf was singled out, especially for the encouragement he had given to male dancers. Ten years before, the ratio of girls to boys in American ballet schools had been 50 to 1; now it was 15 to 1.

There were of course the by-now familiar grumblings from the usual raft of anonymous Royal Ballet dancers who took the opportunity to criticise Rudolf. That year one said that if Rudolf didn't 'push off' soon, he – the anonymous dancer – would have to 'remove my candle from under this particular bushel'. A ballerina said that when Rudolf was charming he could charm the birds out of the trees but that when he was horried he was so horrid she felt sorry for him. A third dancer said that when Rudolf and Margot danced *Giselle* he didn't know which one was the ballerina, while a fourth said that Rudolf was, quite simply, 'the Antichrist'. These opening salvos seemed to have become part of the ritual of the Royal Ballet's season in New York.

One dancer who did not hide behind anonymity was Michael Somes who in an interview said that he thought Rudolf's influence on Margot was not all good. He had, Somes said, improved her technique but not the emotional side of her dancing. Margot was moved to respond, saying in an interview of her own that Rudolf had more natural talent than Somes, and that Michael had in fact 'over-fulfilled' his talents. Whatever else, these spats were good for box office.

The American critics took a different tack this time. They attacked Margot as well as Rudolf, arguing that the publicity for the Royal Ballet concentrated far too much on these two, to the exclusion of others equally talented. Nothing was ever said, but it may well have been that some details of the Gable/Seymour drama had begun to leak. It was a theme that would recur as the years went by.

Rudolf enjoyed some of the publicity, of course, but endured a great deal more. From his point of view, and from Margot's, publicity was more important than for other dancers of the Royal Ballet. He did not live on a salary, his income was not guaranteed and there was always the risk of injury putting a permanent end to his dancing career. As a measure of the link between publicity and earning power, in 1964 Rudolf was earning £500 a performance in Europe, and between $1,000 and $2,800 in the United States, which compares not at all badly with Lynn Seymour's Royal Ballet salary in the same year, which was £40 a week, or about £2,100 a year. Rudolf was always very interested in money – he was mean, or careful, depending on your point of view. He would rarely carry money with him to restaurants, for example. He knew there would usually be some rich hanger-on who would consider it a privilege to pay.

Aside from all the carping, the tour was as great a success as all the others. All three Kennedy sisters attended the first night in New York, when there were thirty-three curtain calls. Ashton was praised for improving the quality of the male dancing even above de Valois's level, and in Toronto the Royal Ballet brought in the biggest gross of any of its tours. On the social side, Margot and Rudolf helped launch the first night of Arthur's, Sybil Burton's new discothèque in Manhattan, during which a health-conscious reporter asked Rudolf how he could dance *and* drink whisky. 'We are not nuns,' sniffed the dancer.

He knew early on the importance of the sound-bite. 'I'm not much in love with the talking,' he once said, but he was. 'If I'm born bastard,' he told one journalist that summer, 'I must be bastard.' To another he said, 'You must sacrifice people to survive.' And to a third, 'Did it all happen too quick?' (He never gave an answer.)

At the same time he was more than ever worried that the Russians might try to kidnap him. Often, because he felt safer with company, he would stay with Joan at her house in Earls Court. One night she had arranged for him to have a massage and they were waiting for the masseur to arrive when the phone rang. It turned out to be a man called John Merry, who told them that their house was being watched by people from the Russian embassy. He said that their phones were being tapped and that their comings and goings were being photographed. Rudolf was inclined to believe this sort of thing, but Joan wasn't – in normal circumstances. However, she had noticed a number of unusual clicks and other noises on her phone recently, so she too listened to what Merry said. He added that he could help them but he wanted to come round himself to explain; when he arrived he would ring the bell three times. This was all very odd, not to say comical. Anyway, Joan agreed but called John Tooley, the assistant manager at Covent Garden, explained the situation, and asked if he would send someone to keep them company. Tooley sent Margot and Keith Money.

They arrived before Merry who, when he did arrive, proposed that he act as Rudolf's bodyguard. Neither Joan nor Rudolf was impressed by him but Margot asked him, there and then, if he did mercenary work. No one present knew what she meant at first, but then it transpired that she wanted Merry to go to Panama and kill Alfredo Jiminez, who had never been prosecuted (underlining the fact that the Panamanians accepted that Tito's shooting was a *crime passionel*). Joan was flabbergasted but remembers that, on a later occasion, Merry served Margot with a bill, which she refused to pay because Jiminez was still alive. As Joan understood it, Merry had indeed gone to Panama, intending to do Margot's bidding, but had been unable to. The bill was for expenses. After Margot refused to pay, Merry tried to run her down in a car – and the whole situation looked like getting out of hand. Fortunately for Joan and the others, Merry was soon afterwards involved in something else, for which he went to jail. It was a bizarre hothouse and the idea of Britain's prima ballerina, also a dame, taking out a contract on a politician was macabre. But Joan had no doubt that the Russians would have kidnapped Rudolf if they'd had the opportunity. Once when the Kirov came to London and a party was given for them in the crush bar at Covent Garden, she suddenly found herself surrounded by the KGB minders of this tour, who wanted to see what she looked like. After that she refused to go to Russia on Rudolf's behalf, in case they kidnapped her and offered to swap her for him.

That summer Margot, Rudolf and Joan Thring spent some time aboard Aristotle Onassis' boat, the *Christina*, with him and his new wife, Jackie. A firm friendship had been struck between Margot and Rudolf and the Onassis' which Joan Thring remembers as extraordinary and down-to-earth all at the same time. On one occasion, when Joan had given a dinner party in London and served puff pastry, Jackie had praised it, adding without any side that it was 'better than General de Gaulle's'. On a later occasion, when Onassis had been called away, and Margot and Rudolf had left the yacht temporarily to dance somewhere, Joan and Jackie had spent several days together, shopping, going to the hairdresser and spending ages deciding whether to have a Greek or a French breakfast (the *Christina* had two kitchens). Jackie had opened up to Joan completely, telling her how part of Jack's brain had landed in her lap in Dallas, and how, over dinner at Lee's, she had told Rose Kennedy, Bobby Kennedy and Ethel Kennedy that she was going to marry Ari. Bobby had replied heatedly, 'Over my dead body'.

Jackie had also told Joan, presciently, that if Bobby were to win the primary, 'they'll kill him'. But she never said who 'they' were. Jackie had her own theory as to who killed the President but she drew the line at discussing it. She did, however, hate (Joan's word) Lyndon Johnson. She conceded, too, that she thought he was involved in the assassination in some way.

That summer, too, there was to be a short tour of Italy. On the way,

Rudolf stopped off at La Turbie, which he was decorating with antique tiles, old beams and fireplaces and, of course, a piano. He then moved to the coast for a few days' vacation in Monte Carlo. Interviewed there, he said, 'Men are like fishes; they meet, they drift apart. The only thing that counts is to love oneself.' Put together with some of his other recent one-liners, this shows he was becoming a bit of a philosopher. What the interviewers did not know was what was happening in his private life. When he said these things he was thinking of Erik, and of what had happened with Margot. He told this interviewer that Margot was 'the best partner I've ever had'. The man assumed he was only talking of dancing.

An Italian photographer turned up one day, keen to take photographs of Rudolf relaxing by the pool. When Rudolf refused, pleading that he was off duty, the photographer pushed him – and Rudolf fell into the water. He was with a boy at the time (one of the reasons why he wanted no photographs) and this young man now turned on the photographer and shoved *him* into the water. The photographer threatened to sue but, as with many incidents on stage, Rudolf was really the wronged party.

While they were in Italy, Margot and Rudolf attended a reception where the Panamanian ambassador was also a guest. Margot buttonholed him and insisted on knowing why the man who had shot her husband had never been charged. Joan was surprised to see the ambassador lose his temper with Margot. 'Madame Fonteyn,' he said, 'you know perfectly well why there have been no charges brought. You really must stop this! Please!' The implication was obvious.

After the Italian tour Rudolf danced with the Australian Ballet in several European cities. In some ways, this tour set a pattern that was to shape a phase of his career. The Australians had come to Britain for the Commonwealth Festival but were offered a European tour on condition that Fonteyn and Nureyev were part of the company. The tour was a great success, save for a much-publicised evening in Paris, when Rudolf turned out to watch the Kirov, which was playing at the same time. He restaged a somewhat rethought *Raymonda*, which showed that he was still maturing his thoughts on all the great classics. He was coming up to twenty-eight and still blossoming.

Erik's situation was less optimistic. He still felt the Royal Danish Ballet was not all it could be, his Danish depressiveness had got the better of him again and he was giving himself a hard time. Erik's feeling was mirrored by the critics, many of whom felt that the Danish company was mired in the Bournonville tradition and needed new works to infuse new life into its repertoire. The old director, Niels Bjorn Larsen, seems to have felt this too, and announced his retirement. Unfortunately, Erik was not offered the job – it went to Flemming Flindt instead. Erik kept his real feelings to himself. But the gulf between him and Rudolf was growing.

CHAPTER FIFTEEN

Rules of Passion

The arbitrary rules of passion
were all the law that I would use;
sharing her in promiscuous fashion
I introduced my saucy Muse.

Nineteen sixty-six did not begin well. Erik experienced a recurrence of his old stomach problem, which deteriorated as the year went on, to the point where he could be suddenly assaulted by violent pains that would require him to remove himself from all company. This depressed him still more. Rudolf was worried by this, and the situation wasn't helped when he learned that his father had died. Joan Thring broke the news. She had taken receipt of the telegram from Rosa which had arrived while Rudolf was abroad and although it was in Russian, Joan was pretty sure of what it said. She drove out to Heathrow in the Mercedes and, on the way back, told Rudolf what had happened. She knew he hated his father and didn't think that the news would upset him greatly. But as he read the telegram he went white, and the scar on his lip stood out. He asked immediately if he could see Fred Ashton and spent a long time with him, talking and drinking. Joan realised then that although Rudolf hated his father, he also hated the fact that he hated him.

Rudolf's other thought was for his mother. How would she cope now? Who would she live with? He realised that he should now make more effort to keep in touch.

While Rudolf and Erik were in the wars emotionally, creatively the outlook was brighter. That year Rudolf was asked to stage three new productions. Two were new productions of the classics (*Sleeping Beauty* and *Don Quixote*) but one was a totally new effort, to be built up from scratch. This was *Tancredi*, at Vienna. *Tancredi* is a strange story, not at all easy to explain. The central, eponymous, figure born of an *Ur* mother, or 'mother of all', meets two female images, which appear to represent sacred and profane love. To cope with this dilemma Tancredi splits into two. Unfortunately the two figures so created fight each other to the death, and return to the womb. The plot is more complicated than this, but since the ballet has only ever been performed five times it is perhaps not essential to spell it out in more detail. First produced in 1952 in Munich, the score of *Tancredi*, was written by Hans Werner Henze and the libretto by Otto Herbst. Withdrawn by the composer after one performance, it was offered to Rudolf, who amended the story and shortened the running time to half an hour from nearly twice that. The costumes, based on the paintings of Dante Gabriel Rossetti, gave the whole production an eerie feel. In Vienna it was produced three times, then withdrawn again, but the important thing from Rudolf's point of view was to discover whether he could create choreography with no previous ideas to fall back on, or build from. He had to devise not only the steps but the *architecture* of the piece. The critics and audience were frankly perplexed but found the standard of dancing high. Rudolf was quietly pleased with his own abilities as a choreographer.

He also staged *Don Quixote* at Vienna. This, always popular with audiences, nonetheless gave Rudolf a few headaches – or rather the Viennese dancers did. The Vienna Opera Ballet is a little like the Paris Opera Ballet in that the dancers are given contracts which last them their creative lifetimes, at the end of which they draw their pensions. This was not the kind of system to suit Rudolf, especially as it meant that many of the more elderly members of the *corps* simply hung around, waiting for the great pension day to arrive. In rehearsing *Don Quixote* (known in the ballet world as 'Donkey Shot'), Rudolf was particularly incensed by one old retainer who simply seemed incapable of getting the steps right in the way that Rudolf wanted.

He called the man over, in front of everyone. The man walked forward.

Rudolf turned to John Lanchbery, the musical director whom Rudolf had requested be sent from London. 'Have you got a piece of paper and a pen?' he asked.

Lanchbery proffered the paper. 'I have a pencil. Will that do?'

Rudolf nodded, took it, and turned back to the dancer. 'Your name?' he asked.

The man told him.

Rudolf wrote it down, or appeared to, scribbled a few extra lines, and pretended to sign it with a flourish. He handed the paper to the man. 'Your pension,' he said.

They all laughed, of course, and, there and then, Rudolf got his way. But it was always an uphill struggle in Vienna.

Rudolf bought his flat in Monaco that spring. He was still stateless, which was a major headache for Joan Thring who had to arrange the paperwork. He had still done nothing about taking out British citizenship and seems at that stage to have considered becoming Monégasque. He had met the Rainiers when he and Margot had performed *Romeo and Juliet* in the Palace courtyard in June, and got on well. It could have been an ideal solution.

On 18 July that year, with impeccable timing, Sol Hurok announced a surprise from New York. He said that his organisation had *already* taken half a million dollars in advance receipts for the Royal Ballet's north American tour which did not begin until 18 April 1967, exactly *nine months* away. This is probably the best indication of how big Fonteyn and Nureyev were at the time.

There were still grouches at Covent Garden (they would never go away). In September Rudolf mounted *Sleeping Beauty* in Milan with Carla Fracci. One local critic said that he had never seen the stalls at La Scala in such a state of ferment. Yet Rudolf was disappointed that no one from the Royal Ballet came to see this production. He felt he was snubbed.

In the same month he mounted *Raymonda* at Covent Garden. It had been refined since Spoleto in 1964 (when Fonteyn had been forced to withdraw, owing to Tito's illness), and he had also mounted it in Australia in 1965. But Rudolf did not accompany the Royal Ballet on its autumn tour of Prague, Bratislava, Belgrade, Sofia, Bucharest and Warsaw. The political situation was still such that his presence would have caused demonstrations, and maybe even cancellation. At the end of the year Margot and Rudolf revived *Giselle* for a few performances; this coincided with the release of Paul Czinner's film of *Romeo and Juliet*, which had been made soon after the ballet's première at Covent Garden. This only fuelled the clamour for still more Fonteyn and Nureyev ballets. With another North American tour the following spring, people realised that a new vehicle for the couple would have to be prepared. Any new work would have to be extra special because, early next year, Margot Fonteyn would be celebrating thirty-five years as a dancer. The new season would kick off with a double gala.

Frederick Ashton responded. The new ballet, he said, would be *Paradise Lost* by the French choreographer, Roland Petit, Fonteyn's one-time lover. She herself records that when Marius Constant, the composer-conductor, took the orchestra rehearsal, he began by addressing the musicians with these words, 'Gentleman, I suppose you have all heard of Milton's *Paradise Lost*?' There were murmurs of approval from the sixty or so in the pit. 'Well gentlemen,' said Constant, 'I just want to tell you that this ballet has nothing whatever to do with Milton's *Paradise Lost*.' Petit had in fact taken a poem by Jean Cau as his theme and, instead of giving Fonteyn and Nureyev yet another classical ballet to dance, mounted a thoroughly modern work, with pop-art décor and flashing neon lights. At the end of the first act, Rudolf, as Adam, was made to dive between a huge pair of scarlet lips of a pin-up, modelled on the paintings of Roy Lichtenstein. Margot's entrance was from a trapdoor in the middle of a ramp at the back of the set. To reach it, she said, she had to crawl on her hands and knees, under the rostrum, from the wings to centre stage, a distance of about thirty feet. She was a very dirty Eve.

Before the première, Tito came out of Stoke Mandeville and Margot took a leave of absence. The double act between them was now as perfectly choreographed as were the bows and curtsies after her performances with Rudolf.

The première of *Paradise Lost* took people by surprise. It was not what the general public expected to see Margot and Rudolf in, and although the applause and critical reaction were good, word of mouth around London was not as ecstatic as usual.

Before the start of the New York season that year, Rudolf went to Toronto for the première of Erik's version of *Swan Lake*. Bruhn's health had improved towards the end of 1966, enough to allow him to work on the ballet in Canada. He introduced a major psychological change in the ballet, in that he altered the role of Von Rothbart, the sorcerer who has turned Odette-Odile into a swan. Usually Von Rothbart is played by a man, but Erik made the character a woman. She was now called the Black Queen. There is nothing intrinsic to the role which says that Von Rothbart *has* to be a man but it was still a fairly major break with tradition. And making evil assume female form could easily be seen in some Freudian way. In any case, the change annoyed many people, Rudolf included. Worse, he accused Erik of stealing his ideas – for music, for new solos for the prince, for the way some of the acting was conceived. Erik had of course seen Rudolf's own *Swan Lake* in Vienna but he always maintained that his version of the ballet owed more to a production he had seen much earlier, in the mid-1950s, staged by Vladimir Bourmeister for the Moscow Stanislavsky Ballet. Nevertheless, it was an awkward moment between the two men. Rudolf was no longer in thrall to Erik. It had been important for him to have someone to look up to. First Margot had turned her back. Now Erik had let him down. Rudolf felt betrayed.

The Royal Ballet's 1967 tour of North America was probably, after the very first in 1949, the most successful ever mounted, certainly in terms of the reception it received. But there was more to it than that. The Met had moved from its old home on Broadway and 39th Street in April 1966 and the new Met was located at Lincoln Centre at Broadway and 65th Street. There, in May, just a few yards from each other, the balletomane could find playing, at the same time, Balanchine's New York City Ballet, with Edward Villella, American Ballet Theatre, with Erik Bruhn, and the Royal Ballet with Rudolf Nureyev. It was, as Rudolf said, a ballet supermarket. Both American Ballet Theatre and the Royal Ballet were offering *Swan Lake*, and both did *Les Noces*.

Members of the different companies took the same classes during the day.

It was an extraordinary time. Fonteyn and Nureyev were given a seventeen-minute ovation on the opening night which was terminated only by the lowering of the asbestos curtain. But ABT took seventeen curtain calls, too, for one of their performances.

So far as the Royal Ballet was concerned, one might have expected New York to respond more warmly to *Paradise Lost* than London had. New Yorkers are much more at home with modern dance. As it turned out, on that tour Petit's ballet was overshadowed by *Romeo and Juliet*, which was new to many Americans. But then, many of these fans were the people who had bought their tickets *nine months* earlier and had waited patiently for the big night. Now, the culmination had arrived.

Moreover, during the New York season, the rumour swept Manhattan that this might be Fonteyn's last tour and so the very last night took on the aura of a farewell. Everyone, the audience included, lived up to such an emotional occasion. It was a Sunday and, after the performance, the entire audience rose to applaud Fonteyn. Flowers rained on to the stage in bunches, one of which she caught, as someone said, as neatly as Joe di Maggio, the baseball star. After half an hour, there were still 1,200 people standing and applauding, and the asbestos curtain was brought down. Although some people left, 500 remained. Margot and Rudolf had now given up bowing and curtsying and just stood on the stage in front of the fire curtain. The orchestra had gone, the electricians and backstage staff had gone; and the applause continued for another ten minutes. Finally, after 42.5 minutes of applause (someone was timing it), they were allowed off stage. It was 12.15 a.m. Only Sol Hurok knew how much it had cost in overtime.

Sol Hurok has been aptly described as the last impresario. Like Nureyev, Hurok was Russian, a poor boy from from Pogar, a town with seven churches and one synagogue, where, as a boy, he stole lilacs in the park. He left Russia to make his fortune, he said, and he left the country singing. 'To be born in Russia is to be born singing.'

He loved to tell the wartime story about the little boy Ivan who follows a Red Army soldier all the way to his village, then calls the police to arrest him because he is a Nazi spy in a stolen uniform. As the spy is led away to be shot, he calls to Ivan. 'Tell me, Ivan,' he says. 'My uniform is perfect, I speak Russian as well as you – how did you know I was not a Red Army man?' 'I followed you a long time,' says Ivan. 'The sun was shining, the birds were chirping, everything was beautiful. And you were not singing. I knew you could not be a Russian.' No gloomy Russia for Hurok.

Hurok arrived in New York in 1906 with three roubles in his pocket, which he exchanged for $1.50. Borrowing another $1.25 from a relative, he travelled to Philadelphia where he got his first job as a streetcar conductor. The first concert he managed was for Mischa Elman, the

Russian violinist but his big break came with Feodor Chaliapin, whom he had worshipped as a boy in Russia (Chaliapin, incidentally, made his first appearance in Ufa). Hurok managed Anna Pavlova and Isadora Duncan. 'He managed anyone who had a name and could be built to higher notoriety,' wrote Agnes de Mille. He went bankrupt twice and was bailed out twice by his assistant Mae Frohman, who paid the rent long enough for him to hire new artists and start again. 'For this service he gave her nothing beyond her weekly salary.'

Every day Hurok gave a lunch at the Russian tearooms on West 57th Street, where he picked up useful gossip from other Russians. He was, in a way, the Lord Duveen of the music world, recognising that Europe had the artists and America the money. Over the years he managed Artur Rubinstein, Isaac Stern, Andrés Segovia, Mstislav Rostropovich and Sviatoslav Richter. He also brought the Ballets Russes, the Bolshoi and the Kirov to America. And it was Hurok, of course, who had imported the Sadler's Wells Ballet in 1949, before it became the Royal Ballet, which made Fonteyn such a star.

Agnes de Mille, the American choreographer who helped created *Rodeo*, *Oklahoma!* and *Brigadoon*, and whose husband worked for Hurok, said that the impresario seemed shorter than he was because he was thick – 'thick hands, thick wrists, thick fingers, thick head, thick neck, square jaw, and a square, baldish crown, so that he looked rather like an unjolly friar.' 'He spoke six languages,' said Isaac Stern, 'and they all turned out to be bad Yiddish.' Like Rudolf he could savage syntax but still end up conveying his meaning better than most people whose native tongue was English. He once dismissed a powerful critic with the remark: 'He has a mind like a claptrap.' His most well-known maxim, as de Mille said, 'has grammarians awestruck'. Referring to fickle audiences, he once remarked – and then repeated it, many times – 'If people don't want to come, nothing will stop them.' He could also be difficult, unfriendly and tyrannical – but he paid well. 'The best in the harlequin business,' is how de Mille charmingly put it.

For every Royal Ballet tour, Hurok gave a welcoming party on the roof of the St Regis Hotel. He himself attended every performance in New York – and then gave the company a farewell party, on the roof of the St Regis Hotel. That year, however, the procedure was reversed at one point, and a dinner was given *for* him. Agnes de Mille was there. In her memoir, *Portrait Gallery*, she wrote,

'How does one appraise his impact on American culture? He is first of all the Great Importer, and the treasures he has brought us from abroad have proved seminal . . . "Hurok Attractions" means not just one thing, but a rich and surprising spanning of activities: the finest among instrumentalists, of course, and singers and conductors, but also, most gratefully and delightfully, booming cavalry officers, chanting children, whirling Russians, bamboo-jumping Filipinos, neck-sliding Hindus, gourd-shaking Mexicans . . . and his special pride, the greatest ballets.

Rudolf and Margot joined the company that year for the end of their stay in New York, before embarking on the usual four-month coast-to-coast excursion. On that tour the company was in Chicago at the same time as a production of *The Philadelphia Story* which had Lee Radziwill in the cast. Rudolf had always encouraged Lee to keep acting although her husband was discouraging. Lee's other great friend, Truman Capote had tried to help her by having the great Hollywood make-up artist, George Martens, attend her though this had only made her more nervous, especially when the two men had thrown all her clothes out of the window, saying they were unsuitable. When she happened to mention that Rudolf was coming to her party after the second night, Capote and Martens forgot all about her and spent hours getting ready, Martens dressing all in white. When Rudolf arrived, he ignored everyone, giving all his attention to Lee, since he knew she had been troubled by criticism of the play. He took her on to the balcony overlooking Lake Erie, while Capote and Martens fretted inside

In San Francisco, Margot led Rudolf astray in fairly spectacular fashion. One evening after performing *Paradise Lost* they had gone on to Trader Vic's for a Chinese supper. (Rudolf was drinking rum in those days.) After eating, Margot said she would like to see the celebrated Haight Ashbury district of the city, where the hippies and 'flower power' people lived. With a couple of friends, therefore, they were dropped off in the area and went for a walk. It was about 3 a.m. Walking near the Golden Gate Park, they came upon a party in full swing. The party-givers, who had been to the ballet early in the evening, invited Margot and Rudolf to join them. The couple climbed up to the roof to look at the stars. No sooner had they arrived than the party was raided. The noise of the music was deafening, especially at three o'clock in the morning. Having been summoned over the noise, the police promptly discovered a number of marijuana cigarettes in use – and equally promptly arrested everyone present, including Margot and Rudolf. A paddy-wagon was sent for and eighteen party-goers were sent down to the city jail. Margot and Rudolf were 'inside' for four hours before being released on bail set at $117. The incident naturally made front-page news all over the world, although the events were fairly innocuous and the charges were immediately dropped. The party-givers explained that Margot and Rudolf did not know about the marijuana and claimed that in any case the party was very law-abiding. There was music but no alcohol and no food (some party!). What annoyed the dancers was the way the police had allowed the press into the jail. Rudolf breathed on the lens of one television camera to make the picture misty.

That summer, as a result of certain changes taking place in the Soviet Union, Rudolf's name was again placed on the KGB's 'wet list', as a candidate for assassination. He had originally been targeted by none other than Nikita Khrushchev. The Soviet President, who had championed him to Ekaterina Furtseva after Rudolf had danced on the afternoon when Voroshilov had sang, had taken Rudolf's defection particularly personally. He had espoused 'selective assassination' as an instrument of Soviet policy since 1959 and had personally authorised the liquidation of several people, including some Ukrainians in Germany. He had first authorised Rudolf's elimination in October/November 1962, a year after the secret trial, when it had become clear that the dancer was not going to heed the judge's 'invitation' to come home for his case to be 're-analysed'. In that same month, Bogdan Stashinsky was sentenced to eight years in Karlsruhe for the murder of Lev Rebet and Stepan Bandera. These were the Ukrainians whose murders Khrushchev had authorised and Stashinsky had carried out the killings. He had defected in the same year as Rudolf, a week before the Berlin wall went up. So assassination was on Khrushchev's mind.

Khrushchev had been deposed in 1964 and his policies largely discredited. But, under Brezhnev, in June 1967, the very time that the Royal Ballet was in America, Yuri Andropov was appointed director of the KGB. He was extremely hardline, and reimposed the sentence on Rudolf.

In June that year, Rudolf was dancing with Claire Motte in Paris in *Notre-Dame de Paris*, by Roland Petit, with music by Maurice Jarre and costumes by Yves Saint-Laurent. Afterwards they all went to eat with Paul Getty Junior (this was just before he was kidnapped and had his ear cut off) and then, in the early hours, returned to the Ritz where Rudolf was staying. Before they turned in, however, Rudolf treated the others to their own private performance, dancing his way across the Place Vendôme in the first rays of dawn – fragments of Petrouchka, Pierrot Lunaire and Apollo. He said he was really trying to woo the woman who was with Paul Getty Junior but in those days Rudolf's wealth could not match the Gettys'.

The break between Rudolf and Erik did not come suddenly. Indeed, it could hardly be called a break. But, beginning in 1967, they did gradually grow apart. Two reasons seem to account for it, or at least to signal it. One, as we have seen, was Erik's production of *Swan Lake*, which contained ideas that Rudolf felt Erik had stolen. At more or less the same time, a plan had been aired for Erik and Rudolf, and Margot and Carla Fracci to dance together. It seems, however, that Margot, who had never danced with Erik, was not over-anxious to appear in the same programme as Carla Fracci who, she felt, might steal some of the glory. Rudolf *had* wanted Erik to dance with Margot, thinking they were ideally suited but Erik, who was thrilled by his partnership with Fracci, cooled towards Fonteyn on Carla's account. The programme never came off, Erik never danced with Margot, and he began to keep his distance from Rudolf, at least when Fonteyn was around.

By now, Fonteyn's own situation had changed. She was still guilt-ridden at bringing Tito back to Britain too soon for his own good. She had spent two years visiting him daily when she wasn't abroad on tour. After her Covent Garden appearances she would take the train to Stoke Mandeville, wish Tito goodnight, sleep in a nearby hotel, then see him for breakfast, before travelling back to London on the early stockbrokers' train, where she had become a familiar sight. When she was on a tour it was a different matter. She was enjoying a highly secret affair with a prominent businessman in London. He was, like many of her personal friends, somewhat dubious, fond of café society, and a member of the Portman Club, home of London's socially prominent bridge set. He was married and so most of their encounters were abroad, in Europe. When Fonteyn was dancing in Milan, Vienna or Munich, say, her lover would fly out on the day of the performance, see Margot afterwards, then fly back to Britain the next day. The press never put two and two together, though the affair was known to her friends.

To the world at large, Margot was the devoted wife, a busy artist, a great star, who doted on her tragically crippled husband. Part of her *was* devoted to Tito, the part that felt guilty and the part that instinctively knew how to live up to her public image (the special curtsies on stage, for instance). For the rest, she had found a man who, like Rudolf, returned her love and affection in the way that she wished and she was grateful. To that extent, she could be said to have again found happiness.

There was an added reason why 1967 was important for Rudolf's private life and, in the long term, his relationship with Erik. In Britain, on 27 July, the Sexual Offences Bill, which legalised homosexual acts between consenting adults over twenty-one, received the Royal Assent. As Rudolf's relationship with Erik cooled, and because he was forever travelling, Rudolf gradually became more promiscuous.

Looking back now, Joan Thring is amazed at how the world was then. Rudolf would pick boys up every night on tour and bring them back to the hotel, often having to smuggle them in by a back door. But much as he wanted sex with them, he hated to wake up with anyone else in his bed in the morning. It was not unknown for him to pick up boys who were actually following Joan, who was very attractive. But Rudolf had the greater appetite. She grew used to the phone call in the early hours, any time between one o'clock and five o'clock. 'Joan,' Rudolf would say, 'Pay boy, please, pay boy.' And Joan would have to get out of bed, put on her dressing gown, and meet the boy by the hotel lift, where she would give him the cash. She admits now that she procured for him – it was the 1960s, after all. She was expected to know how much boys cost in Barcelona, Beirut or Boston.

Often his sexuality got the better of him in the middle of the day, and he would have to act on his urge. On one occasion, a Sunday, the three of them – Margot, Joan and Rudolf – had spent the day with Margot's mother (known as the 'Black Queen') and returned to Joan's house in Earls Court. Joan was cooking when suddenly Rudolf announced that he had to go out and 'find boy'. Margot had tried to mother him, telling him not to go out on an empty stomach, but a terrible row had ensued. In fact, Rudolf was so angry that he had stormed out of the house taking the only key and locking the two women inside. They had to break the door down because, naturally, he didn't come back.

In the autumn of 1967 Rudolf finally bought a house in London. Or rather, Joan Thring bought it for him – and almost at once regretted it. It was a very attractive house although earlier on he had looked at Lionel Bart's place in Fulham, which had a purple lavatory. The house Nureyev decided on, which cost him £45,000, was a six-bedroomed mansion in East Sheen, overlooking Richmond Park. He bought it from John Guillermin, a film director whose most well-known film was *The Blue Max*, and his neighbours were David Jacobs, the disc jockey, and Cyril Smith, the pianist.

What Thring immediately regretted about the house was its location. It was what Rudolf wanted but it was a very long way from Covent Garden. More to the point, there were two bridges to cross and, with London traffic, that was bound to be a problem. Rudolf always carried his shoe bag everywhere. He didn't like new shoes as other dancers did, but instead had his 'Giselle' shoes, his 'Don Quixote' shoes, and his 'Swan Lake' shoes, caked with sweat. His favourite trick was to fight his way through crowds of fans by swiping them with his shoe bag, and he swiped at Joan too when there was a problem. She could see the bridges and the shoe bag becoming inextricably linked. And that, of course, is what happened. They were trapped one day on Putney bridge, and Rudolf, after swiping at Joan, just got out of the car and ran for the tube. He hardly ever went on the tube and never for a moment imagined that the first train he saw might be going in the wrong direction. But it was.

London and New York apart, Nureyev's most successful 'second city' at that stage of his career was Vienna. In the autumn he was invited back to appear – at last – in a Balanchine ballet, a revival of *Apollo*. He was a great success. The movements Balanchine had created – his language – were very different from classical ballet and he himself had doubted that someone with Rudolf's strict training could adapt. But Rudolf was always very adaptable. Another change that autumn was the French début of Petit's *Paradise Lost* in Paris. The French at last seemed to have lost their nervousness about being associated with a defector, and in fact on that occasion, the drama was provided by Covent Garden who induced

Rudolf to fly back to London between the dress rehearsal and the opening night of *Paradise Lost*, because they had a performance of *Swan Lake* and everyone else who could do it was either ill or injured or too far away.

Towards the end of the year Erik, who had settled in Stockholm for a while to help rejuvenate the Royal Swedish Ballet, invited Rudolf to mount his own version of *The Nutcracker*. Rudolf accepted with alacrity – he said he preferred to restage the classics because 'there wasn't enough time' to start new ones from scratch. But he had perhaps not realised, as Erik had, that the Swedish ballet was very run down – which is why Erik was there, after all. *The Nutcracker* is an elaborate production, with a large cast and many technical effects, which requires a big company backstage. This alone made Rudolf nervous but the lethargic Swedish dancers had to be whipped into action – almost literally, at times. (It was a little bit like a re-run of the Vienna 'pensions' business.) Bruhn had been dancing in Oslo when Nureyev arrived in Stockholm and when he returned it was to find the dancers up in arms at Rudolf's treatment, and threatening to strike. One had even accused him of trying strangle her. Though this dispute was real enough, there was also a certain amount of ritual in it. Rudolf did have a temper, as everyone knew, but at the same time he was aware that, provided you have the talent to go with it, temper and box office are related. The disputes he had, whether in Austria, North America or Sweden, never went beyond a certain point. This was because, more often than not, Rudolf exploded for a reason. He over-reacted, perhaps, but to a genuine fault, weakness or shortcoming. This had been true elsewhere, as it was true now. The dispute was settled quickly, the company was given its much-needed shake-up, the Swedish press took a great interest in the whole affair – and *The Nutcracker* was a great success, both critically and commercially.

Because of its success in Sweden, Rudolf was allowed to mount *The Nutcracker* at Covent Garden in February of the following year. Created in 1892, to music by Tchaikovsky, the original choreography by Lev Ivanov had been largely lost, although in one version or another it had always been popular and had been in the Sadler's Wells repertory since 1934. Now, however, Rudolf suggested a newer, grander treatment, as befitted the grand environs of Covent Garden. Nicholas Georgiadis's designs replaced those of Renzo Mongiardino in Stockholm. Rudolf's idea was that the story would be seen through the eyes of a child. The monsters and visions, which reflect the anxieties of the heroine, would come to dominate the work and would make it more like *Sleeping Beauty* or *Giselle* than a Christmas pantomime. (It was also somewhat Freudian, suggesting that, whether he liked it or not, Erik's *Swan Lake*, far from being stolen from Rudolf, actually inspired Rudolf in his own work.) One innovation he required was the use of a large *corps de ballet* made up entirely of young children from the Royal Ballet's school. There was some opposition to this, since he wanted *very* young children and their teachers were worried that their attention span, and stamina, might not meet Rudolf's exacting standards. But once again Rudolf proved the doubters wrong and showed himself able to induce even these young souls to raise their game. When he was doing the teaching, lessons lasted much longer than usual, with no complaints.

Before the opening of *Nutcracker*, he was due to dance in Ashton's new ballet, *Jazz Calendar*, but went down with a bad dose of the flu. When the audience arrived that night, 9 January 1968, they were disappointed to see placards in the foyer announcing the news that Rudolf was indisposed; they were told they could claim a refund, of the difference between the special Fonteyn/Nureyev price and the 'ordinary' price. Seven-thirty arrived and the curtain didn't rise. Five minutes later the house manager, John Collins, appeared on stage. Everyone was thinking the same. 'Now what?' Was it going to be one of those nights when everything went wrong? In fact, Collins announced that Nureyev had appeared at the theatre about an hour before, with a temperature of 102 degrees, but that he *would* dance *Jazz Calendar*. It may have been after this performance that Rudolf acquired his nickname, Neveroff.

This performance apart, the curtain was never held at Covent Garden for Rudolf, who often liked to 'psych' himself up. At other theatres it was a different story. Once, in Amsterdam, the curtain went up forty-five minutes late, just because Rudolf didn't feel that he was ready.

When *Nutcracker* opened, Nureyev danced the opening night, with Merle Park as Marie, the heroine. The couple were very well received and this marked the beginning of the end of his time with Fonteyn. They would still dance together for several years, but now came a crossover period when he also danced a lot with Monica Mason, Antoinette Sibley and Merle Park.

The year had started well, and promised more. It was an in-between year so far as North American tours were concerned but the Royal Ballet's 1967 tour had been such a success that Hurok decided to break the usual rhythm and mount, not a full tour, but a New York season at the time of year the Royal Ballet usually came, prior to travelling on to other cities. The company was accordingly booked for the Metropolitan Opera House, Lincoln Center, from 18 April to 26 May. A European tour, with the smaller touring company, was also planned that year – Spain, Portugal, Monte Carlo, Italy, France, Holland and Switzerland. Despite the fact that *Paradise Lost* had already been dropped from the company's repertoire, Roland Petit was given more commissions, especially to create for Fonteyn and Nureyev.

Behind these public events, however, far more significant developments were taking place backstage at Covent Garden, which in the long run would have important consequences for Rudolf. For some time, Frederick Ashton had let it be known that he was thinking of retiring in 1970. Sir David Webster, the general administrator, had sounded out Kenneth MacMillan about taking over and MacMillan had in principle accepted. However, Webster also had in mind John Field, then in charge of the Royal Ballet's touring company. Matters suddenly came to a head in February 1968, when Sir Donald Albery, director of the London Festival Ballet, announced his resignation. Soon afterwards, his post was offered to Field. Alarmed, Webster persuaded Field to reject the Festival Ballet offer and so Field gained the impression that, by doing so, he would succeed Ashton in 1970. This was a reasonable inference. Why should he pass up one directorship unless he was being promised another, bigger plum? But there was also the offer Webster had made to MacMillan. As a result, Webster felt impelled to offer *co*-directorship to Field and MacMillan. This decision was announced while the company was in New York and seems to have taken not only them, but also Ashton, by surprise. Ashton appeared to take sides when he said that he felt a creative person should be at the head of the Royal Ballet. Margot, if she felt slighted by these manoeuvres, didn't show it. There were those who felt that *she* might follow in Ashton's shoes (Cranko was another candidate). These changes would not take place for another two years yet, but their importance lay in the fact that they ushered in a time of uncertainty after a golden period that had lasted for two decades. Change was coming at the Royal Ballet but what that change would be, exactly, no one could foresee.

Still, in New York, Fonteyn and Nureyev's dancing was as impressive as ever. Their *Swan Lake* was called 'a history-making partnership' and Rudolf's new control as Siegfried was particularly applauded, his black doublet and white tights being seen as symbolic of the 'integration' he had brought to the Royal Ballet. He had infused the company with his fire; they had imposed their reticence on him. Such was their impact that the Cote Basque, Manhattan's snootiest restaurant, admitted Rudolf without a tie and Margot in a pants suit. The film producer Sam Spiegel, who was their host that day, declared himself impressed – and few people impressed Sam.

Naturally, all this pleased Rudolf. However, he was less than happy with the non-dance press. That year, for example, there were certain comments in the New York tabloids about how revealing his tunics were. One said that his micro-costumes showed more of him than did the miniskirts of the girls around town – it was reminiscent of the Leningrad attacks ten years before. At the same time, and more substantially, he was featured in *After Dark* magazine. In an interview he confessed to having regrets about his autobiography. No good came of it, he said. It was a vice of childhood. Being honest on paper, he had concluded, was 'a very dangerous game'. Whether or not he knew it at the time, the interview turned out to be embarrassing for him, because *After Dark* was a gay magazine. That is not quite accurate. In 1968, the gay pride movement had yet to get into its stride, and attitudes were still forming. *After Dark* published articles on culture and entertainment which were of interest to everyone but the editor illustrated the magazine with photographs of men – nude men, men in G-strings, men with their shirts off, men in their underwear, men in very tight jeans. Nureyev's mood wasn't improved when he bumped into George Balanchine at the Russian Tea Room on West 57th Street. In one of his more flamboyant pieces of arrogance, Nureyev always sat at the first table on the right as you go in, with his back to the wall, even if his lunch or dinner companion was a woman. His argument was that people wanted to see *him*, not his companion. When the encounter with Balanchine took place, in the wake of the *After Dark* article, the older man remarked acidly that Rudolf had become 'the Liberace of ballet'.

Rudolf was also featured in *Esquire*, in a long perceptive article by Lee Harris that at last managed to get away from the usual round of familiar questions. Harris had travelled with Rudolf in Europe and North American and observed him on and off stage. He noted that Rudolf bit his nails, read the *International Herald Tribune* for its comics, Peanuts, *BC*, and the *Wizard of Iz* and that he invariably dressed in a strange way – a cross between a sorcerer and Batman. He noted now Rudolf laughed at his – Harris's – haircut. But in doing so Harris drew out of Rudolf the confession that fathers are always jealous of their sons, that they 'want to be beautiful like their sons'. That is why hair is so important, said Rudolf, why older men laugh at young boys' hair so much: they are jealous. Fathers, he said, should teach their sons all they know 'then kick them out of the house'. He left no doubt as to which generation he was part of. Harris tried to draw him on politics more than anyone had yet been able to do. He failed to secure a comment on Vietnam, then so much in the news, but Rudolf did take Cassius Clay's part in his fight against military duty. He said that what the government was doing was 'disgusting. He's world champion. They should show some respect.' This was of course not a million miles from his own situation back in Leningrad in the 1950s. Nureyev also thought the British masochistic and sick. 'Can you imagine any other country where Lady Godiva could only find one peeping tom!' He put it down to too many birchings at school.

Harris mentioned that many people didn't like Rudolf, said bad things about him and that London had recently gone off him. He mentioned Lucia Chase of American Ballet Theatre, who had described Rudolf as a poseur, as too destructive, as attracting to the ballet 'people we don't want'. Rudolf took this in his stride. He acknowledged his nature, saying that 'kindness doesn't help. You have to overpower people. That's how you win.' The world doesn't need parasites, he went on. 'You tell me who your friends are and I'll tell you who you are.' He recognised the pleasures of love, he said, but thought men shouldn't marry. Love had to be mutual, accompanied by respect. Love kills you when it is unwanted, he said.

Harris then moved on to New York, where he had interviewed staff at the Metropolitan Opera House. He found no shortage of people there who were ready to criticise Rudolf. The usherettes thought that Rudolf and Hurok brought out the worst in audiences and revealed that on the evenings when Rudolf danced there the theatre put on more wheelchairs for people injured in the crush during the curtain calls. That year Hurok had refused to announce on which nights Rudolf would be dancing, so people had to buy tickets for more than one night, to improve their chances of seeing him. The usherettes hated the 'savage' people who came only for Rudolf. They were 'sadists', said one, who also objected to the way he 'milked' the curtain calls. It produced overtime but meant she got home too late to do her other, daytime, job properly the next day.

Finally, Harris alluded to Rudolf's personal lifestyle with an indirect but vivid quote from Anton Dolin. 'Rudolf can be as naughty as he likes,' said Dolin, 'but if he's not careful they are going to find him dead some morning in an alley in Soho, his head laid open by a lorry driver's spanner.' This was an extraordinary article of Harris's, *Esquire* at its best. It was the first time a journalist had taken on Rudolf and not been massacred.

Harris had missed however accompanying Rudolf to Verona one night when he wasn't performing in Milan. At Verona, the Ballet Rambert were appearing and performing one of Glen Tetley's ballets called *Embrace Tiger and Return to Mountain*. Rudolf arrived and, with the group he was travelling with, went backstage before the curtain went up to see Rambert's artistic director, Norman Morrice. He told Morrice that he wanted to see the Tetley ballet. 'Well, you will,' replied Morrice. 'It's last on the programme.' 'But you don't understand,' Rudolf now said. 'I want to see it now. If I have to wait till the end of the evening it will be too late to get back to Milan. You must bring it forward.'

Morrice refused but offered instead to have his administrative director find Rudolf a hotel in Verona. Morrice was expecting a fight but Rudolf accepted his offer, adding only that the administrative manager should be discreet because he, Rudolf, was travelling incognito. Morrice was a bit bemused by this when Rudolf was wearing brightly coloured harlequin pants covered with huge coloured diamonds. Sure enough as he took his seat, the audience called out 'Nureyev! Nureyev!' That put him in a good mood, so good that he decided to take the whole Rambert company to dinner after the show. But then he spoiled it all by trying to pick up the waiter. When the waiter refused to be picked up, Rudolf's mood turned very ugly and the evening ended under a cloud. It was a typical roller-coaster Rudolfine evening.

On October 3, Erik turned forty. He was in good shape, technically still flawless and although there were tiny lines around the corners of his eyes and mouth, he certainly did not look his age. He had been honoured that year with *Dance Magazine*'s Award, a most prestigious acknowledgement of his talent and a professional recognition that Rudolf had never received. But Erik knew now that he would never again dance the more strenuous roles (like Don Quixote) and that change had to come. He was an altogether more discreet man than Rudolf and their age difference was, in a sense, greater now than it had ever been. The changing gay scene only made that more marked. Part of Erik still loved Rudolf – would always love Rudolf – but there was no way that Erik could ever have been described as the Liberace of ballet.

That November, Margot and Rudolf were invited to a huge party in Teheran, to celebrate the Shah's birthday. Rudolf had to go to Vienna first and insisted that Joan Thring join him there. The reason was as simple as it was tawdry. Rudolf loved pornographic magazines but knew that, entering Teheran, he might be stopped. Joan therefore was made to fly from London to Iran by way of Vienna so that *she* could pick up the pornography and carry it into Teheran with her. Rudolf couldn't bear to be without these magazines for long.

Though there was truth in Balanchine's comment about Rudolf as Liberace, it was also very unkind. It should never be forgotten that Rudolf had a very impressive range as a dancer. It owed a lot to his memory for steps, and without this he could not have travelled all over the world, dancing at short notice. At around the time that Balanchine was making his barbed remarks, Rudolf was extending his range still more in, perhaps, the most exciting way. He went to Holland and danced with the Dutch National Ballet in Rudi van Dantzig's *Monument for a Dead Boy*. A thoroughly modern ballet, inspired by the death of a young poet, this recounts some of the episodes in his life, including a number of controversial and vivid sequences which depict both heterosexual and homosexual activities.

Whereas in classical ballet all dancers learn the same basic steps, modern dance has developed in such a way that, despite Martha Graham's attempt to codify the steps, most choreographers invent their own language. There is nothing wrong with this – as the popularity of modern dance shows – but for someone like Rudolf to involve himself with van Dantzig there were obvious risks, since he was starting from scratch. Rudolf's solution was simple, but effective. He first danced *Monument* on Christmas Day 1968 but insisted that he also perform *The Nutcracker pas de deux* in the same programme, because audiences would expect to see something they associated with him, as well as something completely new. It was a bold decision because he knew he would be compared with dancers who had spent their entire careers dancing in van Dantzig's style but, in the event, he was a success and Rudolf and Rudi became very good friends. One cannot see Liberace ever taking comparable risks.

Although ten years younger than Erik, Rudolf was also approaching a difficult time. On the one hand he was an established dancer, a formidable presence wherever he went, both creatively and commercially. At the same time, for a dancer the late twenties are different from the early twenties. The muscles no longer allow him to do the feats as he once did – or at least, to do them so often. Because he had been a late starter, Rudolf had been technically imperfect when he defected, as certain critics never tired of pointing out. He had spent his twenties improving – and there is no doubt that he had improved dramatically on that score. But then again, he danced so much, spent so much time cooped up in aeroplanes, and coping with the jet lag and dehydration that ensued. The result was that, around this time, his dancing began to be very uneven. He had always been a good partner – all his prima ballerinas said that – but now he started to be less considerate, and the old rumours about his arrogance and moodiness resurfaced. Landing sweetly after a big jump had never been his strong point, and again he started having problems in that department. He could still rise to the big occasion, but not every night was a big occasion. His favourite phrase for good people who were dancing badly was 'They have galoshes on.' He loved the word galoshes. In early 1968 it applied to him.

But he didn't cut down on the number of performances he gave. His reason was only partly money. He had recently, as we have seen, extended his range with the van Dantzig and Petit ballets. He was still a permanent guest artist with the Royal Ballet but the wholesale changes due there were now only a year away. And Margot couldn't go on for ever. Then what? He *had* to dance with other companies, to form new relationships.

January 1969 found him dancing in Paris. This engagement certainly showed that his appetite, and the strength that had attracted Fonteyn, had not diminished. In Paris his contract stipulated that he have a new partner every night. 'I wear them out,' he said.

In late March there was the double gala at Covent Garden to celebrate Margot's thirty-fifth anniversary as a dancer and to introduce the new work that the company would take to North America. This was Roland Petit's *Pelléas et Mélisande*. Margot's gala was a great success. Tito was there. Erik danced, as did Carla Fracci and Marcia Haydée. Margot herself looked wonderful and announced that, contrary to speculation, she had *no* plans to retire. Tito's illness saw to that.

When the company arrived in New York the St Regis roof party was as glittering as ever. The Jockey Club threw a special celebration for Margot and Rudolf, they grossed $180,000 in Mexico City, the first time they had played there, and their *Giselle* in San Francisco was, according to the *Examiner*, nothing short of 'sensational'. At a star-studded Hollywood party on Malibu Beach, Rudolf spoke Russian with Natalie Wood and threw chicken drumsticks around the room. At the Met in New York, while Rudolf was dancing with Monica Mason, two old women were sitting in the stalls, in front of a friend of Monica's. 'Funny,' the friend heard one of the women say, 'she doesn't *look* fifty.' It was impossible for some people to imagine that, in 1969, Rudolf Nureyev ever danced with anyone other than Margot Fonteyn.

However, this tour was not quite the runaway success that all the others had been. One reason was that Petit's new ballet had been a fairly last-minute production and had worked even less well than *Paradise Lost*. Indeed, it is even described in the official history of the Royal Ballet as 'turgid and overlong'. What success the 1969 North American tour had was due to the redeeming qualities of *Swan Lake*, which was also performed.

In one crucial way, however, at least from Rudolf's point of view, the most significant event during that tour took place on 27 June, while the Royal Ballet were performing at Jones Hall in Houston, Texas. On that night, nine plain-clothes police raided the Stonewall Inn, an illegal gay bar in Christopher Street, Greenwich Village, New York. As the bartender and three transvestites were arrested and led away, fighting erupted outside and there was an attempt to set fire to the bar while some of the policemen were still inside. That night and for two nights afterwards, rioting broke out in the Christopher Street area with police retaliating against homosexuals for the attempt to burn down the Stonewall Inn. Many gays were beaten, and could be seen bruised and bleeding, lying on the sidewalk. Someone said that Seventh Avenue resembled 'a battlefield in Vietnam'. HOMO NEST RAIDED screamed the *Daily News* with all the finesse of a Russian tank. 'Queen bees are stinging mad.'

But the *News* underestimated the force and significance of what had taken place. Two weeks later, the first 'Gay Power' meeting was held in Greenwich Village. The Gay Liberation Movement had begun.

CHAPTER SIXTEEN

Text of Danger

Tatyana, lonely heroine,
roamed the still forest like a ranger,
sought in her book, that text of danger,
and found her dreams, her secret fire,
the full fruit of her heart's desire.

On 10 January 1970, doctors in Frankfurt announced that they had achieved considerable success in treating 'disturbed homosexuals' with an operation that involved disintegrating parts of the brain with an electric shock. Among the 'negligible' side effects reported were amnesia, total loss of libido and potentially dangerous hormone imbalances in the body. A report in *Sexology* magazine concluded that gay men had larger penises than heterosexual men: 3:3 inches when limp, on average, as opposed to three inches exactly. At the same time, 'the first marriage [in America] to legally bind two persons of the same sex' took place in Los Angeles. There was still enormous prejudice against homosexuality, and much nonsense talked about it. Gore Vidal recounted one episode that had happened to him. 'Somebody was asking me,' he said. 'Said he thought Richard Nixon was obviously homosexual. I said: "Why do you think that?" He said: 'You know, that funny, uncoordinated way he moves.' I said: "Yeah, like Nureyev."

A change in attitudes towards homosexuality would gather pace throughout the 1970s. Gay behaviour would change, too, markedly. These changes affected and involved Rudolf more than he would ever acknowledge but, to begin with, in 1970 itself, it was the changes taking place at Covent Garden that concerned him most. On 7 January a press conference was called, presided over by Lord Drogheda, the chairman of the board. He announced formally that, at the end of the season (late spring/early summer), Sir Frederick Ashton – who had been made a

Companion of Honour in the Queen's Birthday honours list – would be retiring and that his place would be taken by two co-directors, Kenneth MacMillan and John Field. Sir David Webster was also about to be replaced as general administrator, by John Tooley. At the same time a drastic reorganisation of the company was outlined. The Sadler's Wells Company was to be merged with the Covent Garden Company, which meant that all performances in London from now on would be at Covent Garden. The size of the company would be reduced though the number of soloists would not. This decision, it was said, was based partly on artistic grounds and partly on financial ones (closing one theatre would save an enormous amount of money). The idea had been considered for fourteen years, said Drogheda, ever since the Bolshoi visit in 1956 had shown what could be done with a monolithic company. Now, at last, it was happening.

In practice, 1970 marked the end of an era. Ashton was the last link with the original group of people who had created the company in the 1930s and he was being replaced by not one, but two, directors. Change was bound to come. Born in Dunfermline, Scotland, in 1929, Kenneth MacMillan was the first major choreographer to have emerged from Dame Ninette de Valois's Royal Ballet School. After leaving the school he spent a few years shuttling between Sadler's Wells and Covent Garden, producing his first works, *Somnambulism* and *Laiderette*, in the mid-1950s. He created *Le Baiser de la fée* and *The Invitation* in 1960, and then *Romeo and Juliet* in 1965. In 1966 he had left London for Berlin to become director of Berlin Opera Ballet. A sensitive and withdrawn man, his ballets showed beautiful use of the stage. Robert Altman, the American film director, once said that MacMillan showed him how to fuse background scenery and foreground action. MacMillan was forty-one when he took over at Covent Garden.

One change appeared almost immediately. A New York season was planned that spring for the Royal Ballet and the new work, which Hurok as usual insisted upon, was to be devised by Rudi van Dantzig, director of the Dutch National Ballet. This, *The Ropes of Time*, did not feature Margot Fonteyn. Instead Rudolf would dance with Monica Mason and Diana Vere. The new administrative team, which had not taken over formally as yet, signalled the new direction the company would take. *The Ropes of Time*, which was premièred on 2 March, was not at all the romantic drama that the public expected, but a piece of modern dance, with the music provided by an electronic tape. Rudolf was able to display his technical virtuosity but, frankly, it was not a success.

In March yet another Nijinsky film was floated, this time with Tony Richardson as director, but for Rudolf the most important news that month was the death of his beloved Pushkin. Rudolf took it badly, partly because the news was announced on the twentieth of the month, four days before an emissary of his was due to fly to Leningrad and make contact with his family and friends there.

The emissary was Monique van Vooren. Van Vooren was Belgian. Her curriculum vitae begins: 'Monique van Vooren is a stellar personality equally at home on either side of the Atlantic, where her friends include achievers, millionaires, superstars, potentates and royalty. Yet this daughter of a well-to-do family (her father was one of the most successful art dealers in Europe) was brought up strictly in a convent. Monique early showed prodigious talents both athletic and intellectual, writing award-winning poetry and placing for three years in a row as Belgium's junior figure skating champion.' She had first met Rudolf in Paris in 1961, before he defected. She did not make much impact at that stage, but later she had moved to Manhattan on a Fulbright scholarship to study philosophy at New York University. However, on a trip to Europe she met Vittorio de Sica, who offered her a part in his film, *Tomorrow Is Too Late*. Back in New York she joined the group around Andy Warhol, appeared in several of his films and took up singing. Bob Colacello, when he was editor of Warhol's *Interview* magazine, described Van Vooren as someone who 'was always heartbroken but she never missed a party'. Monique's first two encounters with Rudolf had been disasters. The first, in Paris in 1961, had been at a party at Raymondo de Larrain's, a friend of hers. Rudolf had smiled at her and approached – and then walked straight by. Clara Saint was standing behind. Then, on the 1964 Royal Ballet tour of North America, when Rudolf was dancing in *Swan Lake*, Monique had sent him some flowers in the form of a swan. Or that is what should have happened. In fact, the florist had made a mistake – and sent a poodle instead. It did not go down well. However, at the opening of Arthur's discotheque, in 1966, she had asked Rudolf to dance and he had replied, 'But of course, you are the most beautiful woman in the room.' They had become good friends after that, so much so that he would stay with Monique when he was performing in New York, in the back room of her apartment on East 66th Street, which overlooked the Soviet embassy to the United Nations.

One reason why Rudolf wanted Monique to go to Russia was because he thought Rosa had married someone Jewish. All his life Rudolf was plagued by accusations of anti-semitism, although he had surrounded himself by people who were Jewish – Gorlinsky, Hurok and, later, Jane Herrman – but Monique has no doubt that, at this point in his life, he did not want Rosa to marry a Jew. In any case, on this occasion it turned out to be a false alarm.

Van Vooren flew to Leningrad via Stockholm. At Stockholm a young woman very like Monique joined the plane and sat next to her. She was a Russian, very beautiful, dressed like Monique in a miniskirt and mink. She spoke English and immediately struck up a conversation. It turned out that her birthday was a few days' away, on the *same* day as Monique's. She had with her a lot of packages, gifts she had bought herself in Stockholm she said, and then asked if, as a non-Russian, Monique would carry some of the packages through the Leningrad customs. As a westerner Monique would be allowed to import them, whereas Russians were not. Knowing how frightened Rudolf still was of being kidnapped by the 'men in civvies', Monique half-thought that this attractive woman must be a KGB 'plant' herself. The coincidence of their birthdays was too much, too corny, surely. She refused to do what the woman asked.

However, her new companion was met at Leningrad airport by her boyfriend, a man called Igor who spoke even better English than she did, and the couple offered to drive Monique to her hotel, the Astoria. This was not without its risks, but she accepted. She was not kidnapped, was helped to her room by Igor and a friendship was struck. Indeed, it was a fortunate meeting because Monique was travelling alone, did not speak Russian, and had only been given addresses by Rudolf of where he *thought* people lived. She attended the girl's birthday party, which turned out to be genuine, and while there she told Igor why she had come to Leningrad. He was wary at first but then agreed to help her track down Rudolf's sister, Rosa, plus several others including Tseniia Iurgenson, Rudolf's old piano teacher, Liuba Miasnikova.

Monique stayed in Leningrad for three weeks. Igor found Rosa, who was still living in the old Sizova flat on Cherny Roszka, with her daughter Guzelle and another family. Rosa acted as Monique's guide, helping her to see Leningrad and they went to the ballet together every night, where Monique's miniskirt and long white sable coat drew almost as much attention as what was happening on stage.

Igor agreed to act as translator so Monique was able to bring Rosa fully up to date on Rudolf's career, and life, and she gave her the clothes she had brought, and some money. But there were three surprises for Monique in Leningrad. The first was that Farida arrived. She had taken the train from Ufa, a journey of three days and, when she arrived, she was wearing what looked like bandages on her feet. She was still poor, still a peasant, who had not adjusted to shoes. Monique found Farida taller and more handsome than she expected. She had a strong face, open, and a stocky, peasant build. Her hands were very strong, too, and her hair, once dark, was going grey. Despite the bandages on her feet, she had a good bearing. The night she arrived, they all went to see the Kirov, where Mikhail Baryshnikov was dancing in *Sleeping Beauty*. The only other time Farida had been to the Kirov had been more than ten years before, to see her son in the same role. She cried throughout the performance.

The second surprise for Monique was to find how friendly the dancers at the Kirov were in regard to Rudolf. Rudolf had given her the name of one dancer in the company, who spoke French. They made contact. Once word spread that Monique and Farida were in the Maryinsky, together, all the members of *Sleeping Beauty* signed a programme and gave it to Monique to take back to Rudolf. She was very touched and so, later, was he.

Monique's third surprise was Tseniia Iurgenson. Although Tseniia was now in her sixties, she was still very attractive, very worldly, full of life even though she had just been widowed. More than anyone, she was proud of what Rudolf had achieved in the west and was proud of her part in his success. She admitted freely to Monique that she and Rudolf had been lovers.

Before she left Leningrad, Farida gave Monique some photographs of Rudolf as a young boy, and a train set he'd had and which she had kept throughout his years in the west. She knew how much he would like to have these things. Monique travelled back from Leningrad via London, where she stayed at Rudolf's house in East Sheen. He was in Argentina at the time so she left the train set and photographs in his house and wrote him a long letter setting out the details of whom she had met and what had been achieved. He wrote back from South America, perhaps the longest letter he ever wrote, thanking her and describing how touched he was at what she had done. He was delighted to have the train set.

A few weeks later he joined Monique in New York. There, the Royal Ballet's new production, the van Dantzig piece, was overshadowed – all but obliterated – by the more traditional ones, the Ashton classics, *Giselle*, MacMillan's *Romeo and Juliet*, *Sleeping Beauty*, Rudolf's own version of *La Bayadère*. Antoinette Sibley, who danced the van Dantzig work with Rudolf, said that the music sounded as if glasses were being thrown against a mirror. She hated it so much and was made so nervous by it that she had to leave for a break in Madeira. Audiences still wanted familiar faces in familiar roles, Fonteyn and Nureyev most of all. And, despite the changes going on around them, they retained the old magic. One critic said they were still 'as explosive as nitroglycerine'. *Newsweek* described Rudolf as 'the ultimate dancer'. At one point the American ballerina Gelsey Kirkland, together with a friend, sneaked backstage into the Met disguised as 'mod' British dancers to watch *Romeo and Juliet*. Kirkland was then working for Balanchine but not enjoying it. That evening changed her sensibility, she later wrote. She was overwhelmed by the romantic spectacle, which provided for her a direction and a model 'that left the New York City Ballet in the dust'. The following day she was almost in tears when she heard Balanchine dismiss the performances and slight the dancers. He criticised Rudolf for always trying to be a prince, and said Margot could not dance at all, that she had 'hands like spoons'. This was too much for Kirkland, who rose in her place and left Balanchine's class for ever.

The perfection of Margot and Rudolf was underlined for many by an incident that took place when Rudolf was dancing *Sleeping Beauty* with Merle Park. That night he was unhappy with the tempos and several times threw fierce looks at the conductor, meaning that he wanted the music slowed down. The conductor appeared to take no notice and, in the second act, Rudolf and Merle collided, he trod on her and they kicked each other. Once more, instead of just carrying on, Rudolf responded by walking off stage. Balletomanes noticed, but Merle Park, to her lasting credit, ad-libbed so brilliantly (with two minutes of 'spaghetti', lots and lots of steps), that many in the audience never realised anything was wrong. After a few moments of throwing vases in the wings Rudolf regained his equilibrium and returned to the stage. He later apologised to Merle and it might have been left at that, had not the *New York Times* critic Anna Kisselgoff (known to Rudolf as 'Anna Piss-me-off'), drawn attention to his lack of manners in her review. Once again, New York was agog at Rudolf's temper and the grin on Sol Hurok's face was broader than ever.

But tension was in the air backstage. More than one critic bemoaned the fact that Rudolf had to seek more work outside the Royal Ballet these days. He had just come back from Australia, noted one, and would be spending a lot of time in the last half of 1970 in Italy, noted another. Clive Barnes took Rudolf's part with a long article in *The Times* in which he said that, after Ninette de Valois and Frederick Ashton, Rudolf was the next most important creative force at the Royal Ballet. This was a view with which Dame Ninette herself concurred but naturally it did not sit well with the new team which was about to take over, especially Kenneth MacMillan, who had been choreographing at the Royal Ballet since 1946 and saw himself as the natural heir to Ashton.

Rudolf felt the tensions, or at least the need to set out his own position a little more clearly. He now began a series of interviews, which would last over the next five years, in which he tried to send signals to the Royal Ballet management, and the public in general. It was a little like a replay of the signals he had sent in Russia when he was ready to defect. This time his message was the exact opposite. He didn't want to move. He told his first interviewer that he had *tried* to be a permanent member of the Royal Ballet but that 'it seems not to be in their interests'. They do what they want to, he added, 'without hurting me too much. I might injure their dancers who are very good.' Coming from Rudolf, this was very revealing and he moved quickly on to other things. He would send out signals but he wouldn't crawl for attention.

One of the topics he moved on to was his private life. Asked yet again if he would get married, he simply said, 'Oh, come *on*!' But he was more forthcoming on why he no longer had a permanent partner. After saying, 'I have a personal life. Something goes on but the public shouldn't know,' he added that any partner would have to put up with one central fact. 'I would think only of myself, my dancing, being up on stage. Who would have the guts to cope with that? And believe me, I don't want surf-riders, people riding the surf from the waves I make.'

In fact, the other dancers in the Royal Ballet, and people like his wardrobe master, Michael Brown, noticed during the New York season that there was now a new man in Rudolf's life. His name was Wallace Potts and he and Rudolf had first met the year before when the Royal Ballet were touring in Atlanta. They had been introduced through Monique van Vooren and Hiram Keller, a friend of Monique's who had appeared in the notorious Fellini film, *Satyricon* and in *Hair*. Monique had watched Rudolf's relationship with Erik change. At one stage, for instance, at La Turbie, Rudolf could not eat and kept asking the time every five minutes, because Erik had not called. After dinner he wouldn't even go to a night club until Erik had phoned. But they had gradually grown apart, at least sexually. On the few occasions that Rudolf slept without a boy in New York he would share Monique's huge bed, but only so that they could talk all night or have midnight feasts of scrambled eggs and vodka, watching old movies. 'If you touch me,' he had told her, 'I'll move to another room.'

But in 1970 Hiram Keller had been in Monique's apartment with an older man with one arm who was keeping Wallace. A couple of weeks later Keller had called Monique and said that, since the Royal Ballet would be performing in Atlanta, Wallace and he would like to give a dinner for Rudolf. Was that acceptable? Rudolf asked what he always asked on occasions like this: how good-looking are they? How old? How young? How attractive? In the end he told Monique to have them come backstage after the show and if he liked them they could give him a dinner. Potts was a maker of pornographic movies, but that paints him blacker than he was. He was tall, good-looking, a rather gentle, soft man who quickly became popular with Rudolf's other friends. He allowed himself to be used by Rudolf, mainly with a good grace, and was very knowledgeable about movies. Rudolf liked that. He always felt that musicals and movies were the art forms that Americans excelled at. When he and Wallace fell out on the first tour, having a fight around the pool at the Royal Ballet's Los Angeles hotel, Frederick Ashton insisted that Rudolf, who had behaved badly, apologise. 'Boys like that come around only rarely,' he said. 'Don't lose him.' Potts told Bob Colacello that 'it was awe at first sight' when he met Rudolf. Early on he had dinner with Margot and Rudolf and they broke his stereotype of ballet dancers as ethereal. 'Both he and Margot could talk about physics, mathematics, philosophy, cosmology.' Wallace would live with Rudolf, who had finally split with Erik in late 1968, for about seven years, mostly at the house in East Sheen.

Another sign of change at the Royal Ballet was that New York was to be the only tour that year. There was a distinct feeling, inside the company and in the Hurok organisation, that enthusiasm for the 'Royal' was waning, certainly outside New York. In view of what happened later this may have been overplayed, but back in London there was a particular treat awaiting everyone. This was the farewell gala at the Garden to Frederick Ashton. It took an unusual form, in that the programme was drawn up in great secrecy and when guests arrived at the theatre on the night they were told simply that the printed order of proceedings would be available *after* the performance.

The curtain rose to reveal Robert Helpmann as the narrator of a three-hour extravaganza which followed the course of Ashton's life, from Guayaquil in Ecuador, via the *eighty* ballets he had created to this very evening. Thirty-five of the ballets, or parts of them, were recreated that night, including six that had not been seen for more than thirty years. No one was announced – the world's greatest dancers were there but the audience was left to recognise who was dancing with whom, in what. Margot danced in three ballets from her extreme youth – *Nocturne, Wise Virgin* and *Apparitions*. Rudolf, who danced in *Les Rendezvous* with Merle Park, was deeply touched by the research and effort that had gone into the gala, and by the depth and variety of Ashton's work. With his own interest in history he always said that the Ashton evening ought to have been preserved in some form, since it was so special. At the end of the evening, the entire cast waltzed to the music from *A Wedding Banquet* and then turned to the choreographer and bowed – Rudolf lower than anyone. But his thanks and admiration were tinged with regret. Now that Ashton had retired, there was no chance at all that he would ever create a new ballet for Rudolf.

In September Rudolf was due in Milan, to perform *Marguerite and Armand* with Margot at La Scala. Just before he left he happened to be walking in the Covent Garden area when he bumped into Natalia Makarova. The Kirov were then appearing in London but at the Festival Hall on the South Bank. At first, Rudolf was wary of Makarova. He was still worried about being kidnapped and would not, at that time, take any aircraft that flew over Cuba – he was convinced that Castro might force the plane down on behalf of his Russian paymasters. So, maybe this chance meeting with Makarova was a set-up. They had not seen each other since 1961. However, after a few moments it seemed as though this was indeed a genuine chance meeting and they struck up a perfectly normal conversation. Makarova was heading for her hotel, the Strand Palace. She was surprised to see him, because she knew there was a party at Fonteyn's that night and she hadn't been invited because he was supposed to be there.

'Why aren't you at the party?' asked Makarova.

Rudolf shook his head. 'Oh, no, I'm going to a movie.' He then said something about the lighting being wrong in *La Bayadère*, one of the ballets the Kirov was doing, and they split up.

A day or so later Rudolf was in Milan, being given a massage by an Italian, Luigi Pignotti, who would loom large in Rudolf's life in later years (he had been recommended by Zubin Mehta). During the massage Luigi happened to mention that he had heard that Makarova had defected in London. Rudolf was surprised, as was the entire Kirov Company.

But their reaction was as nothing compared to the KGB's, who were flabbergasted and embarrassed – *they* had had their eye on someone else, someone called Mikhail Baryshnikov.

Makarova had been a year behind Rudolf at the Vaganova, joining the Kirov in 1959 when she danced with Dolgushin. At the time she defected she said that she didn't remember Nureyev well from Leningrad, though they worked there side by side in 1959 and 1960. What she did remember was that he didn't think much of her. 'Once, at some sort of critique, he came out against my moving up in the company: "Why promote her when she can hardly stand on her legs?" [he is said to have remarked].' She also recalled that he had objected to her make-up – she had so smeared her face with it, to achieve swarthiness in *Don Quixote*, that it came off on the other dancers when she kissed them. So maybe Chelkov had been right all along when he had told her she was wearing too much eye-shadow at the Vaganova.

Makarova had danced with the best male dancers of her day at the Kirov in the 1960s, including Soloviev, Rudolf's room mate on the 1961 tour, and the company's new star, Mikhail Baryshnikov. But she had become disenchanted with the company, finding the insistence on Soviet ballets in the 1960s simply nonsensical. 'The party administration which oversaw the Kirov did not understand that it is impossible to produce a ballet about the construction of a hydro-electric plant.' In some of these ballets real rifles were used on stage, and in one a tractor appeared. 'Such well-intentioned nonsense was not done out of ignorance, but from a serious failure to understand the nature of ballet.' After major disagreements about the aesthetics of dance – at one point Sergeyev told her there were 'western arabesques' and 'Russian arabesques' and that the western variety were 'unnecessary' in Russia – she simply decided the situation was becoming absurd. She realised on the tour of Britain that she had more in common with friends in the west, and more chance to dance the roles she wanted to. She asked those friends to call Scotland Yard.

Her defection really put pressure on Sergeyev, who stayed behind in London after the Kirov had left for Holland, and tried to see her. She refused. Sergeyev was right to be so concerned. Although he and Dudinskaya had not been treated too badly after Rudolf had bolted, this second episode was even more worrying. After his return to Leningrad, both he and Dudinskaya were dismissed.

A new frost settled as a result of the scandal and Maya Plisetskaya was again refused permission to travel, this time to Berlin where she was to have danced at the same time as Rudolf. In Russia it was put about, quite erroneously, that he had lured Makarova to the west. No doubt the chance meeting in Covent Garden had been observed. The Bolshoi released a note saying that Plisetskaya was too ill to travel to Berlin, but on the night she was supposed to have performed she was observed in the audience at a Moscow concert. Rudolf and Makarova (in a blonde wig) rubbed salt in the Russian wounds by dancing a 'pas de defectors' for American Ballet Theatre in November.

The MacMillan–Field regime began in October with a smash hit, in the form of Jerome Robbins's *Dances at a Gathering*. Robbins, who staged *West Side Story*, was a warmer choreographer than Balanchine and this ballet, which had first been performed in New York in 1979 by New York City Ballet, certainly reflected that. The music consisted of assorted Chopin pieces but, though the ballet was plotless, or 'abstract', it was warm, sunny and lyrical, witty and *very* inventive. London audiences loved it. It opened with ten dancers of whom five – Rudolf, Lynn Seymour, Antoinette Sibley, David Wall and Ann Jenner – were Pisces. Antoinette Sibley thought this was one reason why they all clicked immediately.

However, no sooner had this successful start been made, than it was suddenly announced, on Christmas Eve, that John Field had resigned from his position as co-director. He had found it impossible to work with Kenneth MacMillan. A new production, of *Anastasia*, was postponed and crisis was again in the air. Field was not replaced but Peter Wright was appointed associate director, under MacMillan. Wright had worked with John Cranko in Stuttgart for three years, where he had first met Rudolf. He had found him exasperating and devastatingly direct in equal measure, but had admired his appetite for work and his generosity, especially the way he helped Lynn Seymour. A choreographer himself, he was particularly known for stunning stagings of *Giselle* and *Sleeping Beauty*, produced for the Canadians, in Cologne and in Vienna. Most recently, Wright had been running the Royal Ballet's touring company. The combination of MacMillan and Wright was to prove very important for Nureyev.

Rudolf was undoubtedly unsettled by these changes but, as a star and a proud Tartar, he didn't show it. Or at least he didn't wear his heart on his sleeve. But he did send out more signals. He gave three more interviews, unusually for him. In one he let it be known that he had 'worked hard' to be a good member of the Royal Ballet and that he had not insisted on dancing only with Margot. He said that, one year, he had been told that he must dance with every female soloist in the company. He had accepted that, he said, but it had never materialised. He implied it wasn't his fault. In the second interview he said that he felt he still needed to be *discovered* by a choreographer. There was something inside him that hadn't yet been brought out; no one surprised him any more. This was surely aimed at MacMillan. Ashton had created just the one role for Rudolf – he was asking that the same thing should not happen again. In the third interview he replied to a criticism that he had refused to dance on provincial tours. It wasn't true, he said, but when he *had* been asked to dance on a tour it had been so late in the day that his time was already booked. This was an important exchange because of course the new associate director, Peter Wright, had been the person in charge of provincial tours. Rudolf was clearing the air with both the director and the associate director.

And he was right to clear the air and right to be worried. In the first six months of 1971 the new approach became very clear: the Royal Ballet did not stage a single version of a nineteenth-century classic, and attendances began to fall off. During this time, Rudolf danced with the Marseilles Ballet (where Rosella Hightower was now the ballet mistress), with Maurice Béjart in Brussels, with the Australian Ballet in North America, a tiring tour of eighteen cities where he danced every performance. This was what audiences wanted (and Rudolf always said that he danced better when he was tired – because his muscles obeyed him), but there were complaints from the other dancers. In fact, when the tour schedule was announced several leading members of the Australian company threatened to resign. They didn't begrudge Nureyev the limelight, they said, acknowledging that he was 'probably the greatest dancer in the world', but they didn't want to be just a backdrop either.

A different problem surfaced in Düsseldorf where, although the audiences cheered his appearances, they also booed heartily at the end, since they thought they had not seen enough of the star to justify the high prices: he danced only in Aurora's Wedding, the last act of *The Sleeping Beauty*. Rudolf, the consummate theatrical animal, responded on stage by treating the boos as applause, bowing in a dignified way. Backstage, however, he agreed with the booers, and in later towns he also danced earlier in the evening.

Back in London he danced new works by Paul Taylor and was featured in a gala at the Coliseum organised by Richard Buckle to save Titian's *Diana and Actaeon* for the nation and to raise money for a museum of the performing arts in London. The gala also featured works by Henry Moore and David Hockney and an auction run by Andy Warhol. Rudolf could be forgiven for feeling that he was loved everywhere except in Floral Street.

Matters improved towards the end of the year when he danced *Swan Lake* with Monica Mason and Lynn Seymour and the *pas de deux* from *Romeo and Juliet* with Margot. But MacMillan was now getting into his stride. Anastasia, when it premièred on 22 July had proved a great success, especially for Lynn Seymour. But her partners were Anthony Dowell, David Wall or Wayne Eagling, not Rudolf. And not Christopher Gable. He had left the dance world altogether, the loudest complainant that Rudolf's presence at the Royal Ballet had been like the First World War, in that he had destroyed 'an entire generation', of male British dancers. There may have been some substance to this charge so far as he, and possibly Michael Somes, were concerned. But two swallows do not make a summer and Dowell, Wall and Eagling had all benefited from Rudolf's presence. Can it really be that MacMillan had never got over the dramatic events that had occurred behind the scenes when *Romeo and Juliet* was performed in 1965 and Lynn Seymour had had an abortion? Had he harboured a grudge against Rudolf all these years? And was he wreaking revenge now?

By the end of the year, the overall policy of the new regime was nowhere more in evidence than in the stark statistics. In 1969, Rudolf had danced 87 performances with the Royal Ballet. In 1970, the change-over year, he had danced 56 performances. In 1971, the number had fallen to 23.

It was fortunate that his time during the winter was taken up with a film about him, called '*I am a Dancer*.' This had begun life as a TV documentary in France but it was decided to expand it and give it a stronger narrative line so that it could be shown in cinemas, where there was more money. Rudolf had his own ideas for the film but EMI, who were interested in taking it over for the bigger screen, called in Bryan Forbes as the 'rescue' director. Forbes flew to Paris to see what film existed and was shown a few frames of interview with Rudolf and segments of *Marguerite and Armand*. The 'screening room' there was a dingy office, the seats were fruit crates, and the screen a whitewashed wall. There was nowhere near enough material for a film and it was clear that more dance scenes would need to be shot. Forbes was given a budget and, after rather fraught negotiations with Sandor Gorlinsky, Rudolf's agent, the project was given the go-ahead.

Forbes had met Rudolf once. In his memoire he wrote that it was 'at an intimate dinner party given by Lee Radziwill who was then hankering after an acting career. Rudy lounged and pouted throughout the meal, confessing to Lee that he had had a bad day and thrown what he described as "a tiny tantrum". I was aware of his reputation for being difficult.' Nonetheless, the two men managed to agree on enough for the film to go forward. It was decided that Rudolf would dance one complete modern ballet, *Field Figures*, which has music by Stockhausen and choreography by Glen Tetley, and the *pas de deux* from *Sleeping Beauty*. In *Field Figures* his partner would be Deanne Bergsma and in *Sleeping Beauty* Lynn Seymour.

For Seymour this project turned out to be even more important than for Rudolf. Her career just then was going through a bad patch: her marriage wasn't working, she had put on weight and MacMillan had replaced her in one of Balanchine's ballets, *Serenade*, 'for her own good'. She started missing class. One day, she wrote in her memoirs, she was still in bed, instead of at class, when the phone rang. It was Rudolf. By some form of telepathy, he knew she was in a bad way. 'I wearily informed Rudi that my Garden schedule was thin because I was fat. He had already heard of the *Serenade* cancellation.'

'Lil, I want you to do something for me,' he said. 'I need you.' He told her that he needed extra sequences for his film and that he wanted her for the *pas de deux* from *The Sleeping Beauty*.

'Ask someone else. You'll get a hernia trying to lift me.'

'You'll do it Lil,' he laughed, and wouldn't prolong the discussion. They both had to get to class, he said.

It was a thoughtful gesture. It was exactly the kind of fillip Seymour needed and, she said later, the offer saved her from professional and financial disaster. Throughout the filming, she said, he behaved towards Seymour as if the film were about her, not him, and this helped her regain her confidence. It was not the first favour he had done her (he had lent her La Turbie when she needed to escape) but it was probably the biggest.

The new sequences were shot on the Coliseum stage one Sunday, and Forbes did not entirely enjoy the encounter. To begin with, Rudolf lost his temper with the stills photographer. According to Forbes, Rudolf had been dissatisfied with his own performance and took it out on the photographer, saying that the shutter noise from his Nikon had distracted him. 'Had he done it to one of the electricians he would probably have been laid flat on his back and that would have been the end of the film.' But Rudolf apologised and they went on.

More important was the fact that Forbes had had five camera crews at the Coliseum since eight o'clock that morning but Rudolf had not arrived until after lunch, 'strutting on stage tetchy and argumentative, and immediately announcing that all my camera positions were in the wrong position and that furthermore Lynn was too heavy for the lifts'. This does seem to have been a shade insensitive on Rudolf's part, given the background, and it is no surprise that Seymour burst into tears and fled to her dressing-room. In his autobiography, Forbes says he sent out for flowers and then buttonholed Rudolf. 'Look, I admire you extravagantly as a dancer, but we've been hanging around all day waiting for you to show up. Either you get changed and dip your feet in the rosin and we shoot it, or else I'm going to dismiss the crews, who are on double salary, and you'll have to pay them out of your own fee.'

'The mention of money brought about a startling change in him; I had struck where it hurt most. He flounced off to his dressing-room. I dried Lynn's tears and an hour later we were finally able to commence shooting. Rudy was still at the height of his powers, dazzling to watch when he executed his seemingly endless *grands jetés*, giving the impression that his feet never touched the ground. It was a heart-stopping spectacle that made all the previous difficulties fade into insignificance.' It was a fascinating experience, Forbes said, but though he admired Rudolf, 'I could not like him.'

Forbes's name did not appear on the film. The French director, Pierre Jourdain, took all the credit. Nureyev would not allow his name to be used in the title because, he said, it would have been insulting to Margot. Forbes and the critics both thought that the sweaty rehearsal scenes contained some important insights into dance. The close-ups of Margot in *Marguerite and Armand* were criticised as being too painful and taking the romance out of the piece but John Percival's narration was praised as helping provide a structure to the film, being sympathetic without being wholly flattering. However, in an interview with Terry Coleman in the *Guardian*, before the première, Rudolf candidly told his interviewer what he thought was wrong with the film. He also said that he would pay £30,000 to have it destroyed.

Besides van Vooren, who was now making annual trips to Leningrad on Rudolf's behalf, he managed to send three reels of film, showing him dancing with Fonteyn in *Romeo and Juliet*, and with the Paris Opéra Ballet (his films were not only illegal in Russia, but in China as well). In Leningrad itself there was quite a community of dancers and friends who showed illegal eight-millimetre films of his performances – many Kirov dancers loved his free style. But the *Romeo and Juliet* film was something special and it was shown at Baryshnikov's apartment though the Nureyevs were invited. According to Baryshnikov they were in Leningrad at the time visiting Rosa and about twelve of them showed up. They watched one reel, tears streaming down their faces, then had a break for tea for an hour, then watched the next reel. That evening went on until two in the morning.

At the end of April the Royal Ballet was again in New York. It was their thirteenth tour, they had a new director, but still Fonteyn and Nureyev were the great draw. Monique van Vooren gave a party for Margot and Rudolf at the Pen & Pencil. By now Rudolf and she were quite close, to the extent that van Vooren would cast an eye over his contracts. Some of these contracts were very – shall we say – creative. In one, Gorlinsky took no commission but Rudolf gave him the use of his fees for three months. It was up to Gorlinsky to invest the money and make what he could. (Jack Lanchbery once asked Rudolf if he lost any sleep over the amount of money Gorlinsky was swindling out of him. 'I don't think about it,' replied Rudolf. 'I'd rather sleep.')

On that tour, however, there was an argument over the contract and Rudolf took it out on Monique, throwing an ashtray at her in the apartment and cutting her head so badly that she had to be to be given stitches in Lenox Hill Hospital. They didn't speak for four days. Still more signs of the broken-backed nature of the Royal Ballet were in evidence on this tour. For example, Anna Kisselgoff in the *New York Times* remarked that the disappointments in the Royal Ballet (*Field Figures*, *Sideshow*) were offset by Fonteyn and Nureyev. Another critic thought that the Royal's season was for balletomanes only, and a third said that Rudolf's status was undiminished, a reference to the fact that he danced less frequently now for the British company, but not less well. That year there were still stronger rumours that this tour would be Margot's last and so tickets were in greater demand than ever. Rudolf himself cast envious glances in the direction of NYCB where Balanchine and John Taras were planning a special programme to celebrate Stravinsky's ninetieth birthday. But there was still no invitation forthcoming from that direction.

While the Royal Ballet was in New York, Andy Warhol, Robert Mapplethorpe and Bob Colacello went to see Rudolf in rehearsal with the company at Lincoln Centre. Colacello had set up the meeting, to gain material for Warhol's *Interview* magazine. From the first, Colacello had an inkling that all might not go well. When he had called to make the arrangements, he had found Rudolf rather regal, and he had specifically asked that Mapplethorpe be present. Colacello had published some of Mapplethorpe's early work in *Interview* and the two had become firm friends even though Andy didn't like him and Candy Darling thought him a 'sicko'.

During the long taxi ride uptown, neither Warhol nor Mapplethorpe spoke. Each was holding a Polaroid Big Shot camera and the atmosphere was icy. In his book on Warhol, Colacello says he alone chatted on 'like a Washington socialite seated between the ambassadors of Iran and Iraq'. When they arrived, and Rudolf's ego was added to those of Warhol and Mapplethorpe it was more than Colacello could handle and he just stood to one side.

The first thing Warhol asked was, 'What colour are your eyes?'

Rudolf replied, 'The interview is cancelled.' Whereupon he switched off Warhol's tape recorder. Colacello, he said, had never warned him that the visit was to be an interview. Warhol had been persuaded to attend only with difficulty and he now became very angry. He put away his tape recorder but took out his Polaroid, popping its flashes at Rudolf. The first made Rudolf look very handsome. He liked it, and the second, which was also a portrait. He liked them so much that he signed both of them, and Colacello began to breathe a little easier. *Détente* of a sort had been achieved, he thought. He was wrong. Warhol's third shot had been a tight close-up of Rudolf's crotch. 'The most famous crotch in the theatre.'

Rudolf exploded, shouting and snarling, says Colacello, grabbed the Polaroid and threw it to the floor. Warhol bent to pick it up but Rudolf put his foot over it. Now Mapplethorpe joined in, aiming *his* camera at Rudolf's foot. Both Rudolf and Warhol hated this move. Rudolf now grabbed Mapplethorpe's camera, yanked out the photograph and scrunched it up. Since it was still wet, one part stuck to the other.

Mapplethorpe tried to make light of it. 'Don't you like your foot?' he said.

'My foot, yes,' said Rudolf, tapping the tip of Mapplethorpe's nose and staring him down. Then he smiled, turned, and launched into his exercises, 'stretching and arching his taut body'.

He allowed them to take whatever photographs they wanted, provided he could have the final say in what they took away with them. He went through them, one by one, tearing up most of them. Warhol and Mapplethorpe were disappointed rather than angry.

But then the rehearsal proper began, with the rest of the Royal Ballet in attendance. 'Suddenly, Nureyev leapt, and leapt again, and again and again and again in a stunning circle of leaps, each one held for an instant of breathtaking suspension, a flash of beauty fixed in flight.' Warhol was overwhelmed. 'He's so great,' he whispered. 'I didn't know a person could be that great. He should be in movies.' Both he and Mapplethorpe took away even the photos Rudolf had torn up. What Warhol never knew was that Rudolf *hated* him.

Back in London, Rudolf was approached by Harry Saltzman, one of the producers of the James Bond films, about yet another Nijinsky project. Saltzman invited him to dinner to discuss the film with the man he wanted to direct it, Ken Russell. Russell had already made films on Isadora Duncan and Claude Debussy and Rudolf admired his work. However, at the dinner Russell said that if Rudolf was to do the film it would take weeks of his time and he would have to give up the autumn season he planned in North America with the National Ballet of Canada. Rudolf didn't want to give up weeks of dancing for, as he put it, 'just a film'. This was intended to be dismissive; Rudolf found Russell patronising. Also, although he admired the director, he didn't like him personally – so he said no to the project. Russell later claimed that the discussion foundered on Rudolf's fee – he had asked for £1 million. But maybe that was simply a way of saying no. This Nijinsky project went the way of all the others.

The Kirov were in London again that year and this time Rudolf arranged to meet Baryshnikov secretly. Rudolf sent a car for him very early, so as to avoid the KGB (two agents married two ballerinas they met on that tour). Rudolf and Baryshnikov spent the day together, walking in Richmond Park, discussing the Kirov, and dance in general. Rudolf showed Mikhail all his costumes – unlike most dancers he liked costumes to open from the front, since he was terrified of being caught in a fire. Baryshnikov couldn't drink because he was dancing that night so, at lunch, Rudolf drank the whole bottle and became quite tipsy and emotional. At the end, he gave the younger man a book on Michelangelo's drawings, and a scarf. A friendship, rather than a rivalry, had been established.

That summer Rudolf spent more time than usual at La Turbie, where his guests included Franco Rosselini, Dino de Laurentis, Sylvia Mangano, Maria Callas and Monique van Vooren, who had just returned from another trip to Russia. There, in her cavernous room at the Astoria

Hotel in Leningrad, she had gathered Rudolf's family and friends for a marathon phone call, when he had held full-scale conversations with a dozen people at one go. Monique always found La Turbie rather oppressive, the sort of house where *The Story of O* might be set, she said. Rudolf had added a lot of ironwork and Gothic-type furniture. The villa was a sort of upside-down house in that the bedrooms and the living room were on the floor where you entered, and the dining room below. One evening, going down to dinner Maria Callas stopped Rudolf in front of a mirror. She stood there looking at both their reflections. 'Rudolf, you could never be in movies,' she said. 'You just don't have the cheekbones.' She thought his cheekbones paled in comparison with hers.

He also saw quite a bit of Mick Jagger that summer. They had first met in the mid-1960s, when Jagger had been to see him perform and then taken his then girlfriend and fellow singer, Marianne Faithful, backstage. According to Jagger's biographer, Christopher Andersen, Faithful was struck by the physical similarity – the lips and the cheekbones – of the two men.

They saw each other from time to time after that, and in the 1970s, by which time Rudolf was exclusively homosexual and very promiscuous, they both visited the Continental Baths below the Ansonia Hotel on New York's Upper West Side. These baths – described memorably as a cross between Hades and an Esther Williams movie – were where Bette Midler, Barry Manilow and Melissa Manchester first found a public, among the very appreciative gay bathers who visited the Continental for the orgies, S & M and other forms of adventurous sex. It was here, according to Christopher Andersen, that Rudolf met, and had sex with, Giorgio Sant'Angelo, Leonard Bernstein and Anthony Perkins.

Jagger was reputedly as bisexual as Rudolf had once been but the two men seem to have spent a great deal of time just talking. 'Me and Nureyev have flaming rows,' Jagger told Faithful, 'about whether it takes more talent and discipline to be a ballet dancer or a pop singer. He used to put me down a lot, but I think I've converted him.'

That summer they were both at a party at the home of television talk show host, Geraldo Rivera, at his apartment on the Lower East Side. As Rivera told the story, he left the two men in his living room, where they were dancing and smoking marijuana, while he went into the kitchen to mix some drinks:

Suddenly, someone snuggled up behind me. I felt an arm around my waist, and I made a kind of half pivot to see who it was. It was Nureyev, and he was moving in time to the music, pressing himself against me from behind. He was being playfully suggestive, overtly sexual, and before I had a chance to even think how to respond, Jagger approached me from the front and started doing the same thing. They were kidding, and giddy, but there was also something seriously competitive going on between them.

Jagger fondled Rivera's chest while Rudolf ran his fingers through their host's hair. Then Rudolf is alleged to have said to Jagger, 'He's a virgin, you know.'

'Oh well,' replied Jagger, 'we can break him in.'

Rivera remained convinced that, despite the playful nature of the encounter, it was a serious attempt to seduce him.

In June 1972 the first officially proclaimed 'Gay Pride Week' took place in Ann Arbor, Michigan.

CHAPTER SEVENTEEN

Hope's Deceptive Dinner

a sweet beginner,
he fed on hope's deceptive dinner;
the world's *éclat*, its thunder-roll,
still captivated his young soul.

In September 1972 Rudolf opened on a North American tour with the National Ballet of Canada. This was a clever move of Celia Franca, the artistic director of the company. She had danced in Britain before the war and immediately afterwards, before starting the NBC, and had worked with everyone from Erik Bruhn to Antony Tudor, the maverick choreographer. In recent years, she had formed an excellent company of young dancers who, in 1972, had just returned from a triumphant tour of Europe. However, good as they were, the National Ballet of Canada had not broken through on to the major international scene – Toronto did not rival London, Copenhagen, Paris or New York. When they played in the United States, for example, they would dance at the Berkeley Theatre, not the main San Francisco Theatre. This was partly prejudice but partly due to the fact that, although the company had several first-class ballerinas, there was no male star of any standing. Celia Franca was well aware of Rudolf's difficulties in London, and equally aware of his pulling power with North American audiences. Her invitation to him was, for her, a natural extension of the company she was head of.

When Rudolf arrived in Toronto, he found the company very provincial to begin with. Linda Mabeduke, who became a very close friend, remembers that he was feeling very raw about his treatment in London and that his guard was up. But, as they worked together on the new production of *The Sleeping Beauty* which he had been commissioned to produce for Franca, he quickly relaxed. His impact on the Canadians was no less revolutionary than it had been on the Royal Ballet a decade before. His *Sleeping Beauty* was much more athletic than the version they were familiar with, which was the Royal Ballet's, and his instruction was typically Rudolfian: 'Come out gangbusters,' he said.

With Rudolf on board, Sol Hurok had guaranteed every performance for the company, on a tour which saw them open in Ottawa, then take in Montreal, Philadelphia, Boston, Cleveland, Birmingham, Atlanta and Baltimore, before finishing the first leg in Toronto. In the process, Karen Kain and Veronica Tennant became known to a much wider audience.

Wallace was now a permanent fixture in Rudolf's life. Although he lived with Rudolf in the East Sheen house, he travelled a lot too and would accompany him to Toronto for the seasons with the National Ballet of Canada. Wallace was not the intellectual presence in Rudolf's life that Erik had been – he was a comic freak, for instance (as Rudolf was), and one of his jobs was to carry the luggage. If he had a fault, it was to take himself too seriously. Bonnie Prandato Robinson, for example, recalls typing Wallace's 'ghastly pornographic scripts' for his films. But he was popular with everyone, much more so than Erik, and was easy company and not a 'taker'. The Canadians, like Linda Mabeduke, liked his self-deprecating sense of humour.

In the winter of 1972–73 Rudolf also took part in a special series of galas at the Paris Opéra in homage to Serge Diaghilev, whose centenary had fallen a few months before. He danced three contrasting ballets on the one programme, *Les Sylphides, Apollo* and *Petrushka*. As a measure of his versatility and stamina, on the nights that he didn't perform, his roles were taken by two or sometimes three dancers. While in Paris he had dinner with Andy Warhol, who was on a world tour, still collecting material for *Interview* and also hoping to land commissions from people who wanted him to paint their portraits. Rudolf didn't play ball on either score.

The Royal Ballet kicked off 1973 with a programme of three Balanchine ballets: *Prodigal Son*, an early work, *The Four Temperaments*, composed in 1946, and *Agon*, dating from 1957. Rudolf danced in *Prodigal Son* (which Diaghilev had never liked when it was first produced for the Ballets Russes). Its blend of mime and technical virtuosity suited him to perfection and he was well partnered by Deanne Bergsma. One of the evenings was a 'Fanfare for Europe,' dedicated to Britain's entry at long last into the Common Market.

Michael Brown remembers one unusual incident – or set of incidents – from this time. At Covent Garden, Rudolf, as befitted his status, always used dressing-room number nine, which overlooked the Covent Garden fruit and vegetable market in those days (and is now overlooked by the opera block). While he was making up, one of the chores that Brown would do for him was to open his mail. Over a period, quite a few letters were purportedly from Farida – but they were *in English*. Neither

Brown nor Rudolf ever got to the bottom of this. Farida was a Tartar, who couldn't write Russian let alone English. So had these letters been concocted by the KGB and if so, why? Who did they think they were deceiving? The letters always said the same thing, imploring Rudolf to come home. Often he would instruct Brown to throw them away before he had finished reading them. It was very strange.

By now Rudolf was leading an exhausting life. In November he had been in Sydney, with the Australian Ballet, and he had flown there from Toronto. In December he had been in Paris. January saw him in London until the last week, when he flew back to America to resume the second leg of his tour with the National Ballet of Canada, in Vancouver. He was keeping himself company on these long flights by reading *Moby Dick* and *Gulag Archipelago* (this is the man who once said he found words dead things). He told one journalist that if only 5 per cent of the Solzhenitsyn book were true, it was important and that everyone should be given a free copy. He saddled himself with yet more travel, dashing off to Madison and Milwaukee to dance with the Wisconsin Ballet, simply because they were mounting ballets – *Apollo* and *The Moor's Pavane* – that he wanted to dance in; this was the first time he had danced *Apollo* in North America. Wallace was filming Rudolf's performances so that he could observe his faults and correct them. Hitherto, Wallace had travelled with weight-lifting gear. Now, it was Rudolf's cameras.

That winter Rudolf had danced five new roles and a new city – Mexico City – where he had worked with Paul Taylor, performing *Aureole* and *Book of Beasts*. Rudolf was to retain a soft spot for Taylor, whom he had first met in Spoleto all those years ago. Later on, he would go to the trouble of arranging a London theatre for the American choreographer, and would fly to New York from London, for one night, to dance in a Taylor season. And he always adjusted his fee for Taylor's more meagre resources.

On the second leg of the tour with the National Ballet of Canada, the *pas de cinq* from *Sleeping Beauty* often had to be cut because it took the production over the three hours, and Hurok refused to pay overtime. It was in Rudolf's contract that the *pas de cinq*, which was *his* choreography, had to be performed in major cities but in smaller cities it was quite often cut. One of these cities was Vancouver. There was therefore some confusion the following day, when the local critic slated the performance, except for the *pas de cinq* – which he said was wonderful. Since it hadn't been performed, no one knew whether the man had attended the performance or not.

On that leg of the tour, they danced Bruhn's version of *La Sylphide*, so Erik came to watch. This made Rudolf nervous. At the time, Linda Mabeduke was playing second leads and spent a lot of time in *Sleeping Beauty* talking with Rudolf, either on stage or in the wings while they were waiting to dance. According to her, the love–hate relationship between

Rudolf and Erik was 'out in front' for everyone on that tour to see. They were cruel about each other, and to each other, yet couldn't do without each other. Both confessed to Linda that the other man had made him an alcoholic. Rudolf still desperately wanted Erik's approval but, by now, the older man very rarely gave it. In Memphis Rudolf was so nervous that he asked a doctor for some pills (the doctor refused).

When they reached New York, the entire company was nervous. This was the apotheosis of their careers: to be playing the Met was in ballet terms, to be received into heaven. At that point, the American Ballet Theatre had never appeared at the Met. And here Rudolf came into his own. Normally, in *Sleeping Beauty*, he didn't appear until the last act and therefore didn't need to get to the theatre very early. But on this first night he was there well before the curtain went up and called everyone on stage. He told them he realised how nervous they were but, he added, 'You should all know, that if I didn't believe in you, I would never let you go on in New York. I am proud of you – you will be wonderful.' And then, as an afterthought, 'If you each want a tot of whisky, that's not such a bad idea either.'

However, during that New York season one unfortunate event took place, perhaps because in his distress over what was happening at the Royal Ballet, Rudolf had really been doing too much. He injured himself and had to withdraw. Without him, Hurok cancelled the Washington engagement that was to have followed. While this highlighted his phenomenal appeal, it made him few friends.

Nor was the situation helped by an interview which Karen Kain gave while the National Ballet of Canada was in New York. She happened to remark that while the company's ballerinas were playing innocent sylphs and swans and sleeping princesses, the rest of the time they were slipping across Broadway to watch the very pornographic movie, *Deep Throat*, which had recently been released; it was probably the furthest the sexual revolution had yet travelled. Perhaps it ought not to have surprised people that ballet dancers were made of flesh and blood, but it did create a *frisson* of excitement for a while. Kain was also quoted as saying that there was one male dancer in the company who went for long walks after their performances, 'prowling the streets for some hunky stranger in the night'. In paragraph three, the author of the interview had referred to Rudolf, saying that the general public only knew 'well-laundered scraps' about his private life. People appeared frightened to talk openly about Rudolf's private life, but would hint at it endlessly.

In New York he gave out more signals to the ballet board of Covent garden. In an interview headlined 'I AM AN INTRUDER,' he acknowledged that he was an intruder wherever he went – London, Toronto, Sydney, Vienna. But he was unrepentant: 'It is not a pleasant situation but I refuse to be left out,' he said and then he brought up Martha Graham: 'I intend to crash *her* gate.' But it was London he had most in mind. It was London where he wanted not only to be a member of the Royal Ballet but, also, if MacMillan should ever leave, director.

But at least in New York he achieved one aspect of professional *recognition* that he always craved. He was given *Dance Magazine*'s Award, in an elaborate ceremony at the Regency Hotel on Park Avenue in Manhattan. This was the award Erik had received a few years earlier, when Rudolf had so admired his *Giselle*. To make the recognition all the sweeter, it was Erik who, on this occasion, presented the award. The editor of the magazine, William Como, acknowledged that Rudolf had brought a new audience to dance, but Erik spoke of Rudolf the man, how he had helped him through a difficult time in his life, when they first met in 1961:

It was not necessarily because of the youth he had then, nor his drive and ambition, which are the expected ingredients in the career of a professional dancer, that I was affected by knowing Rudolf. It was his burning passion for the art of dance that gave me infinite inspiration and helped me push through a difficult phase of transition as the dancer. Perhaps we all need such inspiration in our lives. I know that I needed it and that Rudolf Nureyev gave it to me. [*Turning to Nureyev*] Rudik, I can only wish you, when you come to need it, a similar inspiration.

In London that spring the Royal Ballet was forced to mount a season at the Coliseum since the Opera had booked the Garden. The new management at least had the sense to stage a real piece of theatre to mark the company's return to its own theatre in June. Natalia Makarova was invited to dance, first, *The Sleeping Beauty* and then *Romeo and Juliet* with Rudolf. The fact that both had trained at the Kirov, that they had overlapped while there, and that she had been given her big chance in London after he defected, made their dancing together seem irresistible. In fact, the encounter was a disappointment. She played a feverish Juliet, the role she had so relished in Leningrad in contrast to all the Marxist ballets of the 1960s, but this hardly suited Rudolf's temperament, and was very different from Margot's interpretation, with which many balletomanes were familiar.

For someone with such a reputation for temperament, Rudolf rarely said anything disparaging about his partners, just as he rarely said anything disparaging about Russia. (In Leningrad, for instance, Dudinskaya and several others felt very betrayed that both Makarova and Baryshnikov, after they defected, criticised aspects of their homeland. They all pointed out that Rudolf, whatever he *felt*, kept his feelings to himself.) In her autobiography, published in 1979, Makarova skipped over *The Sleeping Beauty*, except to say that it had serious flaws.

She had more to say about *Romeo and Juliet* which, she explains, she had to learn in a week, taught by Georgina Parkinson. To begin with, she found the MacMillan choreography uncomfortable and the implied Margot interpretation alien to her – she wasn't English, after all. Juliet-Margot, as she referred to the role, seemed to her too reserved, too cerebral. Instead she used Ulanova as a model.

She did not meet her Romeo-Rudi until the dress rehearsal, when she jumped out on stage with a Renaissance-type hairdo which, she felt, did not sit at all happily with her small frame. And indeed, she felt that she startled Rudolf – 'with the result that the whole rehearsal turned into one continuous misunderstanding'. She mixed up her entrances, the scenery was unsteady, making the dancers nervous, and she thought the balcony was about to collapse beneath her at any moment.

Although others didn't agree with her, she says she had an immediate rapport with Rudolf.

'I was overcome by Romeo-Rudi, who was utterly passionate, untrammelled in his feelings, almost driven by an insanity of sensual desire. His dancing was magnificent, fresh, without even the slightest technical flaws . . . At the end of the first act, in the balcony scene, I rushed down the stairs to meet Romeo, and when he caught my hand, I was astounded by the boyish infatuation and the passion that emanated from Rudi. He gave me immense emotional impetus, and we did not even have to act; we simply became the lovers of Verona . . . In the death scene he jumped upon the platform in front of Juliet's tomb like a wounded beast, and I suddenly was struck almost physically by his inner state.'

One woman with whom Rudolf did have a rapport was the Queen – and not just because, like Margot, he had a soft spot for titles. That year, 1973, he attended a World Wildlife Fund Gala with Antoinette Sibley (the Duke of Edinburgh was the president of WWF). They were presented to the Queen, who spent some time chatting with them. After a little while, Antoinette drew Rudolf's attention to the fact that Her Majesty had taken off her shoes. Like him, she had problems with her feet.

After his London performances with Makarova, Rudolf danced with Paul Taylor's – very modern – company at another theatre in London. Taylor had been on a European tour but without a London engagement. Victor Hochhauser, the impresario, agreed to provide one if Rudolf was included among the cast. After that Rudolf teamed up again with Makarova in Paris during the summer. This turned out to be an extraordinary engagement. The plans called for the Paris Opéra Ballet to give thirteen performances of *Swan Lake* on an open-air stage erected in one of the courtyards of the Louvre. The first night, Bastille Day, was free for the citizens of Paris.

Nureyev was booked to dance every night, but three ballerinas were chosen to star opposite him – Noëlla Pontois and Ghislaine Thesmar, from the Paris company, and Makarova, as a guest.

The first thing that went wrong was the weather. It was cold and windy, so cold that, on occasion, the *corps de ballet* of swans had to wear warm leotards under their tutus. As Rudolf sat on the throne, before dancing, he wrapped a cloak around his legs to keep them from seizing up. Two performances were rained off. Rudolf visited the tent where the *corps de ballet* were holding a meeting to decide whether conditions were too bad to perform. He didn't want to interfere – just to ask them to make up their minds before 8.30, when the good movies were due to start.

Just before she danced on her first night, probably because of the weather, Makarova slipped and fell. Because of this, in her first performance she omitted her solo and other parts of the ballet. On her second night she danced the role completely but the one after that was again abridged, which drew adverse comment both from the audience and from other dancers. Makarova countered by saying that she was not well enough to dance her remaining performances, and these were allotted to the two French ballerinas. This was unfortunate, but it would soon have been forgotten if she had not then made some caustic comments to a journalist on a San Francisco newspaper (she settled in that city). She was quoted as saying that in Paris Rudolf had been very jealous of her when he realised that the crowds had come to see her, not him. This was puzzling to many, since he was the one dancing every night, and the huge auditorium of 6,500 seats was sold out throughout the festival, even for the performances she wasn't dancing in. But she was insistent, saying also that Rudolf much preferred appearing with younger dancers 'who would do what he told them'. Her final insult was to say that 'things are difficult for a man of thirty-five'. Nureyev said nothing.

Makarova's jibe about Nureyev's age was unkind but he couldn't deny the fact that in 1973 he *was* thirty-five. In many respects his age didn't show but his dancing had changed. He hovered in the air somewhat less. He was a less sensational dancer but, many critics felt, a better dancer. Makarova's own reaction to him as Romeo, quoted earlier, shows that he had lost none of his intensity. When they had first danced together, she had said, 'You dance like *them*,' meaning westerners. 'No,' Rudolf had replied, 'I dance like me.'

The mad itinerary continued throughout the 1973–74 winter. He hated to be in London because, in the three-day week brought about by Prime Minister Edward Heath's fight with the miners, there was precious little television. After Paris Nureyev toured Israel, and performed in Copenhagen, Oslo and Milan, where he was kicked out of his hotel for picking up a boy and taking him back to his room. Later there were more trips to France, to Versailles and Monte Carlo, a day trip to New York,

Milan again and Canada again. Perhaps nothing could illustrate Nureyev's busy schedule at this time and his complete domination of the dance world more than two events which followed one another in close proximity at the Metropolitan Opera House theatre in May 1974. On 5 May, the last night of the tour by the National Ballet of Canada took place at the Met. Two days later, the Royal Ballet opened *its* American tour at the same theatre. Rudolf simply went from one company to the other. He used the same dressing-room.

There were two sad events in New York. He was due to see Sol Hurok one day to discuss an idea he had for his own touring company, to be called Nureyev and Friends. Hurok liked the idea and had suggested Radio City Music Hall as a venue. Rudolf turned up at the Hurok offices at 4 p.m. as arranged, only to find that the impresario, who had been visiting David Rockefeller at Chase Manhattan Bank to discuss the financing of Nureyev and Friends, had suffered a massive heart attack and died. It was as serious a blow to Rudolf as it was to the Royal Ballet.

The second sad event in New York that year was Margot Fonteyn's absence from the Royal Ballet's programme. She hadn't been invited.

On 13 May Mary Quant cosmetics announced that it was actively marketing make-up, including eye-shadow, lipstick and mascara, for men. The next day the first federal gay civil rights bill, introducing anti-discrimination legislation relating to gay men and lesbians, was introduced into Congress by Bella Abzug and Edward Koch.

In Leningrad Nureyev's old teacher, Udeltsova, was eighty-four, turning eighty-five that summer. Because of her great age, she had left Ufa to live full time with her daughter who was now a well-known psychiatrist, specialising in the treatment of alcoholism. Udeltsova retained her zest for life and, much as she missed Ufa, was still thrilled by Leningrad. Her daughter was so highly thought of that they had their own apartment, shared with no one else, and a telephone. Anna Ivanovna saw Rosa quite often and kept up a correspondence with Zulfira ('Zoya') Mikhailovna Kogan, one of Rudolf's first partners in Udeltsova's classes. This correspondence evokes life in Russia under Brezhnev when Ufa was a closed city. Airmail letters took thirteen days to travel from one location to the other; Zulfira sent Udeltsova honey for her tea; Udeltsova sent Zulfira news – always a few sentences about Rudolf. That he travelled everywhere – London, New York, Sydney – that he rang Rosa regularly and *always* asked after Anna Ivanovna. She was able to quote from the *New York Times*, about Rudolf. She said that Rosa had, in her youth, been a first-class gymnast, and coming from Udeltsova this was praise indeed. But now, she said, Rosa was a nurse in a kindergarten and had wasted her education – it was a poorly paid and time-consuming job. In one reminiscence with Zulfira, she mentioned how, when Rudolf had first achieved success at the Maryinsky, if he knew she was in the theatre when he was performing, he would always find where she was sitting and be sure to bow especially to her. 'But now he is far away and I will never see him again. Just as you will never see your childhood partner again. And it would be interesting for you to speak with him, wouldn't it? You never argued with him? I think he got on well with girls. For some reason the head of the children's sector conceived a hatred for him and threw him out of the circle. That really hurt me and I left the House of Teachers, although the director tried to make me stay. I couldn't bear it that such a poor, talented boy had been insulted.' She let slip that she believed in God, despite it being 'unfashionable' in Russia, and she prayed that God would look after Rudolf. These were fond words but, underneath it all, she had not forgiven him for defecting. 'I shall not write to him,' she wrote after she read his autobiography, in which she was mentioned. 'Since he left Russia . . . that was unpleasant for me as I taught him differently. Despite his singular fame, and countless riches, I pity him because all his nearest and dearest are left in Russia and world-wide glory does not bring happiness.' Age had not dimmed Udeltsova's acumen.

On 29 June 1974 Mikhail Baryshnikov defected from the Kirov in Toronto. Baryshnikov, from Riga in Latvia, had replaced Rudolf in the affections of Pushkin and so his flight was particularly traumatic for the Kirov. After Makarova had gone, Sergeyev and Dudinskaya had of course been demoted, not to mention several members of the KGB. As a result, the artistic direction of the Kirov, which had been stagnant for much of the late 1960s, collapsed even further. Roland Petit had been to Leningrad a few months earlier and, like Makarova and Rudolf, Baryshnikov could see that opportunities were greater in the west.

Interestingly, the theatre itself had opposed his inclusion on the 1974 tour but had been overruled by Moscow. So, when he defected, the theatre was not held responsible. There were, as a result, few repercussions inside the theatre, and the KGB hushed up the defection in Russia, where at first it was said that Baryshnikov was on extended leave. Only the tour leaders were punished, one of whom, Alexander Lapauris, later got drunk and killed himself by driving into a lamp-post.

After his detection, the initial plan was for Baryshnikov to dance with Makarova, for the National Ballet of Canada, in Rudolf's version of *The Sleeping Beauty*. It is not clear whether Rudolf vetoed this, or if Baryshnikov himself thought such a move would be too provocative. Anyway, it never came off. But Baryshnikov's arrival in the west soon meant that the two ex-Kirov stars would be carefully compared. Just as Rudolf had stimulated others to raise their game, now Baryshnikov, ten years his junior, would do the same to him.

By the autumn of 1974, Rudolf's earning capacity was enviable to someone with Baryshnikov's talent. It was in the region of $5,000–10,000 a performance. One of the people he had met in London was Jacob (later Lord) Rothschild, who helped him invest his money in gold, paintings and property. As a trustee of the National Gallery in London, Rothschild once opened up the gallery after a performance, so that Rudolf could see the pictures by himself. His favourite painter, he said, was 'Rembrandt, probably'. Rudolf liked property as investment and began to think about buying somewhere in Manhattan. He no longer stayed with Monique in New York but with either Christopher Allen, a friend of Erik's, who had a flat on East 72nd Street, or at the Pierre Hotel. Across Central Park from the Pierre he could see the exotic outline of the Dakota building.

When he was in New York he saw a lot of Lee Radziwill now, for she had moved back from London. It was with Lee that he met Baryshnikov in the autumn, together with Rostropovich. However good a friend Lee was, she was forever challenged by Rudolf. She had her own television show at the time and persuaded Rudolf to appear as a guest. But when she asked him if he would ever get married, he snapped back, 'Marry? One doesn't expect such silly questions from an old friend.' He was perhaps being a little harsh on Lee. Many of their mutual friends thought that she was desperately in love with Rudolf and would have married him like a shot had he been the marrying kind. He also attended the first-night party at the Plaza Hotel after David Bowie's Diamond Dogs show at Madison Square Garden. This was the celebrated evening when Jagger, Bowie and Bette Midler disappeared together into one of the bedrooms for an hour by themselves.

On that trip Rudolf danced with Paul Taylor's company. Although the programme was very modern and Rudolf danced bare-chested, and indeed barefoot, he had by now made the transition from prince very successfully. Taylor's season was longer than usual, and in a bigger theatre than usual, but it was nonetheless a complete sell-out. That was all due to Rudolf.

There were more signals to the ballet board. In the autumn he told an interviewer that he now thought in English; he had been dreaming in English, he said, for some time. One couldn't get any more British than that, surely, without actually taking out British citizenship? But, as before, these signals went into the ether, and nothing came back.

Never one to wait for the mountain to come to him, Rudolf took the initiative – and set up his own company. That summer he had tried out Nureyev and Friends, at the Palais des Sports in Paris, with Merle Parke as his partner-in-chief, as it were. He now decided to try it out in New York over Christmas. The Uris Theatre (a big auditorium) was booked, as were Merle Park, Louis Falco, Lisa Bradley and other members of Paul Taylor's Dance Company. The programme consisted of *Apollo*, *The Flower Festival pas de deux*, *The Moor's pavane* and *Aureole* and was a great success. Rudolf was

really on his own now. He was Diaghilev *and* Nijinsky. That only left
Balanchine.

On 31 January 1975, the American Association for the Advancement of
Science passed a resolution deploring discrimination in 'any form' against
gay men and lesbians, and noted that 'homosexuals, transvestites,
transsexuals . . . may be valued members of their profession, capable of
making great contributions to the progress of science and to the national
welfare . . .'

Rudolf was so famous by now that many people believed that his habit
of dancing far more than anyone else could only be due to sheer greed.
That may have been an element but in early 1975, for the first time since
1961, Rudolf was actively seeking work. The nightmare that he had lived
with looked as though it could come true.

The chief culprit here was the Royal Ballet. It had been evident for
some time that MacMillan, Peter Wright, the associate director and the
others had their own agenda (as was perfectly proper) and, whether
it was right or not, that agenda had no big space for Rudolf. The
blunt truth was that, after 22 March that year, when he appeared
in *Dances at a Gathering*, Rudolf was not scheduled to perform at
Covent Garden until 4 December, in *Petrushka*. In 1975 he danced
twenty-one performances at Covent Garden, down again from 1974.
He *was* seen in Britain, with the National Ballet of Canada, which had
enjoyed such success with him in America that it visited London for a
two-week season at the Coliseum. Rudolf danced Franz in *Coppélia* and
Erik played Dr Coppélius – amazingly, this was the first time they had
danced together on the London stage. Seeing that he was being passed
over by the Royal, the Festival Ballet snapped him up, and he led their
tour, in June, to Australia. Rudolf liked Australia. That's where Margot
and he had made love. He liked the openness of the Australians, their
lavatorial sense of humour, and their climate. It was during this tour that
one critic reported back to his London paper more about Rudolf's habits
with boys than about his fellow-dancers. The piece was printed but the
editors telexed the critic that his copy was not exactly what they had in
mind. When Rudolf found out he threw a plate of rice at the critic the
next time he saw him.

But before he left on that tour, Rudolf broke ground at last. He was
nothing if not direct, so he now said openly, in an interview with a reporter
from the London *Evening Standard*, that he wanted to be director of
the Royal Ballet. Strictly speaking, the post was not available: Kenneth
MacMillan was the director. But it was no secret in Covent Garden that
he found the administrative side of his job a great strain. He was a private,
remote man who had had a difficult start, after the sudden resignation of
John Field, and he always knew that Margot would have to be phased out

during his term in charge. One course of action would have been to build up another ballerina to partner Rudolf. But Macmillan wanted to make more changes, particularly to introduce more modern choreography to the Garden, and like Balanchine he saw Rudolf as a prince. It didn't seem to matter that Rudolf was a great success with Béjart, with Paul Taylor, with Murray Louis, or with Rudi van Dantzig. Rudolf lived in hope so far as the Royal Ballet was concerned, but was continually deceived.

In July, Rudolf was attacked from a different quarter. It was a familiar argument but from a new source, John Fraser, the ballet critic of the *Toronto Globe and Mail*. While the National Ballet of Canada was in New York, he published in the *New York Times* a long piece headlined, NUREYEV, LEAVE CANADIAN BALLET ALONE. While conceding that Rudolf had wrought many fine changes on the NBC, Fraser argued that it was now time for him to 'go elsewhere to find his backdrop'. Until Rudolf appeared on the scene, he said, ballet in Canada had been moving ahead slowly, with Erik Bruhn's help. But now it was in a rut, 'thanks in part to too much stargazing'. He didn't deny that Rudolf had helped, especially in being partly responsible for the promotion of two very good Canadian dancers, Frank Augustine and Karen Kain, and in his production of *Sleeping Beauty*, which was 'a gift with nettles but a gift nevertheless'. But the list on the debit side was very much longer, he said. *Sleeping Beauty*, for example, had cost $380,000 to produce, mainly because Nicholas Georgiadis, the designer, had trawled Europe for the most expensive materials for his sets, which had nearly bankrupted the company. Fraser said Rudolf's professional manners were a disgrace, that he shouted at other dancers during the performance and had once overturned a box of nails on the stage during an intermission. During the second act of *Sleeping Beauty* Rudolf was supposed to take off his jacket and give it to a retainer, but he held on to it, toying with the retainer, almost flirting with him. His stage presence was still awesome, Fraser said, but his dancing – at thirty-seven – was beginning to slip. The National Ballet of Canada now needed a focus for all the groundwork that Celia Franca, Erik Bruhn and others had laid, but that focus wasn't Rudolf. The company was drifting, when it should be surging ahead. Nureyev, Fraser said, was doomed to adoration and a lack of appreciation, to using and being used. Once again he had to get used to hearing that he must pack up and move on. Nureyev, he concluded in a strikingly familiar phrase, remained what he was when he left Russia – 'a stranger in strange lands'.

Most Canadians were appalled. *The Times* printed letters from the chairman of the board, from the directors, from all the leading dancers, including Frank Augustine, Karen Kain, Sergio Stefanschi and Veronica Tennant, disavowing Fraser's arguments and stressing how much Rudolf had done for the company. Even Martha Graham weighed in, publicly denouncing a critic for the first time in her long career. Fraser's article was vicious and undignified, she said, and completely unnecessary. She had worked with Rudolf and although at the time 'it was difficult for both of us', he was never unprofessional and always showed her the utmost courtesy. Fraser's own editors at the *Globe and Mail* also seemed appalled, and he was immediately shifted from ballet to drama critic.

Balanchine was less gracious than Graham. He took the opportunity to say, unnecessarily, that Rudolf did not make his name as a dancer 'but for defecting from Russia, for living in Monte Carlo, for being seen in society, and so forth and so on'. Like his comment about Rudolf being the Liberace of ballet, there was a kernel of truth in what he said but, as before, its purpose was not to speak as he found but to wound.

In August Rudolf danced *Le Corsaire* with Gelsey Kirkland. Having seen him dance with Margot five years earlier, when she was still with Balanchine, she had since transferred to the American Ballet Theatre and danced with Baryshnikov. This had given her the courage to invite Rudolf to partner her. She was in awe of him and the encounter was, for her, 'unforgettable'. 'It was,' she said, 'not so much the raw energy on the stage that touched me, but the tender moments that followed the dance. Rudi seemed to be genuinely proud of me as a dancer. I had heard how difficult he could be with his ballerinas, but that night he was the perfect gentleman. He showed me off during curtain calls as if I were an equal sharing in the art, not merely a necessary appendage to his artistry. I wished that he were ten years younger.'

Van Danztig also came to the rescue that year. In October Rudolf danced sixteen performances in a three-week season with the Dutch National Ballet in Amsterdam and Utrecht and made a quick tour with them to Switzerland and Austria. This wasn't all modern – *Le Corsaire* was the staple – but, like the Australians, the Scottish Ballet (which also came to the rescue), the Festival Ballet and the Canadians, the Dutch National Ballet found that it was in great demand if Nureyev happened to be in the cast. In the last six months of 1975 Rudolf danced with nine separate companies in five countries. It was galling that the Royal was the only company to be an unwilling partner.

In October 1975 Rudolf crashed Martha Graham's gate. After Balanchine, this was probably the most illustrious gate in modern dance. Graham was starker than other choreographers, very different from the classical tradition, but Rudolf, ever willing to learn, took her classes in New York. He was determined not to be treated differently from anyone else, just so he could be certain he was being taught the authentic Graham technique. Graham created Lucifer for him. 'He is not Satan,' she said, no doubt contradicting what many people thought. 'He . . . is the Promethean figure that brought light, fire. When he fell through his own pride, which every man and woman endures, he ceased to be a god, to be untroubled, and . . . suffered all the torments a man suffers. And I felt that curious explosive self-mockery, that lament for the piece of nothingness that was part of Lucifer and part of my life and Rudolf's life.' At the gala the ticket prices ranged up to $10,000.

Immediately afterwards, he danced in a four-week run at the Uris Theatre, the largest modern season ever attempted on Broadway. Graham had choreographed three new works, one of them for Rudolf. She had not been easy to win over – it had taken time – but she didn't seem prejudiced against Rudolf, as Balanchine was. As one of the critics noted in reviewing this season, attendances for ballet in America had risen from one million in 1964 to twelve million a decade later. Who could argue with such figures, and which figure, more than any other, was responsible for that jump?

On 1 November, in the United States, Tennessee Williams's autobiography, *Memoirs*, was published. This recounted Williams's tempestuous homosexual love affair with Frankie Merlo and described in some detail how, during the Second World War, Williams used to 'cruise' Times Square in Manhattan, picking up GIs and taking them back to the 'Y' for sex. 'Cruise' was a word coming more and more into view at that time, as was homosexuality itself. Several critics took the same line in reviewing the book, acknowledging that Williams's sexuality had been known about for years but arguing that it was unseemly for him to talk about it in public.

The mid-1970s was a period of transition, sexually speaking. Gay bars and clubs proliferated, as did the gay media. Several US states passed statutes outlawing discrimination against homosexuals. At the same time, many states tenaciously resisted such moves, and more than one gay bar or club was torched. In January 1976 the Pope issued an encyclical on sexual ethics which called homosexuality 'a serious depravity' that 'can in no case be approved of'. In early 1976 Los Angeles police, armed and accompanied by a helicopter escort, raided a gay charity 'slave' auction being held at the Mark IV Baths by the city's 'leather community'. Forty people were arrested for violating the state's 'involuntary servitude' law. Nothing could better illustrate the atmosphere of the times.

In John Fraser's phrase, being gay in the mid-1970s was to inhabit a strange land. Rudolf certainly did. Like Tennessee Williams, he cruised for lovers, not just in Times Square but wherever he happened to be. Like Williams, his homosexuality was known about but with one exception was never talked about in public. The exception was a feature focussed on Rudolf in an early issue of *Christopher Street*, a magazine first published in May 1976 and named after the riots that had sparked the gay liberation movement. The three articles were actually very informative but Rudolf was not happy at being identified with gay life in this manner.

Joan Thring left Rudolf at this point, having rescued him from one fracas too many. One of the last straws was a trip to Beirut where Rudolf would insist on cruising the beach, despite the fact that the bay and harbour were occupied by ships of the Soviet navy. Half of him was worried at being kidnapped by the KGB; the other – now slightly stronger – half was concerned to search out boys wherever they were. Joan decided one night that she had just had enough.

Rufolf's sex drive, his urge for boys, was apt to get the better of him at any moment. The most notorious time of all occurred while he was staying with Franco Zeffirelli, the Italian film director, in Treville, his villa on the cliffs just outside Positano in southern Italy. They were to discuss yet another Nijinsky project. A lot of guests were staying, including Gregory Peck, and this put Rudolf in a difficult mood right away: Peck was a bigger star than he was, and had been given the best guest room. On the night in question, Zeffirelli had given his cook the evening off, since the man needed a break. Instead the host took everyone to a restaurant in Positano. The whole party, of fifteen or twenty, had to descend a series of steps to the water, and be ferried along the coast to the town in Zeffirelli's launch.

The first thing that everyone noted about Rudolf that night was the way he was dressed. He wore a turban, a blouse or loose-fitting shirt, very short shorts, cut like a loincloth, and boots with very high heels. He was also wearing a certain amount of make-up. ('Put make-up on my English,' he would say to interviewers; it was an important part of his life.) There was a boy among the party and, during the course of dinner, Rudolf very obviously flirted with him. After dinner, in the motor launch on the way back to the house, he sat with him in the stern. When they reached Zeffirelli's jetty and began the long climb to the house – there were perhaps a hundred steps – Rudolf lingered at the back with the boy.

A little later, after everyone had reached the house, as he thought, Zeffirelli's butler locked the iron gate at the top of the steps which barred any unwanted intruders who might have arrived by sea. It was only after another hour that Zeffirelli noticed that neither Rudolf nor the boy was among the party. Dyson Lovell, a fellow guest and Hollywood producer, volunteered to look for them. He found them on the wrong side of the locked gate, Rudolf furiously shouting and screaming at being locked out. Lovell found the key and opened the gate but Rudolf would not be mollified. Once inside, he turned to Lovell and said, 'You can tell Zeffirelli *this* is what I think of his villa' – then took down his shorts and defecated on a number of the concrete steps. As he reached the higher steps he came to a terrace with a table-tennis table and, at the edge, a number of valuable antique vases with geraniums in them. Rudolf pushed several of the vases over the edge, so that they fell down the cliff, shattering into pieces.

By this time, Zeffirelli had been told of the events lower down the cliff and had himself come looking for Rudolf. When he realised what had happened to the precious vases, he went for the Russian. Rudolf dodged, and threw one of his host's lamps at him. Zeffirelli erupted and a real scrap ensued. Several of those present thought that Zeffirelli would kill Rudolf, until Dyson Lovell intervened and pulled Zeffirelli away. The dancer was ordered to pack his bags immediately, and leave. Luigi Pignotti, who was also there, packed the cases and called a taxi. Unfortunately, the villa was some way from Positano and it was already past midnight. So a taxi had to be brought from Naples, thirty miles away. Zeffirelli however, wanted Rudolf out of the house at once and insisted he wait in the road. So Dyson Lovell was forced to help Luigi carry Rudolf's case up yet more steps: the villa was as far below the road as it was above the water.

By the time they reached the narrow corniche, it was after 1 a.m., and the road was deserted. What stuck in Dyson Lovell's mind was the last image he had of Rudolf, after all this tumult. When he reached the road, Rudolf had soon got tired of waiting for the taxi and decided to walk along the corniche towards it, in the direction of Naples. His case had a set of wheels and a short chain with which to pull it. 'Come along pony,' Rudolf said to the case and dragged it off. Dyson Lovell watched, half horrified and half enchanted as this famous man, dressed in a turban, short shorts and high-heeled boots, dragged his 'pony' into the night. A stranger in a strange land.

On 10 January, 1976, the most familiar of all Rudolf's landscapes came to a sad end. He danced *Romeo and Juliet* with Margot at Covent Garden. It was their last full performance together on that stage. After almost fourteen years, an era was at an end. After the performance she handed him a single, long-stemmed red rose. He kissed her hand. It was the same gesture he had used after *Giselle* in 1962.

CHAPTER EIGHTEEN

Jealousy's Grim Weather

and after jealousy's grim weather
I'll part them.

Throughout his life, even when he was young, Rudolf always wore a hat, a beret usually, or a cap. He felt the cold and was terrified of being cold. Whether this had something to do with being poor as a boy, with never having enough clothes to keep properly warm during the war, whether he had some illness as a child that no one else knows about, or whether he just grew up that way, he was obsessed with keeping warm. Apart from anything else, for a dancer it helped to minimise the risk of injury. And there was something else. He had a fear of catching pneumonia. In attacking the lungs, pneumonia is especially hard on people with a physical profession, like dancing. When he was young, pneumonia was a killer disease so perhaps he retained his childhood fear of the illness.

So when he was admitted to St John's hospital in Los Angeles, suffering from pneumonia, in the middle of February 1976, he was very distressed. The illness had finally caught up with him. To an extent, he had brought the problem on himself, despite all his precautions. He had flown direct from Paris to Los Angeles, where he was due to open in *Raymonda* with the American Ballet Theatre. He had gone straight from the airport to rehearsal (this was normal for Rudolf). However, the following day, about half an hour before the first performance, he suddenly had difficulty breathing and a doctor was summoned. He was found to have a temperature of 103 degrees, but there were now only thirty minutes to go before the curtain went up so, for Rudolf, there was no question of not dancing. He *never* cancelled. The doctor gave him something that helped the breathing and brought down the temperature, and the performance went ahead as planned.

The next day, he was admitted to hospital, and Fernando Bujones replaced him. Rudolf remained in hospital a week – a long time for him but it may have been too short for a complete cure as there are those, including Michael Brown, the wardrobe master at Covent Garden, who believe that Rudolf was never the same after this episode. They remain convinced that he damaged part of himself during that week, that his elevation, particularly, was never again as good.

He left hospital not to keep some long-arranged dancing engagement but to work on a matter that, as time went by, had grown ever more irritating. This was the blunt refusal by the Soviet authorities to grant his mother, or his sister Rosa, an exit visa to come to the west and visit him. Although Monique had gone to Leningrad on his behalf every year for the past five years, that wasn't enough. He had also just found out that the Soviet authorities took 40 per cent of any money he sent Farida, as a sort of 'defector's tax', which incensed him even more. That spring he set about enlisting the aid of the British Prime Minister, Harold Wilson, and the American President, Gerald Ford, in a campaign to make the Russians change their tune.

May that year was a little like a return to the old days, in that he danced with the Royal Ballet at the Met, partnering Monica Mason, Lesley Collier and Jennifer Penney in *Manon*, *La Fille mal gardée*, *La Bayadère*, *Swan Lake* and certain other ballets. The New York press found him 'compelling', 'better than in years'. The *Washington Post* said that 'This Royal company is crowned by Nureyev the king.' Clearly, not everyone agreed with Michael Brown.

There was no nationwide tour that year but, after New York, the Royal Ballet travelled down to Washington for a two-week season. While he was there, according to the KGB file, Nureyev approached Kolevatov of the Bolshoi, who was also in town, to ask if he could arrange a visit to Russia for him. This meeting, according to the file, was observed by the KGB 'resident' in Washington. The meeting lasted three hours and Rudolf let it be known that he was missing Russia and badly wanted to see his family. According to the interpretation placed on this meeting by the KGB documents, Rudolf was expressing a desire to return to Russia permanently, but this seems unlikely. It is possible of course that his pneumonia had shaken him and that he felt more strongly, as Udeltsova had put it in her letters to Zulfira Mikhailovna, that his nearest and dearest were on the other side of the iron curtain. Or that he had decided the Russians would never allow his mother out, so he would have to go to her. In these circumstances he may really have been sounding out the Russians, to see what their attitude was. Unfortunately the KGB file does not reveal his exact motive.

According to the Soviet criminal code, anyone guilty of treason by defection is the subject of 'executive supervision' by the KGB for fifteen years. Executive supervision appears to mean that the 'target' is watched (rather than followed) by resident KGB agents all over the world, who can move in on the individual whenever they wish to, at the behest of their political masters. Nureyev's executive supervision should therefore have come to an end in 1976. In his case, however, he now became the subject of 'executive checking'. This was subtly different and meant that he was no longer looked after by the KGB as such, but by lesser functionaries – resident Soviet foreign correspondents, heads of trade delegations and so on. He wasn't followed but his basic movements were recorded. This continued from 1976 until 1979 and the reason for the extra three years of surveillance was that the KGB believed that Rudolf was now funding homosexual organisations in Europe and America. The documents made available did not go any further than that just then, but this matter would turn out to be, at least potentially, very important, as we shall see.

By June Rudolf's health was back to normal, if not supranormal. One can state this with some confidence because in that month, back in London, he mounted his second Nureyev season in which he danced forty-eight performances in forty-seven days, using three different ballet companies: the Festival Ballet, Nureyev and Friends, and the Scottish Ballet. The entire seven-week season was sold out, and he was paid $3,000 a performance. It netted him $144,000 which, at today's values, would be $255,000.

Three days after this marathon he opened at the Met in New York with the National Ballet of Canada, and from New York flew straight to Spain for a marathon of a quite different kind. He was to star in Ken Russell's film about Rudolph Valentino.

One day in early 1975 Rudolf had received a telephone call from his manager, Sandor Gorlinsky to ask if Rudolf would consider playing the part of Nijinsky in a new film. To be produced by Robert Chartoff and Irwin Winkler and directed by Ken Russell, it would describe the life of the early screen legend, Rudolph Valentino. This was the fourth project to involve the name of Nijinsky since 1961 so Rudolf did not get too excited. It was a small part, which would mean just a couple of days' filming and Nureyev agreed, provided it could be fitted in with his dancing.

A few days later, Ken Russell himself called back with the more astounding news that, after careful consideration, both the producers and he himself now believed that Nureyev should play the title role of *Valentino*. This was a different proposition altogether. As the star of the film, his presence on set would be required almost every day for five months and his schedule would not allow him that sort of freedom for more than a year. Russell, however, was by now so convinced that Rudolf was perfect for the part that he was willing to wait, the first time he had ever done such a thing.

Nureyev thought it over for a few days and discussed it with Sandor Gorlinsky. Gorlinsky did not see Rudolf every day, as Joan Thring used to, but he was, so to speak, the next best thing.

As a keen film-goer himself, Rudolf was familiar with Russell's work, and liked it, especially his television film, *Isadora* (about Isadora Duncan), *Women in Love*, the director's rendering of D.H. Lawrence's novel starring Glenda Jackson, and *Tommy*, Russell's rock opera. Some time before there had also been the proposal for Russell to make an entire film about Nijinsky, when he had again talked to Nureyev, but the project had fallen through.

Nureyev was no stranger to Valentino either. Not simply because he was a film buff, or because his mother had named him after the actor, but also because he was one of the stars whose films were as well known in Russian as they are in the west. Nureyev recalled that, years before, when he was dancing *Laurencia* with Dudinskaya, he saw part of Valentino's film, *Blood and Sand*. 'In it,' he said,

> 'there's a scene which shows the cruelty of the public towards him. Afterwards I told Dudinskaya how horrible and frightening I thought that would be and how some people did not seem to understand it. She replied, "Well, what about us dancers? People out there are just waiting for us to fall down and break a leg, to get a taste of blood." That was the first time I thought about Valentino.
>
> 'I was very impressed by Valentino's acting . . . At that time I didn't know he had done ballroom dancing, but there is a dance quality in his movement . . . His basic postures are remarkable.'

Nureyev's one problem was that Russell had said his conception for the film was that it was about 'an untalented homosexual actor who was exploited by Hollywood'. Rudolf said, 'It was hard for me to play a homosexual, and nearly impossible to play someone untalented.' Half of this statement was, presumably, a joke.

He agreed to do the film. His own fame, indeed his eminence, was now such that he could bring a certain something to the film; he would not simply interpret the character he was to play, but enlarge it and render it up to date. Like Valentino himself, he was, as Russell himself put it, 'perhaps the most glamorous yet mysterious figure in the world today'.

Once Rudolf had agreed to do the film, he set about learning all he could about the actor and studying the script. Valentino, an Italian from near Taranto in the south of the country, was born in 1895 and emigrated to America in 1913. His first jobs were as gardener and waiter, from where he graduated to ballroom dancer in the halls where wives went to amuse themselves while their husbands were at work. He began to tour as a professional dancer, which took him to Los Angeles and Hollywood, and there he danced as an extra in a film called *Alimony*. As a dark-skinned, smooth Latin, he graduated to small-time villain roles. In 1920 he got his big break when June Mathis, an MGM scriptwriter, was looking for someone to play the lead in a Spanish story she had adapted from a novel by Blasco-Ibanez, called *The Four Horsemen of the Apocalypse*.

As 'Alexander Bland' wrote, 'No actor had ever had such an instant and devastating success, and from then on his career was a triumph.' Valentino exuded a mix of menace, manners and sensuality and became a Great Screen Lover. He spent his earnings flamboyantly, on homes, horses, custom-built cars, antiques and foppish clothes. Underneath it all, however, he despised many of the films he appeared in and desperately tried to extend his range. Neither the studios nor his public wanted him as anything but the character he already was and he became progressively discontented. This was made worse by his first marriage, to a lesbian, and his second, also unconsummated, to Natasha Rambova, an exotic stage designer, who moved in the same lesbian set as his first wife.

The two nullified marriages fuelled speculation about Valentino's sexuality, culminating in the charge by a Chicago journalist that 'American manhood was being undermined by a hero who used a powder puff in the men's room.' Valentino challenged the man, unsuccessfully, to a boxing match but afterwards went down with a severe case of gastric trouble – and died.

The public, having – in a sense – killed him, now turned again and mobbed his remains. Within a few days, 100,000 people filed past his 'powdered and painted corpse'. The fans were inconsolable and the film moguls aghast at the catastrophe they had allowed to happen. With Valentino's death, his legend was born.

There were of course some obvious parallels between the Nureyev and the Valentino stories. Both men were exiles, both had sexual charisma and mystery, both were temperamental and flamboyant. Both were familiar with the rewards, and the cost, of international fame.

But there were differences, too. At first, Nureyev found Valentino unsympathetic as a character, someone who allowed himself to be pushed around without fighting back. He thought he had to make Valentino more positive and less passive. He formed the view that Valentino must really have loved his second wife, Rambova, in order to let her treat him as she did, and that he was a true victim of success. In Valentino's time, he noted, there was no television, so his fame was all the greater – there were few rivals. From this perspective, the powder-puff incident acts as a catalyst to both the public and private side of Valentino's predicament.

All well and good, but the fact was that Nureyev's speciality was dance, a form of theatre in which there is no speech. Therefore, no one knew how, when it came down to it, Nureyev would perform.

Filming began in August 1976 in Almeria in Spain. During the next twenty-one weeks, the company would transfer to other sites in Spain, including Barcelona, to Blackpool in England, and finally to the Elstree Studios near London. Nureyev arrived direct from New York where, the night before, he had danced in a triumphant farewell performance at the

Metropolitan Opera House in his own production of *The Sleeping Beauty*, for the National Ballet of Canada. He had received a standing ovation in the middle of the performance, after a spectacular solo.

There was a tricky moment on the first day when Nureyev had to have his hair cut. In the era in which Valentino lived all men had a 'short back and sides', but this wasn't Nureyev's style at all. It reminded him too much of Ufa during the war. He was with the hairdresser for a long time; she *was* allowed to take off what she wanted, but only under the strictest supervision.

On the second day the tension rose, for now Nureyev was to speak his first lines. There were two reasons, at least, for this tension. In the first place, and very obviously, Nureyev's was a silent art, he was used to expressing himself with his body. Most successful actors, whatever their appearance on stage, have voices that are either remarkable or easy to listen to. Think of Richard Burton, Jack Nicholson, Dustin Hoffmann, Sir John Gielgud, Katharine Hepburn, Anthony Hopkins, Edith Evans, Glenda Jackson. Rudolf's voice was variable at best, what one observer described as 'allegro'.

The second reason was that Valentino's speaking voice was in fact a mixture of Brooklyn and Italian, so it would not be easy to shape Nureyev's Russian tones to this requirement. He had lessons from Marcella Markham, an American actress turned voice coach. To begin with, his voice was rather high, but he soon settled in and Markham was widely congratulated for her work. The real problem emerged only later. Ken Russell was a meticulous director. He had a video camera on set as well as the proper film camera, so that he could immediately get an idea of how a scene looked. He was obsessed as much by the physical appearance of a scene as by the dialogue, with the result that there could be up to twenty takes, just to improve on the look of a scene even if the dialogue was already perfect. Nureyev had a very musical ear. As a result, the more time he spent on a set, the more he was affected by the English and American voices he was surrounded by, and the more his accent deviated from what it ought to be. There is a convention in film-making that all suggestions to actors are made through the director, but Marcella Markham felt she could not keep interrupting Russell's concentration to tell Nureyev where he was going wrong. She set up a system whereby she would send brief instructions to him via the make-up artist or hairdresser, who relayed her messages in whispered tones as they brushed sweat from Nureyev's face or readjusted his hair.

With both Russell and Nureyev having explosive temperaments and massive egos, there was always the possibility of a major clash, which might unsettle the equilibrium of the film crew. But it didn't happen. Nureyev was used to people letting off steam in the ballet. The physical strain is such that minor eruptions are inevitable. So, if Russell did lose his temper, Nureyev was the last to show concern. He knew how he behaved himself, and that the frustration would soon pass. Jonathan Benson, the assistant director, put it this way: 'Russell and Nureyev both behaved very professionally but they didn't get close; Russell was never comfortable with him.'

The site chosen for the first shots, which involved restaging scenes from two of Valentino's big films, *The Four Horsemen* and *The Sheik*, was a stretch of sand, a sort of mini-desert, twenty miles inland from Almeria. Huge palm trees, sixty feet high, were brought 200 miles from Alicante and buried in concrete so that they wouldn't blow over. From Almeria the crew was flown north in a chartered aircraft to Barcelona, for one day's filming in the zoo there. Here Nureyev distinguished himself in a different way. Filming usually finished for the day at 6.45, after which everyone was free to take a shower and have dinner, though the actors would often get together to run through the script for the next day's shooting. This made for long days and people were generally thankful to go to bed as soon as they could. Not Nureyev, however. Wherever they were, he always wanted to explore the nightlife, after which he would go cruising for boys. The morning after they arrived in Barcelona, which had been a relatively easy day since all they had done had been to fly north, Nureyev arrived on set looking very pleased with himself. When pressed, he announced that he had found a unique boy the night before. 'I do believe,' he said, 'that he is the only chimney sweep in all Spain.'

After Barcelona, they flew on to S'Agaro on the Costa Brava for some beach shots. After S'Agaro they all flew to London, where the studio part of the filming was carried out at the Elstree studios in Borehamwood, north of London. From here they made a few trips outside, to the theatre of the Blackpool Tower (a replica of the Eiffel Tower in Paris) where the boxing scene was filmed, to the ballroom of a railway hotel, where Anthony Dowell, as Nijinsky, teaches Valentino the tango, then back to a valley in Spain for a cowboy scene.

Nureyev, who had kept up his dance exercises wherever they were, changed his routine in London. He was staying at the Grosvenor House Hotel on Park Lane, with Luigi Pignotti, who would wake him at 6 a.m. so that he could reach the set by eight. Filming took all day, although Luigi could give Rudolf a massage in the lunch break. After filming he drove into London, to the rehearsal rooms at Covent Garden, and spent ninety minutes there, practising. Of course, Nureyev hoped he might become a film star when *Valentino* was released, but he never forgot, could not forget, his first calling. At the same time, he did some eight performances with the Royal Ballet at Covent Garden, choreographed *Romeo and Juliet* for the London Festival Ballet, and learned Glen Tetley's *Pierrot Lunaire*. For the Covent Garden performances he would go straight from the set to the theatre, at one point not having enough time even to change his hairstyle – he danced in his Valentino curls.

The filming attracted its share of press attention, especially the scene in which Valentino is in prison and forced to urinate in his pants (Rudolf performed like a trouper). Most of the attention, however, focused on Nureyev's relationship, or non-relationship, with his leading lady, Michelle Phillips. She was quite different from Nureyev, in looks, background and temperament. A Californian through and through, she had first become famous as a member of the rock group, the Mamas and the Papas. When the group disbanded in 1969 she had turned to acting, specialising in sexy-but-tough roles, such as the gangster's girlfriend in *Dillinger*.

Several members of the cast were thrown by Rudolf's standoffishness at first and requested a company dinner, where they could all let their hair down. This didn't work as well as had been hoped and, shortly afterwards, in a press interview, Phillips roundly criticised Rudolf. She said that he was small, that she had to wear flat shoes so as not to overwhelm him, that when filming began he was arrogant, rude and self-centred. She said that Russell had warned her Rudolf was a scene-stealer, that he always wanted the camera on him and liked to appear the dominant person even when the script called for something else.

She turned her aggression on him, and the set was soon smouldering. Russell thought this was perfect but it soon got out of hand. Before the film, Phillips had been dating Jack Nicholson and Warren Beatty and was therefore confident that she knew how to handle big egos. So when Rudolf was in a discussion one day about his costume, and she went up to make a suggestion, she was ready for him when he swore at her, but not when he slapped her hand and told her not to interfere. As he walked away, she hit him on his behind and told him that he could say whatever he liked to her, but he couldn't hit her.

Fortunately, as she later said, they had already done their big romantic scene, because they were never close again after this encounter. Rudolf did not apologise. Phillips didn't expect him to, knowing how much it would cost him. At the end of the film there was no exchange of notes, no goodbyes. They just walked off the set. She said she didn't find him sexual or sensual, but did concede he was a very romantic figure. They were chalk and cheese.

On 2 September 1976 the Centers for Disease Control in Atlanta reported the worldwide outbreak of a new strain of penicillin-resistant gonorrhoea. A week later a California court upheld the conviction of two men in their twenties, who had been arrested for 'kissing in public' in a parked car at a motorway rest stop. The men were ordered to register with the state, as 'sex offenders'. In December a San Francisco proctologist reported having recently seen an 'unprecedented upsurge' in the number of men needing to have 'bizarre objects' removed from their rectums. Among the objects were flashlights, light bulbs, chocolate bars and various fruits and vegetables.

At the end of the year, Rudolf was back at the Royal Opera House performing his 'teacosy' role, as he called it, to bolster audiences in the pre-Christmas period, but again he wasn't given any new ballets to dance, which is what he really wanted. That year, overall, he danced eighteen performances at the Garden, down again from the previous year. The number of performances he gave at the Opera House had fallen each year since 1969.

In the early months of 1977 he stepped up his campaign on behalf of his mother and sister, Rosa. The other two sisters were both married and expressed no wish to come to the west. Rosa was not married and her daughter, Guzelle, was sixteen and very keen to see beyond the iron curtain. Rosa had had no any promotion since Rudolf's defection and her prospects in Russia were dim. This campaign was typical of Rudolf because he had been told at the time that the KGB had informed his mother that she would 'definitely' not be allowed to go to the west. According to one account, Farida had actually said goodbye to him in one phone call, never expecting to hear from him again. Perhaps they thought the meeting with Kolevatov of the Bolshoi had been counterproductive. Rudolf couldn't accept this. As part of his campaign, he wrote a letter to *The Times* in which he drew attention to the fact that, the previous year, the Russians had been one of thirty-five nations who had attended a human rights conference in Helsinki at which it had been agreed that more travel would be allowed between eastern and western countries. In 1977 the decisions of the Helsinki Accord were to be reviewed at a Belgrade conference and Rudolf thought there was a slim chance that the Russians might let Farida and Rosa out, to show that they were acting on the Helsinki declaration. There was no response from Russia itself to his letter. The only response was from a Russian embassy official in London who suggested that Nureyev should visit his mother. Asked whether the dancer would be allowed to leave again if he did make such a visit, the official said, 'Nobody could guarantee that.' Rudolf must have considered the possibility that his efforts were actually making the situation worse, not better.

Monique van Vooren, for one, felt that there was an element of charade about this campaign. Or perhaps charade is too strong a word – but there was certainly part of Rudolf that, deep down, didn't want his mother to come to the west. Quite simply, he didn't want his mother to see how he lived – that is, as a homosexual. On her trips to Leningrad, Monique had always posed as Rudolf's girlfriend, promising the family that, one day, the couple would be married. Another woman who helped at this time was Princess Firyal of Jordan, whose former sister-in-law, Princess Dina, the first wife of King Hussein, helped him get messages through.

That year he turned thirty-nine. He was given a birthday party in New

York by the Iranian ambassador to the United Nations. In fact, he and Monique were given a joint birthday party, since her birthday came about a week after his. She went to pick him up at the Uris Theatre on Broadway, where Nureyev and Friends were performing *Pierrot Lunaire* and *The Lesson*, in which he appeared as an old man. She went backstage in the last intermission, to find him dressing in his usual blue dressing gown, surrounded by bottles and jars, Bob Kelly white cake make-up base, hairspray, powder, cups of tea, and Jamie Wyeth sketching him for a portrait. (The Wyeths became good friends.) As Rudolf applied more and more make-up, he gradually acquired the demeanour of an old man. Suddenly a spider appeared on the table, and the dresser went to kill it. Rudolf, *without ceasing to be an old man*, stopped him, saying it would be bad luck.

After the performance, knowing it would be Rudolf's birthday in an hour's time, the Uris theatre management released hundreds of balloons into the auditorium, and the applause went on for twenty minutes. Back in the dressing-room, Monique found he was his usual self in regard to criticism from friends. If they liked the performance, and said so, he was immediately bored by the conversation. But if they hadn't liked it, and remained silent, he wanted to know why they were silent.

Jackie Onassis came backstage – she was the only person he ever stood up for. She looked stunning in a black and white suit. Then the four of them left for the Iranian embassy. That night there were two cakes, one for Rudolf, another for Monique. At the end of the evening, Rudolf's cake was all gone, but Monique's hadn't been touched. 'Why do you think that is?' said Rudolf.

'I don't know. You've got more friends than me? You're more famous?'

He shook his head. 'Your cake's still a virgin. People don't like virgin.'

When she looked puzzled he laughed and pointed to the maraschino on the top of the cake. 'Look, your cake hasn't lost its cherry.' He was delighted with his joke.

In April Studio 54 opened in Manhattan. Almost immediately this disco became, according to a journalist, 'a haven of drugs, lewd dancing, beautiful boys'. Among the regulars were Truman Capote, Halston, Andy Warhol, Roy Cohn, Liza Minelli, Robert Mapplethorpe and Rudolf. Bouncers on the door arrogantly turned away anyone they didn't like the look of.

In the same month, Rudolf announced that he was to mount a production of *Romeo and Juliet* at the Coliseum, for the Festival Ballet. It was to be an entirely new conception. To begin with, Rudolf had even considered using sixteenth-century music, but then got cold feet, and switched back to Prokofiev. But the ballet would have completely new choreography, devised by him.

This was, in its way, a provocative move. *Romeo and Juliet* had been Kenneth MacMillan's first full-length ballet for Covent Garden, the ballet originally devised for Lynn Seymour and Christopher Gable and 'hijacked' for Margot and Rudolf. Rudolf was setting out his stall in London. Baryshnikov was due in London in March to dance *Romeo and Juliet* with the Royal Ballet, while Rudolf's own production had its première three months later. It invited a direct comparison.

Between then and the first night, he and Margot returned briefly to the scene of their former glory, where they danced *Hamlet Prelude*, a specially choreographed piece by Fred Ashton for the Queen's Silver Jubilee Gala on 30 May. At the same time, Rudolf persuaded forty-two US congressmen to petition Moscow to allow his mother to leave Russia. In all, the petition had 108,000 signatures, from 80 countries, including dancers and musicians from 200 companies and orchestras worldwide. The congressmen presented the petition to the Russian embassy in Washington and, simultaneously, Margot presented it to the embassy in London. This was an impressive piece of organisation by Rudolf, and an impressive turnout on his behalf, by all the others. It still did no good.

That spring, Rudolf was astonished and dismayed to learn that Yuri Soloviev, 'Cosmic Yuri', with whom he had shared a room in Paris in 1961, had committed suicide. Soloviev had been with some friends celebrating the birthday of one of them and had then gone to his *dacha* alone. His body was found several days later, a gun nearby. There were dark rumours in Leningrad that the KGB had a hand in this killing, in long-term retaliation for his part in Rudolf's defection. The 'men in civvies' believed he had warned Rudolf that morning when he returned to his hotel room, after being out all night with Clara Saint. If Rudolf had not been primed, so this theory began, he would not have made a dash for it at Le Bourget but would have gone quietly back to Moscow. And if Rudolf hadn't defected, neither would Makarova nor Baryshnikov. And those national treasures, Sergeyev and Dudinskaya, would not have been dismissed, nor the KGB embarrassed, as they had been, repeatedly.

A rival theory was that Soloviev *did* commit suicide, as a result of the games of administrative leapfrog that had taken place at the Kirov since Sergeyev's dismissal in 1971. He had been followed by a triumvirate of Irina Kolpakova, Vladilen Semenov (her husband), and Oleg Vinogradov. Most of the dancers hated this arrangement. In 1973, the triumvirate had been replaced by Igor Belsky, the man who had taught Rudolf his role in Laurencia. It had been Belsky who had pushed him too hard as a young, inexperienced soloist, so that he had injured himself before his second performance with Dudinskaya. Few of the dancers took Belsky seriously as a choreographer – he was a character dancer, with little dignity – and he was soon replaced . . . by Oleg Vinagradov. It was clear to Soloviev, who was also in the running for the post, that the Kirov wasn't going to change, that it seemed set on a course for artistic oblivion. Like Rudolf, he lived for dance but his world was disappearing.

Whichever theory accounted for Soloviev's death, Rudolf was badly shaken. He was not the suicidal type, and found it especially hard to bear in others.

Shortly before the first night of *Romeo and Juliet*, Rudolf gave an interview that was interesting on several grounds. His age was beginning to show in little things, he conceded, not on stage but in other ways. For instance, he couldn't eat steak any more – it was too much to digest. Instead he ate game. And he had to be careful of his drinking – 'Pimm's makes me drunk in no time.' More substantially, he was by now quite peevish about the Royal Ballet. He never mentioned MacMillan or Peter Wright by name, but he was growing increasingly open in his criticism. 'They don't want to give me any new works here,' he said. 'They keep me lingering. This, I think, is a sin. When you have dancers of exceptional quality you don't just shut them out.' He impressed on the interviewer that he had given fourteen years of his life to Covent Garden; no other 'guest artist' could show the same loyalty. The lack of new works that had been created for him really hurt. He mentioned it often.

But he also said two other things which show how difficult it is to work out the details of Rudolf's life in Russia before he defected. He told the journalist that while he was at the Kirov he was made to share a flat with a forty-nine-year-old dancer, and that the flat had only one bedroom. This cannot be true. Alla Sizova was his age – this is confirmed by several sources in Leningrad, including his family. Was he lying? Was he conflating two people into one? Dudinskaya was forty-nine when he first danced with her. Was he deliberately misleading or just bored by the same old questions? This is important, because it was in this interview that he also said his mother had made a three-day bus trip from Ufa to Leningrad in 1961 to wave him goodbye. Why would she have done that if he was coming back a few weeks later?

Even now, he couldn't shake off the Royal Ballet links. Michael Brown, wardrobe master at Covent Garden, was forever being called to the Festival Ballet, or the BBC, to look after Rudolf. It was, whether he liked to admit it or not, home.

Romeo and Juliet, when it appeared, produced an interesting reaction. Clive Barnes thought it revolutionary. Others, though less happy with the choreography, were overwhelmed by the drama and passion that Rudolf had revealed, but thought that the big scenes failed. Still others compared it unkindly with Kenneth MacMillan's version at Covent Garden. In fact, Rudolf had been true to his word, when he had said that his favourite authors were Pushkin and Shakespeare and in this production he showed how closely he had studied the play, and its history. He knew where

Shakespeare had got his ideas from and he offered a much closer retelling of the story than many people were used to. For instance, he was criticised for introducing little observations on certain characters here and there; this was thought inappropriate to the story, but they were lifted from Shakespeare's own words. He was also criticised, in a knowing way, for implying a homosexual relationship between Mercutio and Romeo though this is a perfectly legitimate interpretation, according to some scholars. But most of the public were thrilled by his choice of Patricia Ruanne as Juliet. Here was a controversial new production, a highly athletic and passionate experience, with a new star. Whatever carping there was (and Rudolf did improve some of the choreography as soon as he had the chance to), the Festival Ballet was soon invited to take this production abroad, on tour. There was satisfaction in that. The Royal Ballet again had a worthy rival in London.

Incidentally, since Rudolf had such a reputation for being selfish, it is interesting to record that Jack Lanchbery, when Rudolf asked him for his opinion of *Romeo and Juliet*, remarked that he thought Nureyev's own role was the least distinguished part of the ballet. 'Yes, you're right,' Rudolf replied. 'I had only a few weeks to prepare. I did everyone else's part first, and by the time I came to me all I had in my head was shit.'

Rudolf's *Romeo and Juliet* highlighted one aspect of his impact that was different from anyone else's – his fans. More than any other dancer in the history of ballet, Rudolf had a dedicated following. At one point, early on in his career in London, he suffered because one of his greatest acolytes worked in the department of the telephone service that handled unlisted numbers. No matter how often he changed his number, this woman could always find him. (Eventually, the phone company admitted its mistake and fired her.) By the mid 1970s about sixty or seventy people, worldwide, followed him wherever he performed. Most, but not all, were women. They would telephone Gorlinsky – who always took their calls, because their names were known to him – and find out, up to a year in advance, where Rudolf was dancing. It didn't matter whether it was a glamorous location, like London, Athens, Paris or Jerusalem, or a small city, like Manchester, Düsseldorf or Atlanta, these fans were there. Moreover, they knew by now which hotels Rudolf favoured, so they would make reservations there, too. Depending on his mood, his sex drive, and whether or not he had close friends in the area, he would either nod to them or entertain them more fully. They knew they could not press themselves upon him but it was unique and very flattering for Rudolf to have a small community that travelled the world – literally – to see him dance.

In the middle of the first run of *Romeo and Juliet*, on 13 June 1977, Covent Garden delivered what was, for the public, a bombshell, although people in the ballet world, Rudolf included, had been expecting the news for some time. Kenneth MacMillan was resigning as artistic director of the Royal Ballet.

Here, at last, was Rudolf's chance. He was the biggest name in dance. His performances, whether in classical ballet or modern dance, were a sell-out, not just in London but in Paris, Vienna, Milan, New York, Toronto, Los Angeles, Sydney, even Manila. He was the only ballet figure whose name was instantly recognisable across the world – a newspaper poll that year found that only Frank Sinatra, Grace Kelly, Fred Astaire and Rudolf Nureyev had instant meaning for everyone they had polled. He was thirty-nine, the perfect age to take over a company like the Royal, he would be able to dance character roles in the future, to keep the pot warm when attendance figures needed to be bolstered. He had restaged the classics to great effect for the Royal Ballet, boosting the status of the *corps* in the process, and had shown himself capable, more than capable, of choreographing new ballets, from *Sleeping Beauty* to *Tancredi* to *Romeo and Juliet*, for the world's top companies. He knew, and was respected by, all the great choreographers of the day – Petit, Béjart, van Dantzig, Glen Tetley, Paul Taylor, Martha Graham, Jerome Robbins. He might not be the favourite of Balanchine but you couldn't have everything. He had danced with all the great ballerinas around the world, Carla Fracci, Lucette Aldous, Karen Kain, Veronica Tennant, Cynthia Gregory, Marcia Haydée, Gelsey Kirkland, Patricia Ruanne. He knew and was loved by the great ballerinas in Britain – Merle Park, Lynn Seymour, Antoinette Sibley, Monica Mason, Georgina Parkinson, Jennifer Penney, Lesley Collier. In a very real sense he had helped create Anthony Dowell, David Wall and Wayne Eagling. You did not have to be a dance fanatic to realise that whereas the Royal Ballet had toured the United States with great success in the 1960s, that accolade now went to the National Ballet of Canada. What did those two companies have in common during their heyday? Rudolf Nureyev.

Most important of all: *he wanted the job*.

It must count as one of the greatest scandals that Rudolf was not made director of the Royal Ballet in 1977. He was considered but he made it clear he would continue to dance, even as director, and the ballet board took the view that, in no time, he would dominate the company, obliterating everyone else in terms of publicity. The man chosen instead was called Norman Morrice. For everyone outside the ballet world, and not a few in it, their reaction was: who? It is no disrespect to Morrice to say that he was, beside Rudolf, a complete unknown. He had joined the Ballet Rambert in 1955, working first as a dancer then as a choreographer. He had produced one work for the Royal Ballet, *The Tribute*, in 1965, and had then taken over at Ballet Rambert, transforming it from a classical company into a troupe specialising in modern dance, which he had learned during a spell in New York in the year Rudolf defected. Since 1974 he had been working full-time as a freelance choreographer. His appointment indicated that the Royal Ballet was headed down the road of modern dance with ever greater speed.

Rudolf kept his thoughts to himself, for the time being. That summer he toured Australia with Festival Ballet, took *Marguerite and Armand* to Manila (Margot was very friendly with Imelda Marcos) and was back in North America with the National Ballet of Canada. Among the ballets he danced with the Canadians was *Swan Lake*. This was of course Erik's production, the one Rudolf had once been so angry about, feeling that Erik had stolen some of his own ideas. This time he exchanged two of Erik's *pas de deux* for new pieces he had choreographed himself. Erik didn't seem to mind.

Rudolf and Lynn Seymour had been invited by Jacob Rothschild to his villa in Corfu, situated on top of a small hill overlooking Albania. For the first few days it rained. In fact, it poured. Rudolf, Lynn wrote later, spent the time in bed, wrapped in the autumnal colours he loved so much, listening to Tchaikovsky. When the sun came out, they went swimming and sailing and gorged themselves on wild strawberries. Seeing them do class every day, it wasn't long before the other guests asked them to give a private performance. Rudolf took charge and said that Lynn would dance one of her Isadora Duncan numbers, from an Ashton ballet set to music by Brahms, and that the dance would be performed in moonlight, outside on the terrace. He would organise the lighting. There were two courtyards at the villa and they chose the inner of the two, with the sea as a backdrop. Lynn was just about to start, red and yellow poppy petals in her hands, when a great wailing was heard and her son, Demian, ran on to the stage sobbing, and clutched her leg. What had been intended as a beautiful, ethereal spectacle had turned out to be, for a three-year-old, terrifying.

Rudolf, the Diaghilev of Corfu, said curtly, 'Performance cancelled.'

In Leningrad, Rosa was losing heart. She, like Rudolf, had once entertained great hopes that she could travel to the west with Farida. Rosa didn't want to stay there permanently – she just wanted to visit Rudolf and see the west. She took no holidays from 1973 on, saving up the days when the time came, to spend three or four months away. The cost would have to be borne by Rudolf. Farida's pension was 23 roubles a month (about £17, which would now be about £98 or $155) and Rosa's salary was 110 roubles a month (£85). Rosa was despairing because of the way officialdom was treating her, despite Rudolf's attempts to make waves. She had once, in twenty-five years, been offered promotion but, when they had found out who she was, the offer had been rescinded. One attempt to obtain a visa was turned down because the authorities said the paperwork was outdated, another because it was delivered outside the official postal system, another because the character reference from her *school* was unfavourable (she was exactly forty nine at the time).

Rosa hoped for change but it was slow in coming. Ordinary people in Russia still thought that Rudolf had done wrong. One book published in the late 1970s quoted a female Moscow taxi driver:

> It's always the same kind of people who turn their backs on Russia, and always for the same reason . . . Did [Nureyev] want for anything here? *Anything?* He had everything he wanted. But he was greedy: he had to make a name for himself, to lap up the "hurrahs" of the western press and fancy audiences, and make a million for himself. That's the psychology of the "haves" for you. If you find a man willing to sell his Motherland, you can bet he's a rich type, some intellectual or bureaucrat, someone high up in the Party or in a university.

The ordinary Russian no longer knew who Rudolf was, or had been.

In London, he could contain himself no longer in regard to the changes at Covent Garden. Asked in an interview what his most *un*favourite role was, he replied without hesitation that it was Siegfried in the Royal Ballet's *Swan Lake*. 'You sit on your ass for twenty minutes and then have to move. It's impossible. I'll never dance in *that* production again.' He was getting his remarks in first. He knew that he was due to dance three performances of *Sleeping Beauty* at Covent Garden in November with Lynn Seymour but, after that, the way things were going, he might never dance for the Royal Ballet again.

Things were difficult domestically, too. Wallace had finally decided to move out. There was no sudden break, just as there had been no sudden break with Erik (who got on very well with Wallace, by the way). Wallace wanted his own life, the initial passion had cooled and, as had happened with Gyckova, love had turned into friendship. Wallace made a film in Paris called *Le Beau Mec* (The Handsome Dude), and then moved back to the United States to direct a thriller called *PsychoCop*. But he and Rudolf kept in touch.

Life wasn't made any easier that autumn by the release of *Valentino*. When he saw the rushes, Rudolf had been optimistic about his stage presence coming across on camera. When the actual film appeared his presence was about the only thing the critics found to praise. In London there was a Royal Première with Princess Margaret as the attraction. Rudolf was pictured with Lisa Solitis, allegedly his Greek girlfriend. Rudolf apart, the film was slated mercilessly. Ken Russell's treatment of the story, according to *Time*, was 'feverish, not to say hysterical'. The film offered 'one gaudy cliché after another' and the boxing scene was described as 'a gay *Rocky*'. *Newsweek* was harsher, saying that

Russell had no artistry left in him, that the film resembled a schoolboy black mass and what 'what Senator McCarthy did to reputations was as nothing to what Ken Russell has done'. Valentino's bad luck, it was felt, had extended fifty years beyond the grave. A Canadian review described the film as 'stupefyingly tasteless'. In France it was 'pulverisé'.

Newsweek did not consider Rudolf a great actor, 'but he is never less than a stunning presence'. 'There's a camp devil loose in him. He has a kinky angel grin.' *Time*, finding Rudolf erotic, thought he was the one element in the film that showed what might have been, in the hands of a different director.

Added to all this, in the same month *The Turning Point* was released. This was a ballet drama, indeed a ballet soap opera, which starred Anne Bancroft, Shirley MacLaine – and Baryshnikov, who was nominated for (but did not win) an Oscar as best supporting actor. Neither dancer came out of the filming experience well, but Baryshnikov was embarrassed much less than Nureyev.

The timing of the release of *Valentino* was also unfortunate in that the bad publicity no doubt made the Covent Garden authorities more certain in their own minds that they had made the right decision in not appointing Nureyev as director. It also meant that they got off relatively lightly so far as the critics were concerned.

Nor was Rudolf's position improved when *Women's Wear Daily* observed him 'slumming with the androgynous Bianca Jagger at New York's notorious kinky gay after hours backroom orgy mecca, The Anvil'. This was very unwelcome publicity. The Anvil was probably the apotheosis, or nadir, depending on your point of view, of the sexual revolution. In the 1970s everyone, whether they had been there or not, had heard of Plato's Retreat, the sex club in Manhattan. The Anvil was less well known but took matters far further. Situated on New York's Lower West Side, the club's very name evoked the area in which it was located and its clientele. A predominantly homosexual club, it catered to the tougher, rougher, end of the trade: people who liked to dress in leather and chains and act out, realistically, their tougher, rougher fantasies. There was in The Anvil, for example, a massive urinal where men would lie to be urinated on by others. There was a thin wall, with holes at crotch height, through which men would insert their erect penises, to be fellated by men they never met.

That autumn, too, the actor Sal Mineo's last interview was published, in which he described how he had taught Rudolf the twist at one of his parties in Hollywood. Mineo had recently been stabbed to death, the victim, it was thought at the time, of 'rough trade'. In the autumn of 1977, in the wake of his film and the visits to the Anvil, Rudolf was referred to coarsely in Hollywood as The Great Vaselino. It was not a good time for him.

*   *   *

In December the Castro Steam Baths – the third San Francisco gay bathhouse in less than a year to be hit by arsonists – went up in flames. One man was killed.

In November Rudolf danced the three performances of *Sleeping Beauty* with Lynn Seymour at Covent Garden. He was pleased to be back, but succeeded in drawing attention to himself in an unfortunate way. In one performance, in the first act, he was standing in the wings watching Lynn perform the Rose Adagio, when the princess exacts a rose from each of her four suitors. He was so immersed in her performance that he forgot where he was and wandered forward, on to the stage. The prince had arrived a whole act too early. It appears to have been a genuine oversight but there was no shortage of Nureyev-knockers who were quick to say that he would do anything to get on the Covent Garden stage.

The irony was that he was still, despite his age, adored and respected everywhere else. In early 1978 he took Nureyev and Friends back to New York where the reviews were again ecstatic. 'He has more muscles than Gray's *Anatomy*,' said *Women's Wear Daily*, not perhaps the most exacting of critical journals, but Anna Kisselgoff of the *New York Times* agreed. 'Nureyev is still the champion,' she wrote, 'The lion is still king of the jungle.' An article on 'The New Athleticism in Ballet' referred to Nureyev more than anyone else. In Italy in May, *Corriere della Sera* said that 'Nureyev is again king of the ballet.'

And it was against this background, with Rudolf still drawing the crowds and the rave reviews, that Norman Morrice announced his first policy initiative at Covent Garden: a temporary (two-year) ban on *all* guest artists. This took some nerve. In his first season as director (autumn 1977 to spring 1978) the guest stars had included Margot Fonteyn, Natalia Makarova, Mikhail Baryshnikov and, for those three *Sleeping Beauties*, Rudolf Nureyev. Morrice's argument was that the Royal Ballet needed to be rebuilt, that a new generation of dancers needed to be brought on and that the best way to do this was to have a self-contained unit, undisturbed by outside influences or glamour. The stability, the greater opportunity to dance many roles, the promotion that would stem from this, would all produce results in the long run. There would be a temporary loss of glamour and excitement, but now was a time for rebuilding. Morrice claimed to have been influenced by something Margot Fonteyn herself had said to him. 'By the time I was twenty, I had danced all the classics.' No one at the Royal Ballet could say that now. When he had raised it at the board meeting the idea had gone down 'like a lead balloon'. But Morrice stuck to his guns and got his way.

Many people were furious. They were furious with the policy, for they did not see why they should continue to pay big prices if they weren't to be offered the big stars. But almost as many were furious that Rudolf was included in this list of 'guest artists'. A campaign on his behalf broke out in the columns of *Dance and Dancers*, led by readers who thought it was disloyal of Morrice and the rest of the administration at Covent Garden to lump Rudolf in with the others. He was not really a guest, they argued. It was just a question of nomenclature (a nice Russian allusion). Rudolf might not be technically a member of the Royal Ballet but the loyalty he had shown to the company, the way he had filled in for Anthony Dowell during the latter's illness, the way he had rescued Lynn Seymour on several occasions when her career was suffering, all this showed that he was a *de facto* member of the company.

One correspondent revealed a series of letters she had exchanged, over the years, with members of the Royal Ballet management which showed, she said, the double-dealing and jealousy that had gone on. When she had suggested Rudolf be given a bigger role at the Garden she had received totally different reasons why this couldn't happen, from Ashton, Webster and Tooley. On a separate occasion she had been given quite different reasons, by Claus Moser (chairman of the board) and Kenneth MacMillan, as to why Rudolf was not used more as a dancer. She implied that she had been lied to or misled over a number of years.

One person who was feeling for Rudolf at this time was Margot, who was by now living in retirement in Panama with Tito. When Rudolf opened in New York with *Romeo and Juliet* in summer 1978, Joan Juliet Buck, the novelist, interviewed him for *Spotlight* magazine. As a writer she was overwhelmed by the fact that he had in his dressing-room a whole suitcase full of books that he travelled with. She observed a large card on his dressing table. It showed a vicious-looking shaggy dog, wearing a Viking helmet (a sort of cross between Rudolf and Erik). The dog was holding a club in one paw and a bunch of flowers in the other. Inside were the words, 'Keep dancing, getting flowers and hitting people over the head – love, Margot.'

Someone else who sympathised with him was Violette Verdy, then director of the Paris Opéra Ballet. She drew attention to the fact that Rudolf's *Romeo and Juliet* was much better received in New York than it had been in London. The British critics and audiences 'never understood his ballsy, raunchy *Romeo and Juliet*. Only when he got to New York did it get the acclaim it deserved . . . It demands constant awareness.' As for Rudolf himself, she said that it was 'almost as if he has created another kind of sex altogether. You don't see a male or a female, you see a dancing creature.' This was the man the Royal Ballet did not want.

In June the *Annals of International Medicine* reported that an intestinal parasite – *Giardia lamblia* – previously restricted to parts of the Soviet Union and the Colorado Rocky Mountains, was showing up with alarming frequency in gay men in the United States.

From the time MacMillan announced his resignation at Covent Garden in June 1977 through until the end of 1978, was possibly the roughest period in Rudolf's career. There had been that scare in early 1975, when it had seemed, briefly, that he didn't have enough work, but that had soon passed. There had been the attack on him by John Fraser in 1976, but Fraser had lost more than he gained (and in any case by now had changed his tune and rallied to Rudolf). But Rudolf was very hurt by the decision to choose Norman Morrice over himself. It was the kind of decision the Russians would have made. He never said anything publicly, but to his close friends – Joan Thring, the Goslings, Margot – he couldn't hide how upset he felt, how let down. Part of him never got over it.

But 1979 was brighter. Rudolf felt encouraged by the famous people who lent their names to his latest attempt to 'rescue' his mother from Russia. In America, Eli Wallach, Zubin Mehta, Constance Cummings, Yul Brynner and Tennessee Williams wrote a joint letter to President Brezhnev, urging him to allow Farida to see her son. Simultaneously, in Britain, Yehudi Menuhin, André Previn, Alan Ayckbourn, John Gielgud and Ken Russell (of all people) sent the same letter. As before, there was no immediate reply but Rudolf wasn't too concerned this time, for he had a plan. The Moscow Olympics were little more than a year away. The Soviet Union would surely have to relax travel arrangements for so huge an international event. *That's* when he would get in, he felt sure.

But in early 1979 something momentous happened. Out of the blue, he received an invitation to dance in New York – from Balanchine. It was the only gate left to crash.

CHAPTER NINETEEN

The Threatening Glow

From here, deep-sunk in pensive woe,
he gazed out on the threatening glow.

In the early weeks of 1979 a young German concert pianist died
in Cologne. He was aged forty-two, homosexual, and in the previous
decade had travelled all over Europe playing in one concert hall
after another. His body had first been attacked by a very rare
disease, indeed an old man's disease, a form of skin cancer usually
seen only around the southern European or Middle Eastern shores
of the Mediterranean, and even then benign. It was known as
Kaposi's sarcoma. A few months later the pianist's lymph nodes
had seemed to explode, as if they were fighting some hidden form
of infection. After that his body was racked by one disease after
another until, gaunt, his weight down to half what it had been,
and his skin covered with lesions, he could fight no more. After
his death, doctors reflected that it was as if his immune system
had broken down.

Rudolf's chance to dance for Balanchine had finally come about
as a result of an idea by Julius Riddle and John White for a joint
benefit, for the New York City Opera and the New York City
Ballet. The programme called for a split bill, a first half of *Dido and
Aeneas* and a second half of *Le Bourgeois Gentilhomme*. Balanchine
had devised two early productions of this ballet (based on Molière's
play, with music by Richard Strauss) but he agreed to Riddle and
White's plan because it offered the chance to put the ballet into
the repertoire of the NYCB.
    Balanchine lived on West 67th Street and his assistant, Barbara
Horgan, remembers being called from there early one morning, around

7.30 a.m., by her boss. He had had a heart attack the previous year and she was worried about him. What he said that morning did not so much worry as astound her. 'I've had an idea,' he said. 'I wonder if Rudolf would like to dance *Bourgeois Gentilhomme.*'

'I nearly fell off my chair,' said Horgan. She was aware of course that Balanchine and Rudolf did not see eye to eye on dance matters and that Balanchine had not really changed his view of Rudolf since that early meeting in 1962, at which she had been present, when the two men had discussed princes. In the 1970s, for example, Geraldine Freund, a society matron in Chicago, had approached Balanchine about staging *Apollo*, with Rudolf, for a benefit. Instead of saying an outright 'No', Balanchine had charged $20,000 for the choreography, an outrageous sum for a single performance. The offer had been accepted (and the proceeds went to his school). But that was as far as their collaboration had gone.

Rudolf was delighted. Though he loved Fred Ashton, and felt that his choreography made him feel naked on stage, meaning that all his emotions were exposed, he never felt that Ashton had created a language, whereas Balanchine had. He had, said Rudolf, invented a new way of moving. Another reason why he was flattered was because neither Baryshnikov, who had been working at NYCB, nor Makarova had yet had ballets created on them. Technically, he wasn't free on the date of the benefit but this wasn't an offer that would come twice, and he made himself free. Rehearsals started in February, with the première set for 8 April. Because of Balanchine's heart condition, he asked Jerome Robbins to help, and Peter Martins was also involved in the choreography. Rudolf played Cléonte, Patricia McBride was Lucile, and Jean-Pierre Bonnefous was M. Jourdain. Students of the School of American Ballet served as the *corps*. Susan Hendl also played a part in helping Rudolf develop the role.

The cast called for twelve boys in the *corps* and among the twelve chosen was a twenty-three-year-old student from Boston, called Robert Tracy. He had studied under Melissa Hayden at Skidmore College, where he had majored in classics and dance, and then under Maria Tallchief. In the production, Tracy played a lackey. Later, he was to say, 'I've played a lackey ever since.'

One day while they were rehearsing *Bourgeois Gentilhomme*, Tracy was late for class, arriving at the same time as Rudolf. Tracy had heard that Rudolf had just come back from Greece and, as they went into class, he asked him about his trip. Having studied the classics, he understood Greek and was knowledgeable about Greek culture. This exchange was to prove decisive; after class, Rudolf approached Tracy and asked the young man if he knew where he could buy batteries for his ghetto-blaster: 'You know, those really big ones.' Rudolf always travelled with a ghetto-blaster but he only ever played classical music on it, never rock or disco. Tracy took him off to a pharmacy on Columbus Avenue and they bought the batteries. On the way they talked about Greece. It was an ironic situation because Tracy was better informed but had never been, whereas Rudolf had been several times, knew the ex-King of Greece, Constantine, and many rich Greeks like Niarchos and Perry Embiricos, who invited him to cruise on his yacht almost every summer. Tracy, from a family of academics impressed Rudolf with his knowledge and his general education, so after they had bought the batteries Rudolf invited the young man back to the Navarro Hotel, on Central Park South, for tea. After tea, they went to bed together.

In 1979 both the sexual revolution and the gay movement were at their height. One of the chief features was not just the 'casual promiscuity' that had so marked the 1960s but an astounding appetite for partners on the part of many homosexuals. A company in Los Angeles had that year marketed a personalised towel for gay men, the 'Beach Cruiser', each towel monogrammed with the buyer's name and phone number in huge black letters. A Denver study of bathhouse patrons showed how important a role was still played by the baths in the homosexual world. This study showed that, on average, bathhouse patrons had 2.7 sexual contacts a night. At this time, when Rudolf was in New York, he was a regular visitor to the Anvil, the Continental and the St Patrick Street baths. In San Francisco, he liked the Castro baths and the Bulldog. San Francisco's Bulldog baths, billing itself as the largest in the country, that year held a 'Biggest Cock in San Francisco' contest. The bathhouses of America at the time were a $100 million a year industry.

In the spirit of these times, it was entirely natural for Rudolf to seduce Tracy on the day he met him. Tracy saw nothing unusual in it either. That afternoon, after they had been to bed together, Rudolf was going out with his friend Judy Peabody to see Twyla Tharp dance. Peabody turned up in a limousine and whisked Rudolf away. As he left, he asked Tracy to call him the next day.

Tracy didn't make the call. His was a curious attitude to Rudolf, one which stemmed from his education. Tracy was never in love with Rudolf. Rather, Rudolf was his hero. So, when the star asked that Tracy call him, Tracy simply didn't believe him. He assumed that his hero had lots of boys, which was true, and Tracy wasn't interested in being just an acolyte.

The weekend passed and, on the Monday, he again attended class. Rudolf immediately came over to him. 'Why didn't you call me?'

'You really meant it? Me?'

That night they went out again. It was a typical Rudolf evening, packed with stimulation. They started at the theatre, where they saw a new play by Arthur Kopit, then went on to a new Pasolini film and then, finally, around midnight, to Elaine's, a restaurant on Second Avenue in the high Eighties. This was a great favourite of Rudolf's, for it stayed open late and attracted many celebrities. The food was indifferent to bad, but Rudolf was always more interested in drinking. Afterwards, they returned to the Navarro. Whether it was simply Tracy's good looks or his education, Rudolf immediately invited him to move in.

In the week before the première of *Le Bourgeois Gentilhomme* Rudolf introduced Robert to the glamorous nightlife of Manhattan that was such a part of being a star. On 2 April they attended a party at the Four Seasons where another of the guests was President Carter. Rudolf teased him, but half-seriously, about not doing more to help his aged mother escape Russia. The following night, he himself gave a party for the Joffrey Ballet at Studio 54; he had appeared with members of that company on Broadway in a Homage to Diaghilev. One of the guests was Robert Mapplethorpe who had become notorious for his 'fist-fucking' photographs, studies of predominantly black buttocks with a whole fist inside. That night Mapplethorpe wore a leather bracelet with sharp studs on the inside. As the evening wore on, he tightened the bracelet notch by notch.

It was a heady, raunchy time. One morning in March of that year, Bob Colacello, then editing Andy Warhol's *Interview* magazine, took a call from Ralph Destino, chairman of Cartier's, who were reviving their Santos watch, in celebration of their 75th anniversary. They were holding a big party but wanted a list of celebrities who would be willing to receive a watch, which could be used in their promotion. Destino asked Colacello if he could help line up some celebrities, through Warhol, and Colacello said he would, if Cartier agreed to take advertising in *Interview* for a year. ('There was *no* difference between editorial and advertising at *Interview*,' said Colacello.)

Colacello had in mind, as recipients, Andy, Truman Capote, Paulette Goddard and Rudolf. The watch was to be made in three versions: stainless steel, a combination of stainless steel and gold, and gold. Destino proposed to give the celebrities the stainless and gold combination.

All the others agreed to this, except for Nureyev. When Colacello reached him, via Monique, Rudolf said he would only play ball if he received the all-gold version. Colacello explained that the other celebrities had already agreed but that made no difference to Rudolf. He would only accept an all-gold version; moreover, at the party, which was to be at the Armory in New York, he would arrive after a performance, and must find waiting for him a steak and French champagne. That was the deal – take it or leave it.

Colacello relayed this back to Destino, who accepted Rudolf's offer because he thought, with Rudolf arriving after his performance, he could be given his watch separately and the other celebrities would never notice the difference. Unfortunately, Paulette Goddard *did* notice the difference and was not at all pleased.

On the other hand, Rudolf was delighted. 'Until that point,' says Colacello, 'he had treated me as a lackey of Andy's, but after that he couldn't have been sweeter. He would jump up in restaurants and greet me in a *very* friendly way. He was a lot like Andy – a peasant at heart and very influenced by material things.'

April 1979 was a propitious time for Rudolf to be dancing Balanchine's choreography. Only a week or so before, *Variety*, the showbusiness newspaper, had run a feature devoted to 'Broadway's Ballet Boom Specials', of which Rudolf's own participation in the homage to Diaghilev was an important part.

Le Bourgeois Gentilhomme opened on a Thursday and played throughout the weekend. Although Balanchine was pleased, and thought that the role suited Rudolf, the critics did not agree. Both Anna Kisselgoff, in the *New York Times*, and Arlene Croce in the *New Yorker* gave it a very poor write-up. Croce said that Rudolf was litle more than a quick-change artist and that there was little evidence of collaboration between the dancers and the choreographers.

Rudolf would have been happier with a better reception but at least he now had his experience with Balanchine. In later years he performed *Bourgeois Gentilhomme* in many places, proud that Balanchine had created a role on him. After New York, and despite the poor reviews, Rudolf danced the same part to packed houses at the Kennedy Center in Washington a month later. Robert Tracy was in the cast, and stayed with Rudolf in the Watergate building. He had not agreed with the critics. Rudolf might have just turned forty-one, Tracy observed, but he was still very good.

After Washington Rudolf went back to Europe and sent Tracy a ticket to come to London for the Nureyev festival he was mounting. It was Tracy's first time in Europe, a fulfilment of a dream he had always had. He and Rudolf stayed in the basement flat in the Goslings' house in Kensington. Rudolf still had the house in East Sheen but other friends were living there at the time.

In London Robert was thrown in at the deep end of Rudolf's European lifestyle. One day they flew to Paris for the wedding of a son of Stavros Niarchos, the next day they flew back for Rudolf to dance with Margot at a gala to celebrate her sixtieth birthday. It had been two years since they had been together, at the Silver Jubilee Gala. Rudolf was at the centre of a mutiny at the Festival Ballet – but this time the dancers were on his side. Beryl Grey, artistic director of the Ballet, had left him out of a trip to China, arguing that his presence would detract from the rest of the company – the familiar argument used all over the world. But since 113 dancers had left the company in the past four years, there *was* only one star, Rudolf, and the China trip had not been much of a success without him. The dancers lost confidence in Beryl Grey. Some tunes don't change.

After the London festival Rudolf and Robert flew back to New York together, and Tracy saw for the first time how frightened Rudolf was of flying. On this occasion, he got completely drunk for the take-off and sat with his head between his knees until the aircraft had reached its cruising altitude. In New York Rudolf was mounting Nureyev and Friends at the Lincoln Centre and also dancing with the Joffrey and the National Ballet of Canada. Tracy went back to school.

In July Farida had an operation for a cataract on her left eye. She was also suffering badly from rheumatism. Eye surgery is one of the few specialisms that Soviet medicine can boast of but this was little comfort to Rudolf. He still had hopes of visiting his mother in the year of the Olympics but it was clear that, in the wake of her operation, *she* would not be able to travel for some time.

That summer Rudolf had two holidays. He spent a few days with Monique van Vooren in Sardinia before flying with Robert to Greece to cruise on Perry Embiricos's yacht. Embiricos, who was gay himself, met them in Piraeus. Rudolf travelled with fourteen pieces of luggage. They sailed down the coast of both Turkey and Greece, and spent time with Ahmet and Mica Ertegün in Bodrum.

Seeing Rudolf's friends close up, Robert was struck that, with few exceptions, they were women. Yes, there were rich men – Niarchos, Embiricos, Rothschild – whom he saw quite a bit over the course of a year, but the chief fact was that Rudolf had a woman, a 'nanny' almost, or a sister, who looked after him, in several cities around the world. There was Monique in New York, Linda Mabeduke in Toronto, Jeanette Etheridge in San Francisco (she and her mother owned the Café Tosca where all the opera and ballet and baseball stars ate), there was Douce François in Paris. She, like Clara Saint, was Chilean, had once been in love with Raymondo de Larrain and, like the others, was willing to abnegate her personality completely in favour of Rudolf's.

London was an exception, for in London there were the Goslings, Maude and Nigel. Though Nigel had been educated at Eton and Cambridge, and though Maude had been a dancer, they were not in the Onassis or Rothschild class when it came to money. Their house in London was comfortable but hardly palatial. The friendship here seemed to be the most genuine, based on time, a genuine love of ballet and art and the fact that they had known and championed Rudolf since before he was famous. There was an equality in their friendship that was lacking in others'. Maude looked after Rudolf's needs in London but she was never a 'lackey', as Robert put it, like some of the others.

There was a second raft of friends, again dominated by women, such as Jackie Kennedy, Lee Radziwill, Phyllis Wyeth, wife of the painter, Judy Peabody and Tessa Kennedy, a socially ambitious interior decorator who had decorated Niarchos's yacht and introduced him to Rudolf. What amused and bewildered Tracy was that half these women, half the time – Douce, say, or Lee – seemed to be in love with Rudolf, in a sexual sense. The most curious of all was Jane Herrman. By 1979 Herrman was quite a force in the ballet world. After Sol Hurok's death in 1974 his organisation had been bought by General Electric, which was not a happy move. As a result the Met had decided to take over the impresario function itself and Jane Herrman had been asked by Anthony Bliss, general administrator of the Met, to look into the matter. A graduate of Barnard College, she had become interested in ballet after the birth of her second child, when her gynaecologist had told her she must exercise more and suggested ballet class. Her report had begun with the notorious – and prophetic – words, 'On the assumption that Hurok cannot sustain operations . . .'. By 1979, she was a sort of cross between Hurok and a general administrator, and loomed large in Rudolf's life, holding the keys to the main stage in America. He invited her on several holidays, including the Mediterranean cruises. It was expected to be tit for tat.

Herrman was not unattractive, with wide-apart eyes (like Farida and Jackie Onassis) and wavy blonde hair. She was, however, rather coarse, apt to get drunk and use words or phrases such as 'cunt' and 'shoot their wad' as if joining in male banter, in the hope that it would win Rudolf over. She too appeared to love Rudolf sexually. Paradoxically, this was combined with a hatred of homosexuality in general and she would wonder aloud, 'I don't know *what* I would do if my son went off with a homosexual.' This latter remark was always aimed at Tracy, who was of course the young son who had done just that.

In the summer of 1979 Rudolf also spent time at La Turbie. Robert was there, and Jane Herrman. They had a fight and from that day were always 'boxing'. Rudolf actually preferred it when there was a certain amount of 'needle' between his friends though, on occasion, he would reprimand Robert if he went too far with Herrmann whom he needed. In return he wasn't over-keen on the fact that Herrmann would tell others that she was sleeping with him. She wasn't.

Some of the spats between Rudolf, Tracy and Jane Herrman could be quite vicious, and her presence could on occasion provoke fights between Rudolf and Robert, something that didn't happen in other circumstances. At the same time, Rudolf liked it that Robert would sometimes cry as a result of these fights. He thought it showed the proper form of passion. Rudolf himself only ever cried about one thing – or rather, one person: Erik. Tracy believed that, deep down, Rudolf was still in love with Erik.

In September that year Rick Wellikoff, a New York schoolteacher, was examined by Dr Linda Laubenstein, a blood specialist at New York University. She noted that he had enlarged lymph nodes and a generalised rash on his skin that had resisted treatment. She was told later by a dermatologist that the rash was a rare form of skin cancer called Kaposi's sarcoma. Laubenstein had never heard of Kaposi's sarcoma, and looked it up. The cancer had originally been discovered in 1871 among Mediterranean and Jewish men, and, in the century that followed, between 500 and 800 cases had been documented. It was also seen among the Bantu. It usually struck men in their forties and fifties and was generally benign. The lesions were painless and the victims usually died much later – of something else. Since the cancer was so rare, Laubenstein decided to follow Rick Wellikoff's case closely and mentioned him to several of her colleagues. Maybe she would write him up as a case study. Two weeks later, she received a phone call from a colleague at the Veterans' Administration Hospital, a few blocks south of New York University on First Avenue.

'You're not going to believe it,' said the colleague, 'but there's another one down here.'

Laubenstein hurried round to the VA Hospital to inspect the other Kaposi's patient for herself. Like Wellikoff he was homosexual and, more uncannily, the two men shared several mutual friends. When she discussed these mutual friends, the new patient singled out a Canadian flight attendant. 'You should talk to him,' the new patient said. 'Because he's got this rash too.'

In the later months of 1979, Rudolf and Robert were apart but generally talked every day by phone. This was an arrangement which suited both of them. Tracy was faithful to Rudolf, though Rudolf did not expect it. In fact he would have been relieved if Tracy had been *un*faithful because he himself had no intention of being faithful. He had just discovered Flaubert's *Letters from Egypt*. He himself had made the same journey, when he was at the Kirov, which had produced the same reaction in him, the same feelings. 'I saw the same eroticism in Egypt as Flaubert did,' he said. 'Sex was very liberating for Flaubert – well, for me too.'

This was the time when Nureyev was staging *Manfred* with the Paris Opéra, which he hoped to take to the Met in 1980. In the course of planning the production, and of rehearsals, Rudolf fell heavily in love with Charles Jude. He was living with Douce François on rue Murillo, near the Parc Monceau in Paris, and this further complicated the situation. For Douce, like Lee Radziwill, was in love with Rudolf at the time, as was Jane Herrmann, and all of them hoped to get him into bed. Jude could not have been more different from Rudolf: he was somewhat bourgeois, wanting only the trappings of success – such as swimming pools, expensive cars, and flashy clothes – and in any case did not return Rudolf's feelings. Tracy was in the background, a form of stability and even tenderness in Rudolf's life, but he was 3,500 miles away in New York. The menage was not unlike a film by Chabrol: 'Three Ladies and a Man'.

That November the world première of Rudolf's *Manfred* took place in Paris, with the Ballet of the Paris Opéra but at the Palais des Sports. The story was taken from Byron's poem, a romantic Gothic tale set in the Alps, in which Manfred, in his castle, tries to cheat the fates – and fails. Mstislav Rostropovich had given Rudolf the Tchaikovsky score some months before, after hinting for ages that he had the perfect vehicle, with which the dancer could create a new ballet. When Rostropovich finally told him what he had in mind, Rudolf was struck by the fact that Tchaikovsky himself had been given Byron's poem, in much the way that *he* had been given the score, by someone who thought it would make a good theme. It was, after *Tancredi*, only the second ballet Rudolf had conceived from scratch.

Unfortunately, on 4 November, almost a month before the première, Rudolf broke a metatarsal at a performance of *The Nutcracker* in West Berlin, and was unable to dance. It was a reminder of the time when Hurok had cancelled the National Ballet of Canada's Washington engagement after Rudolf injured himself. This time the performance went ahead, but because of Rudolf's absence the auditorium at the Palais des Sports was half empty. Even when Rudolf was fit enough to dance, on 15 December, the public still stayed away in such numbers that the New Year's Eve performance was cancelled entirely. Word had gone round that the choreography was 'relentlessly difficult'. It was a blow.

Though he was spectacularly unfaithful to Tracy, Rudolf did send the younger man a ticket for him to come to Paris for Christmas that year (He now called him his 'Ganymede.') Rudolf usually spent Christmas with Marie-Hélène de Rothschild at her estate outside Paris, then travelled for New Year to St Moritz where he (and

Tracy and Douce) were guests of either Niarchos or Christina Onassis. Being Muslim and not at all religious, Rudolf did not celebrate Christmas as such but enjoyed the parties and celebrations nonetheless. Gifts were always exchanged with Yves Saint Laurent, who was becoming a good friend.

In 1980 he happened to remark to the producers of *Dance in America*, Emile Ardelino and Judy Kinberg among others, that he had never been invited to dance with them. A programme was accordingly arranged, in which Rudolf danced *Faune* as well as other excerpts. A week's rehearsal in New York was followed by a week's filming in Nashville, at a studio which formed part of the complex of buildings attached to the Grand Ol' Oprey. One day during the actual filming, the cast was encouraged to relax in the Oprey itself, which that day consisted mainly of cowboys and cowgirls dressed in rhinestones and denim (the Oprey is like a cross between a pub and a music hall, when people and performers mingle at tables arrayed around the room). Rudolf arrived at the Oprey still in his *Faune* costume, which included androgynous make-up, figure-hugging tights, body-stocking, and a bunch of fake grapes which covered his crotch. As well as all this, he had swapped his ballet shoes for clogs. The remarks of the cowboys and cowgirls may be imagined.

Early in the same year Rudolf bought an apartment in the Dakota building in New York. On Central Park West, it is dominated by two striking towers and has a famous clientele. Apart from Nureyev, in 1980 the Dakota was home to John and Yoko Lennon, Leonard Bernstein, Lauren Bacall and Paul Goldberger, the architectural critic for the *New York Times*. The fifth-floor apartment cost Rudolf $350,000. Although he had at last bought a home in the United States, Rudolf was not sure he really felt at home with Americans – for two reasons. He felt they had never accepted him when he first danced there, and he felt they had gone overboard for Baryshnikov, partly to spite him.

Even now, with Tracy living in the Dakota (and being very hush-hush about it), there were still plenty of boys around. This was an arrangement which suited Rudolf. He liked the stability of having one partner whom he respected and with whom he could plan holidays, a social life, and discuss books, music and history, but he also liked the variety and excitement of fresh partners every night. Even straight boys who were experimenting with their sexuality would sleep with him (and Rudolf preferred to believe that everyone was basically bisexual). Tracy, not being in love with Rudolf, didn't mind. Rudolf was a hero of his and, as a classics graduate he was also aware of the Greek story of the hero who became the servant. Would that happen with Rudolf?

In those days, Rudolf charged $10,000 a performance, although he would take less for companies he liked or thought needed his support, such as Balanchine's company and the American Ballet Theatre. Other companies appeared determined to do without him. The most notorious was the Paris Opéra which was scheduled to make a North American tour in spring of the following year, with Rudolf and Peter Schaufuss as guest stars. Schaufuss was a young Dane who had danced with New York City Ballet and the National Ballet of Canada. Anticipation of this tour was very great in New York, for it would be the first visit to America by the French since 1948 – since *before* the Royal Ballet's triumphant debut.

The French were looking forward to the visit too, but a fuss blew up when *Le Figaro*, the newspaper that was more hostile to Rudolf than any other, ran an article entitled: 'Paris Opéra Ballet – Tomb of the Unknown Dancer'. The phrase had actually been minted by Maurice Béjart. Who else, the newspaper said sarcastically, would take foreign guests on a tour? It was an insult to France, to have the French dancers overshadowed by foreigners. Furthermore, it was inconceivable that the New York City Ballet would take foreigners on one of *their* tours so why should the French do it? The paper helpfully reminded its readers that the Royal Danish Ballet had refused to take Rudolf with them when they played in New York in 1975.

The mischief worked. Under the French system, with the dancers being government employees, they had the right to strike and 'to create work stoppages'. The company had fifteen *étoiles*, or stars, of its own. The male dancers protested against the inclusion of Rudolf and Schaufuss and were supported by the company when a vote was taken: 112 in favour of shedding the guest stars, six against, and twelve abstaining. Rudolf, the man with the temperament, did not show it on this occasion. By now he was used to the argument. It had been used by the Royal Ballet, the Festival Ballet, the Danes, the Canadians and the Australians at one time or another. Why should the French be any different? Instead he proposed that he only dance on certain nights. The French refused to compromise. It wasn't anything personal, they told Rudolf, and he was very welcome to dance as a guest artist with them in Paris. But on tour the French company should be French.

Matters weren't helped when it emerged that the Met had entered into a separate contract with Rudolf from the one they had with the Paris Opéra Ballet. A personal element surfaced when it further emerged that the dancer who had led the protests against Rudolf in Paris was none other than Charles Jude, whom Rudolf had so assiduously helped and fallen in love with. In the face of these problems, the Met and other American theatres withdrew their offers to the Paris company, despite the embarrassment it caused to the French government. No one wanted to risk the French dancers going on strike in America. A final twist was the fact that the decision to cancel was taken by Jane Herrman. She it was who had entered into a separate contract with the man she loved, Rudolf, who in turn was in love with the man who was leading the protests in Paris.

The tour was cancelled on 7 February, only two weeks before the scheduled opening. This in itself created a fuss of a different kind. The New York press made the very fair point that, if the Met had been so worried about the quality, or reliability, of the French dancers, they should never have entertained hiring them in the first place. It was also the occasion for a fierce attack on the Paris Opéra Ballet by its outgoing director, Violette Verdy, who was moving to Boston and giving way to Rudolf's old friend, Rosella Hightower. Verdy was a distinguished and experienced dancer who had performed with American Ballet Theatre *and* New York City Ballet, including their Russian tour of 1962. (Once, being coached by Balanchine in how to jump, he had given her immortal advice while she was actually in the air: 'Now, stay there!' he said.) Verdy blamed the French system for the problem. This system, she said, prevented anyone firing the older dancers who had made the trouble in the first place. 'They have their country homes,' she said, 'their little cars, their wives, their mistresses . . . They just don't want to come to the United States and work.' She thought the French government should use the occasion to throw out the old dancers and keep the rest. It did no good. The cancellation was confirmed.

The Met replaced the Paris company at the last minute with a Martha Graham series, in the course of which Rudolf danced her famous *Appalachian Spring* ballet, with the Japanese ballerina, Yuriko Kimura. The series was a sell-out. One Texan newspaper, referring to Rudolf's performance, called him the biggest thing since oil. In some quarters the Paris Opéra Ballet was not missed.

No sooner had the French fuss died down than another erupted, this time in Rome in March where Rudolf was supposed to dance in *Swan Lake*. The choreographer on that occasion should have been none other than Yuri Grigorovich, the Soviet colleague who had created *The Stone Flower*, which Rudolf had so admired as a student at the Vaganova, and who had fallen out with Rudolf when he was late for rehearsal. Grigorovich did not mind working with Rudolf after all the years that had elapsed but Moscow did. Yet another performance was cancelled.

Perhaps these rebuffs got to him, for Rudolf then seems to

Modern
choreographers: with
Merce Cunningham
(far left),
Baryshnikov, and
Bob Fosse (far right).

1987: outside the Ufa
theatre of opera and
ballet where he first
watched ballet and
the stage where he
first appeared.

In Ufa, overlooking the Belaya River, in 1987. His return was a disaster from beginning to end. 'They speak a different language there.'

With Linda Mabeduke and **Margot** Fonteyn at his 50th birthday concert in New York.

With Natalia Dudinskaya, St Petersburg, 1989. Unlike **Markarova and** Baryshnikov, she said, Rudolf never bad-mouthed Russia.

St Bart's: the view from Rudolf's house.

The terrace at Rudolf's house in St Bart's.

The living room of his apartment in the Dakota building in New York. As with the Quai Voltaire flat in Paris, it was mainly decorated with male nudes.

Rudolf on stage after
la Bayadere. He
stumbled three times.

An elegant way of
letting his public
know how ill he was.

Honoured by Jack
Lang as a
Commander of Arts
& Letters.

Led away by Luigi Pignotti. Linda
Mabeduke looks on.

Fatally ill, but still handsome and 'very,
very, happy'.

The party attendants: with Marie-Helene
de Rothschild (left) and Pierre Berge.

Conducting at the Met, in New York. A marvellous recovery after his collapse in Kazan. 'Vouloir c'est pouvoir.'

In his box at the Paris Opera, October 8, 1992. The first night of La Bayadere. 'For many people Rudolf died that night.'

Rudolf's funeral. His final exit from the Palais Garnier.

A final farewell – to the music of Giselle.

have embarked on one of his periodic outbursts of temper. In London he threw an ashtray at a mirror when the pianist at a rehearsal decided that it was over before he did. He fell out with John Dexter, the production director of the Met, over a production of Satie's *Parade*, which was to be part of a French evening. Dexter had plenty of theatre experience but little knowledge of ballet – and neither man would give way to the other's ideas. That production too was withdrawn. Then Rudolf had yet another disgreement with the backstage staff at Vienna (was that the sixth or the hundred and sixth?). There had been reports that he was considering becoming the next artistic director of the Vienna Opera Ballet but he insisted he would only take over if the 'fat and lazy' members of the company were fired first. The company was so offended that it refused to attend rehearsals.

The withdrawal of the American – and other – teams from the Moscow Olympics effectively killed any hope Rudolf had of seeing his mother that year. No one was in a forgiving mood.

At the end of the year, Rudolf was gratified when Clive Barnes again took his side against the Royal Ballet. It had now been three years since Norman Morrice had taken over and, Barnes concluded, the company was in bad shape. It had been in bad shape since even before Morrice had been made director, Barnes said, but now the drop in standard was very clear. 'Morrice has tried very hard but apart from the ailing Merle Park it has not a classic ballerina to call its own.' Anthony Dowell and David Wall were now only guest artists and the Royal, for the first time in a very long while, was no longer a company of stars. Morrice, Barnes said, had increased the technical ability of the young dancers but had had '*no* impact on artistic direction or purpose.' Barnes was always kinder to Rudolf than most critics, but there were many who shared his view about the Royal Ballet, not least in Britain.

By now, Rudolf had also made up with Zeffirelli, who gave him a party in New York. Rudolf dressed modestly, and behaved impeccably. He himself had hopes of a new movie career. MGM had just announced plans for a film with Rudolf: *Exposed*, co-starring Nastassja Kinski.

He also behaved impeccably at Imelda Marcos' Thanksgiving Party at the Waldorf Towers, especially in the limousine going home afterwards. His hostess had given everyone a gift and, when Rudolf opened his in the car, he found a pair of diamond cufflinks. Immediately, he handed them to the driver. 'Rudolf!' said Monique. 'What are you doing? Don't you like them?'

'I love them,' he replied. 'But I don't like the source.'

Rudolf and Robert Tracy were still living together in the Dakota

apartment when Rudolf was in New York. Just as Rudolf had liked
to be 'fatherly' with the younger dancers at the National Ballet of
Canada, so there was an element of that in his relation with Robert.
Tracy reminded Rudolf of himself as a younger man. He liked Tracy's
intelligence, his knowledge of dance, his facility with languages, his
awareness of history. He was more interesting than Wallace, easier
than Erik.

They went to Europe for Christmas 1980. Niarchos sent a plane
for them and Douce came too. The paparazzi photographed their
arrival at Christina Onassis's party in St Moritz. In February Rudolf
was to dance in a special show for Yves Saint Laurent, who was
launching a new fragrance for men, Kouros. Rudolf danced three short
ballets and then everyone present adjourned to Maxim's which Saint
Laurent had taken over for the evening. It was a glittering occasion:
the guests included Catherine Deneuve, Jean-Paul Belmondo, Isabel
Adjani, Paloma Picasso, Jerry Hall, Marc Bohan and Isabel Goldsmith.
The evening was notable, however, for the fact that Yves Saint Laurent,
in welcoming his guests, kissed all the women on the cheek, but Rudolf
fully on the lips. Rudolf had had some famous lovers in his time but Yves
had not been mentioned before.

After a short tour of Europe he was back in New York in April for
something out of the ordinary – a performance of *From Sea to Shining
Sea*, with Baryshnikov. Barnes had cleverly billed this evening as an
'exhibition fight' between two heavyweights. When the two dancers
came together on stage afterwards, Barnes observed that Rudolf
extended his hand to the younger man, without waiting for Baryshnikov
to come to him. It was a nice gesture by 'Mr Tantrum'.

He was less accommodating some weeks later when he was interviewed on British television to mark the twentieth anniversary of his
defection. The Royal Ballet were in New York at the time, appearing
before Prince Charles, among others. Rudolf, perhaps emboldened by
Barnes's article on how far the company had sunk, but also because
he now had little to lose, roundly attacked the Royal Ballet, claiming
that they had done all in their power to turn him into a nonentity, that
they had used him to bring in revenue but had not created any ballets
of interest for him. And, when Margot had gone, 'they gave me a kick in
the arse – and out'. Ironically, that year he danced thirty performances
in London, more than he had done for the Royal Ballet in some years
in the 1970s. But these performances were for the Festival Ballet, or
his own Nureyev and Friends and, for Rudolf, it wasn't the same thing.
He had been hurt by the Royal Ballet and although he didn't usually
bear grudges, Covent Garden was an exception. The British, he said,
were 'grey, second rate'. He wouldn't wait around 'for crumbs' from
the Royal. That is how much his rejection hurt.

On 3 July 1981 the *New York Times* reported the outbreak of a rare form of cancer, Kaposi's sarcoma, among forty-one previously healthy gay men. Dr Alvin Friedman-Kien of New York University Medical Center said that at least nine of the men had 'severe defects in their immunological systems'.

Eight weeks later, on 28 August, the Centers for Disease Control in Atlanta revealed that cases of Kaposi's sarcoma, as well as a rare parasitical form of pneumonia – pneumocystis – were inexplicably increasing across the country. More than 90 per cent of the cases had been diagnosed in gay men. One researcher speculated that, perhaps, the disease was linked to the men's sexual lifestyles, or to drug use.

Some people took these reports very seriously. The Royal Ballet, for instance, before their US tour that year, were approached discreetly by one of the staff from the American embassy in London, warning any homosexual members of the company to avoid the gay bars. 'A very peculiar sexual disease is happening,' he said, 'and your dancers should be aware of it.'

However, for many gays, Nureyev included, these reports were too vague, too piecemeal, too technical to break through, while their own promiscuous lifestyles were too glowing, precious and enjoyable to allow anything to spoil the fun. Tracy was different. He was an academic, familiar with the careful ways of science, and he knew that behind the bald headlines and statistics must lie a much more complex, and perhaps more threatening truth. Also he had his ear closer to the ground, and had more time than Rudolf, and he knew that the gay press, particularly the *Sentinel* of San Francisco and the *New York Native*, had published stories about a new killer pneumonia attacking gay men. Friends of Tracy had already died. Something was going on out there.

Tracy decided to change his lifestyle. He looked about him and decided that, however much he might admire Rudolf as a dancer and a strong character, he didn't like his fantastic promiscuity. They had to stop sleeping together. Predictably, the occasion was incendiary. They were in Caracas in August, dancing *Giselle*, when Tracy told Rudolf of his decision. Rudolf exploded and turned on Tracy, beating him around the head and giving him a black eye. The next day they had to fly from Venezuela to Verona, via Portugal. On the flight to Lisbon, Tracy fell asleep and woke up to feel Rudolf stroking his head, anxious to comfort the younger man. When they arrived in Verona, the hotel was not to Tracy's liking and Rudolf made sure it was changed. This made them late for rehearsals but Rudolf accepted the blame, protecting Tracy. As they practised in class together, Rudolf manoeuvred himself near to Tracy and whispered, 'Always you.'

But Tracy was adamant. It was now the last week of August and, in the previous month, yet more gay friends of his had died of the mysterious new cancer that was afflicting so many homosexual men. Something *was* going on; he didn't know what but if sex had something to do with it, then he had to cut that link with Rudolf. His promiscuity wasn't going to change. It might be too late already.

And so, in Verona that night, there was another fight. This time, however, before it came to blows, Tracy packed his things and left. He took a train to Venice and from there flew to Rome where he stayed with a friend, Giovanna Augusta. She and Tracy were lovers, and she was also drawn to Rudolf. There was promiscuity everywhere.

Rudolf tracked Tracy down and tried to persuade him to rejoin the company in Athens, where they were supposed to dance *Sleeping Beauty* at the open-air Herodes Atticus Theatre with the Vienna Opera Ballet. Rudolf was to appear as the Prince and Robert as the Blue Bird. Tracy could emerge as a star.

He refused. He spent the rest of the summer by himself and wouldn't see Rudolf again until they met in class in December. He never slept with Rudolf again.

In the autumn Monique van Vooren published a novel, *Night Sanctuary*. This told the story of a Russian ballet star who had defected to the west, in London, in the 1950s. It was, of course, a rather thinly disguised version of Rudolf's story. Or so people were invited to believe. The *Village Voice* called the novel 'astonishing' but what was astonishing about the book was the way in which a story ostensibly about dance and the theatre reeked of sex. Almost all the characters, male and female, were prostitutes in one form or another. Almost all were bisexual. Almost all, male and female, preferred one or more kinds of exotic sex – bondage, leather, groups, drug-enhanced orgies. The central character, the defecting dancer, was surrounded by admirers of both sexes all of whom wanted to get him into bed. In Russia, the dancer had enjoyed an affair with his music teacher, intended by van Vooren to be a disguised reference to Rudolf's affair with Tseniia Iurgenson.

Rudolf hated the book. He was furious. 'If she really loved me,' he said, 'she would never have published it. How could Rex Reed [a showbusiness journalist] say everyone should read it? It's garbage. Women are more cruel than men.' What he hated of course was the emphasis on sex. For he was still paradoxical about his own sexuality. He never hid his homosexuality or his behaviour from those around him – indeed it would have been difficult to hide the sort of promiscuity Rudolf indulged in. But he didn't want it talked about publicly. He was a private man and it could harm his career. Monique was banished.

Only weeks later, his film with Nastassja Kinski was released, and was roundly trashed. *Exposed* is a cold war terrorist/spy thriller with a complicated plot, in the course of which Rudolf, as a macho Jewish violin virtuoso, captured Kinski, a top model. One reviewer said the film was so bad it could 'damage your mental health'. Mostly, it was James Toback, the writer/director of the movie who was derided (he was the man who had let slip the roster of Rudolf's famous sexual partners). So in that sense *Exposed* was a re-run of *Valentino*. But it did little to improve Rudolf's standing.

In December 1981 he and Robert took class together but didn't speak. In New York Rudolf loved to go to Stanley Williams's class at the Lincoln Center. Williams was British born but Danish trained and his classes in New York have become legendary. His style is very quiet – you can barely hear him in class and the essence of his success is in timing: he teaches dancers to be slightly ahead of the music. That way, their steps have maximum attack, maximum surprise value.

Shortly after this silent encounter in class, Robert, who was appearing in Puerto Rico in a ballet with Marcia Haydée, received a telephone call from Violette Verdy, who was dancing with Rudolf in *Manfred* in Zurich. She had been delegated, she said, to track down Robert. She said that Rudolf was anxious to re-establish some sort of contact so would Robert call Rudolf in Zurich when he had a moment. Tracy recognised that this indirect approach was the only sort of apology Rudolf was capable of, so he made the call. When he got through, Rudolf was very sweet and said that he accepted Tracy's sexual embargo – but still wanted to be with him. Robert moved back into the Dakota.

As he approached forty-four, Rudolf's life had taken on something of the character of a roller-coaster. Good times would be followed by bad in a regular wave. After the unpleasantness of Monique's *Night Sanctuary* and *Exposed*, 1982 began on a distinctly better note. Not only was Robert back in the Dakota but, in January in Vienna, Rudolf was offered Austrian citizenship. Rudolf had decided on Austria partly because of the time he had spent in Vienna with the State Opera House but also because Austria was technically neutral in the political sphere. He still didn't want anything to compromise his standing in Russia. It was during research for the documentation required to satisfy the Austrian authorities that evidence was produced which appeared to show that Rudolf was actually born on 14 March, but that his mother didn't *register* his birth until the seventeenth, when the train reached Razdolnaya. This seems a long time between railway stations. If true, it would be ironic, because Rudolf always said that the number seventeen was important in his life – being the day of the month on which he was born and defected. It now seems he may not have been born on 17 March, and he actually defected on 16 June.

And then, after the Austrians had agreeably surprised him, in Paris, the culture minister Jack Lang first mentioned that Rudolf might be considered for the post of director of the Paris Opéra Ballet. Although

Rosella Hightower had taken over from Violette Verdy, it was still felt that more of a shake-up was needed.

His own company! At last. His satisfaction was complete when he was asked back by the Royal Ballet to dance at Covent Garden. In London it had finally been accepted that the Morrice policy of no guest artists wasn't working. Rudolf was invited back to dance in *Swan Lake* and *La Bayadère*, partnered by Lesley Collier and Lynn Seymour.

It was an emotional time. When he bumped into Norman Morrice in Floral Street before the first rehearsal he flung his arms around him and kissed him – but only because people were watching. It was not how Rudolf felt – far from it. He was still telling anyone who would listen that the Royal Ballet had kicked him in the arse. He did show Morrice his Kermit the Frog neck charm. In the late 1970s, Rudolf had appeared on *The Muppet Show*, starring opposite Miss Piggie in a tutu, dancing 'Swine Lake'. The producers had given him a little silver charm of Kermit as a geasture of thanks. Rudolf had had it altered; adulterated, in fact. As he showed it to Morrice, Kermit now had a penis to which a chain was attached. When the chain was pulled, Kermit had an erection. Rudolf had gone to a lot of trouble with this charm, and laughed uproariously when the chain was pulled.

On the nights Rudolf danced at Covent Garden he was, naturally, keen to show what they had all been missing. And he did. The reviews were wonderful. *The Times* said that even at his age, he jumped higher than anyone. The *Guardian* found him in wonderful physical shape and said he never slipped out of character even when he was just watching others: 'His eyes reflect events before they happen.' The *Daily Telegraph* said that he had proved that he was still a great artist, that he altered the atmosphere on the Covent Garden stage, that there had been 'no diminution' in his charisma. The critic could not remember when he had seen Rudolf give a better performance.

The audience agreed. It was quite like old times, someone wrote. The people cheered, threw flowers and 'generally refused to leave'. They loved it most when Rudolf bowed to an oldish woman in the stalls. Not Udeltsova but Margot Fonteyn. He had made his point.

In fact, he had made it so well that Morrice swallowed humble pie and there and then invited Rudolf back later in the year to choreograph his own ballet. With that gesture, that recognition, the rift was healed.

Since he was obviously going to be spending time in France, and since both he and his mother had finally accepted that she *wasn't* going to come to the west, Rudolf now changed tack. Guzelle, Rosa's daughter, Rudolf's niece, had surprised everyone by marrying a South American – partly as a way to emigrate. For some reason the Soviet authorities were more ready to allow people out who had concluded marriage to a foreigner. This therefore gave Rudolf the idea of arranging a marriage of convenience for Rosa, and Douce Francois' brother, Pierre, was prevailed upon to do the honours. It worked, in the sense that Rosa duly arrived in the west. It didn't work in the sense that Guzelle insisted on being with her mother and proved to be a nightmare, ostensibly trying to become a dancer but in reality only interested in fashion and spending Rudolf's money. Rosa wasn't much better and Rudolf sent her to the South of France. She never mastered French – and in fact was denied a French driving licence because her language was so poor. Later, when Rudolf visited La Turbie, they kept away from each other.

A month after his Covent Garden success, it was confirmed that Rudolf would take over as artistic director of the Paris Opéra Ballet in September 1983, more than a year away. At last, he was head of a major ballet company. It would be the fitting climax to his career. Accordingly, at the end of March 1982 he bought a flat in Paris, at 23 quai Voltaire, overlooking the Seine and the Louvre.

Barely had he moved in, however, than he heard that Nigel Gosling was seriously ill. At the time, Rudolf was in New York, but he interrupted his schedule to visit Gosling in hospital. Gosling had retired from the *Observer* in 1975 but he wasn't such an old man, being seventy-two in 1982. After the visit, Rudolf flew back to the US, where he was to appear with the Boston Ballet in Chicago in *Don Quixote*. There, towards the end of May, he heard the sad news that Gosling had died. For Rudolf, this was in a way like losing a second father, and he was quite upset. (But he didn't go to the funeral; he hated injections, hospitals and funerals.) Robert was then thinking of changing careers, of becoming a writer, and one of the first books he compiled was to be an anthology of Gosling's criticism. Rudolf was touched by that.

That summer Rudolf performed in Turkey and Greece and holidayed with Niarchos. Robert accompanied him. Things were easier between them, for Rudolf now said to Tracy what he had said to Gyckova years before: 'I'm glad we've got the sex over with . . .' Niarchos had for some reason conceived a passion for flying his helicopter at night, a somewhat dangerous practice that was not helped when Rudolf and the Earl of Dudley were forced to make an emergency landing. For a nervous flyer like Rudolf, this episode was nerve-racking.

On holiday Rudolf could make others nervous. Like many famous people he had an ambivalent attitude towards being recognised. He could be angry if he *was* recognised, if it meant people invaded his privacy, but he could be livid if he wasn't. Several people report that, on holiday in Greece or Turkey, Rudolf would pose or position himself by famous ruins until he was recognised. Then, once that part of his ego had been gratified, he would relax properly. It was the same at airports. If the check-in staff did not recognise him, he would 'help' them, talking about ballet, or Russia, until they cottoned on. On one of his Niarchos holidays, Rudolf had been unusually reticent about his companion, presenting him as his osteopath. This had proved a popular choice of profession, for half the ageing women on the holiday had various aches and pains, or said they had. The young man was forced to spend more time in their company than with Rudolf. Or perhaps they were just getting their own back in a clever way.

That summer he bought his second apartment in the Dakota. This was a better choice, being on the second floor overlooking the park. It cost $1.8 million. He kept the fifth-floor apartment for a while, but eventually sold it for $700,000. In London he sold the East Sheen house, also making a good profit – he had paid £45,000 back in the 1960s; now he received £400,000. He hadn't used it in two years, he was leaving London emotionally, and, now that Nigel was dead, Maude would welcome him as a guest even more than before. In fact, she made over the basement of Victoria Road for his use.

In the month that Gosling died, the *New York Native*, New York's gay newspaper, was reporting what appeared to be a new phase in the 'plague' that was affecting the city's gay population. The number of men with lymphadenopathy (disease of the lymph nodes) was increasing alarmingly now. Other gay men seemed listless and 'dragged out'. According to Randy Shilts, in his account of AIDS, *And the Band Played On*, oral candidiasis, or thrush, was the most common precursor of the more serious cases. Shingle-type lesions on the shoulders and face were also appearing more often. Numbers of men would spend their nights drenched in terrifying night sweats which 'left their sheets soaked with perspiration, their hair saturated with the salty fetor, and their bodies limp with exhaustion.'

Tracy, now thoroughly alarmed by what was happening in the gay world, examined his body every day for any of the telltale signs. He had found nothing, so far. Instead, he had a different kind of problem. In December that year he visited Paris. He became very dehydrated in the aircraft and believes he may have had a form of epileptic seizure while he was in the opera house. When he came to he found that Rudolf was holding his hand and that he had lost all his teeth when he fell. 'Go find my teeth,' Tracy croaked. 'My mother paid a fortune for the orthodontic work.' Later, he was taken to the American Hospital in Paris where Douce François, who had become Rudolf's amanuensis now that he was living in Paris, was very helpful. She brought soup every day.

In Russia Rudolf's name was still banned, officially speaking, but after three major defections there was a natural curiosity on the part of most dancers to know what life in the west was like. For some time there had been a thriving underground trade in black-market films and videos of the defectors performing in the west – and there was a bigger demand for films of Rudolf than for Makarova or Baryshnikov. One of the Bolshoi teachers in Moscow, Naum Azarin, operated a sort of illegal salon at his flat. He had a supply of Nureyev tapes and would show them to selected dancers behind closed curtains. Irek Mukhamedov, who had won the Moscow Grand Prix in 1981, twenty-three years after Rudolf won it, was one of those allowed to join Azarin's secret salon. Mukhamedov was fascinated by Rudolf's style. Before he saw the tapes, he had heard only bad things about Rudolf – not just that he had betrayed his country but that he had been cruel to his mother. Being shown the tapes presented Mukhamedov with a problem. He immediately wanted to emulate Rudolf – but didn't dare. Had he imitated any of Rudolf's steps, the authorities would have known he had seen foreign tapes, and that would not have helped his career. For the time being, he sat on his ambition.

Rudolf, meanwhile, confessed to an interviewer in 1982 that he wished he had defected even earlier. He finally admitted that, by the time he was twenty-three, he was imbued with the Kirov style and rather arrogant about it, too. He had been convinced, he said, that the Kirov training was the best in the world and from that two things followed. In the first place, he wasn't as open to other techniques as he might have been (remember the problems with Erik in Copenhagen). Equally important, he thought his attitude had scared away choreographers like Ashton and Balanchine. Had he been younger and more pliable, he felt sure they would have created more for him. 'Without Balanchine you can't live,' he said. The beauty of Margot and Erik, he added, was that they taught him not all ballet was the same; he had thought it was when he left the Kirov. The interviewer had obviously caught Rudolf in a reflective mood, because he also said something he had never admitted before – that he had overshadowed Anthony Dowell and David Wall. Maybe, now that the rift with Covent Garden had been healed, he could admit things – to himself as well as to others.

The second half of 1982 saw the première of *The Tempest* at Covent Garden, and the American première of *Manfred*. Reviews of *The Tempest* were mixed. His 'intriguing theatrical imagination' was praised, but Dowell was generally felt to have outdanced him on this occasion. He had a small tempest of his own when, in October, a twenty-four-year-old Italian woman, Clarita Gatto, claimed he was in love with her and that she was expecting their child. This could have been a big story but fizzled out. The American reaction to *Manfred* mirrored the American reaction to his *Romeo and Juliet*. Anna Kisselgoff thought it 'hardly the disaster that the French and British reviews had implied'. She preferred Nureyev in *Don Quixote* but *Manfred* was well worth the effort, she said. He took seven curtain calls.

What was really remarkable about these performances was the fact that Rudolf was dancing with the Zurich Ballet, who were on their first North American tour. At forty-four, his presence still made all the difference. What had happened with the Royal Ballet, the Festival Ballet, the Canadian, Australian and Paris Ballets had now happened with Zurich.

And with Boston. Throughout 1982 and 1983, until he joined the Paris Opéra Ballet full-time, Rudolf formed new associations – the Ballet Théâtre de Nancy, and the Matsuyama Ballet in Japan, where he danced with Yoko Morishita. But it was his association with the Boston Ballet and Violette Verdy that meant the most to him. Everyone agreed that his presence in Boston had galvanised the company (though Verdy also had something to do with that). His production of *Don Quixote* had cost $250,000 in décor alone but it was worth it, the local critics felt, because the production was 'a comic romp with all the pace of a Marx Brothers movie', this being intended as a compliment. And then a familiar tragedy struck: Rudolf injured himself and the following ten-day season was cancelled. Since the Boston Ballet had predicted a gross revenue of $600,000 for this season, which was a sell-out, it was very bad news indeed, and more than one paper had the Boston company on the brink of financial ruin. Of course, it turned out that they were insured with Lloyd's of London for injury to the principal dancer, so it was nowhere near as serious as that.

Nureyev recovered, and went on a short tour of France with the Ballet Théâtre de Nancy where, in Bordeaux, he caught a chill. Two tiring tours of Japan and South America followed before he caught up with Verdy and her company in Milan for their European tour. George Balanchine had recently died, which may have accounted for Rudolf's reflective mood at this time. In any case, it was on this tour that he spent hours talking with Violette Verdy and baring his soul. She had first seen him in Paris before he defected so had been well positioned to observe the changes that had come over Rudolf. She felt that she had helped him appreciate Balanchine even more. He, in turn, had encouraged her to teach. They had enjoyed several snorkelling holidays together off the Florida coast, one with Henry Ford. Verdy liked Tracy and thought Rudolf and he made a 'harmonious' couple. She saw Rudolf's temper and, once, he had shaped up to hit her but had thought better of it at the last moment. She realised, as dancers in Russia had realised, that his bluntness, roughness and barbaric manners, which he never lost, were all a form of truth, of honesty, and that helped her adjust to them. He told her, as he had told others, that he had made love to Tseniia. He even told Violette that he had loved Tseniia. He had made love to Margot 'once or twice', he said, and had loved her. He could love women, he explained, but affairs with women took so much time, and he didn't have time, he had to dance. With men, sex was over quickly

– and he snapped his fingers. Sex was functional for him; that was one reason he was gay. 'I could feel guilty about some of the boys I have slept with,' he said, 'but I have to do what I have to do. If they follow me, they follow me. It sounds cruel, but there we are.' Violette got the impression that, as he said this, Rudolf was thinking of Wallace.

However, he also said he would like a child.

Do I know the woman? Violette asked.

No, he replied. Douce said she would have my child, but maybe I should just donate my seed to a sperm bank.

Rudolf also confessed to Violette how cruel Erik had been to him. When they had met, Erik hadn't been able to take Rudolf's sincerity; he was too neurotic and unfulfilled. He had felt that Rudolf was devouring him, taking, taking, taking . . . This was something else Rudolf hadn't admitted before. But then, he said, drink got to Erik. Drink and drugs, muscle relaxants especially. That all made him cruel. Erik would tell Rudolf cruel things, true things but cruel nonetheless, and it had killed the feelings they had had for each other. To Violette, Rudolf obviously regretted that. It may well have been the only regret of his life.

One morning in February 1983 a meeting took place in the offices of Professor Luc Montagnier at the Pasteur Institute in Paris. Present at the meeting, besides Montagnier, were Doctors Willy Rosenbaum, Françoise Barre, Française Brun-Vezinet and Jean-Claude Chermann. At the meeting Montagnier announced that a new human virus had been discovered. It was cytopathic, meaning it killed certain types of cell, in this case T-lymphocytes, part of the body's immune system.

His announcement electrified the others at the meeting, Rosenbaum especially. Among the five, Rosenbaum knew most about the new 'plague' affecting gay men, and he told the others all he knew. He had been watching hopelessly, he said, as one disease after another piled up in the bodies of the sufferers. It was little use treating one disease because another would 'erupt' a day or so later and kill the patient. Quietly, he said that the only thing that could explain this set of circumstances was a virus that attacked the body's immune system, rendering it unable to fight any illness that came its way. A virus that attacked the T-lymphocytes made good sense. He had no proof but he felt sure this new virus could explain the outbreak of the disease with which he was becoming all too familiar.

Only days later, on 7 March, the *New York Native* ran a banner headline across its front page, '1,112 AND COUNTING.' This was the number of people so far who had died of the gay plague in the United States. Letters poured into the paper, denouncing the article as 'alarmist' and 'sex-negative'. Other statistical information at the time showed that a gay person having twenty sexual partners a year had a one in ten chance of sleeping with a sufferer from Acquired Immune Deficiency Syndrome, or AIDS, as the disease was now called.

A survey that same month by three gay psychologists in San Francisco produced statistics which were alarming in a different way. Among their results was the finding that while most gay men now knew all about AIDS, and what caused it, 62 per cent still engaged in high-risk sex acts at the same frequency as, or *more* often than, before they had found out about AIDS. The study also showed the continuing importance of bathhouses: men who went to bathhouses were far less likely than other men to use any form of protection. And the form of sex that had changed least of all was oral sex – more than 60 per cent of gays questioned still practised oral sex, unprotected. The chilling thing for Robert Tracy was that, in all these statistics, Rudolf was absolutely typical.

In late summer 1983 Rudolf finally took over at the Paris Opéra Ballet. It was a prestigious but difficult company, in which all the dancers, as Rudolf well knew from experience, were state employees. In existence since 1661, it had evolved a set of practices positively Byzantine in their complexity and as rigid as steel. Even Napoleon had had his problems with the Paris Opéra, where there had been twenty-three administrators in fourteen years while he was Emperor. Since Serge Lifar had resigned as artistic director in 1958 there had been eight artistic directors, one every three years. Two had lasted barely a year and one, Roland Petit, left before he began. It was a challenge but it was also, undoubtedly, an opportunity. Many people thought that if anyone could sort out the Paris Opéra Ballet, Rudolf could.

Two events coincided with Rudolf's appointment in Paris. One was very public, the other extremely private. The public event took place in Manchester when his performance with the Boston Ballet on tour was booed by certain sections of the audience. Rudolf had had his critics before but he had always been a great success with audiences. At forty-five, time was at last beginning to take its toll on his body. Luigi now had to give him not one but two massages a day.

The second, more private event, was that he began to suffer night sweats.

CHAPTER TWENTY

The KGB File: 3 – The Murder of Zoya Federova

On Friday 11 December 1981, on Kutuzovsky Prospekt in Moscow, just after one o'clock in the afternoon, Zoya Federova was shot once in the head while making a telephone call. The bullet entered her skull from behind and exited through one eye. She died instantly. She was seventy-four. Zoya Federova was a famous Russian actress who had led an eventful life which had brought her into conflict with the Soviet authorities on several occasions. According to the KGB file, Rudolf was implicated in her death.

Few documents concerning this matter have been made available and most of those that were were divulged as this book went to press, making it difficult to corroborate the file's contents. The possibility remains, therefore, that the allegations and inferences contained in the KGB file are either wrong or, given Nureyev's history, sheer propaganda aimed at blackening his name even after his death. These possibilities are considered in more detail towards the end of this chapter. But first, some facts.

Zoya Federova was, without question, the most famous and colourful Soviet actress of her day – and the most tragic. Her unsolved murder has puzzled and fascinated Russians for more than a decade. Born in 1907 (or 1909, according to the dictionary you use), she was extremely attractive and rather wild, a Soviet version of Marilyn Monroe crossed with Audrey Hepburn. But the time she entered the Moscow theatre school in 1934 she had already appeared in a number of films. During the 1930s and early 1940s she became one of the most popular Soviet film stars, her most successful movies being *Friends, Harmony, Great Citizen, Man with a Rifle, Friends at the Front*, and *Marriage*, though there were many others. She specialised in rather impudent, insolent roles in which her good looks helped enormously in an authoritarian state. She was made a Merited Artist of the Soviet Union (the highest honour) in 1965, but by then her life had been turned upside down.

Towards the end of the Second World War, Zoya Federova fell in love with an American. His name was Roger Jackson Tait and at the end of the war he was a naval attaché at the United States embassy in Moscow. At the time (1944–45), the Soviet Union and the United States were theoretically allies, but the shape of the post-war world was already clear and love affairs between Russians and Americans were not really welcome to either side. Tait was by all accounts a rather naïve and romantic man; Federova was so famous by that time that she thought the authorities could not touch her.

Zoya was so well known in Russia in fact that she could never leave it permanently, nor would she have wanted to. And so, as 1945 and the end of the war arrived, the couple formulated a plan to live six months of the year in America and six months in Russia, where Zoya could continue to make her films. The couple was so convinced of their future together that, when the war ended, Zoya was pregnant. In celebration of the victory over the Germans, the child was to be called Victor if it was a boy and Victoria if it was a girl.

This was to reckon without Stalin. Overnight, Tait became *persona non grata* in Russia and was given seventy-two hours in which to leave the country. By all accounts, the Americans, although not perhaps the instigators of this policy, nonetheless acceded to it without making too much trouble. Whether Tait was in fact spying for the United States, and Federova was collaborating with him, has never been satisfactorily explained. But Tait was encouraged to go home and to forget all about his Russian girlfriend. Few people realised that Federova was pregnant.

Tait had no choice but to obey his orders, and he returned to North America. But he genuinely loved Federova and after their separation, he sought news of her, writing letters, sending telegrams, hoping she would reply. After two years, he received a letter purportedly from her, which had been posted in Stockholm. Tait had never seen Federova's handwriting and so had no way of knowing if the letter was genuine or not. It was short and, among other things, it said in so many words: 'You really annoy me with your pestering. I am happy. I am married and I have two children.' Tait was amazed that his former love could have changed so much but, in 1947, with the cold war firmly under way, he could not check whether the letter really was from Federova, or was a concoction of the KGB.

In fact, Federova was in prison. Their daughter (called Victoria, as they had planned) had been born in January 1946. When the child was eleven months old, Federova was arrested, following a clutch of articles in the Soviet press claiming that she was a terrorist who had intended to dig a tunnel under the Kremlin in order to blow it up. Federova was, according to these articles, an American spy. As a result she was separated from her daughter, who was sent to an aunt. Shortly after, the aunt, who was divorced and until then had lived in Moscow, was sent away from the capital, with her own two children, a girl and a boy, and Victoria. They were sent to a village called Polugkno in the north of Russia, and allowed just two suitcases between them.

Life in Polugkno in 1947 was not so very different from Ufa, maybe worse. There was no heating in the apartment where they all lived, and the sleeping conditions were very crowded. There were only potatoes to eat, or the peel of potatoes and occasionally, at festivals, milk.

Victoria was brought up to believe that her aunt was her mother. Federova had been sentenced to twenty-five years' imprisonment for espionage and her sister never expected to see her again. Because her mother was in prison for a political offence, other children were forbidden to fraternise with Victoria, who grew up as a solitary child and a great reader.

When Victoria was four she was sent, as a treat, to Moscow, to meet some relatives whom she knew nothing about. One of her cousins took her walking in the centre of old Moscow, along the Arbat, where they chanced upon a cinema in which one of Federova's films was playing. Outside the cinema was a large poster showing Federova as the star of the film. Victoria's cousin pointed to the poster and told her that Federova was her mother. That took some believing but, eventually, Victoria was convinced.

Meanwhile, Federova had been in the notorious Lubyanka prison in Moscow in solitary confinement and was then moved out of the capital to the Mordovia area, between Totma and Termnukax where there were thirty-six camps. This was Stalinism at its worst.

After some time in Polugkno, Federova's sister and her dependants were moved from the countryside back to the city, to Petropavlovsk, in Kazakhstan. This was because of the sister's 'good behaviour'.

However, around the end of 1954 or beginning of 1955, after eight years in jail, Federova was released. It was about eighteen months after Stalin had died, and there had been a new 'investigation' of her case, which had concluded that a mistake had been made. From Moscow, Federova sent a telegram to her sister, saying that she had been released and asking that her daughter be sent to her in Moscow. Federova also sent a food parcel and Victoria saw oranges and apples for the first time in her life. They were so strange that, when they were unpacked, she didn't know what they were.

Aged eight, she was put aboard the train alone for a four-day journey to Moscow. The train was seven hours late but she finally met her mother on the platform when she arrived in the Soviet capital.

The amazing thing was that Federova was *still* famous. She had spent, arguably, the best years of her life in prison – from the age of thirty-three until she was forty-one, exactly the same as the time Hamet spent in the war – but her films still played in all the Russian cinemas and she was recognised in the street or on a train. Officially, she was still despised – left out of important receptions, never allowed to go abroad, or to meet influential foreigners. Naturally, she detested the Soviet authorities for what they had done to her. Her flat on Gorky Street and all her possessions had been confiscated. On her release they should have been returned to her, but never were. In those days famous actors would get large flats to themselves, but that courtesy was never extended to Federova. She was expected to make do with a small room.

At first, when she was asked, Zoya told her daughter that her father was a Russian pilot who had been killed in the war. Then, perhaps to explain why she had been in prison, she sat Victoria down one evening and told her the truth.

'Do you have a photograph?' Victoria asked.

'Everything was taken from me when I was arrested, and never returned,' said her mother.

'Then how will I know what he looked like?'

Zoya smiled. 'Go and look in the mirror.'

Some time in the 1960s, Zoya and Victoria met a visitor from the United States, one Irina Kint, and told her their story. She promised to search for Roger Jackson Tait. It took her rather longer than it should have done, but in 1974 Victoria received an invitation from her father (now an admiral) to come and see him. When she applied for an exit visa she was at first told that she had as much chance of being granted one as of 'seeing my own ears'. Victoria therefore contacted the Moscow correspondents of the *New York Times* and the *Los Angeles Times* and told them her story.

Her mother was very worried by this and started hiding all their intimate possessions again in case she or her daughter should be imprisoned. But after about a year, Victoria was suddenly granted a visa and flew to the United States, courtesy of the *National Inquirer*, which paid her $10,000 for the excusive rights to cover her reunion with her father, in Florida. By this time, Victoria was twenty-eight.

Their meeting took place in 1974. Four years later Tait, who was already ill with cancer when he met his daughter, died. But Victoria had decided to stay in America, and she married and had a child. Zoya travelled to the United States three times between 1976 and her death.

This, then, is the extraordinary background to this singular woman. After Federova had been released from prison she was allowed to make more films, and now began to appear in comedies. During the 1970s she was again given a decent flat on Kutuzovsky Prospekt, which was a sort of protected enclave for Soviet elites of one kind or another.

Her death occurred between 2.30p.m. and 5p.m. She was shot by a

Belgian-made Zauer 38 (7.65 calibre) gun while she was sitting down talking to someone on the telephone. The telephone was found gripped hard in her hand when the body was discovered at 8.30 that evening. Scraps of paper, with telephone numbers on them, were lying on the table next to her. The door to her apartment had not been forced. Fingerprints other than hers were found on cups and saucers, on some Venetian glasses and on her coffee table. There were 2,400 roubles in a purse, as well as jewellery in a few boxes. There was no sign of a scuffle. The investigating authorities formed the view that Zoya Federova knew the person who had killed her and had willingly admitted him, or her, to the apartment.

A neighbour confirmed that she had heard loud music and running water in Federova's apartment shortly after one o'clock, lunchtime. She had knocked on the door but received no reply. The neighbour visited the flat a second time, between three and six that evening and, getting no reply again, put a note for Zoya under the door. But she was worried, and phoned Federova's nephew. He had a key, let himself in, and discovered the body.

Two other witnesses later testified that they had spoken to Federova on the telephone at 1.45 and between 2p.m. and 2.30 repectively. She must have died, therefore, between 2.30 and 8.30 though the pathologist concluded that she had been dead by five o'clock.

Immediately following her killing, two theories became current in the Soviet Union itself. Both had her being killed by some agent of the state. According to one theory, Federova had been allowed three visits to the United States to visit her daughter, Victoria. This was a lot in the days of the cold war and she was allowed to go, according to Russian sources, because the authorities believed that they 'owed' Federova for her years of wrongful imprisonment. However, she was allowed to visit the United States only on the understanding that she would not engage in any anti-Soviet propaganda, must give no interviews and generally keep a low profile, making the trips as a private individual. But in 1978 Victoria published a book in America, describing her and her mother's story. This was scarcely a low-profile act. In addition, Victoria had appeared in a film containing anti-Russian propaganda. In other words, on this theory Federova was felt to have broken her end of the bargain, and she was killed as a result.

On this analysis, Federova would have been killed by agents from Department 19, the emigration department of the KGB. An added gloss is that the special unit set up by the police to investigate her death suffered a strange fate. Three policemen were appointed but in early 1982, within the space of a month and a half, one committed suicide in mysterious circumstances, one died from cirrhosis of the liver, and the third accepted promotion in another area of Russia.

A second theory centred upon Federova's secret life in the clandestine art world. At the time her body was discovered, although many roubles were left on her, and some jewellery, the flat also contained some sixty empty jewellery boxes. It emerged that several neighbours were aware that, for a number of years, Federova had traded in antiques, gold and precious stones. In her address book, which was found with her, there were 2,032 phone numbers and 1,398 addresses, 971 of which were in Moscow and 427 in other towns. By Russian standards this was huge (and not only by Russian standards).

On this analysis, Federova had a long list of extremely well-heeled acquaintances who did business with her, trading art objects and jewellery, and when her request to visit her daughter in America for a fourth time had been turned down she had asked one of these acquaintances to intervene on her behalf. When that acquaintance had refused, Federova had threatened to expose him (or her) as someone who traded illegally in art. Neighbours had observed that Federova was frequently picked up from her flat by someone who was never seen but who arrived in a large black limousine, the type invariably used by high party officials. She would return late at night. Federova never admitted her neighbours to her apartment, conducting all business by shouting through the door. On this theory she had been killed by or on the orders of the big-wig she had threatened to blackmail.

A third theory involves Nureyev. The rest of this chapter has been put together using the KGB reports and comparing them with other details that have emerged in the thirteen years since Federova's death, some of which have appeared in Soviet *samizdat* periodicals, such as *Soversheno Sekretno* ('Top Secret'). This case has so fascinated Russians that a retired police officer, V.R. Kostenko, spent several years trying to get to the bottom of the mystery.

What seems clear is that, throughout the 1970s, Zoya Federova, who had retired from the movies by then, *had* become intimately involved in the smuggling of art and antiques out of Russia. This was a thriving business, since there was virtually no market inside the Soviet Union. Although churches had been disbanded, their decorations, including icons, were often simply left in vaults. Privately owned icons and other objects were hidden, since people were afraid to show evidence of religious feelings. At that time, there was no end to the cold war in sight and hard currency was welcome.

Federova was famous and much-loved, and had been done a great wrong by the state. From this, two things followed. She was a formidable woman and was not prepared to forgive the state. An article which appeared in 1992 in *Krasnozretz*, a periodical, gives a friend's account of Federova's bitterness at the way in which she had been treated. Second, there were a number of fans who would do anything for her, and these included people in official positions and in the national airline, Aeroflot, who helped her to smuggle things to the west.

There have been three waves of emigration from Soviet Russia: the White Russians after the revolution; after the Second World War; and in the 1970s. Many travelled to America, but not a few settled in Paris, as the White Russians did. Federova developed good links with the third-wave emigrants in France.

As the 1970s wore on, Federova developed a system whereby she would take possession of precious metals, jewellery and the smaller antiques at her flat in Kutuzovsky Prospekt. No one ever came to the flat – the antiques were brought in the black limousine. It was the driver she knew, not any big-wig in the back; they had originally got to know each other in the camps when she had been imprisoned. (There were so many of these camps, with so many people imprisoned, that for a while in the 1960s, 1970s and early 1980s, the ex-prisoners formed quite a community.)

Federova would photograph the objects and in the first instance send the photographs to the west, so that prospective buyers could choose what exactly they wanted. As time went by, her strong links with France appear to have been supplemented by equally firm bonds with the United States and Israel (indirect and difficult in the 1970s). The first contact with Nureyev was apparently made in August 1973, while he was dancing in Tel Aviv with Lynn Seymour in *Le Corsaire*.

Nureyev was interested in the art that Federova could offer, for two reasons. Firstly, for himself. He bought some icons, but also a number of larger pictures, especially portraits of Peter the Great, whom he admired. But, as time went by, Nureyev too began to trade in these smuggled art works in order to make money – not for himself, but to help various homosexual organisations. After his death, Rudolf was criticised by some gays for trying to hide his homosexuality from his public, and for not being more politically active in support of gay liberation. In fact, the KGB file claims that Nureyev supported two homosexual organisations: one (unnamed) group with headquarters in Nice, and a second, called LEEV, with headquarters in Los Angeles but whose president is Eugenia Debryanskaya, a Russian who once headed the Libertarian Party in Moscow. According to the file, Debryanskaya visited Nureyev in Paris in 1991 where he gave her $1.5 million to support LEEV. Hitherto, he had 'invested,' as the file puts it, FF 500,000 (£50,000) in the Nice-based group. Two Italian and two French names, of world-famous actresses and fashion designers, are also mentioned in the documents as secret supporters of this group.

According to the file, Federova organised the theft of objects from towns and villages all over the Soviet Union, using a man who now runs a kiosk in central Moscow, selling engravings. He would store the large objects, which she would sometimes collect in the black limousine. She kept all aspects of her organisation separate, and she kept the money she made in her flat. No hard currency was found with the body.

Beginning in 1979, Federova apparently began to outgrow Nureyev. That is to say, she found outlets who would take more art objects and pay more for them, and she preferred to deal with them. She offered Nureyev less and less. When he complained she threatened to expose his part in the traffic and advised him to accept a *fait accompli*. Here, the second theory given above, the 'blackmail' variant, joins up with this one. According to the file, Nureyev realised that his part in the illegal traffic of Russian art could always be divulged while Federova was alive, or she could always try to blackmail him. She was clearly unstable, in his view, and might go public at any time.

Again, according to the file, in early December 1981 Federova told several friends that she was expecting a guest from France on the tenth of the month. She mentioned no names but, according to these friends, the 10 December meeting did take place.

What went on in that meeting no one knows. Was a further rendezvous arranged for the following day? The compiler of the KGB file believes that it was and that two people, not one, attended the meeting. The KGB further believes that one of these individuals was American, the other Israeli, very possibly the person who first 'recruited' Nureyev to the Federova network in 1973. The KGB reaches this conclusion on the basis of a careful analysis of people who left the Soviet Union by plane in the wake of the killing. Contrary to what one might expect, the killer or killers did not murder Federova and then make a dash for it. In fact, he or they stayed in Moscow until January and then left quietly when the immediate fuss had died down. One flew back to the United States, the other to France and then on to Israel. Their actual identities were not made known.

On this scenario, the 'blackmail' element emerged via interrogation of the limousine driver, the man whom Federova had met in the camps and who now runs a kiosk in Moscow. She had apparently mentioned to him that someone was coming to see her from France and that he was an intermediary from Nureyev, who wanted to continue doing business with her.

And there it is. Two points in particular need to be discussed. First, as presented, there does not appear to be much of a motive here for Rudolf to take any drastic action *unless* the blackmail element forms a much stronger part of the story. It would appear that Federova was a forceful, even wilful woman and, in fact, the murder could be better understood if certain elements in the narrative are reversed. What if Rudolf, having got involved with Federova, had second thoughts, and wanted to disengage himself from their business association? If this hadn't suited Federova, she might have responded by threatening to expose him: not merely the fact that he was trafficking in smuggled art, which would surely have killed any chance of his ever seeing his mother again, but also his involvement with gay rights organisations, which would have spoiled his image, as he saw it. That would have provided a much stronger motive.

The second question concerns the sheer convenience of this story from the KGB's point of view. There is no question but that in Russia, in the immediate aftermath of the killing, many people thought it was the work of the KGB. How convenient for them now to put the blame on Nureyev, using forged documents that it is virtually impossible for a western writer to check, and 'clearing' their own name in the process. And Rudolf is not around to contradict their version.

Even this may not be all of the picture. There are those who believe that the murder of Zoya Federova is linked to the mysterious disappearance of the Paris-based art dealer, Garig Basmadjian, in Moscow in 1989. The KGB documents throw a new light on this, too.

Basmadjian was an Armenian, born in Jerusalem, who studied in Armenia, Israel and Moscow. He was a poet with at least a dozen works to his name. Having realised that there was no official or legal way to exhibit Russian art in the west, he took it upon himself to do so, travelling extensively in Russia in the 1970s to see what was available. According to his sister, Vartoshi, he traded in art that was brought out of Russia by foreign diplomats, correspondents, airline staff and so forth. To begin with he operated privately but in 1980 he opened a gallery in Paris.

There was no direct or overt link between Bazmadjian and Nureyev but a circle of artists formed around the Armenian's gallery, which became a focal point – even a sort of bank – for such exiled painters and sculptors as Rimas Bitchunas, Yaroslav Manukhin, Alexandre Vassiliev, Toomas Vint and Valentin Vorobiov. Nureyev certainly knew some of these artists, for example Vorobiov.

In July 1989 Bazmadjian was in Russia at the invitation of the Ministry of Culture. He was staying at the Rossia Hotel. On the twenty-ninth of the month he was met in the lobby of the hotel by two men who took him away in a car. He was never seen again.

Alexandre Gurov, head of the organised crime branch of the Moscow police, later said that his force knew the names of the criminals but that they were 'outside the USSR'. He did not say which country they were in or whether they were Russians or foreigners.

Bazmadjian's disappearance is tantalising. Was he the man who 'recruited' Rudolf to Federova's network in Israel? Was he the man who visited her on 10 December 1981, and perhaps the day after? Is that why he has disappeared? Was it revenge for his part in her death? Why should he have done Rudolf's dirty work for him? Did Rudolf pay him? Was the opening of Bazmadjian's Paris gallery in 1980, and his first sensational exhibition, in 1981, linked in any way to the timing of Federova's death later the same year? Had he taken over her business and was she now in the way?

One final coincidence. The KGB documents say that Nureyev moved some of his art around the world hidden in the costume and scenery cases of his own company. This company was started in 1974, a year after he is said to have been recruited in Israel and to have begun to do business with Federova. Federova's best-known film was called *Friends*. Rudolf's company was, of course, called 'Nureyev and Friends'.

CHAPTER TWENTY-ONE

The Scar of Passion's Knife

But when a later age has found us,
the climacteric of our life,
how sad the scar of passion's knife.

By the summer of 1983, awareness of AIDS was beginning to spread. In May, ABC's *20/20* programme broadcast its first story on the widening crisis. In June the *New York Times* at last put a story about the problem on its front page. And the Hothouse, San Francisco's legendary four-storey, 10,000-square-foot baths, which according to Leigh Rutledge, was 'devoted to the most outré forms of gay sexual expression, including bondage, discipline, water sports and fist-fucking,' closed its doors in the wake of growing concern over the spread of AIDS.

Tracy was distressed when Rudolf began suffering from night sweats, but not really surprised. He – Tracy – had followed the news about the disease in some detail, and was one of the very few homosexuals who had changed his behaviour immediately and had maintained a chaste lifestyle ever since. His behaviour could not have been more different from Rudolf's. At that stage, one of Rudolf's partners was Arthur Mitchell of the Dance Theatre of Harlem, who had also slept with Rock Hudson and Calvin Klein. When he was in New York, Rudolf used to frequent the St Mark's Baths, which billed itself as the world's largest bathhouse and where, in the early 1980s, homosexual orgies regularly took place. Tracy tried to dissuade Rudolf from going, but he wouldn't hear of it. In May 1983 the management put up signs to the effect that 'some' doctors believed that AIDS was sexually transmitted but Bruce Mailman, the proprietor of the baths, took the view that 'People can do what they want to, I have no right to direct their behaviour.' Robert had noticed the survey in the *New York Native* earlier in the year, which had shown that the sexual practice least likely to have changed was oral sex. Rudolf was typical here, too. One evening he picked up a hustler in Rounds, a gay bar. Later, back at the Dakota, Rudolf said to Tracy, 'Do you think I was at risk of AIDS from that guy? He wouldn't take his mouth off my dick.' Knowing Rudolf's habits, and that he was already having night sweats, Tracy's reply was succinct. 'What about *him* Rudolf?' he said. 'What about the risk to him?'

The problems that faced Rudolf at the Paris Opéra Ballet were formidable and did not only involve the huge company of dancers and their unique, and virtually inviolate status. There was also the repertoire, which was limited and somewhat run down. As Rudolf himself put it, they had a series of spectacles but only four real ballets. Although Roland Petit and Maurice Béjart were both distinguished French choreographers, neither had been associated with the Paris Opéra Ballet for any prolonged period, so there was no choreographic tradition in Paris like that of Ashton in London, Bournonville in Copenhagen or Balanchine in New York. Serge Lifar had created many ballets but these too had been allowed to lapse. A final problem was that Rudolf was only going to be in Paris for half a year. The contract that he had successfully negotiated with Jack Lang, the French Minister of Culture (who had really wanted Rudolf), had stipulated he work in Paris for 180 days a year, thus freeing him from any liability to pay French taxes; it also allowed him one new production a year and – this was a clever move on Rudolf's part – certain new physical facilities which would make life easier for all the dancers *and* improve the status of ballet *vis-à-vis* the opera. He was to dance in thirty to forty performances a year and only one out of four first nights.

Rudolf's very first day at the Opéra had hardly been a success. An official at the Ministry of Culture, Paul Paux, had resigned because, at a time of austerity for the rest of France, Rudolf had negotiated *three* salaries for himself – one as director, one as choreographer, and one as dancer. The figure was never revealed but the official regarded it as 'obscene'. Erik, who had recently been appointed artistic director of the National Ballet of Canada (generally regarded as 'a mess' since Rudolf left), rang from Toronto on the first day to wish Rudolf luck and ask him how it had gone. 'Not bad,' Rudolf had replied. 'I only got angry three times.'

But this apart, Rudolf made an excellent start at the Palais Garnier, as the home of the Paris Opéra Ballet was called. The Palais was memorably described by a French dancer, Patrick Dupond, as 'a hippo', a living object that is nine-tenths below the surface. It is also a small city of 3,000 souls, with its own bank, bistro, smell, and very much its own ways of doing things. *Etoiles*, for instance, receive their own dressing-rooms, unthinkable in many theatres.

Rudolf's first three productions were his own *Raymonda*, Pierre

Lacotte's *Marco Spada*, and Balanchine's *Le Bourgeois Gentilhomme*. Each of these had been created for him, but that was good box office. One piece of choreography was his (and it was a revived classic), one was French, and one was by the greatest choreographer of the day. In the first months of his helmsmanship, he also announced that there would soon be a new *Swan Lake*, a new *Don Quixote*, and Petit's ballet, *Phantom of the Opera*. He planned a modern evening, he said, with ballets by Glen Tetley, Rudi van Dantzig and Karol Armitage, the first of a long-term series of programmes which would give the French public a complete view of the development of contemporary ballet. Finally, a trip to the United States was in the works and a number of guest artists would be invited.

By and large, this balanced and intelligent programme went down very well with the domestic critics and with the foreign press, who took a particular interest in Rudolf. Anna Kisselgoff, in the *New York Times*, said that Rudolf was having to 'force feed' the French but she approved. She observed that dance in France was 'in good shape', remarking that the country had eighty-five companies that received some sort of subsidy, and twelve major ones (including Paris, Marseilles and Nancy). There was an anti-Rudolf claque in Paris that waxed and waned in size and noise level throughout his time there, but it never got out of hand.

Rudolf decided to keep the organisation of the dancers created by Rosella Hightower. They were divided into three: a group that danced the traditional roles and also performed at ballets contained in operas; a group of young dancers; and an experimental group, who tried out all the new choreography. But one of Rudolf's main headaches would always be the central fact of life at the Palais Garnier, that out of 142 dancers, less than half that number danced regularly. There was a lot of expensive dead wood.

An early sign of trouble was Roland Petit's announcement that he was withdrawing all his ballets from the Paris Opéra Ballet because Rudolf had insisted on introducing his own steps into *Notre Dame de Paris* while guesting with Petit's own Ballet National de Marseilles the previous year. The old charge of being cavalier with the choreography recurred. But *Phantom of the Opera* was left on the schedule for the time being.

Despite this, Rudolf's first productions for the Paris Opéra Ballet, *Raymonda*, in November 1983, *Don Quixote*, the following month, *Phaedra's Dream* (by Martha Graham), in January 1984, and *Harlequin*, *Le Bourgeois Gentilhomme*, *The Tempest* and *La Bayadère*, all in March, succeeded gloriously. The French press applauded loudly, both the extension of the repertoire and the standard of dancing, which saw a number of stars begin to emerge – Manuel Legris, Laurent Hilaire, Charles Jude, Isabelle Guérin and Elisabeth Platel, among others.

Raymonda especially was a clever choice, with three big leading roles, twelve soloists, and several dances for the *corps*. Rudolf also brought Yvette Chauviré out of retirement to help with the production and dance the character role of the countess. As she was the greatest French dancer of the century, this was an act of respect on Rudolf's part that the French appreciated. *The Times* said that the Paris company was now the biggest and the best in the world.

Nothing epitomised the new mood in France, which Rudolf undoubtedly helped to engender, more than the reception given to Martha Graham in February 1984. She was ninety that year. Hers was the first American dance company to appear on stage at the Paris Opéra Ballet and, thirty years earlier, her works had been roundly booed by French balletomanes when she had appeared at another Paris theatre. This time the chic Parisians lavished applause on her and her dancers (Rudolf played a near-naked Hippolyte in *Phaedra's Dream*), Jack Lang awarded her the Légion d'honneur on the stage of the theatre after the performance, and a gala supper was held in the theatre's vaulted promenade afterwards. Halston was there, as were Marc Bohan and a whole clutch of Rothschilds. A new glitter was already attached to the ballet. And, with the recognition of Martha Graham, a new set of aesthetic values.

Parisian luminaries such as Pierre Cardin and Sonia Rykiel lavished praise on Rudolf, who that month announced that the season for 1984 would contain thirteen different programmes, more than twice as many as the year before, including new works by Merce Cunningham, William Forsythe and Karol Armitage. *Ballet News* wrote that 'Not since the age of Lifar have the prospects in Paris seemed so bright.'

The only problem was the old problem. Rudolf might now be an artistic director, a choreographer, an administrator, and a teacher but he was still, first and foremost, a dancer. On 22 March *Le Figaro* predicted that 'the curtain might not go up tonight'. Rudolf, it said, had provoked 'la cholère' among the *étoiles*, the stars of the Paris Opéra Ballet. His sin, of course, was wanting to dance all the first nights. He was doubly culpable, in the eyes of the dancers, because he had promised *not* to do this when he took over at the Palais Garnier, and the arrangement had been specifically agreed after the previous dispute, at the time the US tour had been called off. Once again, the dancers said this was nothing personal but Rudolf had danced three out of four first nights, in defiance of the contract. He climbed down.

When his six months in Paris came to an end that year he headed for New York and Toronto. In New York he appeared in the gala to celebrate the Met's centenary, a nostalgic evening despite the cost of the tickets – around £1,000 – where Margot, Frederick Ashton, Lynn Seymour, Erik Bruhn and Carla Fracci also appeared. (The evening was produced by Jane Herrman.) He went to Toronto to see how Erik was doing, and danced with Karen Kain in *Sleeping Beauty*. The critics found him 'well-preserved for forty-six', 'a consummate technician *and* athlete,' and 'at peak fitness'. Little did they know.

Rudolf had not been unduly worried when he started to have nightsweats. Although stories were beginning to appear in the mainstream press about AIDS, they were not as numerous or as alarming as they might have been. As was later revealed, the editors of newspapers and television programmes, who were more or less prejudiced against homosexuals, refused at first to acknowledge the seriousness of the situation. What the cost of this was, in lives lost, is anyone's guess now, but in any case many gays themselves did not want to know the full truth, partly for fear that they themselves might already be infected, and partly because they were loath to abandon the so recently acquired freedoms in the sexual sphere.

A third reason arose out of the fact that, at that time, there was no test for AIDS.

But then two things happened within the space of a few weeks in the spring of 1984 which finally got through to Rudolf. On 23 April 1984, Margaret Heckler, the US Secretary of Health and Human Services, announced that the 'probable' cause of AIDS had been discovered. It was, she said, a transmissible virus that had recently been isolated by US and French researchers. There is no doubt that this had a major effect on many gays who, hitherto, had denied the link between sex and AIDS. For many the exchange of bodily fluid, semen especially, had been the supreme erotic act. Now they could not hide from the risks it brought with it. For Rudolf, this public news conference was soon followed by a private communication that affected him even more directly. On 27 May, a month after Secretary Heckler's dramatic news conference, Rock Hudson visited a dermatologist in Beverly Hills, to consult him about a small but persistent growth on the back of his neck. The doctor told him the growth was Kaposi's sarcoma and, a few days later, confirmed that the film star had AIDS.

When he found out about Hudson, with whom he knew he had shared a partner, and now that the scientists had announced they had isolated the cause of the dreaded disease, Rudolf was finally provoked into action. A year earlier, at the beginning of 1983, in Bordeaux on that tour of France with the Ballet Théâtre de Nancy, he had been ill. Through his friend Charles Murdland, a director of London's Festival Ballet, he had been introduced to a French doctor, Michel Canesi, who had treated him successfully. Now, towards the end of 1984, he contacted Canesi again.

Being French, Canesi had certain advantages for Rudolf. In the first place, of course, he was living in Paris, directing the Paris Opéra Ballet. Second, as the Heckler statement had made clear, the French were just as advanced in this branch of medicine as the Americans. Third – and possibly the most important advantage in Rudolf's mind – he wanted to steer clear of American doctors. Should the worst prove to be true, then if the news got out it could bar him from entry to the US, which had to be avoided at all costs.

Canesi, a thirty-year-old dermatologist and venerealogist, was well connected in Paris and well informed. Nureyev told him that he didn't feel right, though he was no more specific about his symptoms than that. To Canesi Nureyev too appeared well informed about the illness, and was clearly worried. Canesi referred him to Dr Willy Rosenbaum, perhaps the most experienced AIDS doctor in France and one of the team at the Pasteur Institute who had been called in by Luc Montagnier when the virus had first been isolated. Rosenbaum worked at Le Salpetrière Hospital.

An official test for AIDS was not licensed until 2 March 1985, but of course for an experienced specialist like Rosenbaum, acting for a celebrity, it was not especially difficult to check Nureyev's blood for what became known as HIV. However, Le Salpetrière was the only place in France where this type of medical examination could take place and it was inevitable that Nureyev was recognised on one of his visits to the clinic. In no time at all the news was all over the Paris gay community that Rudolf Nureyev had AIDS – even before he was given the results of his test. It is a measure of the times, and the Anglo-Saxon self-preoccupation, that this news did not immediately spread to a wider public.

After a few days, Rosenbaum gave Canesi the results of the blood test and it fell to the dermatologist to tell Rudolf the grim truth – that yes, he was HIV positive. Now, although this was scarcely good news, and despite the fact that new statistics were being released all the time, Canesi told Rudolf that, to the best of his knowledge, only 10 per cent of people who tested positive actually became sick. This was high enough in any rational sense, but, looked at another way, Rudolf did have a 90 per cent chance of escaping AIDS.

Rudolf now insisted that Tracy take the test in Paris, which he did. When he tested negative, Rudolf could see, at least in theory, that Tracy had been right and he had been wrong, that a man's lifestyle had a great deal to do with AIDS. At Rosenbaum's suggestion, he agreed to undergo treatment with HPA-23, an experimental drug that Rock Hudson was using.

HPA-23, or antimoniotungstate to give the drug its scientific name, had been developed in France in the early 1970s by Dr Jean-Claude Chermann, one of the team of four doctors who had been present with Willy Rosenbaum when Luc Montagnier had announced the discovery of the virus which caused AIDS. During research with mice, Chermann had found that HPA-23 was successful in preventing the spread of the leukaemia virus. He thought it was worth trying with AIDS patients who, in any case, had nothing to lose. In late 1983 sixty patients had been treated with the drug as an experiment, by means of one or another of two dosage regimes. Either they received relatively massive doses over a short period (of a few weeks), or much longer treatment using much smaller doses. Rudolf was given the former regime.

In early 1984 Rosenbaum's first results looked promising. HPA-23 appeared successful in inhibiting the reproduction of the AIDS virus in humans. The most striking case was that of an AIDS-stricken haemophiliac who had rebounded dramatically after taking HPA-23. Hudson had heard about the drug in San Francisco in August 1983 and had arrived in Paris in September, the month when Rudolf took over at the Palais Garnier. Hudson too was given the massive-dose regime, since he had to get back to America to star in a new series of *Dynasty*. He left Paris believing he was cured of AIDS.

Rudolf received injections at the Salpetrière Hospital to begin with. Then Canesi went with him to Spain with the Ballet Théâtre du Nancy, to Florence, with Sylvie Giullem, and to Germany. Rudolf responded well, so that Canesi cut down the number of injections from one a day to three or four a week. After that, treatment had to be discontinued because the drug itself became too toxic. During that time, Rudolf neither gained nor lost weight and this appears typical of the way HPA-23 worked, if work it did. If it had any effect at all, it worked by preventing the AIDS virus from reproducing. This meant it wasn't a cure as such, but was a way of preventing the disease getting worse.

In Rudolf's case this seemed to be enough, at least at the time. As a dancer he was very fit, as the Toronto critics observed, and he was blessed with fantastic willpower. Like Hudson, after his treatment with HPA-23, Rudolf believed that he was cured.

Back in Paris in late summer 1984, the pressure on Rudolf from the dancers continued. In an interview, the dancer Patrick Dupond described him as a *monstre sacré*, perhaps the only one, he said, now that Callas was dead. He acknowledged Rudolf's accomplishments: that he was a good teacher, that the new studio, the biggest in Europe, the new rehearsal rooms and the new cafeteria had all forced the French government to appreciate and value its dancers. But, he said baldly, Rudolf was dancing too much. And he let it be known that if Rudolf didn't change his behaviour on that score, another strike was threatened.

But Rudolf was a passionate man, and a star. He found it extremely difficult to change his behaviour in any aspect of his life, private or public. No sooner had he returned to Paris and settled in at the quai Voltaire, than he was involved in yet another fight. This time he was teaching a class when Michel Renault, the man giving the following class, entered the room. Renault said nothing until the class had run five minutes over. Then he drew Rudolf's attention to the fact. Rudolf asked for another five minutes. After a further fifteen minutes, Renault simply began giving his class without waiting for Rudolf to stop. Rudolf asked him what he was doing. Renault explained the particular movement he was teaching.

'But that's *shit!*' growled Rudolf.

'Nevertheless, I have been doing it for nineteen years. That's how long I've been a star in this company – '

He got no further. Rudolf cracked him across the jaw and stormed out.

This, of course, was just the episode that the anti-Rudolf claque had been waiting for, especially as an X-ray examination of Renault's jaw showed a slight fracture. He announced that he was suing the company and called for Rudolf to resign or be fired. His case was taken up by the dancers' union, whose chief official released a pompous statement in which he said that the administration of the Paris Opéra Ballet had 'signed a blank cheque when they hired Rudolf Nureyev. Now, they don't have the courage to lance this abscess. We have let a dictator into the Palais Garnier.' He mixed metaphors as well as Rudolf danced. Or punched.

Before this bout was settled, Rudolf was embroiled in another (they always seemed to go in batches) when he was in Edinburgh, to dance *Le Bourgeois Gentilhomme* with Monique Loudières at the Playhouse Theatre. On this occasion the management had allowed an artist, Emilio Coia, backstage to sketch him. Coia was a distinguished portraitist, who had previously sketched Max Beerbohm, G.K. Chesterton, Aldous Huxley and Dmitri Shostakovich, all without trouble. No matter. Rudolf hadn't been warned and when he saw what was happening he exploded, marched up to the man, snatched the drawings from his hand, and tore them up. More front-page headlines.

Despite what the Canadian critics said, the number of bad reviews which Rudolf was beginning to attract for his dancing was growing. At one performance in New York that August, when he was dancing *Apollo* and the *Flower Festival pas de deux* with Nureyev and Friends, the *Wall Street Journal* said he was 'numbingly inept, physically inelastic'. Another critic said his *plié* had gone, and without that he had no jump.

As the winter of 1984–85 approached, new opportunities still opened up for Rudolf. There was, for instance, his first tour of India, Korea and Japan. While he was in Japan he had his blood changed. This was a technique one British pop star was rumoured to have tried, to overcome one of his addictions. Rudolf mentioned *his* transfusions to only a very few close friends.

But in Paris, the glitter was wearing off. Jane Herrman cancelled the tour that had been planned for the following spring. Rudolf and his administrative team had been unable to agree a repertoire that she liked, and without a repertoire she was unable to make a proper budget. Also, the French government had unhelpfully refused to pay for the company's travel to America, so Herrman thought that the Met could lose as much as $500,000 on the arrangement. Rudolf's revival of Serge Lifar's *Icare* had not gone down well, either. This had been a noble attempt to give back to the company some of its own history, but the production had looked dated and had provoked a storm. The *soirées* he had devoted to the music of Stravinsky and Stockhausen had been even less well received and the claque that always sat at the back of the stalls and booed on first nights had found a new voice. The Renault affair had still not been settled when Rudolf threw a bottle at one of the costumiers and now *they* took industrial action, refusing to work for him.

But the big production that autumn was a new version of *Swan Lake*. Ultimately, Rudolf's standing would depend on that. The production opened three days before Christmas and 'le tout Paris' stepped out for the occasion. Marie-Hélène de Rothschild chaired the charity dinner after the performance, Princess Thurn und Taxis, the 'punk Princess', wore her spiky hair and spiky heels, and 780 glitterati ballet-lovers sat down to a dinner decorated with swans made of ice and accompanied by Russian violinists. Part of the Palais Garnier was transformed into a discothèque for the evening. As for the performance, it was given mixed reviews. Marie-Hélène said she 'suffered' because Rudolf was not performing. The company itself had been in two minds about abandoning its traditional version, by Vladimir Bourmeister, and a strike had been called but was faced down by Rudolf. However, the main criticism was that his choreography was generally felt to have been sabotaged by the designs of Ezio Frigerio, who had given the stage austere white walls and transformed the lake into an aquarium. Even Rudolf thought that his interpretation might be too cold, too psychological. The one undoubted success was the emergence of a new star that night, in the form of a tall, willowy, red-headed ballerina, called Sylvie Guillem. The French have a rather touching and very dramatic tradition, in which the artistic director of the company – in this case, Rudolf – appears on stage after the performance from time to time and announces to the assembled company, and to the audience, that such and such a dancer has been promoted. On that December evening, Rudolf made just such a dramatic announcement about Guillem. She was nineteen.

In the New Year, after the company had returned from a tour of India, the Renault affair was finally settled – he received around £6,000 in compensation. Anna Kisselgoff, however, raised a more substantial issue, asking whether the ballet boom, now twenty-five years old (and thus coinciding with Rudolf's arrival in the west) was at last beginning to wane. Kisselgoff paid tribute to Rudolf's unique influence on this boom, and noted that 54 million people in the United States had been to a ballet performance in 1984. But she detected a change. In an age of television, people went to the theatre *for* theatre, and modern and avant-garde dance did not give them that, she said. The death of Hurok had removed one very theatrical person from the scene, who had not really been replaced by the Met's new arrangement, and the death of Balanchine had removed perhaps the one man who could keep modern dance alive. And of course, there had been no sensational defections since 1974, more than a decade earlier . . .

It was a prescient article. Although Kisselgoff didn't make much of it, a number of critics in London at exactly the same time observed that standards were again falling at the Royal Ballet. Both the *Guardian* and the *Evening Standard* devoted several articles to this theme. The glitter had gone, they said, the stars had vanished, the centre of gravity had moved elsewhere, to Paris. Norman Morrice, chiefly, was blamed. Rudolf must have been grimly pleased.

He was less pleased at losing two new ballets that spring, when first David Bintley and then Rudi van Dantzig pulled out of agreements to produce new works for Paris. Both cited the difficulties of working with either the French dancers or the French musicians. The rank and file had safe jobs, and their union power was paramount.

Rudolf was even more annoyed when, in early 1985, rumours began to circulate, in New York, that he had AIDS. He was at work on his new ballet, *Washington Square*, and couldn't really spend as much time as he wanted crushing the rumours. But at least they surfaced via a sympathetic outlet, namely Clive Barnes, in the *New York Post*. Barnes wrote that, for some months, '*chic* New Yorkers' and people in the ballet subculture had been speculating on Rudolf's imminent death. He noted that, of late, Rudolf had missed one or two performances, including one of *Giselle* which had been successfully taken over at the last minute by none other than Baryshnikov. Rudolf had also been off colour earlier in 1985, when his illness had been reported, variously, as mononucleosis and bronchitis. Barnes also added: 'Nureyev-watchers cannot have failed to notice that for the first time in more than twenty years, this summer Nureyev is not making a single appearance in New York.' Barnes therefore announced that he had been to see Rudolf, in Miami – and could confirm that the rumours were wrong. Rudolf, he admitted, had been suffering 'mild bronchitis' but was otherwise 'alive and well' and 'enthusiastically fit'.

It says a lot for Rudolf's willpower, and the loyalty of those around him, that Barnes's investigation (which was really an interview) uncovered so little.

Washington Square premièred on 7 June 1985. In theory it was a good choice, an American story by an American author who had become a naturalised European (Henry James). There were, therefore, elements that would appeal on both sides of the Atlantic – and Rudolf already had plans to take the Paris company to America in 1986. There were also biographical elements. James, like Rudolf, was an exile. And the story concerns an overbearing father who, in trying to blunt his daughter's feelings for an unwelcome suitor, succeeds only in destroying her feelings for him. The production should have blazed with all Rudolf's intelligence and passion.

Unfortunately, many found it tedious, a slight tale inflated to one hour and ten minutes of boredom. On the first night it was booed, with the anti-Rudolf claque in fine voice. The Sloper residence (the Slopers are the main family in the story) was likened to the Bank of England, and Charles Ives's music was likened to American folk music (this was not intended as a compliment). Nor was the production helped by the designs, which divided the set in two so completely that many people could not see the entire stage. One wag called out 'This is the *demi-opera*!' It was the second production in which Rudolf had been let down by the designs. Nonetheless, at the party after the first night, at a new bistrot called L'aurent, Rudolf still ate 'a million' oysters. What did the critics know? Who remembered the critics?

In the autumn of 1985 Rudolf was in Paris less than he had been the previous year. He still loved to travel; he still filled houses. In Cardiff they even sold seats without a full view of the stage, such was the demand. They didn't mind the demi-ballet in Wales. But the complaints continued, too. In Manchester, a Cheshire couple, who had been fans for years, they said, reported him and the Ballet Théâtre de Nancy to the British Trading Standards office, because he had been billed to 'dance' and, they said, he was on stage for thirty-two minutes yet his feet never left the ground. They wanted their £33 back. They didn't get it and no doubt their complaint was in part frivolous, but Rudolf's dancing now began to divide his friends and fans. There were still those who followed him everywhere but there were also those, like Joan Thring and Sergio Stefanschi, who stopped going to see him. Thring had such fond memories of him at his best – she says she feels sorry for people who never saw Margot and Rudolf dance together – that she couldn't bear his dancing now. Or the way he combed his hair forward to hide the fact that he was receding.

After the Manchester engagement, and before he reached London, Rudolf heard that Rock Hudson had died at his home in Los Angeles. The actor was fifty-nine. When mortuary staff arrived to remove the body, they found more than a hundred journalists outside the house. The following day Mario Cuomo, Governor of New York, announced that he was considering closing all gay bathhouses under his jurisdiction.

Nineteen-eighty-six started well. Rudolf was able to announce that the Paris Opéra ballet *would* tour North America that year; the Rotonde Lifar, a new rehearsal room, was opened by Jack Lang in February, amply indicating the improved status of the ballet at the Palais Garnier; and, while the company was in New York, there would be a joint gala between American Ballet Theatre and the Paris Opéra Ballet at which Rudolf and Baryshnikov would dance together in the third act of *Raymonda*. Whatever Kisselgoff might say, Rudolf was still thinking of ways to keep the ballet boom going.

Then two bombshells landed in his lap. The first was a vitriolic attack on him by Maurice Béjart. This came about in a curious way. One night, after a performance of one of his ballets, Béjart had stepped out on to the stage in Paris and promoted to *étoile* status Manuel Legris and Eric Vu An, a Vietnamese dancer. This had immediately been rescinded by Rudolf. In this case, Rudolf was right because such promotions always had to be discussed in advance between the choreographer, artistic director and management, and anyway since a rise in salary was automatic, the overall budget and total number of *étoiles* always had to be considered. Béjart, however, claimed that he had discussed the matter with Rudolf, and called the director a liar. He said he had been deceived by Rudolf. Two nights later Béjart went on television and spoke darkly about 'a figure that haunts the corridors of the opera with sunken cheeks and a leather cap . . . I do not need to tell you who I mean.' He claimed that Rudolf had been responsible for a decline in standards at the Paris Opéra, and he called on him to resign. Nureyev was, he said, in a phrase used before, an intruder.

Rudolf played it down. The management stood by him. In fact, they said it should not be necessary to stand by him, since he was the director and had acted well within his rights. Still, they felt obliged to point out that, as it seemed to them, Béjart was going through 'a psychologically difficult period where he takes his wishes for reality and from which we hope he will recover quickly'. No one bitches better than the French.

Béjart didn't recover quickly. He forbade Rudolf to dance '*Songs of a Wayfarer*,' which had been specifically created for him. He did let the Paris Opéra Ballet keep *Arepo* (opera spelled backwards), mainly it was thought because this had been received very well in Paris at the time *Washington Square* had been scorned. However, this piece had been turned down for the American tour, so relations between the two men were scarcely at their best.

There may have been more to this incident than met the eye. Among the French press, *Le Figaro* had always been Rudolf's leading critic and, following the dismal reviews of *Washington Square*, when *Arepo* had been so favoured, the paper had been running a campaign to replace Rudolf with Béjart when the former's three-year contract with the Paris Opéra Ballet came up for renewal in 1986. Béjart's attack may, therefore, have been part of this campaign. In any event, it was followed by a long letter, splashed across half a page of *Le Figaro*, from Béjart and Petit, arguing that star dancers were quite the wrong people to run major ballet companies. Since Anthony Dowell had just taken over at Covent Garden, Erik Bruhn in Toronto, and Peter Martins at the New York City Ballet, Rudolf was in good company and Béjart's campaign began to look spiteful and silly.

The second blow, which occurred right in the middle of the Béjart fracas, was the death of Erik. The last phase of his illness happened very quickly, in a matter of weeks. Erik was always a heavy smoker and the official cause of his death was given as lung cancer. However, when he was in Toronto he lived with a much younger, Greek-born dancer called Constantine Patsalas, who was to die a few years later from AIDS. Many people, in the ballet world and in Toronto, are convinced that Erik too died of AIDS.

In his last days, Rudolf flew to Toronto. As Erik had grown older, Linda Mabeduke had seen him grow darker and bitter. One evening, they had all been out for dinner when Erik had suddenly turned on Linda – a very gentle, rather innocent woman – and said, 'This company [the National Ballet of Canada] is going to destroy me – but I'll take you all with me.' He had then begun boasting about the money he had made in his life, and the property he had. This had gone on at such length that Rudolf was finally forced to respond. He held up two fingers, and said, 'Two Dakotas, everything you own.' Erik had been humbled. Curiously, in the light of this, while Erik was ill, he made sure that Linda Mabeduke was kept fully informed. They had never been especially close so this was an odd move – unless Erik was hoping Linda would relay the news to Rudolf. In his last days he wanted the company of his old partner.

But Rudolf did not arrive in Toronto for a fight. He visited Erik and later told Linda that Erik was already too far gone mentally for there to be much conversation. At one point, he had tried to get out of bed, thinking he had to go to the theatre. But for most of Rudolf's visit, he just held his former lover. For hours, he just held him. Later that evening, when he had dinner with Linda Mabeduke and her husband, Bill, Rudolf told them what had happened. And then he said, 'You know, I would have been Erik's *dresser*!'

Next morning Bruhn went into a coma. He died later that day.

This sadness would never be fully extinguished for Rudolf. He did, however, have the immense satisfaction of seeing the Paris Opéra Ballet rapturously received that July, at the Met, in New York. They danced *Swan Lake*, *Raymonda* and *Washington Square*, during the course of which Patrick Bart and Sylvie Guillem were acclaimed as real stars in the mould, dare it be said, of Fonteyn and Nureyev. In a nice *coup de théâtre*, Rudolf stepped out after the performance one evening and declared that Manuel Legris was being promoted to *étoile*. Béjart had been humbled. So too was the Royal Ballet, criticised yet again for low standards in the British press, even as Rudolf enjoyed this latest triumph. After New York his next three years in Paris were assured.

*   *   *

Rudolf was now forty-eight and doors were opening and closing at more or less the same rate. In September Claire Motte died. Coming so soon after the death of Erik, it highlighted Rudolf's own mortality and brought him closer to Claire's widower, Mario Bois. Bois, a music publisher, now took over as the agent for Rudolf's choreographic rights.

But the following month saw the première of *Cinderella*. Rudolf chose to set this ballet in Hollywood and it was therefore a high-risk project. The sets included blow-up cardboard photographs of Betty Grable, the size of a skyscraper, wearing high heels and a bathing costume, of King Kong, the Keystone Cops, and much else. Given the failures with his previous sets, this was also a risk. In fact, *Cinderella* was Rudolf's greatest succers yet, universally acclaimed in all departments. Even *Le Figaro* was forced to admit that 'triumph' was not too strong a word.

Cinderella premièred on 24 October and played for about three weeks on the first stint. In the winter Rudolf had a tour in North America with his 'Friends' company and an English tour with English National Ballet and the Northern Ballet. He was still as busy as ever, despite his age and (still secret) illness though, except for the Paris Opéra Ballet, he was playing in smaller towns – Canterbury and Sheffield in Britain, Hamilton in Canada, Danville, Kentucky in the United States. But the (smaller) houses were still full.

Like everyone else, Rudolf had been aware for some time that circumstances were changing in the Soviet Union. Mikhail Gorbachev had followed Andropov and Chernenko to power in March 1985 and the twin policies of *glasnost* and *perestroika* got into their stride the following year. In early 1987 Nureyev was asked by a reporter if he would like to go back to dance in the Soviet Union and he replied that he would if Gorbachev himself sent out the invitation. He let it be known at the same time that as recently as 1983 the Russians had tried to have his appointment as artistic director of the Paris Opéra Ballet overturned, but Mitterand himself had lent his support to Jack Lang.

It was thus something of a snub when he heard, only days later, that the Soviet government had invited Makarova and Baryshnikov to dance at the Bolshoi, but not him. As Rudolf was quick to point out, Baryshnikov had actually made an anti-Soviet film, *White Nights*, so he could only conclude that the invitation had to do with politics: the Soviet Union must be playing 'footsie', as he put it, with the United States. France and/or Austria had to take a back seat.

In March 1987 he spent his forty-ninth birthday in Panama, where he was on a tour with the 'Friends', travelling between Miami and California (and still not overflying Cuba). While he was there, he saw Margot, who took him to meet General Noriega. Rudolf was bewildered. It was like her friendship with Imelda Marcos – the old love of rogues reasserting itself. She and Tito had known Noriega for years. He – the general –

had liked their fame and in 1983 had given her a flashy birthday party. A year later Tito would try again to stand as a deputy, on a platform sympathetic to Noriega.

On that visit Rudolf realised just how much of a drain Tito could be on Margot's resources. When they travelled, to New York say, he thought nothing of hiring a car and muscular help to take him swimming at the Athletic Club. An afternoon like that could easily cost $600 or $700. Margot suffered in other ways, too. Because one of their male servants had to come into the bedroom three or four times a night to turn Tito, she could never undress properly. Rudolf had at one time considered offering her the East Sheen house but Joan Thring had dissuaded him, saying it was too big and too far out of central London for Margot at her age. But he reassured Margot, saying that whatever *she* needed in the way of medical or other financial help, he would be only too happy to help. But he wasn't keen to waste anything on Tito. He was also bitterly disappointed that Margot had done nothing about his birthday. Perhaps she was just too old now.

He then flew on to California where, as well as packing the 6,500-seat Shrine Auditorium, he gave away his friend Natasha Harley's daughter, at her wedding to Reza Badiyi, the director of *Falcon Crest*, the TV soap that starred Jayne Wyman. He insisted to an interviewer that he would live to be seventy.

This may not have been wise, for now the AIDS rumours started again. On that tour the 'Friends' played Detroit, where a reporter asked if it was true that a Chicago sponsor had withdrawn his support for Rudolf because he had AIDS. Rudolf's temper ignited. 'No, it is *not* true!' he hissed. 'Don't harp. I'm alive, I'm very well, I don't have AIDS. Now it is the fashion to have AIDS,' he said bitterly. 'If there are no dogs barking at you, you aren't worth anything.' *Detroit News* ran the interview under the headline, FORTRESS NUREYEV.

In truth, he was very worried though his lifestyle was not much changed. The drug AZT was just beginning to be used in France but Canesi didn't want to give it to him, because he was worried that the side-effects would hamper Rudolf's dancing. But Rudolf insisted, despite knowing that high doses of AZT could be dangerous. He didn't take it regularly, however, just when he felt like it. As Canesi put it, 'He went off with tons of drugs and when I went to see him I found unused packets all over the place.'

AZT is a primitive drug and very toxic but at that stage it appeared to work, again by extending the incubation period between infection and the onset of full-blown AIDS. Governments on both sides of the Atlantic were worried enough about the epidemic by now to fund major research projects.

If Rudolf had a bad day, he made light of it. 'If I were in Russia now,' he told Jack Lanchbery on one occasion, my mother would rub goose grease on my chest and put me to bed. But in retrospect several people recall a slight change in Rudolf's manner which dated from then. On leaving a party, or the theatre, or for the airport, he no longer said 'Goodbye' or 'Au Revoir'. He said 'Stay well, or 'Be well.'

5 May, 1987. San Francisco's last gay bathhouse, the 21st Street Baths, closed its doors.

9 May. Robert Jacobson, editor of *Ballet News*, the magazine which had consistently championed Rudolf and all that he had done for dancing, died of AIDS, aged forty-six.

On 16 June, the Paris Opéra Ballet opened at the Metropolitan Opera House in New York with *Cinderella*. Every evening was a sell-out and both Kisselgoff and Barnes were enthusiastic in their praises. In fact, said Barnes, Rudolf had taken the Paris Opéra Ballet to new heights and it had now taken over from the Bolshoi and the Royal Ballet as the best company in the world. It escaped no one's attention that in the 1960s the Royal Ballet had toured North America, to great acclaim. In the 1970s it had been the turn of the National Ballet of Canada, and in the 1980s it was now the Paris Opéra Ballet. What did those three companies have in common? The answer was obvious. What an opportunity had been missed in London.

2 July. Michael Bennett, director, choreographer and producer of the 1975 Broadway hit musical, *A Chorus Line*, died, of AIDS, aged forty-four.

In October 1987 Rudolf danced again with Baryshnikov, in *Appalachian Spring*, at a gala for Martha Graham who was 93. Maya Plisetskaya was there that night, too, aged sixty-one. So many of her performances had been disrupted by Rudolf that her very presence meant that the world was changing. Rudolf had been trying to get Graham to let him stage *Appalachian Spring* in Paris for years but she had always refused. It was her favourite ballet, which she had created for herself and her husband, and Aaron Copland had written the music especially for her. She didn't think it suited the French. Rudolf may have been unwilling to accept her arguments, for it seems that he overstepped the mark that night, at the dinner after the performance, at the Pierre Hotel. It was attended by Jessye Norman, Judy Peabody, Jerome Robbins and Alice Tully, among others. To begin with, Rudolf was seated between Graham and Plisetskaya but after a while Graham moved. She conceded afterwards that, at dinner, Rudolf had been offensive to her but that wasn't why she moved, she said. At her dinners she always took care to sit next to several of the guests as the meal progressed. But Rudolf obviously felt strongly that night for after Graham had moved, he took offence and directed his aggression at Ron Protas, Graham's associate director. He shouted at Protas that he was an 'ungrateful hypocrite' and proceeded to pour a glass of water over Protas' head. The 'hypocrite' remark was held to be a reference to the Graham company's refusal to grant him *Appalachian Spring*, despite the fact that he had often danced for them without charging a fee. Anyway, after the water-throwing instance, Rudolf swept up Tracy, Jessye Norman and Judy Peabody and left the dinner. After that, of course, he was never going to get *Appalachian Spring*.

Meanwhile, the decline of the ballet boom, so long predicted, did not appear to have materialised; new and very unusual areas were being opened up to the pleasures of dance. At the beginning of November it was announced that Rudolf would dance at Caesars' Palace in Las Vegas later in the year. There had been six months of difficult negotiations to fit in the engagement, which finally involved Rudolf and other members of the Paris Opéra Ballet flying by Concorde to America, to dance at nine in the evening in front of 700 specially invited 'high rollers'. What other dancer, except perhaps Nijinsky, would ever have been given such unusual recognition?

In the summer he had been asked whether he still wanted to see his mother. He had replied that he had tried many times but that Gorbachev, like all the others before him, had refused to help. 'I'm not Jewish,' Rudolf said. 'So there is no political advantage in inviting me.' He had just heard from his friend Jamie Wyeth that a portrait of Rudolf, based on the sketches that Monique van Vooren had seen on the evening of their joint birthday party at the Iranian embassy all those years ago, had been withdrawn from an exhibition of Wyeth's works, which was touring Moscow and Leningrad. Makarova and Baryshnikov had been rehabilitated, but not Nureyev. Baryshnikov felt this as keenly as Rudolf. Interviewed in *Rolling Stone* magazine, he said he thought Rudolf was more attached to Russia than he, Baryshnikov, was, despite Rudolf always saying that his 'country' was the stage. 'He left more people behind than I did,' said Baryshnikov. 'He was much more of a cult figure, with crazy fans following him everywhere.'

Rudolf returned to Paris from North America in the middle of October. He needed to prepare for *The Nutcracker*, which was due to open in the week before Christmas. He was also beginning to think about the 1988 tour, which would begin in New York. Therefore, he wasn't prepared for a bombshell that came his way via the French Ministry of Culture. He had, said the official from the Ministry, been granted a very unusual privilege by the Soviet government. It was a two-day visa to visit Russia. He could go to Ufa and see his mother.

CHAPTER TWENTY-TWO

Days that Doom has Measured Out

> I count each hour the whole day through;
> and yet in vain ennui I squander
> the days that doom has measured out.
> And how they weigh! I know about
> my span, that fortune's jurisdiction
> has fixed.

On the very day that Rudolf arrived in Ufa, the *New York Times* bestseller list featured for the first time a book entitled *And the Band Played On*. This was Randy Shilts's moving account of the AIDS epidemic, recounting eleven years from 1976 to 1987 and showing how sexuality, politics and scientific rivalry had helped allow the epidemic to grow faster and in greater secrecy than should have been the case. That same weekend, the *Wall Street Journal* ran a front-page article detailing how the fear and prejudice in regard to AIDS was disturbing American life. One Texan man had shot his nephew to death because he thought he had AIDS. A public housing official tried to have a woman evicted from her apartment after she had let a friend with AIDS stay there. In Dallas a post office ordered certain postmen to be disinfected every day because they delivered mail to the local AIDS hospice.

When Rudolf landed in Moscow he was more worried about the cold, and he had come well stocked with coats, caps and scarves. He was met at Sheremetevo International Airport by about 600 autograph-seekers, half a dozen television crews and a few staff from the French and Austrian embassies. Although in his dealings with the press Rudolf said that he thought Gorbachev had something to do with the special visa he had been granted, he knew that this was both more and less than the truth. Yes, there was a humanitarian aspect to the visit, in that his mother was undoubtedly ill. But the Soviet authorities were more interested in being seen as humane themselves than in extending any human warmth to Rudolf. He knew, as others were free to observe, though no one did, that he was accompanied by François Léotard, who had replaced Lang as Minister of Culture. Oleg Vinogradov, director of the Kirov, was already in Paris. The fact was, there was an element of politics in this visit, as Rudolf well recognised. An exchange of visits between the Paris Opéra Ballet and one of the leading Russian companies was again on the cards, and Rudolf's forty-eight-hour visa was in reality part of the softening-up process in the negotiations which would be beginning with M. Léotard in Moscow while Rudolf was in Ufa. It was as coldly cynical as that.

After signing autographs and answering press questions, Rudolf transferred from Sheremetevo to Domededovo, well to the south of the city, from where a good many internal flights left.

The trip to Ufa was described in the prologue. Nureyev's companions were a Mr Duval, as bodyguard, who did not speak Russian, and a female interpreter. When he left Ufa, he flew first to Paris and then to Las Vegas for the 'high-roller' peformance, and on to Toronto, where he stayed with Linda Mabeduke. She remembers that he was very upset when he arrived. His mother, he said, had not recognised him. This would clearly have been very upsetting if true, after all the years of pressuring the Soviet government, but Rezida, his sister in Ufa who took him to meet Farida, flatly contradicts this. She herself was surprised and upset by her mother's reaction but, after Rudolf had left Ufa, she asked Farida if she had realised who had been to see her. 'Oh yes,' her mother had replied. 'It was Rudolf.'

One can see why Rudolf did not tell the truth about what had happened in Ufa. It must have been a terrible blow, after the many attempts to bring his mother west, to be snubbed in this fashion. It must have been very shaming. It would have made him embarrassed and angry. His anger showed in one interview he gave after he returned to the west. 'They speak a different language in Ufa,' he said. 'I don't want to say I am superior but we had nothing to say to each other. We didn't speak at all.' Likewise, the family in Ufa were given only forty-eight hours' notice that Rudolf was coming, and had no chance to make proper plans.

More puzzling is Rudolf's mother's behaviour. If she was *not* confused, and Rezida says she was not, why did she refuse to acknowledge him? It was an extraordinary piece of behaviour. The best – perhaps the only – answer lies in Russian psychology. Russians are very proud, loyal and tough people. They are also very deliberate. They regard themselves as very special, not the master race exactly, but certainly foremost in comparison with the other races that surround them. So, when it finally came to a meeting, Farida may simply have done her duty as she saw it, her duty to Russia and to the memory of Hamet, whom she had loved even above Rudolf. There is a parallel to this situation in Rudolf's beloved Pushkin, in *Eugene Onegin*. When Onegin, having killed Lensky in a duel and gone off on his travels, returns to St Petersburg, he meets Tatyana again. She is now the wife of an older man but she is clearly still in love with Onegin. He insists on a meeting, alone, which she grants him. In the west, certainly in Hollywood, this would be a prelude to a happy ending, but not in Pushkin, not in gloomy Russia. Tatyana sends Onegin away. She will abide by her duty to her husband, even though it means that Onegin and she herself will be miserable for the rest of their lives. The parallels with Rudolf's return are there.

Rudolf had little time to adjust to this difficult situation for, a short while after he returned from Ufa, his mother died, early in 1988. Natasha Harley received a phone call from Guzelle, Rosa's daughter, giving her the news and asking her to call Rudolf and look after him that night. He was at the Dakota and came round to her flat on 68th Street straight away. He had only been with her for about half an hour when the doorbell rang again. It was Baryshnikov. He had heard about Farida, knew that Rudolf would need some Russian company, and had a good idea where he would be. The three of them sat talking and drinking vodka until about three in the morning. For Natasha Harley this was the only time she ever heard Rudolf look back. He and Misha spoke the whole time about Leningrad, Pushkin (both Pushkins), the Maryinsky, Sergeyev. Rudolf had finally succumbed, for that one night, to the nostalgia for St Petersburg that he had always said he would avoid.

Farida was distressed at the end that she could not be buried with Hamet. His grave in Ufa had been robbed of its headstone and the family couldn't find the correct plot. The revolution which had once promised so much for Rudolf's parents ultimately failed them.

The year 1988 promised to be one of celebration – for Rudolf would be fifty. Covent Garden got in first, inviting Rudolf to dance in a special gala performance of *Giselle* with Sylvie Guillem. It would be her London début and, it was announced, his farewell to the role of Albrecht. It was not an altogether happy evening. Guillem fell on stage but otherwise completely outdanced him. For many critics her virtuosity simply underlined how bad Rudolf was by this time, how the role was now beyond his technical abilities. He was described as limp, flashy, earthbound, agonisingly laboured. Guillem wrote one critic, had cruelly exposed how much Rudolf had degenerated. Only Clement Crisp, in the *Financial Times*, had anything good to say. 'Nureyev,' he wrote, 'now brought a complete dramatic understanding to the role.' He was an 'icon of romantic fervour'.

At the end of the performance the audience, though moved by Rudolf's last appearance in the role, gave more applause to Guillem.

Rudolf, too, acknowledged that she had outdanced him and, although it was a farewell of sorts for him, and a birthday tribute, he pushed her forward to accept the applause. Later, on their way to dinner with Peter Wright, the director and choreographer who had been associate director of the Royal Ballet under Kenneth MacMillan, they were besieged by fans at the stage door in Floral Street. Instead of fighting through, they stayed for nearly half an hour, giving autographs and chatting.

Rudolf's fiftieth birthday was spent in Hollywood, at the Shrine auditorium, scene of so many Rudolf triumphs. He had recently been in New Zealand and, while there, had received an invitation from Baryshnikov, who was then artistic director of American Ballet Theatre, asking if he would like to dance *Giselle* with them on 17 March, when they would be on tour in Los Angeles. It was another nice gesture of Baryshnikov's and the evening was crowned with a party to which the whole Nureyev set jetted in: Natasha Harley, the Peabodies, the Niarchoses, Douce, Princess Firyal, Jacob Rothschild, Tessa Kennedy, the Wyeths, Robert Tracy, Giovanna Augusta. A week later, at a birthday celebration in Vienna, Rudolf gave what was billed as his last performance in the role of Siegfried in *Swan Lake*. Those doors were closing one by one.

In early June he was back in London to dance in a gala to celebrate Dame Ninette de Valois's ninetieth birthday (she had specially asked that he be there). Then it was on to New York where, inevitably perhaps, the biggest and best birthday tribute took place. Like Baryshnikov, Peter Martins, who had followed Balanchine as artistic director of the New York City Ballet, invited Rudolf to dance with his company. Rudolf danced *Orpheus*, thus completing the Balanchine/Stravinsky trilogy (the others were *Apollo* and *Agon*) and on that evening it was Judy Peabody's turn to give the after-performance party. This was more of a ballet/music crowd; guests included Lincoln Kirstein, Jessye Norman and Jane Herrmann.

The big night at the Met took place on 27 June. This was particularly appropriate as it coincided with the Paris Opéra Ballet's third consecutive North American season, underlining – if it needed underlining – that Paris ballet was to the 1980s what Canadian ballet had been to the 1970s, and the Royal Ballet to the 1960s. Rudolf danced Béjart's *Song of a Wayfarer*, which had been created for him in the early seventies (and had been released after Béjart's recent embargo). He was partnered by Charles Jude – Rudolf always liked to say that, after Margot, Jude was his best partner. The Paris company danced the first part of Harold Lander's *Etudes*, and William Forsythe's new ballet, *In the Middle, Somewhat Elevated*. Jessye Norman sang and James Levine, who had flown in from Salzburg, conducted.

The evening was temporarily spoiled by some hearty booing of the Forsythe offering, though when the dancers came out this turned to cheering, to show that it was the choreography that was disliked, not the dancers. At the end of the performance the company performed its *Grand défilé*, another French speciality, in which the back of the stage was opened up and all the members of the company, dressed in white and accompanied by Berlioz's 'March of the Trojans', emerged from the gloom in order of rank. The Paris Opéra ballet has many official ranks – in ascending order, *stagiaires, quadrilles, coryphées, sujets, premiers danseurs, étoiles.* For this tour Rudolf had also brought over to America eighty-five pupils from the Paris Opéra Ballet school, as well as one hundred dancers, so the *défilé*, the first time it had been performed outside Paris, was especially effective.

Balloons began to fall as the *défilé* concluded and Rudolf's friends appeared – Frederick Ashton, Violette Verdy, Lynn Seymour, Anthony Dowell, the America ballerina Cynthia Gregory, Karen Kain, Baryshnikov, Makarova, Jerome Robbins and, last, to a tremendous ovation, Margot. A huge banner came down with Rudolf's name on it and, as the balloons on the stage reached to the knee, Mayor Ed Koch appeared. In a somewhat rambling but enchanting speech he said that *he* had enjoyed the Forsythe ballet and that those who had booed would 'probably have booed Mozart'. He then proceeded to make 'only two gaffes', as Anna Kisselgoff later put it, saying that the Paris Opéra Ballet was *six* hundred years old, and that it was part of a New York festival then running. Finally he presented Rudolf with a Tiffany Crystal Apple, an award, he said, reserved for distinguished achievers. Then, ahead of a supper party held on the grand tier of the Met, the curtain came down. Even that had been ordered new for the gala.

In the *New York Times* Anna Kisselgoff responded warmly to the celebration. Only a fool would ask why Rudolf kept on performing, she wrote. 'Money is important, but dancing is his life.' Nothing more needed to be said.

Although Rudolf continued to dance, it would appear that his first real thoughts about giving up date from June 1988, when he was in New York with the Paris Opera Ballet. On the third of the month, Mario Bois made a note in his diary that Rudolf had told him he had decided to become a conductor.

Rudolf was back in New York that September for Lee Radziwill's marriage to Herbert Ross, who had produced Baryshnikov's movie *The Turning Point*, and whose latest success was *Steel Magnolias*. The wedding was a small affair which took place in Lee's apartment on 72nd Street. Her sister Jackie was there and the dinner, later, was also attended by Steve Martin, Veronica Tennant, Stephen Sondheim, Bernadette Peters and Robert Tracy. Lee wouldn't wait for Rudolf for ever.

Rudolf's relations with Lee had continued stormy. On one occasion, in an outburst of temper, he had shouted 'Thank god for Auschwitz!', which had not gone down at all well with Herbert Ross and they hadn't spoken for a while. Wallace Potts had arranged a make-up lunch but that had been nearly ruined when Rudolf had called Lee the Princess of Nothing. Part of him didn't want Lee to give herself to another man.

In New York, Rudolf was both the same as always and different. He still 'hijacked' his friends (Monique was back in favour) for his Manhattan Marathons – two Broadway shows and two movies in a single day ending up in the back alcove of Elaine's. But now when he went to the Russian tearoom he ate *côtolette de volaille*, a chicken dish. This, for the man who had scorned chicken lunches as producing chicken performances.

Rudolf at fifty was still, for many people, as big an attraction as ever. That autumn he danced in Austria, Italy, the Bronx, Italy again, and Cairo, as well as fulfilling some of his commitments in Paris. Everywhere he went the same three articles were written about him. The professional critics wrote that he was over the hill. News reporters wrote that, none the less, he filled theatres and enchanted audiences. And someone, sometimes the medical correspondent, would ask: 'How long can he go on?' Rudolf's answer was always the same: 'You don't ask a writer or a painter to stop. Don't pension me off.'

He was becoming fonder of Italy and bought Léonide Massine's old island, Li Galli, off the coast of Positano in Italy. It meant he would now be Zeffirelli's neighbour. He paid $2 million.

At the same time, he showed more signs of becoming settled in Paris. Tracy had moved there, and was writing a column for French *Vogue*. When he had moved into the quai Voltaire apartment, Rudolf had commissioned an acolyte of Renzo Mongiardino, the Italian designer he had met when Erik was in Oslo, to do the decoration, insisting only that he be allowed some Russian birchwood chairs he had already bought. The apartment Mongiardino's assistant designed had three distinctive features. First, the predominant effect was achieved by texture rather than form. Rudolf loved textiles and carpets and these were everywhere, including eighteenth- and nineteenth-century theatrical costumes, some displayed on mannequins. Second, the bathrooms were dominated by enormous, and enormously elaborate brass shower fittings that resembled in some indefinable way Russian samovars. Third, everywhere you looked there were images of male nudes. The walls of the dining room were covered in Old Master paintings of male nudes. The sideboard was festooned with bronzes of male nudes. The bathrooms were lined in Old Master drawings of male nudes. The only exception was the small music room, which had a harpsichord overlooking the Seine and where the walls were filled with prints of old theatres. But even here the texture – of the prints, of the wood on the floors and harpsichord, of the curtains – was paramount.

When Rudolf was asked where was home, he no longer said 'the stage' but 'quai Voltaire'.

For a man who believed in astrology and omens, 1989 began with mixed signs. At the end of the preceding year, three famous ballet figures had died of AIDS – Robert Joffrey, founder and artistic director of the Joffrey Ballet, aged fifty-nine; Arnie Zane, dancer and choreographer, aged thirty-nine; and Gregory Huffmann, formerly lead dancer with the Joffrey and a teacher in its school, aged thirty-five. But Rudolf was still dancing – an American tour with the 'Friends' in January, 1989, Germany in February, Switzerland and the Far East in April. He had been HIV positive now for at least five years, but he appeared to be keeping 'full-blown AIDS', as it was called, at bay. And, at the beginning of the year, he was confirmed in his position at the Palais Garnier for a further three years. He was clearly important to keep his medical status secret.

However, inside the company fresh problems were building. In February he invited Twyla Tharp to the Palais Garnier. They had first met in Spoleto, when he had been with Margot not long after he defected. For some time he had been asking her to produce a ballet for him, as part of his modern dance plans, and she after years of procrastination had finally consented, having been 'smitten', as she put it, by Sylvie Guillem. The contract for her new ballet, *Rules of the Game*, stipulated that she must have Guillem in the main role, and Rudolf had been happy to agree. The problem was Guillem herself. She had fallen out with Rudolf, and suddenly defected to the Royal Ballet. Given the history of Rudolf's own relations with Covent Garden, this act was seen by him as a great betrayal and he badly wanted *Rules of the Game* to go ahead despite the fine print of Twyla Tharp's contract.

She, to her lasting credit, obliged, and painfully rebuilt the piece around Isabelle Guérin. *Rules of the Game* was a great success and, to show his gratitude for avoiding yet another scandal, Rudolf gave Twyla a dinner at Les Halles at which they ate so many oysters and drank so much champagne that they all but passed into oblivion and, for a moment, Rudolf became amorous. He spoiled it, however, by biting Twyla Tharp's arm. She nearly slugged him, she said, but decided to put it down to animal passion. The teeth marks lasted for almost a day.

But the averted scandal over *Rules of the Game* only served as a prelude to a bigger problem: *Swan Lake*, which was due to have its first night on Rudolf's fifty-first birthday, 17 March 1989 and this time he was to appear in the part of van Rothbart. Once again it was to be a gala with the charity dinner hosted by Marie-Hélène de Rothschild.

A week before the première Rudolf was saddened but also shocked to learn that Robert Mapplethorpe had died of AIDS. Yet another of his partners had succumbed. Barely had this news registered, however, than a more immediate problem presented itself – yet another strike by the dancers. This time they had two grievances. There was a plan to force dancers who wanted to become teachers to take a diploma. The *corps* thought this unnecessary and demeaning. Also many of the technical staff were worried by the impending move of the opera part of the company to the new theatre at the Bastille. Job cuts were threatened.

The solution of the dancers was to bite the hand that, at least partly, fed them. They would not dance on the night of the gala. This manoeuvre was desribed by 'Suzy' in the *New York Post* in one of the most extraordinary pieces of journalism ever written. Its flavour can only be given by quoting it at length:

Quelle flap in la belle Paris. Those nasty old strikes are rearing their ugly têtes again. Some sort of general strike in France has been threatened for Saturday but it's not a threat but a fait accompli that the ballet dancers at the Paris Opéra are striking that very day. Pas de paycheques, vous savez, or quelquechose like that. As if that were not already quite horrendous enough the Paris Opéra ballerinas and dancers are grumbling that they might lay down their tights and tutus early and not show up at all on Friday night for the grand and glittering private premiere. Great balls of feu! Do you know what that means? It means that the most dazzling event of the Paris social season so far will be left without a dazzling event and will have to make do with merely the dazzling supper set to follow the performance. Even if they serve lark's tongue sous cloche or ortolan en plumage it will not be the same. The Parise haute monde is praying those leapers and twirlers will see the light and dance, dance, dance for the ravishing six hundred in their fab finery. Still, even without a show the show will go on. You see the chairman of the evening is Baroness Guy de Rothschild, than whom there is no one whomer in all the land.

Then came a list of noted American and other socialites like Sid and Anne Bass, Alfred Taubman, Lynn Wyatt, Oscar de la Renta, Prince and Princess Michael of Kent. It was on an occasion like this that Douce, in order to get back into Rudolf's good books, turned up dressed as a man.

In fact, despite Suzy's admonitions, the dancers did not perform, the supper went ahead, but the following night's ordinary ticket holders had an unexpected first night to themselves. And it was, again, a triumph. The chorus of approval took in the French, British and American press. Once more Rudolf's successes were compared and contrasted with the Royal Ballet. 'Uneven times at Covent Garden', said the *New York Times*, which acknowledged that Anthony Dowell was proving a better director than Norman Morrice, but partly because of Sylvie Guillem. (The French had marked her defection as 'a national catastrophe.') As before, the *Times* noted, it took a foreigner to put the Royal's dancers on their mettle.

Rudolf had surely made his point by now. He was the greatest director the Paris Opéra Ballet had had since Serge Lifar, and how he compared with Lifar was academic. It took a foreigner to keep the Paris Opéra Ballet on its mettle.

His relations with Guillem continued to be awkward. London had been entranced by her virtuosity and she, as the *New York Times* had observed, was responsible for bringing people back to Covent Garden who had deserted it when Rudolf had been pushed out. But, again like Rudolf, Guillem was temperamental, and when, in the summer, Rudolf would not grant her more than three days to rehearse a ballet she already knew, or let the Paris ballet coach and costume fitter come to London to help her prepare, she withdrew from two ballets she was scheduled to appear in.

This was scandal enough, but then Rudolf announced that Kenneth Greves, a Danish dancer who had been with American Ballet Theatre in New York, would be joining the company that summer. The ostensible reason was that Greves was more than six feet tall and the company did not have a tall dancer. At first the dancers accepted this. Pieces were written about him in the French press, praising his experience, his height, his blond hair and blue eyes. He appeared likeable, diffident about his talent. It was only when he arrived in Paris and danced one performance of *Swan Lake* that the dancers realised that (a) he simply wasn't good enough to be an *étoile*, and (b) Rudolf was in love with him. Elisabeth Platel was delegated by the dancers to approach Pierre Bergé, the president of the Opéra, and Bergé told Rudolf 'he couldn't do it'.

But Rudolf wouldn't be told. 'Balanchine wasn't told what to do,' he yelled at Bergé (and, strictly speaking, Bergé later admitted, Rudolf was right). But Rudolf had to give way because what he knew, and no one else in the Palais Garnier did, was that he had appointed Greves not because he was his lover but because he *wasn't*. Rudolf was desperate to seduce the younger man but the younger man was not as easy as, say, Robert Tracy. So Rudolf lavished attention on Greves, and in August gave him a birthday party at the Dakota. But he badly misjudged even that. Greves was twenty-one yet Rudolf invited mostly his own friends. They might be famous but Greves was of a different generation and hated the whole thing – they were all 'geriatrics'. Then the couple went on to Rudolf's farm in Virginia (which he had bought in 1981), the older man still hoping that Greves would sleep with him. It didn't happen, and Rudolf was both angry and hurt. It never seemed to occur to him that Greves might be worried about catching AIDS, or wasn't a committed homosexual.

A complicating factor was the creation, that summer, by Flemming Flindt, of a new ballet based on Gogol's *The Overcoat*. This was specially designed for Rudolf, a role with a lot of dancing but scope for his dramatic gifts, too. It was an enormous success at the Maggio Musicale festival in Florence in June and new possibilities were opened up – a new repertoire which could continue for . . . who knows how long? Either way, all these performances would take him away from Paris.

And then a much bigger problem raised its head. Earlier in the year, ever eager to try new things, Rudolf had signed a contract to star in a twenty-week touring show in North America of the Rodgers and Hammerstein musical, *The King and I*. This of course had been made famous as a movie starring Yul Brynner. Indeed, when the plan for Rudolf to appear in the show had been announced someone had remarked that *The King and I* without Brynner was like a dollar bill without Washington's portrait on it. Still, Rudolf was tempted, by the challenge and by the fee – he was paid $1 million for the first 24-week leg of the contract, which overall envisaged several six-month tours for up to five years.

Friends like Rudi van Dantzig tried to dissuade him from taking on the tour, citing the awful music, the kinds of audience such a show would attract, the jokes people would make. Rudolf went ahead anyway. Everything started well. The show, with Liz Robertson starring opposite him, opened on 18 August in Syracuse, upstate New York, where the reviews were surprisingly good. Surprising because in his role as the King of Siam Rudolf was called upon not only to dance and act but to sing. There had been the usual bickerings in rehearsal, when at first Rudolf wouldn't allow the air-conditioning to be turned on, even though it was 90 degrees in the studio. As ever he was worried about feeling cold. Then the director, Arthur Storch, had suggested they were running out of rehearsal time and that Rudolf should forgo his dance class. 'I believe,' Rudolf replied menacingly, 'that I'll be in a better mood if I don't.'

One early reviewer said that seeing Nureyev in this show was like discovering Alaska. Another claimed he could make people forget Brynner, that he commanded the stage, and was 'Every inch a king.'

This was all highly flattering but among the fan mail was a very different kind of letter. It was from Pierre Bergé, president of the Paris Opéra, and it had been written on 6 September, when Rudolf was in Baltimore, the third city of the *King and I* tour, and six days before he was due back in Paris for the new season at the Opéra. It was the third letter Rudolf had received from Bergé. The first two had been written in July, at the time of the Greves affair and when details about *The King and I* had been released. Bergé could see a confrontation looming and tried to head it off, though Rudolf *had* specified that *The King and I* be organised in 24-week segments so he could keep his other commitments. In his first letters Bergé had referred, ambiguously but pointedly, to the problem of Rudolf's *relationships* with the dancers in his company. Many dancers, he wrote, 'are all ready and willing to love you but you do not provide them with the opportunity'. Everybody was willing to respect Rudolf, he wrote, 'but for that you have to be respectable. Your various misbehaviours, in language or gestures, are simply not up to your standard. Moreover, they tend to separate you from your real family, the ballet.'

This was both tactful and yet forceful of Bergé, a man who knew his own mind, as his sacking of Daniel Barenboim as artistic director of the Opéra a few months before had shown (he was known as the 'Pit Bull of the Fashion World'). But Bergé received no reply. When he wrote again he already knew that Rudolf was due to be in Boston with *The King and I* on 11 September, when the dancers reassembled in Paris after the summer break. He was sad, angry and regretful. Rudolf, he felt, was not keeping his side of the bargain. He couldn't be head of the Paris ballet by spending a few days now and then in the city, even if it did amount to 180 days throughout the year. He needed to spend several months there at a stretch. Rudolf's demands for his new contract were also quite tough – a bilingual secretary, reimbursement for all his airplane tickets, a driver available around the clock.

Rudolf ignored Bergé. He was inaccessible to him but not to others. When Linda Mabeduke gave birth to her daughter, she immediately called Rudolf to give him the news, since he had agreed to be the girl's godfather as he was already to Lynn Seymour's twins. He took Linda's call in an intermission in Boston, and his first question was, 'How can you talk, so soon after the birth?' (The child was one-and-a-half hours old at this point.) Bewildered by the question for a moment, Mabeduke replied, 'But it's not that end, Rudolf!' His second question was, 'How are her insteps?' He had wanted the girl to be called Tatyana, after the heroine in *Eugene Onegin*, but they had settled on Alexandra Nureyeva.

In the second week of *The King and I* tour, Greves walked out on Rudolf. The show was playing in Toronto and one day he just wasn't there. He didn't say goodbye but just disappeared. Rudolf was upset and, after the show that night, called Linda and Bill Mabeduke. They were already in bed but recognised that he was low, and so got up, got dressed, and went out to dinner with Rudolf to keep him company. Though he was upset, he was fatalistic. The Mabedukes were glad it was over. They had always felt that Greves behaved like a young coquette with an older man. 'It was abominable,' Linda said.

A week later the feud with Bergé hit the press, which characterised it as a 'bitter row', true enough on Rudolf's part but less so on Bergé's. Rudolf affected to say that he was bored with the Paris job, and that he would consider taking over as director of the American Ballet

Theatre, if the post were offered. (Baryshnikov had indicated he wished to resign and had appeared in a Broadway show.) The ABT job was not offered, but these were in any case the wrong signals to send Bergé. A meeting was arranged which, though amicable, did not produce agreement and Bergé now replaced Rudolf, temporarily, with Patrick Bart. The situation wasn't helped when, shortly later, Rudolf revealed that he would break into *The King and I* tour for an unscheduled trip – to St Petersburg, where he would dance with the Kirov. It rounded off Rudolf's own story but was hardly flattering to the Paris Opéra Ballet.

One man who did foresee what was happening – on several fronts – was Gorlinsky. He realised that Rudolf would need a savvy lawyer before too long, whatever happened, and he recommended Barry Weinstein, from Chicago, who handled Makarova's affairs. Weinstein would not prove everyone's favourite, but Gorlinsky's action was timely.

In some ways Rudolf's return to the Kirov, in November 1989, was a curious episode. He had always said 'You can't go back', but here he was doing just that. It was understandable but it suggested that Baryshnikov was right and Rudolf had been dissembling all those years. He had left more behind in Russia than he would ever admit, either to others or to himself.

The invitation to the Kirov had arisen casually enough. After Makarova had returned home, Vinogradov issued a parallel invitation to Nureyev. Rudolf chose *La Sylphide*, a sensible choice in that the role of James involves some jumping but not much lifting, and it is one of the shortest classics. The Kirov were quite thoughtful too, in that the ballerina they chose as his partner, Zhanna Ayupova, was not their best dancer. They didn't want to humiliate him.

He arrived in St Petersburg, as it was now once again called, with an entire television film crew from CBS, plus friends and colleagues like Luigi Pignotti, intent on recreating this historic return. He was met at the airport by Tamara Myasciorva, the same Tamara who had first met him at Elizaveta's salons. Her first reaction was to notice that Rudolf arrived drunk (she used a Russian word which means spirits, not beer or wine). She was shocked by that and by the fact that he didn't seem to recognise some of his old friends who had also come to meet him. Rezida, ironically, had been intending to visit him in Paris at the very time he came to St Petersburg, so she had given away the train tickets she had already bought, and travelled from Ufa with her son Yuri to have her holiday there.

The entire circus transferred to the Leningrad Hotel (now the St Petersburg Hotel) where Rudolf was given a wonderful room on the sixth floor, with a sunken bath and a view of the Neva, St Isaac's

Cathedral and the *Aurora*, (the ship whose cannon signalled the start of the revolution in 1917). As was his habit, he asked for plenty of towels, but the management kept an eye on these extras and kept asking for them back. 'Nothing has changed,' grumbled Rudolf, who refused to eat Russian food, concentrating instead on salami and (western) beer.

Tamara was also shocked when she accompanied Rudolf to an interview with the CBS crew, which took place in the Maryinsky Theatre, in a box to the right of the stage. He was still affected by drink, she said. Asked what it felt like to come back to his homeland, he waved to the stage and said, 'Any stage is my home.' This was not at all what Tamara and other Leningraders wanted to hear. Although Rudolf asked to be photographed next to a picture of Pushkin, Tamara, who had been very close to Rudolf's mentor, said he asked *no* questions about him – that surprised her too. She did notice, in rehearsals, that he was very tired, always stopping and drinking what she called a pick-me-up. (She implied it was alcohol but it may well have been tea.) She never suspected then that he might be ill, she was too concerned with Rudolf's vanity, as she saw it. 'He kept saying to the CBS crew, "Put the camera on *me*."'

Nureyev gave one interview to a periodical in St Petersburg, *Smena*, in which he let slip that he had intended to defect, at some stage. At Le Bourget, he said, when they were trying to put him on the Moscow-bound plane, his only thought was for the Royal Ballet. It was the Royal that he had always, secretly, wanted to perform with. (Obviously, this is why his failure to become director had hurt so much; it would have been such a fitting end to his ambitions.)

For Rudolf, the visit to St Petersburg was, he said later, a bitter disappointment. He visited the Vaganova, walked up and down Nevsky Prospekt, organised tickets for Rezida to visit him in Paris after all, looked at the run-down *banias* and saw how the shop 'Noti' had changed (there was no longer a piano there). But he found the Maryinsky Theatre exactly the same as he had left it – the same smell, the same run-down feel to it, the same *babushkas* guarding the same doors. He was scheduled to give three performances but gave only two because he had injured his foot before he arrived and once more it was bandaged. Rudolf forbade any cameras either in rehearsal or in the wings during the performances.

By 1989, after years of communism, and four years of chaos under Gorbachev, the ballet in the Kirov was in decline and many of the old-style balletomanes, like Alexander Mikhailovich, had stopped going. But they all turned out to see Rudolf, as did many famous people from the Leningrad art world. It was, without doubt, an occasion.

Mikhailovich said that watching Rudolf perform was like watching your grandfather dance. This is a characteristically Russian thing to say, because it implies more than age, it implies respect. Rudolf could no longer do the things that the role called for, but you could see that, in his day, he *could* have done them. To Mikhailovich, watching Rudolf in 1989 was like watching Michael Somes, Fonteyn's other partner, in Leningrad on the Royal Ballet's 1961 ballet tour. Somes too was a master past his prime.

The reactions of many were complicated that night. Ayupova, Rudolf's partner, said in a radio interview the next day that she had not realised he would dance so badly, that any dancer in the Kirov company could have danced better than he did. But later she changed her tune and said on television how happy she had been to dance with such a great performer. As Mikhailovich put it, 'He was old but you could see he had a great artistic arsenal.'

When Nureyev first came out on to the stage, he was welcomed with warm applause. As James, he was of course dressed as a Briton, in a kilt. Of course the Misasnikovas were there, as were Dudinskaya, Tamara and Sergei Sorokin. Udelstova, now aged one hundred, sat in the company box. But many people left after the first interval. 'Our feelings were strangely muddled,' wrote Inna Sklarevskaya, a St Petersburg critic. 'Our ovation was not for the performance but for the past. We had come to see one of our own, who was a stranger.' In other words, he was a stranger even in his own land.

Already Nureyev was losing his figure, she wrote, and had sore legs. At the rehearsals, which were also 'chock-a-block', he had played with the audience:

> He merely performed a few individual steps and then sketched the rest out carelessly . . . but the shuffling little gait, the candid butchering of form while putting his partners into position and, to cap it all, the bright yellow shiny clogs on top of his ballet slippers . . . what a good impression it all made! . . . Everything was calculated . . . turning the thing from a rehearsal into a barely disguised farce. "That's as much of my rehearsal as you're going to get" seemed to be the order of the day . . . There was no inclination to take seriously Nureyev's own suggestion of his unique level, and hope remained for some sort of miraculous metamorphosis in the following day's performance.
>
> 'The artistic wonder on the morrow did not materialise, rather the event that evening turned out to be somewhat pathetic. We became the audience of a peculiar solo show, framed as the ballet *Sylphide* . . . watching Nureyev we were simultaneously meeting him and saying goodbye . . . It was as if he wanted to say, "Look how your Nureyev danced, Nureyev, whom you didn't even know!" . . . he was not even bothering to hide his present weaknesses . . . and at some points it was even possible to notice him limping.'

But Sklarevskaya acknowledged that his *interpretation* of the role, whatever its technical shortcomings, was dramatically mature, devoid of clichés, and seemed to grow out of Rudolf rather than be imposed by him. She may have put her finger on it when she concluded by saying that the tragedy of the performance was that it had come too late – not for St Petersburg but for Rudolf. Once again the deliberate, unsentimental Russian thinking, of a piece with Farida's reactions, and Tatyana's in *Eugene Onegin*.

Afterwards there was a party at the French consulate, where Rudolf met Dudinskaya and Udeltsova. There was warmth but here too Udeltsova rebuked him for leaving Russia. She had not taught him to behave in such a way, she said.

Rudolf had been right the first time. You can't go back.

The tour of *The King and I* continued until February 1990. Andrew Grossman, Rudolf's agent at Columbia Artists Management Inc, had helped organise Nureyev and Friends for a number of years and *The King and I* was his response to Rudolf's desire to do 'something special'. But the tour had posed problems. Because of his health – Grossman says Rudolf was infected as early as late 1978 or early 1979 – he refused a medical, which meant that the show hit the road without insurance. But they never had a contract anyway. Grossman had approached Rudolf through Gorlinksy in Berlin and they had simply shaken hands.

Grossman was impressed by Rudolf's professionalism – except in one regard. It had originally been agreed that he would consult Seth Riggs, a respected Hollywood voice coach who had helped to train Liza Minnelli, Cher and Michael Jackson. Riggs was supposed to fly to Li Galli in Italy but Rudolf cancelled at the last minute. So instead of a whole month to practise he had a shorter time in New York – and it showed. There was, so Grossman felt, no voice *projection*. The sing-speak just didn't work. It would, in time, prove decisive.

But during that tour Grossman came very close to Rudolf, mainly because of one of Rudolf's other night-time habits. His contract guaranteed him $1 million, first-class accommodation and a limousine. When there were only 300–500 miles between engagements then Rudolf would drive throught the night, in the limo, rather than take a flight the next morning. On these night-time drives Grossman would be in the car with Rudolf. They would stock up on hamburgers, Heineken and Pouilly-Fuissé and hit the road. Sometimes they would nod off but more often would talk all the way through the journey, arriving at the next hotel at about four o'clock in the morning. Rudolf would immediately take a bath – he was so concerned about his health then, and catching infections, that he would sometimes bathe five times a day. The hotel rooms and the wings at stage right were always dominated by huge piles of towels. Once arrived at the hotel, they would kill the phones and Rudolf would sleep until two or three in the afternoon, when he would have breakfast. He would check out the floor of the theatre (they travelled with their own floor for Nureyev and Friends), then play the piano which he insisted be installed in every hotel room. Already he had one eye on the future.

It was on the all-night drives that Rudolf would grow reflective with Grossman, just as he had grown reflective on tour with Violette Verdy. In this way he admitted to Grossman that he had, as he put it, had a 'full relationship' with Margot, and had loved her. It was through Grossman that Rudolf sent money to Margot, when she was in hospital in Houston. 'I should have married her,' he said one night.

He talked about conductors – he loved Klemperer; critics – he respected John Percival and Clement Crisp and hated Anna Kisselgoff; and he talked about the women in his life. Knowing that he had AIDS, he once said to Grossman, referring to Douce François, Miasnikova, Tessa Kennedy and Jeanette Etheridge, 'Don't let me die surrounded by all these *hens*!'

It was on one of the tours with Grossman that Kisselgoff gave Rudolf a particularly brutal review. When he learned that she was coming to another performance, a few days hence, he called her at the *New York Times* and told her that if he saw her there he would 'knock a bucket of shit on your head'. Grossman was then called by a very pompous editor from the *Times*, pontificating about the protection of critics. Ms Kisselgoff, he said, *would* be attending the performance, accompanied by someone who might *look* very slight but was in fact a judo black belt. Mr Nureyev should be warned. The night in question was a farce, Grossman said, for Rudolf kept peeking through the curtain before the start, to see where Kisselgoff was sitting. He then tried all the emergency exits until he found her. In the end she wrote not a bad review.

The journalist Elisabeth Kaye also accompanied Rudolf on the tour and was surprised by much of what she saw. She quickly noticed what others had noticed before – that Rudolf liked to shock with bad language. He liked the effect it produced. On one occasion, for example, when the conversation turned to a discussion about the merits of a certain Russian diplomat in America, Rudolf's contribution was that the man 'had a big dick'. Also, he liked to talk about sex in a deliberately brutal way. He might not have been an Anvil regular but he liked to talk as though he were. Kaye also remarked on the fact that, wherever he went, Rudolf always carried with him a bag of pornographic films. In some cases he had slept with the 'stars' of these films.

But she was if anything more shocked by his interpretation of the king in *The King and I*. At the point where the governess teaches *him* to dance, he played the role 'very camp'. And Kaye wondered whether the reason he did so was because it was the way he saw himself. She began to wonder whether, deep down, Rudolf hated the fact that he was homosexual. It would certainly explain the promiscuity, the abundance of anonymous sex, the brutality of his sex talk, his need to shock, the secrecy, the occasional longing after marriage. It might even explain the fact that, as someone in Sotheby's (London) said to Bonnie Prandato Robinson, Rudolf was not very good in bed. That year Rudolf gave an interview in which he said that people now didn't try to get too close to him, implying that the reason was because he was so famous. But perhaps they didn't like what they saw. Perhaps he didn't like what *he* saw.

Despite the fact that it was the second or third highest grossing show in theatre history, *The King and I* came to an inglorious end. After Rudolf had cut corners with Seth Riggs, the Rodgers and Hammerstein people were not greatly impressed by his performance but felt that it could only improve. Grossman was given the go-ahead for the first twenty-four week itinerary. Towards the end, however, the Rodgers and Hammerstein people came to see it again and formed the view that Rudolf had not improved enough, and further permissions were withheld. It was a blow, not sweetened when Barbara Horgan did the same with Balanchine's ballets. She was now one of the people controlling the rights in Balanchine's work and shared the view of the Rodgers and Hammerstein group: that Rudolf was simply not up to it any more.

Rudolf stayed in America with Nureyev and Friends until he was due back in London in May for a benefit gala for Margot. Just as his fairy-tale return to the Kirov had been a disappointment, so Margot's fairy-tale life was ending in a far from romantic fashion. Her health had deteriorated, especially since the death of Tito the previous November. Worse, she was not a wealthy woman. What Tito hadn't spent as a playboy and philanderer, he had consumed as a cripple. There was no particular age reason for the gala; she was seventy-one. The benefit had been organised, by John Tooley mainly, to raise £250,000 to provide a trust fund for her, and then to fund scholarships for young ballerinas. It had been revealed that, the previous year, Margot had been forced to sell her jewellery at Christie's. The report had infuriated her, but it was true.

She made the most of it. 'I took my wedding vows seriously,' she said. 'For richer, for poorer. It's not death I'm afraid of, but of living too long.'

Both Princess Margaret and Princess Diana were at the gala, at which Placido Domingo sang Verdi arias and Rudolf danced Mercutio from Kenneth MacMillan's *Romeo and Juliet*, partnered by Sylvie Guillem. But that night was more than a farewell to Margot. It was the last time Rudolf danced on the Covent Garden stage.

In August 1990, Rudolf spent a few days' holiday at a house jointly owned by Mario Bois and Jack Lanchbery near Seville in Spain. After he had unpacked, taken a shower and been given a whisky, Rudolf asked Mario to show him where the boys' pool was. Little realising that this was slang for the location where the gays gathered, Mario led Rudolf to the swimming pool where his own boys often bathed. 'Mario!' Rudolf sighed with smile, 'You know nothing!' And then he explained about the 'Reservoir des garçons' in every town.

In the early part of 1990, Patrick Dupond had replaced Patrick Bart as the new, permanent, head of the Paris Opéra Ballet. Rudolf had settled down by then and had agreed to accept the position of premier choreographer at the Palais Garnier. Many people who loved Rudolf's dancing professed not to like his choreography anywhere near as much, but the fact was that by summer 1990 one of Rudolf's productions was playing somewhere in the world almost every day, sufficient for him to appoint Mario Bois, Claire Motte's widower, as his agent on this matter. Bois had been one of the few people to get the better of Gorlinsky in negotiations, and Rudolf liked that.

Most of the rest of 1990 and 1991 was taken up with performances for the Cleveland Ballet, the National Ballet of Cuba, the Naples Ballet and with extensive Nureyev and Friends tours, in North America, Germany, Spain and Italy. He now danced mainly *The Lesson*, *Song of a Wayfarer*, *The Moor's Pavane*, and a new ballet that had been created especially for him at fifty by Flemming Flindt. This was the aforementioned *The Overcoat* and it proved, even at fifty-two, a great success.

Throughout that period ballet dancers and friends of Rudolf continued to die of AIDS in frightening numbers:

5 January, 1990: Ian Horvath, founder of the Cleveland Ballet and a former Joffrey soloist – aged 46.
2 June, 1990: Demian Acquavella, who danced in several New York companies – aged 32.
13 February, 1991: Burton Taylor, ex-Joffrey leading dancer and contributing editor to *Dance Magazine* – aged 47.
15 February, 1991: Paul Russell, principal dancer with the Dance Theatre of Harlem and San Francisco ballet – aged 43.
8 March, 1991: Edward Stierle, lead dancer with the Joffrey – aged 23.

No one has ever satisfactorily explained the link between ballet and homosexuality. Some people question that it exists universally – the Royal Danish Ballet, for example, is said to be a heterosexual company in the main whereas in one study of the New York City Ballet, six of the eight male principals were gay, half the soloists were practising homosexuals, and the corps was 'overwhelmingly' gay. Clive Barnes addressed the issue in the *New York Times* in 1974, and in 1988, in a book entitled *Dance, Sex and Gender*, Judith Lynne Hanna, an anthropologist at the Univesrity of Maryland, devoted two chapters to the subject.

She pinpoints the French revolution as the point after which men who became professional dancers were increasingly assumed to be homosexual. Her preferred theory appears to be that homosexual men were attracted to the ballet for three reasons – one, as a fringe or marginal activity itself (until very recently), it was more accepting of people who, in some way or another, were marginal themselves. Ballet therefore became a 'sanctuary for "faggots".' Two, as a basically female world, in the nineteenth and early twentieth century, homosexual men, who were assumed to be more sensitive and more expressive than other men, were naturally attracted to the ballet. And three, that the arts in general allowed homosexual men (as others) more freedom to explore their own psychology and their sexuality. Arlene Croce, ballet critic of *The New Yorker*, has said that Nijinsky's three ballets, *Faune*, *Jeux* and *Sacre* can only be understood as a biography of the homosexual orgasm. In more recent years, Judith Hanna says that a fourth reason has been added for the link between homosexuality and ballet. Since Diaghilev and Nijinsky, classical dance in the west has grown increasingly 'respectable' and so many homosexual men were able to achieve 'respectability' as professional dancers.

She also finds that male dancing has become more and more 'masculine' over the past decades, where Nureyev has been a noticeable example. Although he danced certain roles that Nijinsky himself considered too 'pretty', at the same time, she says, Nureyev's wide appeal may well have stemmed from the fact that, as a boy, he learned a great many folk dances to begin with. These, according to Judith Hanna, at least lend dance a male edge and give it a much stronger, more masculine flavour.

In other words, dancing has become both more masculine and more sexual since Nijinsky, and this, according to Hanna, accounts for the greater popularity of ballet in general as well as its appeal for homosexuals in particular – to show that they are not the 'pansies' they were labelled in the French revolution.

Whatever the reason for the link between homosexuality and classical dance (if there *is* one overrriding reason) Nureyev's own place in this debate is complex and even paradoxical. Though he might have been flamboyantly and promiscuously homosexual off-stage, he was nothing of the kind as a performer. There are but two reports of him being 'camp' during a performance, and one of them was in *The King and I*, scarcely a notable dancing role. Though he could be flirtatious with other members of the company – other dancers, stage hands or musicians – the audience never saw this either. In fact, quite the opposite was true. Rudolf was not just a prince on stage, but a very heterosexual, very *masculine* prince. Nureyev understood masculinity – all the early reports show that to be true from the start.

He never jumped like a gazelle or a deer, for example, but like a lion. He gathered his strength, his power, until he was ready. Given his physique, he may have had no choice, but still he exploited what he had to the full: he was above all a *theatrical* being.

In an important sense, Nureyev's homosexuality cannot be separated from his sexuality. Here, his private life and his stage life do coincide – in that for him sex was a very important aspect of life which affected everything. Just as he developed into a promiscuous individual privately, so he infused ballet with sex appeal. He knew he had it, more than almost anyone else, and saw no reason to ignore the fact. At times he took risks with his sexuality on stage – but again rarely. More important, it was there, out in front so to speak, for everyone to see. Here too he was a child of his time. The post-war world of the 1960s was ready for just such a figure as Rudolf and he was only too happy to oblige.

Mostly this influence was good – but not entirely, not in everyone's book. The reassertion of men in ballet, which Rudolf undoubtedly took a leading part in, culminated in the 1970s and 1980s in a number of ballets which derogated women. Anti-women messages are part of Jerome Robbins's *The Cage* (once banned in The Hague for this very reason); William Forsythe's 1982 work, *Love Songs*, suggests that women 'deserve' the violence against them, and works by Antony Tudor, Louis Falco and Maurice Béjart have all attracted similar criticisms. Still other works have stressed homosexual love as a 'rival' to the heterosexual kind (*Triad*, for example, by Kenneth MacMillan), while Vincent Nebrada's *Gemini* was dismissed as 'homosexual propaganda' and *The Relativity of Icarus*, performed by the Joffrey, was simply 'pornographic'. This is a controversial area of dance, with no real equivalent in the other arts. And Rudolf steered clear.

Any discussion of Rudolf's sexuality, or homosexuality, is bound to raise the issue – one might almost say the spectre – of Nijinsky. From his earliest performances, Rudolf was being labelled as the new Nijinsky and, when he reached London in 1961–2, as was seen earlier, comparing the two dancers became almost a national pastime.

Both men came from grinding poverty, where their fathers were either absent and/or a negative force. Both were plucked to stardom by an older woman, Tchessinskaya in Nijinsky's case, Dudinskaya in Rudolf's. Both came under the spell of older men – Diaghilev and Bruhn. Both were blessed by an androgynous kind of beauty and introduced more sex into classical dance, among other things by changing their costumes so as to be more revealing. Both were the toast of Paris and both were exiled from Russia. The coincidences are uncanny but not necessarily any more than that. One does wonder to what extent Dudinskaya tried emulate Tchessinskaya and to what extent Rudolf modelled himself on Nijinsky.

More interesting is the point made by Sir Peter Wright, that the absence of a father in both Nijinsky and Nureyev's life may, in the long run, have been no bad thing. Whether or not this absence was a causative factor in the aetiology of the dancers' homosexuality, it certainly seems to have made them drawn to older men – and this is Wright's point, that young homosexuals are often educated by their lovers, men with far more to teach their 'protégés' (for want of a better word) than the original fathers. In other words, would Nijinsky have been Nijinsky but for Diaghilev, and would Rudolf have been Rudolf but for Erik Bruhn? This is a tantalising theory.

But perhaps the differences between Nijinsky and Nureyev are more revealing, in the long run, than the similarities. Who really knows who jumped better? What we do know is that all the reports of Nijinsky's jump were ecstatic, whereas there are mixed reports about Rudolf's, certainly in the early days. And Rudolf never jumped *off*stage, as Nijinsky did on occasions, and to great effect. So perhaps Nijinsky had the better Jump.

In Nijinsky's short life, he produced at least two works – *Faune* and *Sacre* – that have passed into legend, are still danced, and still have the power to thrill. It may be too soon to judge Rudolf's original choreography but as of now neither *Tancredi*, *Manfred*, nor *Washington Square* seems to have the staying power of the Nijinsky works. So perhaps Nijinsky was a more creative choreographer as well as a better jumper.

But we should not be misled by this. Roger Fry, the art critic and historian, once said after a visit to Venice that Veronese was the greater painter but that Titian was the greater man. He meant that Veronese had greater technical gifts than Titian – he could render perspective better, paint satins with a more realistic sheen, the details of a picture were more meticulous – but that, despite these advantages, Titian still painted better pictures, because he understood the human condition more, which meant that he could infuse his work with more feeling, more emotion. This made Titian's paintings more real – and in the end more moving.

This is the way to look at Nijinsky and Nureyev. Nijinsky never really recovered from his break with Diaghilev; his marriage to Romola seems to have helped push him over the edge into madness. If he was schizophrenic, as seems to have been the case, his illness would almost certainly have shown itself anyway but, if he was a true homosexual, and not a bisexual, his marriage would scarcely have helped his mental health.

In contrast, Rudolf was magnificently sane. Everyone, from Ninette de Valois down, pays tribute to Nureyev's intelligence, his financial acumen, his iron will. He was a man who *controlled* his life as only the very sane, the very bright and the very forceful can.

If there is more to dance than leaping and spinning, and being technically brilliant, then Rudolf is surely the greater of the two men. In *Spectre* and *Faune*, Nijinsky may have given the world two incomparable masterpieces, but Rudolf gave the world his life, his *example*. It is sometimes said that Rudolf was the Maria Callas of ballet – a sacred monster who, by his temperament and brilliance attracted new people to his art form. Perhaps, but in a very real sense a better comparison is with Picasso. Both men were not just promiscuous, but also prolific, producing so much work, in so many different styles, that the whole world can be familiar with the *oeuvre*. They drew people to their art by making it accessible, physically accessible. Picasso and Rudolf also shared an instinctive understanding of the twentieth-century mass media world: they knew that they functioned best as symbols – symbols of what people wish to be. In a mass media world the symbol is all-important.

In some ways it could be said that Rudolf was the greatest artist of them all, because he *moved* people. He knew that people wanted to be moved, he knew that ballet does not film well and that therefore the live performance is all. Ballet – dance – is a form of theatre where, even in the late twentieth century, you really need to *be* there, for the full experience. And so, while film or TV actors rarely face their audiences in a live dramatic context, ballet dancers (as for opera stars to a lesser extent) are engaged every time they dance in a direct emotional encounter – 250 times a year in Rudolf's case. For Rudolf, and for his many fans, this is what mattered: the emotion in the encounter. This is why he danced long past his physical prime. His emotional force remained undimmed and this is what people came to see, to be part *of*.

This is surely why, in any comparison with Nijinsky, Rudolf wins convincingly. We remember Nijinsky, essentially, for his freakish qualities. But Rudolf fulfilled his talent in a way that Nijinsky never did, in a way that people rarely do. Nijinsky, for whatever reasons, *succumbed* to the pressures he was faced with, but Rudolf never did. He never found dancing easy, he never found life easy, but he never gave in and whatever happened he never cancelled a performance.

Nijinsky the freak holds few lessons for us, beyond the fact that some people are exceptional for reasons that are still largely unexplained. But the example of Rudolf is surely the greatest lesson there is – that salvation, redemption, fulfilment, can only come from within, is a function of talent, will power and grey matter and that, properly applied, the rewards can be huge both materially and, for want of a better word, spiritually.

Aged fifty-two now, Rudolf still danced more nights than he didn't and, in *The Overcoat*, he showed no sign of the changes taking place in his body. This ballet is the story of a man who is reviled at work and believes that he can transform his life with a new overcoat. This he commissions at great expense from a tailor, who takes advantage of him. When the coat is made the man wears it to parties, hoping that his status will be improved. Instead, everyone laughs at him and, in the end, because the coat is new, he is taken for a wealthy man by robbers, who set upon him, rob him and steal the coat. He is so distraught that he goes mad and is put into a strait-jacket – another overcoat. Eventually he dies but in the last scene his spirit wreaks revenge. It is a tragic role about an outsider but with many opportunities for Chaplinesque comedy and it suited Rudolf perfectly. The ballet lasted for ninety minutes but he made the time fly. Reviews were excellent and widespread. 'A legend is dressed to advantage,' said one. '*The Overcoat* wears well,' read another.

Margot was not wearing well. In February 1991 she died after a long illness. Rudolf had visited her, and, if anyone still needed proof that they had been lovers, she gave it to them. She was dying of cancer but refused to let Rudolf see her in bed. On the days he visited, she refused the drugs that helped her condition and pain but made her drowsy. She got up, dressed, put on her make-up, and received Rudolf, sitting at a table. She also told him how close to destitution she had been. Had Covent Garden not held the benefit for her in May 1990, her money would have run out two months later. She died on 21 February, the 29th anniversary of their debut in *Giselle*. Ironically, the rumours about Rudolf's health had receded, but it was about now that Canesi first noticed a change in him. He began to lose weight and his skin and hair tone changed. To the trained medical eye, Canesi's patient was beginning to succumb to full AIDS.

A month after Margot died Nureyev turned fifty-three, when he was dancing in Florida. His stamina was amazing but the following month, appearing with Nureyev and Friends in England, the spectacle for many of his non-dancing friends was just too much and they stayed away. By now his tours were in smaller cities – Cambridge, Malvern, Reading, Bristol and Nottingham – there was no scenery and the music was piped. They played in school halls, sports complexes, on a tour organised by Jeffrey Kruger of Hove, who in his time had handled Bill Haley and the Comets and Pat Boone. Rudolf had once said he hated piped music as much as he hated chicken lunches.

Nicholas Dromgoole, in the *Daily Telegraph*, remarked of this tour that it was little short of scandalous, since Rudolf himself was in so little of it. But even that was too much for some people. In Sunderland, at the Empire Theatre, the second of nineteen British venues, fifty people besieged the box office after the performance demanding their money back. The taped music had been faulty and, once again, Rudolf had not left the ground. When he finished in London, the venue was Wembley arena, well away from the West End. Tessa Kennedy, one of the few friends who braved the evening, found that the audience consisted largely of coachloads of provincial housewives who fitted in the show after a day's shopping in London.

In Verona he kicked a fellow dancer so hard that the dancer was kept in hospital for three days for observation. Mario Bois had a different interpretation yet again about this incident. Afterwards, Rudolf had said to him, 'That black cunt, he scratched me twice.' Bois concluded that the dancer must have had AIDS. Rudolf even viewed AIDS solipsistically.

It was a pathetic end for such a magnificent man and, while Rudolf was in Australia, he decided to retire. A final factor may have been that, some time before, he had undergone an operation on his kidneys and for a while needed a catheter. Despite the pain it must have caused, he continued to dance with the catheter inside him. After one Sydney performance, he came off stage bathed in sweat and clearly in agony. All he said was, 'I think I've interfered with the plumbing.' There was another factor in his decision to retire from dancing. About six months earlier he had revealed that he had been taking conducting lessons in secret in June 1991, in the Palais Auersperg in Vienna, where he had conducted music by Mozart, Haydn, Tchaikovsky and Stravinsky. He revealed that he had plans to conduct in Bulgaria and in Kazan in Russia and that he had first thought about conducting ten years before when he had met Herbert von Karajan at Salzburg. Rudolf had not felt well at the time – it may have been when he first contracted the AIDS virus – and he had remarked to von Karajan, who was seventy-three, that he looked very fit. Von Karajan had put it down to the exertions of wielding the baton, and, from then on, Rudolf had always had it in the back of his mind to take up conducting when he finished dancing. It was not merely a question of his health. He had always been very musical and it was a way of continuing to *perform*.

There was also the fact that, in conducting himself, he was still helping ballet to grow. There is a widespread feeling in the ballet world that orchestras do not give of their best when performing for the ballet, certainly in comparison with opera. Certainly, the world's great conductors involve themselves in opera to a much greater extent than they do with ballet. This no doubt has something to do with ballet's more limited repertoire, musically speaking, and the restrictions on *tempi* in ballet, dancers being less flexible on this matter than singers. It also has something to do with the perception that opera is, in some snobbish way, socially preferable to ballet. As a famous ballet conductor, Rudolf was in a position to begin to change this.

None the less, there was a bitter irony – yet again – in his decision to retire just when he did. While he was in Australia, a dancer named Chinko Rafique was in London looking for him. Rafique was half Indian and half English. He had started his career at the Royal Ballet but then moved in exactly the opposite direction to Rudolf – he was now a dancer with the Ufa Ballet. Knowing London and speaking English, he had been sent to Britain with two letters. One was from Shamil Teregeyev, the director of the Ballet Theatre in Ufa, and the other was from the Ministry of Culture in Ufa. Both invited him to dance in the town of his youth.

On 28 January 1992, Clark Tippet, choreographer and principal dancer with the American Ballet Theatre, died of AIDS in New York. He was fifty-seven.

At New Year over 1991–2 Bob Colacello was with a friend, Kevin Farley, on St Bart's, where Rudolf had just bought a house and was fixing it up. They were walking one day on the 'Grand Saline' beach, a quasi-nudist beach where gays would cruise looking for lovers, when they came upon Nureyev, completely alone and completely naked. He came over and said 'Hello', having always been very friendly to Colacello since the latter obtained a gold Cartier watch for him. Rudolf, who was well aware that he was HIV positive, nonetheless immediately started making eyes at Kevin, and then plunged into the sea, showing off his body and ability to move and do acrobatics. 'He looked magnificent,' said Colacello later. The state of Rudolf's own illness did not in any way affect his willingness to get involved with new partners.

Six weeks later, on 24 February, John Wilson, dancer, choreographer and Joffrey Ballet founding member, died of AIDS, aged sixty-four. By then Rudolf was in Berlin, where he danced Carabosse, where again he thought he had displaced the plumbing. From Berlin he flew to Budapest and it was there, playing the angel in Gabor Kevehazi's *Cristoforo*, that Rudolf danced for the last time.

The reviews were warm if not ecstatic – but it was not a particularly sentimental occasion. Rudolf was now much more interested in his new career as a conductor. He had engagements in Kazan, at the Virginia School of Arts, at the Met in May to conduct the American Ballet Theatre and in San Francisco in July. In New York and San Fransisco he would conduct *Romeo and Juliet*. And, further on, there was a new version of *La Bayadère*, which he was choreographing for Dupond in Paris. He would conduct there, too.

In March Rudolf arrived in Kazan, to learn to conduct the music for *Romeo and Juliet* with a Russian orchestra. He took the train from Moscow to Kazan, which is 250 miles west of Ufa, and for much of the journey was closeted in his own compartment with the local conductor, learning the movements. The journey was overnight and it was on the train that he started again to suffer night sweats. Part of the itinerary called for a concert in Yalta and he was going to spend his 54th birthday with the Miasnikovas in Leningrad. Douce François was with him, videotaping the entire trip, as was her practice now that Wallace was no longer around. Such was Rudolf's will, and promiscuity, even at this stage, that, according to the psychiatrist who provided so much of the information on Russia's gay community, Rudolf was rumoured in Kazan to have infected no fewer than four men while he was there. According to Vladimir Nikolaivich Zotov, who worked with Rudolf in Kazan, and Vladimir Alexandreiovich Yahalev, ballet master at Kazan Ballet, he certainly had the strength to go 'carousing' during his three-week stay.

On the day before he was due to leave, he went to the *bania* with some of the musicians from the orchestra and then out into the cold (it was still winter in Russia). He caught a chill. At first he thought it was pneumonia and kept saying, 'Like my father, like my father.' But then he was transferred to the Kirov Military Hospital in Leningrad, where he stayed for a week but did not respond to treatment either for bronchitis or for pneumonia. Two nights before his fifty-fourth birthday, his night sweats turned into a high fever, with a temperature of 40 degrees. Douce called Canesi in Paris, who ordered Rudolf to cut short his trip and fly back to Paris. A private plane was chartered.

Some time later, the Virginia School of Arts announced that Rudolf had cancelled his engagement to conduct its orchestra. Its press people told journalists that Nureyev was ill. They had heard from his agent in Vienna, they said, that he was suffering from extreme fatigue and had a heart problem.

CHAPTER TWENTY-THREE

Twelfth Night's Chillest, Iciest Air

Unheard,
she appears before him, grim and frozen.
No look, no word for him: she's chosen
to encase herself inside a layer
of Twelfth Night's chillest, iciest air.

When Rudolf arrived in Paris he was exhausted. Canesi examined him and found his condition 'catastrophic. I thought he was going to die.' He arranged for Rudolf to be admitted to the Perpétuel-Secours Hospital at Levallois where he was diagnosed within an hour as having a viral infection of the heart lining. This was extremely rare but by no means unknown among people suffering from AIDS. Rudolf was transferred immediately to the Ambroise-Parte clinic at Neuilly where, on 2 April, he was operated on and a pint of fluid drained from the membrane around his heart. Subsequently, he was returned to Perpétuel-Secours and treated with Ganciclovir.

And there then took place the most amazing recovery. Rudolf was due to mount a new production of *La Bayadère* in the autumn and he started work on that. He discussed the set designs with Ezio Frigerio and sounded out the possibility of Ninel Kurgapkina coming from St Petersburg to help him. The choice for this production had originally been between Benjamin Britten's *Prince of the Pagodas*, first performed at Covent Garden in 1957 but not terribly well received, and *La Bayadère*. The latter had two attractions for Rudolf. He had, when he returned to Leningrad in 1989, managed to obtain a photocopy of Minkus's original score. Which meant that he would be able to mount the full four acts, a feat that had not occurred since before the Russian revolution. With the full score available, he felt he could not only produce and direct the ballet but conduct the orchestra as well.

But his next conducting assignment was only a month away. This was *Romeo and Juliet*, at the Met in New York, with the American Ballet Theatre. Even though he was ill, he knew that he wouldn't be allowed short cuts, nor should he expect any special allowances. This was a professional engagement at one of the most prestigious theatres in the world, with one of the best companies. He had to be equal to the occasion.

At first he didn't want to take a nurse, objecting to the cost (£2500). Canesi was irritated, feeling that Rudolf had dispensed with his services now that he was on the mend, as he thought. He actually said to Canesi, 'I don't need you any more.' But, three days later, Rudolf called back and apologised, agreeing that he needed a nurse. Canesi was thrown by Rudolf's apology – like others, he knew how much that took. But he got him the nurse.

Rudolf arrived in New York about two weeks before the performance and rehearsed with the orchestra every morning at 10.30. He would then go home, have a light lunch, nap for half an hour, then study the score for the rest of the afternoon, *willing* himself to overcome his exhaustion. Douce was there to look after his day-to-day needs and to keep distractions to a minimum and Maude Lloyd soon arrived as well. One person who was particularly looking forward to the New York concert was Nicholas Dromgoole, the ballet critic of the *Daily Telegraph* in London. He revealed that, years before as a young man, he had been entertained to lunch at the old Caprice (where Rudolf had dinner with Dietrich and Connery) by Sir David Webster, John Tooley's predecessor as general manager at Covent Garden. Webster had said that when Nureyev, then a young man, gave up dancing, then such was his musical knowledge and creativity that he must surely become one of the world's great conductors. No one, Dromgoole least of all, had expected Rudolf to dance for so long, but at last Rudolf was set to prove Webster right, or wrong.

For anyone searching for omens or meaningful coincidences, the month after Rudolf came out of hospital was an eerie time. In swift succession the deaths occurred of Asaf Messerer, Konstantin Sergeyev, and Vakhtung Chaboukiani, who was eighty-two. Rudolf was not sentimental but even he was struck by this wave of sad news.

Although, strictly speaking, the ABT evening was not Rudolf's début as a conductor, it was the first time many of his friends and fans had had the chance to watch him. His Vienna concert had not been widely publicised and Kazan was hardly a musical mecca like Manhattan. Marilyn La Vine, one of Rudolf's most loyal fans, who was in the audience that night, remembers that, as he approached the rostrum, he was holding on to the music stands and the wall of the pit as he acknowledged his welcome. He wasn't leaning heavily but he did go from support to support. Among the other guests in the audience that evening were Irina Kolpakova, Rudolf's first Giselle, and Alessandra Ferri, his last. Linda Mabeduke had flown down from Toronto.

The main dancers were Sylvie Guillem as Juliet and Laurent Hilaire as Romeo, both protégés of Rudolf's, so the entire evening was close to being a family affair. He took the score at the slower, more majestic pace preferred in Russia (when he had danced at the Maryinsky in 1989 one of the local critics had remarked on how fast he took the music). This Russian pace was not to everyone's taste in Manhattan but it was recognised for what it was, and as legitimate. But many others were completely won over by his reading of the Prokofiev score. One critic said he was a 'baton in a thousand', another that he had given the finest rendition he had ever heard, and Clive Barnes, as loyal as Maude Gosling, said that he had squeezed the best *Romeo and Juliet* out of this particular orchestra that he had witnessed. Anna Kisselgoff found the dancing dull, Nureyev thin but handsome but she didn't mind the protracted ovation he was given at the end.

It had been a good night for Rudolf but afterwards, at the party he gave in the Dakota, his friends who hadn't seen him since he came back from Kazan were shocked. The guest list was as glittering as ever – Jackie Onassis, Jerome Robbins, Natalia Makarova, Pat Buckley, wife of journalist William F. Buckley, Jane Herrmann, Robert Tracy, Peter Martins, director of the NYCB, Monique van Vooren – but Rudolf was too exhausted to sit at the table. He lay on a *chaise-longue* and occasionally rose to get something to eat. Each of his friends was invited into his bedroom, with its heavy oak, Gothic four-poster, for a private chat. Linda Mabeduke was close to tears. A couple of days before the concert, she had gone out with Tracy to buy liquor for the party and on the way back, on the pavement in the street, he had told her that Rudolf had AIDS. That night, she sat with him on the bed, and said, 'Rudolf, we didn't know.' He just nodded. He would not discuss it directly but when Monique took a polaroid of him he would not accept it. 'You keep it,' he said. 'It may be the last.'

In fact, he was still recovering, rather than faltering once more. From New York he went on to Vienna where he indulged in a very public fight with their new artistic director, Elena Tchernichova, and several of the musicians. On her appointment he had withdrawn all his ballets unless he had veto rights over the cast and could choose when he danced himself. This was too much for her in her new position and she decided to do without his ballets altogether. Predictably this infuriated Rudolf, and in an interview he revealed that the Viennese orchestra called Tchernichova Madame Tchernobyl behind her back, on account of her 'catastrophic' organisational abilities. This was too much for the administration who now cancelled his engagement to conduct *Cinderella*. He was allowed to conduct other works but even here there were problems. Some of the musicians dared to speak out, that he was 'ill and incompetent'. Whereupon Franz Moser, the managing director of the company, took Rudolf's part and fired all seven protestors, including the chief conductor.

Rudolf didn't mind. He had invitations from the Australians to conduct there and from the Tokyo Philharmonic. Roland Petit wanted him to conduct *Coppélia* in Marseilles in November, after *La Bayadère*, and before any of this he was booked to conduct the University of California orchestra in San Francisco. When he turned up, in July, he was almost the old Rudolf, wearing to rehearsal one blue and one yellow clog. 'These are my San Francisco shoes,' he said. His performance was well received and afterwards there was a long line of well-wishers standing outside his dressing-room door, like old times. Linda Mabeduke jumped the line because it was late and she had her sons with her who had to be in bed soon. She had brought them to say goodbye. Rudolf kissed them. He knew he wouldn't see them again but still nothing was said.

Continuing to show incredible willpower, in the evening after the performance, Rudolf had dinner in Jeanette Etheridge's Café Tosca and then went out to a night club. The Kirov were in town and although he disapproved of their extended tour, saying they were depriving St Petersburg for nearly a year, he went to see them. He met up again with Zhanna Ayupova, the ballerina he had danced with in Leningrad in 1989. She noticed that, although this was San Francisco in July, Rudolf was wearing a fur coat. She realised then that the rumours in the ballet world that he had AIDS must be true.

The administration at the Paris Opéra arrived at the same conclusion and, very quietly, they moved the date of the première of *La Bayadère* forward. In previous years the big autumn production at the Palais Garnier premièred anywhere between the last week of October and the week before Christmas. This year there were those who thought that, if it were left too late, Rudolf might not make it. The date was set for 8 October.

Rudolf was given the firm date before he set off for a short holiday in St Bart's. It was now that Robert Tracy, worried about Rudolf, but also worried about himself after Rudolf's death, instructed Marvin Mitchelson, America's famous 'palimony' lawyer, to sue for a financial settlement. In the circumstances this did not make Tracy popular but he *had* lived with Rudolf and therefore felt he had a genuine claim. In 1989 a Los Angeles jury had awarded Marc Christian, Rock Hudson's lover, $21.75 million in damages for the emotional distress he suffered on learning that Hudson had AIDS. This was later reduced to $5.5 million. Tracy, who was served with three eviction orders from the Dakota by Barry Weinstein, didn't ask for that much. He received somewhere in the region of $500,000 and Rudolf agreed to settle. Of course, it damaged his relations with both Rudolf and the people around him.

Rudolf arrived back from St Bart's on 3 September. Canesi met him and couldn't hide the fact that he was shocked by Rudolf's appearance. Noticing this, Rudolf asked, 'Is it the end?'

Rehearsals began in the middle of the month, allowing only three weeks with the full cast before the première. The fourth act had been dropped; the designs had proved too expensive and too difficult to stage. By then, Rudolf's life was divided into good days and bad days. He moved only between the quai Voltaire, the Palais Garnier and the Perpétuel-Secours Hospital. Ninel Kurgapkina had arrived from Russia and moved in with Douce at rue Murillo, near Parc Monceau. Rudolf had opted for the three full acts of *La Bayadère*, which he had first danced in Leningrad in 1961, with Moiseeva and Sizova. The truth was that his memory was now deteriorating and he needed Kurgapkina to help in the reconstitution.

Everyone assumed by this point that Rudolf had abandoned all hope of conducting. However, with a week to go before the première he approached Helene Trailine, director of programming at the Paris Opera, to ask when he was supposed to rehearse with the orchestra. Trailine didn't know what to say, so she blustered and promised to get back to him. Instead she immediately telephoned Canesi, begging him to intervene. He did, forbidding Rudolf to take on any more responsibilities. But Rudolf wasn't taken in. When he next saw Trailine, at the dress rehearsal, he was in a rage and pushed away the arm of the man who was helping him down a staircase. He wanted to show that he was still strong and for that day he rejected the use of the chaise longue in favour of a chair, although it clearly exhausted him.

The run-up to the première was not helped by Pierre Bergé. It is true to say that, since he had taken over as president of the Opéra, one form of chaos had followed another. (As Yves Saint Laurent's president, Paris wags described his opera/ballet work as his 'night job'.) First, he fired Daniel Barenboim, then Rudolf, then a number of lesser lights. As a result of the changes brought about by these resignations and sackings, the atmosphere had been poisoned backstage, culminating in an accident while the opera company was on tour that summer in Seville, when a piece of heavy scenery had fallen, killing one stage hand and injuring several others. This delayed a new production of Arthur Honegger's *Jean d'Arc Aubucher*, running it up against *La Bayadère*, which had of course been brought forward.

Rehearsals were particularly trying, with the support staff doubly busy. And Rudolf, having rallied after Kazan right through until his San Francisco performance, was now weakening again. He was forced to give direction from the side of the stage, lying on a *chaise-longue*, since he couldn't stand for more than a minute or two. Even at this stage he hated to talk about his illness, although he always insisted that

Canesi tell him the truth. The only concession he made was to have Barry Weinstein fly to Paris from Chicago so that he could discuss the provisions of his will.

The dancers, aware of his condition as few others appeared to be, responded sympathetically, but only up to a point. At one stage the directions called for the *corps* to dance with stuffed parrots on their wrists. This was too much and they threatened – yet again – to go on strike. This dispute was solved, only for another to take its place concerning the last act. This was less satisfactorily resolved, and cuts had to be made in the choreography. These changes were awkward, meaning a revision that delayed the last two rehearsals, which stretched late on into the night. Tempers, on all sides, became very frayed.

Despite this, despite everything, the world at large did not suspect how ill Nureyev was. The pre-production publicity in the French press described the ballet as a 'Danse d'Amour' on Isabelle Guérin's part with no apparent realisation of what may have lain behind that sentiment. On the morning of the première, in *Le Figaro*, René Sirvin, who had become more and more sympathetic to Rudolf, said that the evening's performance would be the event of the season. Another critic described how Nureyev was tired after all the rehearsals but was 'surmontant' (overcoming) his illness. Yet another said that his face showed how moved he had been by the spectacle he had created. But he coughed a lot.

8 October was one of Rudolf's bad days. When he arrived at the theatre, there were gasps by those who saw his gaunt appearance. He seemed to have forgotten the theatre he knew so well, and needed to be guided to his box. There, a bed or *chaise-longue* had been prepared for him, banked with cushions. From this box he could see the stage over the parapet, but most of the audience couldn't see him. He was exhausted, virtually beyond speech.

Like many in the group of sixty or seventy fans that Nureyev had acquired over the years, and who travelled all over the world to see him, Marilyn La Vine was at the Palais Garnier that night. She had a seat at the front of the stalls and the first thing she noticed, before the lights went down, was that there was a private box, at stage level, stage right, where she could just see the top of Nureyev's head. She knew it was him because he was wearing a black and red turban. People kept coming into the box and would lean down and kiss him.

The lights were lowered and the performance began. *La Bayadère* had been the first ballet with which Rudolf had made his name in the west, when the Kirov had danced it in 1961. Then Rudolf had re-created it for Frederick Ashton. His career had come full circle in more ways than one. Ezio Frigerio's set looked like the interior of his house at Li Galli.

At the interval, Marilyn decided to pay her respects to Rudolf and made her way along the corridor towards his box. As she was doing so, she saw him coming towards her. She stopped, devastated. He was being held up by two people she didn't know and presumably he was bored with lying in his box. He noticed her, and nodded. That nod, the last communication she had with him, was still pure Rudolf. That nod said, yes, it's me. It doesn't look like me, but it is. Yes, I'm ill, dying. But for now I'm still here. He couldn't speak, partly because he was exhausted, partly because his mouth was filled with candidiasis, oral thrush.

He was led away and Marilyn returned to her seat as the lights were going down for the second act.

One of the people with Rudolf, whom Marilyn didn't recognise, was Michel Canesi. During the performance he leaned down to Rudolf and whispered, 'Rudolf, are you happy?'

Rudolf looked up. 'Very, very happy,' he said as best he could.

Canesi fought back the tears.

The last act, of course, contains the famous Kingdom of the Shades scene that had so entranced Olivier Merlin when he had first seen it on the Kirov's 1961 tour. It is also the act where Solor dances for the last time with Nikiya, who is already dead. The parallels were too painful for Marilyn La Vine to dwell on.

After the curtain had come down, and the dancers had taken their bows, there was a call for Rudolf from the audience. There was a delay. Rudolf was being helped through from his box but Michel Canesi told him that he didn't have to go on if he didn't want to.

'No, no,' said Rudolf. 'I must. I want to. But let's make it brief.' It was, thought Canesi, an elegant way of letting his public know what was happening.

Rudolf was led forward by Isabelle Guérin and Laurent Hilaire. Dressed in white tie and tails, with his red and black turban and his scarlet and gold blanket over his left shoulder, he looked elegant and exotic all at the same time, as only Rudolf could look. But he also looked gaunt. His eyes were sunk deep inside his head, making his cheekbones more prominent than ever. He shambled forward. There was a smile somewhere in his face and, yes, the same old proud defiance. But there was something new – the dark, staring, black-eyed look of people who are close to death *and know it*. As he appeared, there was, as Canesi put it, four seconds of absolute silence. It happened after his first *Giselle* at Covent Garden in 1962. But this time there was no Lydia Lopokova in the stalls to murmer 'Lurvely'.

Instead, there was a sudden, thunderous ovation. The audience stood as one as everyone realised, at the same time, that this really was farewell. As the applause rose, a few '*Au revoirs*' could be heard among the clapping. Flowers were thrown but Rudolf was too weak to pick them up. He was too weak even to bow.

He nearly fell three times and had to be supported by the ballerinas.

Three times the curtain rose and fell. By the last time Rudolf's mouth had sagged open, the smile had faded. His dark eyes stared. He looked frightened. The curtain came down for the last time. For many people, Rudolf Nureyev died that night, on stage. As he always said he would do.

Behind the curtain, Rudolf was seated as comfortably as possible. People were lining up to convey their congratulations on the performance. Once again, Michel Canesi said he didn't have to go through with all this, but once again Rudolf insisted that he did. He was a man of the theatre and there would be few nights like this one.

Jack Lang, the Minister of Culture, approached and presented Nureyev with the gold medal and black and white ribbon of a Commander of Arts and Letters. The award sat very well with Rudolf's exotic outfit. After about half an hour the celebrations on stage, if they can be called that, were abandoned and Rudolf was taken out by a rear door. But this was Rudolf Nureyev and he wasn't going home just because a few friends thought it would be best. He still knew how to be forceful and insisted on being taken to the post-première party, where he sat next to Pierre Bergé and discussed their plans for the following year. Amazingly, to those present who had seen him on stage earlier in the evening, he now appeared to rally. Among those at the party was Roland Petit. 'Roland!' Rudolf called out, 'Where's the music?' He meant *Coppélia*.

The next morning there was little thought for the critical reception of *La Bayadère*, though it was well received. The pictures of Rudolf's gaunt features were wired around the world at the same speed, and with the same impact, as those of Rock Hudson a few years before. Indeed the two events seemed to encapsulate the AIDS phenomenon. Rock Hudson had been the first internationally known individual to succumb to the disease, thrusting its existence and extent unavoidably into prominence. The pictures of Rudolf underlined the reach of AIDS, its tenacity, the fact that this epidemic could not be ignored. Rudolf's life had been devoted to the achievement of physical beauty. He had been one of the most beautiful men of his day and conceivably the best dancer of all time. For him to be stricken in this way was tragic beyond measure. For years he had been among the most famous men on earth. Only his manner of leaving it could add immeasurably to that fame.

Not that the Opéra were about to admit that Rudolf had AIDS. There now followed a curious period when what everyone knew to be true was denied officially. The day after the premierè the Paris Opéra Ballet press officer admitted only that Nureyev was very tired, and was still recovering from serious surgery. The press officer then set out a textbook definition of pericarditis and left it at that.

After such an emotional evening, the choreographer John Taras was uncertain whether to call on Rudolf at quai Voltaire the next day, a Friday. In the morning, however, he ran into Luigi Pignotti, who told him that Rudolf had been having good days and bad days since 1985 and not to let that bother him. Accordingly, Taras called in at quai Voltaire that afternoon, where he found a scene 'as if from Lorca'. The flat was simply packed with people – Douce, Charles Jude, Rudi van Dantzig, Canesi – all tiptoeing about because Rudolf was asleep. Taras was about to join in this sombre scene himself when suddenly the door to Rudolf's bedroom opened and in he walked. Immediately, he buttonholed Taras. He had decided, he said, to form a choreographical school in St Petersburg – it would update the Vaganova. Did Taras want to be involved? 'Of course,' was the reply. Next Rudolf turned to van Dantzig and made the same suggestion. He too agreed.

'It was so moving,' said Taras later, 'how he talked about the possibilities, about the people there.' Luigi had been right. 9 October was a good day.

Douce – quietly in love with Rudolf down the years, ready to be a friend and a doormat according to Rudolf's whim, ready to have his child if only he would consent – now sought to prevent what she saw as an outbreak of bad taste in the media, who were speculating on whether Rudolf had AIDS. Hitherto she had kept her silence but now she gave interviews in which she commented, 'What is being said about Rudi is unfair. He is a legend and does not deserve to be treated in this fashion.' She insisted that his emaciated appearance was due to hard work and the effect of his operation. 'We have kept the papers from him but Rudi is beginning to sense something. If he finds out what people are saying it could destroy him.' (Did he not want to read the reviews? Was he not being destroyed anyway?) In fact a German fan had faxed him a rave review in a German newspaper which also discussed his AIDS. This slipped through Douce's protective net and Rudolf was very distressed when he read it. Given time, she insisted in her interviews, he could make a full recovery, and she went on to outline a plan for a tour of South America in December. 'Quite frankly, do you think that I would be spending all this money if Rudi was about to die?'

But what Luigi Pignotti had not told John Taras was that the bad days were increasing in frequency and, a few days after the première of *La Bayadère*, Rudolf, along with Jude, Jude's wife and a large dog, escaped Paris for the sun of St Bart's. The press followed, braving the extraordinary landing on the island's only airstrip, which forces incoming aircraft to stop their engines in mid-air as they pass over a saddle of small hills, and drop like a stone for a moment, to meet the runway at the correct altitude.

Rudolf and his friends stayed for ten days at his wooden house on the island's less fashionable windy Atlantic coast. Each day Rudolf forced himself into the sea. There had been a time when he had paraded his naked body on the beach by his house, showing off to tourists. Not any more. Each day he forced himself to eat oysters and drink Montrachet. He was determined still to live.

But, after the initial excitement of arrival, the bad days resumed. As St Bart's is such a remote spot, it soon became clear that Rudolf would have to return to Paris. His return coincided with the death from AIDS of Melvin Dixon, aged forty-two, author of *Trouble the Waters*. It was 26 October.

A month of tests followed. For these he was taken to Perpétuel-Secours Hospital. Most days Canesi pumped vitamins into him. He, like all others around Rudolf, would not discuss his patient's illness, attributing his frail condition to his surgery.

During November, Rudolf's skin began to acquire a papery texture, and clung more closely to those famous Tartar cheekbones. He felt the cold more than ever now, and wore a woollen bonnet at all times, even on good days, with headphones clamped over it, so that he could hear his beloved Bach and the music of *Coppélia*, which he was due to conduct in Marseilles in a few weeks. Parisian friends dropped by – Pierre Bergé, Charles Jude, Mario Bois – but more touching were the telephone calls from friends from all over the world – Violette Verdy, Natasha Harley, John Lanchbery. When Joan Thring rang she asked Rudolf, gently, if he were in much pain. 'I can't complain,' he managed to say. 'I can't complain.'

One by one, people said goodbye.

He still rallied, and on good days would read the French and English papers, or sit in a chair covered in a coloured textile and look out on the quai Voltaire and across to the Louvre. Not all the papers were shown to him. Rudolf still was not aware that the whole world knew he had AIDS, and his friends had decided that that's how it would remain. Such information, they felt, would have saddened him too much.

In 1984, Mario Bois had been partly responsible for the creation of the Société des Auteurs et Compositeurs Dramatiques, the SACD. This was an organisation designed to protect the rights of choreographers and adaptors, musicians and arrangers, whose ballets or musical pieces might be performed in the grand theatres of the world. Bois was responsible for registering Rudolf's works with SACD, beginning with *Washington Square*. At that point it was not always accepted by theatre managements that they should pay royalties for every performance – just for the initial rights to present a work. But the idea spread fairly rapidly across Europe and north America (with the exception of Italy), and then to Australia and Japan. This was to become an important supplementary form of income for Rudolf. For example, between September 1991 and the autumn of 1992, Rudolf received at least £90,000 in rights payments for *Romeo and Juliet, La Bayadère* and *Don Quixote*. It partly accounted for his closer relationship with Bois from 1984 on.

There were hardly any good days now, and his body was hit by repeated waves of thrush. On 20 November he was admitted to Perpétuel-Secours Hospital in the north-west of Paris under a false name, Monsieur Potts – Wallace was back on the scene and being very helpful, now that Tracy had lost touch. This was the third time in Rudolf's life he had used such a device. (The first had been when he travelled to London to discuss the first gala with Margot; the second was when he had visited Erik in Australia.) At the hospital, he was installed in room 517, on the fifth floor, and placed on a drip even though this risked infection.

To begin with he rallied and impressed his doctors. Then he fell back again. He hated the sheer *boredom* of being ill. Jerome Robbins, who was rehearsing at Palais Garnier, visited him every day. Now, part of him at least seemed to accept the inevitable, in so far as he chose his burial ground, the Rusian Orthodox cemetery of Sainte-Geneviève-des-Bois, an hour outside central Paris. It was the traditional resting place of aristocratic white Russian families exiled in France. His father would have hated it.

Now the 'nannies' – or the pride of lionesses, as Linda Mabeduke put it – began to arrive in Paris to comfort Douce and Marika Bessobrassova, who had borne the brunt of the care of Rudolf so far. Linda was there, from Toronto, Jeanette Etheridge from San Francisco, Natasha Harley and Monique van Vooren from New York, Liuba Miasnikova from St Petersburg. There was a firm pecking order, which everyone recognised (Marika, Douce, Jeanette, etc . . .) 'Then the lioness-in-chief arrived,' said Mabeduke. Maude.

Wallace was there, the only man, the solitary ex-lover. Rudolf had bought a second small flat on the quai Voltaire, which was used by his family, Rosa and Guzelle mainly. Amazingly, they kept their distance. The sad truth was that the Nureyevs were still peasants at heart and didn't know how to behave. Wild animals were still loose on the quai Voltaire. The building rang with the noise and bustle of people except that Rudolf wasn't there. One friend who didn't visit was Clara Saint. She had lost touch years before. Conversely, Madonna decided she *did* want to visit Rudolf even though she didn't know him. The plan came to nothing.

When the Italian writer Ettore Mo visited him at Perpétuel-Secours in the first week of December, he was unable to tell whether Rudolf was about to give out 'or whether his great Tartar soul was really helping him cling to the hope that his vitality would be fully restored'. Rudolf couldn't swallow and was being fed intravenously, yet Mo found that he had plans to stage *The Nutcracker, Sleeping Beauty* and *Romeo and Juliet* in Milan. He couldn't help noticing that Rudolf spoke extremely slowly and that sometimes as long as ten minutes would elapse before he answered a question.

While he was there the phone rang several times. Often, it was the rich and beautiful women who had become his friends – in America, Australia, Japan, Greece, South America. The nurses came in. Rudolf was wearing pure wool pyjamas covered in patterns of autumn browns, reds and ochres. The nurses made him more comfortable on his pillows and he began to recall Fonteyn. 'She was my ideal partner,' he told Mo. 'We had different temperaments, and there was an age difference of twenty years. But our bodies, our movements, our hands and feet always managed to meet and merge wonderfully, and I don't think I ever found such a balanced partnership again.'

Old spaghetti westerns were playing on the TV in the hospital room. Mo asked Rudolf if he wanted to play some of his *own* videos, showing his choreography, or one of his films, *Valentino* maybe, or *Exposed*. Rudolf gestured vaguely, 'as if all of a sudden he wanted to push aside not only his glorious repertoire but the whole of his past'.

Mo's two hours were coming to an end. With the authority that very ill people are granted, Rudolf tried to reassure *him* that he was not starved for affection, that Douce, Marika or Liuba came every day, bringing him his hot tea, still with five sugars, the way he liked it.

Mo asked about Rosa. Did she come? Rudolf hadn't mentioned her. 'No,' whispered Rudolf. 'She doesn't come. We've lost touch.'

He said one other thing. Mo was just leaving and rain was pelting against the hospital windows. Rudolf didn't raise his voice but his words were clear. What he said was: 'I am greater now than ever.'

When Luigi visited him a few days later, he was much weaker. But Luigi had news. He bent down by the bed and asked, 'Rudolf, if you hear me, close your eyes.'

He closed his eyes.

'The San Carlo in Naples changed their mind. They want you to do *Swan Lake* now. If you agree, close your eyes.'

Rudolf closed his eyes.

Michel Canesi said that in those December days Rudolf was like Petrushka 'the disjointed puppet, broken and unhappy'. He reminisced now about Erik. Not the cruelty but the passion they had had for each other, a passion Rudolf had not known before, or since. Once more, he repeated, 'I would have been Erik's *dresser!*'

But Rudolf had a deeper knowledge of the dance, and of the classics, than Canesi and, instead of Petrushka, he may have been reminded at that time of his most romantic role, the one ballet that was created for Margot and him, and which was never danced by anyone else:

Marguerite and Armand. For in the book on which the ballet is based, *La Dame aux Camélias*, the heroine, Marguerite Gautier, approaches her end with an uncanny similarity, at the same time of year, as Rudolf approached his.

The story ends with a letter in the form of a diary, written by Marguerite to Armand to explain her behaviour to him, and to ask his forgiveness.

'Today is the 15th December. I have been ill for three or four days. This morning, I took to my bed; the weather was dull and I feel low. There is no one with me here . . . I may die of my illness, for I always had a feeling that I would die young.

20 December
'The weather is dreadful: it's snowing and I am here alone. For the last three days, a fever has laid me so low that I have been unable to write to you . . . I cough blood all the time . . . Today I got up for a while and, from behind the curtains at my window, I watched the bustle of life in Paris which I do believe I have put behind me once and for all.

25 December
'My doctor has forbidden me to write every day. He is right, for remembering only makes the fever worse . . .

4 January
'I have just come through a succession of racking days. I never knew how much pain our bodies can give us. Oh! my past life! I am now paying for it twice over!

'I have had someone sitting with me each night. I could not breathe. A wandering mind and bouts of coughing share what remains of my sorry existence.

My dining room is crammed full of sweets and presents of all kinds which friends have brought me . . . If they could only see what illness has reduced me to, they would run away in horror.'

In the last entry of her letter/diary, Marguerite rallies enough to be taken to the theatre, her cheeks rouged ('otherwise I should have looked like a corpse'), but is brought home half-dead and coughs up blood all night. 'I cannot speak and can hardly move my arms. God! God! I am going to die! I was expecting it, but I cannot reconcile myself to the thought . . .' The visit to the theatre was Marguerite's last entry in her diary.

Charles Jude was one of the last people to speak to Rudolf. On the morning of 4 January 1993 the two men discussed Rudolf's plans to visit Shanghai the following year, to teach western dance techniques to the Chinese. But, at 4.25 that afternoon, he slipped into a coma. He died two days later, at 3.45 pm on Wednesday, 6 January, the Russian Christmas and the Christian Feast of the Epiphany, the day after Twelfth Night. Unlike Marguerite Gautier, or Margot Fonteyn, his end was peaceful. As Michel Canesi put it, echoing Joan Thring 'He did not complain.' But then, as one of very few people who have lived life to the full, who, with his technical gifts and his dramatic charisma probably *moved* more people than anyone in his generation, who danced more days in his life than he did not, who conquered love to the point where he needed it less than anyone else, yet who had loved, and been loved by, men and women, who successfully resisted the degrading influences of popular culture, who sat in the Oval Office and visited the Anvil, whose friends ranged from Spanish chimney sweeps to Jacqueline Onassis, who remained utterly faithful to his own temper, who was a familar face and yet a stranger with his own private world, whose virgin fire remained undimmed for more than half a century, what on earth did he have to complain about?

Epilogue

An End before His Time

the youthful votary of rhyme,
has found an end before his time.
The storm is over.

Rudolf was buried six days later, on 12 January. It began as a cold, stormy, winter morning. It was raining when the oak coffin arrived at the Palais Garnier in a hearse and was carried into the foyer by six dancers. The steps outside the Paris Opéra were strewn with flowers sent by his public. The coffin was carried into the foyer of the theatre and lifted up to the top of the wide marble staircase, where it was laid. The ceremony took place here, in this more intimate space, rather than in the theatre proper. On a velvet cushion two steps below the coffin were his two principal French awards, the Légion d'honneur, Chevalier's Cross, and his sash as a Commander of Arts and Letters. Along each side of the grand staircase were twenty-four white bouquets of chrysanthemums, laid by the *petits rats*, ballet school students. Hundreds of electric candles blazed with light.

Between his death and his funeral, Rudolf had received many tributes but perhaps the most moving came from Oleg Vinogradov, of the Kirov. He said, quite simply, 'What Nureyev did in the west, he could never have done here.' It was also made known that Rudolf's name had now been re-entered into the history of the Kirov, some of his effects were on display at the theatre museum in Leningrad, and a rehearsal room was to be named after him at the Vaganova (the others are named after Nijinsky and Sergeyev). Recognition at last that the 'traitor' was in fact nothing of the kind.

Leading the mourners on the stairway were Rosa and Rezida, with Rudolf's two nephews Yuri and Victor and his two nieces Guzelle and Alysa. Around them were the *étoiles* and other members of the Paris

Opéra Ballet, many of them weeping openly. At the foot of the stairs beyond a small string ensemble, and in the galleries, stood several hundred friends and distinguished figures from the world of ballet. The forty-five-minute programme began with the first part of Bach's 'Art of the Fugue'. There followed literary selections, chosen by Rudolf, and more music by Bach, Tchaikovsky and Mahler. The poems read out by his friends included an extract from Byron's *Manfred*, Michelangelo's 'Love has ravished me, beauty has enchained me', Goethe's 'I have crossed this world running and have seized every desire by the hair', and one of Rudolf's favourite passages from *Eugene Onegin*:

> We must leave these sad shores,
> the hostility of this country . . .
> and languish for gloomy Russia,
> where I suffered, where I loved, where I buried my heart.

Jack Lang made the eulogy. 'You chose to be interred in the soil of France,' he said, 'which will be sweet and hospitable to you.' He also paid tribute to the manner of Rudolf's last days which, he said, recalled the ancient sages and their 'art of dying'. 'He kept silent but he fought. He suffered but he worked. What a lesson in courage and in greatness.' The gods, he said, had granted Rudolf exceptional gifts.

'La beauté', la puissance, le goût de l'absolu . . . Il atteint une dimension mythique. Comme le phénix, il renaît chaque matin après s'être extenué chaque soir.' Rudolf, Lang said, had once told him, 'Vouloir c'est pouvoir.'

The coffin was then carried down the great staircase a final time. In the foyer below, and in the galleries above, Rudolf's friends and famous colleagues watched sadly: Carla Fracci, Lynn Seymour, Marika Besobrasova, Yvette Chauviré, Franco Zelfirelli, Patrick Dupond, Jean Babilée, Ghislaine Thesmar, Zizi Jeanmaire, Roland Petit, Anthony Dowell, Linda Mabeduke, Jacob Rothschild, Ruggiero Raimondi, John Neumeier, Rudy van Dantzig, John Taras, Leslie Caron, Lee Radziwill, Maude Gosling, Jeanette Etheridge, Amyn Prince Aga Khan, Peter Wright, Antoinette Sibley, Merle Park, Jane Hermann, Nicholas Georgiadis, several members of the Niarchos family, John Tooley, Serge Sorokin and the Swiss lawyers who were to administer the two linked Nureyev Foundations, one in Europe the other in North America, which had been announced between his death and this day. Rudolf's fortune, estimated at between $33 million and $40 million, was to be used to help support the careers of young dancers and to fund unspecified 'scientific and medical research'. The Swiss lawyers, in true Swiss lawyer fashion, later sent a bill to Jacob Rothschild, chairman of the European trust, *charging* for their attendance at the funeral.

Outside the theatre, the weather had changed. The sun shone. At the graveyard of Sainte-Geneviève-du-Bois, where the Russian Orthodox cemetery is located in Paris, and where Serge Lifar is also buried, the silver birches were faintly reminiscent of Ufa, but otherwise this suburban place seemed in some ways more distant from the Opéra than is the Maryinsky, or the Met, or Covent Garden. But Rudolf was now on Russian soil. His exile was over.

As the coffin was lowered into the ground, a quartet played Adam's music from the last act of *Giselle*. Rudolf was buried, like Valentino, in his evening clothes. His ballet shoes were cast down, too, and an armful of white lilies was strewn over them, in remembrance of his Albrecht at Giselle's grave. Whatever else he may have done in his life, Rudolf never forsook his princes. And they never forsook him.

Selected Bibliography

Note: Only major articles have been included

Anonymous, *Konstantin Sergeyev*, Moscow 1978

Alovert, Nina, 'Yuri Grigorovich: An Appreciation,' *Dance Magazine*, July 1987

Andersen, Christopher, *Jagger Unauthorised*, London, Simon & Schuster, 1993

Anderson, Jack, *The One and Only: The Ballet Russe de Monte Carlo*, New York, Dance Horizon, 1981

Andrew, Christopher, and Oleg Gordievsky, *KGB, the Inside Story*, New York, Harper Collins, 1990

Ardoin, John, *The Callas Legacy*, New York, Scribner's, 1977

Balanchine, George, and Francis Mason, *Balanchine's Festival of Ballet*, London, W.H. Allen, 1978

Ballet Review, 'A Tribute to Rudolf Nureyev,' Winter 1993

Barnes, Clive, *Nureyev*, New York, Helene Obolensky Enterprises Inc., 1982

——, *Nureyev: Twenty years in the West*, New York, Putnam, 1982

Barron, John, *KGB, The Secret Work of Soviet Secret Agents*, London, Hodder & Stoughton, 1974

Baryshnikov, Mikhail, 'Memories of Nureyev,' *Vogue*, March, 1993

Beaumont, Cyril, *Complete Book of Ballets*, London, Putnam, 1949

Benedetti, Jean, *Stanislavski*, London, Methuen, 1988

Beschloss, Michael, *The Crisis Years: Kennedy and Khrushchev 1960–1963*, New York, Edward Burlingame Books, 1991

Bland, Alexander, *The Nureyev Image*, London, Studio Vista, 1976

——, *The Royal Ballet – the First Fifty Years*, New York, Doubleday, 1981

Bockris, Victor, *Warhol*, London, Century Hutchinson, 1989

Bois, Mario, *Rudolf Noureev*, Paris, Editions Plume, 1993

Borisoglebsky, Mikhail, *A Documentary History of Russian Ballet*, two volumes, Leningrad, 1938

Borovsky, Victor, *Chaliapin: A Critical Biography*, New York, Knopf, 1988

Buckle, Richard, *Nijinsky*, New York, Simon and Schuster, 1972

——, *Diaghilev*, New York, Atheneum, 1979

——, in collaboration with John Taras, *George Balanchine*, London, Hamish Hamilton, 1988

Bullock, Alan, *Hitler and Stalin: Parallel Lives*, London, Fontana Press, 1993

Byron, Lord, *Complete Poetical Works*, Oxford, Oxford University Press, 1970

Cartier, Jacqueline, 'A Leningrad, Béjart s'amuse en écoutant Léotard parler de Noureev,' *France-Soir*, 29 June 1987

Chujoy, Anatole, *The New York City Ballet*, New York, Knopf, 1963

Churcher, Sharon, *New York Confidential*, New York, Crown, 1986

Colacello, Bob, *Holy Terror: Andy Warhol Close Up*, New York, HarperCollins, 1990

——, 'The last Days of Nureyev,' *Vanity Fair*, March 1993

Coward, Noel, *Diaries*, edited by Graham Payn and Sheridan Morley, London, Weidenfeld and Nicolson, 1982

Crisp, Clement, 'Les Etoiles de Paris,' *Ballet News*, July 1985

Demidov, Alexander, *The Russian Ballet Past & Present*, Moscow, Novosti Press/New York, Doubleday, 1977

Dumas *fils*, Alexandre, *La Dame aux Camélias*, translated by David Coward, Oxford, Oxford University Press, 1986

Dunning, Jennifer, *'But first a school': The First Fifty Years of the School of American Ballet*, New York, Elisabeth Sifton Books/Viking, 1985

Dupuis, Simone, and Nicole Le Caisne, 'Palais Garnier: Eh bien! dansez maintenant,' *L'Express*, 10 March 1989

Eaton, Quaintance, *The Miracle of the Met: An Informal History of the Metropolitan Opera 1883–1967*, New York, Meredith Press, 1968

Fonteyn, Margot, *Autobiography*, London, W.H. Allen, 1975

Forbes, Bryan, *A Divided Life*, London, Heinemann, 1992

Geva, Tamara, *Split Seconds: A Remembrance*, London, Jonathan Cape, 1986

Gosling, Nigel, *Leningrad/St Petersburg*, Studio Vista, 1965

Grey, Antony, *Quest for Justice*, London, Sinclair-Stevenson, 1992

Gruen, John, *Erik Bruhn, Danseur Noble*, New York, The Viking Press, 1979

——, *The Private World of Ballet*, New York, Viking, 1970

Guest, Ivor, *Le Ballet de l'Opéra de Paris*, Paris, Flammarion, 1976

——, *The Romantic Ballet in England*, London, Pheonix House, 1954

Hanna, Judith Lynne, *Dance, Sex and Gender*, Chicago, University of Chicago Press, 1988

Haskell, Arnold, *Ballet*, Harmondsworth, Penguin, 1938

Heymann, C. David, *A Woman Named Jackie*, London, Heinemann, 1989

Higham, Charles, *The Life of Marlene Dietrich*, New York, Norton, 1977

Hinchley, Vernon, *The Defectors*, London, Harrap, 1967

Huckenpahler, Victoria, *Ballerina: A Biography of Violette Verdy*, New York, Marcel Dekker, 1978

Hurok, Sol, in collaboration with Ruth Goode, *Impresario*, London, Macdonald, 1947

Ilicheva, Marina, *Irina Kolpakova*, Leningrad 1979

James, Henry, *Washington Square*, Oxford, Oxford University Press, 1963

Jennings, Luke, 'Rudolf Nureyev, The Final Chapter,' *The (London) Sunday Times Magazine*, 31 January, 1993

Kavanagh, Julie, 'Master of Illusion,' Harpers & Queen, 1986

Kaye, Elizabeth, 'Nureyev: Dancing in his own shadow,' *Esquire*, March 1991

Karsavina, Tamara, *Theatre Street*, New York, Dutton, 1931

Kelley, Kitty, *Elizabeth Taylor: The Last Star*, New York, Simon & Schuster, 1981

Kerensky, Oleg, *Ballet Scene*, London, Hamish Hamilton, 1970

Kirkland, Gelsey, with Greg Lawrence, *Dancing on My Grave*, New York, Doubleday, 1986

Kirstein, Lincoln, *The New York City Ballet*, New York, Knopf, 1973

Krasovskaya, Vera, *Vakhtang Chaboukiani*, Leningrad, 1960

Kremshevskaya, Galina, *Natalia Dudinskaya*, Leningrad, 1964
  Agrippina Vaganova, Leningrad, 1981

Legat, Nicolas, *Ballet Russe*, Translated by Sir Paul Dukes, London, Methuen, 1939

Lemay, Paul, 'Nureyev Now! After Paris,' *Dance magazine*, May 1990

Levinson, André, *Marie Taglioni*, Paris, Editions F. Alcan, 1929

Lifar, Serge, *Serge Diaghilev*, New York, Putnam, 1940
  Ma Vie, Translated by James Holman Mason, London, Hutchinson, 1970
  Les Memoires d'Icare, Paris, Editions Sauret, 1993

Lilly, Doris, *Those Fabulous Greeks: Onassis, Niarchos, and Livanos*, London, W.H. Allen, 1971

Lvov-Anokhin, Boris, *Alla Shelest*, Moscow, 1964

Makarova, Natalia, *A Dance Autobiography*, New York, Knopf, 1979

Markova, Alicia, *Giselle and I*, New York, Vanguard Press, 1960

Martin, John, *American Dancing: The Background and personalities of the Modern Dance*, New York, Dance Horizons, 1968

Martins, Peter, with Robert Cornfield, *Far from Denmark*, Boston, Little Brown, 1982

Massie, Suzanne, *Land of the Firebird: The Beauty of Old Russia*, London, Hamish Hamilton, 1980.

Massine, Léonide, *My Life in Ballet*, Edited by Phyllis Hartnoll and Robert Rubens, London, Macmillan, 1968

McDonagh, Don, *Martha Graham: A Biography*, New York, Praeger, 1973

Messerer, Asaf, *Dance, Idea, Time*, Moscow, 1979

Migel, Parmenia, *The Ballerinas: From the Court of Louis XIV to Pavlova*, New York, Macmillan, 1972

de Mille, Agnes, *Portrait Gallery*, Boston, Houghton Mifflin, 1990

Money, Keith, *Anna Pavlova: her Life and Art*, New York, Knopf, 1982

Neale, Wendy, *Ballet Life Behind the Scenes*, New York, Crown Publishers, 1982

Newman, Barbara, *Antoinette Sibley: Reflections of a Ballerina*, London, Hutchinson, 1986

Nijinsky, Romola, *Nijinsky*, New York, Simon & Schuster, 1934
The Last years of Nijinsky, New York, Simon & Schuster, 1952

Nureyev, Rudolf, *An Autobiography*, London, Hodder & Stoughton, 1962, reissued 1993

Oppenheimer, Jerry, *Barbara Walters, An authorized Biography*, New York, St Martin's Press, 1990

Panov, Valery, with George Feifer, *To Dance*, New York, Knopf, 1978

Pastori, Jean-Pierre, *Patrick Dupond: La Fureur de Danser*, Paris, Editions Pierre-Marcel Favre, 1982

Payne, Charles, *American Ballet Theatre*, New York, Knopf, 1978

Penrose, Barry, and Simon Freeman, *Conspiracy of Silence: The Secret Life of Anthony Blunt*, New York, Vintage, 1988

Percival, John, *Nureyev*, London, Granada, 1979

Perlmutter, Donna, *Shadowplay: The Life of Antony Tudor*, New York, Viking, 1991

Peyser, Joan, *Bernstein, A Biography*, New York, William Morrow, 1987

Philp, Richard, and Mary Whitney, *Danseur: The Male in Ballet*, New York, McGraw Hill, 1977

Prokhorova, Valentina, *Konstantin Sergeyev*, Leningrad, 1974

Pushkin, Alexander, *Eugene Onegin*, Harmondsworth, Penguin, 1979

Richmond, Yale, *U.S.-Soviet Cultural Exchanges, 1958–1986: Who Wins?* London, Westview Press.

Rivera, Geraldo, with Daniel Paisner, *Exposing Myself*; New York, Bantam, 1992

Robinson, Harlow, *The Last Impressario, The Life, Times and legacy of Sol Hurok*, New York, The Viking Press, 1994

Roslavleva, Natalia, *Era of the Russian ballet, 1770–1965*, New York, Dutton, 1966

Rutledge, Leigh W., *The Gay Decades*, New York, Plume/Penguin, 1992

Schonberg, Harold C., 'Metropolitan Opera House Closes 83 years in a Blaze of Elegance,' *New York Times*, 17 April, 1966

Schwarz, Boris, *Music and Musical Life in Soviet Russia*, Bloomington, Indiana, Indiana University Press, 1983

Seymour, Lynn, with Paul Gardner, *Lynn*, London, Granada, 1984

Shilts, Randy, *And the Band Played On: Politics, People and the AIDS Epidemic*, New York, St Martin's Press, 1987

Sirvin, René, 'Opéra: l'affaire Noureev,' *Le Figaro*, 24 September, 1989

Smakov, Gennady, *Baryshnikov, From Russia to the West*, New York, Farrar Strauss Giroux, 1981
The Great Russian Dancers, New York, Knopf, 1984

Sokolova, Lydia, *Dancing for Diaghilev*, Edited by Richard Buckle, London, John Murray, 1960

Spender, Stephen, *Journals: 1939–1983*, London, Faber & Faber, 1985

Stassinopoulos, Arianna, *Maria Callas, The Woman behind the Legend*, New York, Simon & Schuster, 1981

Taper, Bernard, *Balanchine*, New York, Macmillan, 1974

Tharp, Twyla, *Push Comes to Shove*, New York, Bantam, 1992

Tracy, Robert, with Sharon Delano, *Balanchine's Ballerinas: Conversations with the Muses*, New York, Linden Press/Simon & Schuster, 1983

de Valois, Ninette, *Step by Step*, London, W.H. Allen, 1977

Vickers, Hugo, *Cecil Beaton*, London, Weidenfeld and Nicolson, 1985

Volkov, Solomon, *Balanchine's Tchaikovsky*, trans. by Antonina Bouis, New York, Simon & Schuster, 1985

Warhol, Andy and Pat Hackett, *Popism, the Warhol Sixties*, New York, Harcourt Brace Jovanovitch, 1980

Werth, Alexander, *Russia: The Post-War years*, New York, Taplinger, 1971

Willis, Margaret, 'Cinderella in Tinseltown,' *Dance Magazine*, February 1987

Ziegler, Philip, *Diana Cooper, A Biography*, New York, Knopf, 1982

Index